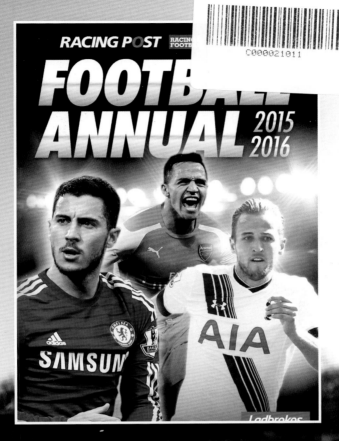

Editor Dan Sait

Contributors Paul Charlton, Dan Childs, Michael Cox, Steve Davies, Alex Deacon, Danny Hayes, Matt Ireland, Glenn Jeffreys, Mark Langdon, James Milton, Kevin Pullein, Dan Sait

Data editor Chris Mann

Cover design Jay Vincent

With additional thanks to Paul Charlton

Published in 2015 by Racing Post Books

27 Kingfisher Court, Hambridge Road, Newbury, Berkshire, RG14 5SJ

Copyright © 2015 Racing Post Books

A catalogue record for this book is available from the British Library.

ISBN 978-1-909471-94-8

Printed and bound in Great Britain by Buxton Press

CONTENTS

Editor's introduction 5
Five things we learnt from 2014-15 6
Mark Langdon

2014-15 betting review 8
James Milton's sideways look at last season

Bookmakers' odds 10
The Betting Jury 12
Zonal Marking 14
Michael Cox talks tactics

Kevin Pullein 16
Working out the value

Important dates 2015-16 18
Premier League 22
Team profiles 24
Stats 44

The Championship 46
Team profiles 48
Stats 60

League One 62
Team profiles 64
Stats 76

League Two 78
Team profiles 80
Stats 92

Non-League 94

Scotland 100
Scottish Premiership 102
Stats *108*
Scottish Championship 110
Stats *113*
Scottish League One 114
Stats *117*
Scottish League Two 118
Stats *121*
Outlook Index 122
Alex Deacon's unique football ratings
Pools results 126
British cup results 127
Europe 136
Italian Serie A *138*
German Bundesliga *144*
Spanish Primera Liga *150*
French Ligue 1 . . . . *156*
Coefficients & minor European tables 162
Champions League & Europa League results 164
Euro 2016 qualifying results, fixtures, tables & odds *176*
2015-16 fixtures 180
Including six-season form guide
Winners & losers 2014-15 250
Profit & loss 2014-15 252
Index of teams 254

EDITOR'S INTRODUCTION

Okay, let's call it how it is – 2014-15 was not a classic. The standard of football in the Premier League was far from excellent, the idea of a title race seemed to fall out of fashion, British sides flopped in the Champions League and Europa League, and pretty much every favourite obliged in each of Europe's top divisions.

But it wasn't a total washout. Barcelona, Bournemouth and Bristol City enjoyed exhilarating seasons, each entertaining their way to glory. Harry Kane's fairytale campaign provided a fascinating subplot to the domestic season. And on the international stage, the heroics of Gareth Bale and his fellow Welshmen gave Euro 2016 qualifying a heartwarming narrative.

So what can we expect of 2015-16? Certainly history would suggest plenty. The seasons following major international tournaments have long carried the tag of hangover campaigns in the Premier League, with serious title races failing to ignite in 2010-11, 2012-13 and last term. But in-between we've had some crackers – the 2009-10 Chelsea v Man United title race went to the final day, 2011-12 was *that* "AgueroooooO!" campaign, while a Luis Suarez-inspired Liverpool treated us to a thrilling title chase in 2013-14.

The omens are good for 2015-16, and so too is the evidence. Louis van Gaal has had a season to unpick the mess at Old Trafford and can now kick on, Arsene Wenger seems to have finally realised that defence is the best form of defence, and Man City look poised to splurge their way to a full refit. It bodes well for the title race and offers genuine hope for a better showing in Europe.

Of course, the climax to a potentially thrilling season is a European Championship for which all four of the home nations are odds-on to qualify, so it really could be a cracking 12 months.

As ever, our top men have every angle covered to deliver you a profitable season. Mark Langdon, Dan Childs and Kevin Pullein are among the best in the business, ably supported by tactics guru Michael Cox and a small army of experts and analysts from the Racing Post and Racing & Football Outlook. Both papers will keep you ahead of the bookies as the season unfolds, but for now we hope the following pages can help you kick-start the season in style.

Dan Sait

For top 2015-16 tips look no further than last term

1. Don't ignore the obvious in Golden Boot battle

It is scandalous that Sergio Aguero has never been included in the PFA Premier League team of the year, but the Manchester City hitman showed his superstar qualities by romping to Golden Boot glory last term and it is becoming depressing how the big clubs are monopolising top scorer honours.

In the past 16 years only five teams – City, Man United, Liverpool, Arsenal and Chelsea – have provided the Premier League Golden Boot winner and even then the Merseysiders claimed only the one when Luis Suarez smashed in 31 goals.

Punters shouldn't even consider backing anyone from outside the elite in terms of the win-only part of their top goalscorer bets and the gulf between the best and the rest is only likely to be extended rather than curtailed.

The days of big Dion Dublin and super Kevin Phillips winning the Boot appear to be over.

2. Chelsea are not great value in big away matches

There's no doubt Chelsea were the best side in the Premier League last season and they won the league by eight points even after easing down for the run-in. But there was a weakness in the Blues ranks and it came in the tough away matches.

Jose Mourinho often adopted defensive tactics on the road, safe in the knowledge his side were always likely to get the job done in their home games, and it resulted in only one away win – at Liverpool – against fellow members of the top seven.

They drew at Man City, Arsenal, United and Southampton, and were stuffed 5-3 away at Tottenham. Over the past two seasons, Chelsea have played 12 away games at top-seven opponents and ten of those finished with under 2.5 goals.

3 Second-season syndrome is alive and kicking

Before last season, a £10 bet on teams to be relegated in their second season would have resulted in a profit of £110.24 and that record was improved when 7-2 shots Hull fell through the trapdoor.

"At the end of August, when I looked at the squad I didn't think we would be in this situation," said Tigers boss Steve Bruce when they were looking down the barrel. It's that sort of complacency that can often set in for teams who begin to get comfortable.

Watch out Leicester...

4 Stoke are a team on the up

The most profitable team in the Premier League this season was Stoke – a £1 bet on the Potters would have resulted in a healthy return of £26.70.

City are often underrated and can still go in at really tasty prices, particularly against the big boys as they showed with wins at the Etihad and White Hart Lane.

5 Pulis is a safe pair of hands

West Brom finished in 13th place but before Tony Pulis arrived on New Year's Day they looked like relegation fodder.

Pulis has never been relegated as a manager and with him at the helm the Baggies should be nowhere near the bottom this time around.

A tough season for backers but the plan came together nicely for the B-Teams...

The summer is a time for football punters to look back on the bets they wish they'd had and, more importantly, the bets they really, really wish they hadn't had. There weren't many fancy prices in the major European leagues as Chelsea (19-10), Juventus (13-10), Barcelona (5-4), Bayern Munich (1-6) and Paris Saint-Germain (1-6) landed the spoils.

You could have boosted your ante-post accumulator with Celtic to win the Scottish Premiership at 1-33 but the real punting gold was located elsewhere.

Forget the A-Team – the B-Teams dominated the Football League as Bournemouth, Bristol City and Burton claimed the Championship, League One and League Two titles. At pre-season odds of 25-1, 8-1 and 16-1, I pity the fool who laid that treble.

Bournemouth boss Eddie Howe is just 3-1 to be named England manager at some point in his career. That bet may require a bit of patience, though – Roy Hodgson was 64 years old when he took the England job so if 37-year-old Howe is appointed at the same age you'll be waiting until 2041 to collect.

Burton's Jimmy Floyd Hasselbaink is another impressive young manager and, with Teddy Sheringham being named Stevenage boss, retired Premier League strikers are flocking to League Two. It won't be long before Dennis Bergkamp is in the Carlisle dugout, screaming at his players to "get it in the bloody mixer!"

Bristol City hacked up in League One after being backed from 18-1 to 8-1 over the summer and the gamble on Blackpool to be relegated from the Championship never looked like going astray.

The Tangerines' nightmare came as no surprise but there were also some major shocks in the relegation markets. Wigan – third-favourites for the Championship at the start of the season and 33-1 to go down – finished second-bottom while Leyton Orient (25-1) and Tranmere (14-1) were unexpected casualties in League One and League Two.

Southampton's summer exodus meant they started the season as short as 7-2 to be relegated from the Premier League. Punters who opposed the Saints at far bigger prices earlier in the close-season were entitled to feel pretty smug... until Ronald Koeman's men won eight of their first 11 games including an 8-0 drubbing of Sunderland – a scoreline available to back at 400-1 in-play.

There was an even more spectacular relegation gamble later in the season. On April 5, before their 1-0 defeat at Sunderland, Newcastle were 250-1 to go down but they went into the final day as 5-1 shots.

A 2-0 home win over West Ham saved the relieved Magpies, condemning Hull to the Championship along with Burnley and wooden-spoon recipients QPR, who had been 6-1 to finish bottom at the start of the season.

Barcelona, 6-1 shots ante-post, won the Champions League, Chelsea picked up the League Cup, and Arsenal retained the FA Cup, thumping Aston Villa 4-0 in the final – a 20-1 shot in the correct-score betting.

Milts takes his new ride for a spin after landing the Football League title treble

In the fourth round of the FA Cup, Middlesbrough won at Manchester City and Bradford shocked Chelsea 4-2. The giant-killing double paid 311-1 while the Bantams were matched at 459-1 in-play after going 2-0 down at Stamford Bridge.

The race for the Premier League Golden Boot proved an intriguing heat as 5-1 ante-post favourite Robin van Persie flopped and a quiet, mild-mannered lad from Chingford turned into a goalscoring superhero.

It takes a good player to keep Roberto Soldado and Emmanuel Adebayor out of the Tottenham team and Harry Kane – matched at 999-1 for the Boot on Betfair – went favourite after his hat-trick against Leicester on March 21.

Harry Hotspur was eventually overhauled by Manchester City's Sergio Aguero – clearly a fluky one-season wonder – but Kane gave his backers a terrific run for their money.

Let's end on a positive note. After in-depth statistical analysis, I can confirm that the best bet of the 2014-15 season was Brentford at 9-2 to finish above 1-7 shots Fulham in the Championship. The Bees had a ten-point lead in the match bet after eight games and ended up 12 places and 26 points above their west-London rivals.

If we can just unearth, say, a dozen ante-post wagers like that one, 2015-16 should be a half-decent season.

Premier League winner

	b365	BFred	Boyle	Coral	Hills	Lads
Chelsea	6-4	11-8	7-5	8-5	6-4	23-20
Man City	11-4	11-4	11-4	12-5	11-4	5-2
Arsenal	9-2	9-2	9-2	9-2	9-2	5
Man Utd	5	5	5	11-2	5	11-2
Liverpool	20	25	22	20	25	28
Tottenham	100	66	100	125	100	125
Everton	250	250	250	300	250	300
Southampton	200	200	250	300	250	250
Crystal Palace	2000	2000	2000	3000	2000	3000
Newcastle	2500	1000	2000	2000	1500	3000
Stoke	1000	1000	1500	2000	1500	3000
Swansea	1500	1000	1500	2000	1500	3000
West Ham	1500	1000	1500	3000	1500	3000
Aston Villa	2500	1500	2000	3000	1000	5000
Leicester	2000	2000	2500	3000	2000	5000
Sunderland	3000	2000	2500	3000	2500	5000
West Brom	2000	2000	2000	5000	2500	5000
Bournemouth	5000	2500	3000	3000	2500	7500
Norwich	5000	2000	5000	5000	2500	7500
Watford	7500	5000	5000	5000	5000	7500

Win or each-way

Premier League relegation

	b365	BFred	Boyle	Coral	Hills	Lads
Watford	8-11	4-6	4-6	8-11	8-13	8-11
Norwich	11-10	11-10	1	6-5	10-11	23-20
Bournemouth	11-10	11-10	11-10	5-4	11-10	23-20
Sunderland	2	9-4	9-4	2	2	9-5
Leicester	3	4	3	4	7-2	4
Aston Villa	9-2	9-2	15-4	10-3	9-2	10-3
West Brom	9-2	9-2	4	9-2	9-2	21-10
Newcastle	9-2	5	9-2	5	4	11-2
Crystal Palace	5	5	5	11-2	11-2	13-2
West Ham	7	13-2	6	9-2	6	11-2
Swansea	8	8	17-2	6	8	9
Stoke	12	12	10	14	14	10
Southampton	40	50	33	40	50	40
Everton	40	66	33	50	40	40
Tottenham	250	250	200	100	100	250
Liverpool	500	500	300	-	100	500
Arsenal	2000	2500	2000	-	500	5000
Man Utd	2000	2500	2000	-	500	4000
Chelsea	5000	5000	5000	-	1000	7500
Man City	5000	5000	5000	-	1000	7500

Win only

Championship winner

	b365	BFred	Boyle	Coral	Hills	Lads
Derby	7	6	7	13-2	6	7
Hull	8	9	8	10	10	8
Middlesbrough	10	10	10	11	9	8
Brentford	12	14	12	9	14	14
Burnley	14	12	14	14	14	14
Wolves	12	14	12	11	14	14
QPR	14	16	14	16	16	14
Ipswich	20	16	18	14	20	16
Bristol City	20	20	20	22	20	16
Nottm Forest	22	20	20	22	20	16
Sheffield Wed	16	20	18	22	20	16
Fulham	18	20	22	22	20	20
Cardiff	25	20	25	22	20	20
Blackburn	28	20	25	18	25	20
Leeds	20	25	25	33	25	25
Brighton	25	25	28	20	16	20
Reading	33	25	33	28	33	25
Birmingham	50	25	40	50	40	33
Preston	50	25	40	40	33	33
Bolton	33	25	28	40	33	33
MK Dons	50	33	33	28	40	33
Charlton	50	50	50	40	40	50
Huddersfield	66	50	66	50	50	50
Rotherham	100	80	100	100	80	80

Win or each-way

League One winner

	b365	BFred	Boyle	Coral	Hills	Lads
Sheffield Utd	5	11-2	5	11-2	5	5
Wigan	13-2	7	13-2	7	13-2	7
Millwall	11	10	10	12	10	8
Peterborough	14	10	12	12	14	12
Bradford	16	14	14	12	16	14
Barnsley	14	16	14	16	14	16
Swindon	12	12	12	18	16	12
Doncaster	20	20	20	16	20	20
Coventry	25	16	22	20	20	20
Chesterfield	25	20	20	25	25	20
Fleetwood	25	25	22	20	20	20
Shrewsbury	28	16	22	20	20	20
Burton	28	25	28	33	25	20
Rochdale	33	25	25	20	25	25
Oldham	33	25	33	33	33	25
Scunthorpe	20	28	33	20	25	33
Bury	20	33	28	25	25	25
Walsall	33	33	33	28	33	33
Gillingham	33	33	33	33	33	25
Southend	40	33	40	33	33	33
Blackpool	33	50	50	66	50	33
Colchester	100	50	100	80	66	66
Port Vale	100	40	66	66	66	40
Crewe	100	66	100	100	80	66

Win or each-way

League Two winner

	b365	BFred	Boyle	Coral	Hills	Lads
Portsmouth	7-2	9-2	4	9-2	4	4
Oxford	9	9	9	8	10	7
Leyton Orient	11	10	10	12	12	12
Luton	12	14	12	10	11	12
Northampton	12	14	14	10	14	12
Bristol Rovers	16	14	14	16	16	14
Cambridge	16	16	16	14	14	16
Plymouth	20	16	18	18	20	16
Wycombe	20	18	20	20	16	16
Stevenage	20	14	18	20	16	16
Notts County	22	16	18	22	20	18
Barnet	25	25	20	25	25	22
Carlisle	28	25	22	25	20	22
Yeovil	33	20	20	33	25	22
Crawley	33	20	20	28	33	25
York	33	33	33	25	25	25
Wimbledon	25	33	28	33	33	33
Hartlepool	40	33	40	33	33	33
Exeter	40	40	33	40	40	33
Mansfield	40	33	50	50	40	40
Newport Co	50	25	33	40	40	40
Dagenham	80	66	66	66	80	80
Morecambe	100	66	66	50	66	66
Accrington	150	66	100	66	80	100

Win or each-way

National League winner

	b365	BFred	Boyle	Coral	Hills	Lads
Tranmere	9-2	9-2	9-2	9-2	4	5
Grimsby	6	6	6	6	5	9-2
Eastleigh	8	15-2	7	7	8	7
Forest Green	8	7	7	8	6	13-2
Cheltenham	10	9	10	11	10	10
Wrexham	12	12	12	12	12	12
Barrow	16	16	16	20	12	16
Woking	16	14	14	14	16	16
Gateshead	20	20	20	16	25	20
Halifax	33	25	28	25	25	25
Lincoln	25	25	25	25	33	22
Macclesfield	33	28	33	25	25	33
Chester	40	33	33	25	33	33
Torquay	40	40	40	40	40	28
Aldershot	50	50	50	40	50	50
Bromley	33	40	40	66	66	50
Dover	33	33	33	40	20	33
Kidderminster	50	40	40	50	25	40
Braintree	66	66	66	80	66	66
Altrincham	100	66	80	100	100	66
Southport	66	80	80	100	100	100
Guiseley	50	80	66	100	100	66
Boreham	100	100	100	200	150	80
Welling	100	100	100	200	150	100

Win or each-way

Scottish Premiership without Celtic

	b365	BFred	Boyle	Coral	Hills	Lads
Aberdeen	4-6	8-11	-	4-6	8-13	4-6
Hearts	9-2	11-2	-	4	5	4
Dundee Utd	12	8	-	10	7	10
Inverness	12	6	-	10	7	10
St Johnstone	12	10	-	10	10	11
Dundee	33	33	-	33	25	28
Motherwell	33	66	-	50	66	40
Partick	66	40	-	50	50	40
Hamilton	66	80	-	80	50	50
Kilmarnock	80	80	-	66	66	66
Ross County	100	50	-	33	80	50

Celtic best-priced 1-20 for the title (Ladbrokes/William Hill)

Scottish Championship

	b365	BFred	Boyle	Coral	Hills	Lads
Rangers	4-6	8-11	8-11	4-5	8-11	4-6
Hibernian	9-4	9-4	9-4	9-4	9-4	21-10
St Mirren	13-2	5	4	10-3	4	11-2
Queen of Sth	33	25	25	25	25	33
Falkirk	22	25	25	33	25	33
Raith Rovers	50	40	40	33	40	40
Morton	125	50	50	50	50	100
Alloa	150	66	80	100	80	150
Dumbarton	150	66	80	100	80	125
Livingston	150	66	66	66	50	125

Win or each-way

Scottish League One

	b365	BFred	Boyle	Coral	Hills	Lads
Dunfermline	9-2	4	4	10-3	4	7-2
Cowdenbeath	7-2	4	4	4	4	4
Stranraer	4	5	4	4	4	4
Ayr	5	9-2	9-2	11-2	11-2	5
Forfar	13-2	6	5	7	5	11-2
Airdrieonians	9	8	15-2	9	8	8
Peterhead	14	10	9	9	8	10
Brechin	14	10	10	14	10	9
Albion	33	28	33	33	33	33
Stenhousemuir	28	25	25	28	33	28

Win or each-way

Scottish League Two

	b365	BFred	Boyle	Coral	Hills	Lads
Clyde	9-4	3	3	5-2	5-2	5-2
Stirling	4	4	4	4	4	4
Arbroath	11-2	11-2	9-2	9-2	9-2	9-2
Queen's Park	5	6	11-2	11-2	4	11-2
East Fife	13-2	9-2	9-2	9-2	5	5
Annan	12	10	9	8	9	9
Berwick	14	11	11	10	10	11
Elgin	20	12	12	12	16	16
Montrose	33	25	25	33	33	33
East Stirling	40	28	28	25	25	33

Win or each-way

ASK THE JURY

Michael Cox
ZonalMarking.net

What was your best bet of last season?
Various Southampton bets. They reinvested wisely, so it was bizarre so many tipped them for relegation. Their Europa League commitments will make it harder this season

Give us your Yankee for the top four English divisions
I'll back Jose Mourinho and his old assistant Aitor Karanka to triumph with Chelsea and Middlesbrough respectively. Wigan could bounce back and Portsmouth look in good shape

Who is set to become this season's Harry Kane?
Newcastle's Ayoze Perez had several excellent performances against good opposition last term. If Newcastle shape up this year, he could score plenty

Will British sides continue to underperform in Europe?
They should improve in the Champions League, but the Premier League coefficient will suffer if Southampton and West Ham struggle in the Europa, or if Liverpool and Tottenham concentrate on the league

Who could outperform expectations at Euro 2016?
England. A 100 percent record in qualifying and encouraging performances. I don't get the negativity – we won't have the star players of ten years ago, but it's more of a team

If you had just one bet all season, what would it be?
Chelsea to win the League Cup at 11-2. Mourinho always takes it seriously and has triumphed in three of his five complete seasons in English football

Dan Childs
Racing Post tipster

What was your best bet of last season?
Watford for the Championship title at 25-1. It didn't kop in the end but there was enough opportunity to bank a sizeable profit before Sheffield Wednesday struck an injury-time equaliser on the final day

Give us your Yankee for the top four English divisions
Chelsea, Wolves, Barnsley and Portsmouth

Who is set to become this season's Harry Kane?
Callum Wilson. The Bournemouth striker took the Championship by storm last season and has the skills, pace and movement to flourish

Will British sides continue to underperform in Europe?
I'm not sure they are underperforming. The reality is that the best attacking players are stockpiled at Barca, Real and Bayern and the English clubs can't compete. Chelsea, thanks to Mourinho's tactical nous, have the best chance

Who could outperform expectations at Euro 2016?
Croatia at 33-1. They look set to finish ahead of Italy in qualifying and have lots of good players, especially in midfield. Poland are worth an interest at 80-1, given how impressive they've been

If you had just one bet all season, what would it be?
Newcastle to be relegated at 11-2. Talk of them spending £25m is all well and good but it will take a lot more to significantly upgrade a side that narrowly escaped last season

Steve Davies
Racing Post tipster

What was your best bet of last season?
The Chelsea-Man City straight forecast was pleasant enough, but for pure profit I'll raise a glass to the Brewers – League Two champions at 16-1

Give us your Yankee for the top four English divisions
Chelsea, Middlesbrough, Millwall, Plymouth

Who is set to become this season's Harry Kane?
Callum Wilson at Bournemouth – if indeed he's at Bournemouth next term. Arsenal were sniffing around the 23-year-old who scored 20 goals for the Cherries last season and is a class act

Will British sides continue to underperform in Europe?
The luck of the draw will determine that, but there's little doubt over two legs you'd fancy Bayern, Barca or Real against any of our elite four. I'd expect a Premier League semi-finalist

Who could outperform expectations at Euro 2016?
There's a real possibility the likes of Wales, Iceland, even Northern Ireland or Albania, will find their way to France for what will be a wide-open tournament. With question marks over the big guns, don't be surprised if a side like Croatia goes all the way

If you had just one bet all season, what would it be?
Crystal Palace to finish in the top half. The Eagles carry excellent form into 2015-16, the bottom ten was full of dross, the three coming up are no great threat and Palace look better than Stoke or Swansea

Mark Langdon
RP Football Editor

What was your best bet of last season?

Hull to be relegated. It's always nice to be right, particularly when there weren't too many others tipping the Tigers to drop. Steve Bruce spent a lot of money on mainly poor players

Give us your Yankee for the top four English divisions

It's never easy to retain the Premier League so I will take a chance on Man City beating Chelsea to the title and Derby are spending a lot of money in the Championship. Sheffield United must go close in League One and I like the look of Luton, who won't need to improve much from last season

Who is set to become this season's Harry Kane?

He is 25 so won't be considered a young breakthrough, but those who only watch the Premier League don't realise how good Bournemouth's Matt Ritchie is. He had 15 goals and 17 assists last term

Will British sides continue to underperform in Europe?

The Champions League entrants aren't as strong as Barca, Real Madrid and Bayern, but I expect them to do better than last term

Who could outperform expectations at Euro 2016?

Croatia have a talented team with Luka Modric, Ivan Perisic, Danijel Subasic, Ivan Rakitic, Mateo Kovacic and Mario Mandzukic all among the ranks

If you had just one bet all season, what would it be?

Ambitious Luton to finish in the top seven of an admittedly strong League Two

Dan Sait
RFO Football Editor

What was your best bet of last season?

Blackpool to be relegated was 13-8 when the Annual came out and had crashed to 8-15 by the time the season kicked off. Not a huge price but the most stress-free bet I've ever had

Give us your Yankee for the top four English divisions

Chelsea, Middlesbrough, Sheffield United, Oxford United. Time for the nearly men to deliver. Well, and Chelsea...

Who is set to become this season's Harry Kane?

Alex Pritchard could be the next Spurs kid to impress if given the game time. It's probably a season too soon for Ruben Loftus-Cheek, but another Chelsea youngster who should impress if loaned to a top-tier club is Patrick Bamford. He has the knack of scoring big goals and looks ready to step up

Will British sides continue to underperform in Europe?

No. Chelsea and Arsenal were both guilty of complacency last season, while Liverpool were not a Champions League side without Luis Suarez. I expect a far better performance this time

Who could outperform expectations at Euro 2016?

The prices for Croatia, Iceland and Poland all look too big. I doubt any will win it but all have great trading potential

If you had just one bet all season, what would it be?

Arsenal in the 'without Chelsea' market at 21-10. The signing of Petr Cech gives them the stability and leadership they've been crying out for at the back

David Wright
Ladbrokes trader

What was your best bet of last season?

Bournemouth to win the Championship at 25-1. Sheffield Wednesday helped me out with a injury-time equaliser on the final day, but I'll take it

Give us your Yankee for the top four English divisions

Chelsea, Derby, Millwall and Cambridge. It's still early days in the transfer market, but these look to be making the best progress

Who is set to become this season's Harry Kane?

It's becoming harder and harder for younger players to break through, especially at the top of the Premier League. With that in mind, it could be a chance for somebody near the bottom to break through. I'm keeping my eye on Callum Wilson of Bournemouth

Will British sides continue to underperform in Europe?

Possibly. Recent poor performances put them lower in the pot for the group stage draw and a second-place finish makes the last-16 match all the harder, as we saw last season

Who could outperform expectations at Euro 2016?

Iceland. They've looked strong in qualifying so far and, with a possible three sides progressing in the group stage, the draw could open up for them

If you had just one bet all season, what would it be?

West Ham top ten finish at 2-1. A good season, all things considered, last time out and some shrewd investment in the summer could prove successful

Tactical tinkering of the challengers points to a mouthwatering title scrap

Chelsea's title victory in 2014-15 was entirely predictable from the outset – in fact, the only surprising aspect was that it took until May for them to confirm the inevitable. Jose Mourinho's side took command while Manchester United and Arsenal were flailing in the first half of the campaign, although those two teams steadily improved, setting themselves up for a title fight this time around.

Both United and Arsenal played in an entirely different manner in the opening weeks compared to the run-in. It's worth remembering that Louis van Gaal was initially determined to use a three-man defence, despite United never appearing comfortable in that system, and only definitively abandoned this approach midway through the campaign.

Van Gaal's first United line-up was unrecognisable by the end of the campaign – Nani and Javier Hernandez both featured on the opening day against Swansea before being loaned out, for example, while various star signings had yet to arrive.

There was plenty of tactical tinkering. Aside from the three-man defence, there was a period with a diamond, for example, and various bizarre uses of players. Ashley Young had a spell at left-back, Wayne Rooney spent far too long in midfield.

By the end of the campaign, Van Gaal had settled upon a 4-3-3 system. There was a period in the spring where everything came together nicely – Rooney returned to his favoured centre-forward role, Young was brilliant down the left, while Juan Mata enjoyed his best spell of form drifting inside from the right and combining with compatriot Ander Herrera.

Michael Carrick and Daley Blind both shone in a deep midfield role, and the only question is about what Van Gaal does in the left-centre midfield slot. Fellaini ended up playing a bizarre role, shuttling forward from midfield to become a target man, and it's a damning indictment of Angel Di Maria's dip in form that he was overlooked for that position, which he'd successfully played for both Benfica and Argentina.

Now Van Gaal has a template. Of course new signings are sure to alter United's starting XI, but the Dutchman has a workable system and can build for the future methodically. The coming campaign won't be spent chopping and changing formations, and if United start well they'll mount a serious title charge.

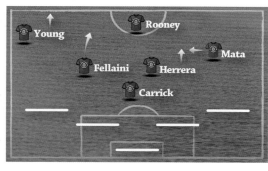

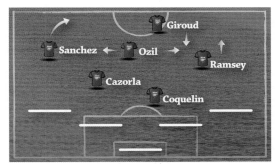

Arsenal had a similar experience. For them it wasn't particularly about changing formations – that's not Arsene Wenger's way – but players breaking into the first team.

The rise of both Hector Bellerin and Francis Coquelin was entirely unexpected, while Nacho Monreal and David Ospina displaced two youth products, Kieran Gibbs and Wojciech Szczesny respectively.

With Santi Cazorla shining in a new deep-lying midfield role, Arsenal's side was transformed midway through the season, and their form in the second half of the campaign was excellent in both league and FA Cup. Again, if they pick up where they left off, Arsenal should be in the mix this season.

Of course, Wenger's side have been in this position many times before – seemingly on the verge of a title challenge which never actually materialises. New signings are needed in key positions along the spine of the side, but, like Van Gaal, Wenger seems to have found a system that works. The onus is now on the players who were excellent for half a season – the aforementioned players, plus Olivier Giroud and Mesut Ozil – to perform for the full duration.

Liverpool and Tottenham, though, appear in the same situation to last term.

Both had a transitional 2014-15 but it wasn't clear what their respective managers had truly discovered over the course of the season. Liverpool's team still required major upgrades in almost every position and Brendan Rodgers was quick to act in this summer's transfer market.

Mauricio Pochettino's Spurs have a clear plan but a squad lacking a proper hierarchy – the back-ups are roughly as good as the first-choice players, but the first-choice players themselves aren't particularly good.

The previous two champions, Chelsea and Man City, still appear the teams to beat. While both have reached the top thanks to a steady stream of expensive recruits over recent years, their strong squads are now acting within clearly defined systems under settled managers. Continuity is the name of the game, and both will start the season with familiar starting XIs.

All this means we start this campaign in a similar situation to last: Chelsea and Man City as the most likely champions, Arsenal and United the closest challengers, then Liverpool and Tottenham the outsiders. The hope is that the latter four have all improved, because after last season's procession the division badly needs a genuine title fight.

Can Arsene finally get the better of Jose?

Every player has their value price, even mighty Lionel Messi

Every player has his price, not just in the transfer market but also in betting markets. Even the best player in the world, Lionel Messi, has a price.

Messi's goal against Athletic Bilbao in the Copa del Rey final was simply breathtaking, with the Barcelona star dribbling around four men before emphatically striking into the near corner.

Anyone who backed Messi to score first in the final won. But backing Messi to score first in every game will be profitable only if the odds are too big – if the chance of him scoring first is higher than the odds suggest.

And what is true of the best is also true of the rest, so what is the chance of a player scoring first in a match?

Before you can answer that question you must ask three others. Will there be a first goal? If there is one, will it be scored by his team? And if it is, will he score it?

Let's go through them in reverse order.

Over time what portion of his team's goals can the player be expected to score? Here are some reference points to help you get started. In the Premier League 54 per cent of goals are scored by forwards, 33 per cent by midfielders and ten per cent by defenders. Three per cent are own goals.

In a team with two forwards of similar skill, each will score approximately 27 per cent of the goals (half of 54 per cent). That share will change with the formation and the relative ability of players.

Sergio Aguero scores 28 per cent of Manchester City's goals. Wayne Rooney scores 25 per cent of Manchester United's goals. You probably thought those numbers would be higher. Messi scores about 40 per cent of Barcelona's goals, but he is one of the best players ever to caress a ball. And note that, for our purposes, saying a player scores X per cent of his team's goals means X per cent of the goals they score when he is on the pitch.

So in this theoretical match, what is the chance of a player's team scoring first if there is a goal?

Barcelona score about 80 per cent of the goals in their La Liga games. Manchester City score about 70 per cent of the goals in their Premier League games. So did Manchester United when they won titles. All teams score more often at home than away, less often against good opponents than bad.

Lionel Messi celebrates his stunning Copa del Rey strike

If Barcelona score 80 per cent of the goals in their games and Messi scores 40 per cent of those goals then Messi should score first in about 32 per cent of Barcelona games where there is a goal (80% x 40% = 32%).

Nearly all Barca games do have a goal, but they are unusually high scoring. In the Premier League 92 per cent of games have at least one goal. The chance is higher in games with good attackers and/or bad defenders, and the other way round.

The chance of a player scoring first in a match is the chance of a goal multiplied by the chance of his team scoring it multiplied by the chance of him being the scorer for his team. If that is higher than the odds imply you have a good bet. Good bets can lose and bad bets can win. But if all your first scorer bets are good ones then over time your winnings will exceed your losses.

The same is true for bets on how and from where goals are scored.

Four out of every five goals are scored with a foot, and twice as many with the right

boot as the left. That is not because the ball falls twice as often to a player's right as his left, it's because most players kick better with their right foot than their left. One who doesn't, of course, is Messi. The simplest way for a player to score more goals would be to become more two-footed.

Five out of every six goals are scored from inside the penalty area. Only one in six is a strike from distance. The aim for every team in possession ought to be to get the ball to one of their players in the box.

Set plays are a significant source of goals, but perhaps not as significant as you might think. One out of every four goals comes from a set piece – from a free kick as often as a corner, and from those a lot more often than from a penalty or a throw.

How much would it cost to buy Messi? There is a price that would represent value for money. Let the accountants work it out. What price Messi – or anyone else – to score the first goal in a match? You can work that out for yourself.

July 2015

Wednesday 1st	Champions League first qualifying round, first leg
Thursday 2nd	Europa League first qualifying round, first leg
Tuesday 7th-8th	Champions League first qualifying round, second leg
Thursday 9th	Europa League first qualifying round, second leg
Tuesday 14th-15th	Champions League second qualifying round, first leg
Thursday 16th	Europa League second qualifying round, first leg
Friday 17th	Champions League third qualifying round draw
	Europa League third qualifying round draw
Tuesday 21st-22nd	Champions League second qualifying round, second leg
Thursday 23rd	Europa League second qualifying round, second leg
Saturday 25th	Scottish Challenge Cup first round
Tuesday 28th-29th	Champions League third qualifying round, first leg
Thursday 30th	Europa League third qualifying round, first leg

August 2015

Saturday 1st	Start of Scottish Premiership season
	Scottish League Cup first round
Sunday 2nd	FA Community Shield
	Arsenal v Chelsea
Tuesday 4th-5th	Champions League third qualifying round, second leg
Thursday 6th	Europa League third qualifying round, second leg
Friday 7th	Champions League playoff round draw
	Europa League playoff round draw
	Start of Dutch Eredivisie season
Saturday 8th	Start of Premier League season
	Start of Football League season
	Start of National League Premier season
	Start of National League North & South season
	Start of Scottish Championship, League One, League Two
	Start of French Ligue 1 season
Monday 10th (week of)	League Cup first round
Tuesday 11th	Uefa Super Cup, Tbilisi
	Barcelona v Seville
Friday 14th	Start of German Bundesliga season
Saturday 15th	FA Cup extra preliminary round
	Scottish Cup first preliminary round
	Start of Spanish Primera Liga season
	Start of Portuguese Primeira Liga season
Tuesday 18th-19th	Champions League playoff round, first leg
	Scottish Challenge Cup second round
Thursday 20th	Europa League playoff round, first leg
Saturday 22nd	Start of Italian Serie A season
Monday 24th (week of)	League Cup second round
Tuesday 25th-26th	Champions League playoff round, second leg
	Scottish League Cup second round
Thursday 27th	Champions League group stage draw
	Europa League playoff round, second leg
Friday 28th	Europa League group stage draw
Saturday 29th	FA Cup preliminary round
Monday 31st (week of)	Football League Trophy first round

September 2015

Thursday 3rd
Euro 2016 qualifiers
Cyprus v Wales

Friday 4th
Euro 2016 qualifiers
Georgia v Scotland
Faroe Islands v Northern Ireland
Gibraltar v Republic of Ireland

Saturday 5th
Euro 2016 qualifiers
San Marino v England
FA Vase first qualifying round
Scottish Cup second preliminary round

Sunday 6th
Euro 2016 qualifiers
Wales v Israel

Monday 7th
Euro 2016 qualifiers
Scotland v Germany
Republic of Ireland v Georgia
Northern Ireland v Hungary

Tuesday 8th
Euro 2016 qualifiers
England v Switzerland

Saturday 12th
FA Cup first qualifying round

Tuesday 15th-16th
Champions League group stage, matchday one

Thursday 17th
Europa League group stage, matchday one

Monday 21st (week of)
League Cup third round

Tuesday 22nd-23rd
Scottish League Cup third round

Saturday 26th
FA Cup second qualifying round
Scottish Cup first round

Tuesday 29th-30th
Champions League group stage, matchday two

October 2015

Thursday 1st
Europa League group stage, matchday two

Saturday 3rd
FA Vase second qualifying round
FA Trophy preliminary round

Monday 5th (week of)
Football League Trophy second round

Thursday 8th
Euro 2016 qualifiers
Scotland v Poland
Republic of Ireland v Germany
Northern Ireland v Greece

Friday 9th
Euro 2016 qualifiers
England v Estonia

Saturday 10th
Euro 2016 qualifiers
Bosnia-Hz v Wales
FA Cup third qualifying round
Scottish Challenge Cup quarter-finals

Sunday 11th
Euro 2016 qualifiers
Gibraltar v Scotland
Poland v Republic of Ireland
Finland v Northern Ireland

Monday 12th
Euro 2016 qualifiers
Lithuania v England

Tuesday 13th
Euro 2016 qualifiers
Wales v Andorra

Tuesday 20th-21st
Champions League group stage, matchday three

Thursday 22nd
Europa League group stage, matchday three

Saturday 24th
FA Cup fourth qualifying round
Scottish Cup second round

Monday 26th (week of)
League Cup fourth round

Tuesday 27th-28th
Scottish League Cup quarter-finals

Saturday 31st
FA Vase first round
FA Trophy first qualifying round

November 2015

Tuesday 3rd-4th	Champions League group stage, matchday four
Thursday 5th	Europa League group stage, matchday four
Saturday 7th	FA Cup first round
Monday 9th (week of)	Football League Trophy area quarter-finals
Thursday 12th-14th	Euro 2016 qualifying playoffs, first leg
Friday 13th	International friendlies
Saturday 14th	FA Trophy second qualifying round
	Scottish Challenge Cup semi-finals
Sunday 15th-17th	Euro 2016 qualifying playoffs, second leg
Tuesday 17th	International friendlies
	England v France
Saturday 21st	FA Vase second round
Tuesday 24th-25th	Champions League group stage, matchday five
Thursday 26th	Europa League group stage, matchday five
Saturday 28th	FA Trophy third qualifying round
	Scottish Cup third round
Monday 30th (week of)	League Cup fifth round

December 2015

Saturday 5th	FA Cup second round
Monday 7th (week of)	Football League Trophy area semi-finals
Tuesday 8th-9th	Champions League group stage, matchday six
Thursday 10th	Europa League group stage, matchday six
	Fifa Club World Cup begins, Japan
Saturday 12th	Euro 2016 finals draw
	FA Trophy first round
	FA Vase third round
Monday 14th	Champions League last 16 draw
	Europa League last 32 & last 16 draw
Sunday 20th	Fifa Club World Cup final, Yokohama

January 2016

Monday 4th (week of)	League Cup semi-finals, first leg
Saturday 9th	FA Cup third round
	FA Vase fourth round
	Scottish Cup fourth round
Monday 11th (week of)	Football League Trophy area finals, first leg
Saturday 16th	FA Trophy second round
Monday 25th (week of)	League Cup semi-finals, second leg
	Football League Trophy area finals, second leg
Saturday 30th	FA Cup fourth round
	FA Vase fifth round
	Scottish League Cup semi-finals

February 2016

Saturday 6th	FA Trophy third round
	Scottish Cup fifth round
Tuesday 16th-17th	Champions League last 16, first leg
Thursday 18th	Europa League last 32, first leg
Saturday 20th	FA Cup fifth round
	FA Vase sixth round
Tuesday 23rd-24th	Champions League last 16, first leg
Thursday 25th	Europa League last 32, second leg
Saturday 27th	FA Trophy fourth round
Sunday 28th	League Cup final

March 2016

Saturday 5th	Scottish Cup quarter-finals
Tuesday 8th-9th	Champions League last 16, second leg
Thursday 10th	Europa League last 16, first leg
Saturday 12th	FA Cup sixth round
	FA Trophy semi-finals, first leg
	FA Vase semi-finals, first leg
Sunday 13th	Scottish League Cup final
Tuesday 15th-16th	Champions League last 16, second leg
Thursday 17th	Europa League last 16, second leg
Friday 18th	Champions League quarter-final draw
	Europa League quarter-final draw
Saturday 19th	FA Vase semi-finals, second leg
	FA Trophy semi-finals, second leg

April 2016

Sunday 3rd	Football League Trophy final
Tuesday 5th-6th	Champions League quarter-final, first leg
Thursday 7th	Europa League quarter-final, first leg
Sunday 10th	Scottish Challenge Cup final
	Scottish Premiership split
Tuesday 12th-13th	Champions League quarter-final, second leg
Thursday 14th	Europa League quarter-final, second leg
Friday 15th	Champions League semi-final draw
	Europa League semi-final draw
Saturday 16th-17th	Scottish Cup semi-finals
Saturday 23rd-24th	FA Cup semi-finals
Tuesday 26th-27th	Champions League semi-final, first leg
Thursday 28th	Europa League semi-final, first leg
Saturday 30th	National League season ends

May 2016

Tuesday 3rd-4th	Champions League semi-final, second leg
	Scottish Premiership playoffs begin
Thursday 5th	Europa League semi-final, second leg
Sunday 8th	Football League season ends
Saturday 14th	National League North & South playoff finals
Sunday 15th	Premier League season ends
	National League Premier playoff final
Wednesday 18th	Europa League final, Basel
Thursday 19th	Scottish Premiership playoff final, first leg
Saturday 21st	FA Cup final
	Scottish Cup final
Sunday 22nd	FA Vase final
	FA Trophy final
	Scottish Premiership playoff final, second leg
Saturday 28th	Champions League final, Milan
	Championship playoff final
Sunday 29th	League 1 playoff final
Monday 30th	League 2 playoff final

June 2016

Friday 3rd	Copa America Centenario begins, USA (*to be confirmed*)
Friday 10th	Euro 2016 begins, France
Sunday 26th	Copa America Centenario final (*to be confirmed*)

July 2016

Sunday 10th	Euro 2016 final, Paris

Powerful squad can help Jose deliver back-to-back titles to Stamford Bridge

J ose Mourinho won consecutive league titles with Chelsea in 2005 and 2006 and he can repeat the trick ten years later, writes Dan Childs. Mourinho will be planning to add further quality to his squad but some advancements can be achieved in-house. Kurt Zouma can expect more game-time – whether in defence or holding midfield – and there is scope for further improvement from Thibaut Courtois and Eden Hazard.

Attacking reinforcements may be seen as a priority. Diego Costa excelled in his first season with 20 goals in 26 league games but has a history of hamstring problems and often struggled to play two full games in a week. Nonetheless, he represented good value for money and if Chelsea are equally successful with this summer's major transfer dealings they are going to be hard to stop.

The biggest challenge could come from Arsenal, who are beginning to reap the reward of Arsene Wenger's patient approach.

By continually qualifying for the Champions League, Wenger has kept the Arsenal coffers in a healthy state and their financial muscle has been flexed over the last two summers with big-money moves for Mesut Ozil and Alexis Sanchez.

Of the two, Sanchez has been the bigger hit, topping the club's league scoring charts in his first season at the club. Olivier Giroud was next best with 14 despite missing the early part of the season through injury, and competition for attacking places could be even fiercer next term with Theo Walcott finishing the campaign in excellent style.

Scoring goals shouldn't be a problem and Arsenal look settled in defence, with right-back Hector Bellerin and centre-backs Laurent Koscielny and Per Mertesacker firmly established.

The goalkeeping position has been addressed and it looks a generally well-balanced squad with room for improvement.

The Gunners were slow starters last term, perhaps due to their involvement in the Champions League playoff round, but have an easier build up to 2015-16 and look primed to improve on their league position of third and points tally of 75.

Man City are second in the outright betting but look a team more likely to get dragged into a battle for Champions League qualification than mount a genuine title challenge.

Yaya Toure's career seems to be in decline and the same applies to Vincent Kompany, who looks a pale shadow of the defensive rock upon which City's 2013-14 title-winning campaign was built.

Sergio Aguero should continue banging in the goals but City seem to have lost the ability to win games without playing well and that may see them come up short in the games that matter most.

They may have just enough about them to finish as top dogs in Manchester though.

Despite massive investment, Louis van Gaal's side struggled to 70 points last term, thanks largely to the contributions of David De Gea and Wayne Rooney. United still lack the depth of their top-four rivals and may end up having to fend off Tottenham and Liverpool in the scrap for fourth.

Key to the data
The table next to every team profile shows head-to-head data for every side they will have to play in the league this season.

1 Every team the club will play in the league in the order they finished last season

2 Results of last season's league meetings **W** win **D** draw **L** loss. Where there was more than one league meeting, the latest is at the right. Regular season only

3 Head-to-head results over the last six seasons at the club's own ground. **P** games played **W** wins **D** draws **L** losses **OV** games with over 2.5 total goals **UN** games with under 2.5 total

goals **BS** games in which both teams scored **CS** number of clean sheets for the home side

4 Promoted and relegated teams shown in fawn in the order in which they finished last season

5 League finishes over the last three seasons

6 Over and under 2.5 and both sides to score stats, including rank in club's division last season. The bar chart shows, horizontally, from top to bottom and rounded to the nearest 5 per cent, the division high, the profiled club and the division low

Leading scorers Numbers in brackets show first goals then 'anytime' goals

	2014-15		Last six seasons at
		H	A	P	W	D	L	OV	UN	BS
Chelsea				6	2	1	3	4	2	4
Man City				6	2	1	3	1	5	2
Arsenal				6	0	2	4	4	2	3
Man United				6	0	3	3	3	3	4
Tottenham			W	6	0	2	4	3	3	4
Liverpool			L	6	1	0	5	1	5	1
Southampton			L	3	0	2	1	0	3	1
Swansea			L	4	1	1	2	0	4	1
Stoke			W	6	1	3	2	2	4	4
Crystal Palace			W	2	0	1	1	0	2	0
Everton			L	6	2	2	2	3	3	4
West Ham			W	D	5	3	1	1	2	3	
West Brom			W	5	3	1	1	4	1	5
Leicester			L	1	1	0	0	1	0	1
Newcastle			L	5	1	2	2	2	3	3
Sunderland			W	6	1	4	1	1	5	2
Aston Villa										
Bournemouth										
Watford										
Norwich				3	2	1	0	2	0	3

Season	Division	Pos	P	W	D	L	F	A	GD
2014-15	Premier League	17	38	10	8	20	31	57	-26
2013-14	Premier League	15	38	10	8	20	39	61	-22
2012-13	Premier League	15	38	10	11	17	47	69	-22

Over/Under 42%/58% 15th   **Both score** 37%/63% 1...

Key stat: Aston Villa were more of a threat after Tim Sherwood arrived but still scored fewer Premi...

ARSENAL

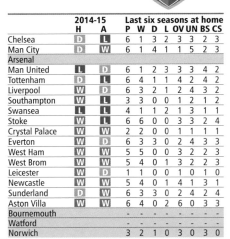

Nickname: The Gunners
Colours: Red and white
Ground: Emirates Stadium
Tel: 020-7619-5003

Capacity: 60,432
www.arsenal.com

Not since 2005 have Arsenal finished in the top two of the Premier League but they look the most likely to give Chelsea a run for their money this season.

Successive FA Cup victories have transformed the mood around the club but Arsene Wenger will have been just as delighted with the third-place finish which ensured the Gunners go straight into the Champions League group stage.

Wenger can get on with planning ahead and has the basis of a strong team with Laurent Koscielny and Francis Coquelin providing serious steel, Petr Cech solving the goalkeeping problem and Alexis Sanchez a world-class attacking outlet.

There is still room for improvement with Mesut Ozil and Jack Wilshere capable of playing more influential roles, but Arsenal are a side on the up.

Longest run without a loss: 10
Longest run without a win: 3
Highest/lowest league position: 2/8
Clean sheets: 13
Yellow cards: 69 **Red cards:** 2
Average attendance: 59,992
Players used: 29
Leading scorer: A Sanchez 16 (8,12)

	2014-15		Last six seasons at home							
	H	A	P	W	D	L	OV	UN	BS	CS
Chelsea	D	L	6	1	3	2	3	3	2	3
Man City	D	W	6	1	4	1	1	5	2	3
Arsenal										
Man United	L	D	6	1	2	3	3	3	4	2
Tottenham	D	L	6	4	1	1	4	2	4	2
Liverpool	W	D	6	3	2	1	2	4	3	2
Southampton	W	L	3	3	0	0	1	2	1	2
Swansea	L	L	4	1	1	2	1	3	1	1
Stoke	W	L	6	6	0	0	3	3	2	4
Crystal Palace	W	W	2	2	0	0	1	1	1	1
Everton	W	D	6	3	3	0	2	4	3	3
West Ham	W	W	5	5	0	0	3	2	2	3
West Brom	W	W	5	4	0	1	3	2	2	3
Leicester	W	D	1	1	0	0	1	0	1	0
Newcastle	W	W	5	4	0	1	4	1	3	1
Sunderland	D	W	6	3	3	0	2	4	2	4
Aston Villa	W	W	6	4	0	2	6	0	3	3
Bournemouth			-	-	-	-	-	-	-	-
Watford			-	-	-	-	-	-	-	-
Norwich			3	2	1	0	3	0	3	0

Season	Division	Pos	P	W	D	L	F	A	GD	Pts
2014-15	Premier League	3	38	22	9	7	71	36	+35	75
2013-14	Premier League	4	38	24	7	7	68	41	+27	79
2012-13	Premier League	4	38	21	10	7	72	37	+35	73

Over/Under 63%/37% 2nd　　**Both score** 58%/42% 1st

Key stat: Arsenal have posted 19 successive top-four finishes since coming fifth in the 1995-96 campaign

2014-15 Premier League appearances

	P	G	Y	R
C Akpom	0 (3)	0	-	-
M Arteta	6 (1)	0	1	-
H Bellerin	17 (3)	2	5	-
J Campbell	0 (4)	0	-	-
S Cazorla	33 (4)	7	5	-
C Chambers	17 (6)	1	8	1
F Coquelin	19 (3)	0	5	-
M Debuchy	10	1	2	-
M Flamini	15 (8)	1	3	-
Gabriel Paulista	4 (2)	0	-	-
K Gibbs	18 (4)	0	3	-
O Giroud	21 (6)	14	5	1
L Koscielny	26 (1)	3	4	-
A Maitland-Niles	0 (1)	0	-	-
D Martinez	3 (1)	0	-	-
P Mertesacker	35	0	2	-
N Monreal	26 (2)	0	3	-
D Ospina	18	0	-	-
A O-Chamberlain	17 (6)	1	4	-
M Ozil	21 (1)	4	-	-
L Podolski	0 (7)	0	-	-

	P	G	Y	R
A Ramsey	23 (6)	6	6	-
T Rosicky	5 (10)	2	1	-
A Sanchez	34 (1)	16	4	-
Y Sanogo	2 (1)	0	-	-
W Szczesny	17	0	1	-
T Walcott	4 (10)	5	-	-
D Welbeck	18 (7)	4	3	-
J Wilshere	9 (5)	2	4	-

Arsenal fans found a new hero in Alexis Sanchez

ASTON VILLA

Nickname: The Villans
Colours: Claret and blue
Ground: Villa Park
Tel: 0121-327-2299

Capacity: 42,788
www.avfc.co.uk

Tim Sherwood was an ideal short-term appointment for Aston Villa, helping them climb away from relegation and inspiring them to reach the FA Cup final.

But there wasn't much long-term thinking behind the move and Sherwood may soon discover, like his predecessors Alex McLeish and Paul Lambert, that a lack of investment will hold him back.

Villa always struggle to hold onto their best players and have been unhealthily reliant on Belgian international striker Christian Benteke, who scored 13 of their 31 league goals last season.

Attacking midfielder Jack Grealish looks one for the future and England under-20 international Callum Robinson could be next to burst onto the scene but Villa are unlikely to significantly improve on last season's 38-point haul.

Longest run without a loss: 5
Longest run without a win: 12
Highest/lowest league position: 10/19
Clean sheets: 10
Yellow cards: 73 **Red cards:** 7
Average attendance: 34,132
Players used: 27
Leading scorer: C Benteke 13 (5,9)

	2014-15		Last six seasons at home							
	H	A	P	W	D	L	OV	UN	BS	CS
Chelsea	L	L	6	2	1	3	4	2	4	2
Man City	L	L	6	2	1	3	1	5	2	1
Arsenal	L	L	6	0	2	4	4	2	3	2
Man United	D	L	6	0	3	3	3	3	4	0
Tottenham	L	W	6	0	2	4	3	3	4	0
Liverpool	L	W	6	1	0	5	1	5	1	1
Southampton	D	L	3	0	2	1	0	3	1	1
Swansea	L	L	4	1	1	2	0	4	1	1
Stoke	L	W	6	1	3	2	2	4	4	2
Crystal Palace	D	W	2	0	1	1	0	2	0	1
Everton	W	L	6	2	2	2	3	3	4	1
West Ham	W	D	5	3	1	1	2	3	1	3
West Brom	W	L	5	3	1	1	5	0	5	0
Leicester	W	L	1	1	0	0	1	0	1	0
Newcastle	D	L	5	1	2	2	2	3	3	2
Sunderland	D	W	6	1	4	1	1	5	2	3
Aston Villa										
Bournemouth			-	-	-	-	-	-	-	-
Watford			-	-	-	-	-	-	-	-
Norwich			3	2	1	0	2	1	3	0

Season	Division	Pos	P	W	D	L	F	A	GD	Pts
2014-15	Premier League	17	38	10	8	20	31	57	-26	38
2013-14	Premier League	15	38	10	8	20	39	61	-22	38
2012-13	Premier League	15	38	10	11	17	47	69	-22	41

Over/Under 42%/58% 15th

Both score 37%/63% 18th

Key stat: Aston Villa were more of a threat after Tim Sherwood arrived but still scored fewer Premier League away goals than any of their top-flight rivals

2014-15 Premier League appearances

	P	G		Y	R
G Agbonlahor	30 (4)	6		7	1
L Bacuna	10 (9)	0		1	-
N Baker	8 (3)	0		-	-
D Bent	0 (7)	0		-	-
C Benteke	26 (3)	13		1	1
Carles Gil	4 (1)	0		1	-
A Cissokho	24 (1)	0		1	-
C Clark	22 (3)	1		9	1
T Cleverley	31	3		6	-
J Cole	3 (9)	1		-	-
F Delph	27 (1)	0		1	1
S Given	3	0		1	-
J Grealish	7 (10)	0		-	-
B Guzan	34	0		2	-
R H-Murphy	0 (1)	0		-	-
A Hutton	27 (3)	1		8	-
M Lowton	8 (4)	0		2	-
C N'Zogbia	19 (8)	0		3	-
J Okore	22 (1)	1		6	-
K Richardson	16 (6)	0		2	1

	P	G		Y	R
C Sanchez	20 (8)	1		7	1
P Senderos	7 (1)	0		2	-
S Sinclair	5 (4)	1		-	-
J Steer	1	0		-	-
R Vlaar	19 (1)	0		4	1
A Weimann	20 (11)	3		5	-
A Westwood	25 (2)	0		4	-

Christian Benteke was at it again for Villa

BOURNEMOUTH

Nickname: The Cherries
Colours: Red and black
Ground: Dean Court
Tel: 0844-576-1910

Capacity: 12,000
www.afcb.co.uk

Bournemouth fully deserved their promotion to the Premier League and could flourish at a higher level.

A lack of goals is often the downfall for promoted clubs but Bournemouth have a top quality striker in Callum Wilson, who has the necessary pace, intelligence and finishing prowess to make a huge impact.

Their energetic midfield plays a high-tempo, attractive brand of football and perhaps the biggest concern is at the back as they can give away cheap goals.

Eddie Howe has bolstered his defence by signing left-back Tyrone Mings from Ipswich, while goalkeeper Artur Boruc has been snapped up on a permanent deal after impressing on loan.

The Cherries are unlikely to feature in many goalless draws but their attacking style could be enough to keep them up.

Longest run without a loss: 14
Longest run without a win: 6
Highest/lowest league position: 1/16
Clean sheets: 19
Yellow cards: 79 **Red cards:** 3
Average attendance: 10,265
Players used: 24
Leading scorer: C Wilson 20 (6,17)

2014-15	H	A	Last six seasons at home							
			P	W	D	L	OV	UN	BS	CS
Chelsea			-	-	-	-	-	-	-	-
Man City			-	-	-	-	-	-	-	-
Arsenal			-	-	-	-	-	-	-	-
Man United			-	-	-	-	-	-	-	-
Tottenham			-	-	-	-	-	-	-	-
Liverpool			-	-	-	-	-	-	-	-
Southampton	1	0	0	1	1	0	1	0
Swansea			-	-	-	-	-	-	-	-
Stoke			-	-	-	-	-	-	-	-
Crystal Palace			-	-	-	-	-	-	-	-
Everton			-	-	-	-	-	-	-	-
West Ham			-	-	-	-	-	-	-	-
West Brom			-	-	-	-	-	-	-	-
Leicester	1	0	0	1	0	1	0	0
Newcastle			-	-	-	-	-	-	-	-
Sunderland			-	-	-	-	-	-	-	-
Aston Villa			-	-	-	-	-	-	-	-
Bournemouth										
Watford	W	D	2	1	1	0	0	2	1	1
Norwich	L	D	1	0	0	1	1	0	1	0

Season	Division	Pos	P	W	D	L	F	A	GD	Pts
2014-15	Championship	1	46	26	12	8	98	45	+53	90
2013-14	Championship	10	46	18	12	16	67	66	+1	66
2012-13	League 1	2	46	24	11	11	76	53	+23	83

Over/Under 57%/43% 6th   **Both score** 54%/46% 10th

Key stat: Championship top scorers Bournemouth were particularly prolific during the run-in, netting two goals or more in nine of their last 12 games

2014-15 Championship appearances

	P	G		Y	R
H Arter	43	9		13	-
A Boruc	37	0		2	-
L Camp	9	0		-	1
S Cook	46	5		10	-
C Daniels	41 (1)	1		4	-
T Elphick	46	1		6	-
D Flahavan	0 (1)	0		-	-
S Francis	42	1		9	1
R Fraser	6 (15)	1		3	-
D Gosling	1 (17)	0		1	-
I Harte	4	0		-	-
K Jones	0 (6)	1		-	-
Y Kermorgant	26 (12)	15		4	1
S MacDonald	3 (2)	0		-	-
E O'Kane	8 (3)	0		-	-
B Pitman	18 (16)	13		3	-
M Pugh	35 (7)	9		3	-
T Rantie	0 (12)	2		-	-
M Ritchie	44 (2)	15		6	-
A Smith	6 (23)	0		5	-

	P	G		Y	R
J Stanislas	6 (7)	1		-	-
A Surman	40 (1)	3		4	-
E Ward	0 (2)	0		-	-
C Wilson	45	20		6	-

Callum Wilson fired the Cherries to promotion

CHELSEA

Nickname: The Blues
Colours: Blue
Ground: Stamford Bridge
Tel: 020-7958-2190

Capacity: 41,841
www.chelseafc.com

Great teams keep trying to improve and Chelsea will be looking to iron out their weaknesses over the summer, ensuring they remain a step ahead of their rivals.

They seemed overly defensive during last season's run-in, scoring 21 goals in 15 league games from the start of February, and more attacking flair may be required to ensure they don't get bogged down in too many tight, low-scoring matches.

The spine of the team is immensely strong with Thibaut Courtois, John Terry, Nemanja Matic and Diego Costa likely to remain key components. And in Eden Hazard they possess arguably the brightest attacking talent in the league.

Hazard could do with some help if Chelsea are to challenge in Europe but Jose Mourinho's men are sufficiently strong to fend off their domestic rivals.

Longest run without a loss: 16
Longest run without a win: 2
Highest/lowest league position: 1/2
Clean sheets: 17
Yellow cards: 74 **Red cards:** 4
Average attendance: 41,546
Players used: 25
Leading scorer: D Costa 20 (5,16)

	2014-15		Last six seasons at home						
	H	A	P	W	D	L	OV UN	BS	CS
Chelsea									
Man City	D	D	6	3	2	1	3 3	4	2
Arsenal	W	D	6	5	0	1	3 3	2	4
Man United	W	D	6	4	1	1	4 2	4	2
Tottenham	W	L	6	4	2	0	5 1	2	4
Liverpool	D	W	6	2	2	2	4 4	4	1
Southampton	D	D	3	1	2	0	2 1	3	0
Swansea	W	W	4	4	0	0	2 2	2	2
Stoke	W	W	6	6	0	0	3 3	1	5
Crystal Palace	W	W	2	2	0	0	1 1	1	1
Everton	W	W	6	4	2	0	3 3	4	2
West Ham	W	W	5	4	1	0	2 3	1	4
West Brom	W	L	5	4	1	0	3 2	2	3
Leicester	W	W	1	1	0	0	0 1	0	1
Newcastle	W	L	5	3	1	1	2 3	1	3
Sunderland	W	D	6	4	0	2	5 1	4	1
Aston Villa	W	W	6	4	1	1	6 0	4	2
Bournemouth	-	-	-	-	-	-	- -	-	-
Watford	-	-	-	-	-	-	- -	-	-
Norwich			3	2	1	0	2 1	2	1

Season	Division	Pos	P	W	D	L	F	A	GD	Pts
2014-15	Premier League	1	38	26	9	3	73	32	+41	87
2013-14	Premier League	3	38	25	7	6	71	27	+44	82
2012-13	Premier League	3	38	22	9	7	75	39	+36	75

Over/Under 45%/55% 11th   **Both score** 53%/47% 9th

Key stat: Chelsea are unbeaten in their last 20 Premier League home games, dating back to a 2-1 loss to Sunderland in April 2014

2014-15 Premier League appearances

	P	G		Y	R
N Ake	0 (1)	0		-	-
C Azpilicueta	29	0		1	1
I Brown	0 (1)	0		-	-
G Cahill	33 (3)	1		5	-
P Cech	6 (1)	0		-	-
A Christensen	0 (1)	0		-	-
D Costa	24 (2)	20		8	-
T Courtois	32	0		1	-
J Cuadrado	4 (8)	0		2	-
D Drogba	8 (20)	4		5	-
C Fabregas	33 (1)	3		11	1
Filipe Luis	9 (6)	0		1	-
E Hazard	38	14		2	-
B Ivanovic	38	4		11	1
R Loftus-Cheek	2 (1)	0		-	-
N Matic	35 (1)	1		10	1
J Mikel	6 (12)	0		1	-
Oscar	26 (2)	6		5	-
Ramires	11 (12)	2		4	-
L Remy	6 (13)	7		-	-

	P	G		Y	R
M Salah	0 (3)	0		-	-
A Schurrle	5 (9)	3		2	-
J Terry	38	5		2	-
Willian	28 (8)	2		3	-
K Zouma	7 (8)	0		-	-

PFA Player of the Year Eden Hazard kept scoring

CRYSTAL PALACE

Nickname: The Eagles
Colours: Red and blue
Ground: Selhurst Park
Tel: 020-8768-6000

Capacity: 26,309
www.cpfc.co.uk

Alan Pardew exceeded expectations by lifting Crystal Palace into the top half, and the main focus as he prepares for his first full season in the Selhurst Park hotseat will be to steer clear of relegation.

Achieving a mid-table finish looks well within the squad's capabilities and some of their best results may be achieved on the road due to a pacy, counter-attacking style which works well against teams playing a high line.

The obvious area for improvement is at Selhurst Park where Palace lost ten of their 19 games last season and conceded 27 goals – the joint-most in the league.

Palace often paid for struggling to unlock well-organised visiting defences and the acquisition of a midfield schemer would seem imperative if they're to provide a better service to the strikers.

Longest run without a loss: 4
Longest run without a win: 8
Highest/lowest league position: 10/18
Clean sheets: 7
Yellow cards: 67 **Red cards:** 4
Average attendance: 24,426
Players used: 30
Leading scorer: G Murray 7 (3,6)

2014-15	H	A	Last six seasons at home							
			P	W	D	L	OV	UN	BS	CS
Chelsea	L	L	2	1	0	1	1	1	1	1
Man City	W	L	2	1	0	1	1	1	1	0
Arsenal	L	L	2	0	0	2	1	1	1	0
Man United	L	L	2	0	0	2	1	1	1	0
Tottenham	W	D	2	1	0	1	1	1	1	0
Liverpool	W	W	2	1	1	0	2	0	2	0
Southampton	L	L	3	0	0	3	1	2	1	0
Swansea	W	D	4	1	0	3	1	3	0	1
Stoke	D	W	2	1	1	0	0	2	1	1
Crystal Palace										
Everton	L	W	2	0	1	1	0	2	0	1
West Ham	L	W	3	1	1	1	2	1	2	1
West Brom	L	D	3	1	1	1	1	2	2	0
Leicester	W	W	5	2	1	2	3	2	3	1
Newcastle	D	D	3	0	1	2	1	2	1	0
Sunderland	L	W	2	1	0	1	2	0	2	0
Aston Villa	L	D	2	1	0	1	0	2	0	1
Bournemouth	-	-	-	-	-	-	-	-	-	-
Watford			4	3	0	1	4	0	2	2
Norwich			2	0	2	0	0	2	1	1

Season	Division	Pos	P	W	D	L	F	A	GD	Pts
2014-15	Premier League	10	38	13	9	16	47	51	-4	48
2013-14	Premier League	11	38	13	6	19	33	48	-15	45
2012-13	Championship	5	46	19	15	12	73	62	+11	72

Over/Under 53%/47% 6th   **Both score** 58%/42% 1st

Key stat: Crystal Palace lost ten Premier League home games last season – more than any of their top-flight rivals

2014-15 Premier League appearances

	P	G		Y	R
S Ameobi	0 (4)	0		-	-
B Bannan	2 (5)	0		1	-
Y Bolasie	31 (3)	4		3	-
F Campbell	13 (7)	4		5	-
M Chamakh	15 (3)	2		4	-
S Dann	34	2		6	-
D Delaney	28 (1)	0		7	1
K Doyle	0 (3)	0		-	-
E Fryers	0 (1)	0		-	-
D Gayle	11 (14)	5		1	-
A Guedioura	0 (7)	0		1	-
B Hangeland	12 (2)	2		2	-
W Hennessey	2 (1)	0		-	-
M Jedinak	24	5		4	1
M Kelly	27 (4)	0		2	-
J Ledley	30 (2)	2		-	-
Lee Chung-Yong	1 (2)	0		-	-
A Mariappa	8 (4)	0		3	-
J McArthur	29 (3)	2		6	-
G Murray	9 (8)	7		4	1
J Mutch	4 (3)	0		2	-

	P	G		Y	R
P N'Diaye Souare	7 (2)	0		1	-
S O'Keefe	1 (1)	0		-	-
J Puncheon	31 (6)	6		8	1
Y Sanogo	3 (7)	0		1	-
J Speroni	36	0		1	-
J Thomas	0 (1)	0		-	-
J Ward	37	1		4	-
J Williams	0 (2)	0		-	-
W Zaha	23 (8)	4		1	-

Murray returned from injury in goalscoring form

EVERTON

Nickname: The Toffees
Colours: Blue and white
Ground: Goodison Park
Tel: 0871-663-1878

Capacity: 40,569
www.evertonfc.com

Last season was a major disappointment for Everton, whose 47-point haul was 25 fewer than in 2013-14, but improvement is on the cards in 2015-16.

Europa League involvement was seen as part of the problem last term although Everton's longest losing run of four games came in midwinter when domestic football was their sole focus.

Sloppy defending was an issue earlier in the season and, in an attacking sense, Everton suffered from poorer than expected contributions from Ross Barkley and club record signing Romelu Lukaku.

However, given their relative youth it is perhaps no surprise that they have struggled for consistency. Both are likely to have learned from the experience and can play their part in ensuring a revival from Roberto Martinez's side.

Longest run without a loss: 6
Longest run without a win: 6
Highest/lowest league position: 9/17
Clean sheets: 10
Yellow cards: 68 **Red cards:** 2
Average attendance: 38,405
Players used: 28
Leading scorer: R Lukaku 10 (5,10)

	2014-15		Last six seasons at home							
	H	A	P	W	D	L	OV	UN	BS	CS
Chelsea	L	L	6	4	0	2	3	3	3	3
Man City	D	L	6	4	1	1	2	4	3	3
Arsenal	D	L	6	1	2	3	4	2	4	1
Man United	W	L	6	4	1	1	3	3	2	3
Tottenham	L	L	6	3	2	1	3	3	3	2
Liverpool	D	D	6	1	3	2	4	2	2	2
Southampton	W	L	3	3	0	0	2	1	2	1
Swansea	D	D	4	2	2	0	1	3	1	3
Stoke	L	L	6	3	1	2	1	5	1	3
Crystal Palace	L	W	2	0	0	2	2	0	2	0
Everton										
West Ham	W	W	5	3	2	0	3	2	3	2
West Brom	D	W	5	2	2	1	3	2	3	3
Leicester	D	D	1	0	1	0	1	0	1	0
Newcastle	W	L	5	3	1	1	4	1	3	1
Sunderland	L	D	6	4	0	2	2	4	1	3
Aston Villa	W	L	6	2	4	0	5	1	5	1
Bournemouth	-	-	-	-	-	-	-	-	-	-
Watford	-	-	-	-	-	-	-	-	-	-
Norwich			3	1	2	0	0	3	2	1

Season	Division	Pos	P	W	D	L	F	A	GD	Pts
2014-15	Premier League	11	38	12	11	15	48	50	-2	47
2013-14	Premier League	5	38	21	9	8	61	39	+22	72
2012-13	Premier League	6	38	16	15	7	55	40	+15	63

Over/Under 47%/53% 9th   **Both score** 50%/50% 11th

Key stat: Everton have not kept a clean sheet in any of their last nine away fixtures

2014-15 Premier League appearances

	P	G	Y	R
A Alcaraz	6 (2)	0	2	1
C Atsu	1 (4)	0	-	-
L Baines	31	2	4	-
R Barkley	22 (7)	2	1	-
G Barry	33	0	11	1
M Besic	15 (8)	0	8	-
T Browning	0 (2)	0	-	-
S Coleman	34 (1)	3	5	-
S Distin	12 (1)	0	-	-
S Eto'o	8 (6)	3	1	-
B Galloway	2	0	1	-
L Garbutt	3 (1)	0	1	-
D Gibson	3 (6)	0	-	-
T Hibbert	4	0	-	-
T Howard	32	0	3	-
P Jagielka	37	4	1	-
A Kone	7 (5)	1	2	-
A Lennon	12 (2)	2	2	-
R Lukaku	32 (4)	10	1	-
J McCarthy	27 (1)	2	7	-

	P	G	Y	R
A McGeady	10 (6)	1	1	-
K Mirallas	18 (11)	7	3	-
S Naismith	22 (9)	6	8	-
L Osman	13 (8)	2	-	-
B Oviedo	2 (4)	0	3	-
S Pienaar	3 (6)	0	1	-
J Robles	6 (1)	0	1	-
J Stones	23	1	1	-

Lukaku will be hoping for more goals next term

LEICESTER

Nickname: The Foxes
Colours: Blue
Ground: King Power Stadium **Capacity:** 32,500
Tel: 0844-815-6000 www.lcfc.co.uk

Leicester were the only promoted side to survive last term and they can avoid a case of second-season syndrome by extending their stay in the top flight.

Nigel Pearson's men were at the foot of the table from the start of December to mid-April but ended up six points clear of the drop zone after winning seven of their final nine matches.

Jamie Vardy, who earned an England call-up, was a key man in their revival and Leonardo Ulloa got back to the form he showed at the start of the season.

They have enough firepower in the side but poor defending remains a concern and their goals-conceded tally of 55 was the fourth-highest in the division.

Another relegation battle looms but the Foxes should carry enough of a threat to remain in the division.

Longest run without a loss: 4
Longest run without a win: 13
Highest/lowest league position: 12/20
Clean sheets: 10
Yellow cards: 50 **Red cards:** 4
Average attendance: 31,692
Players used: 28
Leading scorer: L Ulloa 11 (4,9)

	2014-15		Last six seasons at home							
	H	A	P	W	D	L	OV	UN	BS	CS
Chelsea	L	L	1	0	0	1	1	0	1	0
Man City	L	L	1	0	0	1	0	1	0	0
Arsenal	D	L	1	0	1	0	0	1	1	0
Man United	W	L	1	1	0	0	1	0	1	0
Tottenham	L	L	1	0	0	1	1	0	1	0
Liverpool	L	D	1	0	0	1	1	0	1	0
Southampton	W	L	2	2	0	0	1	1	1	1
Swansea	W	L	3	3	0	0	2	1	2	1
Stoke	L	W	1	0	0	1	0	1	0	0
Crystal Palace	L	L	5	2	1	2	2	3	2	2
Everton	D	D	1	0	1	0	1	0	1	0
West Ham	W	L	2	1	0	1	2	0	2	0
West Brom	L	W	2	0	0	2	1	1	1	0
Leicester										
Newcastle	W	L	2	1	1	0	1	1	0	2
Sunderland	D	D	1	0	1	0	0	1	0	1
Aston Villa	W	L	1	1	0	0	0	1	0	1
Bournemouth			1	1	0	0	1	0	1	0
Watford			5	3	1	1	4	1	4	1
Norwich			1	0	0	1	1	0	1	0

Season	Division	Pos	P	W	D	L	F	A	GD	Pts
2014-15	Premier League	14	38	11	8	19	46	55	-9	41
2013-14	Championship	1	46	31	9	6	83	43	+40	102
2012-13	Championship	6	46	19	11	16	71	48	+23	68

Over/Under 45%/55% 11th   **Both score** 45%/55% 14th

Key stat: Leicester blasted their way to safety with a series of free-scoring performances, scoring two goals or more in seven of their last ten games

2014-15 Premier League appearances

	P	G	Y	R
M Albrighton	10 (8)	2	3	-
E Cambiasso	27 (4)	5	1	-
D Drinkwater	16 (7)	0	1	-
B Hamer	8	0	-	-
D Hammond	9 (3)	0	3	-
R Huth	14	1	2	-
M James	20 (7)	0	2	1
A King	16 (8)	2	1	-
A Knockaert	3 (6)	0	-	-
P Konchesky	26	1	4	2
A Kramaric	6 (7)	2	-	-
T Lawrence	0 (3)	0	-	-
R Mahrez	25 (5)	4	-	-
L Moore	10 (1)	0	4	-
W Morgan	37	2	1	1
D Nugent	16 (13)	5	3	-
N Powell	0 (3)	0	-	-
J Schlupp	30 (2)	3	4	-
K Schmeichel	24	0	-	-
M Schwarzer	6	0	-	-
D Simpson	13 (1)	0	4	-

	P	G	Y	R
G Taylor-Fletcher	0 (1)	0	-	-
L Ulloa	29 (8)	11	3	-
M Upson	5	0	-	-
J Vardy	26 (8)	5	5	-
M Wasilewski	22 (3)	1	6	-
C Wood	0 (7)	1	-	-
R de Laet	20 (6)	0	3	-

Leonardo Ulloa's goals helped keep Leicester up

LIVERPOOL

Nickname: The Reds
Colours: Red
Ground: Anfield **Capacity:** 45,362
Tel: 0151-264-2500 www.liverpoolfc.tv

Finishing in sixth place was seen as a major disappointment for Liverpool but, barring their Luis Suarez-inspired title push in 2013-14, it was a fairly standard performance.

Liverpool's final tally of 62 points is the second highest they have achieved in the last five seasons and there seems little scope for big improvement, with the club either unwilling or unable to compete for the best players on the market.

An injury-free campaign from Daniel Sturridge would be a major boost and there's room for improvement from Lazar Markovic and Adam Lallana, who have made slow starts to their Anfield careers.

Steven Gerrard, their league top scorer last season, has called time on his Reds career and his loss could be keenly felt as Liverpool strive to regain a top-four spot.

Longest run without a loss: 13
Longest run without a win: 4
Highest/lowest league position: 5/12
Clean sheets: 14
Yellow cards: 68 **Red cards:** 3
Average attendance: 44,658
Players used: 25
Leading scorer: S Gerrard 9 (2,8)

	2014-15		Last six seasons at home							
	H	A	P	W	D	L	OV	UN	BS	CS
Chelsea	L	D	6	2	1	3	3	3	3	1
Man City	W	L	6	3	3	0	5	1	5	1
Arsenal	D	L	6	1	2	3	4	2	5	0
Man United	L	L	6	3	1	2	3	3	4	2
Tottenham	W	W	6	4	1	1	3	3	2	3
Liverpool										
Southampton	W	W	3	2	0	1	1	2	1	1
Swansea	W	W	4	3	1	0	3	1	2	2
Stoke	W	L	6	4	2	0	1	5	0	6
Crystal Palace	L	L	2	1	0	1	2	0	2	0
Everton	D	D	6	3	3	0	3	3	2	4
West Ham	W	L	5	4	1	0	3	2	1	4
West Brom	W	D	5	3	0	2	2	3	2	1
Leicester	D	W	1	0	1	0	1	0	1	0
Newcastle	W	L	5	4	1	0	3	2	3	2
Sunderland	D	W	6	3	3	0	4	2	3	3
Aston Villa	L	W	6	1	2	3	4	2	4	1
Bournemouth			-	-	-	-	-	-	-	-
Watford			-	-	-	-	-	-	-	-
Norwich			3	2	1	0	2	1	2	1

Season	Division	Pos	P	W	D	L	F	A	GD	Pts
2014-15	Premier League	6	38	18	8	12	52	48	+4	62
2013-14	Premier League	2	38	26	6	6	101	50	+51	84
2012-13	Premier League	7	38	16	13	9	71	43	+28	61

Over/Under 53%/47% 6th

Both score 53%/47% 9th

Key stat: Liverpool have scored first-half goals in nine of their last 11 Premier League home fixtures

2014-15 Premier League appearances

	P	G		Y	R
J Allen	16 (5)	1		3	-
M Balotelli	10 (6)	1		5	-
F Borini	3 (9)	1		2	1
E Can	23 (4)	1		3	1
P Coutinho	32 (3)	5		3	-
J Enrique	2 (2)	0		-	-
S Gerrard	25 (4)	9		7	1
J Henderson	36 (1)	6		6	-
J Ibe	7 (5)	0		-	-
Javi Manquillo	10	0		3	-
G Johnson	15 (4)	1		2	-
B Jones	3	0		-	-
A Lallana	23 (4)	5		4	-
R Lambert	7 (18)	2		2	-
D Lovren	22 (4)	0		4	-
Lucas	16 (4)	0		4	-
L Markovic	11 (8)	2		-	-
S Mignolet	35 (1)	0		-	-
A Moreno Perez	26 (2)	2		6	-
M Sakho	15 (1)	0		1	-

	P	G		Y	R
J Sinclair	0 (2)	0		-	-
M Skrtel	33	1		8	-
R Sterling	34 (1)	7		5	-
D Sturridge	7 (5)	4		-	-
K Toure	7 (5)	0		-	-

Steven Gerrard waved a fond farewell to Anfield

MAN CITY

Nickname: The Citizens
Colours: Sky blue and white
Ground: Etihad Stadium
Tel: 0161-444-1894

Capacity: 46,708
www.mcfc.co.uk

Six wins from their last six games allowed Man City to finish second but the final flourish doesn't obscure a poor campaign.

Sergio Aguero won the golden boot but Vincent Kompany and Yaya Toure – key components of the 2013-14 title success – were no longer as effective.

Kompany has become increasingly injury prone and his regression helps explain why City went from having the second-best to fifth-best defensive record.

And while Toure's ten-goal haul may seem impressive enough, it was half the number he managed the season before.

At 32, Toure seems unlikely to get back to his peak and his lack of defensive awareness is becoming a problem in the big games. City, like Toure, appear to be a fading force and could be further away from the league summit by May.

Longest run without a loss: 12
Longest run without a win: 4
Highest/lowest league position: 1/4
Clean sheets: 14
Yellow cards: 79 **Red cards:** 2
Average attendance: 45,365
Players used: 24
Leading scorer: S Aguero 26 (10,17)

	2014-15		Last six seasons at home							
	H	A	P	W	D	L	OV	UN	BS	CS
Chelsea	D	D	6	4	1	1	2	4	3	2
Man City										
Arsenal	L	D	6	3	1	2	3	3	3	1
Man United	W	L	6	3	1	2	2	4	2	3
Tottenham	W	W	6	5	0	1	4	2	3	2
Liverpool	W	L	6	4	2	0	5	1	3	3
Southampton	W	W	3	3	0	0	2	1	2	1
Swansea	W	W	4	4	0	0	3	1	1	3
Stoke	L	W	6	5	0	1	3	3	0	5
Crystal Palace	W	L	2	2	0	0	1	1	0	2
Everton	W	D	6	3	1	2	2	4	3	2
West Ham	W	L	5	5	0	0	3	2	3	2
West Brom	W	W	5	5	0	0	4	1	1	4
Leicester	W	W	1	1	0	0	0	1	0	1
Newcastle	W	W	5	5	0	0	5	0	2	3
Sunderland	W	W	6	4	2	0	6	0	4	2
Aston Villa	W	W	6	6	0	0	6	0	3	3
Bournemouth			-	-	-	-	-	-	-	-
Watford			-	-	-	-	-	-	-	-
Norwich			3	2	0	1	3	0	2	1

Season	Division	Pos	P	W	D	L	F	A	GD	Pts
2014-15	Premier League	2	38	24	7	7	83	38	+45	79
2013-14	Premier League	2	38	27	5	6	102	37	+65	86
2012-13	Premier League	2	38	23	9	6	66	34	+32	78

Over/Under 58%/42% 4th

Both score 55%/45% 6th

Key stat: Man City have topped the Premier League scoring charts in three of the last four seasons

2014-15 Premier League appearances

	P	G		Y	R
S Aguero	30 (3)	26		4	-
W Bony	2 (8)	2		1	-
D Boyata	1 (1)	0		1	-
W Caballero	2	0		-	-
G Clichy	23	1		1	-
M Demichelis	28 (3)	1		6	-
E Dzeko	11 (11)	4		1	-
Fernandinho	25 (8)	3		7	-
Fernando	22 (3)	2		6	-
J Hart	36	0		1	-
S Jovetic	9 (8)	5		-	-
A Kolarov	16 (5)	2		4	-
V Kompany	23 (2)	0		7	-
F Lampard	10 (22)	6		1	-
E Mangala	24 (1)	0		4	1
J Milner	18 (14)	5		6	-
S Nasri	18 (6)	2		5	-
J Navas	23 (12)	0		3	-
J Pozo	1 (2)	0		-	-
B Sagna	8 (1)	0		1	-

	P	G		Y	R
D Silva	32	12		8	-
S Sinclair	0 (2)	0		-	-
Y Toure	27 (2)	10		5	-
P Zabaleta	29	1		7	1

Sergio Aguero was the top flight's top scorer

MAN UNITED

Nickname: The Red Devils
Colours: Red and white
Ground: Old Trafford
Tel: 0161-868-8000

Capacity: 75,731
www.manutd.com

Louis van Gaal was in ebullient mood at Man United's end of season awards ceremony but fourth place was nothing much to shout about.

United's 70-point haul was just six better than the number gained by David Moyes and was achieved with the help of massive investment on Daley Blind, Marcos Rojo, Luke Shaw, Ander Herrera, Angel Di Maria and Radamel Falcao.

None of the new arrivals made a significant impact although Van Gaal can take credit for reviving the fortunes of Ashley Young and Marouane Fellaini.

Wayne Rooney topped the scoring charts but only flourished when Van Gaal stopped playing him in midfield. Getting the best out of Rooney is a must if United are to stay in the top four and far more is needed to mount a serious title challenge.

Longest run without a loss: 10
Longest run without a win: 3
Highest/lowest league position: 3/10
Clean sheets: 11
Yellow cards: 66 **Red cards:** 5
Average attendance: 75,334
Players used: 33
Leading scorer: W Rooney 12 (4,10)

	2014-15		Last six seasons at home							
	H	A	P	W	D	L	OV	UN	BS	CS
Chelsea	D	L	6	2	2	2	3	3	4	1
Man City	W	L	6	3	0	3	6	0	5	0
Arsenal	D	W	6	5	1	0	3	3	4	2
Man United										
Tottenham	W	D	6	4	0	2	5	1	3	3
Liverpool	W	W	6	5	0	1	6	0	4	1
Southampton	L	W	3	1	1	1	1	2	2	0
Swansea	L	L	4	3	0	1	2	2	2	2
Stoke	W	D	6	6	0	0	5	1	4	2
Crystal Palace	W	W	2	2	0	0	0	2	0	2
Everton	W	L	6	4	1	1	3	3	2	3
West Ham	W	D	5	5	0	0	4	1	2	3
West Brom	L	D	5	2	1	2	2	3	2	2
Leicester	W	L	1	1	0	0	1	0	1	0
Newcastle	W	W	5	3	1	1	3	2	3	1
Sunderland	W	D	6	4	1	1	2	4	2	3
Aston Villa	W	D	6	5	0	1	5	1	3	2
Bournemouth			-	-	-	-	-	-	-	-
Watford			-	-	-	-	-	-	-	-
Norwich			3	3	0	0	2	1	0	3

Season	Division	Pos	P	W	D	L	F	A	GD	Pts
2014-15	Premier League	4	38	20	10	8	62	37	+25	70
2013-14	Premier League	7	38	19	7	12	64	43	+21	64
2012-13	Premier League	1	38	28	5	5	86	43	+43	89

Over/Under 55%/45% 5th

Both score 58%/42% 1st

Key stat: Man United's tally of six away league wins last season was fewer than eight of the other nine teams that finished in the top half

2014-15 Premier League appearances

	P	G	Y	R
Anderson	0 (1)	0	-	-
T Blackett	6 (5)	0	3	1
D Blind	25	2	4	-
M Carrick	16 (2)	1	1	-
T Cleverley	1	0	1	-
A Di Maria	20 (7)	3	1	-
J Evans	12 (2)	0	1	-
R Falcao	14 (12)	4	2	-
M Fellaini	19 (8)	6	5	1
D Fletcher	4 (7)	0	1	-
J Hernandez	1	0	-	-
A Herrera	19 (7)	6	6	-
A Januzaj	7 (11)	0	-	-
P Jones	22	0	3	-
M Keane	0 (1)	0	-	-
J Lingard	1	0	-	-
J Mata	27 (6)	9	2	-
P McNair	12 (4)	0	2	-
Nani	0 (1)	0	-	-
A Pereira	0 (1)	0	-	-
Rafael Da Silva	6 (4)	0	2	-
M Rojo	20 (2)	0	6	-

	P	G	Y	R
W Rooney	33	12	5	1
L Shaw	15 (1)	0	2	1
C Smalling	21 (4)	4	2	1
T Thorpe	0 (1)	0	-	-
V Valdes	1 (1)	0	-	-
L Valencia	29 (3)	0	4	-
D Welbeck	0 (2)	0	-	-
J Wilson	2 (11)	1	3	-
A Young	23 (3)	2	5	-
D de Gea	37	0	-	-
R van Persie	25 (2)	10	5	-

Rooney helped United through a tricky season

NEWCASTLE

Nickname: The Magpies
Colours: Black and white
Ground: St James' Park
Tel: 0844-372-1892

Capacity: 52,404
www.nufc.co.uk

Mike Ashley breathed a sigh of relief after Newcastle achieved top-flight survival on the last day of the 2014-15 campaign but his joy could prove short-lived.

The Premier League looks a stronger division this season, with Bournemouth, Norwich and Watford all capable of competing on fairly even terms with the rest of the bottom 12 clubs.

And the strength of the promoted trio should be ringing alarm bells at St James' Park, where a lack of investment has contributed to a steady decline in the team's performance – the 2-0 win at home to West Ham on the final day ended a sequence of ten games without a win.

Steve McClaren has been brought in to stop the rot – having been sacked for failing to get Derby promoted – but he'll need all his experience to fix this club.

Longest run without a loss: 6
Longest run without a win: 10
Highest/lowest league position: 5/19
Clean sheets: 8
Yellow cards: 71 **Red cards:** 7
Average attendance: 50,359
Players used: 27
Leading scorer: P Cisse 11 (3,8)

	2014-15		Last six seasons at home							
	H	A	P	W	D	L	OV	UN	BS	CS
Chelsea	W	L	5	3	1	1	3	2	3	1
Man City	L	L	5	0	0	5	2	3	2	0
Arsenal	L	L	5	0	2	3	2	3	2	1
Man United	L	L	5	1	1	3	3	2	0	2
Tottenham	L	W	5	1	2	2	4	1	4	0
Liverpool	W	L	5	3	1	1	3	2	2	2
Southampton	L	L	3	1	1	1	2	1	3	0
Swansea	L	D	5	1	1	3	4	1	3	2
Stoke	D	L	5	3	1	1	4	1	4	1
Crystal Palace	D	D	3	2	1	0	1	2	1	2
Everton	W	L	5	2	0	3	5	0	4	0
West Ham	W	L	4	2	1	1	1	3	0	3
West Brom	D	W	6	2	3	1	5	1	6	0
Leicester	W	L	2	2	0	0	0	2	0	2
Newcastle										
Sunderland	L	L	5	1	1	3	3	2	2	0
Aston Villa	W	D	5	4	1	0	2	3	2	3
Bournemouth	-	-	-	-	-	-	-	-	-	-
Watford			1	1	0	0	0	1	0	1
Norwich			3	3	0	0	1	2	1	2

Season	Division	Pos	P	W	D	L	F	A	GD	Pts
2014-15	Premier League	15	38	10	9	19	40	63	-23	39
2013-14	Premier League	10	38	11	8	19	43	59	-16	49
2012-13	Premier League	16	38	11	8	19	45	68	-23	41

Over/Under 50%/50% 8th

Both score 47%/53% 13th

Key stat: Home form is likely to be key to Newcastle's survival hopes as the Magpies have lost 11 of their last 13 away fixtures

2014-15 Premier League appearances

	P	G		Y	R
R Aarons	0 (4)	1		1	-
M Abeid	7 (6)	0		-	-
J Alnwick	5 (1)	0		-	-
S Ameobi	15 (10)	2		2	-
V Anita	17 (2)	0		3	-
A Armstrong	1 (10)	0		1	-
Ayoze Perez	25 (11)	7		-	-
R Cabella	21 (10)	1		2	-
P Cisse	11 (11)	11		1	-
J Colback	35	4		12	-
F Coloccini	32	1		3	1
P Dummett	24 (1)	0		4	-
R Elliot	3	0		-	-
Y Gouffran	24 (7)	2		3	-
J Gutierrez	6 (4)	1		4	-
M Haidara	12 (3)	0		-	-
D Janmaat	37	1		7	1
T Krul	30	0		1	-
G Obertan	8 (5)	1		-	-
E Riviere	15 (8)	1		-	-

	P	G		Y	R
M Sissoko	34	4		9	2
S Taylor	7 (3)	1		3	1
R Taylor	11 (3)	0		3	-
C Tiote	10 (1)	0		5	-
H Vuckic	0 (1)	0		-	-
M Williamson	27 (4)	1		7	2
S de Jong	1 (3)	1		-	-

Gutierrez celebrates his season saving strike

NORWICH

Nickname: The Canaries
Colours: Yellow and green
Ground: Carrow Road
Tel: 01603-760-760

Capacity: 27,033
www.canaries.co.uk

All three promoted sides have a good chance of staying up but Norwich look the most vulnerable. It's always slightly harder for the playoff winners, who get less time for players to recuperate and for the management to set up transfers.

Head coach Alex Neil was hugely impressive last term, leading the Canaries to 17 wins in his 25 matches at the helm. However, while his squad always had the potential to excel in the Championship, many of them have shown in the past to not be up to Premier League standard.

Cameron Jerome, Norwich's top scorer last term with 18 league goals, is a perfect example given that he amassed a total of 12 goals in his last four top-flight seasons.

Nathan Redmond has the potential to improve but may be one of the few bright aspects in a difficult campaign.

Longest run without a loss: 8
Longest run without a win: 5
Highest/lowest league position: 1/11
Clean sheets: 14
Yellow cards: 89 **Red cards:** 4
Average attendance: 26,342
Players used: 30
Leading scorer: C Jerome 18 (2,15)

	2014-15 H	A	Last six seasons at home P	W	D	L	OV	UN	BS	CS
Chelsea			3	0	1	2	1	2	1	1
Man City			3	0	1	2	2	1	2	1
Arsenal			3	1	0	2	1	2	1	1
Man United			3	1	0	2	1	2	1	1
Tottenham			3	1	1	1	0	3	1	1
Liverpool			3	0	0	3	3	0	2	0
Southampton			3	1	1	1	0	3	0	2
Swansea			4	2	2	0	2	2	3	1
Stoke			3	1	2	0	3	2	1	
Crystal Palace			2	1	0	1	1	1	1	1
Everton			3	1	2	0	3	0	3	0
West Ham			2	1	1	0	1	1	1	1
West Brom			3	1	0	2	1	2	0	1
Leicester			1	1	0	0	1	0	1	0
Newcastle			3	1	2	0	1	2	1	2
Sunderland			3	3	0	0	2	1	2	1
Aston Villa			3	1	0	2	1	2	1	1
Bournemouth	D	W	1	0	1	0	0	1	1	0
Watford	W	W	2	1	0	1	2	0	1	1
Norwich										

Season	Division	Pos	P	W	D	L	F	A	GD	Pts
2014-15	Championship	3	46	25	11	10	88	48	+40	86
2013-14	Premier League	18	38	8	9	21	28	62	-34	33
2012-13	Premier League	11	38	10	14	14	41	58	-17	44

Over/Under 59%/41% 4th   **Both score** 57%/43% 7th

Key stat: Norwich are unbeaten in their last 12 away league games, dating back to a 2-1 defeat at Reading in late December

2014-15 Championship appearances

	P	G	Y	R
A Andreu	0 (6)	0	-	-
S Bassong	18	0	-	-
E Bennett	3 (6)	0	-	-
R Bennett	3 (4)	0	2	-
C Cuellar	8	0	2	-
G Dorrans	12 (3)	3	1	-
L Fer	0 (1)	0	-	-
J Garrido	3 (4)	0	1	-
L Grabban	23 (12)	12	2	1
J Hooiveld	7	0	-	-
W Hoolahan	27 (9)	4	4	-
G Hooper	16 (14)	12	2	-
J Howson	32 (2)	8	4	1
C Jerome	32 (9)	18	7	-
B Johnson	40 (1)	15	13	1
K Lafferty	11 (7)	1	6	-
J Loza	0 (2)	1	1	-
R Martin	45	2	8	-
C McGrandles	0 (1)	0	-	-
C Morris	0 (1)	0	-	-
J Murphy	1 (12)	1	1	-

	P	G	Y	R
G O'Neil	10 (11)	0	2	-
V Odjidja-Ofoe	1 (4)	0	-	-
M Olsson	42	1	9	1
N Redmond	33 (10)	4	1	-
J Ruddy	46	0	2	-
A Surman	1	0	-	-
A Tettey	34 (2)	2	13	-
M Turner	22 (1)	1	5	-
S Whittaker	37	2	3	-

Jerome kicked things off in the playoff final

SOUTHAMPTON

Nickname: The Saints
Colours: Red and white
Ground: St Mary's Stadium
Tel: 0845-688-9448

Capacity: 32,689
www.saintsfc.co.uk

A seventh-place finish was enough to earn European qualification for Southampton and the extra demands needn't prevent them from posting a third-successive top-eight finish.

Having to start their Europa League campaign in late July is far from ideal but Saints have a strong squad and look equipped to perform well on all fronts.

Ronald Koeman has quickly established himself as one of the most respected coaches in the league and can continue to get the best out of a group of players that has room for further improvement.

The fitness of injured goalkeeper Fraser Forster will be a concern but talented youngsters James Ward-Prowse and Sadio Mane should continue to improve and fit-again Jay Rodriguez may be ready to lend a hand to Graziano Pelle in attack.

Longest run without a loss: 6
Longest run without a win: 5
Highest/lowest league position: 2/7
Clean sheets: 15
Yellow cards: 58 **Red cards:** 3
Average attendance: 30,652
Players used: 29
Leading scorer: G Pelle 12 (2,9)

	2014-15		Last six seasons at home							
	H	A	P	W	D	L	OV	UN	BS	CS
Chelsea	D	D	3	1	1	1	2	1	2	0
Man City	L	L	3	1	1	1	2	1	2	0
Arsenal	W	L	3	1	2	0	1	2	2	1
Man United	L	W	3	0	1	2	2	1	3	0
Tottenham	D	L	3	0	1	2	3	0	3	0
Liverpool	L	L	3	1	0	2	2	1	1	0
Southampton										
Swansea	L	W	3	1	1	1	0	3	1	1
Stoke	W	L	3	1	2	0	1	2	2	1
Crystal Palace	W	W	3	3	0	0	0	3	0	3
Everton	W	L	3	2	1	0	1	2	0	3
West Ham	D	W	4	1	3	0	0	4	1	3
West Brom	D	L	3	1	1	1	1	2	0	2
Leicester	W	L	2	1	0	1	0	2	0	1
Newcastle	W	W	3	3	0	0	2	1	0	3
Sunderland	W	L	3	1	1	1	1	2	1	1
Aston Villa	W	D	3	2	0	1	3	0	3	0
Bournemouth			1	1	0	0	0	1	0	1
Watford			1	1	0	0	1	0	0	1
Norwich			3	1	2	0	2	1	3	0

Season	Division	Pos	P	W	D	L	F	A	GD	Pts
2014-15	Premier League	7	38	18	6	14	54	33	+21	60
2013-14	Premier League	8	38	15	11	12	54	46	+8	56
2012-13	Premier League	14	38	9	14	15	49	60	-11	41

Over/Under 37%/63% 17th   **Both score** 34%/66% 20th

Key stat: Southampton struggled for goals towards the end of last season, scoring fewer than two in 12 of their last 16 games

2014-15 Premier League appearances

	P	G		Y	R
T Alderweireld	26	1		3	-
R Bertrand	34	2		3	1
N Clyne	35	2		4	-
J Cork	5 (7)	2		-	-
K Davis	6 (1)	0		-	-
S Davis	32 (3)	0		3	-
F Djuricic	3 (6)	0		1	-
E Elia	9 (7)	2		2	-
J Fonte	37	0		5	-
F Forster	30	0		1	-
D Gape	0 (1)	0		-	-
F Gardos	5 (6)	0		1	-
P Gazzaniga	2	0		-	-
J Hesketh	1 (1)	0		1	-
L Isgrove	0 (1)	0		-	-
S Long	16 (16)	5		2	-
S Mane	24 (6)	10		5	-
E Mayuka	0 (5)	0		-	-
J McCarthy	0 (1)	0		-	-
G Pelle	37 (1)	12		6	-
G Ramirez	0 (1)	0		-	-

	P	G		Y	R
H Reed	5 (4)	0		-	-
M Schneiderlin	24 (2)	4		6	1
R Seager	0 (1)	0		-	-
D Tadic	24 (7)	4		2	-
M Targett	3 (3)	0		-	-
V Wanyama	26 (6)	3		10	-
J Ward-Prowse	16 (9)	1		-	1
M Yoshida	18 (4)	1		3	-

Graziano Pelle got off to a flyer at Southampton

STOKE

Nickname: The Potters
Colours: Red and white
Ground: Britannia Stadium
Tel: 01782-367-598

Capacity: 27,740
www.stokecityfc.com

Mark Hughes has done a great job in lifting Stoke into the top half of the Premier League and he can keep them there in 2015-16.

Given the difficulty in attracting world-class talent to the Britannia it will be hard to improve on ninth place, but Stoke have a well-balanced squad of battle-hardened players who know what it takes to grind out results.

Old hands Peter Crouch and Jonathan Walters should continue to chip in with goals and Mame Biram Diouf will look to build on his most prolific season in English football. And at the other end, Stoke retain enough of the defensive steel that was their hallmark under Tony Pulis.

Hughes's side finished 2014-15 in solid fashion, losing once in seven games, and should enjoy another strong campaign.

Longest run without a loss: 3
Longest run without a win: 4
Highest/lowest league position: 8/16
Clean sheets: 9
Yellow cards: 83 **Red cards:** 1
Average attendance: 27,081
Players used: 25
Leading scorer: M Biram Diouf 12 (5,10)

2014-15	H	A	P	W	D	L	OV	UN	BS	CS
				Last six seasons at home						
Chelsea	L	L	6	1	2	3	3	3	3	1
Man City	L	W	6	0	5	1	1	5	5	1
Arsenal	W	L	6	3	2	1	3	3	4	2
Man United	D	L	6	1	2	3	2	4	4	0
Tottenham	W	W	6	2	0	4	5	1	4	1
Liverpool	W	L	6	4	1	1	3	3	4	2
Southampton	W	L	3	1	2	0	2	1	3	0
Swansea	W	L	4	3	1	0	1	3	2	2
Stoke										
Crystal Palace	L	D	2	1	0	1	2	0	2	0
Everton	W	W	6	2	4	0	0	6	3	3
West Ham	D	D	5	2	2	1	3	2	4	0
West Brom	W	L	5	1	3	1	4	2	3	3
Leicester	L	W	1	0	0	1	0	1	0	0
Newcastle	W	D	5	4	0	1	3	2	2	3
Sunderland	D	L	6	3	2	1	1	5	2	3
Aston Villa	L	W	6	2	2	2	3	3	3	2
Bournemouth			-	-	-	-	-	-	-	-
Watford			-	-	-	-	-	-	-	-
Norwich			3	2	0	1	0	3	0	2

Season	Division	Pos	P	W	D	L	F	A	GD	Pts
2014-15	Premier League	9	38	15	9	14	48	45	+3	54
2013-14	Premier League	9	38	13	11	14	45	52	-7	50
2012-13	Premier League	13	38	9	15	14	34	45	-11	42

Over/Under 45%/55% 11th

Both score 55%/45% 6th

Key stat: Stoke have been more attack-minded under Mark Hughes, scoring in each of their last 12 home fixtures

2014-15 Premier League appearances

	P	G		Y	R
C Adam	15 (14)	7		5	-
M Arnautovic	20 (9)	1		2	-
O Assaidi	1 (8)	0		1	-
P Bardsley	24 (1)	0		6	-
A Begovic	35	0		3	-
M Biram Diouf	28 (6)	12		7	-
J Butland	3	0		-	-
G Cameron	21 (6)	0		4	-
P Crouch	17 (16)	8		4	-
R Huth	0 (1)	0		-	-
S Ireland	11 (7)	0		3	-
B Krkic	14 (2)	4		2	-
V Moses	19	3		3	-
M Muniesa	14 (5)	0		3	-
S Nzonzi	38	3		2	-
P Odemwingie	1 (6)	0		-	-
E Pieters	29 (2)	0		8	-
R Shawcross	32	2		7	-
O Shenton	0 (1)	0		-	-
S Sidwell	5 (7)	0		3	-

	P	G		Y	R
D Teixeira	0 (1)	0		-	-
J Walters	28 (4)	8		5	-
G Whelan	26 (2)	0		6	-
M Wilson	25 (2)	0		5	1
P Wollscheid	12	0		4	-

Diouf made an impressive impact at Stoke

SUNDERLAND

Nickname: Mackems/The Black Cats
Colours: Red and white
Ground: Stadium of Light
Tel: 0871-911-1200

Capacity: 49,000
www.safc.com

Dick Advocaat did well to lead Sunderland out of a very difficult predicament last season but he may find it a lot tougher in his first full year at the Stadium of Light.

Both of Advocaat's predecessors, Paolo Di Canio and Gus Poyet, did good short-term jobs before failing to take the club to the next level. And the same fate may lie in store for Advocaat as Sunderland's squad is simply not good enough to guarantee Premier League survival.

Jermain Defoe scored just about enough goals to help them avoid the drop but the 32-year-old's best days are behind him and no-one else at the club seems capable of getting into double figures.

It's essential that Sunderland defend well but the back-line is weakened by Wes Brown's departure, while John O'Shea is heading towards the end of his career.

Longest run without a loss: 5
Longest run without a win: 7
Highest/lowest league position: 13/18
Clean sheets: 13
Yellow cards: 95 **Red cards:** 2
Average attendance: 43,157
Players used: 25
Leading scorer: Fletcher 5 (2,3) Wickham 5 (4,5)

	2014-15		Last six seasons at home							
	H	A	P	W	D	L	OV	UN	BS	CS
Chelsea	D	L	6	0	1	5	5	5	1	5	1
Man City	L	L	6	4	1	1	1	5	2	4
Arsenal	L	D	6	1	1	4	2	4	3	1
Man United	D	L	6	0	2	4	1	5	2	1
Tottenham	D	L	6	1	2	3	5	1	5	1
Liverpool	L	D	6	2	1	3	1	5	2	2
Southampton	W	L	3	1	2	0	2	1	3	0
Swansea	D	D	4	1	2	1	1	3	1	3
Stoke	W	D	6	4	2	0	2	4	2	4
Crystal Palace	L	W	2	0	1	1	1	1	1	1
Everton	D	W	6	1	4	1	1	5	4	1
West Ham	D	L	5	2	2	1	3	2	3	2
West Brom	D	D	5	1	2	2	3	2	3	2
Leicester	D	D	1	0	1	0	0	1	0	1
Newcastle	W	W	5	2	2	1	1	4	3	1
Sunderland										
Aston Villa	L	D	6	1	1	4	2	4	1	1
Bournemouth			-	-	-	-	-	-	-	-
Watford			-	-	-	-	-	-	-	-
Norwich			3	1	2	0	1	2	1	2

Season	Division	Pos	P	W	D	L	F	A	GD	Pts
2014-15	Premier League	16	38	7	17	14	31	53	-22	38
2013-14	Premier League	14	38	10	8	20	41	60	-19	38
2012-13	Premier League	17	38	9	12	17	41	54	-13	39

Over/Under 34%/66% 20th   **Both score** 45%/55% 14th

Key stat: Sunderland survived despite a desperate lack of goals last season. They notched more than one goal in just two of their last 16 games

2014-15 Premier League appearances

	P	G		Y	R
J Altidore	2 (9)	0		-	-
R Alvarez	5 (8)	0		3	-
L Bridcutt	10 (8)	0		7	1
W Brown	23 (2)	0		5	1
W Buckley	9 (13)	0		2	-
L Cattermole	26 (2)	1		14	-
S Coates	9 (1)	0		1	-
J Defoe	17	4		1	-
S Fletcher	20 (10)	5		4	-
E Giaccherini	2 (6)	0		2	-
J Gomez	22 (7)	4		7	-
D Graham	7 (7)	1		-	-
A Johnson	23 (9)	4		2	-
B Jones	14	0		7	-
S Larsson	36	3		10	-
M Mandron	0 (1)	0		-	-
V Mannone	10	0		-	-
J O'Shea	37	0		4	-
C Pantilimon	28	0		2	-
A Reveillere	15 (1)	0		-	-

	P	G		Y	R
V Roberge	1	0		1	-
J Rodwell	17 (6)	3		5	-
S Vergini	28 (3)	0		6	-
C Wickham	31 (5)	5		8	-
P van Aanholt	26 (2)	0		4	-

A stunning winner set Defoe off on derby day

SWANSEA

Nickname: The Swans
Colours: White
Ground: Liberty Stadium
Tel: 01792-616-600

Capacity: 20,828
www.swanseacity.net

Garry Monk was deservedly in the running for manager of the year after leading Swansea up to eighth, but he may soon discover that he has taken the south Wales club as far as he can.

There is enough quality in the squad to ensure they steer well clear of relegation but since losing Wilfried Bony in January they no longer possess a prolific striker.

That they coped so well without Bony was largely down to the contributions of striker Bafetimbi Gomis and midfielder Gylfi Sigurdsson, both of whom impressed in the second half of the season.

However, Bony still finished the campaign as Swansea's top league scorer and if they are to equal or better last season's performance Monk may need to unearth another striking talent in the summer transfer market.

Longest run without a loss: 3
Longest run without a win: 5
Highest/lowest league position: 5/9
Clean sheets: 13
Yellow cards: 51 **Red cards:** 5
Average attendance: 20,554
Players used: 28
Leading scorer: W Bony 9 (6,8)

	2014-15		Last six seasons at home							
	H	**A**	**P**	**W**	**D**	**L**	**OV**	**UN**	**BS**	**CS**
Chelsea	L	L	4	0	2	2	1	3	2	0
Man City	L	L	4	1	1	2	2	2	2	2
Arsenal	W	W	4	2	0	2	3	1	3	0
Man United	W	W	4	1	1	2	2	2	3	0
Tottenham	L	L	4	0	1	3	3	1	4	0
Liverpool	L	L	4	1	2	1	1	3	1	2
Southampton	L	W	3	0	1	2	0	3	0	1
Swansea										
Stoke	W	L	4	3	1	0	2	2	2	2
Crystal Palace	D	L	4	1	3	0	1	3	2	2
Everton	D	D	4	0	1	3	2	2	2	0
West Ham	D	L	3	1	2	0	1	2	1	2
West Brom	W	L	5	3	0	2	4	1	2	2
Leicester	W	L	3	3	0	0	0	3	0	3
Newcastle	D	W	5	2	2	1	2	3	2	2
Sunderland	D	D	4	1	3	0	2	2	2	2
Aston Villa	W	W	4	2	2	0	2	2	2	2
Bournemouth			-	-	-	-	-	-	-	-
Watford			2	0	2	0	0	2	2	0
Norwich			4	2	0	2	4	0	2	2

Season	Division	Pos	P	W	D	L	F	A	GD	Pts
2014-15	Premier League	8	38	16	8	14	46	49	-3	56
2013-14	Premier League	12	38	11	9	18	54	54	0	42
2012-13	Premier League	9	38	11	13	14	47	51	-4	46

Over/Under 42%/58% 15th   **Both score** 50%/50% 11th

Key stat: Swansea have lost their defensive discipline in matches at the Liberty Stadium, keeping just one clean sheet in their last nine home games

2014-15 Premier League appearances

	P	G		Y	R
J Amat	7 (3)	0		3	-
M Barrow	1 (10)	0		1	-
K Bartley	7	0		2	-
W Bony	16 (4)	9		3	1
L Britton	7 (2)	0		1	-
T Carroll	8 (5)	0		1	-
J Cork	15	1		1	-
N Dyer	23 (9)	3		2	-
M Emnes	3 (14)	0		2	-
L Fabianski	37	0		-	1
F Fernandez	27 (1)	0		-	-
J Fulton	1 (1)	0		-	-
B Gomis	18 (13)	7		-	-
K Gorre	0 (1)	0		-	-
M Grimes	0 (3)	0		-	-
Ki Sung-Yong	30 (3)	8		4	-
J Montero	15 (15)	1		-	-
K Naughton	10	0		1	-
Nelson Oliveira	4 (6)	1		-	-
A Rangel	22 (5)	0		2	1

	P	G		Y	R
A Richards	7 (3)	0		1	-
W Routledge	27 (2)	3		1	1
J Shelvey	28 (3)	3		9	1
G Sigurdsson	32	7		2	-
N Taylor	34	0		9	-
D Tiendalli	1 (2)	0		-	-
G Tremmel	1 (1)	0		-	-
A Williams	37	0		6	-

Gylfi made an impressive return to south Wales

TOTTENHAM

Nickname: Spurs
Colours: White and navy blue
Ground: White Hart Lane
Tel: 0344-499-5000

Capacity: 36,240
www.tottenhamhotspur.com

Tottenham are becoming accustomed to falling just short of the top four and may find history repeats itself in 2015-16.

They've been commendably consistent, finishing between fourth and sixth for six successive seasons, but just one Champions League qualification has been achieved in that time and, if anything, the battle to join the elite is getting tougher.

Mauricio Pochettino is looking to play the long game by developing a young group of players and will rely principally on Christian Eriksen and Harry Kane to make the difference in attack.

Defence was an obvious weakness as Spurs, despite the presence of top-class keeper Hugo Lloris, shipped 53 goals. However, they strengthened the backline over the summer and the signing of Toby Alderweireld could prove inspired.

Longest run without a loss: 6
Longest run without a win: 4
Highest/lowest league position: 5/12
Clean sheets: 9
Yellow cards: 80 **Red cards:** 4
Average attendance: 35,727
Players used: 27
Leading scorer: H Kane 21 (7,15)

	2014-15		Last six seasons at home							
	H	A	P	W	D	L	OV	UN	BS	CS
Chelsea	W	L	6	2	3	1	3	3	6	0
Man City	L	L	6	2	1	3	4	2	3	2
Arsenal	W	D	6	4	1	1	5	1	5	0
Man United	D	L	6	0	4	2	3	3	4	2
Tottenham										
Liverpool	L	L	6	4	0	2	6	0	3	1
Southampton	W	D	3	3	0	0	1	2	1	2
Swansea	W	W	4	4	0	0	2	2	2	2
Stoke	L	L	6	2	2	2	3	3	3	2
Crystal Palace	D	L	2	1	1	0	0	2	0	2
Everton	W	W	6	4	2	0	3	3	4	2
West Ham	D	W	5	2	2	1	3	2	2	2
West Brom	L	W	5	1	3	1	4	3	1	2
Leicester	W	W	1	1	0	0	1	0	1	0
Newcastle	L	W	5	3	0	2	3	2	2	2
Sunderland	W	D	6	5	1	0	2	4	3	3
Aston Villa	L	W	6	4	1	1	2	4	1	4
Bournemouth			-	-	-	-	-	-	-	-
Watford			-	-	-	-	-	-	-	-
Norwich			3	1	1	1	1	2	2	1

Season	Division	Pos	P	W	D	L	F	A	GD	Pts
2014-15	Premier League	5	38	19	7	12	58	53	+5	64
2013-14	Premier League	6	38	21	6	11	55	51	+4	69
2012-13	Premier League	5	38	21	9	8	66	46	+20	72

Over/Under 71%/29% 1st

Both score 58%/42% 1st

Key stat: All of Tottenham's nine Premier League away wins last season were against teams that finished outside of the top seven

2014-15 Premier League appearances

	P	G		Y	R
M Adebayor	9 (4)	2		1	-
N Bentaleb	25 (1)	0		8	-
E Capoue	11 (1)	0		2	-
N Chadli	28 (7)	11		3	-
V Chiriches	8 (2)	0		3	1
B Davies	9 (5)	0		3	-
M Dembele	10 (16)	1		1	-
E Dier	25 (3)	2		4	-
C Eriksen	37 (1)	10		4	-
F Fazio	20	0		2	1
L Holtby	0 (1)	0		-	-
Y Kaboul	11	0		2	-
H Kane	28 (6)	21		4	-
E Lamela	25 (8)	2		6	-
A Lennon	3 (6)	0		1	-
H Lloris	35	0		-	-
R Mason	29 (2)	1		10	-
K Naughton	5	0		-	2
Paulinho	3 (12)	0		3	-
D Rose	27 (1)	3		7	-

	P	G		Y	R
R Soldado	7 (17)	1		1	-
B Stambouli	4 (8)	0		4	-
A Townsend	10 (7)	2		2	-
J Vertonghen	31 (1)	0		6	-
M Vorm	3 (1)	0		-	-
K Walker	15	0		3	-
D Yedlin	0 (1)	0		-	-

It was real Boy's Own stuff from Harry Kane

WATFORD

Nickname: The Hornets
Colours: Yellow and red
Ground: Vicarage Road
Tel: 01923-496-000

Capacity: 20,250
www.watfordfc.com

Each of Watford's previous two Premier League stays have lasted just one season but things could be different this time.

The Hornets were the second-highest scorers in the Championship last season thanks largely to a potent strikeforce featuring Troy Deeney (21 league goals), Matej Vydra (16) and Odion Ighalo (20).

Vydra signed a long-term contract over the summer and, having settled at Vicarage Road, should be more successful than when he joined West Brom on loan for the 2013-14 Premier League season.

Attacking midfielder Almen Abdi can provide the forwards with quality service and the main concern is at the back.

However, the arrival of towering centre-back Sebastian Prodl should help shore things up and the Pozzo scouting network is sure to make further additions.

Longest run without a loss: 9
Longest run without a win: 4
Highest/lowest league position: 1/7
Clean sheets: 15
Yellow cards: 79 **Red cards:** 7
Average attendance: 16,664
Players used: 31
Leading scorer: T Deeney 21 (7,17)

	2014-15		Last six seasons at home							
	H	A	P	W	D	L	OV	UN	BS	CS
Chelsea	-	-	-	-	-	-	-	-	-	-
Man City	-	-	-	-	-	-	-	-	-	-
Arsenal	-	-	-	-	-	-	-	-	-	-
Man United	-	-	-	-	-	-	-	-	-	-
Tottenham	-	-	-	-	-	-	-	-	-	-
Liverpool	-	-	-	-	-	-	-	-	-	-
Southampton	1	0	0	1	1	0	0	0		
Swansea	2	0	0	2	1	1	1	0		
Stoke	-	-	-	-	-	-	-	-	-	-
Crystal Palace	4	0	2	2	2	2	3	0		
Everton	-	-	-	-	-	-	-	-	-	-
West Ham	1	0	0	1	1	0	0	0		
West Brom	1	0	1	0	0	1	1	0		
Leicester	5	3	1	1	5	0	4	0		
Newcastle	1	0	0	1	1	0	1	0		
Sunderland	-	-	-	-	-	-	-	-	-	-
Aston Villa	-	-	-	-	-	-	-	-	-	-
Bournemouth	D	L	2	1	1	0	1	1	2	0
Watford										
Norwich	L	L	2	0	1	1	2	0	1	0

Season	Division	Pos	P	W	D	L	F	A	GD	Pts
2014-15	Championship	2	46	27	8	11	91	50	+41	89
2013-14	Championship	13	46	15	15	16	74	64	+10	60
2012-13	Championship	3	46	23	8	15	85	58	+27	77

Over/Under 57%/43% 6th   **Both score** 50%/50% 12th

Key stat: Attack is the best form of defence when Watford play on the road. They have netted at least two goals in each of their last nine away fixtures

2014-15 Championship appearances

	P	G		Y	R
A Abdi	28 (4)	9		6	-
K Andrews	4 (5)	1		2	-
G Angella	32 (3)	2		5	2
I Anya	27 (8)	0		-	-
S Bassong	11	0		1	-
J Bond	2 (1)	0		-	-
G Byers	0 (1)	0		-	-
C Cathcart	28 (1)	3		7	-
M Connolly	4 (2)	1		1	-
T Deeney	37 (5)	21		7	-
L Doyley	5 (1)	0		2	-
L Dyer	4 (10)	1		-	-
J Ekstrand	23 (1)	1		3	1
D Fabbrini	2	0		1	-
F Forestieri	10 (14)	5		4	-
H Gomes	44	0		2	-
A Guedioura	13 (4)	3		4	-
T Hoban	20 (7)	0		4	1
O Ighalo	22 (13)	20		2	-
M Layun	14 (3)	0		2	-
L McGugan	5 (1)	0		-	-

	P	G		Y	R
B Mensah	0 (1)	0		-	-
M Motta	7 (2)	0		1	1
G Munari	21 (7)	3		5	-
S Murray	2 (4)	0		-	-
J Paredes	32 (7)	0		5	-
D Pudil	19 (4)	0		2	1
G Tamas	6 (1)	0		2	1
D Tozser	34 (11)	5		6	-
M Vydra	31 (11)	16		2	-
B Watson	20 (1)	0		3	-

Watford goal-machine Troy Deeney cut loose

WEST BROM

Nickname: The Baggies/Throstles/Albion
Colours: Navy blue and white
Ground: The Hawthorns
Tel: 0871-271-1100

Capacity: 26,768
www.wba.co.uk

Tony Pulis has never been relegated in over 20 years as a football manager and his knowhow should ensure West Brom steer clear of the bottom three.

Albion enjoyed a decent finish to the season, securing eye-catching wins over Chelsea (3-0) and away at Old Trafford (1-0), and they also kept clean sheets in four of their last six games, showing a defensive aptitude which has often been the hallmark of Pulis's teams.

The Baggies should continue to do the basics right but could do with a few more attacking options, given last season's over-reliance on Saido Berahino.

The second top scorer was Brown Ideye with just four goals while Victor Anichebe managed only three. Anichebe is the type of powerful striker Pulis tends to favour, so he may be prominent in 2015-16.

Longest run without a loss: 5
Longest run without a win: 5
Highest/lowest league position: 11/17
Clean sheets: 16
Yellow cards: 64 **Red cards:** 3
Average attendance: 25,063
Players used: 26
Leading scorer: S Berahino 14 (3,11)

	2014-15		Last six seasons at home							
	H	A	P	W	D	L	OV	UN	BS	CS
Chelsea	W	L	5	3	1	1	3	2	3	2
Man City	L	L	5	0	1	4	3	2	3	1
Arsenal	L	L	5	0	2	3	3	2	4	0
Man United	D	W	5	0	2	3	5	0	4	0
Tottenham	L	W	5	0	2	3	3	2	3	0
Liverpool	D	L	5	2	2	1	2	3	2	2
Southampton	W	D	3	2	0	1	0	3	0	2
Swansea	W	L	5	2	0	3	2	3	2	1
Stoke	W	L	5	1	0	4	2	3	1	1
Crystal Palace	D	W	3	1	1	1	1	2	1	1
Everton	L	D	5	2	1	2	0	5	1	2
West Ham	L	D	4	1	2	1	2	2	2	2
West Brom										
Leicester	L	W	2	1	0	1	2	0	1	1
Newcastle	L	D	6	2	2	2	2	4	4	1
Sunderland	D	D	5	4	1	0	4	1	2	3
Aston Villa	W	L	5	2	3	0	3	2	3	2
Bournemouth			-	-	-	-	-	-	-	-
Watford			1	1	0	0	1	0	0	1
Norwich			3	1	0	2	2	1	2	0

Season	Division	Pos	P	W	D	L	F	A	GD	Pts
2014-15	Premier League	13	38	11	11	16	38	51	-13	44
2013-14	Premier League	17	38	7	15	16	43	59	-16	36
2012-13	Premier League	8	38	14	7	17	53	57	-4	49

Over/Under 45%/55% 11th **Both score** 37%/63% 18th

Key stat: Tony Pulis's teams are often defensive-minded and West Brom were no different, scoring fewer than two goals in 11 of their last 14 matches

2014-15 Premier League appearances

	P	G		Y	R
V Anichebe	11 (10)	3		-	-
C Baird	9 (10)	0		2	-
S Berahino	32 (6)	14		2	-
S Blanco	0 (3)	0		1	-
I Brown	13 (11)	4		2	-
C Brunt	33 (1)	2		5	-
J Davidson	1 (1)	0		-	-
C Dawson	29	2		6	-
G Dorrans	19 (2)	1		5	-
D Fletcher	15	1		2	-
B Foster	28	0		2	-
C Gamboa	1 (9)	0		1	-
C Gardner	30 (5)	3		10	-
J Lescott	34	1		3	-
G McAuley	24	1		2	1
C McManaman	5 (3)	0		1	-
J Morrison	29 (4)	2		3	-
Y Mulumbu	10 (7)	0		1	1
B Myhill	10 (1)	0		1	-
J Olsson	9 (4)	1		2	-

	P	G		Y	R
S Pocognoli	15	0		1	-
G Samaras	0 (5)	0		-	-
S Sessegnon	20 (8)	1		5	-
S Varela	3 (4)	1		1	-
A Wisdom	22 (2)	0		1	-
C Yacob	16 (4)	0		5	1

Berahino's goals were crucial to West Brom

WEST HAM

Nickname: The Hammers/Irons
Colours: Claret and blue
Ground: Boleyn Ground   **Capacity:** 35,016
Tel: 0871-529-1966   www.whufc.com

A vital season is in store for West Ham who will be anxious to steer well clear of relegation in their final year before moving to the Olympic Stadium.

There are one or two potential pitfalls ahead with new manager Slaven Bilic needing to adjust to the division and the Europa League a potential distraction.

But West Ham have built up a powerful squad in recent years and it's not unreasonable to expect them to improve.

They were unlucky last season with injuries to forwards Andy Carroll and Diafra Sakho, who when fit and firing are capable of causing problems for most top-flight defences.

Defensively they look solid, conceding the fewest goals among last season's bottom 11, and that strong foundation should stand them in good stead.

Longest run without a loss: 5
Longest run without a win: 7
Highest/lowest league position: 4/12
Clean sheets: 9
Yellow cards: 65 **Red cards:** 2
Average attendance: 34,871
Players used: 28
Leading scorer: D Sakho 10 (3,10)

	2014-15 H	A	Last six seasons at home P	W	D	L	OV	UN	BS	CS
Chelsea	L	L	5	1	1	3	3	2	3	0
Man City	W	L	5	1	2	2	3	2	4	1
Arsenal	L	L	5	0	1	4	5	0	4	0
Man United	D	L	5	0	2	3	3	2	3	0
Tottenham	L	D	5	2	0	3	2	3	2	2
Liverpool	W	L	5	2	0	3	5	0	5	0
Southampton	L	D	4	2	1	1	3	1	4	0
Swansea	W	D	3	3	0	0	1	2	1	2
Stoke	D	D	5	1	2	2	1	4	2	1
Crystal Palace	L	W	3	0	1	2	1	2	1	1
Everton	L	L	5	0	1	4	4	1	5	0
West Ham										
West Brom	D	W	4	1	3	0	3	1	4	0
Leicester	W	L	2	2	0	0	1	1	1	1
Newcastle	W	L	4	1	1	2	2	2	2	2
Sunderland	W	D	5	2	2	1	1	4	1	3
Aston Villa	D	L	5	2	2	1	2	3	2	3
Bournemouth	-	-	-	-	-	-	-	-	-	-
Watford			1	0	1	0	0	1	1	0
Norwich			2	2	0	0	1	1	1	1

Season	Division	Pos	P	W	D	L	F	A	GD	Pts
2014-15	Premier League	12	38	12	11	15	44	47	-3	47
2013-14	Premier League	13	38	11	7	20	40	51	-11	40
2012-13	Premier League	10	38	12	10	16	45	53	-8	46

Over/Under 47%/53% 9th   **Both score** 55%/45% 6th

Key stat: West Ham have gone 12 away league games without a victory since a 2-1 success at West Brom in early December

2014-15 Premier League appearances

	P	G	Y	R
Adrian	38	0	3	1
M Amalfitano	14 (10)	3	3	-
R Burke	4 (1)	0	-	-
A Carroll	12 (2)	5	2	-
C Cole	8 (15)	2	2	-
J Collins	21 (6)	0	6	1
A Cresswell	38	2	5	-
G Demel	3 (3)	0	-	-
M Diame	0 (3)	0	-	-
S Downing	37	6	3	-
J Jaaskelainen	0 (1)	0	-	-
M Jarvis	4 (7)	0	-	-
C Jenkinson	29 (3)	0	2	-
C Kouyate	30 (1)	4	5	-
E Lee	0 (1)	0	-	-
R Morrison	0 (1)	0	-	-
Nene	0 (8)	0	-	-
M Noble	27 (1)	2	4	-
K Nolan	19 (10)	1	2	-
J O'Brien	6 (3)	0	2	-

	P	G	Y	R
D Poyet	1 (2)	0	1	-
W Reid	29 (1)	1	10	-
D Sakho	20 (3)	10	2	-
A Song	25 (3)	0	4	-
J Tomkins	20 (2)	1	6	-
E Valencia	25 (7)	4	2	-
R Vaz Te	3 (1)	0	-	-
M Zarate	5 (2)	2	1	-

Sakho enjoyed a solid debut season at West Ham

Premier League stats 2014-15

Key Points in all tables (except the league table) do not include any deductions imposed by the league.
POS H A Overall league position, rank from home games only, rank from away games only **Sup** Average match supremacy **GFA** Goals For Average **GAA** Goals Against Average **PGA** Points Gained Average

Pos	H	A	Premier League 2014-15	P	W	D	L	F	A	W	D	L	F	A	GD	Pts
					Home					**Away**						
1	1	1	Chelsea	38	15	4	0	36	9	11	5	3	37	23	+41	87
2	2	2	Man City	38	14	3	2	44	14	10	4	5	39	24	+45	79
3	4	3	Arsenal	38	12	5	2	41	14	10	4	5	30	22	+35	75
4	3	7	Man Utd	38	14	2	3	41	15	6	8	5	21	22	+25	70
5	8	4	Tottenham	38	10	3	6	31	24	9	4	6	27	29	+5	64
6	6	6	Liverpool	38	10	5	4	30	20	8	3	8	22	28	+4	62
7	5	9	Southampton	38	11	4	4	37	13	7	2	10	17	20	+21	60
8	9	8	Swansea	38	9	5	5	27	22	7	3	9	19	27	-3	56
9	7	10	Stoke	38	10	3	6	32	22	5	6	8	16	23	+3	54
10	16	5	Crystal Palace	38	6	3	10	21	27	7	6	6	26	24	-4	48
11	11	11	Everton	38	7	7	5	27	21	5	4	10	21	29	-2	47
12	10	15	West Ham	38	9	4	6	25	18	3	7	9	19	29	-3	47
13	14	12	West Brom	38	7	4	8	24	26	4	7	8	14	25	-13	44
14	12	17	Leicester	38	7	5	7	28	22	4	3	12	18	33	-9	41
15	13	19	Newcastle	38	7	5	7	26	27	3	4	12	14	36	-23	39
16	19	13	Sunderland	38	4	8	7	16	27	3	9	7	15	26	-22	38
17	17	14	Aston Villa	38	5	6	8	18	25	5	2	12	13	32	-26	38
18	18	16	Hull	38	5	5	9	19	24	3	6	10	14	27	-18	35
19	20	18	Burnley	38	4	7	8	14	21	3	5	11	14	32	-25	33
20	15	20	QPR	38	6	5	8	23	24	2	1	16	19	49	-31	30

Best attack

		GF	GFA
1	Man City	83	2.18
2	Chelsea	73	1.92
3	Arsenal	71	1.87
4	Man Utd	62	1.63
5	Tottenham	58	1.53
6	Southampton	54	1.42
7	Liverpool	52	1.37
8	Stoke	48	1.26
9	Everton	48	1.26
10	Crystal Palace	47	1.24
11	Swansea	46	1.21
12	Leicester	46	1.21
13	West Ham	44	1.16
14	QPR	42	1.11
15	Newcastle	40	1.05
16	West Brom	38	1
17	Hull	33	0.87
18	Sunderland	31	0.82
19	Aston Villa	31	0.82
20	Burnley	28	0.74

Best defence

		GA	GAA
1	Chelsea	32	0.84
2	Southampton	33	0.87
3	Arsenal	36	0.95
4	Man Utd	37	0.97
5	Man City	38	1
6	Stoke	45	1.18
7	West Ham	47	1.24
8	Liverpool	48	1.26
9	Swansea	49	1.29
10	Everton	50	1.32
11	Crystal Palace	51	1.34
12	West Brom	51	1.34
13	Hull	51	1.34
14	Tottenham	53	1.39
15	Sunderland	53	1.39
16	Burnley	53	1.39
17	Leicester	55	1.45
18	Aston Villa	57	1.5
19	Newcastle	63	1.66
20	QPR	73	1.92

Top scorers

	Team	Goals scored	
S Aguero	Man City	26	▓▓▓▓▓▓▓▓▓▓▓▓▓▓▓▓▓▓▓▓▓▓▓▓▓▓
H Kane	Tottenham	21	▓▓▓▓▓▓▓▓▓▓▓▓▓▓▓▓▓▓▓▓▓
D Costa	Chelsea	20	▓▓▓▓▓▓▓▓▓▓▓▓▓▓▓▓▓▓▓▓
C Austin	QPR	18	▓▓▓▓▓▓▓▓▓▓▓▓▓▓▓▓▓▓
A Sanchez	Arsenal	16	▓▓▓▓▓▓▓▓▓▓▓▓▓▓▓▓
S Berahino	West Brom	14	▓▓▓▓▓▓▓▓▓▓▓▓▓▓
O Giroud	Arsenal	14	▓▓▓▓▓▓▓▓▓▓▓▓▓▓
E Hazard	Chelsea	14	▓▓▓▓▓▓▓▓▓▓▓▓▓▓
C Benteke	Aston Villa	13	▓▓▓▓▓▓▓▓▓▓▓▓▓
M Biram Diouf	Stoke	12	▓▓▓▓▓▓▓▓▓▓▓▓
G Pelle	Southampton	12	▓▓▓▓▓▓▓▓▓▓▓▓
W Rooney	Man Utd	12	▓▓▓▓▓▓▓▓▓▓▓▓
D Silva	Man City	12	▓▓▓▓▓▓▓▓▓▓▓▓
W Bony	Man City*	11	▓▓▓▓▓▓▓▓▓▓▓
N Chadli	Tottenham	11	▓▓▓▓▓▓▓▓▓▓▓
P Cisse	Newcastle	11	▓▓▓▓▓▓▓▓▓▓▓
D Ings	Burnley	11	▓▓▓▓▓▓▓▓▓▓▓
L Ulloa	Leicester	11	▓▓▓▓▓▓▓▓▓▓▓
C Eriksen	Tottenham	10	▓▓▓▓▓▓▓▓▓▓
R Lukaku	Everton	10	▓▓▓▓▓▓▓▓▓▓

Over 2.5 goals

	H	A	%
Tottenham	12	15	71%
Arsenal	13	11	63%
QPR	9	15	63%
Man City	10	12	58%
Man United	13	8	55%

Under 2.5 goals

	H	A	%
Sunderland	12	13	66%
Burnley	13	11	63%
Hull	12	12	63%
Southampton	11	13	63%
Swansea, Aston Villa			58%

Both to score

	H	A	%
Arsenal	10	12	58%
Crystal Palace	12	10	58%
Man United	11	11	58%
QPR	10	12	58%
Tottenham	10	12	58%

Both not to score

	H	A	%
Southampton	14	11	66%
Aston Villa	9	15	63%
West Brom	12	12	63%
Burnley	11	12	61%
Hull	11	12	61%

Premier League results 2014-15

	Arsenal	Aston Villa	Burnley	Chelsea	Crystal Palace	Everton	Hull	Leicester	Liverpool	Man City	Man United	Newcastle	QPR	Southampton	Stoke	Sunderland	Swansea	Tottenham	West Brom	West Ham
Arsenal		5-0	3-0	0-0	2-1	2-0	2-2	2-1	4-1	2-2	1-2	4-1	2-1	1-0	3-0	0-0	0-1	1-1	4-1	3-0
Aston Villa	0-3		0-1	1-2	0-0	3-2	2-1	2-1	0-2	0-2	1-1	0-0	3-3	1-1	1-2	0-0	0-1	1-2	2-1	1-0
Burnley	0-1	1-1		1-3	2-3	1-3	1-0	0-1	0-1	1-0	0-0	1-1	2-1	1-0	0-0	0-0	0-1	0-0	2-2	1-3
Chelsea	2-0	3-0	1-1		1-0	1-0	2-0	2-0	1-1	1-1	1-0	2-0	2-1	1-1	2-1	3-1	4-2	3-0	2-0	2-0
Crystal Palace	1-2	0-1	0-0	1-2		0-1	0-2	2-0	3-1	2-1	1-2	1-1	3-1	1-3	1-1	1-3	1-0	2-1	0-2	1-3
Everton	2-2	3-0	1-0	3-6	2-3		1-1	2-2	0-0	1-1	3-0	3-0	3-1	1-0	0-1	0-2	0-0	0-1	0-0	2-1
Hull	1-3	2-0	1-0	2-3	2-0	2-0		0-1	1-0	2-4	0-0	0-3	2-1	0-1	1-1	1-1	1-0	1-2	0-0	2-2
Leicester	1-1	1-0	2-2	1-3	0-1	2-2	0-0		1-3	0-1	5-3	3-0	5-1	2-0	0-1	0-0	2-0	1-2	0-1	2-1
Liverpool	2-2	0-1	2-0	1-2	1-3	1-1	0-0	2-2		2-1	1-2	2-0	2-1	2-1	1-0	0-0	4-1	3-2	2-1	2-0
Man City	0-2	3-2	2-2	1-1	3-0	1-0	1-1	2-0	3-1		1-0	5-0	6-0	2-0	0-1	3-2	2-1	4-1	3-0	2-0
Man United	1-1	3-1	3-1	1-1	1-0	2-1	3-0	3-1	3-0	4-2		3-1	4-0	0-1	2-1	2-0	1-2	3-0	0-1	2-1
Newcastle	1-2	1-0	3-3	2-1	3-3	3-2	2-2	1-0	1-0	0-2	0-1		1-0	1-2	1-1	0-1	2-3	1-3	1-1	2-0
QPR	1-2	2-0	2-0	0-1	0-0	1-2	0-1	3-2	2-3	2-2	0-2	2-1		0-1	2-2	1-0	1-1	1-2	3-2	0-0
Southampton	2-0	6-1	2-0	1-1	1-0	3-0	2-0	2-0	0-2	0-3	1-2	4-0	2-1		1-0	8-0	0-1	2-2	0-0	0-0
Stoke	3-2	0-1	1-2	0-2	1-2	0-1	1-0	1-0	6-1	1-4	1-1	1-0	3-1	2-1		1-1	2-1	3-0	2-0	2-2
Sunderland	0-2	0-4	2-0	0-0	1-4	1-1	1-3	0-0	0-1	1-4	1-1	1-0	0-2	2-1	3-1		0-0	2-2	0-0	1-1
Swansea	2-1	1-0	1-0	0-5	1-1	1-1	3-1	2-0	0-1	2-4	2-1	2-2	2-0	0-1	2-0	1-1		1-2	3-0	1-1
Tottenham	2-1	0-1	2-1	5-3	0-0	2-1	2-0	4-3	0-3	0-1	0-0	1-2	4-0	1-0	1-2	2-1	3-2		0-1	2-2
West Brom	0-1	1-0	4-0	3-0	2-2	0-2	1-0	2-3	0-0	1-3	2-2	0-2	1-4	1-0	1-0	2-2	2-0	0-3		1-2
West Ham	1-2	0-0	1-0	0-1	1-3	1-2	3-0	2-0	3-1	2-1	1-1	1-0	2-0	1-3	1-1	1-0	3-1	0-1	1-1	

Record when first to score

		P	W	D	L	F	A	Sup	PGA	Pts
1	Man City	26	22	3	1	67	21	+1.77	2.7	69
2	Man Utd	23	19	2	2	49	19	+1.30	2.6	59
3	Southampton	20	17	2	1	35	9	+1.30	2.6	53
4	Chelsea	28	21	6	1	60	22	+1.36	2.5	69
5	Arsenal	26	21	3	2	61	21	+1.54	2.5	66
6	Tottenham	18	14	2	2	35	17	+1.00	2.4	44
7	Stoke	16	12	3	1	32	12	+1.25	2.4	39
8	Liverpool	23	17	3	3	43	21	+0.96	2.3	54
9	QPR	8	5	3	0	19	12	+0.88	2.3	18
10	Swansea	19	13	2	4	26	12	+0.74	2.2	41
11	West Brom	16	11	2	3	25	11	+0.88	2.2	35
12	Crystal Palace	11	7	3	1	23	12	+1.00	2.2	24
13	West Ham	17	10	5	2	27	17	+0.59	2.1	35
14	Aston Villa	14	9	3	2	21	11	+0.71	2.1	30
15	Newcastle	13	8	3	2	21	11	+0.77	2.1	27
16	Burnley	11	7	2	2	15	12	+0.27	2.1	23
17	Everton	19	11	5	3	37	23	+0.74	2	38
18	Leicester	14	9	1	4	24	13	+0.79	2	28
19	Hull	13	7	5	1	20	10	+0.77	2	26
20	Sunderland	15	7	5	3	24	29	-0.33	1.7	26

Record when keeping a clean sheet

		P	W	D	F	Sup	PGA	Pts
1	Man City	14	14	0	34	+2.43	3.0	42
2	Chelsea	17	15	2	30	+1.76	2.8	47
3	Stoke	9	8	1	12	+1.33	2.8	25
4	Newcastle	8	7	1	11	+1.38	2.8	22
5	Southampton	15	13	2	29	+1.93	2.7	41
6	Arsenal	13	11	2	26	+2.00	2.7	35
7	Swansea	13	11	2	16	+1.23	2.7	35
8	Man Utd	11	8	3	19	+1.73	2.5	27
9	West Brom	16	11	5	18	+1.13	2.4	38
10	Liverpool	14	10	4	17	+1.21	2.4	34
11	Everton	10	7	3	14	+1.40	2.4	24
12	Leicester	10	7	3	11	+1.10	2.4	24
13	Tottenham	9	6	3	12	+1.33	2.3	21
14	West Ham	9	6	3	10	+1.11	2.3	21
15	QPR	6	4	2	7	+1.17	2.3	14
16	Hull	10	6	4	10	+1.00	2.2	22
17	Aston Villa	10	6	4	9	+0.90	2.2	22
18	Burnley	10	5	5	5	+0.50	2.0	20
19	Crystal Palace	7	3	4	4	+0.57	1.9	13
20	Sunderland	13	4	9	6	+0.46	1.6	21

Watertight Middlesbrough can navigate a safe route through treacherous waters

Bournemouth did the bookies a favour by claiming the Championship title at 25-1 last season, and many will be wondering whether they should go for another dark horse this year or play it safe, writes Dan Sait. Of course, that ignores the fact that there is no safe play in a division that hasn't seen a favourite oblige since 2002, and there's a case to be made for simply avoiding any team at single-figure odds in this section.

Certainly odds of 11-2 and 8-1 for Derby and Hull lack appeal. Both are big clubs with strong squads but there must be doubts over Derby's ability to go again after suffering consecutive promotion meltdowns, while the Tigers went down with a whimper in May and their squad may yet get picked apart.

Another market leader to be wary of are Brentford who impressed last term but have since changed both manager and direction.

Middlesbrough, however, look a fair price at 11-1. They misfired in the playoff final but have shown steady progression under Aitor Karanka. The former Real Madrid assistant has built from the back since taking charge and Boro's record of just 37 goals conceded last season was eight better than second-best Bournemouth. A little more guile needs adding to the squad and a bit more bravery is required on the road, but Boro start from a solid base and last term's impressive FA Cup win at Man City highlights their potential.

The 9-2 for Burnley to win promotion also looks very reasonable. They only finished two points below Hull last term and always seemed to be treating their season in the top tier as an opportunity to cash in and build for the future. Danny Ings' departure will be felt but the club is stable, superbly managed by Sean Dyche and should now be able to throw a few quid at strengthening the front line.

At the other end of the division, things look wide open. All three promoted teams are capable of staying up, while the second and third favourites for the drop, Huddersfield and Charlton, also lack appeal at the prices.

The Terriers started 2014-15 in shambolic fashion but finished a comfortable 16th after Chris Powell came in and turned things around, while Charlton simply look far too short at 5-2. The Addicks may swap managers with every full moon but that hasn't stopped them finishing well clear of the drop in each of the last three seasons.

Birmingham are another side to swerve as they have thrived under Gary Rowett, but one favourite who look worth their place is Rotherham. Whether you want to wait all season for a 7-4 return is a different question.

The lack of appeal among the favourites opens the door for a big-name casualty, and it could be Bolton who struggle.

Wanderers have regressed steadily since their relegation in 2012, finishing seventh, 14th and then 18th. Money is an issue and morale at the club appears fragile, so 6-1 about Bolton dropping looks attractive.

At 12-1, QPR may be of interest to big-price hunters. A troubled club facing a huge amount of rebuilding must be of interest but, admittedly, it would still take quite a collapse for them to go down. However, they'll be a team to get after on a game-by-game basis as the bookies have long overrated Rangers.

Boro's George Friend revels in last season's victory over Derby

BIRMINGHAM

Nickname: Blues
Colours: Blue
Ground: St Andrews (29,409)
Tel: 0844-557-1875   www.bcfc.com

Lee Clark rarely convinced as Birmingham boss and the club was second-bottom and smarting from an 8-0 home defeat when Gary Rowett replaced him in October.

It was a no-lose situation for the new man but Rowett instantly reversed Blues' fortunes and eventually finished tenth.

This campaign will be a truer test of Rowett's fledgling managerial credentials but he hasn't put a foot wrong so far and there's even hope that the long-running ownership issue might finally be resolved.

Longest run without win/loss: 8/6
High/low league position: 10/23
Clean sheets: 12 **Yellows:** 57 **Reds:** 6
Avg attendance: 16,334 **Players used:** 31
Leading scorer: C Donaldson 15 (6,11)
Key stat: Birmingham's points-per-game average rose from 0.79 before Rowett arrived to 1.63 under him

	2014-15 H	A	P	W	D	L	OV	UN	BS	CS
Hull			3	0	2	1	1	2	1	2
Burnley			4	2	2	0	4	0	4	0
QPR			1	0	0	1	0	1	0	0
Middlesbrough	D	L	4	2	2	0	3	1	3	1
Brentford	W	D	1	1	0	0	0	1	0	1
Ipswich	D	L	4	1	2	1	2	2	3	0
Wolves	W	D	4	2	1	1	3	1	4	0
Derby	L	D	4	1	2	1	4	0	3	0
Blackburn	D	L	5	2	2	1	4	1	5	0
Birmingham										
Cardiff	D	L	3	0	2	1	0	3	1	1
Charlton	W	D	3	1	1	1	0	3	1	1
Sheffield Weds	L	D	3	1	1	1	1	2	1	1
Nottm Forest	W	W	4	2	1	1	3	1	3	1
Leeds	D	D	4	2	1	1	1	3	2	2
Huddersfield	D	W	3	0	1	2	1	2	2	0
Fulham	L	D	3	1	0	2	1	2	1	1
Bolton	L	W	5	2	0	3	4	1	4	0
Reading	W	W	3	2	0	1	2	1	2	1
Brighton	W	L	4	1	2	1	1	3	1	2
Rotherham	W	W	1	1	0	0	1	0	1	0
Bristol City			2	1	1	0	1	1	1	1
MK Dons			-	-	-	-	-	-	-	-
Preston			-	-	-	-	-	-	-	-

Season	Division	Pos	P	W	D	L	F	A	GD	Pts
2014-15	Championship	10	46	16	15	15	54	64	-10	63
2013-14	Championship	21	46	11	11	24	58	74	-16	44
2012-13	Championship	12	46	15	16	15	63	69	-6	61

Over/Under 41%/59% 19th   **Both score** 50%/50% 12th

BLACKBURN

Nickname: Rovers
Colours: Blue and white
Ground: Ewood Park (31,154)
Tel: 01254-372-001   www.rovers.co.uk

After finishing two points and two places outside the top six in 2014, Blackburn underachieved last season, dropping back to finish 11 points off the playoffs.

It was a missed opportunity as a talented but relatively inexperienced side failed to pick up a lot of the easier points, claiming just 23 of a possible 42 against the bottom seven sides.

Transfer plans will be hampered by the club's Financial Fair Play restrictions but a fairly young squad should improve.

Longest run without win/loss: 5/9
High/low league position: 6/13
Clean sheets: 10 **Yellows:** 71 **Reds:** 2
Avg attendance: 16,047 **Players used:** 30
Leading scorer: J Rhodes 21 (7,18)
Key stat: Wolves were the only top-ten team to secure fewer points against the bottom seven sides than Blackburn

	2014-15 H	A	P	W	D	L	OV	UN	BS	CS
Hull			2	2	0	0	0	2	0	2
Burnley			3	1	1	1	2	1	3	0
QPR			2	2	0	0	1	1	1	1
Middlesbrough	D	D	3	1	1	1	1	2	1	2
Brentford	L	L	1	0	0	1	1	0	1	0
Ipswich	W	D	3	3	0	0	1	2	1	2
Wolves	L	L	5	2	0	3	3	2	2	1
Derby	L	L	3	1	1	1	1	2	2	1
Blackburn										
Birmingham	W	D	5	2	2	1	2	3	4	1
Cardiff	D	D	2	0	1	1	1	1	2	0
Charlton	W	W	3	1	0	2	1	2	1	1
Sheffield Weds	L	W	3	1	1	1	1	2	1	2
Nottm Forest	D	W	3	1	1	1	2	1	1	1
Leeds	W	W	3	2	1	0	1	2	1	2
Huddersfield	D	D	3	1	2	0	0	3	0	3
Fulham	W	W	4	3	1	0	2	2	3	1
Bolton	W	L	6	4	0	2	4	2	3	3
Reading	W	D	2	1	1	0	1	1	1	1
Brighton	L	D	3	0	2	1	1	2	2	0
Rotherham	W	L	1	1	0	0	1	0	1	0
Bristol City			1	1	0	0	0	1	0	1
MK Dons			-	-	-	-	-	-	-	-
Preston			-	-	-	-	-	-	-	-

Season	Division	Pos	P	W	D	L	F	A	GD	Pts
2014-15	Championship	9	46	17	16	13	66	59	+7	67
2013-14	Championship	8	46	18	16	12	70	62	+8	70
2012-13	Championship	17	46	14	16	16	55	62	-7	58

Over/Under 54%/46% 9th   **Both score** 67%/33% 1st

BOLTON

Nickname: The Trotters
Colours: White and blue
Ground: The Macron Stadium (28,100)
Tel: 0844-871-2932   www.bwfc.co.uk

Bolton are still struggling with the financial fallout of their 2012 relegation as they can no longer offer the same wages or fees as many of their competitors.

Also limiting ambition is a habit of starting the season in first gear, and a return of just five points from Bolton's first ten games cost Dougie Freedman his job. Neil Lennon came in and steered the club clear of the drop, but his honeymoon period wore off to leave Bolton claiming just three wins from their final 16 games.

Longest run without win/loss: 6/8
High/low league position: 13/24
Clean sheets: 10 **Yellows:** 79 **Reds:** 2
Avg attendance: 16,455 **Players used:** 44
Leading scorer: A Le Fondre 8 (1,7)
Key stat: Bolton had the second-worst away record in the division, losing 15 games

	2014-15 H	2014-15 A	P	W	D	L	OV	UN	BS	CS
Hull			2	1	1	0	2	0	2	0
Burnley			3	2	0	1	1	2	1	1
QPR			2	1	0	1	1	1	1	0
Middlesbrough	L	L	3	1	1	1	3	0	3	0
Brentford	W	D	1	1	0	0	1	0	1	0
Ipswich	D	L	3	0	2	1	1	2	2	1
Wolves	D	L	5	3	2	0	1	4	2	3
Derby	L	L	3	1	1	1	2	1	1	1
Blackburn	W	L	6	5	0	1	4	2	3	2
Birmingham	L	W	5	2	2	1	4	1	4	0
Cardiff	W	W	2	2	0	0	2	0	1	1
Charlton	D	L	3	1	2	0	0	3	2	1
Sheffield Weds	D	W	3	0	2	1	0	3	1	1
Nottm Forest	D	L	3	0	3	0	2	1	3	0
Leeds	D	L	3	0	2	1	1	2	2	0
Huddersfield	W	L	3	2	0	1	0	3	0	2
Fulham	W	L	4	1	2	1	2	2	1	2
Bolton										
Reading	D	D	2	0	2	0	0	2	2	0
Brighton	W	L	3	2	0	1	0	3	0	2
Rotherham	W	L	1	1	0	0	1	0	1	0
Bristol City			1	1	0	0	1	0	1	0
MK Dons			-	-	-	-	-	-	-	-
Preston			-	-	-	-	-	-	-	-

Season	Division	Pos	P	W	D	L	F	A	GD	Pts
2014-15	Championship	18	46	13	12	21	54	67	-13	51
2013-14	Championship	14	46	14	17	15	59	60	-1	59
2012-13	Championship	7	46	18	14	14	69	61	+8	68

Over/Under 54%/46% 9th   **Both score** 57%/43% 7th

BRENTFORD

Nickname: The Bees
Colours: Red
Ground: Griffin Park (12,763)
Tel: 0845-3456-442   www.brentfordfc.co.uk

Brentford impressed last season and very nearly achieved successive promotions.

A new stadium is on the horizon and owner Matthew Benham is a willing investor, but the club will have to adapt to a significant change in style after Benham dismissed manager Mark Warburton.

A lack of agreement over recruitment policy was a major cause of the split but Benham's statistics-led approach also seems to favour long-ball tactics and set pieces to Warburton's slick passing style.

Longest run without win/loss: 4/5
High/low league position: 3/14
Clean sheets: 11 **Yellows:** 75 **Reds:** 2
Avg attendance: 14,334 **Players used:** 25
Leading scorer: A Gray 16 (5,15)
Key stat: Griffin Park saw an average of 3.21 goals per game in 2014-15 – the equal-most in the division

	2014-15 H	2014-15 A	P	W	D	L	OV	UN	BS	CS
Hull			-	-	-	-	-	-	-	-
Burnley			-	-	-	-	-	-	-	-
QPR			-	-	-	-	-	-	-	-
Middlesbrough	L	L	1	0	0	1	0	1	0	0
Brentford										
Ipswich	L	D	1	0	0	1	1	0	1	0
Wolves	W	L	2	1	0	1	2	0	0	1
Derby	W	D	1	1	0	0	1	0	1	0
Blackburn	W	W	1	1	0	0	1	0	1	0
Birmingham	D	L	1	0	0	1	0	1	1	0
Cardiff	L	W	1	0	0	1	1	0	1	0
Charlton	D	L	4	1	2	1	1	3	3	0
Sheffield Weds	D	L	3	1	1	1	1	2	1	2
Nottm Forest	D	W	1	0	1	0	1	0	1	0
Leeds	W	W	2	1	1	0	0	2	0	2
Huddersfield	W	L	4	2	0	2	3	1	1	1
Fulham	W	W	1	1	0	0	1	0	1	0
Bolton	D	L	1	0	1	0	1	0	1	0
Reading	W	W	1	1	0	0	1	0	1	0
Brighton	W	W	3	1	1	1	1	2	1	1
Rotherham	W	W	2	1	0	1	0	2	0	1
Bristol City			1	1	0	0	1	0	1	0
MK Dons			5	2	2	1	4	1	4	0
Preston			-	-	-	-	-	-	-	-

Season	Division	Pos	P	W	D	L	F	A	GD	Pts
2014-15	Championship	5	46	23	9	14	78	59	+19	78
2013-14	League 1	2	46	28	10	8	72	43	+29	94
2012-13	League 1	3	46	21	16	9	62	47	+15	79

Over/Under 65%/35% 2nd   **Both score** 61%/39% 3rd

BRIGHTON

Nickname: The Seagulls
Colours: Blue and white
Ground: Falmar Stadium (30,750)
Tel: 0344-324-6282   www.seagulls.co.uk

After two seasons contesting the playoffs, Brighton regressed to the point that they struggled against relegation last term.

Mere survival isn't what Tony Bloom would have expected from his significant investment but his appointment of Sami Hyypia as manager always looked like a gamble that might not pay off.

Replacement Chris Hughton looks a far better bet but he has plenty of damage to repair and there's no guarantee he will propel Brighton back into the playoff mix.

Longest run without win/loss: 11/4
High/low league position: 16/22
Clean sheets: 14 **Yellows:** 93 **Reds:** 5
Avg attendance: 25,645 **Players used:** 35
Leading scorer: Joao Teixeira 6 (2,4)
Key stat: Chris Hughton won just six of his 22 matches as Brighton manager, losing ten

BRISTOL CITY

Nickname: The Robins
Colours: Red and white
Ground: Ashton Gate (13,414)
Tel: 0117-963-0600   www.bcfc.co.uk

Robins fans enjoyed a glorious 2014-15 as their team treated them to an attractive brand of attacking football that claimed the League One title with relative ease.

A Football League Trophy success was the cherry on top of a wonderful season and a huge amount of credit must go to manager Steve Cotterill, who entered the dugout in December 2013 when the club was second-bottom in League One.

It would be no surprise if City's upward trajectory continued in the second tier.

Longest run without win/loss: 2/16
High/low league position: 1/2
Clean sheets: 20 **Yellows:** 47 **Reds:** 2
Avg attendance: 12,056 **Players used:** 24
Leading scorer: A Wilbraham 18 (6,16)
Key stat: Bristol City finished 2014-15 on a 16-match unbeaten run

| | 2014-15 | | Last six seasons at home | | | | | | | |
	H	A	P	W	D	L	OV	UN	BS	CS
Hull			2	1	1	0	0	2	0	2
Burnley			3	2	0	1	0	3	0	2
QPR			1	1	0	0	0	1	0	1
Middlesbrough	L	D	4	0	1	3	1	3	2	0
Brentford	L	L	3	2	0	1	1	2	0	2
Ipswich	W	L	4	2	1	1	2	2	2	1
Wolves	D	D	2	1	1	0	0	2	1	1
Derby	W	L	4	3	0	1	2	2	2	2
Blackburn	D	W	3	1	2	0	1	2	2	1
Birmingham	W	L	4	2	1	1	1	3	2	1
Cardiff	D	D	3	0	3	0	1	2	2	1
Charlton	D	W	5	1	3	1	2	3	2	2
Sheffield Weds	L	D	4	2	1	1	1	3	1	2
Nottm Forest	L	D	4	1	1	2	2	2	2	2
Leeds	W	W	5	2	2	1	3	2	2	2
Huddersfield	D	D	5	1	3	1	2	3	2	3
Fulham	L	W	1	0	0	1	1	0	1	0
Bolton	W	L	3	2	1	0	2	1	3	0
Reading	D	L	3	0	2	1	1	2	2	0
Brighton										
Rotherham	D	L	1	0	1	0	0	1	1	0
Bristol City			2	2	0	0	0	2	0	2
MK Dons			2	1	0	1	0	2	0	1
Preston			-	-	-	-	-	-	-	-

Season	Division	Pos	P	W	D	L	F	A	GD	Pts
2014-15	Championship	20	46	10	17	19	44	54	-10	47
2013-14	Championship	6	46	19	15	12	55	40	+15	72
2012-13	Championship	4	46	19	18	9	69	43	+26	75

Over/Under 30%/70% 24th   **Both score** 43%/57% 21st

| | 2014-15 | | Last six seasons at home | | | | | | | |
	H	A	P	W	D	L	OV	UN	BS	CS
Hull			3	1	1	1	2	1	2	1
Burnley			3	2	0	1	2	1	2	1
QPR			2	1	1	0	0	2	1	1
Middlesbrough			4	2	0	2	2	2	1	1
Brentford			1	0	0	1	1	0	1	0
Ipswich			4	1	1	2	2	1	1	1
Wolves			2	0	0	2	2	0	2	0
Derby			4	2	1	1	1	3	2	1
Blackburn			1	0	0	1	1	0	1	0
Birmingham			2	0	0	2	0	2	0	0
Cardiff			4	2	0	2	4	0	2	1
Charlton			1	0	0	1	0	1	0	0
Sheffield Weds			2	0	2	0	2	0	2	0
Nottm Forest			4	1	2	1	1	3	2	2
Leeds			3	0	0	3	2	1	1	0
Huddersfield			1	0	0	1	1	0	1	0
Fulham			-	-	-	-	-	-	-	-
Bolton			1	0	0	1	1	0	1	0
Reading			3	1	1	1	1	2	2	1
Brighton			2	0	1	1	0	2	0	1
Rotherham			1	0	0	1	1	0	1	0
Bristol City										
MK Dons	W	D	2	1	1	0	2	0	2	0
Preston	L	D	4	1	2	1	1	3	3	0

Season	Division	Pos	P	W	D	L	F	A	GD	Pts
2014-15	League 1	1	46	29	12	5	96	38	+58	99
2013-14	League 1	12	46	13	19	14	70	67	+3	58
2012-13	Championship	24	46	11	8	27	59	84	-25	41

Over/Under 59%/41% 3rd   **Both score** 50%/50% 14th

BURNLEY

Nickname: The Clarets
Colours: Claret and blue
Ground: Turf Moor (21,401)
Tel: 0871-221-1882   www.burnleyfootballclub.com

The finances weren't quite in place for Burnley to survive in the top tier but last season sets them up nicely for the future.

Danny Ings' departure further weakens a lightweight attack but Burnley now have the cash to rebuild the front line, and the stability of the club and excellence of manager Sean Dyche means the Clarets will be optimistic of bouncing back.

The combination of Dyche's managerial skills with a few quality squad additions should make Burnley serious challengers.

Longest run without win/loss: 10/4
High/low league position: 17/20
Clean sheets: 10 **Yellows:** 65 **Reds:** 2
Avg attendance: 19,131 **Players used:** 24
Leading scorer: D Ings 11 (3,10)
Key stat: Burnley only lost by more than two goals in two of their 38 Premier League games last season

	2014-15 H	A	P	W	D	L	OV	UN	BS	CS
Hull	W	W	5	4	0	1	1	4	0	4
Burnley										
QPR	W	L	3	2	1	0	1	2	1	2
Middlesbrough			4	1	1	2	1	3	1	1
Brentford			-	-	-	-	-	-	-	-
Ipswich			4	3	0	1	2	2	1	3
Wolves			2	1	0	1	1	1	1	1
Derby			4	3	0	1	0	1	3	3
Blackburn			3	0	2	1	0	3	2	0
Birmingham			4	2	0	2	4	0	3	1
Cardiff			3	0	3	0	0	3	3	0
Charlton			2	1	0	1	1	1	0	1
Sheffield Weds			2	0	2	0	1	1	2	0
Nottm Forest			4	3	1	0	2	2	3	1
Leeds			4	2	0	2	3	1	3	1
Huddersfield			2	1	0	1	1	1	1	0
Fulham			1	0	1	0	0	1	1	0
Bolton			3	1	2	0	0	3	2	1
Reading			3	1	0	2	2	1	1	0
Brighton			3	1	1	1	1	2	1	2
Rotherham			-	-	-	-	-	-	-	-
Bristol City			3	1	2	0	1	2	2	1
MK Dons			-	-	-	-	-	-	-	-
Preston			1	1	0	0	1	0	1	0

Season	Division	Pos	P	W	D	L	F	A	GD	Pts
2014-15	Premier League	19	38	7	12	19	28	53	-25	33
2013-14	Championship	2	46	26	15	5	72	37	+35	93
2012-13	Championship	11	46	16	13	17	62	60	+2	61

Over/Under 37%/63% 17th   **Both score** 39%/61% 16th

CARDIFF

Nickname: The Bluebirds
Colours: Blue
Ground: Cardiff City Stadium (33,280)
Tel: 0845-365-1115   www.cardiffcityfc.co.uk

The return to blue bought owner Vincent Tan a truce with rebellious Cardiff fans but they simply turned their ire on Russell Slade who was accused of implementing an ugly, direct style of football after he replaced Ole Gunnar Solskjaer.

However, the squad seems to be behind Slade and he is probably better judged after a full summer to implement his methods. The wage bill needs reducing, which could hinder Slade's progress, but he has a solid base to work from.

Longest run without win/loss: 7/5
High/low league position: 8/17
Clean sheets: 10 **Yellows:** 68 **Reds:** 4
Avg attendance: 21,124 **Players used:** 38
Leading scorer: K Jones 11 (2,10)
Key stat: Cardiff were the only Championship team outside the bottom nine not to manage more than two consecutive wins last season

	2014-15 H	A	P	W	D	L	OV	UN	BS	CS
Hull			4	2	0	2	3	1	1	1
Burnley			3	1	2	0	1	2	1	2
QPR			2	0	1	1	1	1	1	0
Middlesbrough	L	L	5	2	0	3	2	3	1	2
Brentford	L	W	1	0	0	1	1	0	1	0
Ipswich	W	L	5	1	2	2	3	2	3	1
Wolves	L	L	2	1	0	1	1	1	1	0
Derby	L	D	5	3	1	1	2	3	3	1
Blackburn	D	D	2	1	1	0	1	1	1	1
Birmingham	W	D	3	3	0	0	1	2	1	2
Cardiff										
Charlton	L	D	2	0	1	1	1	1	1	1
Sheffield Weds	W	D	3	3	0	0	2	1	2	1
Nottm Forest	W	W	5	3	1	1	2	3	2	2
Leeds	W	W	4	3	1	0	3	1	4	0
Huddersfield	W	D	2	2	0	0	1	1	1	1
Fulham	W	D	2	2	0	0	1	1	1	1
Bolton	L	L	2	0	1	1	1	1	1	0
Reading	W	D	4	2	2	0	3	1	3	1
Brighton	D	D	3	0	1	2	1	2	1	1
Rotherham	D	W	1	0	1	0	0	1	0	1
Bristol City			4	4	0	0	4	0	3	1
MK Dons			-	-	-	-	-	-	-	-
Preston			2	1	1	0	0	2	1	1

Season	Division	Pos	P	W	D	L	F	A	GD	Pts
2014-15	Championship	11	46	16	14	16	57	61	-4	62
2013-14	Premier League	20	38	7	9	22	32	74	-42	30
2012-13	Championship	1	46	25	12	9	72	45	+27	87

Over/Under 48%/52% 14th   **Both score** 61%/39% 3rd

CHARLTON

Nickname: Addicks
Colours: Red and white
Ground: The Valley (27,111)
Tel: 020-8333-4000   www.cafc.co.uk

Addicks fans don't get long to familiarise themselves with their managers, but that doesn't seem to be hurting the team.

Bob Peeters had Charlton flirting with the playoff places but a slew of injuries and a drop in form saw Charlton go nine games without a win and Peeters sacked.

Replacement Guy Luzon did help push up the points-per-game ratio marginally (from 1.19 to 1.45) but it's worth noting that six of Luzon's eight wins as Charlton manager came against bottom-half sides.

Longest run without win/loss: 13/11
High/low league position: 5/20
Clean sheets: 10 **Yellows:** 62 **Reds:** 2
Avg attendance: 16,708 **Players used:** 32
Leading scorer: I Vetokele 11 (4,10)
Key stat: Only Sheffield Wednesday could match Charlton's 18 draws last term. They shared identical W14, D18, L14, GD -6 records

	2014-15 H	A	Last six seasons at home P	W	D	L	OV	UN	BS	CS
Hull			1	0	1	0	0	1	0	1
Burnley			2	0	0	2	1	1	0	0
QPR			1	1	0	0	0	1	0	1
Middlesbrough	D	L	3	0	1	2	1	2	1	1
Brentford	W	D	4	3	0	1	1	3	0	3
Ipswich	L	L	3	0	0	3	1	2	1	0
Wolves	D	D	2	1	1	0	1	1	2	0
Derby	W	L	3	1	1	1	1	2	2	0
Blackburn	L	L	3	0	1	2	2	1	3	0
Birmingham	D	L	3	0	2	1	0	3	2	0
Cardiff	D	W	2	1	1	0	1	1	2	0
Charlton										
Sheffield Weds	D	D	5	1	3	1	1	4	4	1
Nottm Forest	W	D	3	1	1	1	1	2	2	0
Leeds	W	D	4	3	0	1	3	1	3	1
Huddersfield	W	D	6	3	2	1	2	4	2	3
Fulham	D	L	1	0	1	0	0	1	1	0
Bolton	W	D	3	2	1	0	2	1	2	1
Reading	W	W	2	1	0	1	1	1	1	0
Brighton	L	D	5	1	1	3	4	1	3	0
Rotherham	D	D	1	0	1	0	0	1	1	0
Bristol City			1	1	0	0	1	0	1	0
MK Dons			3	3	0	0	2	1	2	1
Preston			1	1	0	0	1	0	1	0

Season	Division	Pos	P	W	D	L	F	A	GD	Pts
2014-15	Championship	12	46	14	18	14	54	60	-6	60
2013-14	Championship	18	46	13	12	21	41	61	-20	51
2012-13	Championship	9	46	17	14	15	65	59	+6	65

Over/Under 48%/52% 14th   **Both score** 57%/43% 7th

DERBY

Nickname: The Rams
Colours: White and black
Ground: Pride Park Stadium (33,597)
Tel: 0871-472-1884   www.dcfc.co.uk

After two years of promotion heartbreak there must now be question marks over the psychological impact of that failure.

Derby spent 56 days at the top of the table before capitulating, with a run of just two wins from their final 13 games leaving them a point outside the playoffs.

An injury crisis, the loss of loanee Jordon Ibe and run-in nerves all played a part but Steve McClaren paid with his job. Former Real Madrid and PSG assistant manager Paul Clement replaces him.

Longest run without win/loss: 7/10
High/low league position: 1/9
Clean sheets: 17 **Yellows:** 77 **Reds:** 3
Avg attendance: 29,232 **Players used:** 31
Leading scorer: C Martin 18 (8,14)
Key stat: Derby were in the top six every day of the season from September until the very last day, when they dropped to eighth

	2014-15 H	A	Last six seasons at home P	W	D	L	OV	UN	BS	CS
Hull			3	0	0	3	1	2	1	0
Burnley			4	0	0	4	4	0	3	0
QPR			3	1	1	1	2	1	2	1
Middlesbrough	L	L	6	3	1	2	4	2	4	0
Brentford	D	L	1	0	1	0	0	1	1	0
Ipswich	D	W	6	0	3	3	3	3	4	1
Wolves	W	L	2	1	1	0	1	1	0	2
Derby										
Blackburn	W	W	3	1	2	0	0	3	2	1
Birmingham	D	W	4	2	2	0	3	1	4	0
Cardiff	D	W	5	1	2	2	3	2	3	1
Charlton	W	L	3	3	0	0	2	1	1	2
Sheffield Weds	W	D	4	3	1	0	4	0	2	2
Nottm Forest	L	D	6	3	1	2	2	4	2	3
Leeds	W	L	5	5	0	0	3	2	3	2
Huddersfield	W	L	3	3	0	0	3	0	2	1
Fulham	W	L	1	1	0	0	1	0	1	0
Bolton	W	W	3	1	2	0	1	2	2	1
Reading	L	W	5	1	0	4	4	1	3	0
Brighton	W	L	4	2	1	1	3	0	3	
Rotherham	W	D	1	1	0	0	0	1	0	1
Bristol City			4	3	0	1	2	2	1	2
MK Dons			-	-	-	-	-	-	-	-
Preston			2	2	0	0	2	0	1	1

Season	Division	Pos	P	W	D	L	F	A	GD	Pts
2014-15	Championship	8	46	21	14	11	85	56	+29	77
2013-14	Championship	3	46	25	10	11	84	52	+32	85
2012-13	Championship	10	46	16	13	17	65	62	+3	61

Over/Under 52%/48% 12th   **Both score** 48%/52% 18th

FULHAM

Nickname: The Cottagers
Colours: White and black
Ground: Craven Cottage (25,700)
Tel: 0843-208-1222   www.fulhamfc.com

Felix Magath took Fulham down in 2014 and that trajectory continued in the second tier, with his side taking just one point from their first eight games, so it was no surprise when he was sacked.

Kit Symons impressed sufficiently as caretaker boss to land his first permanent role in management, but results tailed off after Christmas and Fulham won just six of their final 24 matches.

Symons' priority must be to shore up a defence that leaked a massive 83 goals.

Longest run without win/loss: 8/6
High/low league position: 13/24
Clean sheets: 9 **Yellows:** 71 **Reds:** 7
Avg attendance: 18,376 **Players used:** 37
Leading scorer: R McCormack 17 (4,12)
Key stat: Fulham conceded three goals or more in over a quarter of their league games last season

	2014-15 H	A	P	W	D	L	OV	UN	BS	CS
Hull			2	1	1	0	1	1	1	1
Burnley			1	1	0	0	1	0	0	1
QPR			2	2	0	0	2	0	1	1
Middlesbrough	W	L	1	1	0	0	1	0	1	0
Brentford	L	L	1	0	0	1	1	0	1	0
Ipswich	L	L	1	0	0	1	1	0	1	0
Wolves	L	L	4	2	1	1	2	2	1	2
Derby	W	L	1	1	0	0	0	1	0	1
Blackburn	L	L	4	2	1	1	2	2	2	1
Birmingham	D	W	3	1	2	0	1	2	3	0
Cardiff	D	L	2	0	1	1	1	1	2	0
Charlton	W	D	1	1	0	0	1	0	0	1
Sheffield Weds	W	D	1	1	0	0	1	0	0	1
Nottm Forest	W	L	1	1	0	0	1	0	1	0
Leeds	L	W	1	0	0	1	1	0	0	0
Huddersfield	W	W	1	1	0	0	1	0	1	0
Fulham										
Bolton	W	L	4	3	1	0	2	2	1	3
Reading	W	L	2	1	0	1	2	0	2	0
Brighton	L	W	1	0	0	1	0	1	0	0
Rotherham	D	D	1	0	1	0	0	1	1	0
Bristol City			-	-	-	-	-	-	-	-
MK Dons			-	-	-	-	-	-	-	-
Preston			-	-	-	-	-	-	-	-

Season	Division	Pos	P	W	D	L	F	A	GD	Pts
2014-15	Championship	17	46	14	10	22	62	83	-21	52
2013-14	Premier League	19	38	9	5	24	40	85	-45	32
2012-13	Premier League	12	38	11	10	17	50	60	-10	43

Over/Under 59%/41% 4th   **Both score** 54%/46% 10th

HUDDERSFIELD

Nickname: The Terriers
Colours: Blue and white
Ground: John Smith's Stadium (24,500)
Tel: 01484-484-112   www.htafc.com

Huddersfield endured a rocky start to 2014-15 as manager Mark Robins was sent packing after the very first match – a 4-0 home defeat to Bournemouth.

It meant the Terriers kicked off from an unsteady platform as Chris Powell entered the dugout six games into the season with the Terriers having already lost four times, but the team regrouped well to stay clear of relegation thereafter.

Given a full pre-season of preparation, Powell will hope to push the team on.

Longest run without win/loss: 7/7
High/low league position: 12/22
Clean sheets: 10 **Yellows:** 70 **Reds:** 4
Avg attendance: 13,613 **Players used:** 36
Leading scorer: N Wells 11 (4,9)
Key stat: Only Blackpool, Fulham and Millwall conceded more goals than Huddersfield last season

	2014-15 H	A	P	W	D	L	OV	UN	BS	CS
Hull			1	0	0	1	0	1	0	0
Burnley			2	2	0	0	1	1	1	1
QPR			1	0	1	0	0	1	1	0
Middlesbrough	L	L	3	1	1	1	3	0	3	0
Brentford	W	L	4	2	2	0	3	1	3	1
Ipswich	W	D	3	1	1	1	2	1	1	1
Wolves	L	W	2	1	0	1	2	0	2	0
Derby	D	L	3	1	2	0	1	2	2	1
Blackburn	D	D	3	0	2	1	3	0	3	0
Birmingham	L	D	3	0	1	2	1	2	2	0
Cardiff	D	L	2	0	2	0	0	2	0	2
Charlton	D	L	6	3	2	1	2	4	4	1
Sheffield Weds	D	D	5	1	2	2	0	5	0	3
Nottm Forest	W	W	3	1	1	1	2	1	1	1
Leeds	L	L	4	1	1	2	4	0	4	0
Huddersfield										
Fulham	L	L	1	0	0	1	0	1	0	0
Bolton	W	L	3	1	1	1	2	1	2	0
Reading	W	W	2	1	0	1	1	0	1	1
Brighton	D	D	5	2	2	1	3	2	5	0
Rotherham	L	D	1	0	0	1	0	1	0	0
Bristol City			1	1	0	0	0	1	0	1
MK Dons			3	2	1	0	1	2	2	1
Preston			1	1	0	0	0	1	0	1

Season	Division	Pos	P	W	D	L	F	A	GD	Pts
2014-15	Championship	16	46	13	16	17	58	75	-17	55
2013-14	Championship	17	46	14	11	21	58	65	-7	53
2012-13	Championship	19	46	15	13	18	53	73	-20	58

Over/Under 61%/39% 3rd   **Both score** 59%/41% 6th

HULL

Nickname: The Tigers
Colours: Amber and black
Ground: The KC Stadium (25,586)
Tel: 01482-504-600   www.hullcityafc.net

Hull were well-organised but toothless as they were relegated from the top flight, and the likely departure of key players won't help their goalscoring troubles.

Injury to Nikica Jelavic was a factor but no-one stepped up to the plate and Hull's lack of goals highlighted the poor return the club have received for a significant transfer outlay in recent years.

However, while the personnel may change, the club remains on a sound financial footing and should regroup.

Longest run without win/loss: 10/3
High/low league position: 10/19
Clean sheets: 10 **Yellows:** 74 **Reds:** 6
Avg attendance: 23,557 **Players used:** 29
Leading scorer: N Jelavic 8 (4,8)
Key stat: Hull only once scored more than two goals in a Premier League game last term – only Burnley matched that poor record

	2014-15 H	A	P	W	D	L	OV	UN	BS	CS
Hull										
Burnley	L	L	5	0	0	5	2	3	2	0
QPR	W	W	2	1	1	0	1	1	1	1
Middlesbrough			3	2	0	1	2	1	2	1
Brentford			-	-	-	-	-	-	-	-
Ipswich			3	2	1	0	2	1	2	1
Wolves			2	1	1	0	2	0	2	0
Derby			3	2	0	1	2	1	1	1
Blackburn			2	1	1	0	0	2	0	2
Birmingham			3	2	0	1	2	1	2	0
Cardiff			4	1	2	1	2	2	3	0
Charlton			1	1	0	0	0	1	0	1
Sheffield Weds			1	0	0	1	1	0	1	0
Nottm Forest			3	1	1	1	2	1	2	1
Leeds			3	1	2	0	1	2	1	2
Huddersfield			1	1	0	0	0	1	0	1
Fulham			2	2	0	0	1	1	0	2
Bolton			2	2	0	0	1	1	1	1
Reading			2	1	1	0	0	2	1	1
Brighton			2	1	1	0	0	2	0	2
Rotherham			-	-	-	-	-	-	-	-
Bristol City			3	2	1	0	1	2	0	3
MK Dons			-	-	-	-	-	-	-	-
Preston			1	1	0	0	0	1	0	1

Season	Division	Pos	P	W	D	L	F	A	GD	Pts
2014-15	Premier League	18	38	8	11	19	33	51	-18	35
2013-14	Premier League	16	38	10	7	21	38	53	-15	37
2012-13	Championship	2	46	24	7	15	61	52	+9	79

Over/Under 37%/63% 17th   **Both score** 39%/61% 16th

IPSWICH

Nickname: Town/Tractor Boys
Colours: Blue and white
Ground: Portman Road (30,311)
Tel: 01473-400-500   www.itfc.co.uk

Mick McCarthy again inspired a club to overachieve, improving Ipswich's league position for a third-successive year. It did end with a galling playoff loss to Norwich but that shouldn't define a superb season.

McCarthy fully deserves his reputation as one of the division's top managers and while his team may not be the prettiest to watch, it is hardworking and effective.

It's unlikely 32-year Daryl Murphy will repeat his stunning goal return but there is depth to McCarthy's attacking options.

Longest run without win/loss: 5/11
High/low league position: 2/10
Clean sheets: 12 **Yellows:** 73 **Reds:** 0
Avg attendance: 19,603 **Players used:** 31
Leading scorer: D Murphy 27 (11,21)
Key stat: Ipswich had the second-best home record but only the tenth-best away record

	2014-15 H	A	P	W	D	L	OV	UN	BS	CS
Hull			3	0	1	2	1	2	2	0
Burnley			4	2	1	1	3	2	1	
QPR			3	1	0	2	3	0	1	1
Middlesbrough	W	L	6	3	3	0	3	3	4	2
Brentford	D	W	1	0	1	0	0	1	1	0
Ipswich										
Wolves	W	D	2	1	0	1	1	1	1	0
Derby	L	D	6	3	0	3	2	4	2	2
Blackburn	D	L	3	1	2	0	1	2	3	0
Birmingham	W	D	4	3	1	0	2	2	3	1
Cardiff	W	L	5	4	0	1	3	2	2	3
Charlton	W	W	3	1	1	1	2	1	2	1
Sheffield Weds	W	D	4	2	1	1	3	1	2	1
Nottm Forest	W	D	6	2	2	2	3	3	5	0
Leeds	W	L	5	4	0	1	5	0	4	1
Huddersfield	D	L	3	1	2	0	3	0	3	0
Fulham	W	W	1	1	0	0	1	0	1	0
Bolton	W	D	3	3	0	0	0	3	0	3
Reading	L	L	5	2	0	3	3	2	3	1
Brighton	W	L	4	3	0	1	2	2	1	2
Rotherham	W	L	1	1	0	0	0	1	0	1
Bristol City			4	2	2	0	1	3	1	3
MK Dons			-	-	-	-	-	-	-	-
Preston			2	1	1	0	1	2	0	

Season	Division	Pos	P	W	D	L	F	A	GD	Pts
2014-15	Championship	6	46	22	12	12	72	54	+18	78
2013-14	Championship	9	46	18	14	14	60	54	+6	68
2012-13	Championship	14	46	16	12	18	48	61	-13	60

Over/Under 50%/50% 13th   **Both score** 61%/39% 3rd

LEEDS

Nickname: United
Colours: White
Ground: Elland Road (39,460)
Tel: 0871-334-1919   www.leedsunited.com

A chaotic season saw owner Massimo Cellino banned from Elland Road in December – reinstated in May – and saw the club go through three managers, with both David Hockaday and Darko Milanic lasting just six matches each.

Academy coach Neil Redfearn stepped up and guided the club from the fringes of the relegation fight to a 15th-place finish but he, too, was then dismissed. It would be impressive if Uwe Rosler could make headway in such unstable surroundings.

Longest run without win/loss: 8/5
High/low league position: 11/21
Clean sheets: 13 **Yellows:** 92 **Reds:** 5
Avg attendance: 24,276 **Players used:** 34
Leading scorer: M Antenucci 10 (4,9)
Key stat: There were just 46 goals scored at Elland Road last season – the second-fewest in the division

	2014-15 H	A	Last six seasons at home P	W	D	L	OV	UN	BS	CS
Hull			3	1	1	1	3	0	3	0
Burnley			4	3	0	1	2	2	2	2
QPR			2	1	0	1	2	0	2	0
Middlesbrough	W	W	5	3	1	1	2	3	3	1
Brentford	L	L	2	0	1	1	0	2	1	0
Ipswich	W	L	5	3	2	0	2	3	3	2
Wolves	L	L	2	1	0	1	1	1	1	1
Derby	W	L	5	1	1	3	2	3	3	1
Blackburn	L	L	3	0	1	2	3	0	2	0
Birmingham	D	D	4	1	1	2	2	2	2	1
Cardiff	L	L	4	0	1	3	2	2	2	0
Charlton	D	L	4	0	3	1	1	3	2	1
Sheffield Weds	D	W	3	1	2	0	1	2	3	0
Nottm Forest	D	D	5	2	1	2	3	2	3	1
Leeds										
Huddersfield	W	W	4	2	1	1	4	0	3	1
Fulham	L	W	1	0	0	1	0	1	0	0
Bolton	W	D	3	2	0	1	2	1	2	2
Reading	D	W	4	0	2	2	1	3	1	2
Brighton	L	L	5	1	1	3	3	2	4	0
Rotherham	D	L	1	0	1	0	0	1	0	1
Bristol City			3	3	0	0	2	1	2	1
MK Dons			1	1	0	0	1	0	1	0
Preston			1	0	0	1	1	0	1	0

Season	Division	Pos	P	W	D	L	F	A	GD	Pts
2014-15	Championship	15	46	15	11	20	50	61	-11	56
2013-14	Championship	15	46	16	9	21	59	67	-8	57
2012-13	Championship	13	46	17	10	19	57	66	-9	61

Over/Under 41%/59% 19th   **Both score** 50%/50% 12th

MIDDLESBROUGH

Nickname: Boro
Colours: Red and white
Ground: Riverside Stadium (34,998)
Tel: 0844-499-6789   www.mfc.co.uk

A disappointing playoff final display saw Boro miss out on promotion but they've made huge strides under Aitor Karanka.

He clearly learnt plenty from former mentor Jose Mourinho, tightening up Boro's defence impressively in his first full season in charge before making it the meanest in the division last term.

They also boasted the best home record but were slightly over-cautious on the road, dropping silly points that may have seen them nick automatic promotion.

Longest run without win/loss: 3/9
High/low league position: 1/9
Clean sheets: 21 **Yellows:** 84 **Reds:** 4
Avg attendance: 19,562 **Players used:** 30
Leading scorer: P Bamford 17 (9,16)
Key stat: Middlesbrough kept 21 clean sheets during the regular league season – that's 46 per cent of their games

	2014-15 H	A	Last six seasons at home P	W	D	L	OV	UN	BS	CS
Hull			3	2	1	0	1	2	1	2
Burnley			4	3	0	1	2	2	2	1
QPR			3	1	0	2	2	1	1	1
Middlesbrough										
Brentford	W	W	1	1	0	0	1	0	0	1
Ipswich	W	L	6	4	1	1	3	3	3	3
Wolves	W	L	2	2	0	0	1	1	1	1
Derby	W	W	6	5	1	0	2	4	2	4
Blackburn	D	D	3	1	2	0	0	3	1	2
Birmingham	W	D	4	3	0	1	2	2	2	1
Cardiff	W	W	5	3	0	2	2	3	2	1
Charlton	W	D	3	2	1	0	2	1	2	1
Sheffield Weds	L	L	4	2	1	1	2	2	3	1
Nottm Forest	W	L	6	3	3	0	2	4	4	2
Leeds	L	L	5	1	1	3	1	4	1	2
Huddersfield	W	W	3	2	1	0	1	2	1	2
Fulham	W	L	1	1	0	0	0	1	0	1
Bolton	W	W	3	3	0	0	1	2	1	2
Reading	L	D	5	2	1	2	2	3	2	1
Brighton	D	W	4	1	1	2	0	4	0	2
Rotherham	W	W	1	1	0	0	0	1	0	1
Bristol City			4	0	2	2	2	2	3	1
MK Dons			-	-	-	-	-	-	-	-
Preston			2	1	1	0	0	2	1	1

Season	Division	Pos	P	W	D	L	F	A	GD	Pts
2014-15	Championship	4	46	25	10	11	68	37	+31	85
2013-14	Championship	12	46	16	16	14	62	50	+12	64
2012-13	Championship	16	46	18	5	23	61	70	-9	59

Over/Under 39%/61% 21st   **Both score** 37%/63% 24th

MK DONS

Nickname: The Dons
Colours: White
Ground: stadium:mk (30,500)
Tel: 01908-622-922 www.mkdons.co.uk

The Dons timed their promotion push to perfection, nicking an automatic slot on the final day having been stuck outside the top two for the previous 12 matches.

And while their first ever promotion to the second tier was the headline act, 2014-15 will also be remembered as the season they thrashed Man United 4-0.

Holding on to manager Karl Robinson is a priority and new signings are needed following the loss of midfielder Dele Alli, but the club seems willing to invest.

Longest run without win/loss: 4/12
High/low league position: 2/8
Clean sheets: 22 **Yellows:** 88 **Reds:** 3
Avg attendance: 9,452 **Players used:** 28
Leading scorer: W Grigg 20 (5,16)
Key stat: MK Dons were the highest scorers in the top seven divisions with 101 goals

	2014-15		Last six seasons at home							
	H	A	P	W	D	L	OV	UN	BS	CS
Hull			-	-	-	-	-	-	-	-
Burnley			-	-	-	-	-	-	-	-
QPR			-	-	-	-	-	-	-	-
Middlesbrough			-	-	-	-	-	-	-	-
Brentford			5	1	2	2	2	3	3	1
Ipswich			-	-	-	-	-	-	-	-
Wolves			1	0	0	1	0	1	0	0
Derby			-	-	-	-	-	-	-	-
Blackburn			-	-	-	-	-	-	-	-
Birmingham			-	-	-	-	-	-	-	-
Cardiff			-	-	-	-	-	-	-	-
Charlton			3	1	1	1	0	3	1	1
Sheffield Weds			2	0	1	1	1	2	0	
Nottm Forest										
Leeds			1	0	0	1	0	1	0	0
Huddersfield			3	0	1	2	2	1	3	0
Fulham			-	-	-	-	-	-	-	-
Bolton			-	-	-	-	-	-	-	-
Reading			-	-	-	-	-	-	-	-
Brighton			2	1	1	0	0	2	0	2
Rotherham			1	1	0	0	1	0	1	0
Bristol City	D	L	2	0	2	0	1	1	1	1
MK Dons										
Preston	L	D	4	0	2	2	0	4	1	1

Season	Division	Pos	P	W	D	L	F	A	GD	Pts
2014-15	League 1	2	46	27	10	9	101	44	+57	91
2013-14	League 1	10	46	17	9	20	63	65	-2	60
2012-13	League 1	8	46	19	13	14	62	45	+17	70

Over/Under 59%/41% 3rd   **Both score** 48%/52% 19th

NOTTM FOREST

Nickname: Forest
Colours: Red and white
Ground: City Ground (30,576)
Tel: 0115-982-4444 www.nottinghamforest.co.uk

It was sadly predictable that Stuart Pearce would fail to transmit his playing success to the dugout and while chairman Fawaz Al-Hasawi was fairly restrained by his standards, he finally snapped when a 23-game run returned just three victories.

Replacement Dougie Freedman won seven and drew two of his first ten games in charge but then slumped to take just two points from Forest's last eight games.

Any continuation of that form could see Al-Hasawi back in sacking mode.

Longest run without win/loss: 9/11
High/low league position: 1/14
Clean sheets: 12 **Yellows:** 70 **Reds:** 3
Avg attendance: 23,492 **Players used:** 33
Leading scorer: B Assombalonga 15 (4,12)
Key stat: Forest have gone backwards under Al-Hasawi, finishing eighth, 11th and then 14th and going through six managers

	2014-15		Last six seasons at home							
	H	A	P	W	D	L	OV	UN	BS	CS
Hull			3	0	0	3	1	2	1	0
Burnley			4	2	1	1	0	4	1	2
QPR			3	2	1	0	1	2	0	3
Middlesbrough	W	L	6	4	2	0	2	4	2	4
Brentford	L	D	1	0	0	1	1	0	1	0
Ipswich	D	L	6	4	2	0	3	3	2	4
Wolves	L	W	2	1	0	1	2	0	2	0
Derby	D	W	6	3	1	2	3	3	4	1
Blackburn	L	D	3	1	1	1	2	1	2	1
Birmingham	L	L	4	1	1	2	3	1	3	1
Cardiff	L	L	5	2	1	2	3	2	3	1
Charlton	D	L	3	1	1	1	1	2	2	0
Sheffield Weds	L	W	4	2	1	1	2	2	2	1
Nottm Forest										
Leeds	D	D	5	2	2	1	3	2	4	0
Huddersfield	L	L	3	2	0	1	1	2	1	1
Fulham	W	L	1	1	0	0	1	0	1	0
Bolton	W	D	3	2	1	0	2	1	2	1
Reading	W	W	5	3	0	2	4	1	3	2
Brighton	D	W	4	0	3	1	2	2	3	1
Rotherham	W	D	1	1	0	0	0	1	0	1
Bristol City			4	2	1	1	0	4	1	2
MK Dons			-	-	-	-	-	-	-	-
Preston			2	1	1	0	2	0	1	1

Season	Division	Pos	P	W	D	L	F	A	GD	Pts
2014-15	Championship	14	46	15	14	17	71	69	+2	59
2013-14	Championship	11	46	16	17	13	67	64	+3	65
2012-13	Championship	8	46	17	16	13	63	59	+4	67

Over/Under 70%/30% 1st   **Both score** 63%/37% 2nd

PRESTON

Nickname: The Lilywhites/North End
Colours: White and navy blue
Ground: Deepdale (23,408)
Tel: 0870-442-1964   www.pnefc.co.uk

Playoff winners are often considered to have snuck in through the back door but Preston kicked it down, loud and proud.

They finished a full ten points ahead of fourth-placed Swindon and made light work of the playoffs beating Chesterfield 4-0 over two legs and thrashing Swindon by the same scoreline at Wembley.

Preston also impressed in the cups, beating Norwich en route to a fifth-round exit to Man United and reaching the area finals of the Football League Trophy.

Longest run without win/loss: 5/18
High/low league position: 2/12
Clean sheets: 21 **Yellows:** 69 **Reds:** 1
Avg attendance: 10,852 **Players used:** 29
Leading scorer: J Garner 25 (5,16)
Key stat: Preston were second in League Two for nine weeks before slipping to third place on the final day of the season

	2014-15		Last six seasons at home							
	H	A	P	W	D	L	OV	UN	BS	CS
Hull			1	0	0	1	0	1	0	0
Burnley			1	0	0	1	1	0	1	0
QPR			2	0	2	0	1	1	2	0
Middlesbrough			2	0	1	1	2	0	2	0
Brentford			3	0	1	2	2	1	2	0
Ipswich			2	2	0	0	0	2	0	2
Wolves			1	0	1	0	0	1	0	1
Derby			2	0	1	1	1	1	1	1
Blackburn			-	-	-	-	-	-	-	-
Birmingham			-	-	-	-	-	-	-	-
Cardiff			2	1	0	1	1	1	0	1
Charlton			1	0	1	0	1	0	1	0
Sheffield Weds			2	0	1	1	1	1	1	0
Nottm Forest			2	1	0	1	2	0	2	0
Leeds			1	0	0	1	0	1	0	0
Huddersfield			1	1	0	0	0	1	0	1
Fulham			-	-	-	-	-	-	-	-
Bolton			-	-	-	-	-	-	-	-
Reading			2	0	1	1	1	1	2	0
Brighton			-	-	-	-	-	-	-	-
Rotherham			1	0	1	0	1	0	1	0
Bristol City	D	W	4	1	2	1	2	2	2	1
MK Dons	D	W	4	0	4	0	1	3	3	1
Preston										

Season	Division	Pos	P	W	D	L	F	A	GD	Pts
2014-15	League 1	3	46	25	14	7	79	40	+39	89
2013-14	League 1	5	46	23	16	7	72	46	+26	85
2012-13	League 1	14	46	14	17	15	54	49	+5	59

Over/Under 39%/61% 22nd   **Both score** 48%/52% 19th

QPR

Nickname: The R's
Colours: Blue and white
Ground: Loftus Road (18,489)
Tel: 020-8743-0262   www.qpr.co.uk

The attempt to build a top-flight defence around 36-year-old Rio Ferdinand was typical of a club too busy star-gazing to see where they were going. And when the going got really tough, Harry Redknapp clutched his knee and jumped ship.

Chris Ramsey stepped up but he has a daunting rebuilding job on his hands.

A whole slew of first-teamers have left and it seems owner Tony Fernandes, who could face a huge Financial Fair Play fine, has tired of throwing money at the club.

Longest run without win/loss: 7/2
High/low league position: 15/20
Clean sheets: 6 **Yellows:** 77 **Reds:** 3
Avg attendance: 17,809 **Players used:** 32
Leading scorer: C Austin 18 (3,15)
Key stat: QPR's points per game average dropped after Ramsey took charge, down from 0.83 to 0.73

	2014-15		Last six seasons at home							
	H	A	P	W	D	L	OV	UN	BS	CS
Hull	L	L	2	0	1	1	0	2	1	0
Burnley	W	L	3	1	2	0	1	2	2	1
QPR										
Middlesbrough			3	2	0	1	2	1	1	2
Brentford			-	-	-	-	-	-	-	-
Ipswich			3	2	0	1	1	2	1	2
Wolves			1	0	0	1	1	0	1	0
Derby			3	1	2	0	1	2	2	1
Blackburn			2	0	2	0	0	2	1	1
Birmingham			1	1	0	0	0	1	0	1
Cardiff			2	1	0	1	1	1	1	0
Charlton			1	1	0	0	0	1	0	1
Sheffield Weds			2	1	1	0	1	1	2	0
Nottm Forest			3	1	2	0	1	2	3	0
Leeds			2	0	1	1	1	1	2	0
Huddersfield			1	1	0	0	1	0	1	0
Fulham			2	1	0	1	1	1	1	0
Bolton			2	1	0	1	2	0	1	0
Reading			4	2	1	1	3	1	4	0
Brighton			1	0	1	0	0	1	0	1
Rotherham			-	-	-	-	-	-	-	-
Bristol City			2	1	1	0	2	0	2	0
MK Dons			-	-	-	-	-	-	-	-
Preston			2	2	0	0	2	0	1	1

Season	Division	Pos	P	W	D	L	F	A	GD	Pts
2014-15	Premier League	20	38	8	6	24	42	73	-31	30
2013-14	Championship	4	46	23	11	12	60	44	+16	80
2012-13	Premier League	20	38	4	13	21	30	60	-30	25

Over/Under 63%/37% 2nd   **Both score** 58%/42% 1st

READING

Nickname: The Royals
Colours: Blue and white
Ground: Madejski Stadium (24,161)
Tel: 0118 968-1100   www.readingfc.co.uk

Arsenal needed a lucky break to beat Reading in their FA Cup semi-final, and Wembley observers will have wondered how a side boasting such an impressive midfield could struggle in the second tier.

A lack of promotion-class strikers is the obvious answer but so too was a defence that conceded far too freely on the road.

Nigel Adkins was sacked after a humiliating 6-1 defeat to Birmingham but replacement Steve Clarke also struggled to get much of a tune out of his team.

Longest run without win/loss: 9/3
High/low league position: 6/20
Clean sheets: 13 **Yellows:** 82 **Reds:** 2
Avg attendance: 17,022 **Players used:** 38
Leading scorer: G Murray 8 (3,6) S Cox 8 (2,6)
Key stat: Reading's points-per-game average dropped from 1.19 to 1.0 after Steve Clarke entered the dugout

	2014-15 H	A	Last six seasons at home P	W	D	L	OV	UN	BS	CS
Hull			2	0	1	1	0	2	1	0
Burnley			3	2	1	0	2	1	2	1
QPR			4	1	2	1	0	4	1	2
Middlesbrough	D	W	5	2	2	1	1	4	1	3
Brentford	L	L	1	0	0	1	0	1	0	0
Ipswich	W	W	5	4	1	0	1	4	2	3
Wolves	D	W	1	0	1	0	1	0	1	0
Derby	L	W	5	2	2	1	4	1	3	1
Blackburn	D	L	2	0	1	1	0	2	0	1
Birmingham	L	L	5	2	1	2	1	4	2	2
Cardiff	D	L	4	0	2	2	1	3	3	0
Charlton	L	L	2	1	0	1	0	2	0	1
Sheffield Weds	W	L	3	2	0	1	1	2	0	2
Nottm Forest	L	L	5	1	3	1	1	4	2	2
Leeds	L	D	4	2	1	1	0	4	0	3
Huddersfield	L	L	2	0	1	1	1	1	2	0
Fulham	W	L	2	1	1	0	2	0	1	1
Bolton	D	D	2	1	1	0	1	1	1	1
Reading										
Brighton	W	D	3	2	1	0	2	1	1	2
Rotherham	W	L	1	1	0	0	1	0	0	1
Bristol City			3	3	0	0	1	2	1	2
MK Dons			-	-	-	-	-	-	-	-
Preston			2	2	0	0	2	0	2	0

Season	Division	Pos	P	W	D	L	F	A	GD	Pts
2014-15	Championship	19	46	13	11	22	48	69	-21	50
2013-14	Championship	7	46	19	14	13	70	56	+14	71
2012-13	Premier League	19	38	6	10	22	43	73	-30	28

Over/Under 57%/43% 6th   **Both score** 43%/57% 21st

ROTHERHAM

Nickname: The Millers
Colours: Red and white
Ground: New York Stadium (12,021)
Tel: 08444-140-733   www.themillers.co.uk

Rotherham's fourth-bottom finish wasn't quite as hairy as it looked as the Millers spent just one week in the bottom three and would have finished in 20th if not for a three-point deduction.

A period of consolidation was to be expected after consecutive promotions, but progress could be slow. The team is well-organised and competitive but short of midfield guile and attacking threat. The loss of captain Craig Morgan could impact on their defensive solidity too.

Longest run without win/loss: 9/6
High/low league position: 15/22
Clean sheets: 10 **Yellows:** 75 **Reds:** 2
Avg attendance: 10,240 **Players used:** 42
Leading scorer: M Derbyshire 9 (4,9)
Key stat: Rotherham scored just 15 away goals – the lowest tally in the division

	2014-15 H	A	Last six seasons at home P	W	D	L	OV	UN	BS	CS
Hull			-	-	-	-	-	-	-	-
Burnley			-	-	-	-	-	-	-	-
QPR			-	-	-	-	-	-	-	-
Middlesbrough	L	L	1	0	0	1	1	0	0	0
Brentford	L	L	2	1	0	1	1	1	0	1
Ipswich	W	L	1	1	0	0	1	0	0	1
Wolves	W	L	2	1	1	0	1	1	1	1
Derby	D	L	1	0	1	0	1	0	1	0
Blackburn	W	L	1	1	0	0	0	1	0	1
Birmingham	L	L	1	0	0	1	1	0	0	0
Cardiff	L	D	1	0	0	1	1	0	1	0
Charlton	D	D	1	0	1	0	0	1	1	0
Sheffield Weds	L	D	1	0	0	1	1	0	1	0
Nottm Forest	D	L	1	0	1	0	0	1	0	1
Leeds	W	D	1	1	0	0	1	0	1	0
Huddersfield	D	W	1	0	1	0	1	0	1	0
Fulham	D	D	1	0	1	0	1	0	1	0
Bolton	W	L	1	1	0	0	1	0	1	0
Reading	W	L	1	1	0	0	1	0	1	0
Brighton	W	D	1	1	0	0	0	1	0	1
Rotherham										
Bristol City			1	1	0	0	1	0	1	0
MK Dons			1	0	1	0	1	0	1	0
Preston			1	0	1	0	0	1	0	1

Season	Division	Pos	P	W	D	L	F	A	GD	Pts
2014-15	Championship	21	46	11	16	19	46	67	-21	46
2013-14	League 1	4	46	24	14	8	86	58	+28	86
2012-13	League 2	2	46	24	7	15	74	59	+15	79

Over/Under 39%/61% 21st   **Both score** 50%/50% 12th

SHEFFIELD WEDS

Nickname: The Owls
Colours: Blue and white
Ground: Hillsborough (39,732)
Tel: 0871-995-1867   www.swfc.co.uk

The Owls improved their league position for a fifth-consecutive season but new owner Dejphon Chansiri clearly thought the progress wasn't rapid enough as he sacked manager Stuart Gray in June.

Gray leaves a solid defensive unit, with Kieren Westwood particularly impressive in goal, and fans will be excited by the promise of Chansiri to "invest in the club to get them to the Premier League."

It could be that the rate of progress is about to speed up at Hillsborough.

Longest run without win/loss: 10/4
High/low league position: 6/14
Clean sheets: 17 **Yellows:** 91 **Reds:** 3
Avg attendance: 21,993 **Players used:** 31
Leading scorer: C Maguire 8 (4,8) A Nuhiu 8 (4,7)
Key stat: Wednesday had the fourth-best defensive record in the Championship but the fourth-worst attack

	2014-15 H	A	P	W	D	L	OV	UN	BS	CS
Hull			1	0	0	1	0	1	0	0
Burnley			2	0	0	2	1	1	1	0
QPR			2	1	0	1	2	0	1	1
Middlesbrough	W	W	4	3	0	1	1	3	1	3
Brentford	W	D	3	1	1	1	1	2	1	2
Ipswich	D	L	4	0	3	1	0	4	3	0
Wolves	L	L	2	0	1	1	0	2	0	1
Derby	D	L	4	0	3	1	1	3	1	2
Blackburn	L	W	3	1	1	1	3	0	3	0
Birmingham	D	W	3	2	1	0	2	1	2	1
Cardiff	D	L	3	1	1	1	1	2	2	0
Charlton	D	D	5	1	2	2	2	3	3	1
Sheffield Weds										
Nottm Forest	L	W	4	0	1	3	0	4	1	0
Leeds	L	D	3	1	1	1	2	1	2	1
Huddersfield	D	D	5	0	2	3	3	2	4	0
Fulham	D	L	1	0	1	0	0	1	1	0
Bolton	L	D	3	0	0	3	3	0	3	0
Reading	W	L	3	2	0	1	1	2	1	1
Brighton	D	W	4	3	1	0	1	3	1	3
Rotherham	D	W	1	0	1	0	0	1	0	1
Bristol City			2	0	0	2	1	1	1	0
MK Dons			2	1	1	0	2	0	2	0
Preston			2	1	0	1	1	1	1	1

Season	Division	Pos	P	W	D	L	F	A	GD	Pts
2014-15	Championship	13	46	14	18	14	43	49	-6	60
2013-14	Championship	16	46	13	14	19	63	65	-2	53
2012-13	Championship	18	46	16	10	20	53	61	-8	58

Over/Under 33%/67% 23rd   **Both score** 46%/54% 19th

WOLVES

Nickname: Wolves
Colours: Gold and black
Ground: Molineux Stadium (31,700)
Tel: 0871-222-2220   www.wolves.co.uk

Following successive relegations, Wolves fell just short of bouncing back with successive promotions, only missing out on the playoffs on goal difference.

A November five-match losing streak to highflying rivals proved Wolves' undoing and Kenny Jackett must look to instil a little more tactical nous after his team lost seven of nine visits to top-ten opponents.

There's enough quality in the squad to compete but the purse strings might have to be loosened to replace Bakary Sako.

Longest run without win/loss: 6/8
High/low league position: 3/13
Clean sheets: 18 **Yellows:** 74 **Reds:** 4
Avg attendance: 22,419 **Players used:** 27
Leading scorer: B Sako 15 (4,13)
Key stat: Wolves conceded 2.43 goals per game when visiting fellow top-eight sides

	2014-15 H	A	P	W	D	L	OV	UN	BS	CS
Hull			2	1	1	0	0	2	1	1
Burnley			2	1	0	1	1	1	1	1
QPR			1	0	0	1	1	0	0	0
Middlesbrough	W	L	2	2	0	0	1	1	1	1
Brentford	W	L	2	1	1	0	1	1	1	1
Ipswich	D	L	2	0	1	1	0	2	1	0
Wolves										
Derby	W	L	2	1	1	0	0	2	1	1
Blackburn	W	W	5	1	2	2	2	3	4	0
Birmingham	D	L	4	2	1	1	0	4	0	3
Cardiff	W	W	2	1	0	1	1	1	1	1
Charlton	D	D	2	0	2	0	0	2	1	1
Sheffield Weds	W	W	2	2	0	0	1	1	0	2
Nottm Forest	L	W	2	0	0	2	2	0	1	0
Leeds	W	W	2	1	1	0	2	0	2	0
Huddersfield	L	W	2	0	0	2	2	0	2	0
Fulham	W	W	4	3	1	0	2	2	2	2
Bolton	W	D	5	2	1	2	4	1	4	1
Reading	L	D	1	0	0	1	1	0	1	0
Brighton	D	D	2	0	2	0	1	1	2	0
Rotherham	W	L	2	2	0	0	0	2	1	1
Bristol City			2	2	0	0	2	0	2	0
MK Dons			1	0	0	1	0	1	0	0
Preston			1	1	0	0	0	1	0	1

Season	Division	Pos	P	W	D	L	F	A	GD	Pts
2014-15	Championship	7	46	22	12	12	70	56	+14	78
2013-14	League 1	1	46	31	10	5	89	31	+58	103
2012-13	Championship	23	46	14	9	23	55	69	-14	51

Over/Under 54%/46% 9th   **Both score** 50%/50% 12th

Championship stats 2014-15

Key Points in all tables (except the league table) do not include any deductions imposed by the league.
POS H A Overall league position, rank from home games only, rank from away games only **Sup** Average match supremacy **GFA** Goals For Average **GAA** Goals Against Average **PGA** Points Gained Average

			Championship 2014-15		Home					Away						
Pos	H	A		P	W	D	L	F	A	W	D	L	F	A	GD	Pts
1	4	1	Bournemouth	46	13	7	3	48	25	13	5	5	50	20	+53	90
2	3	3	Watford	46	14	4	5	48	22	13	4	6	43	28	+41	89
3	7	2	Norwich	46	12	6	5	50	24	13	5	5	38	24	+40	86
4	1	5	Middlesbrough	46	15	5	3	42	12	10	5	8	26	25	+31	85
5	8	4	Brentford	46	12	6	5	46	28	11	3	9	32	31	+19	78
6	2	10	Ipswich	46	15	5	3	40	18	7	7	9	32	36	+18	78
7	5	8	Wolves	46	13	6	4	42	23	9	6	8	28	33	+14	78
8	6	6	Derby	46	12	7	4	48	24	9	7	7	37	32	+29	77
9	9	9	Blackburn	46	11	6	6	37	28	6	10	7	29	31	+7	67
10	10	13	Birmingham	46	10	7	6	29	31	6	8	9	25	33	-10	63
11	13	12	Cardiff	46	10	5	8	31	30	6	9	8	26	31	-4	62
12	11	15	Charlton	46	9	9	5	32	27	5	9	9	22	33	-6	60
13	21	7	Sheff Wed	46	5	11	7	16	20	9	7	7	27	29	-6	60
14	14	11	Nottm Forest	46	9	5	9	37	32	6	9	8	34	37	+2	59
15	18	14	Leeds	46	8	6	9	22	24	7	5	11	28	37	-11	56
16	15	17	Huddersfield	46	8	8	7	34	34	5	8	10	24	41	-17	55
17	16	20	Fulham	46	9	5	9	36	38	5	5	13	26	45	-21	52
18	12	23	Bolton	46	9	8	6	35	27	4	4	15	19	40	-13	51
19	19	19	Reading	46	8	5	10	24	25	5	6	12	24	44	-21	50
20	20	18	Brighton	46	6	8	9	26	29	4	9	10	18	25	-10	47
21	17	22	Rotherham	46	8	7	8	31	34	3	9	11	15	33	-21	46*
22	22	21	Millwall	46	5	7	11	25	40	4	7	12	17	36	-34	41
23	24	16	Wigan	46	3	8	12	18	29	6	4	13	21	35	-25	39
24	23	24	Blackpool	45	4	7	12	18	35	0	7	16	18	56	-55	26

Rotherham deducted 3pts

Best attack

		GF	GFA
1	Bournemouth	98	2.13
2	Watford	91	1.98
3	Norwich	88	1.91
4	Derby	85	1.85
5	Brentford	78	1.7
6	Ipswich	72	1.57
7	Nottm Forest	71	1.54
8	Wolves	70	1.52
9	Middlesbrough	68	1.48
10	Blackburn	66	1.43
11	Fulham	62	1.35
12	Huddersfield	58	1.29
13	Cardiff	57	1.24
14	Birmingham	54	1.17
15	Charlton	54	1.17
16	Bolton	54	1.17
17	Leeds	50	1.09
18	Reading	48	1.04
19	Rotherham	46	1
20	Brighton	44	0.96
21	Sheff Wed	43	0.93
22	Millwall	42	0.91
23	Wigan	39	0.85
24	Blackpool	36	0.8

Best defence

		GA	GAA
1	Middlesbrough	37	0.8
2	Bournemouth	45	0.98
3	Norwich	48	1.04
4	Sheff Wed	49	1.07
5	Watford	50	1.09
6	Ipswich	54	1.17
7	Brighton	54	1.17
8	Wolves	56	1.22
9	Derby	56	1.22
10	Brentford	59	1.28
11	Blackburn	59	1.28
12	Charlton	60	1.3
13	Cardiff	61	1.33
14	Leeds	61	1.33
15	Birmingham	64	1.39
16	Wigan	64	1.39
17	Bolton	67	1.46
18	Rotherham	67	1.46
19	Nottm Forest	69	1.5
20	Reading	69	1.5
21	Millwall	76	1.65
22	Huddersfield	75	1.67
23	Fulham	83	1.8
24	Blackpool	91	2.02

Top scorers

	Team	Goals scored
D Murphy	Ipswich	27
T Deeney	Watford	21
J Rhodes	Blackburn	21
R Gestede	Blackburn	20
O Ighalo	Watford	20
C Wilson	Bournemouth	20

Over 2.5 goals

	H	A	%
Nottm Forest	14	18	70%
Brentford	17	13	65%
Huddersfield	15	13	62%
Fulham	14	13	59%
Norwich	13	14	59%

Under 2.5 goals

	H	A	%
Brighton	15	17	70%
Sheff Weds	18	13	67%
Middlesbrough	14	14	61%
Rotherham	12	16	61%
Birmingham	12	15	59%
Leeds	15	12	59%

Both to score

	H	A	%
Blackburn	15	16	67%
Nottm Forest	15	14	63%
Brentford	15	13	61%
Cardiff	13	15	61%
Ipswich	12	16	61%

Both not to score

	H	A	%
Middlesbrough	15	14	63%
Brighton	11	15	57%
Reading	17	9	57%
Wigan	14	12	57%
Millwall	11	14	54%
Sheff Weds	13	12	54%

SOCCERBASE.COM

Championship results 2014-15

	Birmingham	Blackburn	Blackpool	Bolton	Bournemouth	Brentford	Brighton	Cardiff	Charlton	Derby	Fulham	Huddersfield	Ipswich	Leeds	Middlesbrough	Millwall	Norwich	Nottm Forest	Reading	Rotherham	Sheffield Wed	Watford	Wigan	Wolves
Birmingham		2-2	1-0	0-1	0-8	1-0	1-0	0-0	1-0	0-4	1-2	1-1	2-2	1-1	1-1	0-1	0-0	2-1	6-1	2-1	0-2	2-1	3-1	2-1
Blackburn	1-0		1-1	1-0	3-2	2-3	0-1	1-1	2-0	2-3	2-1	0-0	3-2	2-1	0-0	2-0	1-2	3-3	3-1	2-1	1-2	2-2	3-1	0-1
Blackpool	1-0	1-2		1-1	1-6	1-2	1-0	0-3	0-1	0-1	0-0†	0-2	1-1	1-2	1-0	1-3	4-4	1-1	1-1	0-1	0-1	1-3	0-0	
Bolton	0-1	2-1	1-1		1-2	3-1	1-0	3-0	1-0	0-0	1-1	1-2	2-0	1-2	2-2	1-1	3-2	0-0	3-4	3-1	2-2			
Bournemouth	4-2	0-0	4-0	3-0		1-0	3-2	5-3	1-0	2-2	2-0	1-1	2-2	1-3	3-0	2-2	1-2	1-2	3-0	1-1	2-2	2-0	2-0	2-1
Brentford	1-1	3-1	4-0	2-2	3-1		3-2	1-2	1-1	2-1	2-1	4-1	2-4	2-0	0-1	2-2	0-3	2-2	3-1	1-0	0-0	1-2	3-0	4-0
Brighton	4-3	1-1	0-0	2-1	0-2	0-1		1-1	2-2	2-0	1-2	0-0	3-2	2-0	1-2	0-1	0-1	2-3	2-2	1-1	0-1	0-2	1-0	1-1
Cardiff	2-0	1-1	3-2	0-3	1-1	2-3	0-0		1-2	0-2	1-0	3-1	3-1	3-1	0-1	0-0	2-4	2-1	2-1	0-0	2-1	2-4	1-0	0-1
Charlton	1-1	1-3	2-2	2-1	0-3	3-0	0-1	1-1		3-2	1-1	3-0	0-1	2-1	0-0	0-0	2-3	2-1	3-2	1-1	1-1	1-0	2-1	1-1
Derby	2-2	2-0	4-0	4-1	2-0	1-1	3-0	2-2	2-0		5-1	3-2	1-1	2-0	0-1	0-0	2-2	1-2	0-3	1-0	3-2	2-2	1-2	5-0
Fulham	1-1	0-1	2-2	4-0	1-5	1-4	0-2	1-1	3-0	2-0		3-1	1-2	0-3	4-3	0-1	1-0	3-2	2-1	1-1	4-0	0-5	2-2	0-1
Huddersfield	0-1	2-2	4-2	2-1	0-4	2-1	1-1	0-0	1-1	4-4	0-2		2-1	1-2	1-2	2-1	2-2	3-0	3-0	0-2	0-0	3-1	0-0	1-4
Ipswich	4-2	1-1	3-2	1-0	1-1	1-1	2-0	3-1	3-0	0-1	2-1	2-2		4-1	2-0	2-0	0-1	2-1	0-1	2-0	2-1	1-0	0-0	2-1
Leeds	1-1	0-3	3-1	1-0	1-0	0-1	0-2	1-2	2-2	2-0	0-1	3-0	2-1		1-0	1-0	0-2	0-0	0-0	0-0	1-1	2-3	0-2	1-2
Middlesbrough	2-0	1-1	1-1	1-0	0-0	4-0	0-2	3-1	2-0	2-0	2-0	4-1	0-1			3-0	4-0	3-0	0-1	2-0	2-3	1-1	1-0	2-1
Millwall	1-3	2-2	2-1	0-1	0-2	2-3	0-0	1-0	1-3	1-3	2-0	1-5	1-4	0-0	0-0		1-1	0-3	1-3	0-2	2-0	3-3		
Norwich	2-2	3-1	4-0	2-1	1-1	1-2	3-3	3-2	0-1	1-1	4-2	5-0	2-0	1-1	0-1	6-1		3-1	1-2	1-1	2-0	3-0	0-1	2-0
Nottm Forest	1-3	1-3	2-0	4-1	2-1	1-3	0-0	1-2	1-1	1-1	5-3	0-1	2-2	1-1	2-1	0-1	2-1		4-0	2-0	0-2	1-3	3-0	1-2
Reading	0-1	0-0	3-0	0-0	0-1	0-2	2-1	1-1	0-1	0-3	3-0	1-2	1-0	0-2	0-0	3-2	2-1	0-3		3-0	2-0	0-1	0-1	3-3
Rotherham	0-1	2-0	1-1	4-2	0-2	0-2	1-0	1-3	1-1	3-3	3-3	2-2	2-0	2-1	0-3	2-1	1-1	0-0	2-1		2-3	0-2	1-2	1-0
Sheffield Wed	0-0	1-2	1-0	1-2	0-2	1-0	0-0	1-1	1-1	0-0	1-1	1-1	1-1	1-2	2-0	1-1	0-0	0-1	1-0	0-0		0-3	2-1	0-1
Watford	1-0	1-1	0-1	7-2	3-0	1-1	0-1	1-0	5-0	1-2	1-0	4-2	0-1	4-1	2-0	3-1	0-3	2-2	4-1	3-0	1-1		2-1	0-1
Wigan	4-0	1-1	1-0	1-1	1-3	0-0	2-1	0-1	0-3	0-2	3-3	0-1	1-2	0-1	1-1	0-0	0-0	2-2	1-2	0-1	0-2			0-1
Wolves	0-0	3-1	2-0	1-0	1-2	2-1	1-1	1-0	0-0	2-0	3-0	1-3	1-1	4-3	2-0	4-2	1-0	0-3	1-2	5-0	3-0	2-2	2-2	

† Match abandoned after 48 minutes and subsequently ruled a 0-0 draw. This result has not been included in any goals-related stats

Record when first to score

		P	W	D	L	F	A	Sup	PGA	Pts
1	Middlesbrough	28	24	3	1	57	11	+1.64	2.7	75
2	Watford	27	22	5	0	65	18	+1.74	2.6	71
3	Brentford	23	19	2	2	56	21	+1.52	2.6	59
4	Wolves	26	20	4	2	52	20	+1.23	2.5	64
5	Norwich	26	20	4	2	62	20	+1.62	2.5	64
6	Huddersfield	16	12	4	0	35	15	+1.25	2.5	40
7	Reading	16	12	3	1	35	16	+1.19	2.4	39
8	Bournemouth	35	24	7	4	82	27	+1.57	2.3	79
9	Ipswich	27	19	6	2	51	24	+1.00	2.3	63
10	Derby	26	19	4	3	60	20	+1.54	2.3	61
11	Nottm Forest	13	9	3	1	36	13	+1.77	2.3	30
12	Birmingham	24	15	7	2	40	22	+0.75	2.2	52
13	Fulham	18	12	4	2	37	17	+1.11	2.2	40
14	Millwall	12	8	2	2	18	11	+0.58	2.2	26
15	Cardiff	22	14	5	3	37	28	+0.41	2.1	47
16	Bolton	16	10	3	3	27	13	+0.88	2.1	33
17	Wigan	13	8	3	2	22	14	+0.62	2.1	27
18	Charlton	20	11	8	1	34	16	+0.90	2	41
19	Blackburn	24	13	6	5	43	30	+0.54	1.9	45
20	Sheff Wed	23	12	8	3	33	20	+0.57	1.9	44
21	Leeds	22	13	2	7	36	29	+0.32	1.9	41
22	Brighton	17	9	6	2	30	21	+0.53	1.9	33
23	Rotherham	17	9	6	2	31	20	+0.65	1.9	33
24	Blackpool	15	4	7	4	22	27	-0.33	1.3	19

Record when keeping a clean sheet

		P	W	D	F	Sup	PGA	Pts
1	Watford	15	15	0	34	+2.27	3	45
2	Bournemouth	19	17	2	45	+2.37	2.8	53
3	Derby	17	15	2	36	+2.12	2.8	47
4	Fulham	9	8	1	18	+2.00	2.8	25
5	Wolves	18	15	3	26	+1.44	2.7	48
6	Norwich	14	12	2	29	+2.07	2.7	38
7	Ipswich	12	10	2	17	+1.42	2.7	32
8	Brentford	11	9	2	20	+1.82	2.6	29
9	Middlesbrough	21	16	5	33	+1.57	2.5	53
10	Leeds	13	10	3	16	+1.23	2.5	33
11	Bolton	10	7	3	12	+1.20	2.4	24
12	Charlton	10	7	3	15	+1.50	2.4	24
13	Birmingham	12	8	4	8	+0.67	2.3	28
14	Blackpool	7	4	3	4	+0.67	2.14	15
15	Reading	13	8	5	17	+1.31	2.2	29
16	Nottm Forest	12	7	5	18	+1.50	2.2	26
17	Blackburn	10	6	4	10	+1.00	2.2	22
18	Rotherham	10	6	4	9	+0.90	2.2	22
19	Sheff Wed	17	9	8	12	+0.71	2.1	35
20	Brighton	14	7	7	11	+0.79	2	28
21	Wigan	10	5	5	9	+0.90	2	20
22	Cardiff	10	5	5	6	+0.60	2	20
23	Millwall	15	7	8	9	+0.60	1.9	29
24	Huddersfield	9	4	5	8	+0.89	1.9	17

Long-suffering Blades can finally cut themselves clear of troublesome third tier

Favourites have a terrible record in England's third tier, with only one of the last 20 coming good, but market leaders Sheffield United can finally escape League One at the fifth attempt, writes Mark Langdon. A change of manager may make the difference, although Nigel Clough will feel he could have got the job done prior to being replaced by Nigel Adkins, who has three times previously gained promotion at this level.

The Blades' run to the semi-finals of the League Cup was definitely a distraction for them last season but they still managed to finish fifth and a defensive injury crisis was partly to blame for the 7-6 aggregate defeat in the playoff semi-finals.

It looks a weaker division this time around and money was spent in January with the cup windfall so it's only logical to expect better from the likes of Matty Done now they have had time to settle.

At 11-2 the Blades certainly look a rock-solid each-way bet with challengers thin on the ground.

Relegated duo Wigan and Millwall should feature, but both have novice managers and the same is also true of a Peterborough side who were only good enough to grab ninth last season.

Yorkshire trio Bradford, Doncaster and Barnsley are respected without being overly feared and Swindon need to rebuild after a difficult summer of player departures.

This division has thrown up some crazy winners in the past with Scunthorpe and Luton obliging at 66-1 and 33-1 respectively, while in 2005-06 Southend, who were 50-1, went up automatically with 66-1 Colchester.

If there is to be another monster shock then Bury, who have signed Leon Clarke and Tom Pope, could be the sort of side who improve at a higher level and Shrewsbury should also be comfortable in the third tier after gaining promotion alongside the Shakers last season.

However, for a second bet head to the relegation market where local rivals Crewe and Port Vale could easily be playing League Two football in the 2016-17 campaign.

Crewe should be odds-on for the drop so odds of 11-8 appeal, but there's always the concern they could have a few talented youngsters coming through the academy. Therefore, preference goes to Vale for the drop at a juicy 13-8.

The Valiants finished only four points off relegation last term and ended that campaign in woeful fashion, collecting just six points from the last 33 available.

Since then they have lost both of their strikers, with leading scorer Pope heading to Bury and Ben Williamson departing for Gillingham, and finding replacements won't be easy with manager Rob Page working on a smaller budget this term.

Another to consider at a bigger price is the 8-1 being offered about Chesterfield.

The Spireites reached the playoffs last season but manager Paul Cook left for Portsmouth and there must be a big question mark over replacement Dean Saunders.

The Welshman has already suffered relegations while manager of Doncaster, Wolves and Crawley and he needs to make a good start to get the fans on side.

Defender Robert Harris enjoys Sheffield United's FA Cup win over Premier League hosts QPR

BARNSLEY

Nickname: Tykes
Colours: Red and white
Ground: Oakwell (23,009)
Tel: 01226-211-333   www.barnsleyfc.co.uk

Last term was disappointing for Barnsley, and manager Danny Wilson paid the price by losing his job, but they did show signs of promise during Lee Johnson's honeymoon period in the dugout.

Six straight wins briefly propelled the Tykes into the playoff spots but they went on to draw six of their final ten games.

If Marley Watkins, an energetic striker brought in from Inverness, can turn some of those stalemates into wins, Johnson could lead Barnsley into the top six.

Longest run without win/loss: 9/9
High/low league position: 6/21
Clean sheets: 13 **Yellows:** 67 **Reds:** 6
Avg attendance: 9,768 **Players used:** 42
Leading scorer: C Hourihane 13 (3,12)
Key stat: Barnsley lost only three of their 14 matches after Lee Johnson arrived at the club in late February

BLACKPOOL

Nickname: Seasiders/Tangerines
Colours: Tangerine and white
Ground: Bloomfield Road (16,750)
Tel: 01253-685-000   www.blackpoolfc.co.uk

New managers are usually bullish in their first press conference as they look to get the fans on side, so it could be telling that upon his unveiling Neil McDonald told Blackpool supporters not to dream of a swift return to the Championship.

Blackpool were hopeless last season, conceding 91 goals in the second tier, and unless much-criticised chairman Karl Oyster allows funds to be spent it is entirely possible the club could be sucked into another relegation dogfight.

Longest run without win/loss: 18/4
High/low league position: 23/24
Clean sheets: 7 **Yellows:** 85 **Reds:** 4
Avg attendance: 10,928 **Players used:** 50
Leading scorer: S Davies 5 (1,5)
Key stat: The Seasiders had a goal difference of -55 in the Championship – at least 21 worse than any other side in the section

	2014-15 H	A	P	W	D	L	OV	UN	BS	CS
Millwall			4	3	0	1	1	3	1	3
Wigan			1	0	0	1	1	0	0	0
Blackpool			4	2	1	1	1	3	2	2
Swindon	L	L	1	0	0	1	1	0	0	0
Sheffield United	L	W	3	1	1	1	1	2	1	1
Chesterfield	D	L	1	0	1	0	0	1	1	0
Bradford	W	L	1	1	0	0	1	0	1	0
Rochdale	W	W	1	1	0	0	1	0	0	1
Peterborough	D	L	4	1	2	1	1	3	2	1
Fleetwood Town	L	D	1	0	0	1	1	0	1	0
Barnsley										
Gillingham	W	W	1	1	0	0	1	0	1	0
Doncaster	D	L	5	1	3	1	1	4	2	2
Walsall	W	L	1	1	0	0	1	0	0	0
Oldham	W	W	1	1	0	0	1	0	1	0
Scunthorpe	L	W	3	1	1	1	2	1	3	0
Coventry	W	D	4	3	0	1	1	3	1	2
Port Vale	W	L	1	1	0	0	1	0	1	0
Colchester	W	L	1	1	0	0	1	0	1	0
Crewe	W	W	1	1	0	0	0	1	0	1
Burton			-	-	-	-	-	-	-	-
Shrewsbury			-	-	-	-	-	-	-	-
Bury			-	-	-	-	-	-	-	-
Southend			-	-	-	-	-	-	-	-

Season	Division	Pos	P	W	D	L	F	A	GD	Pts
2014-15	League 1	11	46	17	11	18	62	61	+1	62
2013-14	Championship	23	46	9	12	25	44	77	-33	39
2012-13	Championship	21	46	14	13	19	56	70	-14	55

Over/Under 48%/52% 14th   **Both score** 54%/46% 6th

	2014-15 H	A	P	W	D	L	OV	UN	BS	CS
Millwall	W	L	4	4	0	0	1	3	1	3
Wigan	L	L	3	1	0	2	2	1	2	1
Blackpool										
Swindon			-	-	-	-	-	-	-	-
Sheffield United			1	1	0	0	1	0	0	1
Chesterfield			-	-	-	-	-	-	-	-
Bradford			-	-	-	-	-	-	-	-
Rochdale			-	-	-	-	-	-	-	-
Peterborough			3	2	0	1	1	2	1	1
Fleetwood Town			-	-	-	-	-	-	-	-
Barnsley			4	1	1	2	2	2	3	1
Gillingham			-	-	-	-	-	-	-	-
Doncaster			3	2	1	0	1	2	2	1
Walsall			-	-	-	-	-	-	-	-
Oldham			-	-	-	-	-	-	-	-
Scunthorpe			1	1	0	0	1	0	1	0
Coventry			2	2	0	0	2	0	1	1
Port Vale			-	-	-	-	-	-	-	-
Colchester			-	-	-	-	-	-	-	-
Crewe			-	-	-	-	-	-	-	-
Burton			-	-	-	-	-	-	-	-
Shrewsbury			-	-	-	-	-	-	-	-
Bury			-	-	-	-	-	-	-	-
Southend			-	-	-	-	-	-	-	-

Season	Division	Pos	P	W	D	L	F	A	GD	Pts
2014-15	Championship	24	46	4	14	28	36	91	-55	26
2013-14	Championship	20	46	11	13	22	38	66	-28	46
2012-13	Championship	15	46	14	17	15	62	63	-1	59

Over/Under 46%/54% 16th   **Both score** 50%/50% 12th

BRADFORD

Nickname: The Bantams
Colours: Claret and amber
Ground: Valley Parade (25,136)
Tel: 0871-978-1911 www.bradfordcityfc.co.uk

Knockout kings Bradford created one of the stories of the season as they recorded a stunning 4-2 triumph at Chelsea en route to the last eight of the FA Cup.

That distraction possibly derailed Phil Parkinson's promotion hopes, although the awful Valley Parade pitch was another factor in finishing just outside the top six.

Sheffield United were rebuffed in their bid to lure Parkinson from City, which highlights the ambition at the club, and Bradford should be in the playoff mix.

Longest run without win/loss: 5/7
High/low league position: 5/13
Clean sheets: 13 **Yellows:** 67 **Reds:** 7
Avg attendance: 13,353 **Players used:** 29
Leading scorer: B Clarke 13 (4,12)
Key stat: Bradford won more away matches (nine) than they did at home (eight) in League One last season

	2014-15 H	A	Last six seasons at home P	W	D	L	OV	UN	BS	CS
Millwall			-	-	-	-	-	-	-	-
Wigan			-	-	-	-	-	-	-	-
Blackpool			-	-	-	-	-	-	-	-
Swindon	L	L	3	0	2	1	1	2	2	1
Sheffield United	L	D	2	1	0	1	0	2	0	1
Chesterfield	L	W	4	1	1	2	1	3	0	2
Bradford										
Rochdale	L	W	3	0	0	3	3	0	2	0
Peterborough	L	L	2	1	0	1	0	2	0	1
Fleetwood Town	D	W	2	1	1	0	1	1	1	1
Barnsley	W	L	1	1	0	0	1	0	1	0
Gillingham	D	L	5	1	3	1	1	4	3	1
Doncaster	L	W	1	0	0	1	1	0	1	0
Walsall	D	D	2	0	1	1	0	2	1	0
Oldham	W	L	2	1	0	1	1	1	1	1
Scunthorpe	D	D	1	0	1	0	0	1	1	0
Coventry	W	D	2	1	1	0	2	0	2	0
Port Vale	D	D	6	1	3	2	0	6	2	2
Colchester	D	D	2	0	2	0	1	2	0	
Crewe	W	W	5	2	1	2	4	1	3	2
Burton			4	1	3	0	0	4	3	1
Shrewsbury			4	2	0	2	4	0	4	0
Bury			2	1	0	1	0	2	0	1
Southend			3	1	1	1	1	2	1	1

Season	Division	Pos	P	W	D	L	F	A	GD	Pts
2014-15	League 1	7	46	17	14	15	55	55	0	65
2013-14	League 1	11	46	14	17	15	57	54	+3	59
2012-13	League 2	7	46	18	15	13	63	52	+11	69

Over/Under 41%/59% 21st   **Both score** 54%/46% 6th

BURTON

Nickname: The Brewers
Colours: Yellow and black
Ground: Pirelli Stadium (6,912)
Tel: 01283-565938 www.burtonalbionfc.co.uk

Jimmy Floyd Hasselbaink carried on the fine work started by Gary Rowett, with Burton winning League Two and now preparing to embark on their debut season in the third tier.

However, despite winning the title Albion failed to score more than once in 24 of their 46 games in the fourth division. They did still finish as the section's most potent side but the Brewers often filled their boots against opponents towards the bottom of the league.

Longest run without win/loss: 2/13
High/low league position: 1/5
Clean sheets: 17 **Yellows:** 60 **Reds:** 4
Avg attendance: 3,237 **Players used:** 36
Leading scorer: L Akins 10 (4,8)
Key stat: There were nine 1-0 wins for Burton last season in League Two and six of those came at the Pirelli Stadium

	2014-15 H	A	Last six seasons at home P	W	D	L	OV	UN	BS	CS
Millwall			-	-	-	-	-	-	-	-
Wigan			-	-	-	-	-	-	-	-
Blackpool			-	-	-	-	-	-	-	-
Swindon			1	1	0	0	0	1	0	1
Sheffield United			-	-	-	-	-	-	-	-
Chesterfield			4	1	1	2	1	3	1	1
Bradford			4	2	2	0	2	2	2	2
Rochdale			3	3	0	0	1	2	1	2
Peterborough			-	-	-	-	-	-	-	-
Fleetwood Town			2	0	0	2	1	1	1	0
Barnsley			-	-	-	-	-	-	-	-
Gillingham			3	2	1	0	1	2	2	1
Doncaster			-	-	-	-	-	-	-	-
Walsall			-	-	-	-	-	-	-	-
Oldham			-	-	-	-	-	-	-	-
Scunthorpe			1	0	1	0	1	0	1	0
Coventry			-	-	-	-	-	-	-	-
Port Vale			4	1	3	0	0	4	2	2
Colchester			-	-	-	-	-	-	-	-
Crewe			3	1	1	1	1	2	2	1
Burton										
Shrewsbury	W	L	4	1	3	0	0	4	2	2
Bury	W	L	4	1	2	1	2	2	2	2
Southend	W	D	5	3	0	2	2	3	2	1

Season	Division	Pos	P	W	D	L	F	A	GD	Pts
2014-15	League 2	1	46	28	10	8	69	39	+30	94
2013-14	League 2	6	46	19	15	12	47	42	+5	72
2012-13	League 2	4	46	22	10	14	71	65	+6	76

Over/Under 39%/61% 16th   **Both score** 50%/50% 10th

BURY

Nickname: The Shakers
Colours: White and blue
Ground: Gigg Lane (11,640)
Tel: 0871-221-1885   www.buryfc.co.uk

A storming finish in which Bury won 13 of their last 16 matches allowed them to seal automatic promotion on the final day, and they also ended with eight straight away victories. That will have pleased David Flitcroft immensely as travel sickness was a major problem for the Shakers earlier in the campaign.

Peter Clarke and Leon Clarke were notable early summer signings and Bury could be one to watch on the handicap getting a hefty start from the bookmakers.

Longest run without win/loss: 5/8
High/low league position: 1/10
Clean sheets: 20 **Yellows:** 71 **Reds:** 4
Avg attendance: 3,774 **Players used:** 33
Leading scorer: D Nardiello 10 (4,8) D Rose 10 (2,10)
Key stat: Bury won only two away matches against teams who finished in the top ten of League Two last season

	2014-15 H	A	Last six seasons at home P	W	D	L	OV	UN	BS	CS
Millwall			-	-	-	-	-	-	-	-
Wigan			-	-	-	-	-	-	-	-
Blackpool			-	-	-	-	-	-	-	-
Swindon			1	0	0	1	0	1	0	0
Sheffield United			2	0	0	2	1	1	0	0
Chesterfield			4	1	2	1	1	3	3	0
Bradford			2	1	0	1	1	1	1	0
Rochdale			3	1	1	1	1	2	1	2
Peterborough			-	-	-	-	-	-	-	-
Fleetwood Town			1	0	1	0	1	0	1	0
Barnsley			-	-	-	-	-	-	-	-
Gillingham			1	1	0	0	1	0	1	0
Doncaster			1	1	0	0	0	1	0	1
Walsall			2	1	1	0	1	1	2	0
Oldham			2	0	1	1	0	2	0	1
Scunthorpe			3	1	2	0	2	1	2	1
Coventry			1	0	0	1	0	1	0	0
Port Vale			2	0	1	1	0	2	1	0
Colchester			2	1	0	1	2	0	2	0
Crewe			3	2	1	0	3	0	2	1
Burton	W	L	4	3	1	0	2	2	1	3
Shrewsbury	W	L	4	3	1	0	1	3	1	3
Bury										
Southend	L	D	3	1	1	1	0	3	1	1

Season	Division	Pos	P	W	D	L	F	A	GD	Pts
2014-15	League 2	3	46	26	7	13	60	40	+20	85
2013-14	League 2	12	46	13	20	13	59	51	+8	59
2012-13	League 1	22	46	9	14	23	45	73	-28	41

Over/Under 37%/63% 18th   **Both score** 39%/61% 21st

CHESTERFIELD

Nickname: Spireites
Colours: Blue and white
Ground: The Proact Stadium (10,400)
Tel: 01246-209-765   www.chesterfield-fc.co.uk

Few gave Chesterfield a serious chance of finishing in the top six last season due to financial constraints, but they made the playoffs despite the January departure of top scorer Eoin Doyle to Cardiff.

Doyle scored 21 times in League One and nobody else hit double figures. The Spireites have since lost manager Paul Cook to Portsmouth and replaced him with Dean Saunders, who has three relegations on his CV since 2011. A fourth can't be dismissed at a nice price.

Longest run without win/loss: 7/7
High/low league position: 3/14
Clean sheets: 14 **Yellows:** 78 **Reds:** 5
Avg attendance: 6,925 **Players used:** 31
Leading scorer: E Doyle 21 (4,13)
Key stat: Chesterfield won the same amount of away matches (seven) as relegated duo Notts County and Leyton Orient last season

	2014-15 H	A	Last six seasons at home P	W	D	L	OV	UN	BS	CS
Millwall			-	-	-	-	-	-	-	-
Wigan			-	-	-	-	-	-	-	-
Blackpool			-	-	-	-	-	-	-	-
Swindon			1	0	0	1	1	0	0	0
Sheffield United	W	D	2	1	0	1	1	1	1	0
Chesterfield										
Bradford	L	W	4	0	3	1	2	2	3	0
Rochdale	W	L	5	3	2	0	3	2	4	1
Peterborough	W	L	1	1	0	0	1	0	1	0
Fleetwood Town	W	D	3	2	0	1	3	0	2	1
Barnsley	W	D	1	1	0	0	1	0	1	0
Gillingham	W	W	3	2	0	1	2	1	1	1
Doncaster	D	L	1	0	1	0	1	0	1	0
Walsall	W	L	2	1	1	0	0	2	1	1
Oldham	D	D	2	0	2	0	0	2	2	0
Scunthorpe	W	L	3	1	1	1	2	1	3	0
Coventry	L	D	1	0	0	1	0	1	0	0
Port Vale	W	W	4	2	1	1	3	1	1	2
Colchester	W	L	2	1	0	1	1	1	0	1
Crewe	W	D	3	1	1	1	2	1	2	0
Burton			4	1	1	2	2	2	3	0
Shrewsbury			2	1	0	1	1	1	1	0
Bury	W	L	4	3	0	1	2	2	1	3
Southend			3	2	0	1	2	1	2	0

Season	Division	Pos	P	W	D	L	F	A	GD	Pts
2014-15	League 1	6	46	19	12	15	68	55	+13	69
2013-14	League 2	1	46	23	15	8	71	40	+31	84
2012-13	League 2	8	46	18	13	15	60	45	+15	67

Over/Under 52%/48% 10th   **Both score** 50%/50% 14th

LEAGUE ONE

COLCHESTER

COLCHESTER UNITED FC

Nickname: The U's
Colours: Blue and white
Ground: Weston Homes Community Stadium (10,105)
Tel: 01206-755-100   www.cu-fc.com

It needed a minor miracle but Colchester just about maintained their League One status on a dramatic final day that saw them deny Preston automatic promotion and all other results going their way. In the end, eight points taken from their last four games was just enough for the U's.

Tony Humes's faith in homegrown youngsters did eventually pay off and, in theory at least, they will be better for the experience. But money is tight and staying up remains the primary ambition.

Longest run without win/loss: 6/4
High/low league position: 14/23
Clean sheets: 11 **Yellows:** 56 **Reds:** 4
Avg attendance: 3,886 **Players used:** 43
Leading scorer: F Sears 10 (2,10)
Key stat: Colchester conceded 77 goals last term, with only Crawley shipping more. On ten occasions they conceded at least three times

	2014-15 H	A	Last six seasons at home P	W	D	L	OV	UN	BS	CS
Millwall			1	0	0	1	1	0	1	0
Wigan	-	-	-	-	-	-	-	-	-	-
Blackpool	-	-	-	-	-	-	-	-	-	-
Swindon	D	D	5	2	1	2	3	2	3	1
Sheffield United	L	L	4	0	2	2	1	3	3	0
Chesterfield	W	L	2	1	0	1	2	0	2	0
Bradford	D	D	2	0	1	1	0	2	0	1
Rochdale	L	L	3	1	1	1	1	2	1	2
Peterborough	L	W	3	2	0	1	2	1	2	1
Fleetwood Town	W	W	1	1	0	0	1	0	1	0
Barnsley	W		1	1	0	0	1	0	1	0
Gillingham	L	D	3	2	0	1	3	0	2	1
Doncaster	L	L	2	0	0	2	1	1	1	0
Walsall	L	D	6	4	1	1	1	5	2	3
Oldham	D	W	6	3	1	2	2	4	2	2
Scunthorpe	D	D	3	0	2	1	2	1	3	0
Coventry	L	L	3	1	0	2	2	1	2	0
Port Vale	L	W	2	1	0	1	1	1	1	1
Colchester										
Crewe	L	W	3	0	0	3	3	0	3	0
Burton	-	-	-	-	-	-	-	-	-	-
Shrewsbury			2	1	1	0	0	2	0	2
Bury			2	2	0	0	1	1	1	1
Southend			1	1	0	0	0	1	0	1

Season	Division	Pos	P	W	D	L	F	A	GD	Pts
2014-15	League 1	19	46	14	10	22	58	77	-19	52
2013-14	League 1	16	46	13	14	19	53	61	-8	53
2012-13	League 1	20	46	14	9	23	47	68	-21	51

Over/Under 57%/43% 7th   **Both score** 57%/43% 5th

COVENTRY

COVENTRY CITY FOOTBALL CLUB

Nickname: The Sky Blues
Colours: Sky blue
Ground: Ricoh Arena (32,500)
Tel: 02476-992-326   www.ccfc.co.uk

Tony Mowbray was appointed in March as Coventry's 12th manager in 14 years and he managed to secure their safety with a decent run of results which included an unbeaten away run.

However, Mowbray likes to play a possession-based game and said himself that it was less than ideal having to share a pitch with rugby side Wasps. That is likely to be a continued source of annoyance for the cash-strapped Sky Blues, particularly in the latter months of the season.

Longest run without win/loss: 7/6
High/low league position: 9/21
Clean sheets: 14 **Yellows:** 77 **Reds:** 4
Avg attendance: 9,332 **Players used:** 36
Leading scorer: J O'Brien 6 (4,5) F Nouble 6 (3,6)
Key stat: Coventry won just two of their 12 home matches after rugby union side Wasps moved in to the Ricoh

	2014-15 H	A	Last six seasons at home P	W	D	L	OV	UN	BS	CS
Millwall			2	1	0	1	1	1	1	0
Wigan	-	-	-	-	-	-	-	-	-	-
Blackpool			2	0	2	0	1	1	2	0
Swindon	L	D	3	0	0	3	3	0	2	0
Sheffield United	W	D	5	3	2	0	2	3	3	2
Chesterfield	D	W	1	0	1	0	0	1	0	1
Bradford	D	L	2	0	2	0	0	2	1	1
Rochdale	D	L	1	0	1	0	1	0	1	0
Peterborough	W	W	4	3	1	0	4	0	4	0
Fleetwood Town	D	L	1	0	1	0	0	1	1	0
Barnsley	D	L	4	3	1	0	3	1	2	2
Gillingham	W	L	2	2	0	0	1	1	1	1
Doncaster	L	L	5	3	0	2	2	3	2	2
Walsall	D	L	3	2	1	0	2	1	2	1
Oldham	D	L	3	1	2	0	1	2	3	0
Scunthorpe	D		4	1	2	1	2	2	4	0
Coventry										
Port Vale	L	W	2	0	1	1	2	0	2	0
Colchester	W	W	3	2	1	0	1	2	1	2
Crewe	L	L	3	0	1	2	3	0	3	0
Burton	-	-	-	-	-	-	-	-	-	-
Shrewsbury			2	0	1	1	0	2	0	1
Bury			1	0	1	0	1	0	1	0
Southend	-	-	-	-	-	-	-	-	-	-

Season	Division	Pos	P	W	D	L	F	A	GD	Pts
2014-15	League 1	17	46	13	16	17	49	60	-11	55
2013-14	League 1	18	46	16	13	17	74	77	-3	51
2012-13	League 1	15	46	18	11	17	66	59	+7	55

Over/Under 43%/57% 19th   **Both score** 52%/48% 9th

CREWE

Nickname: The Railwaymen
Colours: Red and white
Ground: Gresty Road (10,066)
Tel: 01270-213-014   www.crewealex.net

The footballing gods smiled on Crewe last season. They were in the relegation zone going into the last weekend but, despite their final day defeat, they still snuck to safety when other results went their way.

Crewe looked doomed early on after taking just four points from their opening ten games, so staying up was a bonus from that disastrous position. However, manager Steve Davis is snookered by a small budget and the famous academy will need to work its magic again.

Longest run without win/loss: 6/4
High/low league position: 18/24
Clean sheets: 10 **Yellows:** 57 **Reds:** 3
Avg attendance: 4,732 **Players used:** 32
Leading scorer: N Ajose 8 (5,7)
Key stat: Crewe conceded 660 shots in League One last season – 57 more than the next worst which was Fleetwood with 603

	2014-15 H	A	P	W	D	L	OV	UN	BS	CS
Millwall			-	-	-	-	-	-	-	-
Wigan			-	-	-	-	-	-	-	-
Blackpool			-	-	-	-	-	-	-	-
Swindon	D	L	4	2	2	0	1	3	2	2
Sheffield United	L	W	3	2	0	1	1	2	0	2
Chesterfield	D	L	3	1	1	1	0	3	0	2
Bradford	L	L	5	2	1	2	1	4	1	2
Rochdale	L	L	2	0	1	1	2	0	2	0
Peterborough	W	D	2	1	1	0	1	1	1	1
Fleetwood Town	W	L	1	1	0	0	0	1	0	1
Barnsley	L	L	1	0	0	1	1	0	1	0
Gillingham	W	L	4	1	1	2	3	1	3	0
Doncaster	D	L	2	0	1	1	1	1	2	0
Walsall	D	W	3	1	1	1	1	2	1	1
Oldham	L	W	3	0	1	2	0	3	1	0
Scunthorpe	W	L	2	2	0	0	0	2	0	2
Coventry	W	W	3	2	0	1	2	1	2	1
Port Vale	W	W	5	2	1	2	4	1	5	0
Colchester	L	W	3	1	1	1	2	1	1	1
Crewe										
Burton			3	3	0	0	3	0	3	0
Shrewsbury			5	0	3	2	2	3	4	0
Bury			3	2	0	1	2	1	1	2
Southend			2	1	0	1	1	1	1	1

Season	Division	Pos	P	W	D	L	F	A	GD	Pts
2014-15	League 1	20	46	14	10	22	43	75	-32	52
2013-14	League 1	19	46	13	12	21	54	80	-26	51
2012-13	League 1	13	46	18	10	18	54	62	-8	64

Over/Under 46%/54% 16th   **Both score** 50%/50% 14th

DONCASTER

Nickname: Rovers
Colours: Red and white
Ground: Keepmoat Stadium (15,231)
Tel: 01302-764-664 www.doncasterroversfc.co.uk

If there is to be a potential improver from those who finished in the bottom half of last season's League One then Doncaster could be that team.

They were much better than their 13th-place finish suggests and for spells were one of the best footballing sides in the division, with Richie Wellens pulling the strings in midfield. Paul Dickov bemoaned a weak mentality from his players in the latter stages, but this was a side who started March in sixth.

Longest run without win/loss: 4/7
High/low league position: 6/20
Clean sheets: 14 **Yellows:** 67 **Reds:** 2
Avg attendance: 6,884 **Players used:** 31
Leading scorer: N Tyson 12 (2,10)
Key stat: Both teams scored in only nine of Doncaster's 46 League One matches last season

	2014-15 H	A	P	W	D	L	OV	UN	BS	CS
Millwall			3	1	1	1	2	1	1	1
Wigan			1	1	0	0	1	0	0	1
Blackpool			3	0	1	2	3	0	3	0
Swindon	L	W	2	1	0	1	1	1	1	1
Sheffield United	L	L	4	1	2	1	1	3	2	1
Chesterfield	W	D	1	1	0	0	1	0	1	0
Bradford	L	W	1	0	0	0	0	0	0	0
Rochdale	D	W	1	0	1	0	0	1	1	0
Peterborough	W	D	3	1	1	1	1	2	2	0
Fleetwood Town	D	L	1	0	1	0	1	0	1	0
Barnsley	W	D	5	2	1	2	1	4	1	2
Gillingham	L	D	1	0	0	1	1	0	1	0
Doncaster										
Walsall	L	L	2	0	0	2	1	1	1	0
Oldham	L	D	2	1	0	1	0	2	0	1
Scunthorpe	W	W	4	4	0	0	4	0	2	2
Coventry	W	W	5	1	3	1	1	4	3	2
Port Vale	L	L	1	0	0	1	1	0	1	0
Colchester	W	W	2	2	0	0	2	0	2	2
Crewe	W	D	2	1	0	1	1	1	1	0
Burton			-	-	-	-	-	-	-	-
Shrewsbury			1	1	0	0	0	1	0	1
Bury			1	1	0	0	1	0	1	0
Southend			-	-	-	-	-	-	-	-

Season	Division	Pos	P	W	D	L	F	A	GD	Pts
2014-15	League 1	13	46	16	13	17	58	62	-4	61
2013-14	Championship	22	46	11	11	24	39	70	-31	44
2012-13	League 1	1	46	25	9	12	62	44	+18	84

Over/Under 54%/46% 9th   **Both score** 48%/52% 19th

FLEETWOOD TOWN

Nickname: The Cod Army
Colours: Red and white
Ground: Highbury Stadium (5,311)
Tel: 01253 775080 www.fleetwoodtownfc.com

It was a solid debut season in League One for Fleetwood, as they finished with a decent 63-point haul.

However, the Cod Army defied the statistics as they kept 14 clean sheets and conceded just 52 goals, but they also allowed 603 shots – the second-worst record in the division behind Crewe.

Over time that cannot continue. Either Fleetwood must improve their defending or this season will see them concede far more goals than they did in 2014-15.

Longest run without win/loss: 7/5
High/low league position: 7/14
Clean sheets: 14 **Yellows:** 95 **Reds:** 3
Avg attendance: 3,522 **Players used:** 29
Leading scorer: D Ball 8 (3,7) J Proctor 8 (3,8)
Key stat: Fleetwood's matches produced the fewest goals (101) in League One last season, an average of just 2.2

	2014-15 H	A	Last six seasons at home P	W	D	L	OV	UN	BS	CS
Millwall			-	-	-	-	-	-	-	-
Wigan			-	-	-	-	-	-	-	-
Blackpool			-	-	-	-	-	-	-	-
Swindon	D	L	1	0	1	0	1	0	1	0
Sheffield United	D	W	1	0	1	0	0	1	1	0
Chesterfield	D	L	3	0	2	1	1	2	2	1
Bradford	L	D	2	0	1	1	1	1	1	0
Rochdale	W	W	3	1	1	1	1	2	0	2
Peterborough	D	L	1	0	1	0	0	1	1	0
Fleetwood Town										
Barnsley	D	W	1	0	1	0	0	1	0	1
Gillingham	W	W	2	1	1	0	1	1	1	1
Doncaster	W	D	1	1	0	0	1	0	1	0
Walsall	L	L	1	0	0	1	0	1	0	0
Oldham	L	L	1	0	0	1	0	1	0	0
Scunthorpe	D	W	2	0	1	1	1	1	1	0
Coventry	L	D	1	0	0	1	0	1	0	0
Port Vale	W	W	2	1	0	1	1	1	1	1
Colchester	L	L	1	0	0	1	0	1	0	0
Crewe	W	L	1	1	0	0	1	0	1	0
Burton			2	0	0	2	2	0	1	0
Shrewsbury			-	-	-	-	-	-	-	-
Bury			1	1	0	0	1	0	1	0
Southend			2	0	2	0	0	2	1	1

Season	Division	Pos	P	W	D	L	F	A	GD	Pts
2014-15	League 1	10	46	17	12	17	49	52	-3	63
2013-14	League 2	4	46	22	10	14	66	52	+14	76
2012-13	League 2	13	46	15	15	16	55	57	-2	60

Over/Under 37%/63% 23rd   **Both score** 41%/59% 23rd

GILLINGHAM

Nickname: The Gills
Colours: Blue and white
Ground: Priestfield Stadium (11,582)
Tel: 01634-300-000 www.gillinghamfootballclub.com

Gillingham looked genuine relegation candidates for the first part of the season but Justin Edinburgh's arrival in place of Peter Taylor in the dugout saw a dramatic improvement. The Gills even hit the dizzy heights of ninth in April before eventually settling for 12th.

From Edinburgh's arrival on February 7 to the end of the season, the side averaged 1.67 points per game, with only promoted trio Preston (2.21), Bristol City (2.1) and MK Dons (1.89) averaging more.

Longest run without win/loss: 8/7
High/low league position: 10/22
Clean sheets: 9 **Yellows:** 74 **Reds:** 2
Avg attendance: 5,694 **Players used:** 33
Leading scorer: C McDonald 16 (4,13)
Key stat: Gillingham gained 30 points from 18 matches after Justin Edinburgh was appointed as manager

	2014-15 H	A	Last six seasons at home P	W	D	L	OV	UN	BS	CS
Millwall			1	1	0	0	0	1	0	1
Wigan			-	-	-	-	-	-	-	-
Blackpool			-	-	-	-	-	-	-	-
Swindon	D	W	4	3	1	0	3	1	2	2
Sheffield United	W	L	2	1	0	1	0	2	0	1
Chesterfield	L	L	3	0	1	2	1	2	2	0
Bradford	W	D	5	3	1	1	1	4	1	3
Rochdale	W	D	2	1	0	1	1	1	1	1
Peterborough	W	W	2	1	1	0	2	0	2	0
Fleetwood Town	L	L	2	0	1	1	1	1	1	0
Barnsley	L	L	1	0	0	1	0	1	0	0
Gillingham										
Doncaster	D	W	1	0	1	0	0	1	1	0
Walsall	D	D	3	0	3	0	1	2	1	2
Oldham	W	D	3	2	0	1	1	2	1	1
Scunthorpe	L	L	1	0	0	1	1	0	0	0
Coventry	W	L	2	2	0	0	2	0	2	0
Port Vale	D	L	5	2	2	1	4	1	4	1
Colchester	D	L	3	0	2	1	1	2	1	1
Crewe	W	L	4	1	0	3	3	1	3	1
Burton			3	3	0	0	2	1	2	1
Shrewsbury			3	1	1	1	0	3	1	1
Bury			1	0	1	0	0	1	1	0
Southend			4	2	1	1	2	2	1	3

Season	Division	Pos	P	W	D	L	F	A	GD	Pts
2014-15	League 1	12	46	16	14	16	65	66	-1	62
2013-14	League 1	17	46	15	8	23	60	79	-19	53
2012-13	League 2	1	46	23	14	9	66	39	+27	83

Over/Under 59%/41% 3rd   **Both score** 63%/37% 3rd

MILLWALL

Nickname: The Lions
Colours: Blue and white
Ground: The Den (20,146)
Tel: 020-7232-1222   www.millwallfc.co.uk

Most Millwall fans blame Ian Holloway for their relegation and not even the appointment of club legend Neil Harris could save the Lions, who finished five points adrift of a Rotherham side that had been hit with a three-point deduction.

Millwall were particularly poor against the stronger Championship sides, taking just five points from 16 games against the eventual top eight. However, they won't face that calibre of opponent in a soft-looking League One this season.

Longest run without win/loss: 9/4
High/low league position: 12/23
Clean sheets: 15 **Yellows:** 89 **Reds:** 5
Avg attendance: 10,902 **Players used:** 40
Leading scorer: L Gregory 9 (3,7)
Key stat: Millwall have finished in the top six in four of their last six seasons in the third tier

| | 2014-15 | | Last six seasons at home | | | | | | | |
	H	A	P	W	D	L	OV	UN	BS	CS
Millwall										
Wigan	W	D	2	2	0	0	1	1	1	1
Blackpool	W	L	4	2	1	1	3	1	3	0
Swindon			1	1	0	0	1	0	1	0
Sheffield United			1	0	0	1	0	1	0	0
Chesterfield			-	-	-	-	-	-	-	-
Bradford			-	-	-	-	-	-	-	-
Rochdale			-	-	-	-	-	-	-	-
Peterborough			2	0	1	1	2	0	2	0
Fleetwood Town			-	-	-	-	-	-	-	-
Barnsley			4	2	1	1	1	3	1	3
Gillingham			1	1	0	0	1	0	0	1
Doncaster			3	2	1	0	1	2	1	2
Walsall			1	1	0	0	1	0	1	0
Oldham			1	1	0	0	0	1	0	1
Scunthorpe			1	1	0	0	1	0	0	1
Coventry			2	2	0	0	2	0	1	1
Port Vale			-	-	-	-	-	-	-	-
Colchester			1	1	0	0	1	0	1	0
Crewe			-	-	-	-	-	-	-	-
Burton			-	-	-	-	-	-	-	-
Shrewsbury			-	-	-	-	-	-	-	-
Bury			-	-	-	-	-	-	-	-
Southend			1	1	0	0	0	1	0	1

Season	Division	Pos	P	W	D	L	F	A	GD	Pts
2014-15	Championship	22	46	9	14	23	42	76	-34	41
2013-14	Championship	19	46	11	16	20	46	74	-28	48
2012-13	Championship	20	46	15	11	20	51	62	-11	56

Over/Under 46%/54% 16th   **Both score** 46%/54% 19th

OLDHAM

Nickname: The Latics
Colours: Blue
Ground: Boundary Park (10,638)
Tel: 0161-624-4972 www.oldhamathletic.co.uk

It's fair to say Darren Kelly is a man under pressure, despite the new Oldham manager only being appointed in May.

Some fans threatened to boycott Boundary Park, those who had bought season tickets were offered a refund and two people were arrested for death threats sent to Kelly over his support for former IRA member Martin McGuinness.

A fast start will be essential for Kelly to calm the disquiet, but the 2014-15 squad needs improvement.

Longest run without win/loss: 8/11
High/low league position: 5/16
Clean sheets: 12 **Yellows:** 50 **Reds:** 4
Avg attendance: 4,349 **Players used:** 37
Leading scorer: J Forte 15 (6,13)
Key stat: Oldham won just three of their final 17 League One fixtures last season

| | 2014-15 | | Last six seasons at home | | | | | | | |
	H	A	P	W	D	L	OV	UN	BS	CS
Millwall			1	0	0	1	0	1	0	0
Wigan			-	-	-	-	-	-	-	-
Blackpool			-	-	-	-	-	-	-	-
Swindon	W	D	5	3	1	1	3	2	3	1
Sheffield United	D	D	4	0	2	2	1	3	2	0
Chesterfield	D	D	2	1	1	0	1	1	1	1
Bradford	W	L	2	1	1	0	1	1	2	0
Rochdale	W	W	3	2	0	1	2	1	1	2
Peterborough	D	D	3	1	1	1	2	1	2	0
Fleetwood Town	W	W	1	1	0	0	0	1	0	1
Barnsley	L	L	1	0	0	1	1	0	1	0
Gillingham	D	L	3	2	1	0	0	3	0	3
Doncaster	D	W	2	0	1	1	2	0	2	0
Walsall	W	L	6	3	2	1	2	4	4	1
Oldham										
Scunthorpe	W	W	3	1	1	1	2	1	3	0
Coventry	W	W	3	1	1	1	1	2	1	1
Port Vale	D	W	2	1	1	0	1	1	2	0
Colchester	L	D	6	0	4	2	1	5	3	1
Crewe	L	W	3	0	1	2	2	1	3	0
Burton			-	-	-	-	-	-	-	-
Shrewsbury			2	1	0	1	1	1	1	1
Bury			2	0	0	2	1	1	1	0
Southend			1	0	1	0	1	0	1	0

Season	Division	Pos	P	W	D	L	F	A	GD	Pts
2014-15	League 1	15	46	14	15	17	54	67	-13	57
2013-14	League 1	15	46	14	14	18	50	59	-9	56
2012-13	League 1	19	46	14	9	23	46	59	-13	51

Over/Under 50%/50% 13th   **Both score** 50%/50% 14th

PETERBOROUGH

Nickname: The Posh
Colours: Blue
Ground: London Road (14,319)
Tel: 01733-563 947   www.theposh.com

Owner Darragh MacAnthony is rarely afraid to share his opinions on Twitter and it's pretty clear from reading his posts that he wants a return to Peterborough's free-scoring days, notably when they scored 106 goals at this level in 2010-11.

Things had gone stale under Darren Ferguson, but novice replacement Dave Robertson has much to prove and other sides are preferred in the outright betting as United aim to improve on last season's disappointing ninth-placed finish.

Longest run without win/loss: 6/4
High/low league position: 2/15
Clean sheets: 12 **Yellows:** 69 **Reds:** 8
Avg attendance: 6,227 **Players used:** 33
Leading scorer: C Washington 13 (4,11)
Key stat: Peterborough scored 53 goals last season, 19 fewer than in the 2013-14 campaign

| | 2014-15 | | Last six seasons at home | | | | | | | |
	H	A	P	W	D	L	OV	UN	BS	CS
Millwall			2	0	0	2	2	0	1	0
Wigan			-	-	-	-	-	-	-	-
Blackpool			3	1	0	2	2	1	2	0
Swindon	L	L	3	2	0	1	2	1	2	1
Sheffield United	L	W	3	1	1	1	1	2	1	2
Chesterfield	W	L	1	1	0	0	0	1	0	1
Bradford	W	W	2	2	0	0	1	1	1	1
Rochdale	W	W	2	2	0	0	2	0	2	0
Peterborough										
Fleetwood Town	W	D	1	1	0	0	0	1	0	1
Barnsley	W	D	4	2	0	2	4	0	4	0
Gillingham	L	L	2	1	0	1	1	1	1	1
Doncaster	D	W	3	0	1	2	2	1	2	1
Walsall	D	D	3	1	2	0	1	2	1	2
Oldham	D	D	3	2	1	0	3	0	3	0
Scunthorpe	L	L	2	1	0	1	2	0	1	1
Coventry	L	L	4	2	0	2	0	4	0	2
Port Vale	W	L	2	1	1	0	1	1	1	1
Colchester	L	W	3	1	1	1	0	3	1	1
Crewe	D	L	2	1	1	0	1	1	2	0
Burton			-	-	-	-	-	-	-	-
Shrewsbury			1	1	0	0	0	1	0	1
Bury			-	-	-	-	-	-	-	-
Southend			-	-	-	-	-	-	-	-

Season	Division	Pos	P	W	D	L	F	A	GD	Pts
2014-15	League 1	9	46	18	9	19	53	56	-3	63
2013-14	League 1	6	46	23	5	18	72	58	+14	74
2012-13	Championship	22	46	15	9	22	66	75	-9	54

Over/Under 46%/54% 16th   **Both score** 50%/50% 14th

PORT VALE

Nickname: The Valiants
Colours: White and black
Ground: Vale Park (18,947)
Tel: 0871-221-1876   www.port-vale.co.uk

Port Vale suffered a poor finish to the 2014-15 campaign and with budget cuts expected for this season it could be difficult for manager Rob Page to get the club back to winning ways.

Chairman Norman Smurthwaite has revealed that the club spent £2.45m on players last season, but that outlay is being slashed to £1.7m for this campaign unless there is a serious upturn in season-ticket sales. That leaves Vale vulnerable and among the relegation favourites.

Longest run without win/loss: 9/4
High/low league position: 8/23
Clean sheets: 6 **Yellows:** 80 **Reds:** 6
Avg attendance: 5,313 **Players used:** 31
Leading scorer: T Pope 8 (5,7)
Key stat: Port Vale won just one of their final 11 matches last season, losing seven, and that came against relegated Yeovil

| | 2014-15 | | Last six seasons at home | | | | | | | |
	H	A	P	W	D	L	OV	UN	BS	CS
Millwall			-	-	-	-	-	-	-	-
Wigan			-	-	-	-	-	-	-	-
Blackpool			-	-	-	-	-	-	-	-
Swindon	L	L	3	0	0	3	1	2	1	0
Sheffield United	W	L	2	1	0	1	2	0	2	0
Chesterfield	W	L	4	0	1	3	2	2	3	0
Bradford	D	D	6	4	2	0	5	1	5	1
Rochdale	W	L	3	1	2	0	1	2	2	1
Peterborough	W	L	2	1	0	1	1	1	1	0
Fleetwood Town	L	L	2	0	0	2	1	1	1	0
Barnsley	W	L	1	1	0	0	1	0	1	0
Gillingham	W	D	5	3	1	1	3	2	3	1
Doncaster	W	W	1	1	0	0	1	0	0	1
Walsall	D	W	2	1	1	0	0	2	1	1
Oldham	L	D	2	1	0	1	0	2	0	1
Scunthorpe	D	D	1	0	1	0	1	0	1	0
Coventry	L		2	1	0	1	1	1	1	0
Port Vale										
Colchester	L	W	2	1	0	1	1	1	1	1
Crewe	L	L	5	1	1	3	2	3	3	0
Burton			4	4	0	0	4	0	3	1
Shrewsbury			4	2	1	1	2	2	3	1
Bury			2	0	1	1	0	2	0	1
Southend			3	0	1	2	2	1	3	0

Season	Division	Pos	P	W	D	L	F	A	GD	Pts
2014-15	League 1	18	46	15	9	22	55	65	-10	54
2013-14	League 1	9	46	18	7	21	59	73	-14	61
2012-13	League 2	3	46	21	15	10	87	52	+35	78

Over/Under 59%/41% 3rd   **Both score** 59%/41% 4th

ROCHDALE

Nickname: The Dale
Colours: Blue and black
Ground: Spotland Stadium (10,249)
Tel: 01706-644-648   www.rochdaleafc.co.uk

Keith Hill worked wonders to get Rochdale to eighth last season but he'll have to pull something out of the bag once again after losing influential Matty Done in January and loan star Jack O'Connell, who is now at Brentford.

Dale's win percentage dropped from 50 to 32 without Connell last season and it was exactly the same for Done, who looked a real class act when Hill shrewdly converted him from a midfielder to forward.

Longest run without win/loss: 4/4
High/low league position: 5/16
Clean sheets: 9 **Yellows:** 63 **Reds:** 5
Avg attendance: 3,309 **Players used:** 31
Leading scorer: I Henderson 22 (4,19)
Key stat: Rochdale won 11 and drew one of their 12 matches against the bottom six last season

	2014-15		Last six seasons at home							
	H	A	P	W	D	L	OV	UN	BS	CS
Millwall	-	-	-	-	-	-	-	-	-	-
Wigan	-	-	-	-	-	-	-	-	-	-
Blackpool	-	-	-	-	-	-	-	-	-	-
Swindon	L	W	2	0	1	1	2	0	2	0
Sheffield United	L	L	2	0	0	2	2	0	2	0
Chesterfield	W	L	5	1	3	1	2	3	4	1
Bradford	L	W	3	0	1	2	1	2	1	1
Rochdale										
Peterborough	L	L	2	0	1	1	1	1	1	0
Fleetwood Town	L	L	3	0	1	2	1	2	1	1
Barnsley	L	L	1	0	0	1	0	1	0	0
Gillingham	D	L	2	0	2	0	0	2	2	0
Doncaster	L	D	1	0	0	1	1	0	1	0
Walsall	W	L	3	2	1	0	3	0	2	1
Oldham	L	L	3	1	1	1	2	1	2	0
Scunthorpe	W	L	3	2	0	1	2	1	1	1
Coventry	W	D	1	1	0	0	0	1	0	1
Port Vale	W	L	3	1	2	0	1	2	1	2
Colchester	W	W	3	1	1	1	3	0	3	0
Crewe	W	W	2	2	0	0	1	1	0	2
Burton			3	0	1	2	1	2	2	0
Shrewsbury			1	1	0	0	1	0	0	1
Bury			3	3	0	0	2	1	0	3
Southend			2	1	0	1	2	0	1	0

Season	Division	Pos	P	W	D	L	F	A	GD	Pts
2014-15	League 1	8	46	19	6	21	72	66	+6	63
2013-14	League 2	3	46	24	9	13	69	48	+21	81
2012-13	League 2	12	46	16	13	17	68	70	-2	61

Over/Under 63%/37% 2nd   **Both score** 52%/48% 9th

SCUNTHORPE

Nickname: The Iron
Colours: Claret and blue
Ground: Glanford Park (9,183)
Tel: 0871-221 1899   www.scunthorpe-united.co.uk

Tightening up the defence will be the top priority for Scunthorpe after they kept just three clean sheets in 2014-15 and became a banker bet for punters who like to get involved in 'both teams to score' wagers.

The Iron made a terrible start last season and were rock-bottom at the end of October. However, sacked manager Russ Wilcox had been unlucky with a horrendous injury list and Scunny should do better than 16th this time around.

Longest run without win/loss: 9/7
High/low league position: 14/24
Clean sheets: 3 **Yellows:** 82 **Reds:** 3
Avg attendance: 3,646 **Players used:** 40
Leading scorer: P Madden 14 (4,13)
Key stat: Both sides scored in 32 of Scunny's 46 league games last term. That 70 per cent figure increased to 74 on the road (17 of 23)

	2014-15		Last six seasons at home							
	H	A	P	W	D	L	OV	UN	BS	CS
Millwall			1	0	0	1	1	0	1	0
Wigan	-	-	-	-	-	-	-	-	-	-
Blackpool			1	0	0	1	1	0	1	0
Swindon	W	L	2	2	0	0	2	0	2	0
Sheffield United	D	L	5	2	3	0	2	3	5	0
Chesterfield	W	L	3	1	2	0	1	2	2	1
Bradford	D	D	1	0	1	0	0	1	1	0
Rochdale	W	L	3	3	0	0	2	1	1	2
Peterborough	W	W	2	2	0	0	1	1	0	2
Fleetwood Town	L	D	2	0	1	0	2	0	1	1
Barnsley	L	W	3	1	1	1	2	1	1	1
Gillingham	W	W	1	1	0	0	1	0	1	0
Doncaster	L	L	4	0	1	3	4	0	4	0
Walsall	W	W	3	1	1	1	2	1	2	0
Oldham	L	L	3	0	1	2	2	1	2	0
Scunthorpe										
Coventry	W	D	4	2	0	2	2	2	2	1
Port Vale	D	D	1	0	1	0	0	1	1	0
Colchester	D	D	3	1	2	0	0	3	2	1
Crewe	W	L	2	1	0	1	2	0	2	0
Burton			1	1	0	0	0	1	0	1
Shrewsbury			1	0	1	0	0	1	0	1
Bury			3	0	1	2	3	0	3	0
Southend			1	0	1	0	1	0	1	0

Season	Division	Pos	P	W	D	L	F	A	GD	Pts
2014-15	League 1	16	46	14	14	18	62	75	-13	56
2013-14	League 2	2	46	20	21	5	68	44	+24	81
2012-13	League 1	21	46	13	9	24	49	73	-24	48

Over/Under 57%/43% 7th   **Both score** 70%/30% 1st

SHEFFIELD UNITED

Nickname: The Blades
Colours: Red and white
Ground: Bramall Lane (32,702)
Tel: 0871-995-1899   www.sufc.co.uk

Last season's ante-post title favourites fell short of promotion, losing 6-5 on aggregate to Swindon in the playoff semi-finals, and Nigel Clough paid the price for that failure despite leading the Blades to the semi-finals of the League Cup.

The cup distraction understandably took a toll, but United have everything in place for a push this time. New manager Nigel Adkins has won promotion three times at this level, twice with Scunthorpe and once with Southampton.

Longest run without win/loss: 6/6
High/low league position: 5/11
Clean sheets: 10 **Yellows:** 65 **Reds:** 4
Avg attendance: 19,805 **Players used:** 33
Leading scorer: J Murphy 11 (3,10)
Key stat: Sheffield United have scored in 21 of their last 22 matches in all competitions

SHREWSBURY

Nickname: The Shrews
Colours: Blue and amber
Ground: Greenhous Meadow (9,875)
Tel: 01743-289-177   shrewsburytown.com

They didn't win the league but plenty of League Two judges felt that Shrewsbury were the best side in the division and bookmakers are rightly giving them plenty of respect for this campaign.

The Shrews had the second-best attack, scoring 67 goals, and managed 23 clean sheets, with the Salop side losing just twice at home, winning 17 times. Town won at Leicester in the League Cup and also knocked Walsall out of the FA Cup so they should be fine at a higher level.

Longest run without win/loss: 3/7
High/low league position: 1/12
Clean sheets: 23 **Yellows:** 68 **Reds:** 6
Avg attendance: 5,343 **Players used:** 30
Leading scorer: J Collins 15 (5,12)
Key stat: Shrewsbury lost all of their away matches 1-0 to fellow top-seven teams in League Two last season

	2014-15 H	A	Last six seasons at home P	W	D	L	OV	UN	BS	CS
Millwall			1	0	1	0	0	1	1	0
Wigan			-	-	-	-	-	-	-	-
Blackpool			1	1	0	0	1	0	0	1
Swindon	W	L	3	3	0	0	0	3	0	3
Sheffield United										
Chesterfield	D	L	2	1	1	0	1	1	2	0
Bradford	D	W	2	0	2	0	1	1	2	0
Rochdale	W	W	2	2	0	0	1	1	0	2
Peterborough	L	W	3	2	0	1	1	2	1	2
Fleetwood Town	L	D	1	0	0	1	1	0	1	0
Barnsley	L	W	3	0	2	1	1	2	1	1
Gillingham	W	L	2	1	0	1	2	0	2	0
Doncaster	W	W	4	1	3	0	2	2	3	1
Walsall	D	D	4	2	2	0	1	3	3	1
Oldham	D	D	4	0	3	1	1	3	4	0
Scunthorpe	W	D	5	3	0	2	4	1	1	2
Coventry	D	L	5	2	1	2	3	2	3	1
Port Vale	W	L	2	2	0	0	1	1	1	1
Colchester	W	W	4	3	1	0	3	1	2	2
Crewe	L	W	3	1	1	1	3	0	3	0
Burton			-	-	-	-	-	-	-	-
Shrewsbury			2	2	0	0	0	2	0	2
Bury			2	1	1	0	1	1	1	1
Southend			-	-	-	-	-	-	-	-

Season	Division	Pos	P	W	D	L	F	A	GD	Pts
2014-15	League 1	5	46	19	14	13	66	53	+13	71
2013-14	League 1	7	46	18	13	15	48	46	+2	67
2012-13	League 1	5	46	19	18	9	56	42	+14	75

Over/Under 43%/57% 19th   **Both score** 65%/35% 2nd

	2014-15 H	A	Last six seasons at home P	W	D	L	OV	UN	BS	CS
Millwall			-	-	-	-	-	-	-	-
Wigan			-	-	-	-	-	-	-	-
Blackpool			-	-	-	-	-	-	-	-
Swindon			3	2	0	1	1	2	1	1
Sheffield United			2	1	0	1	1	1	1	1
Chesterfield			2	0	2	0	0	2	1	1
Bradford			4	3	0	1	3	1	3	1
Rochdale			1	0	0	1	0	1	0	0
Peterborough			1	0	0	1	1	0	1	0
Fleetwood Town			-	-	-	-	-	-	-	-
Barnsley			-	-	-	-	-	-	-	-
Gillingham			3	2	1	0	0	3	0	3
Doncaster			1	0	0	1	1	0	1	0
Walsall			2	1	0	1	0	2	0	1
Oldham			2	1	0	1	1	1	1	1
Scunthorpe			1	0	0	1	0	1	0	0
Coventry			2	1	1	0	1	1	2	0
Port Vale			4	1	2	1	1	3	1	2
Colchester			2	0	2	0	1	1	2	0
Crewe			5	3	0	2	1	4	1	3
Burton	W	L	4	4	0	0	2	2	1	3
Shrewsbury										
Bury	W	L	4	1	2	1	2	2	1	2
Southend	D	L	3	1	2	0	1	2	3	0

Season	Division	Pos	P	W	D	L	F	A	GD	Pts
2014-15	League 2	2	46	27	8	11	67	31	+36	89
2013-14	League 2	23	46	9	15	22	44	65	-21	42
2012-13	League 1	16	46	13	16	17	54	60	-6	55

Over/Under 35%/65% 20th   **Both score** 33%/67% 25th

SOUTHEND

Nickname: The Shrimpers
Colours: Blue
Ground: Roots Hall (12,392)
Tel: 01702-304-050 www.southendunited.co.uk

Southend certainly know how to put their supporters through the mill. They won seven games in a row to move into the top three but then blew automatic promotion on the final day at Morecambe. They then needed a last-gasp equaliser in the playoff final before beating Wycombe on penalties to secure a spot in League One.

It was a deserved success for Phil Brown, who organised the team superbly, and there should be enough talent in the squad for them to stay in the division.

Longest run without win/loss: 5/10
High/low league position: 3/10
Clean sheets: 23 **Yellows:** 68 **Reds:** 7
Avg attendance: 6,024 **Players used:** 28
Leading scorer: B Corr 14 (8,13)
Key stat: Southend have lost two of their last 17 matches and suffered just one defeat at Roots Hall in 2015

	2014-15		Last six seasons at home							
	H	A	P	W	D	L	OV	UN	BS	CS
Millwall			1	0	1	0	0	1	0	1
Wigan			-	-	-	-	-	-	-	-
Blackpool			-	-	-	-	-	-	-	-
Swindon			2	0	1	1	2	0	2	0
Sheffield United			-	-	-	-	-	-	-	-
Chesterfield			3	2	0	1	3	0	1	2
Bradford			3	1	1	1	2	1	1	1
Rochdale			2	1	1	0	1	1	2	0
Peterborough			-	-	-	-	-	-	-	-
Fleetwood Town			2	1	1	0	0	2	1	1
Barnsley			-	-	-	-	-	-	-	-
Gillingham			4	2	1	1	1	3	1	2
Doncaster			-	-	-	-	-	-	-	-
Walsall			1	1	0	0	1	0	0	1
Oldham			1	0	0	1	0	1	0	0
Scunthorpe			1	0	0	1	0	1	0	0
Coventry			-	-	-	-	-	-	-	-
Port Vale			3	1	1	1	2	1	1	2
Colchester			1	0	0	1	1	0	1	0
Crewe			2	1	0	1	0	2	0	1
Burton	D	L	5	1	2	2	0	5	1	2
Shrewsbury	W	D	3	2	0	1	1	2	0	2
Bury	D	W	3	0	3	0	0	3	2	1
Southend										

Season	Division	Pos	P	W	D	L	F	A	GD	Pts
2014-15	League 2	5	46	24	12	10	54	38	+16	84
2013-14	League 2	5	46	19	15	12	56	39	+17	72
2012-13	League 2	11	46	16	13	17	61	55	+6	61

Over/Under 26%/74% 26th   **Both score** 39%/61% 21st

SWINDON

Nickname: The Robins
Colours: Red and white
Ground: County Ground (15,728)
Tel: 0871-876-1969 www.swindontownfc.co.uk

Few League One teams received as many plaudits as Swindon last season, but it all counted for nothing as they were blown away in the playoff final against Preston.

The squad has since been stripped with high-profile players falling out of contract and key midfielders Ben Gladwin and Massimo Luongo heading to QPR.

Swindon have built solid relationships with Premier League clubs so could still secure quality loan youngsters, but other teams make more betting appeal.

Longest run without win/loss: 5/9
High/low league position: 1/7
Clean sheets: 14 **Yellows:** 81 **Reds:** 4
Avg attendance: 7,940 **Players used:** 32
Leading scorer: A Williams 21 (5,18)
Key stat: 17 of Swindon's 23 league away matches last season produced over 2.5 goals – the highest in the division

	2014-15		Last six seasons at home							
	H	A	P	W	D	L	OV	UN	BS	CS
Millwall			1	0	1	0	0	1	1	0
Wigan			-	-	-	-	-	-	-	-
Blackpool			-	-	-	-	-	-	-	-
Swindon										
Sheffield United	W	L	3	2	1	0	2	1	2	1
Chesterfield	W	W	1	1	0	0	1	0	1	0
Bradford	W	W	3	2	1	0	1	2	1	2
Rochdale	L	W	2	0	1	1	1	1	2	0
Peterborough	W	W	3	2	1	0	1	2	2	1
Fleetwood Town	W	D	1	1	0	0	1	0	1	0
Barnsley	W	W	1	1	0	0	0	1	0	1
Gillingham	L	D	4	2	1	1	3	1	2	1
Doncaster	L	W	2	0	1	1	0	2	1	0
Walsall	D	W	5	0	4	1	3	2	4	1
Oldham	D	L	5	1	2	2	2	3	3	0
Scunthorpe	W	L	2	1	1	0	1	1	2	0
Coventry	D	W	3	1	2	0	2	1	3	0
Port Vale	W	W	3	3	0	0	2	1	1	2
Colchester	D	D	5	1	3	1	2	3	3	1
Crewe	W	D	4	4	0	0	3	1	1	3
Burton			1	1	0	0	0	1	0	1
Shrewsbury			3	3	0	0	2	1	2	1
Bury			1	0	0	1	0	1	0	0
Southend			2	2	0	0	1	1	1	1

Season	Division	Pos	P	W	D	L	F	A	GD	Pts
2014-15	League 1	4	46	23	10	13	76	57	+19	79
2013-14	League 1	8	46	19	9	18	63	59	+4	66
2012-13	League 1	6	46	20	14	12	72	39	+33	74

Over/Under 65%/35% 1st   **Both score** 52%/48% 9th

WALSALL

Nickname: The Saddlers
Colours: Red and white
Ground: Banks's Stadium (11,300)
Tel: 01922-622-791   www.saddlers.co.uk

A 14th-place finish hints at a mundane season and for much of Walsall's League One campaign that was true with the club involved in 17 draws, eight of which finished goalless.

However, the Saddlers made it to Wembley for the first time in their history and that provided a moment of joy, despite their Football League Trophy final loss to Bristol City. More excitement could follow this season, with the club set to work on a slightly bigger budget.

Longest run without win/loss: 6/7
High/low league position: 10/23
Clean sheets: 18 **Yellows:** 46 **Reds:** 0
Avg attendance: 4,392 **Players used:** 29
Leading scorer: T Bradshaw 17 (4,15)
Key stat: Walsall won only four of the 19 matches that top scorer Tom Bradshaw failed to start last season

	2014-15 H	A	P	W	D	L	OV	UN	BS	CS
Millwall			1	0	1	0	1	0	1	0
Wigan	-	-	-	-	-	-	-	-	-	-
Blackpool	-	-	-	-	-	-	-	-	-	-
Swindon	L	D	5	0	2	3	2	3	4	0
Sheffield United	D	D	4	2	2	0	2	2	4	0
Chesterfield	W	L	2	2	0	0	1	1	1	1
Bradford	D	D	2	0	1	1	0	2	0	1
Rochdale	W	L	3	1	2	0	1	2	1	2
Peterborough	D	D	3	1	1	1	1	2	1	2
Fleetwood Town	W	W	1	1	0	0	0	1	0	1
Barnsley	W	L	1	1	0	0	1	0	1	0
Gillingham	D	D	3	0	3	0	0	3	2	1
Doncaster	W	W	2	1	0	1	2	0	0	1
Walsall										
Oldham	W	L	6	4	1	1	2	4	2	3
Scunthorpe	L	L	3	0	1	2	3	0	3	0
Coventry	L	D	3	1	0	2	1	2	0	1
Port Vale	L	L	2	0	0	2	0	2	0	0
Colchester	D	W	6	3	1	2	1	5	1	3
Crewe	L	D	3	0	2	1	1	2	2	0
Burton	-	-	-							
Shrewsbury			2	2	0	0	1	1	1	1
Bury			2	0	1	1	1	1	2	0
Southend			1	0	1	0	1	0	1	0

Season	Division	Pos	P	W	D	L	F	A	GD	Pts
2014-15	League 1	14	46	14	17	15	50	54	-4	59
2013-14	League 1	13	46	14	16	16	49	49	0	58
2012-13	League 1	9	46	17	17	12	65	58	+7	68

Over/Under 35%/65% 24th   **Both score** 41%/59% 23rd

WIGAN

Nickname: The Latics
Colours: Blue and white
Ground: DW Stadium (25,023)
Tel: 01942-774-000   www.wiganlatics.co.uk

Only two sides were shorter than Wigan in the Championship outright ante-post betting and they were 33-1 to go down. But the Latics crashed through the trapdoor, sacking two managers – Uwe Rosler and Malky Mackay – in the process.

Changes have been made behind the scenes and much will depend on whether inexperienced manager Steven Caldwell proves to be the right choice at the helm because in terms of talent, Wigan should be fighting for the title at this level.

Longest run without win/loss: 8/6
High/low league position: 15/23
Clean sheets: 10 **Yellows:** 83 **Reds:** 5
Avg attendance: 12,882 **Players used:** 41
Leading scorer: J McClean 6 (0,5)
Key stat: Wigan won only three home matches last season and scored just 18 goals in the process

	2014-15 H	A	P	W	D	L	OV	UN	BS	CS
Millwall	D	L	2	0	1	1	0	2	0	1
Wigan										
Blackpool	W	W	3	1	0	2	1	2	0	1
Swindon	-	-	-	-	-	-	-	-	-	-
Sheffield United	-	-	-	-	-	-	-	-	-	-
Chesterfield	-	-	-	-	-	-	-	-	-	-
Bradford	-	-	-	-	-	-	-	-	-	-
Rochdale	-	-	-	-	-	-	-	-	-	-
Peterborough	-	-	-	-	-	-	-	-	-	-
Fleetwood Town	-	-	-	-	-	-	-	-	-	-
Barnsley	1	1	0	0	0	1	0	1		
Gillingham	-	-	-	-	-	-	-	-	-	-
Doncaster	1	0	1	0	1	0	1	0		
Walsall	-	-	-	-	-	-	-	-	-	-
Oldham	-	-	-	-	-	-	-	-	-	-
Scunthorpe	-	-	-	-	-	-	-	-	-	-
Coventry	-	-	-	-	-	-	-	-	-	-
Port Vale	-	-	-	-	-	-	-	-	-	-
Colchester	-	-	-	-	-	-	-	-	-	-
Crewe	-	-	-	-	-	-	-	-	-	-
Burton	-	-	-	-	-	-	-	-	-	-
Shrewsbury	-	-	-	-	-	-	-	-	-	-
Bury	-	-	-	-	-	-	-	-	-	-
Southend	-	-	-	-	-	-	-	-	-	-

Season	Division	Pos	P	W	D	L	F	A	GD	Pts
2014-15	Championship	23	46	9	12	25	39	64	-25	39
2013-14	Championship	5	46	21	10	15	61	48	+13	73
2012-13	Premier League	18	38	9	9	20	47	73	-26	36

Over/Under 46%/54% 16th   **Both score** 43%/57% 21st

League One stats 2014-15
Key Points in all tables (except the league table) do not include any deductions imposed by the league.
POS H A Overall league position, rank from home games only, rank from away games only **Sup** Average match supremacy **GFA** Goals For Average **GAA** Goals Against Average **PGA** Points Gained Average

Pos	H	A	League One 2014-15	P	W	D	L	F	A	W	D	L	F	A	GD	Pts
					Home					Away						
1	1	1	Bristol City	46	16	5	2	48	17	13	7	3	48	21	+58	99
2	2	3	MK Dons	46	16	3	4	60	19	11	7	5	41	25	+57	91
3	3	2	Preston	46	13	9	1	43	21	12	5	6	36	19	+39	89
4	4	4	Swindon	46	12	5	6	38	28	11	5	7	38	29	+19	79
5	8	6	Sheff Utd	46	10	7	6	35	24	9	7	7	31	29	+13	71
6	5	9	Chesterfield	46	12	4	7	42	26	7	8	8	26	29	+13	69
7	17	5	Bradford	46	8	6	9	26	33	9	8	6	29	22	0	65
8	9	14	Rochdale	46	11	3	9	36	29	8	3	12	36	37	+6	63
9	10	12	Peterborough	46	10	5	8	27	26	8	4	11	26	30	-3	63
10	11	8	Fleetwood	46	8	9	6	28	27	9	3	11	21	25	-3	63
11	7	19	Barnsley	46	11	5	7	41	29	6	6	11	21	32	+1	62
12	6	20	Gillingham	46	11	6	6	37	29	5	8	10	28	37	-1	62
13	19	7	Doncaster	46	7	6	10	24	29	9	7	7	34	33	-4	61
14	14	15	Walsall	46	8	8	7	28	24	6	9	8	22	30	-4	59
15	15	18	Oldham	46	8	8	7	32	34	6	7	10	22	33	-13	57
16	12	21	Scunthorpe	46	9	6	8	27	28	5	8	10	35	47	-13	56
17	20	11	Coventry	46	6	9	8	25	33	7	7	9	24	27	-11	55
18	18	17	Port Vale	46	8	5	10	31	31	7	4	12	24	34	-10	54
19	21	16	Colchester	46	7	4	12	30	36	7	6	10	28	41	-19	52
20	16	22	Crewe	46	8	7	8	21	28	6	3	14	22	47	-32	52
21	24	10	Notts County	46	5	6	12	24	33	7	8	8	21	30	-18	50
22	13	24	Crawley	46	9	6	8	30	33	4	5	14	23	46	-26	50
23	23	13	Leyton Orient	46	5	6	12	30	34	7	7	9	29	35	-10	49
24	22	23	Yeovil	46	5	7	11	17	33	5	3	15	19	42	-39	40

Best attack

		GF	GFA
1	MK Dons	101	2.2
2	Bristol City	96	2.09
3	Preston	79	1.72
4	Swindon	76	1.65
5	Rochdale	72	1.57
6	Chesterfield	68	1.48
7	Sheff Utd	66	1.43
8	Gillingham	65	1.41
9	Barnsley	62	1.35
10	Scunthorpe	62	1.35
11	Leyton Orient	59	1.28
12	Doncaster	58	1.26
13	Colchester	58	1.26
14	Bradford	55	1.2
15	Port Vale	55	1.2
16	Oldham	54	1.17
17	Peterborough	53	1.15
18	Crawley	53	1.15
19	Walsall	50	1.09
20	Fleetwood	49	1.07
21	Coventry	49	1.07
22	Notts County	45	0.98
23	Crewe	43	0.93
24	Yeovil	36	0.78

Best defence

		GA	GAA
1	Bristol City	38	0.83
2	Preston	40	0.87
3	MK Dons	44	0.96
4	Fleetwood	52	1.13
5	Sheff Utd	53	1.15
6	Walsall	54	1.17
7	Chesterfield	55	1.2
8	Bradford	55	1.2
9	Peterborough	56	1.22
10	Swindon	57	1.24
11	Coventry	60	1.3
12	Barnsley	61	1.33
13	Doncaster	62	1.35
14	Notts County	63	1.37
15	Port Vale	65	1.41
16	Rochdale	66	1.43
17	Gillingham	66	1.43
18	Oldham	67	1.46
19	Leyton Orient	69	1.5
20	Scunthorpe	75	1.63
21	Crewe	75	1.63
22	Yeovil	75	1.63
23	Colchester	77	1.67
24	Crawley	79	1.72

Top scorers

		Team	Goals scored
J Garner	Preston	25	|||||||||||||||||||||||||
I Henderson	Rochdale	22	||||||||||||||||||||||
E Doyle	Chesterfield	21	|||||||||||||||||||||
A Williams	Swindon	21	|||||||||||||||||||||
W Grigg	MK Dons	20	||||||||||||||||||||

Over 2.5 goals

	H	A	%
Swindon	13	17	65%
Rochdale	13	16	63%
Bristol City	13	14	59%
Gillingham	12	15	59%
MK Dons	15	12	59%
Port Vale	15	12	59%

Under 2.5 goals

	H	A	%
Walsall	15	15	65%
Fleetwood	14	15	63%
Preston	14	14	61%
Bradford	13	14	59%
Coventry	12	14	57%
Sheff Utd	12	14	57%

Both to score

	H	A	%
Scunthorpe	15	17	70%
Sheff Utd	15	15	65%
Gillingham	13	16	63%
Port Vale	13	14	59%
Colchester	14	12	57%
Barnsley, Bradford			54%
Crawley			

Both not to score

	H	A	%
Fleetwood	12	15	59%
Walsall	13	14	59%
Yeovil	13	13	57%
Doncaster	14	10	52%
MK Dons	13	11	52%
Preston	10	14	52%

SOCCERBASE.COM

League One results 2014-15

	Barnsley	Bradford	Bristol City	Chesterfield	Colchester	Coventry	Crawley Town	Crewe	Doncaster	Fleetwood	Gillingham	Leyton Orient	MK Dons	Notts County	Oldham	Peterborough	Port Vale	Preston	Rochdale	Scunthorpe	Sheffield United	Swindon	Walsall	Yeovil
Barnsley		3-1	2-2	1-1	3-2	1-0	0-1	2-0	1-1	1-2	4-1	2-0	3-5	2-3	1-0	1-1	2-1	1-1	5-0	1-2	0-2	0-3	3-0	2-0
Bradford	1-0		0-6	0-1	1-1	3-2	1-0	2-0	1-2	2-2	1-1	3-1	2-1	1-0	2-0	0-1	1-1	0-3	1-2	1-1	0-2	1-2	1-1	1-3
Bristol City	2-2	2-2		3-2	2-1	0-0	1-0	3-0	3-0	2-0	0-0	0-0	3-2	4-0	1-0	2-0	3-1	0-1	1-0	2-0	1-3	3-0	8-2	2-1
Chesterfield	2-1	0-1	0-2		6-0	2-3	3-0	1-0	2-2	3-0	3-0	2-3	0-1	1-1	1-1	3-2	3-0	0-2	2-1	4-1	3-2	0-3	1-0	0-0
Colchester	3-1	0-0	3-2	2-1		0-1	2-3	2-3	0-1	2-1	1-2	2-0	0-1	0-1	2-2	1-3	1-2	1-0	1-4	2-2	2-3	1-1	0-2	2-0
Coventry	2-2	1-1	1-3	0-0	1-0		2-2	1-3	1-3	1-1	1-0	0-1	2-1	0-1	1-1	3-2	2-3	0-2	2-2	1-1	1-0	0-3	0-0	2-1
Crawley Town	5-1	1-3	1-2	1-1	0-0	1-2		1-1	0-5	1-0	1-2	1-0	2-2	2-0	2-0	1-4	1-2	2-1	0-4	2-2	1-1	1-0	1-0	2-0
Crewe	1-2	0-1	1-0	0-0	2-0	0-0	1-1		2-0	3-1	1-1	0-5	0-3	0-1	1-0	2-1	1-2	1-2	5-2	0-1	0-0	1-1	1-0	1-0
Doncaster	1-0	0-3	1-3	3-2	2-0	2-0	0-0	2-1		0-0	1-2	0-0	0-0	0-2	0-2	1-3	1-1	1-1	5-2	0-1	1-2	0-2	3-0	
Fleetwood	0-0	0-2	3-3	0-0	2-3	0-2	1-0	2-1	3-1		1-0	1-1	0-3	2-1	0-2	1-1	1-0	1-1	1-0	2-2	1-1	2-2	0-1	4-0
Gillingham	0-1	1-0	1-3	2-3	2-2	3-1	1-1	2-0	1-1	0-1		3-2	4-2	3-1	3-2	2-1	2-2	0-1	1-0	0-3	2-0	2-2	0-0	2-0
Leyton Orient	0-0	0-2	1-3	1-2	0-2	2-2	4-1	4-1	0-1	0-1	3-3		0-0	0-1	3-0	1-2	3-1	0-2	2-3	1-4	1-1	1-2	0-0	3-0
MK Dons	2-0	1-2	0-0	1-2	6-0	0-0	2-0	6-1	3-0	2-1	4-2	6-1		4-1	7-0	3-0	1-0	0-2	2-2	2-0	1-0	2-1	0-3	5-1
Notts County	1-1	1-1	1-2	0-1	2-1	0-0	5-3	2-1	2-1	0-1	1-0	1-1	0-1		0-0	1-2	0-1	1-3	1-2	2-2	1-2	0-3	1-2	1-1
Oldham	1-3	2-1	1-1	0-0	0-1	4-1	1-1	1-2	2-2	1-0	0-0	1-3	1-3	3-0		1-1	1-1	0-4	3-0	3-2	2-2	2-1	2-1	0-4
Peterborough	2-1	2-0	0-3	1-0	0-2	0-1	4-3	1-1	0-0	1-0	1-2	1-0	3-2	0-0	2-2		3-1	0-1	2-1	1-2	1-2	1-2	0-0	1-0
Port Vale	2-1	2-2	0-3	1-2	1-2	0-2	2-3	0-1	3-0	1-2	2-1	3-0	0-0	0-2	0-1	2-1		2-2	1-0	2-2	2-1	0-1	1-1	4-1
Preston	1-0	1-2	1-1	3-3	4-2	1-0	2-0	5-1	2-2	3-2	2-2	2-2	1-1	1-1	1-0	2-0	2-0		1-0	2-0	1-1	3-0	1-0	1-1
Rochdale	0-1	0-2	1-1	1-0	2-1	1-0	4-1	4-0	1-3	0-2	1-1	1-0	2-3	2-2	0-3	0-1	1-0	3-0		3-1	1-2	2-4	4-0	2-1
Scunthorpe	0-1	1-1	0-2	2-0	1-1	2-1	2-1	2-1	1-2	0-2	2-1	1-2	1-1	0-1	0-1	2-0	1-0	0-4	2-1		1-1	3-1	2-1	1-1
Sheffield United	0-1	1-1	1-2	1-1	4-1	2-2	1-0	1-2	3-2	1-2	2-1	2-2	0-1	1-1	1-1	1-2	1-0	2-1	1-0	4-0		2-0	1-1	2-0
Swindon	2-0	2-1	1-0	3-1	2-2	1-1	1-2	2-0	0-1	1-0	0-3	2-2	0-3	3-0	2-2	1-0	1-0	1-0	2-3	3-1	5-2		3-3	0-1
Walsall	3-1	0-0	1-1	1-0	0-0	0-2	5-0	0-1	3-0	1-0	1-1	0-2	1-1	0-0	2-0	0-0	0-1	3-1	3-2	1-4	1-1	1-4		1-2
Yeovil	1-1	1-0	0-3	2-3	0-1	0-0	2-1	1-1	0-3	0-1	2-2	0-3	0-2	1-1	2-1	1-0	1-2	0-2	0-3	1-1	1-0	1-1	0-1	

Record when first to score

		P	W	D	L	F	A	Sup	PGA	Pts
1	Rochdale	18	16	1	1	44	12	+1.78	2.7	49
2	MK Dons	28	24	2	2	81	20	+2.18	2.6	74
3	Swindon	25	21	1	3	58	21	+1.48	2.6	64
4	Bristol City	32	25	6	1	72	21	+1.59	2.5	81
5	Chesterfield	20	16	2	2	48	18	+1.25	2.5	50
6	Preston	32	23	9	0	62	16	+1.44	2.4	78
7	Sheff Utd	21	15	5	1	35	13	+1.05	2.4	50
8	Peterborough	18	14	2	2	32	17	+0.83	2.4	44
9	Walsall	17	13	2	2	32	21	+0.65	2.4	41
10	Gillingham	18	13	2	3	36	21	+0.83	2.3	41
11	Doncaster	16	11	3	2	29	11	+1.13	2.3	36
12	Bradford	25	16	6	3	40	18	+0.88	2.2	54
13	Fleetwood	22	15	4	3	36	18	+0.82	2.2	49
14	Port Vale	20	13	5	2	38	22	+0.80	2.2	44
15	Barnsley	24	15	3	6	40	22	+0.75	2	48
16	Crewe	23	13	7	3	34	22	+0.52	2	46
17	Oldham	23	12	9	2	40	21	+0.83	2	45
18	Crawley	18	11	3	4	31	21	+0.56	2	36
19	Colchester	20	11	4	5	37	26	+0.55	1.9	37
20	Leyton Orient	17	9	6	2	38	20	+1.06	1.9	33
21	Yeovil	14	7	6	1	21	11	+0.71	1.9	27
22	Coventry	22	11	7	4	35	28	+0.32	1.8	40
23	Scunthorpe	22	10	9	3	38	32	+0.27	1.8	39
24	Notts County	21	11	5	5	34	26	+0.38	1.8	38

Record when keeping a clean sheet

		P	W	D	F	Sup	PGA	Pts
1	Preston	21	21	0	40	+1.90	3	63
2	Sheff Utd	10	10	0	17	+1.70	3	30
3	Rochdale	9	9	0	22	+2.44	3	27
4	Scunthorpe	3	3	0	7	+2.33	3	9
5	Swindon	14	13	1	25	+1.79	2.9	40
6	Bradford	13	11	2	18	+1.38	2.7	35
7	Barnsley	13	11	2	20	+1.54	2.7	35
8	Port Vale	6	5	1	9	+1.50	2.7	16
9	Bristol City	20	16	4	41	+2.05	2.6	52
10	Fleetwood	14	11	3	16	+1.14	2.6	36
11	MK Dons	22	17	5	44	+2.00	2.5	56
12	Oldham	12	9	3	17	+1.42	2.5	30
13	Crawley	11	8	3	11	+1.00	2.5	27
14	Colchester	11	8	3	14	+1.27	2.5	27
15	Crewe	10	7	3	9	+0.90	2.4	24
16	Yeovil	7	5	2	8	+1.14	2.4	17
17	Doncaster	14	9	5	19	+1.36	2.3	32
18	Chesterfield	14	9	5	22	+1.57	2.3	32
19	Peterborough	12	8	4	10	+0.83	2.3	28
20	Gillingham	9	6	3	11	+1.22	2.3	21
21	Notts County	12	7	5	10	+0.83	2.2	26
22	Leyton Orient	10	6	4	14	+1.40	2.2	22
23	Walsall	18	10	8	21	+1.17	2.1	38
24	Coventry	14	8	6	11	+0.79	2.1	30

Coffer-boosting cup run gives new boys the means to escape a tough division

Two teams who came up from the Conference in 2014 could be the answer in finding the winner of a tricky League Two betting heat, writes Mark Langdon. Several ambitious clubs are showing enormous determination to escape from the Football League's basement division, but it's relative newcomers Luton (at 16-1) and Cambridge (20-1) who are fancied to go well.

Portsmouth have to be favourites given they are a huge club at this level and manager Paul Cook not only lifted Chesterfield out of this division in 2014 but nearly took the Spireites up to the Championship.

However the Pompey outfit he now joins isn't exactly flying under the radar of the bookies and the south coast side could finish only 16th last season, so much improvement is needed if they are to justify the hype.

Of the other market leaders Oxford are still feared, but Leyton Orient, Bristol Rovers and Northampton make much less appeal, while Luton look solid for a promotion push.

The Hatters were flying for much of last season until injury problems and a crisis in confidence saw them drop from fourth to ninth on the back of seven straight defeats.

Wily manager John Still has done well in the transfer market, bringing in hungry youngsters Jack Marriott from Ipswich, Dan Potts (West Ham) and Cameron McGeehan (Norwich). Warrior defender Scott Cuthbert is a tremendous signing from Orient, too.

Town are solid defensively and if they can improve in the attacking third Luton have to go close, while Cambridge have been one of the big market movers over the summer.

It's easy to see why Cambridge have been all the rage with value seekers. Fresh from last season's cash boost following their two ties with Manchester United, Richard Money has been able to strengthen the side considerably.

Centre-backs Leon Legge and Mark Roberts have dropped down from League One clubs Gillingham and Fleetwood respectively, while Southend were stunned when leading scorer Barry Corr opted for a move to the Abbey Stadium rather than move up with the Essex boys.

Experienced Keith Keane is a consistent type in midfield, Elliot Omozusi should be a decent right-back at this level and Luke Berry, so impressive when Cambridge came up from the Conference, returns to the club following a spell with Barnsley.

Cambridge finished 19th last season but they basically gave up after the trip to Old Trafford and this is a side with potential – United won at champions Burton as well as drawing away at Shrewsbury and Southend, who were both promoted.

So many teams are having a right go this season that it means the division will be ultra-competitive and the relegation market is incredibly tight.

Don't be surprised if some sides get sucked in at bigger prices and three to consider are 11-1 pokes Barnet, who didn't look the most impressive of Conference winners last season, as well as Crawley and Newport.

Money is tight at Crawley and Newport were awful after Justin Edinburgh departed.

Cambridge and Luton will again do battle in League Two but this time they could fighting for the title

ACCRINGTON

Nickname: Stanley
Colours: Red
Ground: Crown Ground (5,057)
Tel: 01254-356-950   www.accringtonstanley.co.uk

Survival represents success for a smaller club like Accrington and they did it easily enough once John Coleman returned to the dugout to fix the mess that James Beattie had left behind.

Accy eventually finished 17th and something similar looks on the cards this time around, although shrewd cookie Coleman could do with improving on a defence that was the worst in League Two last season with 77 goals conceded and just one away clean sheet.

Longest run without win/loss: 8/5
High/low league position: 11/21
Clean sheets: 5 **Yellows:** 70 **Reds:** 5
Avg attendance: 1,478 **Players used:** 38
Leading scorer: P Mingoia 8 (3,7)
Key stat: Accrington's matches produced 135 goals – five more than any other side in League Two

AFC WIMBLEDON

Nickname: The Dons
Colours: Blue and yellow
Ground: Kingsmeadow Stadium (4,850)
Tel: 0208-547-3528   www.afcwimbledon.co.uk

The Wombles were rated lively outsiders in last year's League Two betting but from the start of September they were never higher than tenth and it was a fairly forgettable season, despite an emotional third-round FA Cup tie against Liverpool.

Top goalscorer Adebayo Akinfenwa has signed a new contract, which is a boost, and manager Neal Ardley is once again talking of making a promotion bid with rumoured cash to spend, but others appear more likely in a hot division.

Longest run without win/loss: 8/4
High/low league position: 10/17
Clean sheets: 15 **Yellows:** 61 **Reds:** 3
Avg attendance: 4,073 **Players used:** 35
Leading scorer: A Akinfenwa 13 (6,10)
Key stat: AFC Wimbledon won only two of their final 15 matches of the 2014-15 season

	2014-15 H	A	Last six seasons at home P	W	D	L	OV	UN	BS	CS
Notts County			1	0	0	1	1	0	0	0
Crawley Town			1	0	0	1	0	1	0	0
Leyton Orient			-	-	-	-	-	-	-	-
Yeovil			-	-	-	-	-	-	-	-
Wycombe	D	D	4	0	3	1	0	4	3	0
Stevenage	D	L	2	1	1	0	1	1	1	1
Plymouth	W	L	4	1	2	1	1	3	2	1
Luton	D	L	1	0	1	0	1	0	1	0
Newport County	L	D	2	0	1	1	1	1	1	0
Exeter	L	W	3	0	0	3	3	0	2	0
Morecambe	W	D	6	4	2	0	3	3	5	1
Northampton	W	W	6	2	0	4	5	1	4	0
Oxford	W	L	5	1	2	2	1	4	0	3
Dag & Red	L	L	5	1	0	4	3	2	2	1
AFC Wimbledon	W	L	4	4	0	0	3	1	2	2
Portsmouth	D	W	2	0	2	0	1	1	2	0
Accrington										
York	D	L	3	0	2	1	1	2	2	0
Cambridge U	W	D	1	1	0	0	1	0	1	0
Carlisle	W	L	1	1	0	0	1	0	1	0
Mansfield	W	W	2	1	1	0	1	1	2	0
Hartlepool	W	D	2	1	1	0	1	1	1	1
Barnet			4	3	0	1	3	1	2	1
Bristol Rovers			3	3	0	0	2	1	2	1

Season	Division	Pos	P	W	D	L	F	A	GD	Pts
2014-15	League 2	17	46	15	11	20	58	77	-19	56
2013-14	League 2	15	46	14	15	17	54	56	-2	57
2012-13	League 2	18	46	14	12	20	51	68	-17	54

Over/Under 61%/39% 1st   **Both score** 65%/35% 2nd

	2014-15 H	A	Last six seasons at home P	W	D	L	OV	UN	BS	CS
Notts County			-	-	-	-	-	-	-	-
Crawley Town			3	1	1	1	2	1	3	0
Leyton Orient			-	-	-	-	-	-	-	-
Yeovil			-	-	-	-	-	-	-	-
Wycombe	D	L	3	1	2	0	1	2	1	2
Stevenage	L	L	2	0	0	2	2	0	1	0
Plymouth	D	D	4	0	3	1	1	3	3	1
Luton	W	W	3	1	2	0	1	2	2	1
Newport County	W	L	3	1	2	0	2	1	2	1
Exeter	W	L	3	2	1	0	3	0	3	0
Morecambe	W	D	4	2	1	1	1	3	1	2
Northampton	D	L	4	0	2	2	2	2	2	0
Oxford	D	D	5	0	1	4	1	4	0	1
Dag & Red	W	L	4	2	2	0	2	2	3	1
AFC Wimbledon										
Portsmouth	W	W	2	2	0	0	1	1	0	2
Accrington	W	L	4	1	1	2	2	3	0	0
York	W	W	5	3	0	2	2	3	2	1
Cambridge U	L	D	3	1	1	1	2	1	1	2
Carlisle	L	D	1	0	0	1	1	0	1	0
Mansfield	L	L	4	2	1	1	1	3	1	2
Hartlepool	L	L	2	1	0	1	2	0	2	0
Barnet			2	0	1	1	0	2	1	0
Bristol Rovers			3	1	1	1	2	1	2	1

Season	Division	Pos	P	W	D	L	F	A	GD	Pts
2014-15	League 2	15	46	14	16	16	54	60	-6	58
2013-14	League 2	20	46	14	14	18	49	57	-8	53
2012-13	League 2	20	46	14	11	21	54	76	-22	53

Over/Under 43%/57% 10th   **Both score** 50%/50% 10th

BARNET

Nickname: The Bees
Colours: Amber and black
Ground: The Hive Stadium (5,233)
Tel: 020-8381-3800   www.barnetfc.com

A fast start that saw Barnet win six of their first seven games enabled the Bees to find a way back up to the Football League, but Martin Allen will need to inspire a big improvement against the better sides after they gained promotion on the back of a solid record in matches against the Conference's cannon fodder.

Barnet picked up 44 of their 92 points against the bottom eight and despite winning the title they look unlikely to make a splash in League Two.

Longest run without win/loss: 2/9
High/low league position: 1/2
Clean sheets: 18 **Yellows:** 60 **Reds:** 3
Avg attendance: 1,683 **Players used:** 27
Leading scorer: J Akinde 31 (12,23)
Key stat: Barnet had only the sixth-best record in the Conference over the second half of the season

	2014-15		Last six seasons at home							
	H	A	P	W	D	L	OV	UN	BS	CS
Notts County			1	1	0	0	0	1	0	1
Crawley Town			1	0	0	1	1	0	1	0
Leyton Orient			-	-	-	-	-	-	-	-
Yeovil			-	-	-	-	-	-	-	-
Wycombe			2	1	0	1	0	2	0	1
Stevenage			1	0	0	1	1	0	0	0
Plymouth			2	1	0	1	1	1	1	1
Luton			1	0	0	1	1	0	1	0
Newport County			-	-	-	-	-	-	-	-
Exeter			1	0	0	1	1	0	1	0
Morecambe			4	2	0	2	2	2	2	1
Northampton			4	2	1	1	3	1	2	2
Oxford			3	0	2	1	2	1	2	0
Dag & Red			3	1	2	0	1	2	1	2
AFC Wimbledon			2	1	1	0	1	1	1	1
Portsmouth			-	-	-	-	-	-	-	-
Accrington			4	1	2	1	1	3	2	2
York			1	0	0	1	1	0	1	0
Cambridge U			1	0	1	0	1	0	1	0
Carlisle			-	-	-	-	-	-	-	-
Mansfield			-	-	-	-	-	-	-	-
Hartlepool			-	-	-	-	-	-	-	-
Barnet										
Bristol Rovers	W	L	3	2	1	0	0	3	1	2

Season	Division	Pos	P	W	D	L	F	A	GD	Pts
2014-15	Conference	1	46	28	8	10	94	46	+48	92
2013-14	Conference	8	46	19	13	14	58	53	+5	70
2012-13	League 2	23	46	13	12	21	47	59	-12	51

Over/Under 65%/35% 2nd   **Both score** 57%/43% 7th

BRISTOL ROVERS

Nickname: The Pirates/The Gas
Colours: Blue and white
Ground: Memorial Stadium (12,011)
Tel: 01179-909-648   www.bristolrovers.co.uk

Trends are there to be broken and Bristol Rovers did just that last season as they became the first team to successfully bounce immediately back from demotion to the Conference thanks to their playoff final penalty shootout win over Grimsby.

Few could deny that the Gas deserved to go up as they motored their way through the division in the final months. However, bookmakers are hugely respectful of the Pirates and others around a similar price are much preferred.

Longest run without win/loss: 3/20
High/low league position: 1/15
Clean sheets: 22 **Yellows:** 61 **Reds:** 5
Avg attendance: 4,535 **Players used:** 28
Leading scorer: M Taylor 18 (6,17)
Key stat: Including playoffs, Bristol Rovers lost just one of their last 32 matches in the Conference

	2014-15		Last six seasons at home							
	H	A	P	W	D	L	OV	UN	BS	CS
Notts County			1	1	0	0	1	0	1	0
Crawley Town			1	0	1	0	0	1	0	0
Leyton Orient			2	0	0	2	2	0	1	0
Yeovil			2	1	0	1	2	0	2	0
Wycombe			3	1	0	2	1	2	1	1
Stevenage			-	-	-	-	-	-	-	-
Plymouth			4	2	0	2	4	0	4	0
Luton			-	-	-	-	-	-	-	-
Newport County			1	1	0	0	1	0	1	0
Exeter			4	3	0	1	1	3	1	2
Morecambe			3	2	0	1	2	1	1	1
Northampton			3	3	0	0	2	1	2	1
Oxford			3	0	2	1	0	3	1	1
Dag & Red			4	1	0	3	1	3	1	1
AFC Wimbledon			3	3	0	0	1	2	0	3
Portsmouth			1	1	0	0	0	1	0	1
Accrington			3	1	0	2	1	2	1	0
York			2	1	1	0	1	1	1	1
Cambridge U			-	-	-	-	-	-	-	-
Carlisle			2	1	1	0	1	1	2	0
Mansfield			1	0	0	1	0	1	0	0
Hartlepool			3	1	2	0	1	2	1	2
Barnet	W	L	3	2	0	1	2	1	2	0
Bristol Rovers										

Season	Division	Pos	P	W	D	L	F	A	GD	Pts
2014-15	Conference	2	46	25	16	5	73	34	+39	91
2013-14	League 2	23	46	12	14	20	43	54	-11	50
2012-13	League 2	14	46	16	12	18	60	69	-9	60

Over/Under 39%/61% 27th   **Both score** 46%/54% 22nd

CAMBRIDGE UTD

Nickname: The U's
Colours: Yellow and black
Ground: Abbey Stadium (9,617)
Tel: 01223-566500   cambridge-united.co.uk

They didn't win the league, but the U's did win the lottery by holding Man United in the FA Cup to force a money-spinning replay at Old Trafford. That windfall has granted the club a war chest for Richard Money to dip into as he looks to make strides with his team this season.

The league campaign fell apart after that trip to Old Trafford but the early-summer signings of Barry Corr, Keith Keane, Leon Legge and Mark Roberts hints at a significant improvement.

Longest run without win/loss: 7/3
High/low league position: 10/19
Clean sheets: 10 **Yellows:** 43 **Reds:** 3
Avg attendance: 5,108 **Players used:** 41
Leading scorer: R Simpson 8 (1,7) T Elliott 8 (3,7)
Key stat: Cambridge won just three of their final 23 matches – a run that started with the FA Cup tie against Man United

CARLISLE

Nickname: Cumbrians/The Blues
Colours: Blue
Ground: Brunton Park (18,202)
Tel: 01228-526-237   www.carlisleunited.co.uk

Most of the off-season in Cumbria has been spent talking about a potential takeover from a mystery billionaire and it must be a relief for Carlisle's supporters to have something positive to focus on after a disappointing season that saw United finish a lowly 20th.

Carlisle rarely played decent football and were never higher than 16th, but they should be thankful of staying up following a return of three points from a possible 27 in the opening nine matches.

Longest run without win/loss: 9/3
High/low league position: 19/24
Clean sheets: 12 **Yellows:** 66 **Reds:** 8
Avg attendance: 4,376 **Players used:** 39
Leading scorer: K Dempsey 10 (2,9)
Key stat: Carlisle took one point away to last season's top ten in League Two

Cambridge Utd

	2014-15 H	A	P	W	D	L	OV	UN	BS	CS
Notts County	-	-	-	-	-	-	-	-	-	-
Crawley Town			2	0	1	1	1	1	1	0
Leyton Orient	-	-	-	-	-	-	-	-	-	-
Yeovil	-	-	-	-	-	-	-	-	-	-
Wycombe	L	L	1	0	0	1	0	1	0	0
Stevenage	D	L	2	0	1	1	1	1	2	0
Plymouth	W	L	1	1	0	0	0	1	0	1
Luton	L	L	6	0	4	2	2	4	4	1
Newport County	W	D	4	1	2	1	1	3	1	2
Exeter	L	D	1	0	0	1	1	0	1	0
Morecambe	L	W	1	0	1	0	1	0	1	0
Northampton	W	W	1	1	0	0	1	0	1	0
Oxford	W	L	2	1	1	0	1	1	2	0
Dag & Red	L	D	1	0	1	0	0	1	1	0
AFC Wimbledon	D	W	3	0	2	1	2	1	2	1
Portsmouth	L	L	1	0	0	1	1	0	1	0
Accrington	D	L	1	0	1	0	1	0	1	0
York	L	D	4	1	0	3	2	2	1	0
Cambridge U										
Carlisle	W	W	1	1	0	0	1	0	0	1
Mansfield	W	D	5	3	0	2	5	0	5	0
Hartlepool	W	L	1	1	0	0	1	0	1	0
Barnet			1	0	1	0	0	1	1	0
Bristol Rovers	-	-	-	-	-	-	-	-	-	-

Season	Division	Pos	P	W	D	L	F	A	GD	Pts
2014-15	League 2	19	46	13	12	21	61	66	-5	51
2013-14	Conference	2	46	23	13	10	72	35	+37	82
2012-13	Conference	14	46	15	14	17	68	69	-1	59

Over/Under 54%/46% 3rd   **Both score** 59%/41% 3rd

Carlisle

	2014-15 H	A	P	W	D	L	OV	UN	BS	CS
Notts County			4	2	0	2	3	1	1	1
Crawley Town			2	0	1	1	0	2	1	0
Leyton Orient			5	1	1	3	4	1	4	0
Yeovil			4	2	1	1	2	2	2	1
Wycombe	L	L	3	1	1	1	2	1	2	1
Stevenage	W	L	4	3	1	0	2	2	1	3
Plymouth	W	L	2	1	1	0	0	2	1	1
Luton	L	L	1	0	0	1	0	1	0	0
Newport County	L	L	1	0	0	1	0	1	1	0
Exeter	L	L	4	1	1	2	3	1	3	0
Morecambe	D	W	1	0	1	0	0	1	1	0
Northampton	W	W	1	1	0	0	1	0	1	0
Oxford	W	L	1	1	0	0	0	1	1	0
Dag & Red	W	L	2	1	0	1	0	2	0	1
AFC Wimbledon	D	W	1	0	1	0	1	0	1	0
Portsmouth	D	L	2	1	1	0	2	0	2	0
Accrington	W	L	1	1	0	0	0	1	0	1
York	L	D	1	0	0	1	1	0	0	0
Cambridge U	L	L	1	0	0	1	0	1	0	0
Carlisle										
Mansfield	W	L	1	1	0	0	1	0	1	0
Hartlepool	D	W	5	3	1	1	4	1	3	2
Barnet	-	-	-	-	-	-	-	-	-	-
Bristol Rovers			2	2	0	0	2	0	1	1

Season	Division	Pos	P	W	D	L	F	A	GD	Pts
2014-15	League 2	20	46	14	8	24	56	74	-18	50
2013-14	League 1	22	46	11	12	23	43	76	-33	45
2012-13	League 1	17	46	14	13	19	56	77	-21	55

Over/Under 54%/46% 3rd   **Both score** 48%/52% 14th

CRAWLEY TOWN

Nickname: The Red Devils
Colours: Red and white
Ground: Broadfield Stadium (5,996)
Tel: 01293-410000   www.crawleytownfc.com

It's all change at Crawley this summer. Mark Yates was appointed as manager and he claims the playoffs are his target despite the playing budget being slashed after last season's relegation under first John Gregory and then Dean Saunders.

The influential Asian betting market was against the Red Devils most weeks and they were proven right. Yates needs to work on a defence that conceded a whopping 79 goals, while Town also need to massively improve on their away form.

Longest run without win/loss: 13/6
High/low league position: 13/24
Clean sheets: 11 **Yellows:** 84 **Reds:** 2
Avg attendance: 2,709 **Players used:** 34
Leading scorer: I McLeod 19 (9,16)
Key stat: Crawley's tally of four road successes was the fewest away wins in League One last season

| | 2014-15 | | Last six seasons at home | | | | | | | |
	H	A	P	W	D	L	OV	UN	BS	CS
Notts County	W	L	3	2	1	0	0	3	0	3
Crawley Town										
Leyton Orient	W	L	3	3	0	0	1	2	1	2
Yeovil	W	L	2	1	0	1	0	2	0	1
Wycombe			-	-	-	-	-	-	-	-
Stevenage			3	0	2	1	1	2	2	0
Plymouth			1	1	0	0	0	1	0	1
Luton			2	1	1	0	1	1	2	0
Newport County			1	0	0	1	1	0	1	0
Exeter			-	-	-	-	-	-	-	-
Morecambe			1	0	1	0	0	1	1	0
Northampton			1	1	0	0	1	0	1	0
Oxford			2	1	0	1	2	0	2	0
Dag & Red			1	1	0	0	1	0	1	0
AFC Wimbledon			3	2	1	0	2	1	3	0
Portsmouth			1	0	0	1	1	0	0	0
Accrington			1	0	1	0	0	1	1	0
York			2	1	1	0	1	1	2	0
Cambridge U			2	2	0	0	1	1	0	2
Carlisle			2	0	2	0	0	2	1	1
Mansfield			2	1	0	1	0	2	0	1
Hartlepool			1	0	1	0	0	1	1	0
Barnet			1	1	0	0	0	1	0	1
Bristol Rovers			1	1	0	0	1	0	1	0

Season	Division	Pos	P	W	D	L	F	A	GD	Pts
2014-15	League 1	22	46	13	11	22	53	79	-26	50
2013-14	League 1	14	46	14	15	17	48	54	-6	57
2012-13	League 1	10	46	18	14	14	59	58	+1	68

Over/Under 52%/48% 10th   **Both score** 54%/46% 6th

DAGENHAM & RED

Nickname: Daggers
Colours: Red and white
Ground: Victoria Road (6,000)
Tel: 020-8592-1549   www.daggers.co.uk

Dagenham are usually ranked among the relegation favourites but have defied their critics every season since gaining promotion to the Football League, finishing 20th, eighth, seventh, 19th, 22nd, ninth and then 14th last season.

The small Essex club will need another big campaign from 19-goal Jamie Cureton but if the veteran forward, who turns 40 in August, can stay fit then the Daggers can once again maintain their place in the Football League.

Longest run without win/loss: 5/5
High/low league position: 13/23
Clean sheets: 15 **Yellows:** 65 **Reds:** 3
Avg attendance: 2,041 **Players used:** 31
Leading scorer: J Cureton 19 (8,16)
Key stat: Dagenham won ten of their final 19 League Two matches last season

| | 2014-15 | | Last six seasons at home | | | | | | | |
	H	A	P	W	D	L	OV	UN	BS	CS
Notts County			2	1	0	1	2	0	1	0
Crawley Town			1	0	1	0	0	1	1	0
Leyton Orient			1	1	0	0	0	1	0	1
Yeovil			1	1	0	0	1	0	1	0
Wycombe	L	D	3	2	0	1	1	2	0	2
Stevenage	L	W	1	0	0	1	0	1	0	0
Plymouth	W	L	5	1	1	3	2	3	2	2
Luton	D	L	1	0	1	0	0	1	0	1
Newport County	L	W	2	0	1	1	0	2	1	0
Exeter	L	L	4	0	3	1	1	3	4	0
Morecambe	L	W	5	0	2	3	3	2	4	0
Northampton	L	L	5	0	0	5	1	4	0	0
Oxford	D	D	4	1	1	2	0	4	0	2
Dag & Red										
AFC Wimbledon	W	L	4	2	0	2	1	3	0	2
Portsmouth	D	L	2	0	1	1	1	1	1	1
Accrington	W	W	5	3	2	0	3	2	3	2
York	W	W	3	2	0	1	0	3	0	2
Cambridge U	L	D	1	0	0	1	1	0	1	0
Carlisle	W	L	2	2	0	0	2	0	1	1
Mansfield	W	L	2	1	1	0	0	2	0	2
Hartlepool	W	W	3	1	1	1	0	3	1	1
Barnet			3	3	0	0	2	1	1	2
Bristol Rovers			4	2	0	2	3	1	1	2

Season	Division	Pos	P	W	D	L	F	A	GD	Pts
2014-15	League 2	14	46	17	8	21	58	59	-1	59
2013-14	League 2	9	46	15	15	16	53	59	-6	60
2012-13	League 2	22	46	13	12	21	55	62	-7	51

Over/Under 46%/54% 6th   **Both score** 41%/59% 19th

EXETER

Nickname: The Grecians
Colours: Black and white
Ground: St James' Park (8,830)
Tel: 01392-411-243   www.exetercityfc.co.uk

A slow start and a poor finish ruined Exeter's playoff chances, but there were at least excuses for the early dropped points as boss Paul Tisdale was forced to work under a transfer embargo.

The Grecians ultimately fell seven points short of the playoffs, but it's worth noting they took points from every member of the top ten bar local rivals Plymouth. Signings like keeper Bobby Olejnik suggests Exeter are a solid bet at odds-against to finish in the top half.

Longest run without win/loss: 7/9
High/low league position: 7/23
Clean sheets: 6 **Yellows:** 45 **Reds:** 1
Avg attendance: 3,873 **Players used:** 28
Leading scorer: T Nicholls 15 (6,13)
Key stat: Both teams scored in 32 of Exeter's 46 League Two matches last season

	2014-15 H	2014-15 A	P	W	D	L	OV	UN	BS	CS
Notts County			2	1	1	0	1	1	2	0
Crawley Town			-	-	-	-	-	-	-	-
Leyton Orient			3	2	1	0	2	1	1	2
Yeovil			3	0	2	1	1	2	3	0
Wycombe	W	L	5	2	1	2	3	2	4	0
Stevenage	D	L	2	0	2	0	0	2	1	1
Plymouth	L	L	4	2	1	1	2	2	3	1
Luton	D	W	1	0	1	0	0	1	1	0
Newport County	W	D	2	1	0	1	0	2	0	1
Exeter										
Morecambe	D	W	3	0	2	1	1	2	2	0
Northampton	L	L	3	1	0	2	1	2	0	1
Oxford	D	D	3	0	2	1	1	2	2	1
Dag & Red	W	W	4	2	1	1	3	1	3	0
AFC Wimbledon	W	L	3	3	0	0	1	2	1	2
Portsmouth	D	L	2	0	2	0	0	2	2	0
Accrington	L	W	3	1	0	2	1	2	1	1
York	D	D	3	1	2	0	1	2	3	0
Cambridge U	D	W	1	0	1	0	1	0	1	0
Carlisle	W	W	4	2	1	1	2	2	2	2
Mansfield	L	W	2	0	0	2	1	1	1	0
Hartlepool	L	L	5	1	1	3	4	1	3	1
Barnet			1	0	1	0	1	0	1	0
Bristol Rovers			4	2	1	1	3	1	3	1

Season	Division	Pos	P	W	D	L	F	A	GD	Pts
2014-15	League 2	10	46	17	13	16	61	65	-4	64
2013-14	League 2	16	46	14	13	19	54	57	-3	55
2012-13	League 2	10	46	18	10	18	63	62	+1	64

Over/Under 57%/43% 2nd   **Both score** 70%/30% 1st

HARTLEPOOL

Nickname: Pools
Colours: White and blue
Ground: Victoria Park (7,856)
Tel: 01429-272-584   hartlepoolunited.co.uk

It was third time lucky in Hartlepool's search for a manager, with Ronnie Moore guiding the club to safety after the poor reigns of Colin Cooper and Paul Murray.

Moore arrived with Hartlepool six points adrift of safety in December and they were still bottom in March, but four straight victories helped to turn things around. Moore has wasted little time in completely overhauling the club this summer and a better season is anticipated without troubling the playoffs.

Longest run without win/loss: 12/5
High/low league position: 20/24
Clean sheets: 9 **Yellows:** 61 **Reds:** 3
Avg attendance: 3,736 **Players used:** 38
Leading scorer: S Fenwick 6 (3,6)
Key stat: Hartlepool lost away without scoring at all members of the top eight last season

	2014-15 H	2014-15 A	P	W	D	L	OV	UN	BS	CS
Notts County			3	2	1	0	2	1	2	1
Crawley Town			1	0	0	1	0	1	0	0
Leyton Orient			4	3	0	1	2	2	2	1
Yeovil			4	1	2	1	1	3	2	1
Wycombe	L	L	4	0	1	3	3	1	4	0
Stevenage	L	L	3	0	1	2	1	2	1	1
Plymouth	W	L	3	3	0	0	1	2	1	2
Luton	L	L	1	0	0	1	1	0	1	0
Newport County	D	D	2	1	1	0	2	0	1	1
Exeter	W	W	5	2	1	2	2	3	3	1
Morecambe	L	W	2	1	0	1	1	1	1	0
Northampton	W	W	2	2	0	0	0	2	0	2
Oxford	D	W	2	0	1	1	1	1	2	0
Dag & Red	L	L	3	1	0	2	1	2	1	0
AFC Wimbledon	W	W	2	2	0	0	1	1	1	1
Portsmouth	D	L	3	0	3	0	0	3	0	3
Accrington	D	L	2	1	1	0	1	1	2	0
York	L	L	2	1	0	1	1	1	1	1
Cambridge U	W	L	1	1	0	0	1	0	1	0
Carlisle	L	D	5	2	0	3	5	0	2	1
Mansfield	W	D	2	1	0	1	1	1	1	0
Hartlepool										
Barnet			-	-	-	-	-	-	-	-
Bristol Rovers			3	1	1	1	3	0	2	1

Season	Division	Pos	P	W	D	L	F	A	GD	Pts
2014-15	League 2	22	46	12	9	25	39	70	-31	45
2013-14	League 2	19	46	14	11	21	50	56	-6	53
2012-13	League 1	23	46	9	14	23	39	67	-28	41

Over/Under 41%/59% 14th   **Both score** 41%/59% 19th

LEYTON ORIENT

Nickname: The O's
Colours: Red
Ground: Brisbane Road (9,271)
Tel: 0871-310-1881   www.leytonorient.com

Only three sides started last season's League One outright betting at a shorter price than Orient to gain promotion but instead the east London boys suffered a relegation at ante-post odds of 25-1.

The takeover of an Italian billionaire was supposed to move Orient to the next level but manager Russell Slade left for Cardiff, there were constant rumours of dressing-room unrest and untried boss Ian Hendon will have a difficult summer getting the club to fit into FFP rules.

Longest run without win/loss: 7/4
High/low league position: 15/24
Clean sheets: 10 **Yellows:** 89 **Reds:** 4
Avg attendance: 5,042 **Players used:** 35
Leading scorer: C Dagnall 11 (3,10)
Key stat: Relegated Orient's -10 goal difference was 22 superior to Crewe, who survived, and the same as 18th-placed Port Vale

	2014-15 H	A	Last six seasons at home P	W	D	L	OV	UN	BS	CS
Notts County	L	D	5	3	0	2	3	2	2	1
Crawley Town	W	L	3	1	0	2	2	1	2	0
Leyton Orient										
Yeovil	W	W	5	3	1	1	4	1	3	2
Wycombe			2	1	0	1	1	1	1	1
Stevenage			3	1	1	1	0	3	0	2
Plymouth			1	1	0	0	0	1	0	1
Luton			-	-	-	-	-	-	-	-
Newport County			-	-	-	-	-	-	-	-
Exeter			3	2	1	0	2	1	1	2
Morecambe			-	-	-	-	-	-	-	-
Northampton			-	-	-	-	-	-	-	-
Oxford			-	-	-	-	-	-	-	-
Dag & Red			1	0	1	0	0	1	1	0
AFC Wimbledon			-	-	-	-	-	-	-	-
Portsmouth			1	1	0	0	0	1	0	1
Accrington			-	-	-	-	-	-	-	-
York			-	-	-	-	-	-	-	-
Cambridge U			-	-	-	-	-	-	-	-
Carlisle			5	2	2	1	4	1	3	2
Mansfield			-	-	-	-	-	-	-	-
Hartlepool			4	2	1	1	1	3	2	2
Barnet			-	-	-	-	-	-	-	-
Bristol Rovers			2	2	0	0	2	0	1	1

Season	Division	Pos	P	W	D	L	F	A	GD	Pts
2014-15	League 1	23	46	12	13	21	59	69	-10	49
2013-14	League 1	3	46	25	11	10	85	45	+40	86
2012-13	League 1	7	46	21	8	17	55	48	+7	71

Over/Under 52%/48% 10th   **Both score** 52%/48% 9th

LUTON

Nickname: The Hatters
Colours: Orange, navy and white
Ground: Kenilworth Road (10,356)
Tel: 01582-411-622   www.lutontown.co.uk

Most newly promoted teams would be happy enough with eighth place the next season at a higher level, but for Luton there was a sense of disappointment that the return to the Football League wasn't capped off by another promotion.

The Hatters looked good for a while, leading the table in November and going on a run of just two defeats in 24, but that was followed by a shocking set of results which included seven straight defeats in one season-ending month.

Longest run without win/loss: 7/11
High/low league position: 1/17
Clean sheets: 18 **Yellows:** 71 **Reds:** 6
Avg attendance: 8,702 **Players used:** 33
Leading scorer: M Cullen 13 (7,10)
Key stat: Only six of Luton's 23 away League Two matches produced over 2.5 goals

	2014-15 H	A	Last six seasons at home P	W	D	L	OV	UN	BS	CS
Notts County			-	-	-	-	-	-	-	-
Crawley Town			2	1	0	1	2	0	1	1
Leyton Orient			-	-	-	-	-	-	-	-
Yeovil			-	-	-	-	-	-	-	-
Wycombe	L	D	1	0	0	1	1	0	1	0
Stevenage	W	W	2	1	0	1	0	2	0	1
Plymouth	L	W	1	0	0	1	0	1	0	0
Luton										
Newport County	W	L	4	2	2	0	2	2	2	2
Exeter	W	D	1	0	0	1	1	0	1	0
Morecambe	L	L	1	0	0	1	1	0	1	0
Northampton	W	L	1	1	0	0	0	1	0	1
Oxford	W	D	2	2	0	0	1	1	1	1
Dag & Red	W	D	1	1	0	0	1	0	1	0
AFC Wimbledon	L	L	3	1	0	2	2	1	1	1
Portsmouth	D	L	1	0	1	0	0	1	1	0
Accrington	W	D	1	1	0	0	0	1	0	1
York	D	D	4	1	2	1	3	1	3	1
Cambridge U	W	W	6	3	2	1	3	3	3	2
Carlisle	W	W	1	1	0	0	0	1	0	1
Mansfield	W	L	5	3	1	1	3	2	2	3
Hartlepool	W	W	1	1	0	0	1	0	0	1
Barnet			1	1	0	0	1	0	1	0
Bristol Rovers			-	-	-	-	-	-	-	-

Season	Division	Pos	P	W	D	L	F	A	GD	Pts
2014-15	League 2	8	46	19	11	16	54	44	+10	68
2013-14	Conference	1	46	30	11	5	102	35	+67	101
2012-13	Conference	7	46	18	13	15	70	62	+8	67

Over/Under 33%/67% 23rd   **Both score** 37%/63% 24th

MANSFIELD

Nickname: The Stags
Colours: Yellow and blue
Ground: Field Mill (10,000)
Tel: 01623-482 482   www.mansfieldtown.net

There was no party for the Stags last season, with Mansfield failing to get 50 points, and the club could be forgiven for feeling apprehensive this term having finished with eight defeats in nine.

Town were terrible in front of goal and awful on the road, winning just three away games. But manager Paul Murray has attempted to solve the scoring issue by bringing Matt Green, who flopped at Birmingham but was prolific for the Stags in the Conference, back to Field Mill.

Longest run without win/loss: 8/4
High/low league position: 8/23
Clean sheets: 11 **Yellows:** 90 **Reds:** 7
Avg attendance: 3,064 **Players used:** 40
Leading scorer: V Oliver 7 (5,7)
Key stat: Mansfield were the lowest-scoring team in League Two last season

	2014-15 H	A	Last six seasons at home P	W	D	L	OV	UN	BS	CS
Notts County			-	-	-	-	-	-	-	-
Crawley Town			2	1	0	1	2	0	1	1
Leyton Orient			-	-	-	-	-	-	-	-
Yeovil			-	-	-	-	-	-	-	-
Wycombe	D	L	2	0	2	0	1	1	1	1
Stevenage	W	L	2	1	0	1	1	1	1	1
Plymouth	W	L	2	1	0	1	0	2	0	1
Luton	W	L	5	1	4	0	1	4	2	3
Newport County	W	W	5	3	1	1	4	1	3	2
Exeter	L	W	2	0	1	1	1	1	1	1
Morecambe	W	L	2	1	0	1	1	1	1	1
Northampton	D		2	1	1	0	1	1	1	1
Oxford	W	L	3	2	0	1	3	0	3	0
Dag & Red	W	L	2	2	0	0	2	0	1	1
AFC Wimbledon	W	W	4	2	0	2	2	2	2	1
Portsmouth	L	D	2	0	1	1	2	0	2	0
Accrington	L	L	2	0	0	2	1	1	1	0
York	L	D	5	1	1	3	2	3	2	1
Cambridge U	D	L	5	3	1	1	3	2	3	2
Carlisle	W	L	1	1	0	0	1	0	1	0
Mansfield										
Hartlepool	D	L	2	0	1	1	1	1	2	0
Barnet			-	-	-	-	-	-	-	-
Bristol Rovers			1	0	1	0	0	1	1	0

Season	Division	Pos	P	W	D	L	F	A	GD	Pts
2014-15	League 2	21	46	13	9	24	38	62	-24	48
2012-13	Conference	1	46	30	5	11	92	52	+40	95

Over/Under 43%/57% 10th   **Both score** 50%/50% 10th

MORECAMBE

Nickname: The Shrimps
Colours: Red and white
Ground: The Globe Arena (6,476)
Tel: 01524-411-797   www.morecambefc.com

It's unlikely Morecambe can push for promotion given their limited resources but they may be a team to follow at big prices on a match-by-match basis if last season's evidence is anything to go by.

The 11th-placed Shrimps won at champions Burton as well as Wycombe, Luton and Newport, while also doing the double over promoted Bury and Southend. Jim Bentley's men lost just once away at sides who finished above them yet struggled in the easier fixtures.

Longest run without win/loss: 6/6
High/low league position: 4/14
Clean sheets: 12 **Yellows:** 70 **Reds:** 4
Avg attendance: 1,998 **Players used:** 28
Leading scorer: K Ellison 11 (8,10) J Redshaw 11 (6,10)
Key stat: Morecambe won more matches away (nine) than they did at home (eight) last season

	2014-15 H	A	Last six seasons at home P	W	D	L	OV	UN	BS	CS
Notts County			1	1	0	0	1	0	1	0
Crawley Town			1	1	0	0	1	0	0	1
Leyton Orient			-	-	-	-	-	-	-	-
Yeovil			-	-	-	-	-	-	-	-
Wycombe	L	W	4	0	1	3	2	2	2	0
Stevenage	D	D	2	0	2	0	2	0	2	0
Plymouth	W	D	4	2	1	1	4	0	4	0
Luton	W	W	1	1	0	0	1	0	0	1
Newport County	W	W	2	2	0	0	2	0	2	0
Exeter	L	D	3	1	0	2	1	2	0	1
Morecambe										
Northampton	L	L	6	0	2	4	3	3	5	0
Oxford	W	D	5	1	3	1	4	2	2	
Dag & Red	L	W	5	2	1	2	4	1	4	1
AFC Wimbledon	D	L	4	1	2	1	2	2	4	0
Portsmouth	W	L	2	1	1	0	2	0	2	0
Accrington	D	L	6	0	2	4	4	2	5	1
York	D	L	3	0	3	0	1	2	1	0
Cambridge U	L	W	1	0	0	1	0	1	0	0
Carlisle	L	D	1	0	0	1	0	1	0	0
Mansfield	W	L	2	1	0	1	1	1	1	0
Hartlepool	L	W	2	0	0	2	1	1	1	0
Barnet			4	2	1	1	3	1	3	0
Bristol Rovers			3	1	1	1	2	1	3	0

Season	Division	Pos	P	W	D	L	F	A	GD	Pts
2014-15	League 2	11	46	12	17	17	53	52	+1	63
2013-14	League 2	18	46	13	15	18	52	64	-12	54
2012-13	League 2	16	46	15	13	18	55	61	-6	58

Over/Under 41%/59% 14th   **Both score** 54%/46% 8th

NEWPORT COUNTY

Nickname: The Exiles
Colours: Yellow and black
Ground: Rodney Parade (7,012)
Tel: 01633-670-690   newport-county.co.uk

Commuting from Essex took its toll on manager Justin Edinburgh and when he decided to move to Gillingham the wheels fell off the Newport promotion train.

Edinburgh exited in early February, although his head had been turned prior to that, and from sitting third in January, Newport had to settle for ninth.

New manager Terry Butcher has work to do if Newport are to challenge in a strong-looking division and County's relegation odds are worth a second look.

Longest run without win/loss: 5/9
High/low league position: 3/18
Clean sheets: 14 **Yellows:** 78 **Reds:** 7
Avg attendance: 3,213 **Players used:** 33
Leading scorer: A O'Connor 10 (3,8)
Key stat: Newport lost 12 League Two games in 2015, only bottom-four outfits Cheltenham, Mansfield and Tranmere suffered more defeats

NORTHAMPTON

Nickname: The Cobblers
Colours: Claret and white
Ground: Sixfields Stadium (7,653)
Tel: 01604-683-700   www.ntfc.co.uk

It has been suggested that top goalscorer Marc Richards' two spells out with injury ruined Northampton's hopes of reaching the playoffs and, while it could be pointed out that it's cobblers to believe one man holds so much sway, it clearly hurt Town.

Northampton won only two of the seven games he missed between September 27 and November 1 and then lost six of 13 during the two-month absence later in the campaign, so Richards' wellbeing is crucial to Northampton.

Longest run without win/loss: 6/6
High/low league position: 5/20
Clean sheets: 13 **Yellows:** 90 **Reds:** 6
Avg attendance: 4,599 **Players used:** 35
Leading scorer: M Richards 18 (5,15)
Key stat: Northampton scored in 23 of the 26 league matches that Marc Richards started last season

	2014-15 H	A	Last six seasons at home P	W	D	L	OV	UN	BS	CS
Notts County			-	-	-	-	-	-	-	-
Crawley Town			1	0	0	1	0	1	0	0
Leyton Orient			-	-	-	-	-	-	-	-
Yeovil			-	-	-	-	-	-	-	-
Wycombe	L	W	2	1	0	1	0	2	0	1
Stevenage	W	L	1	1	0	0	0	1	0	1
Plymouth	W	D	2	1	0	1	1	1	1	1
Luton	W	L	4	2	1	1	1	3	2	1
Newport County										
Exeter	D	L	2	0	2	0	1	1	2	0
Morecambe	L	L	2	0	0	2	1	1	1	0
Northampton	W	L	2	1	0	1	2	0	2	0
Oxford	L	L	2	1	0	1	1	1	1	0
Dag & Red	L	W	2	0	0	2	2	0	2	0
AFC Wimbledon	W	L	3	1	1	1	3	0	3	0
Portsmouth	W	W	2	1	0	1	1	1	1	1
Accrington	D	W	2	1	1	0	1	1	2	0
York	W	W	4	4	0	0	4	0	2	2
Cambridge U	D	L	4	1	2	1	1	3	3	0
Carlisle	W	W	1	1	0	0	1	0	1	0
Mansfield	L	L	5	3	1	1	0	5	1	3
Hartlepool	D	D	2	1	1	0	1	1	1	1
Barnet			-	-	-	-	-	-	-	-
Bristol Rovers			1	1	0	0	0	1	0	1

Season	Division	Pos	P	W	D	L	F	A	GD	Pts
2014-15	League 2	9	46	18	11	17	51	54	-3	65
2013-14	League 2	14	46	14	16	16	56	59	-3	58
2012-13	Conference	3	46	25	10	11	85	60	+25	85

Over/Under 35%/65% 20th   **Both score** 39%/61% 21st

	2014-15 H	A	Last six seasons at home P	W	D	L	OV	UN	BS	CS
Notts County			1	0	0	1	0	1	0	0
Crawley Town			1	0	0	1	0	1	0	0
Leyton Orient			-	-	-	-	-	-	-	-
Yeovil			-	-	-	-	-	-	-	-
Wycombe	L	D	4	1	1	2	3	1	4	0
Stevenage	W	L	2	2	0	0	0	2	0	2
Plymouth	L	L	4	1	1	2	1	3	1	2
Luton	W	L	1	1	0	0	1	0	1	0
Newport County	W	L	2	2	0	0	2	0	1	1
Exeter	W	W	3	2	0	1	2	1	1	2
Morecambe	W	W	6	3	2	1	3	3	2	3
Northampton										
Oxford	L	D	5	4	0	1	4	1	4	1
Dag & Red	W	W	5	4	1	0	3	2	3	2
AFC Wimbledon	W	D	4	3	1	0	1	3	1	3
Portsmouth	W	L	2	1	0	1	0	2	0	1
Accrington	L	W	6	3	2	1	2	4	1	5
York	W	D	3	1	0	2	1	2	0	1
Cambridge U	L	L	1	0	0	1	0	1	0	0
Carlisle	L	L	1	0	0	1	0	1	0	0
Mansfield	W	D	2	1	1	0	0	2	1	1
Hartlepool	W	L	2	2	0	0	1	1	1	1
Barnet			4	1	1	2	2	2	2	2
Bristol Rovers			3	2	1	0	1	2	1	2

Season	Division	Pos	P	W	D	L	F	A	GD	Pts
2014-15	League 2	12	46	18	7	21	67	62	+5	61
2013-14	League 2	21	46	13	14	19	42	57	-15	53
2012-13	League 2	6	46	21	10	15	64	55	+9	73

Over/Under 48%/52% 5th   **Both score** 57%/43% 6th

NOTTS COUNTY

Nickname: The Magpies
Colours: Black and white
Ground: Meadow Lane (20,300)
Tel: 0115-952-9000   www.nottscountyfc.co.uk

If you want to know why understanding the Asian market is so important then check out the plight of Notts County. Even when Notts made a blistering start of two defeats in 14, they drifted almost weekly because their key performance indicators (KPIs) were mainly horrendous.

They were being dominated in the shot and possession stats and, sure enough, those who look beyond the results were rewarded as County were relegated with only four wins in their last 30 matches.

Longest run without win/loss: 11/9
High/low league position: 4/22
Clean sheets: 12 **Yellows:** 90 **Reds:** 7
Avg attendance: 5,351 **Players used:** 45
Leading scorer: G Thompson 12 (5,10)
Key stat: County used 45 players last season – only Tranmere and Blackpool (who were also relegated) used more in the Football League

OXFORD UTD

Nickname: The U's
Colours: Yellow
Ground: The Kassam Stadium (12,500)
Tel: 01865-337533   www.oufc.co.uk

Finishing 13th wasn't unlucky for Oxford in their debut campaign under Michael Appleton and plenty of punters have jumped on the United bandwagon for this season after a strong finish to 2014-15.

Appleton was happy to play the long game, blooding youngsters who will be stronger for their second season. Season-ticket sales are up, good players have been brought in and there's thought to be a big budget to attract talent. No wonder Oxford have been cut in the title betting.

Longest run without win/loss: 7/8
High/low league position: 13/23
Clean sheets: 16 **Yellows:** 64 **Reds:** 1
Avg attendance: 6,154 **Players used:** 41
Leading scorer: D Hylton 14 (5,12)
Key stat: Oxford lost just four of their final 20 matches in League Two and finished unbeaten in eight with five wins in that period

	2014-15 H	A	Last six seasons at home P	W	D	L	OV	UN	BS	CS
Notts County										
Crawley Town	W	L	3	2	1	0	1	2	2	1
Leyton Orient	D	W	5	1	3	1	2	3	4	1
Yeovil	L	D	4	2	0	2	4	0	3	1
Wycombe			1	0	1	0	0	1	1	0
Stevenage			3	1	0	2	1	2	1	1
Plymouth			1	1	0	0	0	1	0	1
Luton			-	-	-	-	-	-	-	-
Newport County			-	-	-	-	-	-	-	-
Exeter			2	1	0	1	1	1	1	0
Morecambe			1	1	0	0	1	0	1	0
Northampton			1	1	0	0	1	0	1	0
Oxford			-	-	-	-	-	-	-	-
Dag & Red			2	2	0	0	1	1	0	2
AFC Wimbledon			-	-	-	-	-	-	-	-
Portsmouth			1	1	0	0	1	0	0	1
Accrington			1	0	0	1	1	0	1	0
York			-	-	-	-	-	-	-	-
Cambridge U			-	-	-	-	-	-	-	-
Carlisle			4	3	0	1	1	3	1	2
Mansfield			-	-	-	-	-	-	-	-
Hartlepool			3	3	0	0	2	1	0	3
Barnet			1	1	0	0	0	1	0	1
Bristol Rovers			1	0	0	1	0	1	0	0

Season	Division	Pos	P	W	D	L	F	A	GD	Pts
2014-15	League 1	21	46	12	14	20	45	63	-18	50
2013-14	League 1	20	46	15	5	26	64	77	-13	50
2012-13	League 1	12	46	16	17	13	61	49	+12	65

Over/Under 48%/52% 14th   **Both score** 52%/48% 9th

	2014-15 H	A	Last six seasons at home P	W	D	L	OV	UN	BS	CS
Notts County			-	-	-	-	-	-	-	-
Crawley Town			2	1	1	0	1	1	2	0
Leyton Orient			-	-	-	-	-	-	-	-
Yeovil			-	-	-	-	-	-	-	-
Wycombe	L	W	4	0	2	2	3	1	3	0
Stevenage	D	W	3	1	1	1	2	1	2	1
Plymouth	D	W	4	2	1	1	3	1	3	1
Luton	D	L	2	1	1	0	0	2	1	1
Newport County	W	W	2	1	1	0	0	2	0	2
Exeter	D	D	3	0	2	1	2	1	2	1
Morecambe	D	L	5	2	2	1	3	2	3	2
Northampton	D	W	5	4	1	0	2	3	3	2
Oxford										
Dag & Red	D	D	4	2	1	1	4	0	4	0
AFC Wimbledon	D	D	5	4	1	0	2	3	2	3
Portsmouth	L	D	2	0	1	1	0	2	0	1
Accrington	W	L	5	2	2	1	3	2	3	2
York	D	W	4	1	2	1	1	3	1	2
Cambridge U	W	L	2	1	1	0	0	2	0	2
Carlisle	W	L	1	1	0	0	1	0	1	0
Mansfield	W	L	3	3	0	0	2	1	0	3
Hartlepool	L	D	2	1	0	1	0	2	0	1
Barnet			3	3	0	0	2	1	2	1
Bristol Rovers			3	1	0	2	1	2	0	1

Season	Division	Pos	P	W	D	L	F	A	GD	Pts
2014-15	League 2	13	46	15	16	15	50	49	+1	61
2013-14	League 2	8	46	16	14	16	53	50	+3	62
2012-13	League 2	9	46	19	8	19	60	61	-1	65

Over/Under 35%/65% 20th   **Both score** 46%/54% 15th

LEAGUE TWO

PLYMOUTH

Nickname: The Pilgrims
Colours: Green and white
Ground: Home Park (16,388)
Tel: 01752-562 561   www.pafc.co.uk

There was the infamous headline from one newspaper when Arsenal announced their new manager – Arsene Who? – and Plymouth fans had a similar question to ask when Derek Adams was brought in to replace John Sheridan, who took them to the playoff semi-finals last season.

Adams led Ross County to promotion to the Scottish Premiership and stabalised them in the top flight before a slow start last term saw him surplus to requirements so Argyle are difficult to judge.

Longest run without win/loss: 7/7
High/low league position: 5/14
Clean sheets: 21 **Yellows:** 66 **Reds:** 3
Avg attendance: 7,412 **Players used:** 30
Leading scorer: R Reid 18 (9,13)
Key stat: Plymouth kept 21 clean sheets last season – the best of any side that did not claim promotion

	2014-15 H	A	P	W	D	L	OV	UN	BS	CS
Notts County			1	0	1	0	0	1	1	0
Crawley Town			1	0	1	0	0	1	1	0
Leyton Orient			1	0	0	1	1	0	1	0
Yeovil			1	0	1	0	0	1	0	1
Wycombe	L	W	3	0	0	3	1	2	0	0
Stevenage	D	L	1	0	1	0	0	1	1	0
Plymouth										
Luton	L	W	1	0	0	1	0	1	0	0
Newport County	D	L	2	0	2	0	0	2	0	2
Exeter	W	W	4	3	0	1	2	2	1	3
Morecambe	D	L	4	2	2	0	2	2	3	1
Northampton	W	W	4	4	0	0	2	2	2	2
Oxford	L	D	4	0	1	3	1	3	2	0
Dag & Red	W	L	5	3	2	0	3	2	2	3
AFC Wimbledon	D	D	4	0	1	3	2	2	3	0
Portsmouth	W	L	2	1	1	0	1	1	1	1
Accrington	W	L	4	1	3	0	1	3	1	3
York	D	D	3	1	1	1	1	2	1	1
Cambridge U	W	L	1	1	0	0	0	1	0	1
Carlisle	W	L	2	1	1	0	0	2	1	1
Mansfield	W	L	2	1	1	0	1	1	2	0
Hartlepool	W	L	3	1	1	0	3	1	1	1
Barnet			2	1	1	0	1	1	1	1
Bristol Rovers			4	2	2	0	1	3	3	1

Season	Division	Pos	P	W	D	L	F	A	GD	Pts
2014-15	League 2	7	46	20	11	15	55	37	+18	71
2013-14	League 2	10	46	16	12	18	51	58	-7	60
2012-13	League 2	21	46	13	13	20	46	55	-9	52

Over/Under 30%/70% 25th   **Both score** 33%/67% 25th

PORTSMOUTH

Nickname: Pompey
Colours: Blue and white
Ground: Fratton Park (20,700)
Tel: 023-9273-1204   www.portsmouthfc.co.uk

Another season in League Two and another season where Portsmouth are considered title favourites, but the 2008 FA Cup winners have failed to even finish in the top half on the two previous occasions they've been market leaders.

Paul Cook dropped down from League One Chesterfield to move to Fratton Park and eventually the size of the club and budget available should bring promotion.

However, Pompey have won only eight away games in two League Two seasons.

Longest run without win/loss: 9/7
High/low league position: 8/18
Clean sheets: 13 **Yellows:** 70 **Reds:** 4
Avg attendance: 15,242 **Players used:** 37
Leading scorer: J Wallace 14 (6,13)
Key stat: Portsmouth won only three away matches last season, the joint fewest in League Two

	2014-15 H	A	P	W	D	L	OV	UN	BS	CS
Notts County			1	0	0	1	0	1	0	0
Crawley Town			1	0	0	1	1	0	1	0
Leyton Orient			1	0	0	1	1	0	1	0
Yeovil			1	0	0	1	1	0	1	0
Wycombe	D	D	2	0	2	0	1	1	2	0
Stevenage	W	L	2	1	1	0	1	1	1	1
Plymouth	W	L	2	1	1	0	2	0	2	0
Luton	W	D	1	1	0	0	0	1	0	1
Newport County	L	L	2	0	0	2	0	2	0	0
Exeter	W	D	2	2	0	0	1	1	1	1
Morecambe	W	L	2	2	0	0	2	0	0	2
Northampton	W	L	2	1	1	0	0	2	0	2
Oxford	D	W	2	0	1	1	1	1	1	1
Dag & Red	W	D	2	2	0	0	1	1	0	2
AFC Wimbledon	L	L	2	1	0	1	0	2	0	1
Portsmouth										
Accrington	L	D	2	1	0	1	1	1	1	1
York	D	D	2	0	1	1	0	2	1	0
Cambridge U	W	W	1	1	0	0	1	0	1	0
Carlisle	W	D	2	1	1	0	1	1	1	1
Mansfield	D	W	2	0	2	0	0	2	2	0
Hartlepool	W	D	3	2	0	1	1	2	1	2
Barnet			-	-	-	-	-	-	-	-
Bristol Rovers			1	1	0	0	1	0	1	0

Season	Division	Pos	P	W	D	L	F	A	GD	Pts
2014-15	League 2	16	46	14	15	17	52	54	-2	57
2013-14	League 2	13	46	14	17	15	56	66	-10	59
2012-13	League 1	24	46	10	12	24	51	69	-18	32

Over/Under 39%/61% 16th   **Both score** 46%/54% 15th

STEVENAGE

Nickname: The Boro
Colours: White and red
Ground: Broadhall Way (6,920)
Tel: 01438-223223   www.stevenagefc.com

Stevenage suffered a near miss last term, losing in extra-time of the playoff semi-finals. And while the building blocks seemed in place under Graham Westley, who signed a lot of non-league players who improved as the season progressed, the club has now moved in a totally different direction by appointing Teddy Sheringham as Westley's replacement.

Sheringham has promised a more attractive playing style but it remains to be seen if the players are suitable.

Longest run without win/loss: 5/8
High/low league position: 6/19
Clean sheets: 15 **Yellows:** 66 **Reds:** 3
Avg attendance: 3,191 **Players used:** 37
Leading scorer: C Lee 9 (4,9)
Key stat: Stevenage won 15 home matches in League Two last season and seven of those finished 1-0

| | 2014-15 | | Last six seasons at home | | | | | | | |
	H	A	P	W	D	L	OV	UN	BS	CS
Notts County			3	1	0	2	0	3	0	1
Crawley Town			3	2	0	1	1	2	1	2
Leyton Orient			3	0	0	3	0	3	0	0
Yeovil			2	0	1	1	0	2	0	1
Wycombe	L	D	3	0	1	2	1	2	2	0
Stevenage										
Plymouth	W	D	1	1	0	0	0	1	0	1
Luton	L	L	2	0	0	2	1	1	1	0
Newport County	W	L	1	1	0	0	1	0	1	0
Exeter	W	D	2	1	1	0	0	2	0	2
Morecambe	D	D	2	1	1	0	0	2	1	1
Northampton	W	L	2	1	0	1	1	1	1	0
Oxford	L	D	3	1	1	1	0	3	0	2
Dag & Red	L	W	1	0	0	1	0	1	0	0
AFC Wimbledon	W	W	2	1	1	0	1	1	1	1
Portsmouth	W	L	2	2	0	0	1	1	1	1
Accrington	W	D	2	1	1	0	2	0	2	0
York	L	W	2	1	0	1	1	1	1	1
Cambridge U	W	D	2	2	0	0	2	0	2	0
Carlisle	W	L	4	2	1	1	3	2	2	
Mansfield	W	L	2	2	0	0	2	0	1	1
Hartlepool	W	W	3	2	1	0	1	2	1	2
Barnet			1	1	0	0	1	0	1	0
Bristol Rovers			-	-	-	-	-	-	-	-

Season	Division	Pos	P	W	D	L	F	A	GD	Pts
2014-15	League 2	6	46	20	12	14	62	54	+8	72
2013-14	League 1	24	46	11	9	26	46	72	-26	42
2012-13	League 1	18	46	15	9	22	47	64	-17	54

Over/Under 46%/54% 6th   **Both score** 50%/50% 10th

WYCOMBE

Nickname: The Chairboys
Colours: Sky and navy blue
Ground: Adams Park (10,300)
Tel: 01494-472-100   www.wwfc.com

Gareth Ainsworth will have had a summer thinking 'if only'. If only Wycombe had held on to the top-three position they occupied from September until losing their penultimate match of the season. If only they had held on for one more minute of their playoff final defeat to Southend, who equalised in the 121st minute and then won on penalties.

Unfortunately for Wycombe, their rise came with the help of classy loan signings so a repeat performance is unlikely.

Longest run without win/loss: 3/12
High/low league position: 1/5
Clean sheets: 15 **Yellows:** 77 **Reds:** 2
Avg attendance: 4,144 **Players used:** 24
Leading scorer: P Hayes 12 (3,12)
Key stat: Wycombe lost just two League Two away games last season and scored seven more goals (37) on the road than at home

| | 2014-15 | | Last six seasons at home | | | | | | | |
	H	A	P	W	D	L	OV	UN	BS	CS
Notts County			1	0	0	1	1	0	1	0
Crawley Town			-	-	-	-	-	-	-	-
Leyton Orient			2	1	0	1	1	1	1	0
Yeovil			2	0	0	2	2	0	2	0
Wycombe										
Stevenage	D	W	3	0	1	2	1	2	1	0
Plymouth	L	W	3	0	1	2	0	3	1	0
Luton	D	W	1	0	1	0	0	1	1	0
Newport County	L	W	2	0	0	2	1	1	1	0
Exeter	W	L	5	2	2	1	3	2	4	0
Morecambe	L	W	4	2	1	1	1	3	1	2
Northampton	D	W	4	0	4	0	1	3	3	1
Oxford	L	W	4	0	1	3	2	2	2	1
Dag & Red	D	W	3	2	1	0	0	3	1	2
AFC Wimbledon	W	D	3	1	0	2	1	2	0	1
Portsmouth	D	D	2	0	1	1	0	2	0	1
Accrington	D	D	4	0	2	2	2	2	2	1
York	W	D	3	2	1	0	1	2	1	2
Cambridge U	W	W	1	1	0	0	0	1	0	1
Carlisle	W	W	3	1	2	0	1	2	2	1
Mansfield	W	D	2	1	0	1	1	1	1	0
Hartlepool	W	W	4	4	0	0	2	2	1	3
Barnet			2	1	1	0	1	1	1	1
Bristol Rovers			3	2	0	1	2	1	2	1

Season	Division	Pos	P	W	D	L	F	A	GD	Pts
2014-15	League 2	4	46	23	15	8	67	45	+22	84
2013-14	League 2	22	46	12	14	20	46	54	-8	50
2012-13	League 2	15	46	17	9	20	50	60	-10	60

Over/Under 46%/54% 6th   **Both score** 59%/41% 3rd

YEOVIL

Nickname: The Glovers
Colours: Green and white
Ground: Huish Park (9,665)
Tel: 01935-423-662   www.ytfc.net

What comes up, must come down. Yeovil's remarkable rise up the Football League ladder started when they gained promotion from the Conference in 2003 and the Glovers made it all the way to the Championship by 2013 before now finding themselves back in the fourth tier.

Last season was a shocker. Yeovil finished bottom of League One with 40 points and a goal difference of minus 39, scoring only 36 goals, and new boss Paul Sturrock has a tough job on his hands.

Longest run without win/loss: 8/4
High/low league position: 13/24
Clean sheets: 7 **Yellows:** 79 **Reds:** 3
Avg attendance: 4,346 **Players used:** 40
Leading scorer: J Hayter 5 (3,5) G Ugwu 5 (3,5)
Key stat: Yeovil failed to score in 21 of their 46 League One matches last season

	2014-15 H	2014-15 A	P	W	D	L	OV	UN	BS	CS
Notts County	D	W	4	2	2	0	1	3	2	2
Crawley Town	W	L	2	1	1	0	2	0	2	0
Leyton Orient	L	L	5	2	2	1	5	0	3	1
Yeovil										
Wycombe			2	2	0	0	1	1	0	2
Stevenage			2	0	0	2	2	0	1	0
Plymouth			1	1	0	0	0	1	0	1
Luton			-	-	-	-	-	-	-	-
Newport County			-	-	-	-	-	-	-	-
Exeter			3	1	1	1	3	0	3	0
Morecambe			-	-	-	-	-	-	-	-
Northampton			-	-	-	-	-	-	-	-
Oxford			-	-	-	-	-	-	-	-
Dag & Red			1	0	0	1	1	0	1	0
AFC Wimbledon			-	-	-	-	-	-	-	-
Portsmouth			1	0	0	1	1	0	1	0
Accrington			-	-	-	-	-	-	-	-
York			-	-	-	-	-	-	-	-
Cambridge U			-	-	-	-	-	-	-	-
Carlisle			4	2	0	2	3	1	2	1
Mansfield			-	-	-	-	-	-	-	-
Hartlepool			4	2	0	2	1	3	0	2
Barnet			-	-	-	-	-	-	-	-
Bristol Rovers			2	0	0	2	1	1	0	0

Season	Division	Pos	P	W	D	L	F	A	GD	Pts
2014-15	League 1	24	46	10	10	26	36	75	-39	40
2013-14	Championship	24	46	8	13	25	44	75	-31	37
2012-13	League 1	4	46	23	8	15	71	56	+15	77

Over/Under 46%/54% 16th   **Both score** 43%/57% 22nd

YORK

Nickname: Minstermen
Colours: Red, white and blue
Ground: Bootham Crescent (7,872)
Tel: 01904-624447   yorkcityfootballclub.co.uk

Punters who use shot statistics to compile their ratings will have been flummoxed by York last season – how is it possible for a team to have 547 shots (second-highest in the division behind Shrewsbury's 563) but score only 46 goals?

The Minstermen often dominated but couldn't score and it was the main reason why they finished with so many draws and an 18th-place finish. However, if their attacking efficiency improves so will York and it could be a drastic improvement.

Longest run without win/loss: 9/6
High/low league position: 16/23
Clean sheets: 14 **Yellows:** 47 **Reds:** 7
Avg attendance: 4,167 **Players used:** 32
Leading scorer: J Hyde 9 (1,9)
Key stat: York were stalemate specialists last season with a league-high 19 draws

	2014-15 H	2014-15 A	P	W	D	L	OV	UN	BS	CS
Notts County			-	-	-	-	-	-	-	-
Crawley Town			2	1	1	0	0	2	1	1
Leyton Orient			-	-	-	-	-	-	-	-
Yeovil			-	-	-	-	-	-	-	-
Wycombe	D	L	3	1	1	1	1	2	1	2
Stevenage	L	W	2	0	1	1	0	2	1	0
Plymouth	D	D	3	1	2	0	0	3	1	2
Luton	D	D	4	2	2	0	1	3	0	4
Newport County	L	L	4	2	1	1	1	3	2	1
Exeter	D	D	3	1	1	1	2	1	2	1
Morecambe	W	D	3	2	0	1	2	1	2	1
Northampton	D	L	3	1	2	0	0	3	2	1
Oxford	L	D	4	1	2	1	1	3	2	1
Dag & Red	L	L	3	2	0	1	2	1	2	0
AFC Wimbledon	L	L	5	2	0	3	4	1	2	1
Portsmouth	D	D	2	1	1	0	1	1	1	1
Accrington	W	D	3	1	2	0	0	3	2	1
York										
Cambridge U	D	W	4	0	4	0	3	1	3	1
Carlisle	D	W	1	0	1	0	0	1	0	1
Mansfield	D	W	5	2	2	1	4	1	4	1
Hartlepool	W	W	2	1	1	0	0	2	0	2
Barnet			1	0	0	1	1	0	1	0
Bristol Rovers			2	1	1	0	1	1	1	1

Season	Division	Pos	P	W	D	L	F	A	GD	Pts
2014-15	League 2	18	46	11	19	16	46	51	-5	52
2013-14	League 2	7	46	18	17	11	52	41	+11	71
2012-13	League 2	17	46	12	19	15	50	60	-10	55

Over/Under 33%/67% 23rd   **Both score** 43%/57% 17th

League Two stats 2014-15

Key Points in all tables (except the league table) do not include any deductions imposed by the league.
POS H A Overall league position, rank from home games only, rank from away games only **Sup** Average match supremacy **GFA** Goals For Average **GAA** Goals Against Average **PGA** Points Gained Average

| League Two 2014-15 | | | | Home | | | | Away | | | | | | |
Pos	H	A		P	W	D	L	F	A	W	D	L	F	A	GD	Pts
1	2	2	Burton	46	16	4	3	34	13	12	6	5	35	26	+30	94
2	1	5	Shrewsbury	46	17	4	2	43	11	10	4	9	24	20	+36	89
3	5	3	Bury	46	14	3	6	33	20	12	4	7	27	20	+20	85
4	11	1	Wycombe	46	10	7	6	30	25	13	8	2	37	20	+22	84
5	6	4	Southend	46	12	8	3	25	9	12	4	7	29	29	+16	84
6	3	15	Stevenage	46	15	3	5	37	23	5	9	9	25	31	+8	72
7	4	12	Plymouth	46	13	6	4	34	14	7	5	11	21	23	+18	71
8	7	14	Luton	46	13	4	6	37	19	6	7	10	17	25	+10	68
9	14	9	Newport County	46	9	7	7	30	25	9	4	10	21	29	-3	65
10	15	7	Exeter	46	8	8	7	30	29	9	5	9	31	36	-4	64
11	19	6	Morecambe	46	8	6	9	26	28	9	6	8	27	24	+1	63
12	8	16	Northampton	46	13	2	8	39	27	5	5	13	28	35	+5	61
13	18	8	Oxford	46	7	9	7	27	24	8	7	8	23	25	+1	61
14	17	10	Dagenham & Red	46	9	3	11	30	26	8	5	10	28	33	-1	59
15	10	17	AFC Wimbledon	46	10	8	5	34	25	4	8	11	20	35	-6	58
16	9	19	Portsmouth	46	11	6	6	34	23	3	9	11	18	31	-2	56
17	12	18	Accrington	46	10	6	7	33	32	5	5	13	25	45	-19	56
18	22	11	York	46	5	10	8	16	21	6	9	8	30	30	-5	52
19	21	13	Cambridge Utd	46	7	5	11	34	33	6	7	10	27	33	-5	51
20	16	20	Carlisle	46	9	5	9	35	37	5	3	15	21	37	-18	50
21	13	24	Mansfield	46	10	5	8	24	23	3	4	16	14	38	-24	48
22	20	23	Hartlepool	46	8	5	10	22	30	4	4	15	17	40	-31	45
23	23	21	Cheltenham	46	5	8	10	22	30	4	6	13	18	37	-27	41
24	24	22	Tranmere	46	5	7	11	26	34	4	5	14	19	33	-22	39

Best attack

		GF	GFA
1	Burton	69	1.5
2	Shrewsbury	67	1.46
3	Wycombe	67	1.46
4	Northampton	67	1.46
5	Stevenage	62	1.35
6	Exeter	61	1.33
7	Cambridge	61	1.33
8	Bury	60	1.3
9	Dag & Red	58	1.26
10	Accrington	58	1.26
11	Carlisle	56	1.22
12	Plymouth	55	1.2
13	Southend	54	1.17
14	Luton	54	1.17
15	Wimbledon	54	1.17
16	Morecambe	53	1.15
17	Portsmouth	52	1.13
18	Newport Co	51	1.11
19	Oxford	50	1.09
20	York	46	1
21	Tranmere	45	0.98
22	Cheltenham	40	0.87
23	Hartlepool	39	0.85
24	Mansfield	38	0.83

Best defence

		GA	GAA
1	Shrewsbury	31	0.67
2	Plymouth	37	0.8
3	Southend	38	0.83
4	Burton	39	0.85
5	Bury	40	0.87
6	Luton	44	0.96
7	Wycombe	45	0.98
8	Oxford	49	1.07
9	York	51	1.11
10	Morecambe	52	1.13
11	Stevenage	54	1.17
12	Newport Co	54	1.17
13	Portsmouth	54	1.17
14	Dag & Red	59	1.28
15	Wimbledon	60	1.3
16	Northampton	62	1.35
17	Mansfield	62	1.35
18	Exeter	65	1.41
19	Cambridge	66	1.43
20	Cheltenham	67	1.46
21	Tranmere	67	1.46
22	Hartlepool	70	1.52
23	Carlisle	74	1.61
24	Accrington	77	1.67

Top scorers

		Team	Goals scored	
M Tubbs	Portsmouth	21	|||||||||||||||||||||
J Cureton	Dag & Red	19	|||||||||||||||||||
R Reid	Plymouth	18	||||||||||||||||||
M Richards	Northampton	18	||||||||||||||||||
J Collins	Shrewsbury	15	|||||||||||||||
T Nicholls	Exeter	15	|||||||||||||||

Over 2.5 goals

	H	A	%
Accrington	13	15	61%
Exeter	11	15	57%
Carlisle	14	11	54%
Cambridge	14	11	54%
Northampton	11	11	48%

Under 2.5 goals

	H	A	%
Southend	21	13	74%
Plymouth	16	16	70%
Luton	14	17	67%
York	19	12	67%
Shrewsbury	14	16	65%
Newport Co	16	14	65%
Oxford	14	16	65%

Both to score

	H	A	%
Exeter	17	15	70%
Accrington	16	14	65%
Cambridge	13	14	59%
Wycombe	13	14	59%
Cheltenham	14	12	57%
Northampton	11	15	57%

Both not to score

	H	A	%
Plymouth	15	16	67%
Shrewsbury	16	15	67%
Luton	15	14	63%
Bury	12	16	61%
Newport Co	11	17	61%
Southend	18	10	61%

League Two results 2014-15

	Accrington	AFC Wimbledon	Burton	Bury	Cambridge Utd	Carlisle	Cheltenham	Dagenham & R	Exeter	Hartlepool	Luton	Mansfield	Morecambe	Newport County	Northampton	Oxford	Plymouth	Portsmouth	Shrewsbury	Southend	Stevenage	Tranmere	Wycombe	York
Accrington		1-0	1-0	0-1	2-1	3-1	1-1	1-2	2-3	3-1	2-2	2-1	2-1	0-2	1-5	1-0	1-0	1-1	1-2	0-1	2-2	3-2	1-1	2-2
AFC Wimbledon	2-1		3-0	3-2	1-2	1-3	1-1	1-0	4-1	1-2	3-2	0-1	1-0	2-0	2-2	0-0	0-0	1-0	2-2	0-0	2-3	2-2	0-0	2-1
Burton	3-0	0-0		1-0	1-3	1-1	1-0	2-1	1-0	4-0	1-0	2-1	0-2	0-1	3-1	2-0	1-1	2-0	1-0	2-1	1-1	2-0	1-0	2-0
Bury	2-1	2-0	3-1		2-0	2-1	0-1	0-2	1-1	1-0	1-0	2-0	1-2	1-3	2-1	0-1	2-1	3-0	1-0	0-1	2-1	2-0	1-1	2-2
Cambridge Utd	2-2	0-0	2-3	0-2		5-0	1-2	1-1	1-2	2-1	0-1	3-1	1-2	4-0	5-1	1-0	2-6	0-0	0-1	1-1	1-2	0-1	0-3	
Carlisle	1-0	4-4	3-4	0-3	0-1		1-0	1-0	1-3	3-3	0-1	2-1	1-1	2-3	2-1	2-1	2-0	2-2	1-2	1-1	3-0	1-0	2-3	0-3
Cheltenham	2-1	1-1	1-3	1-2	3-1	0-0		1-1	1-2	1-0	1-1	1-1	1-1	0-1	3-2	1-1	0-3	1-1	0-1	0-1	0-1	2-0	1-4	0-1
Dagenham & R	4-0	4-0	1-3	1-0	2-3	4-2	3-1		1-2	2-0	0-3	0-1	0-2	0-0	2-0	0-0	1-2	1-3	0-2	0-1	0-1	2-0		
Exeter	1-2	3-2	1-1	2-1	2-2	2-0	1-0	2-1		1-2	1-1	1-2	1-1	2-0	0-2	1-1	1-3	3-2	2-0	0-0	1-2	2-1	1-1	
Hartlepool	1-1	1-0	0-1	0-2	2-1	0-3	2-0	0-2	2-1		1-2	1-0	0-2	2-2	1-0	1-1	3-2	0-0	2-0	0-1	1-3	0-0	1-3	1-3
Luton	2-0	0-1	0-1	1-1	3-2	1-0	1-0	3-1	2-3	3-0		3-0	2-3	3-0	1-0	2-0	0-1	1-1	0-0	2-0	2-0	1-0	2-3	2-2
Mansfield	0-1	2-1	1-2	0-1	0-0	3-2	1-1	2-1	2-3	1-1	1-0		1-0	1-0	1-1	2-1	1-0	1-2	0-1	1-2	1-0	1-0	0-0	1-4
Morecambe	1-1	1-1	1-2	1-0	0-2	0-1	0-0	2-3	0-2	0-1	3-0	2-1		3-2	0-1	1-0	2-1	3-1	1-4	3-1	0-0	0-0	1-3	1-1
Newport County	1-1	4-1	1-1	1-2	1-1	2-3	2-2	2-2	1-0	0-1	0-1		3-2		0-1	2-0	1-0	1-0	2-0	1-1	0-2	3-1		
Northampton	4-5	2-0	1-2	2-3	0-1	0-2	2-0	1-0	1-0	5-1	2-1	1-0	2-1	3-0		1-3	2-3	1-0	1-1	1-1	1-0	0-2	3-3	3-0
Oxford	3-1	0-0	0-1	2-1	2-0	2-1	1-2	3-3	2-2	0-2	1-1	3-0	1-1	1-0	1-1		0-0	0-1	0-2	2-3	0-0	2-0	1-2	0-0
Plymouth	1-0	1-1	1-1	0-2	2-0	1-0	3-0	3-0	3-0	2-0	0-1	2-1	1-1	0-0	2-0	1-2		3-0	1-0	2-0	1-1	3-2	0-1	1-1
Portsmouth	2-3	0-2	1-1	0-1	2-1	3-0	2-2	3-0	1-0	1-0	2-0	1-1	3-0	0-1	2-0	0-0	2-1		0-2	1-2	3-2	3-2	1-1	1-1
Shrewsbury	4-0	2-0	1-0	5-0	1-1	1-0	3-1	2-0	4-0	3-0	2-0	2-0	1-0	0-0	1-2	2-0	0-2	2-1		1-1	3-2	2-1	0-0	1-0
Southend	1-2	0-1	0-0	1-1	0-2	2-0	0-0	1-1	1-0	1-0	2-0	0-1	2-0	0-1	1-0	2-0	1-0	1-0	1-0		2-0	1-0	2-2	1-0
Stevenage	2-1	2-1	1-0	0-0	3-2	1-0	5-1	0-1	1-0	1-0	1-2	3-0	1-1	2-1	2-1	0-2	1-0	1-0	1-0	4-2		2-2	1-3	2-3
Tranmere	3-0	1-1	1-4	0-1	1-1	0-2	2-3	2-3	1-2	1-1	0-1	0-0	2-1	0-3	0-1	3-1	2-1	1-2	2-2		1-2		1-1	
Wycombe	2-2	2-0	1-3	0-0	1-0	3-1	2-1	1-1	2-1	1-0	1-1	2-1	0-1	1-2	1-1	2-3	0-2	0-0	1-0	4-1	2-2	0-2		1-0
York	1-0	2-3	1-1	0-1	2-2	0-0	1-0	0-2	0-0	1-0	0-0	1-1	2-1	0-2	1-1	0-1	0-0	0-0	0-1	2-3	0-2	2-0	0-0	

Record when first to score

		P	W	D	L	F	A	Sup	PGA	Pts
1	Burton	28	25	3	0	54	17	+1.32	2.8	78
2	Bury	27	22	3	2	44	12	+1.19	2.6	69
3	Plymouth	24	20	3	1	47	11	+1.50	2.6	63
4	Shrewsbury	24	20	3	1	46	8	+1.58	2.6	63
5	Newport County	19	16	2	1	35	15	+1.05	2.6	60
6	Luton	24	19	3	2	41	13	+1.17	2.5	60
7	Wycombe	24	18	5	1	43	21	+0.92	2.5	59
8	Southend	30	22	6	2	44	18	+0.87	2.4	72
9	Morecambe	21	15	3	3	36	21	+0.71	2.3	48
10	Portsmouth	17	12	3	2	34	14	+1.18	2.3	39
11	Hartlepool	15	11	2	2	21	16	+0.33	2.3	35
12	Northampton	23	16	2	5	38	17	+0.91	2.2	50
13	Accrington	20	13	5	2	37	26	+0.55	2.2	44
14	Exeter	17	11	5	1	29	17	+0.71	2.2	38
15	Stevenage	28	18	6	4	46	25	+0.75	2.1	60
16	Dagenham & R	22	15	2	5	42	21	+0.95	2.1	47
17	Mansfield	20	13	4	3	27	19	+0.40	2.1	43
18	Cambridge Utd	15	9	5	1	31	13	+1.20	2.1	32
19	AFC Wimbledon	24	14	5	5	45	32	+0.54	2	47
20	York	17	9	7	1	29	15	+0.82	2	34
21	Carlisle	20	11	5	4	32	19	+0.65	1.9	38
22	Oxford	18	11	2	5	33	22	+0.61	1.9	35
23	Tranmere	14	8	3	3	27	20	+0.50	1.9	27
24	Cheltenham	18	7	9	2	23	21	+0.11	1.7	30

Record when keeping a clean sheet

		P	W	D	F	Sup	PGA	Pts
1	Northampton	13	13	0	21	+1.62	3	39
2	Accrington	5	5	0	5	+1.00	3	15
3	Bury	20	18	2	30	+1.50	2.8	56
4	Burton	17	15	2	24	+1.41	2.8	47
5	Shrewsbury	23	19	4	38	+1.65	2.7	61
6	Luton	18	15	3	25	+1.39	2.7	48
7	Carlisle	12	10	2	17	+1.42	2.7	32
8	Southend	23	18	5	25	+1.09	2.6	59
9	Newport County	14	11	3	15	+1.07	2.6	36
10	Hartlepool	9	7	2	10	+1.11	2.6	23
11	Plymouth	21	16	5	32	+1.52	2.5	53
12	Stevenage	15	11	4	15	+1.00	2.5	37
13	Dagenham & R	15	11	4	24	+1.60	2.5	37
14	Morecambe	12	9	3	15	+1.25	2.5	30
15	Mansfield	11	8	3	8	+0.73	2.5	27
16	Exeter	6	4	2	7	+1.17	2.3	14
17	Wycombe	15	9	6	11	+0.73	2.2	33
18	Portsmouth	13	8	5	16	+1.23	2.2	29
19	Cambridge Utd	10	6	4	14	+1.40	2.2	22
20	Cheltenham	5	3	2	4	+0.80	2.2	11
21	Oxford	16	9	7	16	+1.00	2.1	34
22	AFC Wimbledon	15	8	7	12	+0.80	2.1	31
23	York	14	7	7	12	+0.86	2	28
24	Tranmere	7	3	4	6	+0.86	1.9	13

Ace marksmen can help Spitfires deliver a real Rolls-Royce performance

Football on the south coast is thriving thanks to the exploits of Southampton and Bournemouth in the upper echelons, and Eastleigh look a good bet to extend the region's feelgood factor by winning the newly rebranded National League, writes Danny Hayes. The Spitfires enjoyed an excellent first season at this level, finishing fourth with an impressive 82 points, before succumbing to Grimsby in the playoffs.

There was no disgrace in that reverse at the end of a long season and there's every reason to expect the ambitious club to improve upon last season's performance now that they have that experience under their belt.

Fleetwood had a similar profile in 2011-12, strolling to the title after a season of acclimatisation in the top tier of non-league football, and Eastleigh are more than capable of following suit.

Richard Hill is looking to keep the nucleus of last season's squad in place, and scoring goals shouldn't be an issue for a team that can boast excellent forward men in James Constable and Jack Midson. And if Hill can tighten up a defence that shipped a rather damaging 61 goals last season, then his outfit should be major players in the title race.

Tranmere will also fancy their title chances as they will hope emulate Bristol Rovers – a club of similar size and stature who went back up at the first time of asking last term.

A second-successive relegation meant Tranmere dropped into non-league football for the first time in their history but they've conducted some shrewd business in the close season, not least the appointment of Gary Brabin, a manager with a wealth of experience at this level.

However, it's notoriously difficult for teams dropping out of the Football League to adapt – Bristol Rovers were the first club in ten years to bounce straight back up – and Tranmere will be regarded as a major scalp for every other side in the division. They look opposable at a short price.

The 2015 playoff final losers, Grimsby, are respected but that was the third-successive playoff failure and their squad is weaker for the loss of forward Lenell John-Lewis. Another nervous playoff tilt may the best the Mariners can hope for.

Wrexham should be right in the mix for promotion despite finishing 11th last season, as they have since recruited wisely by bringing Gary Mills in as manager.

Mills did an excellent job at Gateshead and has been quick to re-energise his squad, wasting no time in doing some shrewd work in the transfer market. If the new recruits bed in quickly and adapt to Mills' expansive style, then Wrexham should enjoy a strong season.

Forest Green, Macclesfield and last season's Conference North champions Barrow are others to consider for the playoff places.

In the relegation market, Welling, who only survived on goal difference last season, might not be so fortunate this time around in a stronger-looking division. Guiseley and Boreham Wood will also do well to avoid the drop following their respective playoff promotions last season.

A team who may reward at a bigger price are Kidderminster, who seem to be on the

Yemi Odubade will be hoping to help Eastleigh to title glory in 2015-16

downgrade. They struggled with financial troubles last season and endured a terrible second half to their campaign, winning just three league games in 2015. The playing budget has been halved so the Harriers' small squad look set for another tough season.

In the National League North, FC United of Manchester look a good bet to claim back-to-back titles after topping the Northern Premier last season.

They wouldn't be the first team to thrive after being promoted to this division, with Chorley, AFC Flyde and Guiseley all reaching the playoffs immediately after coming up in recent seasons, and FC United have the infrastructure in place to go one better.

Basingstoke get the vote in the National League South. They've made good progress in recent seasons, culminating in a third-place finish last year. With the same squad in place and reinforcements likely, they look well placed for a promotion bid.

Conference 2014-15

Pos	H	A		P	W	D	L	F	A	W	D	L	F	A	GD	Pts
					Home					**Away**						
1	2	2	Barnet	46	16	2	5	54	21	12	6	5	40	25	+48	92
2	1	6	Bristol Rovers	46	17	4	2	47	14	8	12	3	26	20	+39	91
3	7	1	Grimsby	46	12	4	7	36	20	13	7	3	38	20	+34	86
4	6	3	Eastleigh	46	12	6	5	45	28	12	4	7	42	33	+26	82
5	5	4	Forest Green	46	12	7	4	42	27	10	9	4	38	27	+26	79*
6	3	9	Macclesfield	46	14	7	2	34	14	7	8	8	26	32	+14	78
7	8	5	Woking	46	11	7	5	39	24	10	6	7	38	28	+25	76
8	4	14	Dover	46	13	4	6	38	18	6	7	10	31	40	+11	68
9	9	12	Halifax	46	11	7	5	38	27	6	8	9	22	27	+6	66
10	12	8	Gateshead	46	10	6	7	38	34	7	9	7	28	28	+4	66
11	14	7	Wrexham	46	9	8	6	27	22	8	7	8	29	30	+4	66
12	13	10	Chester	46	11	3	9	35	36	8	3	12	29	40	-12	63
13	10	16	Torquay	46	10	7	6	35	26	6	6	11	29	34	+4	61
14	15	13	Braintree	46	10	4	9	28	25	8	1	14	28	32	-1	59
15	11	20	Lincoln	46	11	4	8	35	28	5	6	12	27	43	-9	58
16	16	18	Kidderminster	46	9	6	8	31	30	6	6	11	20	30	-9	57
17	17	19	Altrincham	46	9	5	9	29	34	7	3	13	25	39	-19	56
18	19	17	Aldershot	46	8	5	10	27	28	6	6	11	24	33	-10	53
19	22	11	Southport	46	6	6	11	21	33	7	6	10	26	39	-25	51
20	18	23	Welling	46	7	8	8	29	27	4	4	15	23	46	-21	45
21	21	21	Alfreton	46	6	8	9	33	40	6	1	16	16	50	-41	45
22	23	22	Dartford	46	4	9	10	26	34	4	6	13	18	40	-30	39
23	24	15	Telford	46	3	5	15	27	44	7	4	12	31	40	-26	36*
24	20	24	Nuneaton	46	7	6	10	25	33	3	3	17	13	43	-38	36*

Forest Green deducted 3pts, Nuneaton deducted 3pts, Telford deducted 3pts

Conference results

	Aldershot	Alfreton	Altrincham	Barnet	Braintree	Bristol Rovers	Chester	Dartford	Dover	Eastleigh	Forest Green	Gateshead	Grimsby	Halifax	Kidderminster	Lincoln	Macclesfield	Nuneaton	Southport	Telford	Torquay	Welling	Woking	Wrexham
Aldershot		2-0	3-1	1-3	1-3	2-2	0-1	1-1	3-1	0-2	1-1	1-2	2-1	1-1	0-1	1-0	0-1	1-0	1-2	1-2	2-0	2-1	0-1	1-1
Alfreton	2-3		1-1	1-1	0-2	0-0	1-1	0-0	2-3	3-2	2-2	1-2	0-2	0-2	2-0	0-0	1-5	1-0	4-2	3-2	4-2	2-2	1-3	2-3
Altrincham	1-0	0-1		1-3	1-0	2-1	4-1	2-1	2-2	3-3	2-2	0-1	1-1	0-0	2-1	1-2	1-0	0-1	2-0	1-2	2-1	0-4	0-3	1-4
Barnet	1-0	2-1	5-0		3-0	2-0	3-0	4-0	2-2	1-0	1-3	2-0	1-3	3-0	3-3	1-2	3-1	1-0	4-0	3-1	2-3	5-0	2-1	0-1
Braintree	1-1	2-1	4-2	1-1		2-0	1-3	3-0	0-1	1-5	1-2	0-0	0-0	0-1	3-1	0-1	2-0	0-2	0-2	2-0	1-0	0-0	1-0	1-0
Bristol Rovers	3-1	7-0	1-0	2-1	2-1		5-1	1-0	1-1	1-2	0-1	3-2	0-0	2-1	1-1	2-0	4-0	3-1	2-0	1-0	1-1	2-0	2-0	1-0
Chester	1-0	2-1	0-2	0-5	2-3	2-2		1-2	3-1	0-1	1-4	1-0	2-2	0-3	1-0	4-0	1-0	5-3	2-0	2-0	0-2	1-1	2-3	2-1
Dartford	1-1	0-1	1-2	0-1	0-2	2-2	2-4		2-1	2-2	1-2	1-1	1-1	1-2	0-0	1-1	3-1	1-1	2-1	0-0	2-1	1-3	1-3	1-2
Dover	3-0	1-0	2-1	0-3	1-0	1-1	2-0	6-1		2-1	0-0	1-0	0-1	0-1	1-2	0-1	5-0	2-2	1-0	2-2	4-0	2-1	2-0	
Eastleigh	1-0	3-1	0-2	1-2	1-0	1-1	3-2	2-0	0-1		2-2	2-2	0-1	4-1	2-1	4-0	4-0	2-1	2-1	3-3	1-2	3-1	2-2	2-2
Forest Green	1-3	2-0	1-0	1-2	1-1	2-1	1-0	0-0	1-1		1-1	2-2	0-2	3-3	3-3	1-0	5-3	3-0	2-1	4-1	2-1	0-1		
Gateshead	1-1	2-0	1-0	0-2	3-1	0-1	2-1	1-0	1-2	2-3	2-4		1-6	2-2	2-0	3-3	2-1	1-2	1-1	4-1	3-1	1-1	0-0	3-1
Grimsby	3-1	7-0	0-0	3-1	1-0	0-1	3-0	3-0	1-1	2-1	2-1	2-2		1-0	0-2	1-3	1-2	0-0	0-1	1-0	0-2	2-0	3-1	0-1
Halifax	1-0	2-0	1-3	1-1	1-0	2-2	0-2	0-0	3-2	0-2	1-0	2-2	1-1		2-0	3-2	2-2	2-0	3-1	5-0	0-2	3-0	1-3	2-2
Kidderminster	0-2	3-0	4-0	1-1	3-1	0-3	2-2	1-0	0-2	1-3	2-4	2-1	0-1	0-0		2-1	0-2	3-1	0-1	1-1	2-1	2-1	1-1	1-1
Lincoln	3-0	3-2	1-2	4-1	3-2	2-3	0-1	1-0	1-0	1-2	1-2	1-1	3-2	1-1	0-0		2-0	3-1	1-0	2-0	1-3	0-2	0-2	1-1
Macclesfield	0-0	2-0	2-1	2-1	1-0	0-0	3-1	2-0	1-0	2-0	2-2	1-1	0-1	1-1	0-0	0-1		0-1	3-0	1-0	1-0	3-2	2-1	2-2
Nuneaton	1-1	0-1	2-1	0-0	0-2	3-2	1-2	3-0	2-3	0-3	1-0	0-2	0-2	1-2	0-0	2-1	1-1		2-3	4-4	0-0	1-0	1-1	2-0
Southport	1-3	0-2	2-1	0-2	0-2	0-1	0-0	2-0	2-2	1-2	0-1	1-1	2-2	1-0	3-3	1-1	0-0		0-3	2-1	1-0	2-5	0-1	
Telford	0-2	0-1	2-1	2-2	1-3	0-1	1-2	2-3	1-4	3-4	0-1	0-1	1-1	0-1	1-1	1-0	2-3	0-0	3-3		4-3	1-2	1-3	1-2
Torquay	1-1	1-1	2-0	1-2	1-5	1-2	0-1	1-1	2-0	2-0	3-3	2-2	2-3	2-1	2-1	1-0	1-1	4-0	0-0	0-1		3-0	1-0	2-1
Welling	3-1	2-3	0-1	1-2	2-1	0-0	1-3	2-2	0-2	1-2	1-1	1-1	0-2	2-1	3-0	2-0	0-0	4-1	0-1	1-1	0-0		1-1	2-1
Woking	1-2	3-0	2-0	1-1	1-0	0-0	1-0	1-1	6-1	1-1	1-0	3-0	1-2	3-2	2-3	3-1	0-0	1-0	1-2	1-3	3-2	2-2		1-1
Wrexham	3-1	4-0	2-3	1-0	3-0	0-0	1-0	1-3	1-1	3-0	0-0	0-3	0-1	0-0	1-0	1-1	2-2	1-0	0-0	0-4	0-0	2-1	1-2	

Conference North 2014-15

Pos	H	A		P	W	D	L	F	A	W	D	L	F	A	GD	Pts
					Home					Away						
1	1	2	Barrow	42	16	3	2	45	16	10	6	5	36	27	+38	87
2	2	1	AFC Fylde	42	14	5	2	51	23	11	5	5	42	20	+50	85
3	5	6	Boston Utd	42	12	5	4	47	25	8	7	6	28	26	+24	72
4	4	8	Chorley	42	11	8	2	42	19	9	3	9	34	36	+21	71
5	6	5	Guiseley	42	12	2	7	40	27	8	8	5	28	22	+19	70
6	8	3	Oxford City	42	9	7	5	29	32	11	2	8	52	35	+14	69
7	3	12	Tamworth	42	13	4	4	40	23	6	8	7	26	34	+9	69
8	13	9	Hednesford	42	9	5	7	34	28	8	5	8	29	22	+13	61
9	11	10	Worcester	42	9	6	6	32	30	7	6	8	22	24	0	60
10	12	11	North Ferriby	42	8	8	5	38	31	6	8	7	27	32	+2	58
11	7	17	Stockport	42	12	2	7	37	28	4	7	10	19	31	-3	57
12	19	4	Solihull Moors	42	6	4	11	31	36	10	3	8	37	27	+5	55
13	17	14	Bradford PA	42	8	6	7	27	31	6	5	10	25	35	-14	53
14	16	15	Gloucester	42	8	6	7	26	28	6	4	11	37	47	-12	52
15	10	18	Harrogate Town	42	9	6	6	30	27	5	4	12	20	35	-12	52
16	9	19	Lowestoft Town	42	8	9	4	31	24	4	6	11	23	42	-12	51
17	15	16	Gainsborough	42	8	6	7	33	27	6	2	13	26	40	-8	50
18	14	20	Brackley	42	9	4	8	17	23	4	4	13	22	39	-23	47
19	20	13	Stalybridge	42	6	4	11	31	39	6	5	10	23	31	-16	45
20	22	7	Colwyn Bay	42	4	3	14	22	43	7	9	5	37	39	-23	45
21	18	21	Leamington	42	7	5	9	33	35	3	5	13	26	39	-15	40
22	21	22	Hyde	42	3	8	10	31	42	0	4	17	18	64	-57	21

Conference North results

	AFC Fylde	Barrow	Boston Utd	Brackley	Bradford PA	Chorley	Colwyn Bay	Gainsborough	Gloucester	Guiseley	Harrogate Town	Hednesford	Hyde	Leamington	Lowestoft Town	North Ferriby	Oxford City	Solihull Moors	Stalybridge	Stockport	Tamworth	Worcester
AFC Fylde		3-2	3-0	4-0	2-1	1-3	6-2	2-1	6-4	0-0	1-2	3-1	1-1	3-1	3-1	1-0	2-1	2-2	3-0	0-0	1-1	4-0
Barrow	1-2		1-0	3-1	0-0	4-0	3-1	3-1	5-0	1-0	1-1	2-1	3-1	2-1	2-0	4-1	2-2	1-3	1-0	1-0	4-1	1-0
Boston Utd	3-1	2-1		1-1	5-0	0-0	5-0	2-1	2-0	5-1	5-2	0-2	3-1	0-0	5-3	0-1	2-7	1-2	1-1	1-1	2-0	2-0
Brackley	0-2	1-0	0-1		2-1	0-1	1-1	3-2	1-0	0-3	1-0	1-0	1-0	2-1	2-3	1-1	0-5	0-1	1-0	0-1	0-0	0-0
Bradford PA	0-1	1-3	0-0	3-2					2-1	1-2	1-1	0-0	1-2	3-2	2-1	1-1	0-5	2-3	1-0	2-0	2-4	0-1
Chorley	2-2	0-0	1-2	2-1	2-1		0-0	4-1	1-2	1-0	4-0	2-0	3-2	2-2	2-2	1-0	1-1	0-0	2-0	3-0	6-0	3-3
Colwyn Bay	0-5	0-1	2-3	1-0	0-0	0-2		4-1	3-1	1-3	0-1	0-3	3-3	1-5	0-1	0-0	3-5	1-4	0-1	1-2	2-0	0-2
Gainsborough	0-0	0-2	1-1	1-2	1-0	3-4	6-3		2-2	1-2	0-1	1-0	3-3	1-0	0-0	3-0	1-2	3-1	2-1	2-0	1-1	1-2
Gloucester	0-2	2-0	0-1	2-1	3-3	2-1	1-1	0-1		1-3	1-0	0-0	1-1	3-1	2-0	1-1	1-7	1-1	0-1	2-1	1-2	2-0
Guiseley	3-1	2-3	2-0	3-1	1-2	2-1	1-1	1-3	1-4		4-2	0-2	2-0	1-0	2-0	2-3	4-0	3-0	0-2	3-0	2-2	1-0
Harrogate Town	1-4	2-2	2-1	5-0	0-2	4-1	0-2	0-0	2-1	0-0		0-2	4-1	1-1	1-1	4-1	1-0	0-4	1-0	2-1	0-0	0-3
Hednesford	2-0	1-1	1-2	4-1	1-1	2-1	0-2	2-1	3-1	1-1	3-2		4-1	1-2	2-0	1-3	0-2	2-1	1-2	1-1	2-3	0-0
Hyde	1-1	4-4	1-3	1-2	1-3	3-3	2-4	1-2	4-0	0-1	1-0	0-1		2-2	5-1	1-0	0-1	1-0	2-4	1-1	2-2	0-3
Leamington	1-4	0-2	1-1	2-1	4-3	1-3	0-3	2-1	4-1	0-1	1-4	0-1	1-2		2-2	4-0	1-1	0-1	0-2	1-2	3-2	1-1
Lowestoft Town	1-0	2-3	1-1	0-1	3-2	3-1	1-1	2-0	0-3	0-0	0-0	2-2	3-0	1-1		1-2	2-1	2-0	1-1	2-2	3-2	1-1
North Ferriby	1-1	2-2	2-0	1-1	0-0	3-4	2-4	2-1	2-2	4-4	1-0	0-2	3-0	3-1	1-2		4-3	1-3	2-0	1-1	0-0	3-0
Oxford City	1-8	0-3	0-0	2-1	1-2	0-0	3-1	2-0	2-2	4-2	1-1	0-3	2-0	3-1	2-1	1-1		1-4	1-1	2-1	1-0	0-0
Solihull Moors	0-1	3-4	1-4	1-0	4-1	3-1	0-0	2-0	0-2	0-1	0-1	1-1	3-0	2-0	3-3	2-4	2-3		1-2	2-2	0-2	1-4
Stalybridge	3-0	0-1	1-1	1-5	0-1	0-1	1-2	4-4	2-1	1-3	2-1	0-5	7-1	0-1	1-1	2-2	0-2	0-3		3-2	3-1	0-1
Stockport	0-0	0-1	3-2	2-1	3-1	0-2	1-1	1-3	5-3	0-3	2-1	3-0	2-0	4-2	3-0	0-1	1-2	1-0	4-3		0-2	2-0
Tamworth	0-3	1-1	1-1	2-1	2-0	0-3	1-1	0-1	2-1	1-0	3-0	3-1	5-0	3-2	2-0	2-2	4-3	3-1	4-1	0-1		1-0
Worcester	0-4	0-2	1-1	0-1	2-0	3-5	2-0	1-2	1-1	2-0	2-2	4-1	2-1	2-1	2-1	1-0	1-4	2-2	2-0	1-1		

Conference South 2014-15

Pos	H	A		P	Home					Away					GD	Pts
					W	D	L	F	A	W	D	L	F	A		
1	6	1	Bromley	40	11	2	7	33	23	12	6	2	46	23	+33	77
2	1	3	Boreham Wood	40	12	4	4	39	20	11	2	7	40	24	+35	75
3	8	2	Basingstoke	40	10	4	6	27	22	12	3	5	40	21	+24	73
4	2	7	Whitehawk	40	12	3	5	32	18	10	3	7	30	29	+15	72
5	3	8	Havant & W	40	12	3	5	34	21	9	4	7	27	20	+20	70
6	7	6	Gosport Borough	40	9	7	4	30	19	10	3	7	33	21	+23	67
7	5	9	Concord Rangers	40	10	5	5	39	24	8	6	6	21	20	+16	65
8	9	10	Ebbsfleet	40	9	5	6	29	20	8	4	8	31	21	+19	60
9	13	5	Hemel	40	6	8	6	30	33	10	4	6	34	27	+4	60
10	12	11	Chelmsford	40	8	4	8	36	34	9	1	10	29	37	-6	56
11	4	19	Eastbourne	40	11	5	4	33	21	3	8	9	18	29	+1	55
12	18	4	Wealdstone	40	5	5	10	22	32	9	7	4	34	24	0	54
13	11	15	St Albans	40	9	4	7	29	25	7	2	11	24	28	0	54
14	10	17	Bath City	40	9	4	7	31	26	6	4	10	28	31	+2	53
15	14	13	Sutton Utd	40	7	4	9	25	28	6	7	7	25	26	-4	50
16	17	12	Bishop's Stortford	40	4	8	8	29	38	8	2	10	26	31	-14	46
17	16	16	Weston-s-Mare	40	6	3	11	30	45	7	2	11	25	41	-31	44
18	19	14	Maidenhead	40	5	4	11	24	35	5	9	6	30	35	-16	43
19	15	18	Hayes & Yeading	40	6	3	11	21	29	5	6	9	18	29	-19	42
20	20	21	Farnborough	40	4	3	13	19	46	4	3	13	23	55	-5 9	30
21	21	20	Staines	40	3	1	16	18	44	4	3	13	21	38	-43	25

Conference South results

	Basingstoke	Bath City	Bishop's St	Boreham W	Bromley	Chelmsford	Concord R	Eastbourne	Ebbsfleet	Farnborough	Gosport	Havant & W	Hayes & Y	Hemel	Maidenhead	St Albans	Staines	Sutton Utd	Wealdstone	Weston-s-M	Whitehawk
Basingstoke		3-2	0-1	2-1	1-2	1-2	0-0	1-0	1-0	3-1	1-1	0-0	2-0	0-1	3-2	0-1	2-1	2-2	2-4	2-1	1-0
Bath City	0-4		0-1	2-0	2-2	0-0	1-1	2-0	2-1	7-4	1-3	1-2	0-0	1-0	4-0	2-0	2-1	0-2	0-1	3-0	1-4
Bishop's St	2-3	1-1		0-5	1-1	2-3	3-1	1-1	1-1	2-2	0-1	2-2	1-3	1-3	2-1	2-1	0-0	2-2	3-4	3-1	
Boreham Wood	0-4	1-2	2-0		1-1	4-0	0-0	5-2	1-3	2-0	1-1	1-2	3-0	1-0	2-1	2-1	3-0	2-0	2-1	4-0	2-2
Bromley	0-3	1-0	3-2	2-1		0-1	1-2	2-1	1-2	5-0	0-3	2-0	1-1	0-1	4-2	1-0	0-1	2-1	1-1	3-0	4-1
Chelmsford	1-1	2-1	4-2	3-4	1-2		0-1	3-2	1-5	6-2	0-1	0-1	1-1	4-0	1-1	2-1	1-3	1-1	0-2	3-2	2-1
Concord R	2-3	3-0	3-3	1-1	1-4	2-1		1-3	1-0	7-0	0-0	3-2	0-1	0-1	2-2	3-1	1-0	0-0	4-2	2-0	3-0
Eastbourne	3-0	0-1	3-0	4-1	1-4	2-0	1-0		1-1	0-0	1-0	1-3	2-1	0-2	2-2	1-0	4-2	1-0	1-1	3-1	2-2
Ebbsfleet	1-5	0-0	4-0	1-1	0-1	0-2	2-0	0-0		3-0	0-3	1-0	1-2	2-2	1-0	4-1	3-2	3-0	0-0	0-1	3-0
Farnborough	2-1	2-7	0-1	0-3	1-2	1-3	0-3				1-4	0-5	1-0	2-2	1-1	0-3	1-1	0-1	1-1	2-3	2-0
Gosport	0-0	3-1	0-0	2-1	0-1	1-1	1-1	2-2	2-1			3-1	1-0	4-0	1-1	1-2	2-1	3-2	0-0	1-1	1-2
Havant & W	2-0	2-0	0-1	2-1	1-3	2-3	0-1	2-1	2-0	1-0	3-2		4-2	2-0	1-1	0-0	3-1	2-2	3-1	1-0	1-2
Hayes & Yeading	0-1	2-0	2-1	0-3	1-2	2-1	3-1	0-1	0-2	2-0	2-3	0-1		2-4	1-1	0-3	0-0	1-1	2-1	1-2	0-1
Hemel	4-3	0-3	0-3	0-6	1-1	3-1	1-2	0-0	1-1	4-1	2-1	1-1	1-1		1-1	3-1	5-1	1-2	1-1	1-1	0-2
Maidenhead	0-3	1-1	1-3	0-1	4-4	2-0	1-2	0-0	0-4	0-1	1-2	0-2	2-0	0-2		1-1	2-0	2-1	1-4	6-2	0-2
St Albans	1-1	1-0	2-1	0-2	2-2	0-2	2-0	3-0	1-0	2-3	2-1	1-0	0-1	1-1	4-1		0-0	2-4	1-3	2-0	2-3
Staines	0-3	1-1	1-0	2-1	0-6	3-5	0-2	0-1	0-2	1-2	2-1	1-2	2-3	0-4	1-2	2-3		0-1	1-2	0-1	1-2
Sutton Utd	2-1	1-3	2-2	1-3	1-2	1-0	1-1	1-1	2-1	2-0	0-1	1-0	0-1	1-2	1-2	2-1	4-2		1-1	1-2	0-2
Wealdstone	0-1	1-2	1-4	0-1	0-4	4-2	1-0	1-0	1-2	3-0	2-2	2-2	1-1	0-3	1-0	1-1				1-3	0-2
Weston-s-Mare	1-2	4-2	0-1	1-4	0-1	3-1	1-2	2-2	3-2	4-3	0-5	2-1	2-2	1-6	0-2	0-2	1-2	3-2	1-2		1-1
Whitehawk	0-1	2-1	1-0	3-0	2-1	5-1	1-1	2-0	1-0	1-1	1-0	0-0	2-0	3-1	3-4	2-1	1-2	0-2	0-1	2-1	

Kilmarnock could struggle but Hearts worth a flutter to prove best of the rest

B eing owners of an artificial pitch didn't give Kilmarnock the home advantage they hoped for last term and that spells more trouble this time round, writes Steve Davies. They flirted with relegation in 2013-14, did so again last season and it could be third time unlucky for a Killie side who have finished in the bottom half in each of the past four seasons and dropped away sharply after a decent start to 2014-15.

SCOTTISH PREMIERSHIP

If the Rugby Park plastic was supposed to offer an edge it manifestly didn't. They lost nine of their final 13 home games of the season, only just doing enough to pip Motherwell for tenth spot.

Manager Gary Locke wasn't universally popular after succeeding Allan Johnston and key players left, one or two with a few barbs aimed at the club and the manager. Even some of Locke's recruits hardly seem to be chomping at the bit with Kallum Higginbotham signing despite revealing a dislike of plastic pitches.

Manny Pascali will be missed and a cut in Locke's budget means the problems that plagued Kilmarnock last season – the club was hit by a bonus row in October – have made a radical rebuild awkward.

At the other end of the Premiership, Aberdeen were best of the rest in 2014-15, ten points better off than Inverness despite trailing Celtic by 17 points. But Hearts might represent a bit of value in betting without Celtic.

The jump from the Championship to Premiership has historically been a daunting one, but last season's second tier featured very decent Hibernian and Rangers sides and Hearts still won by a country mile, so maybe the gulf won't prove quite so big this time.

Last term relative minnows Hamilton were very much in the mix for top-two honours

prior to the departure of manager Alex Neil during the winter, and Hearts under Robbie Neilsen look far better equipped to stay competitive until the very end.

The Championship looks a straight fight between Rangers and Hibs, and on the evidence of last season there is probably less between them than the prices imply. The Edinburgh side might be a bit of value to frustrate the Gers.

Livingston's prospects of avoiding being dragged into another relegation scrap have been boosted by the lifting of a second transfer embargo. Players had left but Mark Burchill has started recruiting, and if they can carry their spring form into the new season, Livi should be fine. Part-timers Alloa continue to punch above their weight but last season's narrow escape may be a hint at what's likely to be coming next.

League One is a wide-open book, with money coming in for Ayr but also plenty of support for Cowdenbeath, Stranraer and Dunfermline, who burned a few fingers last term and may not have quite the funds to throw around if they falter again.

One to watch might be Airdrieonians, who came from way downtown last season to finish fifth. They have made a string of interesting signings over the summer and could be a decent each-way alternative to the main contenders.

Hearts players congratulate Jamie Walker on his Edinburgh derby equaliser

ABERDEEN

Nickname: The Dons
Colours: Red
Ground: Pittodrie (20,961)
Tel: 01224 650-400   www.afc.co.uk

Aberdeen are on an upward curve – ninth in 2011-12, eighth a year later, third and now second – which should mean a title challenge next. With 17 points to find on Celtic that's unlikely so second prize and a more realistic one, is holding on to second spot, which looks manageable.

Derek McInnes's men responded well to last season's European heartache, with the highlight an eight-match league winning run. Once Hamilton faded, the Dons were rarely threatened for second.

Longest run without win/loss: 4/13
High/low league position: 1/6
Clean sheets: 19 **Yellows:** 43 **Reds:** 1
Avg attendance: 12,981 **Players used:** 28
Leading scorer: A Rooney 18 (10,15)
Key stat: Aberdeen enjoyed 18 wins to nil last season, including eight in a row, which was only one fewer than Celtic achieved

	2014-15 H	A	Last six seasons at home P	W	D	L	OV	UN	BS	CS
Celtic	L L	L L	10	1	2	7	5	5	5	0
Aberdeen										
Inverness CT	W W	W W	9	5	0	4	4	5	4	3
St Johnstone	W L	L D	12	4	4	4	2	10	3	6
Dundee United	L W	W L	10	4	4	2	5	5	6	2
Dundee	D	W D D	3	2	1	0	1	2	1	2
Hamilton	W	L W	5	3	0	2	4	1	2	3
Partick	W D	W	3	2	1	0	1	2	0	3
Ross County	W W	W	5	3	1	1	2	3	0	4
Kilmarnock	W	W W	11	6	2	3	5	6	4	5
Motherwell	W W	W	10	2	3	5	5	5	4	3
Hearts			9	1	5	3	1	8	3	4

Season	Division	Pos	P	W	D	L	F	A	GD	Pts
2014-15	Premiership	2	38	23	6	9	57	33	+24	75
2013-14	Premiership	3	38	20	8	10	53	38	+15	68
2012-13	Premiership	8	38	11	15	12	41	43	-2	48

Over/Under 45%/55% 8th   **Both score** 32%/68% 11th

Top league scorers	P	G		Y	R
A Rooney	32 (5)	18		4	-
D Goodwillie	21 (10)	6		2	-
P Pawlett	28 (8)	6		4	-
N McGinn	34 (2)	5		-	-
J Hayes	32	3		3	-
R Jack	30 (2)	3		5	-
S Logan	35	3		4	-
A Taylor	31 (1)	3		-	-
A Considine	36 (1)	2		4	-
M Reynolds	37	2		2	-
C Smith	5 (19)	2		-	-

CELTIC

Nickname: The Bhoys
Colours: Green and white
Ground: Celtic Park (60,411)
Tel: 0871-226-1888   www.celticfc.net

Predictably, Celtic blew the field away domestically and wrapped up a fourth-successive title with three rounds of games to go. They conceded just 17 goals, the best top-flight record for almost a century, and won 29 of 38 league games.

The Bhoys remain a long way short of cracking Europe, though. Celtic lost twice in the Champions League preliminaries, illegally to Legia, legally to Maribor, and were pipped by Inter Milan after scraping through their Europa League group.

Longest run without win/loss: 2/11
High/low league position: 1/6
Clean sheets: 22 **Yellows:** 43 **Reds:** 1
Avg attendance: 43,951 **Players used:** 33
Leading scorer: L Griffiths 14 (4,10)
Key stat: Celtic conceded just five goals in 21 Premiership games after Christmas, and only one of those came in the first half of a game

	2014-15 H	A	Last six seasons at home P	W	D	L	OV	UN	BS	CS
Celtic										
Aberdeen	W W	W W	10	10	0	0	8	2	5	5
Inverness CT	W W	L D	10	7	2	1	6	4	3	6
St Johnstone	L	W W D	11	8	1	2	5	6	3	6
Dundee United	W W	L W	12	9	3	0	8	4	9	3
Dundee	W W	D W	4	4	0	0	3	1	1	3
Hamilton	L W	W	5	4	0	1	2	3	1	3
Partick	W W	W	3	3	0	0	0	3	0	3
Ross County	D	W W	4	2	2	0	2	2	2	2
Kilmarnock	W W	W	9	7	1	1	6	3	5	3
Motherwell	D W	W	12	10	2	0	6	6	2	10
Hearts			9	9	0	0	5	4	2	7

Season	Division	Pos	P	W	D	L	F	A	GD	Pts
2014-15	Premiership	1	38	29	5	4	84	17	+67	92
2013-14	Premiership	1	38	31	6	1	102	25	+77	99
2012-13	Premiership	1	38	24	7	7	92	35	+57	79

Over/Under 53%/47% 5th   **Both score** 34%/66% 10th

Top league scorers	P	G		Y	R
L Griffiths	14 (10)	14		1	-
K Commons	20 (9)	10		3	-
S Johansen	33 (1)	9		5	-
J Guidetti	19 (5)	8		1	-
A Stokes	18 (3)	7		1	-
J Denayer	29	5		1	-
S Brown	31 (1)	4		9	1
G Mackay-Steven	11 (3)	4		1	-
S Scepovic	4 (14)	4		-	-
V van Dijk	35	4		3	-

DUNDEE

Nickname: The Dark Blues
Colours: Blue and white
Ground: Dens Park (11,506)
Tel: 01382-889966   www.dundeefc.co.uk

Dundee will hope their form at the end of 2014-15 isn't carried through to the start of 2015-16, as a solid enough season saw them into the top six at the split, but their last seven games yielded just one point.

A disappointing end perhaps, but boss Paul Hartley will have been thrilled that the promoted Dark Blues managed a top-half finish. The low points were three humbling defeats to Dundee United, one of them a 6-2 mauling, and the challenge this season will be staying in the top six.

Longest run without win/loss: 6/8
High/low league position: 6/8
Clean sheets: 7 **Yellows:** 64 **Reds:** 4
Avg attendance: 7,131 **Players used:** 30
Leading scorer: G Stewart 13 (4,12)
Key stat: In 12 league meetings with last season's eventual top three, Dundee didn't manage a single victory

	2014-15		Last six seasons at home							
	H	A	P	W	D	L	OV	UN	BS	CS
Celtic	D L	L L	3	0	1	2	1	2	2	0
Aberdeen	L D D	D D	5	0	3	2	2	3	5	0
Inverness CT	L L	D D	6	0	3	3	4	2	5	0
St Johnstone	D L	W L	4	0	2	2	2	2	3	0
Dundee United	L W	L L	3	1	0	2	3	0	2	0
Dundee										
Hamilton	W D	L	6	2	3	1	1	5	2	3
Partick	D W	D	8	5	1	2	3	5	3	3
Ross County	D	L L	9	2	3	4	1	8	3	3
Kilmarnock	D W	W	4	1	2	1	1	3	2	2
Motherwell	W	W W	3	1	0	2	3	0	2	0
Hearts			2	2	0	0	0	2	0	2

Season	Division	Pos	P	W	D	L	F	A	GD	Pts
2014-15	Premiership	6	38	11	12	15	46	57	-11	45
2013-14	Championship	1	36	21	6	9	54	26	+28	69
2012-13	Premiership	12	38	7	9	22	28	66	-38	30

Over/Under 45%/55% 8th   **Both score** 66%/34% 1st

Top league scorers	P	G		Y	R
G Stewart	32 (2)	13		8	1
D Clarkson	18 (5)	8		4	-
G Harkins	21 (7)	4		2	1
G Irvine	25 (1)	4		5	-
J McAlister	34 (3)	2		3	-
J McPake	34	2		6	-
L Tankulic	12 (14)	2		2	-

I Davidson, A Harris, P Heffernan, T Konrad, P MacDonald, P McGinn, S McGinn, P McGowan, C Wighton all 1 goal

DUNDEE UNITED

Nickname: The Terrors
Colours: Orange and black
Ground: Tannadice Park (14,223)
Tel: 01382-833-166   dundeeunitedfc.co.uk

When Dundee United beat Motherwell 3-1 at the end of January, they were locked in a thrilling four-way battle for second place. Four months later, they signed off in fifth following a run of three wins in 15, missing out on Europe and fully 19 points adrift of Aberdeen.

The January sales of Gary Mackay-Steven and Stuart Armstrong to Celtic were the catalysts for that frustrating climax and it leaves Jackie McNamara needing to rebuild once again.

Longest run without win/loss: 7/5
High/low league position: 1/5
Clean sheets: 9 **Yellows:** 73 **Reds:** 2
Avg attendance: 7,895 **Players used:** 30
Leading scorer: N Ciftci 14 (8,12)
Key stat: United haven't been involved in a 0-0 draw since September 2013 and Tannadice last staged a goalless draw in September 2012

	2014-15		Last six seasons at home							
	H	A	P	W	D	L	OV	UN	BS	CS
Celtic	W L	L L	12	3	1	8	7	5	5	1
Aberdeen	L W	W L	10	4	1	5	5	5	6	2
Inverness CT	D	L L L	8	4	2	2	5	3	4	2
St Johnstone	W L	L D	10	4	3	3	2	8	2	5
Dundee United										
Dundee	W W	W L	4	3	1	0	3	1	2	2
Hamilton	D W	W	5	2	2	1	2	3	3	1
Partick	W L	D	3	2	0	1	1	2	1	1
Ross County	W L	W	5	2	2	1	2	3	3	2
Kilmarnock	W	L L	9	5	4	0	5	4	6	3
Motherwell	W W	L	13	7	2	4	9	4	8	4
Hearts			9	7	1	1	5	4	4	4

Season	Division	Pos	P	W	D	L	F	A	GD	Pts
2014-15	Premiership	5	38	17	5	16	58	56	+2	56
2013-14	Premiership	4	38	16	10	12	65	50	+15	58
2012-13	Premiership	6	38	11	14	13	51	62	-11	47

Over/Under 61%/39% 2nd   **Both score** 50%/50% 4th

Top league scorers	P	G		Y	R
N Ciftci	34 (2)	14		8	1
S Armstrong	17 (3)	6		1	-
C Erskine	27 (7)	6		2	-
G Mackay-Steven	15 (7)	5		1	-
J Fojut	36	4		9	-
C Telfer	13 (8)	4		2	-

M Bilate, R Dow, R Muirhead, P Paton, J Rankin, B Spittal all 2 goals

HAMILTON

Nickname: The Accies
Colours: Red and white
Ground: New Douglas Park (6,018)
Tel: 01698-368-650   www.acciesfc.co.uk

If ever there was a tale of two halves, this was it. The promoted Accies started irresistibly, top after ten games with the plaudits flying for manager Alex Neil. After a 1-0 win at St Johnstone in early January they were still in the top three.

But Neil was lured to Norwich and then the wheels came loose. Martin Canning stepped up to player-manager and found life tough, with Hamilton embarking on a 13-game winless streak which saw them condemned to a bottom-half finish.

Longest run without win/loss: 13/9
High/low league position: 1/7
Clean sheets: 14 **Yellows:** 82 **Reds:** 5
Avg attendance: 2,912 **Players used:** 28
Leading scorer: A Andreu 12 (6,10)
Key stat: Early pacesetters Hamilton picked up 36 points in the first half of last season but just 17 points in the second half

	2014-15 H	A	Last six seasons at home P	W	D	L	OV	UN	BS	CS
Celtic	L	W L	4	0	1	3	1	3	2	0
Aberdeen	W L	L	6	1	2	3	3	3	2	1
Inverness CT	L L	L	4	0	0	4	2	2	2	0
St Johnstone	W D	W	6	2	2	2	1	5	2	3
Dundee United	L	D L	4	0	1	3	1	3	2	0
Dundee	W	L D	5	2	1	2	4	1	4	0
Hamilton										
Partick	D D	W L	6	2	3	1	2	4	3	2
Ross County	W D	W L	4	2	1	1	3	1	2	1
Kilmarnock	D D	L W L	6	1	5	0	2	4	2	4
Motherwell	W W	W L	5	2	3	0	2	3	1	4
Hearts			3	1	0	2	2	1	1	0

Season	Division	Pos	P	W	D	L	F	A	GD	Pts
2014-15	Premiership	7	38	15	8	15	50	53	-3	53
2013-14	Championship	2	36	19	10	7	68	41	+27	67
2012-13	Championship	5	36	14	9	13	52	45	+7	51

Over/Under 50%/50% 6th   **Both score** 32%/68% 11th

Top league scorers	P	G		Y	R
A Andreu	21 (2)	12		1	-
A Crawford	37 (1)	11		5	-
M Antoine-Curier	20 (2)	8		1	-
J Scotland	12 (12)	5		1	-
M Canning	22 (1)	3		8	1
D MacKinnon	27 (3)	3		13	-
D Imrie	33 (1)	2		6	1
D Redmond	20 (3)	2		1	-

G Docherty, N Hasselbaink, Lucas, J Tena all 1 goal

HEARTS

Nickname: Jambos
Colours: Claret and white
Ground: Tynecastle (17,529)
Tel: 0871-663-1874   www.heartsfc.co.uk

The runaway Championship winners are back after a one-year exile and, according to the bookies at least, will be nearer the top three than bottom three come May.

They couldn't have bounced back up much more emphatically, failing to win just seven of 36 league games, and even a failure to beat Hibs three times out of four was of little concern in the bigger picture.

Far tougher tests lie ahead but this is a very different Hearts set-up to the one that left the Premiership just over a year ago.

Longest run without win/loss: 1/20
High/low league position: 1/2
Clean sheets: 16 **Yellows:** 61 **Reds:** 4
Avg attendance: 15,985 **Players used:** 29
Leading scorer: G Zeefuik 12 (3,8)
Key stat: Hearts have only failed to score in two of their last 47 league games and scored two or more in 27 league games last term

	2014-15 H	A	Last six seasons at home P	W	D	L	OV	UN	BS	CS
Celtic			9	3	0	6	3	3	2	
Aberdeen			7	5	1	1	5	2	2	4
Inverness CT			5	1	2	2	3	2	4	0
St Johnstone			8	4	1	3	2	6	3	4
Dundee United			9	2	4	3	3	6	4	3
Dundee			2	1	0	1	0	2	0	1
Hamilton			3	3	0	0	1	2	1	2
Partick			2	0	0	2	1	1	1	0
Ross County			4	2	2	0	3	1	3	1
Kilmarnock			9	3	0	6	5	4	1	3
Motherwell			10	3	2	5	2	8	2	4
Hearts										

Season	Division	Pos	P	W	D	L	F	A	GD	Pts
2014-15	Championship	1	36	29	4	3	96	26	+70	91
2013-14	Premiership	12	38	10	8	20	45	65	-20	23
2012-13	Premiership	10	38	11	11	16	40	49	-9	44

Over/Under 67%/33% 3rd   **Both score** 53%/47% 3rd

Top league scorers	P	G		Y	R
G Zeefuik	13 (2)	12		2	-
J Keatings	15 (14)	11		2	-
O Sow	20 (2)	11		2	1
J Walker	26 (6)	11		3	-
B King	22 (9)	8		1	-
C Paterson	27 (2)	6		5	1
S Nicholson	21 (8)	5		-	-
D Wilson	31	5		6	-
Alim Ozturk	33	4		9	-
P Buaben	21	4		4	1
S El Hassnaoui	10 (8)	4		-	-

INVERNESS CT

Nickname: Caley
Colours: Blue and red
Ground: Caledonian Stadium (7,800)
Tel: 01463-222-880   www.ictfc.com

Finishing third was impressive but add a first-ever Scottish Cup win and last term was about as good as it gets for Caley.

Expectations weren't exactly sky-high, despite a fifth-place finish in 2014, with many fans still unsure over manager John Hughes. His "play like Barcelona" mantra invited a few comments, but he had the last laugh after a phenomenal campaign.

A shot at Europa League qualification was the reward and, after twice bloodying Celtic's nose last term, confidence is high.

Longest run without win/loss: 9/9
High/low league position: 2/5
Clean sheets: 12 **Yellows:** 63 **Reds:** 5
Avg attendance: 3,699 **Players used:** 25
Leading scorer: B McKay 10 (4,8)
Key stat: Inverness played Celtic five times in 2014-15, winning twice – including a cup semi-final win – and drawing one of the others

KILMARNOCK

Nickname: Killie
Colours: Blue and white
Ground: Rugby Park (17,921)
Tel: 01563 545-300   www.kilmarnockfc.co.uk

Killie only narrowly avoided relegation in 2013-14 and suffered a similar ordeal last season. And many at Rugby Park are bracing themselves for more of the same.

Their end-of-season malaise was in contrast to last autumn where six wins in their first ten games had Allan Johnston's side in good shape. But it was form they couldn't sustain. Results suffered, Johnston was fired and Gary Locke was entrusted to see out the season, which he managed despite some poor results.

Longest run without win/loss: 7/7
High/low league position: 3/10
Clean sheets: 8 **Yellows:** 83 **Reds:** 3
Avg attendance: 4,106 **Players used:** 25
Leading scorer: T Obadeyi 9 (4,7)
Key stat: Free-scoring Kilmarnock scored in each of their last nine Premiership games but somehow found a way of losing eight of them

	2014-15 H	2014-15 A	Last six seasons at home P W D L OV UN BS CS
Celtic	W D	L L	8 2 1 5 3 5 4 1
Aberdeen	L L	L L	10 3 2 5 4 6 4 3
Inverness CT			
St Johnstone	W W	L D	9 5 3 1 1 8 3 5
Dundee United	W W W	D	10 4 3 3 5 5 5 4
Dundee	D D	W W	5 2 3 0 1 4 3 2
Hamilton	W	W W	3 1 1 1 1 2 2 0
Partick	L	L L	5 2 0 3 4 1 3 1
Ross County	D D	W	7 3 2 2 5 2 6 1
Kilmarnock	W D	W	8 3 4 1 4 4 7 1
Motherwell	W	W L	8 4 0 4 7 1 6 2
Hearts			7 2 4 1 1 6 4 3

Season	Division	Pos	P	W	D	L	F	A	GD	Pts
2014-15	Premiership	3	38	19	8	11	52	42	+10	65
2013-14	Premiership	5	38	16	9	13	44	44	0	57
2012-13	Premiership	4	38	13	15	10	64	60	+4	54

Over/Under 42%/58% 11th   **Both score** 50%/50% 4th

Top league scorers	P	G		Y	R
B McKay	22 (1)	10		-	-
M Watkins	29 (4)	7		7	-
A Doran	15 (18)	6		3	-
E Ofere	7 (3)	5		3	-
R Christie	26 (9)	4		3	1
G Tansey	36	4		8	-
J Meekings	37	3		4	-
N Ross	13 (13)	3		1	-
G Shinnie	37	2		4	-
G Warren	36	2		5	1
D Williams	27 (7)	2		1	-

	2014-15 H	2014-15 A	Last six seasons at home P W D L OV UN BS CS
Celtic	L	L L	10 1 1 8 7 3 4 1
Aberdeen	L L	L	10 3 3 4 2 8 5 3
Inverness CT	L	L D	8 2 1 5 6 2 7 1
St Johnstone	L	W D	10 2 3 5 6 4 7 2
Dundee United	W W	L	10 3 3 4 6 4 8 1
Dundee	L	D L	3 0 1 2 2 1 2 1
Hamilton	W L	D D	5 3 0 2 4 1 2 3
Partick	W D	D W	4 2 1 1 4 0 3 1
Ross County	L L	W L	5 2 1 2 4 1 2 2
Kilmarnock			
Motherwell	W L	D L	10 4 1 5 4 6 3 4
Hearts			9 3 3 3 4 5 5 3

Season	Division	Pos	P	W	D	L	F	A	GD	Pts
2014-15	Premiership	10	38	11	8	19	44	59	-15	41
2013-14	Premiership	9	38	11	6	21	45	66	-21	39
2012-13	Premiership	9	38	11	12	15	52	53	-1	45

Over/Under 55%/45% 4th   **Both score** 58%/42% 3rd

Top league scorers	P	G		Y	R
T Obadeyi	28 (1)	9		2	-
J Magennis	38	8		3	-
A Eremenko	17 (10)	4		7	-
C Slater	23 (3)	4		7	1
M Pascali	29 (2)	3		8	1
L Ashcroft	20 (2)	2		2	-
S Clingan	22 (2)	2		2	-
M Connolly	25 (1)	2		8	-
G Kiltie	2 (6)	2		-	-
R Muirhead	7 (13)	2		-	-

MOTHERWELL

Nickname: The Well/The Steelmen
Colours: Amber and claret
Ground: Fir Park (13,677)
Tel: 01698-333-333   www.motherwellfc.co.uk

After back-to-back second-place finishes, few expected Motherwell to be scrabbling around for survival in May. The ultimate indignity would have been relegation but they were spared that courtesy of a playoff success over Rangers – managed, ironically, by Stuart McCall, the man who had brought the good times to Fir Park.

It was hard to pinpoint what went wrong but that well-earned triumph over the Gers should encourage them to think that last term was something of a one-off.

Longest run without win/loss: 8/3
High/low league position: 10/12
Clean sheets: 7 **Yellows:** 58 **Reds:** 8
Avg attendance: 4,341 **Players used:** 33
Leading scorer: J Sutton 12 (4,10)
Key stat: Motherwell suffered more defeats (15) and conceded more goals (42) on their travels than any of their top-flight rivals

	2014-15 H	A	Last six seasons at home P	W	D	L	OV	UN	BS	CS
Celtic	L	DL	11	3	1	7	7	4	5	1
Aberdeen	L	LL	9	4	3	2	4	5	6	2
Inverness CT	LW	L	9	6	1	2	5	4	3	4
St Johnstone	LD	L	11	6	2	3	8	3	7	2
Dundee United	W	LL	10	3	2	5	5	5	4	2
Dundee	LL	L	3	0	1	2	1	2	2	0
Hamilton	LW	LL	5	3	0	2	2	3	0	3
Partick	WD	LL	4	3	1	0	1	3	1	3
Ross County	DD	WL	6	4	2	0	4	2	5	1
Kilmarnock	DW	L W	10	4	4	2	5	5	7	2
Motherwell										
Hearts			8	6	1	1	5	3	4	4

Season	Division	Pos	P	W	D	L	F	A	GD	Pts
2014-15	Premiership	11	38	10	6	22	38	63	-25	36
2013-14	Premiership	2	38	22	4	12	64	60	+4	70
2012-13	Premiership	2	38	18	9	11	67	51	+16	63

Over/Under 50%/50% 6th   **Both score** 47%/53% 6th

Top league scorers	P	G		Y	R
J Sutton	27 (11)	12		1	-
L Ainsworth	19 (15)	6		-	-
L Erwin	20 (14)	5		3	-
S McDonald	11	5		2	1
H Ojamaa	16 (2)	3		3	1
I Vigurs	10 (1)	2		4	-

C Grant, F Kerr, L Laing, S Pearson, S Ramsden all 1 goal

PARTICK

Nickname: The Jags
Colours: Yellow and red
Ground: Firhill Stadium (10,102)
Tel: 0141-579-1971   www.ptfc.co.uk

Manager Alan Archibald recognised that a solid defence would be the key to survival, and 12 clean sheets in 2014-15 compares favourably to the four they mustered a year earlier. They conceded 65 goals in that first season after promotion, just 44 last term. The progress is clear.

A team that was good enough to beat Inverness all three times they met in the league can clearly shape up in the top flight and, despite an eighth-place finish, they were never in danger of relegation.

Longest run without win/loss: 5/4
High/low league position: 7/9
Clean sheets: 12 **Yellows:** 70 **Reds:** 4
Avg attendance: 3,516 **Players used:** 29
Leading scorer: K Doohlan 9 (3,6)
Key stat: Partick failed to score in 11 of their 19 away games. They were unbeaten on the eight occasions when they did find the net

	2014-15 H	A	Last six seasons at home P	W	D	L	OV	UN	BS	CS
Celtic	L	LL	3	0	1	2	0	3	2	0
Aberdeen	L	LD	3	1	0	2	2	1	1	0
Inverness CT	WW	W	5	3	1	1	2	3	2	2
St Johnstone	DW	W	3	1	1	1	1	2	0	2
Dundee United	D	LW	3	0	3	0	1	2	2	1
Dundee	D	DL	7	1	3	3	0	7	1	3
Hamilton	LW	DD	6	4	1	1	3	3	2	4
Partick										
Ross County	WL	LW	10	2	4	4	5	5	6	2
Kilmarnock	DL	LD	4	0	3	1	1	3	4	0
Motherwell	WW	LD	3	2	0	1	2	1	2	1
Hearts			2	0	1	1	1	1	2	0

Season	Division	Pos	P	W	D	L	F	A	GD	Pts
2014-15	Premiership	8	38	12	10	16	48	44	+4	46
2013-14	Premiership	10	38	8	14	16	46	65	-19	38
2012-13	Championship	1	36	23	9	4	76	28	+48	78

Over/Under 45%/55% 8th   **Both score** 37%/63% 8th

Top league scorers	P	G		Y	R
K Doohlan	18 (17)	9		2	-
S O Donnell	34	5		4	-
R Stevenson	28 (4)	5		4	-
C Balatoni	32	3		2	-
S Bannigan	34 (2)	3		8	-
G Fraser	13 (10)	3		2	-
S Lawless	28 (5)	3		5	-
L Taylor	10 (5)	3		2	-

J Craigen, C Elliott, F Frans, K Higginbotham all 2 goals

ROSS COUNTY

Nickname: County
Colours: Blue, red and white
Ground: Victoria Park (6,541)
Tel: 01349-860860 rosscountyfootballclub.co.uk

County started with seven straight losses and were tailed off by Christmas, so it was astonishing that they weren't relegated.

The incredible turnaround began on Valentine's Day, when Ross fell back in love with the top division thanks to a 3-2 victory against Motherwell, the first of eight wins in nine matches.

Manager Jim McIntyre's end-of-season response was to release 12 players and start rebuilding a squad that he will hope can further extend their Premiership stay.

Longest run without win/loss: 11/9
High/low league position: 9/12
Clean sheets: 6 **Yellows:** 74 **Reds:** 5
Avg attendance: 3,573 **Players used:** 34
Leading scorer: L Boyce 10 (2,8)
Key stat: Ross County went the whole season without a single home draw. They haven't had a stalemate at Victoria Park since March 2014

	2014-15 H	A	Last six seasons at home P	W	D	L	OV	UN	BS	CS
Celtic	L L	D	6	1	2	3	3	3	4	0
Aberdeen	L	L L	4	2	1	1	1	3	2	1
Inverness CT	L	D D	7	2	2	3	4	3	3	3
St Johnstone	L W	L	5	3	0	2	2	3	2	3
Dundee United	L	L W	5	2	0	3	4	1	3	2
Dundee	W W	D	9	3	3	3	3	6	4	2
Hamilton	L W	L D	4	3	0	1	2	2	2	1
Partick	W L	L W	10	2	4	4	6	4	6	3
Ross County										
Kilmarnock	L W	W W	6	2	1	3	4	2	4	1
Motherwell	L W	D D	5	2	1	2	4	1	3	2
Hearts			3	1	1	1	3	0	3	0

Season	Division	Pos	P	W	D	L	F	A	GD	Pts
2014-15	Premiership	9	38	12	8	18	46	63	-17	44
2013-14	Premiership	7	38	11	7	20	44	62	-18	40
2012-13	Premiership	5	38	13	14	11	47	48	-1	53

Over/Under 71%/29% 1st   **Both score** 63%/37% 2nd

Top league scorers	P	G	Y	R
L Boyce	17 (13)	10	2	1
M Gardyne	22 (2)	6	2	-
C Curran	17 (2)	5	1	-
J Jervis	10 (17)	4	1	-
R De Vita	13 (1)	3	2	-
P Quinn	28 (1)	3	4	-

Y Arquin, G Carey, T Dingwall, J Irvine, D Maatsen, M Woods all 2 goals

ST JOHNSTONE

Nickname: The Saints
Colours: Blue and white
Ground: McDiarmid Park (10,696)
Tel: 01738-459090 perthstjohnstonefc.co.uk

A side that failed to score more than two goals in any game should have been struggling but that was far from the case with St Johnstone.

The key to survival for a team that can't score is a rock-solid defence, and that's exactly what Saints had – 34 goals scored and 34 conceded resulted in fourth place and a fourth-successive top-six finish.

That means fans of the Perth club have a fourth successive Europa League qualifying campaign to look forward to.

Longest run without win/loss: 6/8
High/low league position: 4/9
Clean sheets: 15 **Yellows:** 72 **Reds:** 2
Avg attendance: 4,526 **Players used:** 22
Leading scorer: B Graham 9 (5,9)
M O'Halloran 9 (3,7)
Key stat: None of St Johnstone's 46 matches last season produced more than three goals

	2014-15 H	A	Last six seasons at home P	W	D	L	OV	UN	BS	CS
Celtic	L D	W	11	1	3	7	6	5		1
Aberdeen	W D	L W	10	3	3	4	3	7	5	3
Inverness CT	W D	L L	10	5	3	2	2	8	1	7
St Johnstone										
Dundee United	W D	L W	12	3	5	4	5	7	6	4
Dundee	L W	D W	3	2	0	1	0	3	0	2
Hamilton	L	L D	5	2	1	2	1	4	2	2
Partick	W	D L	3	1	2	0	0	3	2	1
Ross County	W	W	5	2	2	1	3	2	3	1
Kilmarnock	L D	W	9	4	2	3	4	5	3	4
Motherwell	W	W D	10	5	1	4	6	4	4	4
Hearts			8	4	3	1	4	4	4	3

Season	Division	Pos	P	W	D	L	F	A	GD	Pts
2014-15	Premiership	4	38	16	9	13	34	34	0	57
2013-14	Premiership	6	38	15	8	15	48	42	+6	53
2012-13	Premiership	3	38	14	14	10	45	44	+1	56

Over/Under 26%/74% 12th   **Both score** 37%/63% 8th

Top league scorers	P	G	Y	R
B Graham	17 (7)	9	4	-
M O'Halloran	30 (8)	9	1	-
S Anderson	37	3	7	-
M Davidson	17 (6)	3	5	-
S MacLean	23 (1)	2	6	-
D Swanson	8 (3)	2	4	-
C Kane	4 (11)	1	1	-
S Lappin	19 (8)	1	6	-
D MacKay	34	1	6	1
J McFadden	8 (9)	1	4	1
C Millar	32	1	4	-

Scottish Premiership stats 2014-15
Key Points in all tables (except the league table) do not include any deductions imposed by the league.
POS H A Overall league position, rank from home games only, rank from away games only **Sup** Average match supremacy **GFA** Goals For Average **GAA** Goals Against Average **PGA** Points Gained Average

Scottish Premiership 2014-15					Home						Away						
Pos	H	A		P	W	D	L	F	A	W	D	L	F	A	GD	Pts
1	1	1	Celtic	38	15	2	2	50	8	14	3	2	34	9	+67	92
2	2	2	Aberdeen	38	12	3	4	32	15	11	3	5	25	18	+24	75
3	4	3	Inverness CT	38	10	6	3	29	19	9	2	8	23	23	+10	65
4	6	4	St Johnstone	38	8	5	6	19	17	8	4	7	15	17	0	57
5	3	11	Dundee Utd	38	12	2	5	32	20	5	3	11	26	36	+2	56
6	9	7	Dundee	38	5	8	7	25	27	6	4	8	21	30	-11	45
7	5	6	Hamilton	38	8	6	5	30	20	7	2	10	20	33	-3	53
8	7	10	Partick	38	8	4	7	32	22	4	6	9	16	22	+4	46
9	11	5	Ross County	38	7	0	12	21	31	5	8	6	25	32	-17	44
10	10	8	Kilmarnock	38	7	1	10	23	27	4	7	9	21	32	-15	41
11	8	12	Motherwell	38	7	5	7	23	21	3	1	15	15	42	-25	36
12	12	9	St Mirren	38	3	2	14	14	30	6	1	12	16	36	-36	30

Best attack

		GF	GFA
1	Celtic	84	2.21
2	Dundee Utd	58	1.53
3	Aberdeen	57	1.5
4	Inverness CT	52	1.37
5	Hamilton	50	1.32
6	Partick	48	1.26
7	Dundee	46	1.21
8	Ross County	46	1.21
9	Kilmarnock	44	1.16
10	Motherwell	38	1
11	St Johnstone	34	0.89
12	St Mirren	30	0.79

Best defence

		GA	GAA
1	Celtic	17	0.45
2	Aberdeen	33	0.87
3	St Johnstone	34	0.89
4	Inverness CT	42	1.11
5	Partick	44	1.16
6	Hamilton	53	1.39
7	Dundee Utd	56	1.47
8	Dundee	57	1.5
9	Kilmarnock	59	1.55
10	Ross County	63	1.66
11	Motherwell	63	1.66
12	St Mirren	66	1.74

Top scorers

	Team	Goals scored
A Rooney	Aberdeen	18
N Ciftci	Dundee Utd	14
L Griffiths	Celtic	14
G Stewart	Dundee	13
A Andreu	Hamilton	12
J Sutton	Motherwell	12

SOCCERBASE.COM
SMARTERBETTING

Record when first to score

		P	W	D	L	F	A	Sup	PGA	Pts
1	Celtic	28	27	1	0	75	9	+2.36	2.9	82
2	Aberdeen	24	20	3	1	46	11	+1.46	2.6	63
3	St Johnstone	17	14	2	1	23	6	+1.00	2.6	44
4	St Mirren	8	6	1	1	15	7	+1.00	2.4	19
5	Dundee Utd	23	17	3	3	53	23	+1.30	2.3	54
6	Hamilton	19	13	4	2	40	16	+1.26	2.3	43
7	Inverness CT	22	15	4	3	35	18	+0.77	2.2	49
8	Ross County	15	10	3	2	28	16	+0.80	2.2	33
9	Dundee	17	10	6	1	27	12	+0.88	2.1	36
10	Partick	16	10	4	2	35	10	+1.56	2.1	34
11	Motherwell	14	9	2	3	27	12	+1.07	2.1	29
12	Kilmarnock	16	9	2	5	26	17	+0.56	1.8	29

Record when keeping a clean sheet

		P	W	D	F	Sup	PGA	Pts
1	Dundee Utd	9	9	0	18	+2.00	3.0	27
2	St Mirren	2	2	0	2	+1.00	3.0	6
3	Aberdeen	19	18	1	35	+1.84	2.9	55
4	Celtic	22	20	2	54	+2.45	2.8	62
5	Inverness CT	12	11	1	18	+1.50	2.8	34
6	Hamilton	14	12	2	28	+2.00	2.7	38
7	Dundee	7	6	1	7	+1.00	2.7	19
8	Motherwell	7	6	1	13	+1.86	2.7	19
9	Ross County	6	5	1	9	+1.50	2.7	16
10	St Johnstone	15	12	3	16	+1.07	2.6	39
11	Partick	12	9	3	25	+2.08	2.5	30
12	Kilmarnock	8	5	3	9	+1.13	2.3	18

Over 2.5 goals

	H	A	%
Ross County	13	14	71%
Dundee Utd	10	13	61%
St Mirren	9	13	58%
Kilmarnock	11	10	55%
Celtic	11	9	53%

Under 2.5 goals

	H	A	%
St Johnstone	12	16	74%
Inverness CT	11	11	58%
Aberdeen	9	12	55%
Dundee	12	9	55%
Partick	7	14	55%

Both to score

	H	A	%
Dundee	15	10	66%
Ross County	12	12	63%
Kilmarnock	9	13	58%
Inverness CT	10	9	50%
Dundee Utd	8	11	50%

Both not to score

	H	A	%
Aberdeen	14	12	68%
Hamilton	13	13	68%
Celtic	13	12	66%
St Johnstone	10	14	63%
Partick	10	14	63%

Scottish Premiership results 2014-15

	Aberdeen	Celtic	Dundee	Dundee United	Hamilton	Inverness CT	Kilmarnock	Motherwell	Partick	Ross County	St Johnstone	St Mirren
Aberdeen		1-2/0-1	3-3	0-3/1-0	3-0	3-2/1-0	1-0	1-0/2-1	2-0/0-0	3-0/4-0	2-0/0-1	2-2/3-0
Celtic	2-1/4-0		2-1/5-0	6-1/3-0	0-1/4-0	1-0/5-0	2-0/4-1	1-1/4-0	1-0/2-0	0-0	0-1	4-1
Dundee	2-3/1-1/1-1	1-1/1-2		1-4/3-1	2-0/1-1	1-2/0-1	1-1/1-0	4-1	1-1/1-0	1-1	1-1/0-2	1-3
Dundee Utd	0-2/1-0	2-1/0-3	6-2/3-0		2-2/1-0	1-1	3-1	1-0/3-1	1-0/0-2	2-1/1-2	2-0/0-2	3-0
Hamilton	3-0/0-3	0-2	2-1	2-3		0-2/0-2	0-0/0-0	5-0/2-0	3-3/1-1	4-0/2-2	1-0/1-1	3-0/1-0
Inverness CT	0-1/1-2	1-0/1-1	0-0/1-1	1-0/2-1/3-0	4-2		2-0/3-3	3-1	0-4	1-1/1-2	2-1/2-0	1-0
Kilmarnock	0-2/1-2	0-2	1-3	2-0/3-2	1-0/2-3	1-2		2-0/1-2	3-0/2-2	0-3/1-2	0-1	2-1/1-0
Motherwell	0-2	0-1	1-3/0-1	1-0	0-4/4-0	0-2/2-1	1-1/3-1		1-0/0-0	2-2/1-1	0-1/1-1	1-0/5-0
Partick	0-1	0-3	1-1	2-2	1-2/5-0	3-1/1-0	1-1/1-4	3-1/2-0		4-0/1-3	0-0/3-0	1-2/0-1/3-0
Ross County	0-1	0-5/0-1	2-1/1-0	2-3	0-1/2-1	1-3	1-2/2-1	1-2/3-2	1-0/1-2		1-2/1-0	1-2/1-2
St Johnstone	1-0/1-1	0-3/1-2/0-0	0-1/1-0	2-1/1-1	0-1	1-0/1-1	1-2/0-0	2-1	2-0	2-1		1-2/2-0
St Mirren	0-2	1-2/0-2	0-1/1-2	0-3/1-1	0-2/1-0	0-1/1-2	1-2/4-1	0-1/2-1	0-1	2-2/0-3	0-1	

New Celtic gaffer Ronny Deila shows off his bling

ALLOA

Nickname: The Wasps Recreation Park
Web: www.alloaathletic.co.uk

Danny Lennon's challenge with part-timers Alloa is to improve their league finish by one place so as to avoid another playoff ordeal.

The Challenge Cup finalists drew three times with Rangers last term and are set for a third-straight season in the Championship.

	2014-15		Last six seasons at home							
	H	A	P	W	D	L	OV	UN	BS	CS
St Mirren	-	-	-	-	-	-	-	-	-	-
Hibernian	W L	L L	2	1	0	1	1	1	1	0
Rangers	D L	D D	2	0	1	1	0	2	1	0
Queen of Sth	D D	L L	6	1	2	3	3	3	3	1
Falkirk	L L	L L	4	1	1	2	3	1	2	2
Raith	L D	D L	4	1	1	2	0	4	0	2
Dumbarton	L W	L L	8	1	1	6	6	2	5	2
Livingston	W D	L D	6	2	2	2	4	2	3	2
Alloa										
Morton			2	2	0	0	0	2	0	2

Season	Division	Pos	P	W	D	L	F	A	GD	Pts
2014-15	Championship	9	36	6	9	21	34	56	-22	27
2013-14	Championship	8	36	11	7	18	34	51	-17	40
2012-13	League One	2	36	20	7	9	62	35	+27	67

Over/Under 47%/53% 10th Bothscore 44%/56% 9th

DUMBARTON

Nickname: The Sons Dumbarton Football Stadium
Web: www.dumbartonfootballclub.com

It's all change at the Rock with miracle worker Ian Murray off to lead St Mirren.

Stephen Aitken comes in from Stranraer to try to extend the Sons' record of four straight mid-table campaigns and he knows he's got a hard act to follow.

	2014-15		Last six seasons at home							
	H	A	P	W	D	L	OV	UN	BS	CS
St Mirren	-	-	-	-	-	-	-	-	-	-
Hibernian	L L	D L	2	0	0	2	2	0	2	0
Rangers	L L	L L	2	0	0	2	2	0	2	0
Queen of Sth	L D	L L	4	0	1	3	2	2	0	1
Falkirk	L W	D D	6	2	1	3	2	4	2	1
Raith	W D	L L	6	2	2	2	6	0	6	0
Dumbarton										
Livingston	W L	W W	8	1	1	6	7	1	5	1
Alloa	W W	W L	8	5	2	1	6	2	7	1
Morton			4	2	0	2	3	1	2	1

Season	Division	Pos	P	W	D	L	F	A	GD	Pts
2014-15	Championship	7	36	9	7	20	36	79	-43	34
2013-14	Championship	5	36	15	6	15	65	64	+1	51
2012-13	Championship	7	36	13	4	19	58	83	-25	43

Over/Under 75%/25% 1st Bothscore 56%/44% 2nd

FALKIRK

Nickname: The Bairns Falkirk Stadium
Web: www.falkirkfc.co.uk

Scottish Cup runners-up Falkirk would swap knockout glory for a promotion push after they narrowly missed out on the playoffs.

A slow start last season of three wins from their first 13 matches cannot be repeated if they want to stay the pace.

	2014-15		Last six seasons at home							
	H	A	P	W	D	L	OV	UN	BS	CS
St Mirren			3	1	1	1	2	1	3	0
Hibernian	W L	W D	4	1	0	3	3	1	2	1
Rangers	L D	L D	3	0	1	2	1	2	2	0
Queen of Sth	D D	L L	8	5	2	1	4	4	4	3
Falkirk										
Raith	L W	D D	10	5	2	3	4	6	5	3
Dumbarton	D D	W L	6	1	2	3	4	2	5	1
Livingston	D W	W L	8	4	2	2	4	4	5	3
Alloa	W W	W W	4	3	1	0	2	2	2	2
Morton			8	5	1	2	3	5	4	2

Season	Division	Pos	P	W	D	L	F	A	GD	Pts
2014-15	Championship	5	36	14	11	11	48	48	0	53
2013-14	Championship	3	36	17	9	8	59	33	+26	66
2012-13	Championship	3	36	15	8	13	52	48	+4	53

Over/Under 50%/50% 8th Bothscore 44%/56% 9th

HIBERNIAN

Nickname: The Hibees Easter Road
Web: www.hibernianfc.co.uk

Runners-up to Hearts, then pipped by Rangers in the playoffs, Alan Stubbs' men will be eager to take the title this time.

Stubbs insists his side will be champions but a repeat of last season, where Hibs lost four of their first six games, must be avoided.

	2014-15		Last six seasons at home							
	H	A	P	W	D	L	OV	UN	BS	CS
St Mirren			10	5	3	2	6	4	7	3
Hibernian										
Rangers	W L	W W	7	1	0	6	3	4	1	1
Queen of Sth	D L	L W	2	0	1	1	0	2	0	1
Falkirk	L D	L W	3	1	1	1	2	1	1	1
Raith	D D	W L	2	0	2	0	0	2	2	0
Dumbarton	D W	W W	2	1	1	0	1	1	0	2
Livingston	W W	W W	2	2	0	0	2	0	2	0
Alloa	W W	L W	2	2	0	0	1	1	1	1
Morton	-	-	-	-	-	-	-	-	-	-

Season	Division	Pos	P	W	D	L	F	A	GD	Pts
2014-15	Championship	2	36	21	7	8	70	32	+38	70
2013-14	Premiership	11	38	8	11	19	31	51	-20	35
2012-13	Premiership	7	38	13	12	13	49	52	-3	51

Over/Under 53%/47% 6th Bothscore 50%/50% 5th

LIVINGSTON

Nickname: Livi Lions   Almondvale Stadium
Web: www.livingstonfc.co.uk

Livi won just four of their first 30 games and were hampered by a points deduction, but they produced an unlikely four-match winning burst at the death to avoid the drop.

Lifting the Challenge Cup was the catalyst behind their late, great escape.

	2014-15 H A	Last six seasons at home P W D L OV UN BS CS
St Mirren	- -	- - - - - - - -
Hibernian	L L L L	2 0 0 2 2 0 1 0
Rangers	L D L D	2 0 1 1 0 2 1 0
Queen of Sth	D W D L	6 1 4 1 5 1 5 1
Falkirk	L W D L	8 2 1 5 5 3 5 0
Raith	L L W W	8 4 1 3 4 4 3 3
Dumbarton	L L L W	8 2 1 5 6 2 6 2
Livingston		
Alloa	W D L D	6 4 2 0 4 2 2 4
Morton		6 0 4 2 2 4 3 1

Season	Division	Pos	P	W	D	L	F	A	GD	Pts
2014-15	Championship	8	36	8	8	20	41	53	-12	27
2013-14	Championship	6	36	13	7	16	51	56	-5	46
2012-13	Championship	6	36	14	10	12	58	56	+2	52

Over/Under 50%/50% 8th   Bothscore 50%/50% 5th

MORTON

Nickname: The Ton   Cappielow Park
Web: www.gmfc.net

Morton came up as League One champions but averaged under two points per game.

Indeed, the four teams immediately below them all lost fewer games than the Ton but they did finish the season in flying form and can carry that momentum into 2015-16.

	2014-15 H A	Last six seasons at home P W D L OV UN BS CS
St Mirren		- - - - - - - -
Hibernian		- - - - - - - -
Rangers		- - - - - - - -
Queen of Sth		8 1 4 3 5 3 5 1
Falkirk		8 2 4 2 3 5 4 3
Raith		10 3 5 2 2 8 4 5
Dumbarton		4 3 0 1 3 1 0 3
Livingston		6 3 1 2 5 1 5 1
Alloa		2 0 0 2 0 2 0 0
Morton		

Season	Division	Pos	P	W	D	L	F	A	GD	Pts
2014-15	League One	1	36	22	3	11	65	40	+25	69
2013-14	Championship	10	36	6	8	22	32	71	-39	26
2012-13	Championship	2	36	20	7	9	73	47	+26	67

Over/Under 56%/44% 3rd   Bothscore 53%/47% 5th

QUEEN OF THE SOUTH

Nickname: The Doonhamers   Palmerston Park
Web: www.qosfc.com

Rangers and Hibs both lost on the Palmerston plastic, where the Doonhamers were superb.

But it's away from home that Queen of the South need to improve – they registered only four wins on the road last term, the same number as bottom club Cowdenbeath.

	2014-15 H A	Last six seasons at home P W D L OV UN BS CS
St Mirren		- - - - - - - -
Hibernian	W L D W	2 1 0 1 0 2 0 1
Rangers	W W L D	2 2 0 0 1 1 0 2
Queen of Sth		
Falkirk	W W D D	8 3 1 4 4 4 3 4
Raith	W W W L	10 5 1 4 4 6 4 4
Dumbarton	W W W D	4 3 0 1 4 0 3 1
Livingston	D W D L	6 2 2 2 3 3 3 1
Alloa	W W D D	6 4 2 0 1 5 1 5
Morton		8 5 0 3 6 2 5 3

Season	Division	Pos	P	W	D	L	F	A	GD	Pts
2014-15	Championship	4	36	17	9	10	58	41	+17	60
2013-14	Championship	4	36	16	7	13	53	39	+14	55
2012-13	League One	1	36	29	5	2	92	23	+69	92

Over/Under 53%/47% 6th   Bothscore 47%/53% 8th

RAITH

Nickname: The Rovers   Stark's Park
Web: www.raithrovers.net

A late plunge cost Raith any chance of a playoff shot and Grant Murray his job.

Ray McKinnon has arrived from Brechin to mastermind a promotion push, which will only be achieved if they improve last season's home tally of six wins.

	2014-15 H A	Last six seasons at home P W D L OV UN BS CS
St Mirren		- - - - - - - -
Hibernian	L W D D	2 1 0 1 2 0 2 0
Rangers	L L L L	2 0 0 2 2 0 1 0
Queen of Sth	L W L L	10 5 1 4 5 5 4 4
Falkirk	D D W L	10 3 5 2 6 4 7 3
Raith		
Dumbarton	W W L D	6 4 1 1 6 0 6 0
Livingston	L L W W	8 1 1 6 4 4 2 2
Alloa	D W D W	4 2 2 0 2 2 4 0
Morton		10 6 3 1 8 2 7 3

Season	Division	Pos	P	W	D	L	F	A	GD	Pts
2014-15	Championship	6	36	12	7	17	42	65	-23	43
2013-14	Championship	7	36	11	9	16	48	61	-13	42
2012-13	Championship	6	36	11	13	12	45	48	-3	46

Over/Under 64%/36% 4th   Bothscore 58%/42% 1st

RANGERS

Nickname: The Gers — Ibrox Stadium
Web: www.rangers.co.uk

Mark Warburton entered the dugout to mixed reviews, but Brentford fans will reassure Rangers that they've landed a gem.

Warburton should lift a decent Gers' squad, who were poor from Christmas onwards and must surely improve.

	2014-15 H A	Last six seasons at home P	W	D	L	OV	UN	BS	CS
St Mirren		5	4	1	0	4	1	5	0
Hibernian	L L L W	7	3	1	3	4	3	2	3
Rangers									
Queen of Sth	W D L L	2	1	1	0	1	1	2	0
Falkirk	W D W D	4	3	1	0	4	0	2	2
Raith	W W W W	2	2	0	0	2	0	1	1
Dumbarton	W W W W	2	2	0	0	2	0	2	0
Livingston	W D W D	2	1	1	0	0	2	1	1
Alloa	D D D W	2	0	2	0	1	1	2	0
Morton		-	-	-	-	-	-	-	-

Season	Division	Pos	P	W	D	L	F	A	GD	Pts
2014-15	Championship	3	36	19	10	7	69	39	+30	67
2013-14	League One	1	36	33	3	0	106	18	+88	102
2012-13	League Two	1	36	25	8	3	87	29	+58	83

Over/Under 56%/44% 5th   Bothscore 53%/47% 3rd

ST MIRREN

Nickname: The Saints — St Mirren Park
Web: www.saintmirren.net

Two point out of a possible 36 against the Premiership's top four showed that the Buddies couldn't live with the big guns.

Relegation always looked likely once Ross County found their feet and new manger Ian Murray has already made big changes.

	2014-15 H A	Last six seasons at home P	W	D	L	OV	UN	BS	CS
St Mirren									
Hibernian		9	3	2	4	2	7	3	4
Rangers		4	1	0	3	2	2	2	0
Queen of Sth		-	-	-	-	-	-	-	-
Falkirk		1	0	1	0	0	1	1	0
Raith		-	-	-	-	-	-	-	-
Dumbarton		-	-	-	-	-	-	-	-
Livingston		-	-	-	-	-	-	-	-
Alloa		-	-	-	-	-	-	-	-
Morton		-	-	-	-	-	-	-	-

Season	Division	Pos	P	W	D	L	F	A	GD	Pts
2014-15	Premiership	12	38	9	3	26	30	66	-36	30
2013-14	Premiership	8	38	10	9	19	39	58	-19	39
2012-13	Premiership	11	38	9	14	15	47	60	-13	41

Over/Under 58%/42% 3rd   Bothscore 42%/58% 7th

Hibs beat Rangers four times last term but lost out to them in the playoffs

Scottish Championship results 2014-15

	Alloa	Cowd'beath	Dumbarton	Falkirk	Hearts	Hibernian	Livingston	Queen of Sth	Raith	Rangers
Alloa		2-3/3-0	0-1/3-0	2-3/1-3	0-1/1-4	2-1/0-1	1-0/2-2	1-1/2-2	0-1/0-0	1-1/0-1
Cowdenbeath	0-3/0-2		1-3/3-0	2-2/0-1	0-2/1-2	1-2/0-2	1-0/1-2	2-1/0-5	1-3/0-1	0-3/0-0
Dumbarton	3-1/1-0	0-0/1-2		0-3/1-0	0-0/1-5	3-6/1-2	1-0/1-5	0-4/0-0	2-1/2-2	0-3/1-3
Falkirk	2-1/1-0	6-0/1-0	1-1/3-3		1-2/0-3	1-0/0-3	0-0/2-0	1-1/1-1	0-1/1-0	0-2/1-1
Hearts	2-0/3-0	5-1/10-0	5-1/4-0	4-1/2-3		2-1/1-1	5-0/1-0	4-1/2-0	1-0/2-1	2-0/2-2
Hibernian	2-0/4-1	3-2/5-0	0-0/3-0	0-1/3-3	1-1/2-0		2-1/2-1	0-0/0-1	1-1/1-1	4-0/0-2
Livingston	4-0/0-0	2-1/1-1	1-2/1-2	0-1/2-1	0-1/2-3	0-4/1-3		2-2/1-0	0-1/0-2	0-1/1-1
Queen of Sth	2-0/1-0	1-2/4-1	3-0/2-1	3-0/1-0	0-3/1-2	1-0/0-2	1-1/3-1		2-0/2-1	2-0/3-0
Raith	1-1/2-1	2-1/1-3	3-1/2-1	0-0/2-2	0-4/1-3	1-3/2-1	1-5/0-4	3-4/3-0		0-4/1-2
Rangers	1-1/2-2	1-0/4-1	4-1/3-1	4-0/2-2	1-2/2-1	1-3/0-2	2-0/1-1	4-2/1-1	6-1/4-0	

Scottish Championship 2014-15

Pos	H	A		P	W	D	L	F	A	W	D	L	F	A	GD	Pts
															Home ← → Away	
1	1	1	Hearts	36	15	2	1	57	12	14	2	2	39	14	+70	91
2	4	2	Hibernian	36	9	6	3	33	15	12	1	5	37	17	+38	70
3	3	3	Rangers	36	10	5	3	43	21	9	5	4	26	18	+30	67
4	2	6	Queen of Sth	36	13	1	4	32	14	4	8	6	26	27	+17	60
5	5	4	Falkirk	36	7	6	5	22	19	7	5	6	26	29	0	53
6	6	5	Raith	36	6	3	9	25	40	6	4	8	17	25	-23	43
7	7	8	Dumbarton	36	5	4	9	18	37	4	3	11	18	42	-43	34
8	9	7	Livingston	36	4	4	10	18	26	4	4	10	23	27	-12	27*
9	8	10	Alloa	36	4	5	9	21	25	2	4	12	13	31	-22	27
10	10	9	Cowdenbeath	36	3	2	13	13	34	4	2	12	18	52	-55	25

Livingston deducted 5pts

Best attack

		GF	GFA
1	Hearts	96	2.67
2	Hibernian	70	1.94
3	Rangers	69	1.92
4	Queen of Sth	58	1.61
5	Falkirk	48	1.33
6	Raith	42	1.17
7	Livingston	41	1.14
8	Dumbarton	36	1
9	Alloa	34	0.94
10	Cowdenbeath	31	0.86

Best defence

		GA	GAA
1	Hearts	26	0.72
2	Hibernian	32	0.89
3	Rangers	39	1.08
4	Queen of Sth	41	1.14
5	Falkirk	48	1.33
6	Livingston	53	1.47
7	Alloa	56	1.56
8	Raith	65	1.81
9	Dumbarton	79	2.19
10	Cowdenbeath	86	2.39

Top scorers

		Team	Goals scored	
J Cummings	Hibernian	18																		
D Lyle	Queen of Sth	15													
L Buchanan	Alloa	14												
D Malonga	Hibernian	13											
G Reilly	Queen of Sth	12										
G Zeefuik	Hearts	12										

Key Points in all tables (except the league table) do not include any deductions imposed by the league. **POS H A** Position, home/away rank **Sup** Average supremacy **GFA/GAA** Goals For/ Against Average **PGA** Pts Gained Average

Record when first to score

		P	W	D	L	F	A	Sup	PGA	Pts
1	Hearts	28	27	0	1	87	16	+2.54	2.9	81
2	Raith	12	11	0	1	22	8	+1.17	2.8	33
3	Hibernian	26	20	5	1	65	21	+1.69	2.5	65
4	Rangers	21	16	5	0	51	11	+1.90	2.5	53
5	Falkirk	17	13	4	0	32	10	+1.29	2.5	43
6	Queen of Sth	23	17	4	2	50	17	+1.43	2.4	55
7	Livingston	11	7	2	2	28	11	+1.55	2.1	23
8	Alloa	10	5	5	0	20	8	+1.20	2	20
9	Dumbarton	12	7	2	3	26	16	+0.33	1.9	23
10	Cowdenbeath	10	6	1	3	19	13	+0.60	1.9	19

Record when keeping a clean sheet

		P	W	D	F	Sup	PGA	Pts
1	Hearts	16	15	1	44	+2.75	2.9	46
2	Rangers	12	11	1	27	+2.25	2.8	34
3	Queen of Sth	14	12	2	28	+2.00	2.7	38
4	Hibernian	13	11	2	30	+2.31	2.7	35
5	Falkirk	12	10	2	18	+1.50	2.7	32
6	Raith	8	6	2	9	+1.13	2.5	20
7	Alloa	7	5	2	12	+1.71	2.4	17
8	Livingston	5	3	2	9	+1.80	2.2	11
9	Dumbarton	8	4	4	4	+0.50	2	16
10	Cowdenbeath	4	2	2	4	+1.00	2	8

Over 2.5 goals

	H	A	%
Dumbarton	12	15	75%
Cowdenbeath	11	14	69%
Hearts	12	12	67%

Under 2.5 goals

	H	A	%
Alloa	9	10	53%
Falkirk	12	6	50%
Livingston	9	9	50%

Both to score

	H	A	%
Raith	13	8	58%
Dumbarton	9	11	56%
Rangers, Hearts			53%

Both not to score

	H	A	%
Alloa	9	11	56%
Falkirk	11	9	56%
Queen of Sth	11	8	53%

AIRDRIEONIANS

Nickname: The Diamonds   Excelsior Stadium
Web: www.airdriefc.com

For the second season running, a sparkling end to the campaign wasn't quite enough to get Airdrieonians into the playoffs.

If manager Gary Bollan can improve on last season's start of two points from the first six matches, they could be in the mix.

	2014-15		Last six seasons at home							
	H	A	P	W	D	L	OV	UN	BS	CS
Cowdenbeath			4	0	2	2	2	2	3	0
Stranraer	D D	L L	4	1	3	0	2	2	4	0
Forfar	L W	D L	8	5	1	2	6	2	5	2
Brechin	W D	D D	8	4	3	1	6	2	7	1
Airdrieonians										
Peterhead	L L	D W	4	1	1	2	2	2	2	1
Dunfermline	W W	L D	8	3	2	3	5	3	5	1
Ayr	W W	W W	8	4	2	2	5	3	3	3
Stenhousemuir	W W	L W	8	4	2	2	4	4	4	2
Albion			2	2	0	0	1	1	0	2

Season	Division	Pos	P	W	D	L	F	A	GD	Pts
2014-15	League One	5	36	16	10	10	53	39	+14	58
2013-14	League One	6	36	12	9	15	47	57	-10	45
2012-13	Championship	10	36	5	7	24	41	89	-48	22

Over/Under 44%/56% 10th   **Both score** 50%/50% 7th

ALBION

Nickname: The Wee Rovers   Cliftonhill Stadium
Web: www.albionroversfc.com

Albion return after two years in the bottom tier, and player-manager Darren Young has brought in former Scotland Under-21 coach Billy Stark to help keep the Wee Rovers up.

Albion averaged 1.97 points per match but, impressively, won 12 of 18 away games.

	2014-15		Last six seasons at home							
	H	A	P	W	D	L	OV	UN	BS	CS
Cowdenbeath			2	1	1	0	1	1	1	1
Stranraer			6	3	1	2	4	2	4	2
Forfar			6	1	2	3	3	3	4	1
Brechin			4	1	0	3	3	1	3	0
Airdrieonians			2	1	0	1	1	1	1	0
Peterhead			2	0	1	1	1	1	1	1
Dunfermline			-	-	-	-	-	-	-	-
Ayr			2	1	0	1	1	1	1	1
Stenhousemuir			4	2	2	0	2	2	3	1
Albion										

Season	Division	Pos	P	W	D	L	F	A	GD	Pts
2014-15	League Two	1	36	22	5	9	61	33	+28	71
2013-14	League Two	7	36	12	8	16	41	54	-13	44
2012-13	League One	10	36	7	3	26	45	82	-37	24

Over/Under 47%/53% 8th   **Both score** 42%/58% 10th

Dunfermline's 11,904-seater East End Park dwarfs most League One stadiums

AYR

Nickname: The Honest Men   Somerset Park
Web: www.ayrunitedfc.co.uk

If the Honest Men are true to their nickname, they'll agree last season was pretty grim.

Just five wins from September saw them finish eighth and prompted a summer overhaul from Ian McCall. That, in turn, had punters all over fancy early title odds.

	2014-15 H	A	Last six seasons at home P	W	D	L	OV	UN	BS	CS
Cowdenbeath			-	-	-	-	-	-	-	-
Stranraer	L L	L L	6	3	0	3	4	2	3	1
Forfar	W W	L W	8	5	0	3	4	4	4	3
Brechin	L D	W L	8	2	2	4	5	3	4	2
Airdrieonians	L L	L L	8	3	2	3	5	3	5	2
Peterhead	D L	L L	4	0	3	1	3	1	4	0
Dunfermline	L L	L L	6	1	1	4	2	4	3	1
Ayr										
Stenhousemuir	L D	D D	8	3	3	2	3	5	3	6 2
Albion			2	2	0	0	2	0	2	0

Season	Division	Pos	P	W	D	L	F	A	GD	Pts
2014-15	League One	8	36	9	7	20	45	60	-15	34
2013-14	League One	4	36	14	7	15	65	66	-1	49
2012-13	League One	7	36	12	5	19	53	65	-12	41

Over/Under 47%/53% 7th   **Both score** 50%/50% 7th

BRECHIN

Nickname: The City   Glebe Park
Web: www.brechincity.com

A 17-match unbeaten run in mid-season had Brechin dreaming of promotion, but ultimately they fell short in the playoffs.

Top-scoring midfielder Alan Trouten and boss Ray McKinnon have left, leaving rookie manager Darren Dods to pick up the pieces.

	2014-15 H	A	Last six seasons at home P	W	D	L	OV	UN	BS	CS
Cowdenbeath			4	2	2	0	3	1	3	1
Stranraer	L L	D W	6	1	2	3	5	1	5	1
Forfar	D L	L W	10	3	2	5	7	3	7	1
Brechin										
Airdrieonians	D D	L D	8	2	5	1	3	5	7	1
Peterhead	D D	D L	6	3	2	1	5	1	5	1
Dunfermline	D W	D W	4	2	2	0	2	2	3	1
Ayr	L W	W D	8	5	1	2	6	2	6	1
Stenhousemuir	W W	W D	12	7	2	3	6	6	6	5
Albion			4	3	0	1	2	2	2	2

Season	Division	Pos	P	W	D	L	F	A	GD	Pts
2014-15	League One	4	36	15	14	7	58	46	+12	59
2013-14	League One	8	36	12	6	18	57	71	-14	42
2012-13	League One	3	36	14	17	5	72	59	+13	61

Over/Under 56%/44% 3rd   **Both score** 61%/39% 2nd

COWDENBEATH

Nickname: The Blue Brazil   Central Park
Web: www.cowdenbeathfc.com

A season forever remembered for that 10-0 drubbing at Hearts ended in relegation.

Colin Nish, signed in January to score goals, has now been promoted from player to player-manager and the Blue Brazil were duly installed as title jollies.

	2014-15 H	A	Last six seasons at home P	W	D	L	OV	UN	BS	CS
Cowdenbeath										
Stranraer			-	-	-	-	-	-	-	-
Forfar			2	2	0	0	1	1	1	1
Brechin			4	3	1	0	2	2	1	3
Airdrieonians			4	2	2	0	1	3	2	2
Peterhead			2	1	0	1	2	0	1	1
Dunfermline			4	1	0	3	3	1	1	0
Ayr			-	-	-	-	-	-	-	-
Stenhousemuir			4	3	1	0	1	3	1	3
Albion			2	2	0	0	2	0	1	1

Season	Division	Pos	P	W	D	L	F	A	GD	Pts
2014-15	Championship	10	36	7	4	25	31	86	-55	25
2013-14	Championship	9	36	11	7	18	50	72	-22	40
2012-13	Championship	8	36	8	12	16	51	65	-14	36

Over/Under 69%/31% 2nd   **Both score** 50%/50% 5th

DUNFERMLINE

Nickname: The Pars   East End Park
Web: www.dafc.co.uk

Even-money favourites for the 2014-15 title, the Pars had a shocker. Top in mid-October, they eventually finished seventh.

Allan Johnston, a success at Kilmarnock in the top flight, will clearly be his own man after axing 18 players in his first week.

	2014-15 H	A	Last six seasons at home P	W	D	L	OV	UN	BS	CS
Cowdenbeath			4	4	0	0	3	1	1	3
Stranraer	L W	W L	4	3	0	1	2	2	2	1
Forfar	D L	L L	4	0	3	1	3	2	2	2
Brechin	D L	D L	4	2	1	1	2	2	2	1
Airdrieonians	W D	L L	8	4	1	3	5	3	4	3
Peterhead	W D	D D	2	1	1	0	1	1	1	1
Dunfermline										
Ayr	W W	W W	6	5	0	1	5	1	4	1
Stenhousemuir	W W	L W	4	3	1	0	2	2	2	2
Albion			-	-	-	-	-	-	-	-

Season	Division	Pos	P	W	D	L	F	A	GD	Pts
2014-15	League One	7	36	13	9	14	46	48	-2	48
2013-14	League One	2	36	19	6	11	68	54	+14	63
2012-13	Championship	9	36	14	7	15	62	59	+3	34

Over/Under 47%/53% 7th   **Both score** 47%/53% 10th

FORFAR

Nickname: The Loons Station Park
Web: www.forfarathletic.co.uk

Pipped for the title on the last day, the Loons then blew a 3-1 lead against Alloa in the playoff final.

It was a heartbreaking finish to a superb campaign but it won't take many tweaks for Dick Campbell's men to challenge again.

	2014-15 H A	Last six seasons at home P	W	D	L	OV	UN	BS	CS
Cowdenbeath		2	1	1	0	1	1	1	1
Stranraer	D W D L	8	6	1	1	3	5	3	5
Forfar									
Brechin	W L D W	10	5	3	2	4	6	6	3
Airdrieonians	D W W L	8	2	3	3	5	3	7	1
Peterhead	W W	4	3	1	0	2	2	3	1
Dunfermline	W W D W	4	3	0	1	2	2	1	3
Ayr	W L L L	8	6	0	2	6	2	6	1
Stenhousemuir	W W W W	10	5	2	3	7	3	6	4
Albion		6	3	2	1	4	2	4	1

Season	Division	Pos	P	W	D	L	F	A	GD	Pts
2014-15	League One	3	36	20	6	10	59	41	+18	66
2013-14	League One	7	36	12	7	17	55	62	-7	43
2012-13	League One	4	36	17	3	16	67	74	-7	54

Over/Under 47%/53% 7th **Both score** 50%/50% 7th

PETERHEAD

Nickname: The Blue Toon Balmoor Stadium
Web: www.montrosefc.co.uk

Well fancied after winning League Two, it just never happened for Peterhead last term.

A three-match winning streak in January was the highlight of a stop-start season that ended with a sixth-place finish and Jim McInally promising his side will improve.

	2014-15 H A	Last six seasons at home P	W	D	L	OV	UN	BS	CS
Cowdenbeath		2	1	0	1	0	2	0	1
Stranraer	L L L L	4	0	1	3	3	1	4	0
Forfar	W W L L	4	2	1	1	2	3	1	4
Brechin	D W D D	6	2	2	2	3	3	2	2
Airdrieonians	D L W W	4	1	1	2	2	2	3	0
Peterhead									
Dunfermline	D D L D	2	0	2	0	0	2	2	0
Ayr	W W D W	4	2	0	2	2	2	2	2
Stenhousemuir	W W W L	6	2	2	2	3	3	2	2
Albion		2	1	1	0	0	2	1	1

Season	Division	Pos	P	W	D	L	F	A	GD	Pts
2014-15	League One	6	36	14	9	13	51	54	-3	51
2013-14	League Two	1	36	23	7	6	74	38	+36	76
2012-13	League Two	2	36	17	8	11	52	28	+24	59

Over/Under 53%/47% 5th **Both score** 64%/36% 1st

STENHOUSEMUIR

Nickname: Warriors Ochilview Park
Web: www.stenhousemuirfc.com

Having ended the regular campaign with six defeats in seven, few fancied Stenhousemuir would survive the relegation playoffs.

However, they bravely saw off East Fife and then Queen's Park to retain League One status for a seventh-successive season.

	2014-15 H A	Last six seasons at home P	W	D	L	OV	UN	BS	CS
Cowdenbeath		4	1	1	2	1	3	1	1
Stranraer	D W W L	6	2	3	1	2	4	3	3
Forfar	L L L L	10	3	1	6	6	4	5	2
Brechin	L D L L	12	4	5	3	8	4	10	1
Airdrieonians	W L L L	8	2	2	4	3	5	4	2
Peterhead	L W L L	6	4	1	1	4	2	5	1
Dunfermline	W L L L	4	1	0	3	2	2	2	1
Ayr	D D W D	8	3	5	0	3	5	7	1
Stenhousemuir									
Albion		4	2	0	2	2	2	1	2

Season	Division	Pos	P	W	D	L	F	A	GD	Pts
2014-15	League One	9	36	8	5	23	42	63	-21	29
2013-14	League One	5	36	12	12	12	57	66	-9	48
2012-13	League One	6	36	12	13	11	59	59	0	49

Over/Under 53%/47% 5th **Both score** 53%/47% 5th

STRANRAER

Nickname: The Blues Stair Park
Web: www.stranraerfc.org

Knocked off top spot on the penultimate weekend and then beaten in the playoffs by Forfar, a fantastic campaign ended in bitter disappointment for the Blues.

New manager Brian Reid has a tough act to follow after Stevie Aitken left for Dumbarton.

	2014-15 H A	Last six seasons at home P	W	D	L	OV	UN	BS	CS
Cowdenbeath		-	-	-	-	-	-	-	-
Stranraer									
Forfar	D W D L	8	5	1	2	5	3	4	2
Brechin	D L W W	6	2	1	3	4	2	3	1
Airdrieonians	W W D D	4	3	1	0	1	3	2	2
Peterhead	W W W W	4	3	0	1	3	1	1	2
Dunfermline	L W W L	4	2	0	2	4	0	4	0
Ayr	W W W W	6	4	1	1	2	4	2	3
Stenhousemuir	L W D L	6	2	3	1	5	1	6	0
Albion		6	3	2	1	4	2	6	0

Season	Division	Pos	P	W	D	L	F	A	GD	Pts
2014-15	League One	2	36	20	7	9	59	38	+21	67
2013-14	League One	3	36	14	9	13	57	57	0	51
2012-13	League One	8	36	10	7	19	43	71	-28	37

Over/Under 39%/61% 11th **Both score** 44%/56% 11th

SCOTTISH LEAGUE ONE

Scottish League One results 2014-15

	Airdrieonians	Ayr	Brechin	Dunfermline	Forfar	Morton	Peterhead	Stenhousemuir	Stirling	Stranraer
Airdrieonians		3-0/2-0	4-0/1-1	3-1/3-2	1-2/3-1	0-1/2-1	0-2/1-3	2-0/2-1	0-0/4-1	3-3/1-1
Ayr	2-3/0-1		0-2/2-2	0-1/0-2	2-0/1-0	1-0/1-1	3-3/2-4	2-3/0-0	2-2/4-0	0-2/0-2
Brechin	1-1/0-0	2-4/2-1		1-1/3-0	3-3/2-3	3-1/1-1	1-1/2-2	1-2/1-1	2-1/2-1	1-2/1-3
Dunfermline	3-0/2-2	4-2/2-1	0-0/0-1		0-0/1-3	1-2/0-4	3-0/1-1	2-0/3-2	4-0/1-1	0-1/1-0
Forfar	1-1/2-0	2-0/1-3	3-1/0-2	2-0/1-0		3-2/1-2	1-0/3-1	3-0/1-0	2-1/4-0	1-1/1-0
Morton	2-1/0-1	0-1/2-1	2-2/0-2	2-1/2-0	2-0/0-2		0-1/3-1	3-1/3-2	2-0/4-0	4-0/2-0
Peterhead	1-1/0-1	2-0/2-0	1-1/3-0	1-1/1-1	3-2/1-0	1-2/1-3		1-0/2-0	1-1/2-1	1-4/1-2
Stenhousemuir	1-0/0-2	1-1/1-1	0-2/2-2	1-0/0-1	0-2/1-3	2-1/2-3	1-2/2-1		4-5/1-2	2-2/1-0
Stirling	2-2/0-2	1-3/1-4	0-5/0-1	0-2/2-2	2-2/0-1	3-4/0-2	2-3/2-1	0-4/3-2		1-1/0-1
Stranraer	1-0/1-0	3-1/1-0	2-2/0-2	1-2/5-1	1-1/4-2	2-0/0-2	5-0/2-0	0-2/3-2	2-0/1-0	

Scottish League One 2014-15

Pos	H	A		P	W	D	L	F	A	W	D	L	F	A	GD	Pts
						Home						Away				
1	3	1	Morton	36	12	1	5	33	16	10	2	6	32	24	+25	69
2	2	3	Stranraer	36	12	2	4	34	17	8	5	5	25	21	+21	67
3	1	4	Forfar	36	13	2	3	32	14	7	4	7	27	27	+18	66
4	7	2	Brechin	36	7	7	4	30	26	8	7	3	28	20	+12	59
5	4	5	Airdrieonians	36	10	4	4	35	20	6	6	6	18	19	+14	58
6	6	6	Peterhead	36	8	5	5	25	20	6	4	8	26	34	-3	51
7	5	7	Dunfermline	36	8	5	5	28	20	5	4	9	18	28	-2	48
8	9	8	Ayr	36	4	5	9	22	28	5	2	11	23	32	-15	34
9	8	9	Stenhousemuir	36	5	4	9	22	30	3	1	14	20	33	-21	29
10	10	10	Stirling	36	2	4	12	19	42	2	4	12	16	42	-49	20

Best attack

		GF	GFA
1	Morton	65	1.81
2	Stranraer	59	1.64
3	Forfar	59	1.64
4	Brechin	58	1.61
5	Airdrieonians	53	1.47
6	Peterhead	51	1.42
7	Dunfermline	46	1.28
8	Ayr	45	1.25
9	Stenh'semuir	42	1.17
10	Stirling	35	0.97

Best defence

		GA	GAA
1	Stranraer	38	1.06
2	Airdrieonians	39	1.08
3	Morton	40	1.11
4	Forfar	41	1.14
5	Brechin	46	1.28
6	Dunfermline	48	1.33
7	Peterhead	54	1.5
8	Ayr	60	1.67
9	Stenh'semuir	63	1.75
10	Stirling	84	2.33

Top scorers

		Team	Goals scored	
D McManus	Morton	20	|||||||||||||||||||
C McMenamin	Stenh'semuir	15	||||||||||||||
A Trouten	Brechin	15	||||||||||||||
B Prunty	Airdrieonians	14	|||||||||||||
A Jackson	Brechin	11	||||||||||
J Longworth	Stranraer	11	||||||||||
G Swankie	Forfar	11	||||||||||

Key POS H A Overall league position, rank from home games, rank from away games **Sup** Avg match supremacy **GFA** Goals For Avg **GAA** Goals Against Avg **PGA** Points Gained Avg

Record when first to score

		P	W	D	L	F	A	Sup	PGA	Pts
1	Morton	16	14	1	1	36	7	+1.81	2.7	43
2	Forfar	20	17	1	2	41	14	+1.35	2.6	52
3	Stranraer	22	17	5	0	46	15	+1.41	2.5	56
4	Airdrieonians	18	14	2	2	36	13	+1.28	2.4	44
5	Dunfermline	19	12	5	2	34	14	+1.05	2.2	41
6	Brechin	24	14	8	2	47	24	+0.96	2.1	50
7	Peterhead	17	10	2	5	28	20	+0.47	1.9	32
8	Ayr	14	7	4	3	28	20	+0.57	1.8	25
9	Stenhousemuir	17	7	2	8	32	30	+0.12	1.4	23
10	Stirling	8	1	4	3	12	16	-0.50	0.9	7

Record when keeping a clean sheet

		P	W	D	F	Sup	PGA	Pts
1	Stranraer	12	12	0	21	+1.75	3	36
2	Morton	10	10	0	25	+2.50	3	30
3	Peterhead	8	8	0	14	+1.75	3	24
4	Forfar	13	12	1	22	+1.69	2.8	37
5	Brechin	12	10	2	21	+1.75	2.7	32
6	Ayr	6	5	1	9	+1.50	2.7	16
7	Stenhousemuir	6	5	1	9	+1.50	2.7	16
8	Dunfermline	11	9	2	19	+1.73	2.6	29
9	Airdrieonians	11	9	2	18	+1.64	2.6	29
10	Stirling	1	0	1	0	0.00	1	1

Over 2.5 goals

	H	A	%
Stirling	11	12	64%
Brechin	12	8	56%
Morton	9	11	56%

Under 2.5 goals

	H	A	%
Stranraer		11	11	61%
Airdrieonians	7	13	56%
Ayr, Dunfermline			53%

Both to score

	H	A	%
Peterhead	11	12	64%
Brechin	15	7	61%
Stirling	10	10	56%

Both not to score

	H	A	%
Stranraer	11	9	56%
Dunfermline	10	9	53%
Airdrieonians, Ayr, Forfar			50%

ANNAN

Nickname: Galabankies   Galabank
Web: www.annanathleticfc.com

Annan took advantage of their artificial pitch at Galabank to post the best home record in League Two.

However, they failed to win on grass until their very final away game of the season, at Elgin, which cost them a playoff spot.

	2014-15 H	A	P	W	D	L	OV	UN	BS	CS
Stirling			4	1	1	2	3	1	3	0
Queens Park	L W	D L	12	6	1	5	7	5	8	2
Arbroath	L W	L D	4	2	0	2	2	2	1	2
East Fife	W W	D L	2	2	0	0	2	0	2	0
Annan										
Clyde	W L	D L	10	4	0	6	3	7	3	3
Elgin	D L	D W	12	3	6	3	6	6	8	2
Berwick	W W	L D	12	5	5	2	7	5	9	2
East Stirling	W W	W W	12	7	1	4	10	2	9	2
Montrose	D W	L L	12	7	4	1	8	4	9	3

Season	Division	Pos	P	W	D	L	F	A	GD	Pts
2014-15	League Two	5	36	14	8	14	56	56	0	50
2013-14	League Two	2	36	19	6	11	69	49	+20	63
2012-13	League Two	8	36	11	10	15	54	65	-11	43

Over/Under 53%/47% 6th   **Both score** 61%/39% 1st

ARBROATH

Nickname: The Red Lichties   Gayfield Park
Web: www.arbroathfc.co.uk

Six points clear in January, Arbroath ended up settling for a playoff place after winning just two of their last 18 matches.

Queens Park beat them in the playoffs leaving new boss Todd Lumsden to oversee the summer refit.

	2014-15 H	A	P	W	D	L	OV	UN	BS	CS
Stirling			4	2	0	2	3	1	3	1
Queens Park	L D	W L	4	1	2	1	2	2	3	1
Arbroath										
East Fife	L D	W L	10	4	4	2	5	5	5	3
Annan	W D	W L	4	2	1	1	2	2	3	0
Clyde	W W	W D	6	5	0	1	4	2	2	3
Elgin	W D	D L	4	2	1	1	2	2	2	2
Berwick	W W	W L	4	4	0	0	3	1	2	2
East Stirling	W L	W L	4	2	0	2	2	2	1	2
Montrose	W D	W L	4	3	1	0	4	0	3	1

Season	Division	Pos	P	W	D	L	F	A	GD	Pts
2014-15	League Two	3	36	16	8	12	65	46	+19	56
2013-14	League One	10	36	9	4	23	52	75	-23	31
2012-13	League One	5	36	15	7	14	47	57	-10	52

Over/Under 53%/47% 6th   **Both score** 58%/42% 2nd

BERWICK

Nickname: The Borderers   Shielfield Park
Web: www.berwickrangersfc.co.uk

An already poor season ended pitifully, with a pair of drubbings leaving Berwick eighth.

A run to the quarter-finals of the Scottish Cup added some welcome gloss to a dreary campaign, but fans are demanding a promotion push under Colin Cameron.

	2014-15 H	A	P	W	D	L	OV	UN	BS	CS
Stirling			4	3	1	0	2	2	2	2
Queens Park	D D	L L	12	7	4	1	4	8	6	6
Arbroath	L W	L L	4	2	0	2	4	0	3	0
East Fife	L L	W W	2	0	0	2	2	0	1	0
Annan	W D	L L	12	4	2	6	8	4	8	1
Clyde	W D	D W	10	5	3	2	6	4	4	4
Elgin	D L	L D	12	5	4	3	7	5	8	3
Berwick										
East Stirling	W W	W W	12	8	2	2	6	6	3	7
Montrose	D D	L W	12	4	4	4	7	5	6	4

Season	Division	Pos	P	W	D	L	F	A	GD	Pts
2014-15	League Two	8	36	11	10	15	60	57	+3	43
2013-14	League Two	5	36	15	7	14	63	49	+14	52
2012-13	League Two	4	36	14	7	15	59	55	+4	49

Over/Under 61%/39% 2nd   **Both score** 50%/50% 6th

CLYDE

Nickname: The Bully Wee   Broadwood Stadium
Web: www.clydefc.co.uk

Nine new faces had arrived at Broadwood by the middle of June as Barry Ferguson shook up the Bully Wee.

Ferguson, now retired as a player, is hoping that last term's joint-lowest scorers can get the goals to justify favouritism.

	2014-15 H	A	P	W	D	L	OV	UN	BS	CS
Stirling			6	3	0	3	4	2	4	1
Queens Park	L W	D W	10	2	0	8	6	4	4	2
Arbroath	L D	L	6	1	2	3	2	4	3	1
East Fife	W W	W D	4	3	0	1	3	1	3	1
Annan	D W	L W	10	3	3	4	4	6	5	2
Clyde										
Elgin	W L	L L	10	3	4	3	6	4	7	1
Berwick	D L	L D	10	4	3	3	8	2	7	2
East Stirling	L D	L W	10	6	1	3	5	5	5	4
Montrose	L W	W	10	4	2	4	4	6	5	4

Season	Division	Pos	P	W	D	L	F	A	GD	Pts
2014-15	League Two	6	36	13	8	15	40	50	-10	47
2013-14	League Two	4	36	17	6	13	50	48	+2	57
2012-13	League Two	3	36	14	2	20	42	66	-24	40

Over/Under 42%/58% 10th   **Both score** 44%/56% 9th

EAST FIFE

Nickname: The Fifers   New Bayview Stadium
Web: www.eastfifefc.info

Gary Naysmith says it's been a frustrating summer trying to bring new faces to Methil.

The former Everton left-back had been hoping to continue the momentum from a decent run-in to the last campaign which ended in playoff defeat.

	2014-15 H A	Last six seasons at home P	W	D	L	OV	UN	BS	CS
Stirling		4	2	0	2	2	2	1	2
Queens Park	D D L L	2	0	2	0	1	1	1	1
Arbroath	L W W D	10	5	2	3	6	4	7	2
East Fife									
Annan	D W L L	2	1	1	0	1	1	2	0
Clyde	L D L L	4	1	2	1	0	4	2	1
Elgin	D W L W	2	1	1	0	1	1	2	0
Berwick	L L W W	2	0	0	2	2	0	2	0
East Stirling	W W D L	2	2	0	0	2	0	2	0
Montrose	W W W W	2	2	0	0	2	0	0	2

Season	Division	Pos	P	W	D	L	F	A	GD	Pts
2014-15	League Two	4	36	15	8	13	56	48	+8	53
2013-14	League One	9	36	9	5	22	31	69	-38	32
2012-13	League One	9	36	8	8	20	50	65	-15	32

Over/Under 56%/44% 5th   **Both score** 53%/47% 4th

EAST STIRLING

Nickname: The Shire   Ochilview Park
Web: www.eaststirlingshirefc.co.uk

It's been hard work for Craig Tully to get a squad together this summer for what looks sure to be a relegation battle.

East Stirling haven't been out of the bottom three in the last five seasons and finished the last campaign badly.

	2014-15 H A	Last six seasons at home P	W	D	L	OV	UN	BS	CS
Stirling		4	2	2	0	2	2	3	1
Queens Park	L W L D	12	3	1	8	7	5	7	1
Arbroath	L W L W	4	1	0	3	3	1	3	1
East Fife	D W L L	2	1	1	0	0	2	1	1
Annan	L L L L	12	4	2	6	8	4	8	2
Clyde	W L W D	10	4	2	4	4	6	3	5
Elgin	W W W D	12	7	3	2	7	5	7	4
Berwick	L L L L	12	5	2	5	5	7	4	4
East Stirling									
Montrose	W L L W	12	5	2	5	9	3	8	3

Season	Division	Pos	P	W	D	L	F	A	GD	Pts
2014-15	League Two	9	36	13	4	19	40	66	-26	43
2013-14	League Two	8	36	12	8	16	45	59	-14	44
2012-13	League Two	10	36	8	5	23	49	97	-48	29

Over/Under 58%/42% 3rd   **Both score** 50%/50% 6th

ELGIN

Nickname: The Black And Whites   Borough Briggs
Web: www.elgincity.com

Jim Weir's men were involved in very few dull matches last season, with a leaky defence costing Elgin any chance of securing a playoff place.

They scored 55 goals but conceded 58 – only the bottom two teams let in more.

	2014-15 H A	Last six seasons at home P	W	D	L	OV	UN	BS	CS
Stirling		4	2	0	2	4	0	3	1
Queens Park	L L L D	12	3	2	7	6	6	7	1
Arbroath	D W L D	4	2	1	1	3	1	4	0
East Fife	W L D L	2	1	0	1	1	1	1	1
Annan	D L D W	12	4	3	5	8	4	8	4
Clyde	W W L W	10	6	1	3	4	6	4	3
Elgin									
Berwick	W D D W	12	6	2	4	11	1	10	2
East Stirling	L D L D	12	6	1	5	6	6	5	4
Montrose	L W W L	12	8	1	3	9	3	8	2

Season	Division	Pos	P	W	D	L	F	A	GD	Pts
2014-15	League Two	7	36	12	9	15	55	58	-3	45
2013-14	League Two	9	36	9	9	18	62	73	-11	36
2012-13	League Two	5	36	13	10	13	67	69	-2	49

Over/Under 58%/42% 3rd   **Both score** 58%/42% 2nd

MONTROSE

Nickname: The Gable Endies   Links Park Stadium
Web: www.montrosefc.co.uk

Paul Hegarty was appointed in March but couldn't stop Montrose finishing bottom, and relegation looked a real possibility after his side lost the first leg of the playoff 1-0.

However, they turned it round on home soil against Brora and will hope to kick on.

	2014-15 H A	Last six seasons at home P	W	D	L	OV	UN	BS	CS
Stirling		4	1	2	1	3	1	3	1
Queens Park	L D L L	12	2	2	8	8	4	9	1
Arbroath	L W L D	4	2	0	2	4	0	1	2
East Fife	L L L L	2	0	0	2	2	0	0	0
Annan	W W D L	12	4	4	4	5	7	7	3
Clyde	L L W L	10	4	1	5	6	4	4	2
Elgin	L W W L	12	4	3	5	9	3	7	2
Berwick	W L D D	12	2	6	4	5	7	10	1
East Stirling	W L L W	12	7	1	4	7	5	5	3
Montrose									

Season	Division	Pos	P	W	D	L	F	A	GD	Pts
2014-15	League Two	10	36	9	6	21	42	78	-36	33
2013-14	League Two	6	36	12	10	14	44	56	-12	46
2012-13	League Two	6	36	12	11	13	60	68	-8	47

Over/Under 72%/28% 1st   **Both score** 47%/53% 8th

QUEENS PARK

Nickname: The Spiders   Hampden Park
Web: www.queensparkfc.co.uk

Gus McPherson's side finished second but, after beating Arbroath in the playoff semi, found Stenhousemuir too strong in the final.

However, having finished bottom of the division 12 months earlier, the season was an unmitigated triumph for Queen's Park.

	2014-15 H	A	Last six seasons at home P	W	D	L	OV	UN	BS	CS
Stirling			4	1	1	2	2	2	2	0
Queens Park										
Arbroath	L W	W D	4	2	1	1	2	2	3	0
East Fife	W W	D D	2	2	0	0	1	1	0	2
Annan	D W	W L	12	4	5	3	5	7	4	6
Clyde	L D	W L	10	5	2	3	6	4	5	4
Elgin	W D	W W	12	4	4	4	5	7	6	3
Berwick	W W	D D	12	5	3	4	6	6	7	3
East Stirling	W D	W L	12	8	2	2	5	7	5	7
Montrose	W W	W D	12	8	2	2	8	4	7	4

Season	Division	Pos	P	W	D	L	F	A	GD	Pts
2014-15	League Two	2	36	17	10	9	51	34	+17	61
2013-14	League Two	10	36	5	9	22	36	68	-32	24
2012-13	League Two	3	36	16	8	12	60	54	+6	56

Over/Under 44%/56% 9th   **Both score** 53%/47% 4th

STIRLING

Nickname: The Binos   Forthbank Stadium
Web: www.stirlingalbionfc.co.uk

Stirling dropped into the basement division after a third relegation in five seasons but they should be in the mix to bounce back up.

The first Scottish club to be owned by its fans, the Binos have cleared out the dead wood and gone on a big recruitment drive.

	2014-15 H	A	Last six seasons at home P	W	D	L	OV	UN	BS	CS
Stirling										
Queens Park			4	1	1	2	4	0	3	1
Arbroath			4	0	3	1	2	2	3	0
East Fife			4	2	1	1	2	2	1	2
Annan			4	2	1	1	2	2	3	0
Clyde			6	3	2	1	1	5	3	2
Elgin			4	0	3	1	2	2	4	0
Berwick			4	4	0	0	3	1	3	1
East Stirling			4	2	1	1	3	1	4	0
Montrose			4	2	1	1	4	0	4	0

Season	Division	Pos	P	W	D	L	F	A	GD	Pts
2014-15	League One	10	36	4	8	24	35	84	-49	20
2013-14	League Two	3	36	16	10	10	60	50	+10	58
2012-13	League Two	7	36	12	9	15	59	58	+1	45

Over/Under 64%/36% 1st   **Both score** 56%/44% 4th

The Borderers celebrate beneath the dreaming spires of Berwick's massive grain silos

Scottish League Two results 2014-15

	Albion	Annan	Arbroath	Berwick	Clyde	East Fife	East Stirling	Elgin	Montrose	Queen's Park
Albion		2-1/2-0	2-1/1-1	2-1/2-0	2-2/0-2	2-0/2-3	1-2/0-1	3-0/0-3	0-0/3-0	1-0/2-1
Annan	2-1/1-3		0-1/2-0	2-0/4-2	2-1/0-1	2-1/2-1	4-3/3-2	3-3/2-3	2-2/4-3	0-1/2-0
Arbroath	1-0/0-2	3-2/1-1		2-0/5-0	4-0/3-1	0-2/1-1	4-0/0-1	1-0/3-3	3-1/2-2	1-2/1-1
Berwick	1-1/0-2	2-0/2-2	1-2/3-1		4-0/0-0	2-3/0-3	5-0/3-0	1-1/0-2	2-2/3-3	0-0/1-1
Clyde	0-1/2-3	1-1/1-0	2-5/1-1	3-3/0-3		3-1/1-0	0-1/1-1	2-1/0-2	1-2/2-0	0-2/2-0
East Fife	0-0/1-0	1-1/2-1	1-5/2-0	2-3/1-4	0-1/1-1		3-1/2-1	1-1/3-1	3-0/3-0	2-2/0-0
East Stirling	1-4/1-5	0-1/1-3	2-3/1-0	0-2/0-4	1-0/1-2	1-1/2-0		2-1/1-0	4-0/0-1	1-3/3-1
Elgin	0-4/2-0	0-0/4-5	1-1/2-1	2-1/3-3	1-0/2-0	1-0/3-5	1-2/0-0		0-1/4-0	1-4/1-2
Montrose	0-2/3-4	2-1/1-1	1-5/3-0	2-1/0-2	0-3/0-1	0-4/0-3	4-1/0-1	2-3/2-1		1-2/2-2
Queen's Park	0-1/0-1	0-0/2-0	0-2/2-1	2-0/2-1	1-2/1-1	3-0/1-0	3-0/1-1	2-1/1-1	2-0/4-1	

Scottish League Two 2014-15

Pos	H	A		P	W	D	L	F	A	W	D	L	F	A	GD	Pts
					Home					Away						
1	3	1	Albion	36	10	3	5	27	18	12	2	4	34	15	+28	71
2	2	2	Queen's Park	36	10	4	4	27	13	7	6	5	24	21	+17	61
3	4	4	Arbroath	36	9	5	4	35	19	7	3	8	30	27	+19	56
4	5	5	East Fife	36	8	6	4	28	22	7	2	9	28	26	+8	53
5	1	9	Annan	36	11	2	5	37	28	3	6	9	19	28	0	50
6	8	3	Clyde	36	6	4	8	22	27	7	4	7	18	23	-10	47
7	6	7	Elgin City	36	7	4	7	28	29	5	5	8	27	29	-3	45
8	7	8	Berwick	36	5	8	5	30	23	6	2	10	30	34	+3	43
9	9	6	East Stirling	36	7	1	10	22	31	6	3	9	18	35	-26	43
10	10	10	Montrose	36	6	1	11	24	36	3	5	10	18	42	-36	33

Best attack

		GF	GFA
1	Arbroath	65	1.81
2	Albion	61	1.69
3	Berwick	60	1.67
4	East Fife	56	1.56
5	Annan	56	1.56
6	Elgin City	55	1.53
7	Queen's Park	51	1.42
8	Montrose	42	1.17
9	Clyde	40	1.11
10	East Stirling	40	1.11

Best defence

		GA	GAA
1	Albion	33	0.92
2	Queen's Park	34	0.94
3	Arbroath	46	1.28
4	East Fife	48	1.33
5	Clyde	50	1.39
6	Annan	56	1.56
7	Berwick	57	1.58
8	Elgin City	58	1.61
9	East Stirling	66	1.83
10	Montrose	78	2.17

Top scorers

	Team	Goals scored	
P Weatherson	Annan	21	
S Murray	Arbroath	19	
C Gunn	Elgin	13	
B Linn	Arbroath	13	
D McKenna	East Stirling	12	
K Smith	East Fife	12	

Key POS H A Overall league position, rank from home games only, rank from away games only **Sup** Avg match supremacy **GFA** Goals For Avg **GAA** Goals Against Avg **PGA** Points Gained Avg

Record when first to score

		P	W	D	L	F	A	Sup	PGA	Pts
1	East Stirling	12	11	1	0	18	3	+1.25	2.8	34
2	Albion	21	19	0	2	47	11	+1.71	2.7	57
3	Queen's Park	18	15	2	1	38	11	+1.50	2.6	47
4	East Fife	18	13	4	1	43	16	+1.50	2.4	43
5	Arbroath	22	15	5	2	55	21	+1.55	2.3	50
6	Annan	19	13	2	4	42	28	+0.74	2.2	41
7	Clyde	17	11	5	1	24	12	+0.71	2.2	38
8	Montrose	11	7	3	1	25	16	+0.82	2.2	24
9	Berwick	18	10	6	2	45	18	+1.50	2	36
10	Elgin City	16	10	2	4	34	19	+0.94	2	32

Record when keeping a clean sheet

		P	W	D	F	Sup	PGA	Pts
1	Arbroath	8	8	0	20	+2.50	3	24
2	Clyde	10	9	1	14	+1.40	2.8	28
3	East Stirling	10	9	1	13	+1.30	2.8	28
4	Albion	15	13	2	26	+1.73	2.7	41
5	Berwick	10	8	2	25	+2.50	2.6	26
6	East Fife	10	8	2	21	+2.10	2.6	26
7	Elgin City	10	8	2	17	+1.70	2.6	26
8	Montrose	5	4	1	7	+1.40	2.6	13
9	Queen's Park	11	8	3	16	+1.45	2.5	27
10	Annan	6	4	2	7	+1.17	2.3	14

Over 2.5 goals

	H	A	%
Montrose	13	13	72%
Berwick	10	12	61%
East Stirling, Elgin			58%

Under 2.5 goals

	H	A	%
Clyde	11	10	58%
Queen's Park	11	9	56%
Albion	8	11	53%

Both to score

	H	A	%
Annan	12	10	61%
Arbroath	9	12	58%
Elgin	9	12	58%

Both not to score

	H	A	%
Albion	10	11	58%
Clyde	9	11	56%
Montrose	9	10	53%

Under-pressure Rodgers will do well to survive a tough start to the season

With the dull as ditchwater 'summer of sport' not quite a distant memory it's time to get on with the real business – the start of 2015-16 and build-up to Euro 2016, writes Alex Deacon. Long-term readers of the Racing & Football Outlook will know that I'm the resident expert in creating and maintaining the RFO's football ratings and the forecasted prices we derive from them.

Week-in, week-out the focus is given to match betting, but one of the greatest benefits of using a ratings system is in their ability to offer a truer, more accurate source of outright market pricing, particularly for the Premier League where the hype is at is shrillest.

If we look back over the past 20 or so years of football, the narrative has changed radically. Historically focus was placed on the players, whereas now the guys kicking the ball round the pitch are at best co-stars, with their managers the true centre of attention.

This means that while the footballing conversation superficially runs on a game-by-game cycle, the glue of the story is actually what happens between matches.

One of the most obvious manifestations of this – outside of betting on pure outright markets – is the increasing popularity of the football specials markets and, most notably, betting on the sack race.

Betting on someone to lose their job may not seem the nicest way to cheer on a winner, but given that none of the guys at the top of the game struggle to put food on the table even when things are going wildly wrong, let's not shed too many tears for these chaps.

The sack race odds at the beginning of the season reflect the broad narrative of the back pages – namely that the shoo-in for the first dismissal is Liverpool manager Brendan Rodgers. In their opening game, the Reds face Stoke, the side who inflicted Liverpool's heaviest defeat in over 50 years on the final day of last season.

Tempting as it might be to take advantage – not least because Liverpool have a difficult start to the season with the six away trips after their visit to the Britannia Stadium taking in each of last season's top five – it's hard to get excited about odds of 7-2.

However, it's also hard to imagine that Rodgers' season will start spectacularly well and it's difficult to ignore the fact that change looks likely to come to Anfield sooner rather than later.

Now, what price the quick return from the MLS of Steven Gerrard?

About the Outlook Index

Our unique ratings provide an objective view of every club. Each team has a rating, roughly on a scale of 0 to 1,000, which goes up or down with league results and takes into account the relative strength of the opposition. The tables show each team's overall rating, plus ratings for home and away form (a separate ratings system) and a Trend rating (-20 to +20). The Last 40 column shows the change, in graphical form, over the last 40 league matches — approximately a season's worth of games running chronologically from left to right, with the scale relative to each individual team's highest and lowest ratings during that time — while the red and blue bars show the the Trend value, based on the last 60 matches but weighted towards more recent games, to help identify the teams in form. Red is hot, blue is not. The tables show final ratings for 2014-15.

Premier League

	Current	Last 40	H	A	Trend	
Chelsea	972		1007	950		-2
Man City	962		997	936		1
Arsenal	959		963	949		3
Man Utd	936		953	923		-2
Liverpool	928		950	916		-11
Tottenham	922		930	923		-4
Southampton	904		916	872		-8
Stoke	903		923	876		2
Everton	902		927	887		-2
Swansea	902		892	881		4
Crystal Palace	900		868	882		7
Leicester	892		887	859		13
WBA	890		886	874		7
Sunderland	881		863	879		4
Burnley	872		866	846		3
West Ham	871		895	860		-12
Aston Villa	866		871	864		0
Newcastle	861		883	851		-8
Hull	860		866	835		2
QPR	852		872	812		0

Championship

	Current	Last 40	H	A	Trend	
Bournemouth	876		860	849		8
Watford	872		853	854		9
Norwich	870		876	859		4
Middlesbro	860		871	829		-1
Wolves	857		854	834		7
Brentford	848		843	814		2
Ipswich	847		875	820		-2
Birmingham	842		832	818		9
Derby	839		854	827		-11
Blackburn	838		844	831		2
Cardiff	832		833	836		4
Huddersfield	832		829	809		6
Sheff Wed	824		813	833		1
Fulham	818		835	820		0
Nottm Forest	817		815	825		-6
Rotherham	815		809	785		3
Charlton	815		824	814		-4
Leeds	814		808	810		-6
Bolton	814		836	796		-6
Brighton	811		817	812		-6
Reading	807		815	814		-5
Millwall	802		808	796		0
Wigan	798		796	818		-4
Blackpool	766		793	761		-6

Leicester's great escape left them with a sky-high Index Trend figure

Jimmy Floyd Hasselbaink's Burton head into League One with a healthy Outlook Index rating

League One

	Current	Last 40	H	A	Trend	
Bristol City	819		811	796		8
MK Dons	802		792	784		9
Preston	800		812	784		-1
Gillingham	767		772	732		4
Chesterfield	767		769	755		3
Sheff Utd	766		783	755		-5
Swindon	765		780	763		-9
Barnsley	762		787	745		-5
Walsall	761		757	757		4
Fleetwood	760		751	746		1
Bradford	758		752	762		3
Oldham	756		751	744		0
Coventry	754		740	756		1
Colchester	754		745	746		11
Peterborough	754		782	753		-2
Doncaster	753		755	770		-5
Crewe	753		757	732		0
Scunthorpe	748		762	729		-3
Leyton Orient	743		740	756		0
Rochdale	743		761	726		-5
Port Vale	741		746	732		-3
Crawley	736		760	716		-2
Notts Co	734		744	732		-4
Yeovil	728		744	730		-3

League Two

	Current	Last 40	H	A	Trend	
Burton	765		768	736		8
Shrewsbury	751		770	726		2
Southend	751		742	735		5
Bury	748		741	739		10
Wycombe	737		708	747		-1
Stevenage	728		756	704		2
Plymouth	723		732	702		3
Oxford Utd	719		711	722		9
Morecambe	716		702	716		7
Exeter	714		713	712		-1
Dag & Red	708		701	712		2
Luton	707		733	688		-4
York	707		706	722		-1
Wimbledon	704		724	684		-2
Accrington	704		716	686		-1
Northampton	702		725	691		-5
Portsmouth	702		726	695		-2
Newport Co	700		704	706		-10
Hartlepool	697		708	674		7
Carlisle	696		722	688		0
Cambridge	686		692	678		-4
Mansfield	674		707	674		-12
Cheltenham	673		684	681		-5
Tranmere	671		695	684		-14

Conference

	Current	Last 40	H	A	Trend	
Bristol Rovers	708		736	688		5
Grimsby	704		680	710		2
Barnet	698		705	679		3
Forest Green	692		681	682		4
Eastleigh	690		663	689		10
Woking	687		685	676		5
Wrexham	680		669	655		5
Dover	680		679	654		5
Macclesfield	676		691	654		-8
Chester	662		656	654		3
Braintree	657		661	655		1
Halifax	654		694	634		-9
Gateshead	654		670	662		-8
Torquay	652		673	656		2
Lincoln	647		659	642		-13
Southport	646		640	643		2
Aldershot	645		653	652		0
Altrincham	645		648	634		-11
Kidderminster	639		675	637		-12
Alfreton	638		653	626		-3
Welling	635		644	629		-1
Dartford	631		629	623		2
Telford	630		606	636		10
Nuneaton	626		648	613		0

Scottish Premiership

	Current	Last 40	H	A	Trend	
Celtic	917		951	892		2
Aberdeen	860		849	843		-8
Inverness CT	848		846	826		1
St Johnstone	842		842	817		6
Dundee Utd	824		844	794		-4
Ross County	812		796	802		9
Motherwell	807		833	774		0
Partick	807		799	793		1
Hamilton	806		800	772		1
Dundee	804		796	783		-4
Kilmarnock	783		781	782		-9
St Mirren	778		780	771		3

Scottish Championship

	Current	Last 40	H	A	Trend	
Hearts	830		829	815		-3
Rangers	821		898	824		-2
Hibernian	805		792	805		6
Queen Of Sth	773		791	725		1
Falkirk	763		773	748		-6
Livingston	730		722	726		11
Raith	728		734	721		-5
Dumbarton	722		726	715		-5
Alloa	710		716	686		6
Cowdenbeath	703		706	702		-4

Scottish League One

	Current	Last 40	H	A	Trend	
Morton	719		728	704		7
Airdrieonians	717		711	692		10
Stranraer	706		709	677		1
Forfar	697		707	681		2
Brechin	692		684	693		-3
Peterhead	678		685	675		-4
Dunfermline	675		702	687		-6
Ayr	650		664	655		4
Stenhsemuir	634		657	644		-9
Stirling	622		643	620		-3

Scottish League Two

	Current	Last 40	H	A	Trend	
Albion	642		645	641		4
East Fife	632		651	629		3
Annan	620		651	607		2
Clyde	620		622	630		5
Arbroath	620		652	624		-7
Queen's Park	613		631	626		-7
Berwick	612		627	607		-1
Elgin	607		618	611		-5
East Stirling	605		606	602		2
Montrose	584		604	596		-2

Italian Serie A

	Current	Last 40	H	A	Trend	
Juventus	980		1027	977		-3
Roma	935		973	942		-6
Lazio	926		943	926		4
Fiorentina	924		932	942		4
Napoli	920		981	920		-7
Inter	914		928	922		5
Torino	908		929	906		-2
Genoa	905		925	890		5
Verona	900		905	887		7
Sassuolo	900		905	897		8
Milan	897		947	906		2
Sampdoria	894		922	908		-6
Palermo	891		914	878		-1
Empoli	890		912	876		-2
Chievo	887		889	899		-2
Atalanta	881		895	885		0
Udinese	870		918	886		-10
Parma	866		904	860		4
Cagliari	864		878	877		3
Cesena	820		869	836		-30

German Bundesliga

	Current	Last 40	H	A	Trend	
B Munich	986		1004	984		-13
Wolfsburg	958		969	925		0
B M'gladbach	956		966	925		9
Leverkusen	945		965	932		2
Dortmund	935		950	924		3
Augsburg	917		924	896		-2
Schalke	917		968	886		-10
Cologne	908		905	877		9
Mainz	907		918	889		1
Stuttgart	903		896	888		9
W Bremen	903		910	880		-5
Frankfurt	902		928	868		1
Hoffenheim	900		922	878		-3
Hamburg	892		900	870		4
Hannover	892		912	874		3
Freiburg	890		896	881		-3
Hetha Berlin	885		884	888		-4
Paderborn	876		878	879		-5

Spanish Primera Liga

	Current	Last 40	H	A	Trend	
Barcelona	1028		1062	1014		7
Real Madrid	1020		1049	1003		4
Atl Madrid	989		1017	977		-7
Seville	986		995	946		4
Valencia	977		1002	940		3
Ath Bilbao	962		962	944		8
Celta Vigo	945		943	925		8
Villarreal	943		970	922		-5
Real Sociedad	936		964	915		1
Rayo Vallecano	932		925	930		5
Espanyol	926		938	921		0
Elche	921		920	920		0
Malaga	920		941	917		-10
Granada	920		926	907		8
Levante	918		925	900		2
Deportivo	912		916	896		2
Almeria	903		906	887		-4
Getafe	901		910	895		-8
Eibar	896		903	913		-6
Cordoba	871		881	898		-15

French Ligue 1

	Current	Last 40	H	A	Trend	
Paris St-G	946		974	934		7
Monaco	924		916	930		2
St Etienne	917		933	895		6
Lyon	912		927	910		-2
Marseille	896		918	895		2
Bordeaux	887		936	873		6
Lille	886		938	878		0
Montpellier	872		898	864		-2
Guingamp	865		876	863		2
Bastia	863		900	836		1
Rennes	863		870	878		-6
Caen	862		866	845		9
Nice	861		874	861		0
Lorient	856		874	858		-1
Toulouse	852		883	842		0
Nantes	851		876	853		-8
Reims	848		866	844		0
Evian TG	839		855	842		-10
Lens	829		854	829		-7
Metz	821		835	813		-5

Bayern won the Bundesliga title again but finished with a negative Index Trend figure

Pools draws chart 2014-15 　　　　　　　　　　　　　　**X score-draw, 0 goalless draw**

Pools No.	Sept	Oct	Nov	Dec	Jan	Feb	Mar	Apr	May	X	0

```
Pools              Sept        Oct       Nov        Dec        Jan        Feb       Mar      Apr       May
No.   9 16 23 30  6 13 20 27  4 11 18 25  1  7 15 22 29  6 13 20 26 28  3 10 17 24 31  7 14 21 28  7 14 21 28  4 11 18 25  2  9 16 23   X  0
 1    X  -  0  -  X  -  X  -  -  X  -  -  -  -  -  X  -  -  X  -  0  X  -  -  -  -  -  -  -  -  -  -  -  -  -  -  0  -  -  0  -   7  4
 2    -  -  -  0  -  -  0  -  -  -  -  0  -  -  0  -  -  0  -  -  -  -  -  -  -  -  X  X  -  X  -  -  -  -  X  0  -  -  -  -  -   4  6
 3    -  X  -  -  0  -  -  -  -  X  -  X  -  -  0  -  -  X  -  -  -  -  0  -  -  X  -  -  -  -  -  -  -  -  X  X  -   7  3
 4    -  -  X  X  0  -  X  -  -  0  -  -  -  X  -  -  -  -  X  -  -  X  -  -  -  -  -  -  -  -  -  -  -  -  -   6  2
 5    -  -  X  -  X  -  -  -  X  -  -  -  -  0  X  X  -  0  -  X  -  -  -  -  -  -  -  -  -  -  -  -  -  -  -   6  2
 6    -  -  -  X  -  X  -  0  -  -  0  0  -  -  -  X  -  -  -  -  X  -  -  0  -  X  -  -  -  -  0  0   5  6
 7    -  -  0  -  -  0  -  -  -  -  X  -  X  -  -  -  X  -  -  0  -  -  -  -  X  X  0  -  -  -  -   5  4
 8    -  -  X  -  -  X  X  -  X  X  -  -  -  -  -  -  0  -  -  X  -  X  -  0  -  -  -  X  X  -  -  -   9  2
 9    -  X  -  -  X  -  -  -  -  -  0  0  -  -  0  -  X  -  -  -  -  -  -  0  -  X  -  -   7  4
10    X  -  -  -  0  X  -  -  -  -  -  0  -  -  -  0  X  -  -  -  X  -  0  -  -   5  5
11    -  -  -  X  -  X  -  0  X  -  X  -  X  -  X  -  0  -  X  -  -  X  -  -  X  X  -  -  X  -   13  2
12    -  -  X  X  0  0  -  -  -  -  X  X  -  -  -  -  X  -  -  -  X  -  -  -  0  X  -   7  3
13    -  X  -  X  -  0  -  -  -  X  X  -  0  -  0  -  X  -  X  -  X  -  X  X  -  -  0  X  -  -  X   11  4
14    X  -  -  X  -  X  -  -  X  X  -  X  -  -  X  -  -  -  0  -  X  X  -  -  X   12  1
15    -  -  X  -  X  -  0  -  0  -  X  X  -  0  -  -  -  X  -  -  -  X  -  -  0  -  X  -  -  X   8  4
16    -  -  -  X  0  -  -  -  -  -  X  0  -  X  X  -  X  0   5  3
17    -  -  X  -  X  X  -  -  X  X  -  0  X  X  -  -  X  -  X  -  X  0  -  -  0  -  0  X   11  5
18    X  -  -  -  X  -  0  0  -  -  X  -  X  -  -  0  -  0  -  -  X  X  X  0  -  -   8  5
19    X  -  -  -  0  X  -  X  -  0  -  X  X  X  -  0  -  -  0  -  X  -  -  X  -  X  -  X  X  -   11  4
20    -  -  -  -  0  X  X  X  -  X  -  X  -  -  0  -  -  0  -  -  X  -  -  0  X  X   9  4
21    -  -  -  -  0  -  X  -  0  -  0  -  X  X  -  -  X  X  -  X  0  -  X   7  4
22    -  0  -  X  -  X  X  -  0  -  -  0  -  X  -  -  X  -  X   6  3
23    X  -  -  X  -  -  0  X  X  -  X  -  -  X  -  0  X  X  -  X  -  X   10  2
24    -  -  -  0  -  0  X  -  X  -  X  -  0  -  X  X  0  -  X  X  -  X  -  X  0  -  X   10  5
25    -  -  X  -  X  -  -  -  -  X  X  -  X  X  -  X  -  9  0
26    -  0  -  0  X  -  -  X  X  -  -  X  -  0  -  X  -  -  0  -  X   5  4
27    -  0  -  X  X  -  X  -  X  -  X  0  -  X  X  X  X   9  2
28    -  0  -  X  X  -  X  -  -  0   3  2
29    X  -  X  -  X  X  -  X  -  X  -  X  -  X  -  X  X   11  0
30    -  X  0  X  -  X  -  -  X  -  6  1
31    -  X  -  0  X  X  X  -  X  -  X  -  X  -  7  1
32    -  X  -  X  X  X  X  -  7  0
33    -  X  -  X  -  X  -  0  X  X  X  X  0  X  X  X  10  2
34    X  0  X  X  X  X  X  0  X  X  0  0  X  0  10  5
35    -  X  X  0  X  X  X  X  X  7  1
36    X  X  X  0  X  X  X  X  0  X  10  2
37    0  X  0  0  X  X  3  3
38    X  0  X  X  4  2
39    X  0  0  0  X  X  X  X  X  7  3
40    X  X  X  0  0  X  X  0  X  7  3
41    X  X  X  X  0  X  X  0  X  0  X  X  11  4
42    X  0  X  X  0  X  5  2
43    X  X  X  0  4  1
44    0  0  X  X  X  X  7  2
45    X  X  0  X  0  4  2
46    0  X  0  X  0  0  X  X  X  0  6  5
47    X  X  0  0  X  X  X  X  X  X  X  X  11  2
48    X  X  X  X  X  X  7  0
49    X  X  X  0  0  X  X  X  X  0  9  4
```

X	12 5 12 12 3 6 8 5 14 8 15 10 7 9 7 11 4 7 12 6 6 10 5 5 13 11 12 6 8 3 7 10 7 11 13 12 13 6 8 10 6 5	**347**
0	1 2 5 2 4 6 10 4 4 2 3 4 3 8 4 3 2 5 3 0 0 10 0 4 0 2 3 2 0 3 5 3 5 2 2 4 3 5 3 3 0 3 3	**134**

British weekend results only. European and international games were used in some weeks.

SCOTTISH CHALLENGE CUP

First round

Friday July 25, 2014
Queen's Park...(1) 1-1 (1)......... Berwick
AET 1-1 after 90 mins,
Berwick won 4-3 on pens

Saturday July 26, 2014
Arbroath.........(0) 1-4 (1)...............Alloa
East Fife..........(2) 2-1 ()............... Forfar
Montrose........(0) 0-3 (3)......... Peterhead
Elgin................(0) 0-3 (0)...........Stirling
Cowdenbeath.(1) 1-3 (0)........... Brechin
AET 1-1 after 90 mins
East Stirling ....(0) 1-7 (1).............Falkirk
Brora Rangers.(1) 3-1 (0)...Stenh'semuir
AET 1-1 after 90 mins
Stranraer.........(0) 3-2 (1).....Dumbarton
Hearts.............(3) 3-1 (0)............Annan
Airdrieonians..(1) 2-2 (1)............Albion
AET 2-2 after 90 mins,
Albion won 4-2 on pens
Queen of Sth...(1) 3-4 (0).......Livingston
AET 2-2 after 90 mins
Morton ....(1) 1-0 (0)......... Spartans
Clyde ....(2) 2-0 (0)................. Ayr

Tuesday August 5
Dunfermline....(0) 1-0 (0)...............Raith
Rangers ....(1) 2-1 (0).......Hibernian
AET 1-1 after 90 mins

Second round

Monday August 18, 2014
Rangers ....(5) 8-1 (0).............. Clyde

Tuesday August 19, 2014
Brechin ....(0) 0-2 (1)...... Peterhead
Brora Rangers.(2) 2-3 (2)........East Fife
Dunfermline....(0) 1-2 (0)............Falkirk
Morton ....(2) 5-2 (1)........ Berwick
AET 2-2 after 90 mins
Stirling............(0) 1-2 (0)...............Alloa
Stranraer.........(2) 2-1 (0)............Albion

Wednesday August 20, 2014
Livingston.......(1) 4-1 (0).............Hearts

Quarter-finals

Saturday September 6, 2014
Morton ....(0) 0-1 (0)...............Alloa
Peterhead ....(0) 0-1 (0)......Livingston
AET 0-1 after 90 mins
Stranraer.........(1) 1-0 (0).............Falkirk

Tuesday October 21, 2014
East Fife..........(0) 0-2 (1)......... Rangers

Semi-finals

Sunday October 12, 2014
Livingston.......(0) 1-1 (1).........Stranraer
AET 1-1 after 90 mins,
Livingston won 5-4 on pens

Wednesday December 3, 2014
Alloa..............(0) 3-2 (0)......... Rangers

Final

Sunday April 5, 2015
Livingston.......(1) 4-0 (0)...............Alloa

SCOTTISH LEAGUE CUP

First round

Saturday August 2, 2014
Airdrieonians ..(0) 1-3 (2)...Stenh'semuir
Albion.............(0) 0-0 (0).......Livingston
AET 0-0 after 90 mins,
Livingston won 4-3 on pens
Alloa..............(1) 1-0 (0)...........Stirling
Brechin ....(0) 0-1 (0).....Dumbarton
Clyde...............(1) 1-2 (0).Cowdenbeath
Dundee...........(2) 4-0 (0)....... Peterhead
Dunfermline....(2) 5-1 (0).............Annan
East Stirling ....(0) 0-4 (0)................. Ayr
Hamilton.........(1) 2-1 (0)........Arbroath
Montrose........(1) 1-3 (2)............Falkirk
Morton ....(1) 2-1 (0)......... Berwick
Queen of Sth...(2) 5-0 (0)...... Elgin City
Raith...............(1) 4-2 (1)............ Forfar
AET 2-2 after 90 mins
Stranraer.........(0) 1-0 (0).........East Fife

Tuesday August 26, 2014
Queen's Park...(1) 1-2 (1)......... Rangers

Second round

Tuesday August 26, 2014
Dundee...........(2) 4-0 (0)...............Raith
Falkirk.............(0) 0-0 (0).Cowdenbeath
AET 0-0 after 90 mins,
Falkirk won 4-3 on pens
Hamilton.........(1) 4-1 (1)...............Alloa
Hibernian........(0) 3-2 (0).....Dumbarton
Kilmarnock......(0) 1-0 (0)................. Ayr
Livingston.......(0) 1-0 (0)...Queen of Sth
AET 0-0 after 90 mins

Morton ....(0) 0-1 (1)............ Partick
St Mirren ....(0) 2-1 (1)....Dunfermline
Stenh'semuir...(1) 1-2 (2)............Hearts
Stranraer.........(1) 1-2 (1)....Ross County

Tuesday September 16, 2014
Rangers ....(0) 1-0 (0)... Inverness CT

Third round

Tuesday September 23, 2014
Aberdeen........(1) 4-0 (0)......Livingston
Falkirk.............(1) 1-3 (1).......... Rangers
Kilmarnock......(0) 0-1 (0)... St Johnstone
Partick ....(0) 1-0 (0)........ St Mirren
AET 1-0 after 90 mins
Ross County....(0) 0-2 (2)........Hibernian

Wednesday September 24, 2014
Celtic ....(1) 3-0 (0)...........Hearts
Dundee Utd ....(0) 1-0 (0)...........Dundee
Hamilton.........(0) 0-0 (0).....Motherwell
AET 0-0 after 90 mins,
Hamilton won 6-5 on pens

Quarter-finals

Tuesday October 28, 2014
Rangers ....(0) 1-0 (0)... St Johnstone

Wednesday October 29, 2014
Aberdeen........(1) 1-0 (0)........Hamilton
Celtic ....(1) 6-0 (0)........... Partick
Hibernian........(1) 3-3 (2).... Dundee Utd
AET 3-3 after 90 mins,
Dundee Utd won 7-6 on pens

Semi-finals

Saturday January 31, 2015
Dundee Utd ....(0) 2-1 (0)........Aberdeen

Sunday February 1, 2015
Celtic ....(2) 2-0 (0).......... Rangers

Final

Sunday March 15, 2015
Dundee Utd ....(0) 0-2 (1)............. Celtic

Kris Commons opens the scoring for Celtic in the League Cup final

Ladbrokes

BACKING SCOTTISH FOOTBALL

GOOD LUCK TO ALL 42 TEAMS

LEAGUE CUP

First round

Monday August 11, 2014

Carlisle .... (0) 0-2 (0) .... Derby

Tuesday August 12, 2014

Barnsley.......... (0) 0-2 (1) ....Crewe
Birmingham.... (1) 3-1 (1) .. Cambridge U
AET 1-1 after 90 mins
Blackburn .... (0) 0-1 (1) ..... Scunthorpe
Bolton............. (0) 3-2 (1) ....Bury
AET 1-1 after 90 mins
Brighton .... (0) 2-0 (0) .... Cheltenham
Bristol C.......... (1) 1-2 (0) .... Oxford
Burton .... (1) 2-1 (1) ....Wigan
Charlton .... (1) 4-0 (0) ....Colchester
Chesterfield .... (2) 3-5 (0) ... Huddersfield
AET 3-3 after 90 mins
Crawley .... (0) 1-0 (0) ....Ipswich
AET 0-0 after 90 mins
Dag & Red ...... (2) 6-6 (3) .... Brentford
AET 4-4 after 90 mins,
Brentford won 4-2 on pens
Exeter .... (0) 0-2 (0) ..Bournemouth
Leeds.............. (2) 2-1 (0) ...... Accrington
Luton.............. (0) 1-2 (0) .... Swindon
MK Dons......... (1) 3-1 (0) .AFC W'bledon
Millwall .... (1) 1-0 (0) .... Wycombe
Morecambe ..... (0) 0-1 (0) .... Bradford
Oldham .... (0) 0-3 (1) ..... Middlesbro
Plymouth .... (1) 3-3 (2) .. Leyton Orient
AET 2-2 after 90 mins,
Leyton Orient won 6-5 on pens
Port Vale .... (3) 6-2 (1) ....Hartlepool
Portsmouth ..... (1) 1-0 (0) ..Peterborough
Reading .... (1) 3-1 (0) .... Newport Co
Rochdale .... (0) 0-2 (1) .... Preston
Rotherham....... (0) 1-0 (0) .... Fleetwood
AET 0-0 after 90 mins
Sheff Wed....... (2) 3-0 (0) .... Notts Co
Shrewsbury .... (1) 1-0 (0) ....Blackpool
Southend .... (0) 1-2 (0) .... Walsall
Stevenage....... (0) 0-1 (0) .... Watford
Tranmere .... (0) 0-1 (1) ...Nottm Forest
Wolves .... (0) 2-3 (0) ..Northampton
Yeovil............. (0) 1-2 (1) ...... Gillingham
York .... (0) 0-1 (0) .... Doncaster

Wednesday August 13, 2014

Coventry......... (0) 1-2 (1) .... Cardiff
Sheff Utd .... (0) 2-1 (0) .... Mansfield

Second round

Tuesday August 26, 2014

Bournemouth .. (2) 3-0 (0) ..Northampton
Brentford .... (0) 0-1 (0) .... Fulham
Burnley .... (0) 0-1 (0) .... Sheff Wed
Crewe............. (1) 2-3 (1) ....Bolton
AET 2-3 after 90 mins
Derby .... (0) 1-0 (0) .... Charlton
Gillingham....... (0) 0-1 (1) ....Newcastle
Huddersfield ... (0) 0-2 (0) ...Nottm Forest
Leicester .... (1) 1-3 (1) ..... Shrewsbury
MK Dons......... (1) 4-0 (0) ...... Man Utd
Middlesbro ..... (0) 3-1 (0) .... Preston
Millwall .... (0) 0-2 (0) ..Southampton

John Terry gets Chelsea off the mark in the League Cup final

Norwich.......... (1) 3-1 (0) .... Crawley
Port Vale .... (1) 2-3 (1) .... Cardiff
Scunthorpe ..... (0) 0-1 (0) .... Reading
Swansea.......... (1) 1-0 (0) .....Rotherham
Swindon .... (0) 2-4 (1) .... Brighton
AET 1-1 after 90 mins
Walsall .... (0) 0-3 (3) ....C Palace
Watford .... (1) 1-2 (1) ...... Doncaster
West Brom....... (1) 1-1 (0) .... Oxford
AET 1-1 after 90 mins,
West Brom won 7-6 on pens
West Ham........ (1) 1-1 (0) .... Sheff Utd
AET 1-1 after 90 mins,
Sheff Utd won 5-4 on pens

Wednesday August 27, 2014

Aston Villa ...... (0) 0-1 (0) .. Leyton Orient
Birmingham..... (0) 0-3 (0) ..... Sunderland
Bradford .... (0) 2-1 (0) ....Leeds
Burton .... (0) 1-0 (0) .... QPR
Stoke .... (1) 3-0 (0) .....Portsmouth

Third round

Tuesday September 23, 2014

Arsenal .... (1) 1-2 (2) ..Southampton
Cardiff .... (0) 0-3 (3) ..Bournemouth
Derby .... (0) 2-0 (0) .... Reading
Fulham .... (2) 2-1 (0) ...... Doncaster
Leyton Orient.. (0) 0-1 (1) .... Sheff Utd
Liverpool .... (1) 2-2 (0) ..... Middlesbro
AET 1-1 after 90 mins,
Liverpool won 14-13 on pens
MK Dons......... (1) 2-0 (0) .... Bradford
Shrewsbury .... (1) 1-0 (0) ....Norwich
Sunderland ..... (1) 1-2 (1) .... Stoke
Swansea......... (1) 3-0 (0) .... Everton

Wednesday September 24, 2014

Burton .... (0) 0-3 (2) .... Brighton
C Palace.......... (1) 2-3 (1) ....Newcastle
AET 2-2 after 90 mins
Chelsea........... (1) 2-1 (1) ....Bolton
Man City......... (0) 7-0 (0) ..... Sheff Wed

Tottenham ...... (0) 3-1 (0) ...Nottm Forest
West Brom...... (1) 3-2 (1) .... Hull

Fourth round

Tuesday October 28, 2014

Bournemouth .. (0) 2-1 (0) .....West Brom
Fulham .... (2) 2-5 (1) .... Derby
Liverpool .... (0) 2-1 (0) .... Swansea
MK Dons......... (0) 1-2 (0) .... Sheff Utd
Shrewsbury .... (0) 1-2 (0) ....Chelsea

Wednesday October 29, 2014

Man City......... (0) 0-2 (1) ......Newcastle
Stoke .... (0) 2-3 (2) ..Southampton
Tottenham ...... (0) 2-0 (0) .... Brighton

Quarter-finals

Tuesday December 16, 2014

Derby .... (0) 1-3 (1) ....Chelsea
Sheff Utd .... (0) 1-0 (0) ..Southampton

Wednesday December 17, 2014

Bournemouth .. (0) 1-3 (2) .... Liverpool
Tottenham ...... (1) 4-0 (0) ....Newcastle

Semi-finals

Tuesday January 20, 2015

Liverpool .... (0) 1-1 (1) ....Chelsea

Wednesday January 21, 2015

Tottenham ...... (0) 1-0 (0) .... Sheff Utd

Second legs

Tuesday January 20, 2015

Chelsea........... (0) 1-0 (0) .... Liverpool
AET 0-0 after 90 mins, aggregate: 2-1

Tuesday January 20, 2015

Sheff Utd .... (0) 2-2 (1) ...... Tottenham
Aggregate: 2-3

Final

Tuesday January 20, 2015

Chelsea........... (1) 2-0 (0) ...... Tottenham

Northern Section first round
Tuesday September 2, 2014
Accrington ......(1) 1-3 (1)............ Carlisle
Barnsley..........(0) 2-0 (0)................York
Crewe..............(0) 0-3 (1)........ Rochdale
Fleetwood ......(1) 1-3 (2).... Morecambe
Notts Co ....(1) 2-0 (0)....... Mansfield
Oldham ....(0) 1-0 (0)......... Bradford
Preston ....(0) 1-0 (0)...... Shrewsbury
Scunthorpe .....(2) 2-0 (0).... Chesterfield

Southern Section first round
Tuesday September 2, 2014
AFC W'bledon (1) 2-2 (1).......Southend
AET 2-2 after 90 mins,
AFC W'bledon won 4-2 on pens
Cheltenham ....(1) 2-0 (0)............ Oxford
Crawley ....(0) 2-0 (0).. Cambridge U
Peterborough..(1) 2-3 (1)..Leyton Orient
Stevenage.......(0) 0-1 (1)......Gillingham
Wycombe ....(0) 0-1 (0)........Coventry
Yeovil..............(0) 1-3 (0).....Portsmouth

Tuesday September 23, 2014
Newport Co....(0) 1-2 (1)......... Swindon

Northern Section second round
Tuesday October 7, 2014
Burton ....(0) 0-3 (2)....... Doncaster
Bury................(2) 3-1 (0).... Morecambe
Hartlepool......(0) 1-2 (1)...... Sheff Utd
Oldham ....(2) 2-2 (0).......Barnsley
AET 2-2 after 90 mins,
Oldham won 4-2 on pens
Preston ....(1) 3-2 (1)........Port Vale
Rochdale ....(0) 0-1 (1)......... Walsall
Scunthorpe .....(1) 1-2 (2)......... Notts Co
Tranmere.........(1) 1-1 (0)........ Carlisle
AET 1-1 after 90 mins,
Tranmere won 5-4 on pens

Southern Section second round
Tuesday October 7, 2014
Colchester.......(2) 3-3 (1)......Gillingham
AET 3-3 after 90 mins,
Gillingham won 4-2 on pens
Coventry.........(2) 3-1 (0)............. Exeter
Dag & Red ......(0) 0-2 (1)..Leyton Orient
Luton..............(0) 1-0 (0)......... Crawley
MK Dons.........(2) 2-3 (1)..AFC W'bledon
Plymouth ....(3) 3-2 (0)......... Swindon
Portsmouth .....(1) 1-2 (1)..Northampton

Wednesday October 8, 2014
Cheltenham ....(0) 1-3 (1)..........Bristol C

Northern Section quarter-finals
Tuesday November 11, 2014
Bury................(1) 1-2 (1)........ Tranmere

Wednesday November 12, 2014
Walsall ....(0) 1-0 (0)........ Sheff Utd

Tuesday November 25, 2014
Oldham ....(0) 2-2 (1)........... Preston
AET , Preston won 10-9 on pens

Tuesday December 9, 2014
Doncaster ....(0) 0-1 (0)......... Notts Co

Southern Section quarter-finals
Tuesday November 11, 2014
Bristol C..........(0) 2-1 (0).AFC W'bledon
Crawley ....(1) 1-2 (0)......Gillingham
Leyton Orient..(1) 2-0 (0)..Northampton

Wednesday November 12, 2014
Coventry.........(0) 2-0 (0)........Plymouth

Northern Section semi-finals
Tuesday December 9, 2014
Tranmere ....(2) 2-2 (1)......... Walsall
AET , Walsall won 5-4 on pens

Tuesday December 16, 2014
Notts Co ....(0) 0-1 (1)........... Preston

Southern Section semi-finals
Saturday December 6, 2014
Gillingham......(0) 1-0 (0)..Leyton Orient

Wednesday December 10, 2014
Bristol C..........(1) 2-0 (0)........Coventry

Northern Area final
Wednesday January 7, 2015
Preston ....(0) 0-2 (0)........... Walsall

Second leg
Tuesday January 27, 2015
Walsall ....(0) 0-0 (0)........... Preston
Aggregate: 2-0

Southern Area final
Tuesday January 6, 2015
Gillingham......(1) 2-4 (2).........Bristol C

Second leg
Thursday January 29, 2015
Bristol C..........(1) 1-1 (1)......Gillingham
Aggregate: 5-3

Final
Sunday March 22, 2015
Bristol C..........(1) 2-0 (0)........... Walsall

SCOTTISH CUP
First round
Saturday September 13, 2014
Auchinleck......(1) 5-0 (0)..Buckie Thistle
Clachnacuddin (1) 1-7 (1)........ Hurlford
Cove Rangers..(5) 9-0 (0)Hawick Royal A
Culter ....(3) 4-2 (0)......Strathspey T
Deveronvale ...(0) 0-1 (1).. Nairn County
Edinburgh C....(1) 2-1 (0).....Coldstream
Forres Mech....(1) 4-1 (1) Civil Serv Strol
Fraserburgh ....(0) 0-0 (0)Linlithgow Rose
Golspie ....(0) 1-4 (2) Dalbeattie Star
Gretna 2008 ...(1) 2-1 (1) Gala Fairydean
Huntly..............(0) 2-1 (1) Wick Academy
Keith...............(0) 1-3 (2)Formartine Utd
Lossiemouth ...(0) 0-4 (1)......... Turriff U
Lothian Thistle (0) 0-1 (0)....East Kilbride

Preston Ath.....(1) 1-2 (0)Threave Rovers
Rothes ....(0) 0-4 (3)... Banks O'Dee
Selkirk.............(0) 0-4 (2)..... Boness Utd
Whitehill W .....(2) 3-1 (0)............ Girvan

First-round replay
Saturday September 20, 2014
Linlithgow Rose(1) 2-1 (1).... Fraserburgh

Second round
Saturday October 4, 2014
Arbroath ....(2) 2-2 (1)........Montrose
Berwick ....(2) 2-0 (0)Formartine Utd
Boness Utd ......(5) 7-1 (1)............. Culter
Brora Rangers. (4) 5-0 (0)....Banks o'Dee
Cove Rangers..(1) 1-2 (2).............Annan
East Fife..........(4) 7-0 (0)Threave Rovers
Edinburgh C....(2) 2-1 (1)....Auchinleck
Elgin City ....(0) 0-0 (0)....Forres Mech
Gretna 2008 ...(0) 0-1 (0)..Queen's Park
Inverurie Locos(0) 0-3 (2)......... Hurlford
Linlithgow Rose(1) 5-1 (0) Dalbeattie Star
Nairn County ..(2) 2-1 (0)..........Huntly
Spartans ....(1) 3-3 (2)....East Kilbride
Turriff U ....(0) 0-3 (1)............. Clyde
Whitehill W .....(0) 0-1 (0)... East Stirling

Sunday October 5, 2014
Stirling Univ....(1) 1-4 (2)...........Albion

Second-round replays
Saturday October 11, 2014
East Kilbride...(1) 1-5 (1).........Spartans
Forres Mech....(0) 1-3 (0)........ Elgin City
Montrose........(1) 1-3 (1).........Arbroath
AET 1-1 after 90 mins

Third round
Saturday November 1, 2014
Annan.............(2) 3-2 (1)......Livingston
Arbroath ....(1) 2-1 (0).. Nairn County
Ayr ....(1) 1-1 (1)...............Alloa
Dumbarton .....(0) 1-2 (1).......... Rangers
East Fife..........(2) 2-3 (2)........... Berwick
Edinburgh C....(1) 2-3 (3).Brora Rangers
Elgin City ....(3) 4-4 (0)..... Boness Utd
Forfar ....(1) 1-3 (2).Cowdenbeath
Hurlford ....(1) 1-1 (0)........... Stirling
Linlithgow Rose(0) 0-2 (0)............Raith
Morton ....(0) 0-0 (0).. Airdrieonians
Peterhead ....(0) 0-1 (0).........Stranraer
Queen's Park...(0) 1-2 (1)............Albion
Spartans ....(1) 2-0 (0)............. Clyde
Stenh'semuir...(1) 1-2 (0).......... Brechin

Sunday November 2, 2014
East Stirling ....(0) 1-4 (1)....Dunfermline

Third-round replays
Saturday November 8, 2014
Boness Utd .....(3) 5-4 (2)........ Elgin City
Stirling............(0) 2-2 (1).......... Hurlford
AET 2-2 after 90 mins,
Stirling won 13-12 on pens

Tuesday November 11, 2014
Airdrieonians ..(0) 0-2 (1)........... Morton

Alloa...............(3) 4-0 (0)................ Ayr

Fourth round

Saturday November 29, 2014
Alloa...............(1) 1-2 (2).......Hibernian
Annan..............(0) 1-1 (1)..........Brechin
Berwick ....(1) 1-1 (0)............Albion
Boness Utd .....(0) 0-5 (1)........Arbroath
Dundee...........(1) 2-1 (1)........Aberdeen
Falkirk.............(0) 1-0 (0).Cowdenbeath
Motherwell.....(1) 1-2 (0)....Dundee Utd
Partick ....(1) 2-0 (0)........Hamilton
Queen of Sth..(1) 4-1 (0).Brora Rangers
Spartans ....(0) 2-1 (1)..........Morton
St Johnstone...(2) 2-1 (0)....Ross County
St Mirren ....(1) 1-1 (0)..Inverness CT
Stirling.............(0) 0-2 (1)............Raith
Stranraer.........(0) 2-2 (1)....Dunfermline

Sunday November 30, 2014
Hearts.............(0) 0-4 (1)............Celtic
Rangers ....(1) 3-0 (0).....Kilmarnock

Fourth-round replays

Tuesday December 2, 2014
Inverness CT...(2) 4-0 (0)........ St Mirren

Tuesday December 9, 2014
Albion.............(0) 0-1 (0)........ Berwick
Brechin ....(3) 4-2 (0).............Annan
Dunfermline....(0) 1-3 (1)........Stranraer

Fifth round

Saturday February 7, 2015
Dundee...........(0) 0-2 (1)..............Celtic
Falkirk.............(1) 2-1 (0)..........Brechin
Hibernian........(1) 3-1 (1)........Arbroath
Partick ....(0) 1-2 (2)...Inverness CT
Queen of Sth..(0) 2-0 (0)...St Johnstone
Spartans ....(0) 1-1 (1)..........Berwick

Sunday February 8, 2015
Rangers ....(0) 1-2 (1)..............Raith
Stranraer.........(0) 0-3 (3)....Dundee Utd

Fifth-round replays

Tuesday February 17, 2015
Berwick ....(1) 1-0 (0)......... Spartans

Quarter-finals

Friday March 6, 2015
Queen of Sth...(0) 0-1 (1).............Falkirk

Sunday March 8, 2015
Dundee Utd ....(1) 1-1 (0)..............Celtic
Hibernian........(2) 4-0 (0).......... Berwick

Tuesday March 10, 2015
Inverness CT...(0) 1-0 (0)...............Raith

Quarter-final replay

Wednesday March 18, 2015
Celtic ....(1) 4-0 (0)....Dundee Utd

Semi-finals

Saturday March 18, 2015
Hibernian........(0) 0-1 (0).............Falkirk

Sunday March 19, 2015
Inverness CT...(0) 3-2 (1)..............Celtic
AET 1-1 after 90 mins

Final

Saturday May 30, 2015
Falkirk.............(1) 2-1 (0)... Inverness CT

First round proper

Friday November 7, 2014
Warrington T ..(1) 1-0 (0).............Exeter

Saturday November 8, 2014
Barnet.............(1) 1-3 (1).......Wycombe
Barnsley..........(2) 5-0 (0)...........Burton
Basingstoke ....(0) 1-1 (1)...........Telford
Bromley ....(1) 3-4 (0).........Dartford
Bury................(1) 3-1 (1)............Hemel
Cambridge U ..(0) 1-0 (0)...... Fleetwood
Cheltenham ....(2) 5-0 (0).........Swindon
Crewe..............(0) 0-0 (0)......Sheff Utd
Dag & Red ......(0) 0-0 (0)........Southport
Dover ....(1) 1-0 (0)......Morecambe
Eastleigh.........(1) 2-1 (0)............Lincoln
Gillingham.......(0) 1-2 (1).........Bristol C
Grimsby...........(0) 1-3 (2)...........Oxford
Hartlepool.......(1) 2-0 (0)...... E Thurrock

Luton...............(1) 4-2 (0)....Newport Co
Northampton ..(0) 0-0 (0)........Rochdale
Oldham ....(1) 1-0 (0)..Leyton Orient
Peterborough..(1) 2-1 (1)...........Carlisle
Plymouth........(1) 2-0 (0).......AFC Fylde
Port Vale ....(2) 3-4 (2).........MK Dons
Southend.........(1) 1-2 (1)...........Chester
Tranmere ....(0) 1-0 (0)...........Bristol R
Walsall ....(0) 2-2 (1)....Shrewsbury
Yeovil...............(1) 1-0 (0)...........Crawley
York ....(1) 1-1 (1).AFC W'bledon

Sunday November 9, 2014
Blyth Sptns .....(1) 4-1 (0)......Altrincham
Braintree..........(0) 0-6 (3)....Chesterfield
Coventry..........(0) 1-2 (1).......Worcester
Forest Green ...(0) 0-2 (1).....Scunthorpe
Gosport Bor ....(1) 3-6 (4).....Colchester
Halifax.............(1) 1-2 (0).........Bradford
Norton U ....(0) 0-4 (3)......Gateshead
Notts Co ....(0) 0-0 (0)......Accrington
Portsmouth.....(1) 2-2 (1).........Aldershot
Stevenage.......(0) 0-0 (0)........Maidstone
Wrexham.........(3) 3-0 (0)...........Woking

Monday November 10, 2014
Havant & W....(0) 0-3 (2)...........Preston

Tuesday November 18, 2014
Mansfield ....(1) 1-1 (1).......Concord R

Weston S-M....(0) 1-4 (3).......Doncaster

First-round replays

Tuesday November 18, 2014
AFC W'bledon (0) 3-1 (1)................York
Accrington ......(1) 2-1 (1).........Notts Co
Rochdale ....(0) 2-1 (1)..Northampton
Sheff Utd ....(1) 2-0 (0).............Crewe
Shrewsbury ....(0) 1-0 (0)..........Walsall
Southport ......(0) 2-0 (0).....Dag & Red
Telford ....(2) 2-1 (0)....Basingstoke

Wednesday November 19, 2014
Aldershot........(0) 1-0 (0).....Portsmouth

Thursday November 20, 2014
Maidstone ......(1) 2-1 (0).......Stevenage

Tuesday November 25, 2014
Concord R.......(0) 0-1 (0)........Mansfield

Second round

Friday December 5, 2014
Hartlepool.......(1) 1-2 (0).....Blyth Sptns

Saturday December 6, 2014
Accrington ......(0) 1-1 (1)..............Yeovil
Bury................(0) 1-1 (0)................Luton
Cambridge U ..(1) 2-2 (1).......Mansfield
MK Dons..........(0) 0-1 (0)....Chesterfield
Oldham ....(0) 0-1 (0).......Doncaster

Oxford ....(0) 2-2 (1)........Tranmere
Preston ....(1) 1-0 (0)....Shrewsbury
Sheff Utd ....(0) 3-0 (0)........Plymouth
Wrexham........(1) 3-1 (0)......Maidstone

Sunday December 7, 2014
Aldershot........(0) 0-0 (0)........Rochdale
Barnsley..........(0) 0-0 (0).........Chester
Bradford ....(2) 4-1 (0).........Dartford
Bristol C..........(0) 1-0 (0)..........Telford
Cheltenham ....(0) 0-1 (0)............Dover
Colchester.......(0) 1-0 (0)..Peterborough
Gateshead ......(1) 2-0 (0)..Warrington T
Scunthorpe .....(1) 1-1 (0).......Worcester
Southport ....(1) 2-1 (1).........Eastleigh
Wycombe ....(0) 0-1 (0)..AFC W'bledon

Second-round replays

Tuesday December 16, 2014
Chester ....(0) 0-3 (1).........Barnsley
Luton...............(0) 1-0 (0)...............Bury
Mansfield ....(0) 0-1 (1).. Cambridge U
Rochdale ....(1) 4-1 (0).........Aldershot
Tranmere ....(1) 2-1 (1)...........Oxford
Yeovil..............(0) 2-0 (0)......Accrington

Wednesday December 17, 2014
Worcester ....(0) 1-1 (1)..... Scunthorpe
AET 1-1 after 90 mins,
Scunthorpe won 14-13 on pens

Friday January 2, 2015
MK Dons.........(0) 0-1 (1)....Chesterfield

Third round

Friday January 2, 2015
Cardiff ....(1) 3-1 (0).......Colchester

Saturday January 3, 2015
Barnsley..........(0) 0-2 (0).....Middlesbro
Blyth Sptns .....(2) 2-3 (0)....Birmingham
Bolton.............(0) 1-0 (0).............Wigan
Brentford ....(0) 0-2 (0)..........Brighton
Cambridge U ..(1) 2-1 (0)..............Luton
Charlton ....(0) 1-2 (1).......Blackburn
Derby ....(0) 1-0 (0).........Southport
Doncaster ....(0) 1-1 (0).........Bristol C
Fulham ....(0) 0-0 (0)..........Wolves
Huddersfield ...(0) 0-1 (0).........Reading
Leicester ....(1) 1-0 (0)......Newcastle
Millwall ....(1) 3-3 (1).........Bradford
Preston ....(0) 2-0 (0)..........Norwich
Rochdale ....(1) 1-0 (0)....Nottm Forest
Rotherham......(1) 1-5 (1)..Bournemouth
Tranmere ....(0) 2-6 (1).........Swansea
West Brom.......(2) 7-0 (0)......Gateshead

Sunday January 4, 2015
Arsenal ....(1) 2-0 (0)................ Hull
Aston Villa ......(0) 1-0 (0)........Blackpool
Chelsea...........(0) 3-0 (0)..........Watford
Dover ....(0) 0-4 (1).........C Palace
Man City.........(0) 2-1 (1)......Sheff Wed
QPR ....(0) 0-3 (1)........Sheff Utd
Southampton...(1) 1-1 (1)...........Ipswich
Stoke ....(0) 3-1 (0).........Wrexham
Sunderland .....(1) 1-0 (0)..............Leeds
Yeovil..............(0) 0-2 (0).........Man Utd

Monday January 5, 2015
AFC W'bledon (1) 1-2 (1)........Liverpool
Burnley ....(0) 1-1 (0)......Tottenham

Tuesday January 6, 2015
Everton...........(0) 1-1 (0).......West Ham
Scunthorpe .....(2) 2-2 (0)....Chesterfield

Third-round replays

Tuesday January 13, 2015
Bristol C..........(1) 2-0 (0).......Doncaster
Chesterfield ....(0) 2-0 (0).....Scunthorpe
AET 0-0 after 90 mins
West Ham.......(0) 2-2 (0).........Everton
AET 1-1 after 90 mins,
West Ham won 9-8 on pens
Wolves ....(0) 3-3 (1)...........Fulham
AET 2-2 after 90 mins,
Fulham won 5-3 on pens

Friday January 2, 2015
Bradford ....(3) 4-0 (0).........Millwall
Ipswich...........(0) 1-0 (1)..Southampton
Tottenham ......(2) 4-2 (2)..........Burnley

Fourth round

Friday January 23, 2015
Cambridge U ..(0) 0-0 (0).........Man Utd

Saturday January 24, 2015
Birmingham....(1) 1-2 (2)......West Brom
Blackburn ....(1) 3-1 (1).........Swansea

*Scottish Cup
winners Inverness*

Cardiff .... (1) 1-2 (0) .... Reading
Chelsea........... (2) 2-4 (1) .... Bradford
Derby .... (1) 2-0 (0) .... Chesterfield
Liverpool .... (0) 0-0 (0) .... Bolton
Man City......... (0) 0-2 (0) ..... Middlesbro
Preston .... (1) 1-1 (0) .... Sheff Utd
Southampton.. (2) 2-3 (3) .... C Palace
Sunderland ..... (0) 0-0 (0) .... Fulham
Tottenham ...... (1) 1-2 (0) .... Leicester

Sunday January 25, 2015
Aston Villa ...... (0) 2-1 (0) .. Bournemouth
Brighton .... (0) 2-3 (2) .... Arsenal
Bristol C.......... (0) 0-1 (0) ...... West Ham

Monday January 26, 2015
Rochdale .... (0) 1-4 (1) .... Stoke

Fourth-round replays

Tuesday February 3, 2015
Fulham .... (1) 1-3 (0) ..... Sunderland
Man Utd .... (2) 3-0 (0) .. Cambridge U
Sheff Utd .... (1) 1-3 (0) .... Preston

Wednesday February 4, 2015
Bolton............. (0) 1-2 (0) .... Liverpool

Fifth round

Saturday February 14, 2015
Blackburn .... (2) 4-1 (1) .... Stoke
C Palace.......... (1) 1-2 (0) .... Liverpool
Derby .... (0) 1-2 (0) .... Reading
West Brom....... (2) 4-0 (0) ...... West Ham

Sunday February 15, 2015
Arsenal .... (2) 2-0 (0) ..... Middlesbro
Aston Villa ...... (0) 2-1 (0) .... Leicester
Bradford .... (1) 2-0 (0) ..... Sunderland

Sunday February 16, 2015
Preston .... (0) 1-3 (0) .... Man Utd

Sixth round

Saturday March 7, 2015
Aston Villa ...... (0) 2-0 (0) ...... West Brom
Bradford .... (0) 0-0 (0) .... Reading

Sunday March 8, 2015
Liverpool .... (0) 0-0 (0) .... Blackburn

Monday March 9, 2015
Man Utd .... (1) 1-2 (1) .... Arsenal

Sixth-round replays

Monday March 16, 2015
Reading .... (2) 3-0 (0) .... Bradford

Wednesday April 8, 2015
Blackburn .... (0) 0-1 (0) .... Liverpool

Semi-finals

Saturday April 18, 2015
Reading .... (0) 1-2 (1) .... Arsenal
AET 1-1 after 90 mins

Sunday April 19, 2015
Aston Villa ...... (1) 2-1 (1) .... Liverpool

Final

Saturday May 30, 2015
Arsenal .... (1) 4-0 (0) ...... Aston Villa

Theo Walcott enjoys the moment after breaking the deadlock in the FA Cup final

FA TROPHY

First round

Saturday December 13, 2014
AFC Fylde ...... (1) 3-0 (0) . Gainsborough
Aldershot........ (0) 0-1 (1) .. Burgess Hill T
Altrincham...... (1) 1-0 (0) .... Macclesfield
Basingstoke .... (1) 2-2 (1) .... Gosport Bor
Bishop's St...... (0) 0-5 (2) .... Torquay
Braintree......... (0) 1-0 (0) ... AFC Sudbury
Bristol R.......... (0) 0-2 (0) ...... Bath City
Bromley .... (1) 2-0 (0) .... Leiston
Concord R....... (0) 0-0 (0) .... Barnet
Dartford.......... (0) 2-0 (0) Solihull Moors
Ebbsfleet .... (1) 1-1 (1) .... Welling
FC Utd .... (2) 4-0 (0) .... Harrogate T
Forest Green ... (0) 2-2 (0) ... Didcot Town

Gateshead ...... (1) 2-0 (0) ...... Halesowen
Guiseley.......... (0) 0-2 (2) .... Chorley
Hemel............. (0) 1-0 (0) ...... Sutton Utd
Hyde............... (3) 4-2 (0) Spennymoor T
Lincoln............ (0) 0-2 (1) .... Alfreton
Lowestoft T .... (1) 1-3 (1) .... Dover
Maidenhead ... (0) 2-1 (1) ..... Poole Town
Nth Ferriby...... (0) 1-1 (0) ...... Boston Utd
Nuneaton .... (0) 0-2 (1) .... Grimsby
Ramsbottom... (0) 0-3 (2) .... Stockport
Southport .... (0) 1-1 (1) .... Wrexham
Telford .... (1) 1-1 (1) .... Chester
Wealdstone ..... (0) 1-0 (0) ...... Hayes & Y
Weston S-M..... (1) 1-3 (2) .. Farnborough
Weymouth...... (0) 1-1 (0) .... Havant & W
Wimborne Town(0)0-3 (1) .... Oxford C
Woking........... (1) 2-0 (0) .... Eastleigh

Stockport .... (2) 2-2 (0) .... Wrexham
Torquay .... (2) 4-0 (0) .... Bromley
Wealdstone ... (1) 1-3 (3) .... Bath City

Tuesday January 20, 2015
AFC Fylde .... (1) 4-0 (0) .... Telford

Second-round replays
Monday January 12, 2015
Farnborough ... (0) 1-0 (0) ... Maidenhead

Tuesday January 13, 2015
FC Utd .... (0) 1-0 (0) .... Chorley
Woking .... (1) 2-1 (1) .... Oxford C
Wrexham .... (2) 6-1 (1) .... Stockport

Wednesday January 21, 2015
Gateshead ...... (1) 3-2 (1) .... Grimsby
AET 2-2 after 90 mins

Third round

Saturday January 24, 2015
Bath City .... (0) 1-0 (0) ...... Altrincham
Dartford .... (0) 2-2 (2) .... Halifax
Hemel .... (0) 0-2 (1) .... Torquay
Woking .... (2) 3-3 (1) .... Dover
Wrexham .... (1) 1-1 (1) ..... Gateshead

Tuesday January 27, 2015
Braintree .... (1) 1-1 (1) .... Ebbsfleet

Third-round replays

Tuesday January 27, 2015
Dover .... (0) 1-0 (0) .... Woking

Tuesday February 3, 2015
Ebbsfleet .... (1) 2-0 (0) .... Braintree

Saturday February 7, 2015
Gateshead ...... (1) 2-2 (1) .... Wrexham
AET 2-2 after 90 mins,
Wrexham won 5-3 on pens
Halifax .... (2) 3-1 (0) .... Dartford

Quarter-finals

Saturday February 7, 2015
Dover .... (1) 3-3 (0) .... Bath City
Nth Ferriby ...... () 1-0 () .... Ebbsfleet
Torquay .... () 1-0 () .... FC Utd

Tuesday February 10, 2015
Halifax .... (0) 0-1 (1) .... Wrexham

Quarter-final replay

Tuesday February 10, 2015
Bath City .... (2) 2-1 (1) .... Dover

Semi-finals

Saturday February 21, 2015
Bath City .... (0) 2-2 (1) ..... Nth Ferriby
Wrexham .... (1) 2-1 (0) .... Torquay

Second legs

Saturday February 28, 2015
Nth Ferriby ...... (0) 1-1 (1) .... Bath City
AET 1-1 after 90 mins,
Nth Ferriby won 4-2 on pens
Torquay .... (0) 0-3 (0) .... Wrexham

Final

Sunday March 29, 2015
Nth Ferriby ...... (0) 3-3 (1) .... Wrexham
AET 2-2 after 90 mins,
Nth Ferriby won 5-4 on pens

Monday December 15, 2014
Bradford PA .... (0) 1-4 (2) . Kidderminster

Tuesday December 23, 2014
Barnet .... (1) 2-6 (1) .... Concord R

Tuesday December 23, 2014
Worcester .... (0) 0-1 (0) .... Halifax

First-round replays

Tuesday December 16, 2014
Boston Utd ..... (0) 0-2 (0) .....Nth Ferriby
Didcot Town ... (0) 0-3 (2) ... Forest Green
Gosport Bor .... (1) 2-1 (0) .... Basingstoke
Havant & W .... (3) 5-0 (0) ...... Weymouth
Wrexham .... (1) 2-0 (0) .... Southport

Monday December 22, 2014
Chester .... (1) 1-1 (0) .... Telford

Tuesday December 23, 2014
Welling .... (2) 2-3 (0) .... Ebbsfleet

Second round

Saturday January 10, 2015
Burgess Hill T .. (1) 1-2 (1) .... Dartford
Chorley .... (2) 3-3 (0) .... FC Utd
Ebbsfleet .... (1) 1-0 (0) ... Forest Green
Gosport Bor .... (0) 0-2 (1) .... Braintree
Grimsby .... (0) 0-0 (0) ...... Gateshead
Halifax .... (2) 5-3 (2) .... Alfreton
Havant & W .... (0) 0-1 (0) .... Dover
Hemel .... (1) 3-1 (0) .... Concord R
Kidderminster . (0) 0-1 (1) ...... Altrincham
Maidenhead ... (0) 2-2 (1) .... Farnborough
Nth Ferriby ...... (0) 2-0 (0) .... Hyde
Oxford C .... (0) 2-2 (1) .... Woking

Last term's treble hopefuls look primed to hang on to their domestic trophies

Upsets were scarce in Europe's major leagues, with Gent's first ever title in Belgium the only major surprise in Uefa's top-ranked competitions, writes Paul Charlton. Chelsea, Dynamo Kiev and PSV ended five-, six- and seven-year waits for the titles but none of the other winners of Europe's top 12 leagues – those with automatic Champions League group stage qualification – had waited more than three years.

And it would be no surprise to see Barcelona, Spanish champions for the fifth time in seven seasons, go in again. Although they only beat Real Madrid to the title by two points, they finished the campaign so strongly that's it hard to imagine they trailed at the winter break, with Real having a game in hand.

Luis Enrique landed a league, cup and Champions League treble in his first season in the dugout, but it's worth noting that on the four occasions that Real Madrid or Barcelona have contested the Fifa Club World Cup in its current format, only Barcelona, in 2009-10, won the domestic championship that season.

There are other factors counting against the champions, too – the transfer embargo, Lionel Messi's upcoming court case on charges of tax evasion (not that it's held him back so far) and another busy summer for Messi and Neymar in the Copa America.

There is an obvious case that Real are the value at odds-against in a two-horse race, but Luis Suarez will surely hit the ground running now that he has clicked very firmly with his Barcelona teammates, and there are question marks surrounding Real Madrid too, with the appointment of new manager Rafa Benitez not a popular choice.

There's no reason to oppose Juventus either, as they bid for a fifth straight Serie A title to match the record they set in the 1930s. The Old Lady had a difficult start to the season after Antonio Conte left in the

summer, but under Massimiliano Allegri Juve won the league by 17 points – as they did in 2013-14 – lifted the cup and reached the Champions League final.

Carlos Tevez, Juve's leading scorer in both his seasons at the club, is off to Boca, Andrea Pirlo is off to New York and, as we go to press, there is plenty of speculation about Paul Pogba. Even so it's hard to see where a sustained challenge to Juve will come from.

Best odds of around 8-13 hardly set the pulse racing but a double with Barcelona, paying out at a little under the 7-4 mark, will provide some interest over the season.

For more competitive betting heats, it could pay to look to the relegation markets.

In France, things could be settled early after the LFP voted to reduce the number of Ligue 1 relegation places to two. The newly promoted sides head the betting, with Troyes having only ever spent one season in the top flight (in 2012-13), Angers having spent just one season in the top flight and two in the third tier since their last sustained stint at the top level ended in 1981, and Gazelec Ajaccio.

Gazelec's Corsican base, Stade Ange Casanova, has a tiny capacity of around 5,000. They won a second-successive promotion last term, but most of the last two decades has been spent in the amateur fourth tier of French football.

This will be their first campaign in the top flight and they look a good relegation bet at

Evens. That said, Thierry Laurey is obviously a shrewd coach to have taken GFCA up and it's possible that they can cause a few upsets at home. The pitch looks pretty rough and their city rivals, AC Ajaccio, were markedly stronger in Corsica during their recent stints in Ligue 1, although their record off the island set the bar very low.

However, while Metz and Lens went straight back down last season and Evian Thonon-Gaillard's four-season stint in the top flight came to an end, six of the nine teams promoted since Evian went up in 2011 are still playing in Ligue 1.

If an established Ligue 1 outfit is to get involved in the relegation scrap, Guingamp might fit the bill at around 5-1. Although the Breton club lost top scorer Mustapha Yatabare last summer and did well, the attack looks pretty thin without Lyon-bound Claudio Beauvue. Beauvue scored 17 league goals, 41 per cent of their total, to match Didier Drogba's club record last season and although Christophe Mandanne weighed in with 11 goals last term, his career scoring record does not inspire huge confidence. Sylvain Marveaux is also set to leave after a decent season on loan from Newcastle.

EAG finished tenth last term but were closer to the drop zone than the European places and with a defence that's nothing to write home about and a goal difference of -14, their third campaign back in the top flight could be hard going.

GFCA won't be the only minnows competing in Europe's top divisions this term. Darmstadt have had two seasons in the Bundesliga, the last in 1981-82, but have had their ups and downs since then and only avoided relegation from the third tier three seasons ago when financial problems meant Kickers Offenbach went down in their place.

Carpi, who can rival Gazelec's status as minnows' minnows, will take their place in Serie A for the first time with a capacity of just over 4,000 at Stadio Sandro Cabassi.

Frosinone, who followed them up as Serie B runners-up, are hardly giants, either. This will also be their first top-flight campaign.

However, in each of the seven seasons since Juve returned to Serie A, only one of the newly promoted sides has gone straight back down, and Udinese, who have been in Serie A since 1995-96, could find themselves dragged into the relegation fight. They finished the last campaign meekly, ending up two places above the drop zone.

Antonio Di Natale was their top scorer for the sixth season in succession but, at 37, his best days are behind him. Star midfielder Allan is also being linked with a number of bigger clubs.

There's a new coach in the dugout, Stefano Colantuono, latterly in charge of Atalanta, and the club is famed for its extensive scouting network which has allowed Udinese to buy and sell a remarkable array of talent.

But if owner Giampaolo Pozzo, who also owns Watford, decides to target the bigger financial rewards on offer in the Premier League, Udinese might struggle.

Watford have already made a high-profile managerial appointment, with Quique Sanchez Flores, who steered Atletico Madrid to the Europa League in 2010, taking charge, and at double-figure odds in the relegation betting it's worth a bet that the Pozzos might be spreading their resources a bit thin.

*Lionel Messi and
Andrea Pirlo work
their magic in the
Champions League final*

ATALANTA

Atleti Azzurri d'Italia — www.atalanta.it

	2014-15 H	A	Last six seasons at home P	W	D	L	OV	UN	BS	CS
Juventus	L	L	5	0	0	5	3	2	2	0
Roma	L	L	5	1	1	3	4	1	5	0
Lazio	D	L	5	2	1	2	2	3	2	1
Fiorentina	L	L	5	2	0	3	1	4	1	1
Napoli	D	D	5	2	2	1	1	4	2	2
Genoa	L	D	5	1	1	3	1	4	2	1
Sampdoria	L	L	4	1	1	2	2	2	1	2
Inter	L	L	5	1	3	1	2	3	5	0
Torino	L	D	4	2	0	2	3	1	3	1
Milan	L	W	5	1	1	3	2	3	3	0
Palermo	D	W	4	2	1	1	2	2	2	2
Sassuolo	W	D	3	2	0	1	1	2	1	1
Hellas Verona	D	L	2	0	1	1	1	1	1	1
Chievo	D	D	5	2	2	1	2	3	3	1
Empoli	D	D	2	0	1	1	2	0	2	0
Udinese	D	L	5	1	4	0	0	5	1	4
Atalanta										
Carpi			-	-	-	-	-	-	-	-
Frosinone			1	0	1	0	0	1	0	1
Bologna			4	2	2	0	1	3	3	1

Season	Division	Pos	P	W	D	L	F	A	GD	Pts
2014-15	Serie A	17	38	7	16	15	38	57	-19	37
2013-14	Serie A	11	38	15	5	18	43	51	-8	50
2012-13	Serie A	15	38	11	9	18	39	56	-17	40

Over/Under 50%/50% 12th **Both score** 61%/39% 7th

BOLOGNA

Renato Dall'Ara — www.bolognafc.it

	2014-15 H	A	Last six seasons at home P	W	D	L	OV	UN	BS	CS
Juventus			5	0	2	3	1	4	2	1
Roma			5	0	1	4	1	4	1	0
Lazio			5	1	2	2	3	2	2	2
Fiorentina			5	2	2	1	2	3	3	1
Napoli			5	2	1	2	3	2	2	1
Genoa			5	2	2	1	2	3	3	2
Sampdoria			4	0	4	0	1	3	4	0
Inter			5	0	2	3	3	2	4	1
Torino			2	0	1	1	2	0	2	0
Milan			5	0	3	2	4	1	3	1
Palermo			4	3	0	1	3	1	2	2
Sassuolo			1	0	1	0	0	1	0	1
Hellas Verona			1	0	0	1	1	0	1	0
Chievo			5	2	2	1	3	2	2	2
Empoli			-	-	-	-	-	-	-	-
Udinese			5	2	1	2	3	2	4	0
Atalanta			4	2	1	1	3	1	3	0
Carpi	D	L	1	0	1	0	0	1	0	1
Frosinone	D	L	1	0	1	0	1	0	1	0
Bologna										

Season	Division	Pos	P	W	D	L	F	A	GD	Pts
2014-15	Serie B	4	42	17	17	8	49	35	+14	68
2013-14	Serie A	19	38	5	14	19	28	58	-30	29
2012-13	Serie A	13	38	11	11	16	46	52	-6	44

Over/Under 38%/62% 17th **Both score** 45%/55% 19th

CARPI

Stadio Sandro Cabassi — www.carpifc1909.it

	2014-15 H	A	Last six seasons at home P	W	D	L	OV	UN	BS	CS
Juventus			-	-	-	-	-	-	-	-
Roma			-	-	-	-	-	-	-	-
Lazio			-	-	-	-	-	-	-	-
Fiorentina			-	-	-	-	-	-	-	-
Napoli			-	-	-	-	-	-	-	-
Genoa			-	-	-	-	-	-	-	-
Sampdoria			-	-	-	-	-	-	-	-
Inter			-	-	-	-	-	-	-	-
Torino			-	-	-	-	-	-	-	-
Milan			-	-	-	-	-	-	-	-
Palermo			1	1	0	0	0	1	0	1
Sassuolo			-	-	-	-	-	-	-	-
Hellas Verona			-	-	-	-	-	-	-	-
Chievo			-	-	-	-	-	-	-	-
Empoli			1	0	0	1	0	1	0	0
Udinese			-	-	-	-	-	-	-	-
Atalanta			-	-	-	-	-	-	-	-
Carpi										
Frosinone	D	L	1	0	1	0	0	1	0	1
Bologna	W	D	1	1	0	0	1	0	0	1

Season	Division	Pos	P	W	D	L	F	A	GD	Pts
2014-15	Serie B	1	42	22	14	6	59	28	+31	80
2013-14	Serie B	12	42	16	11	15	50	49	+1	59
2012-13	Lega Pro	3	32	14	9	9	38	30	+8	51

Over/Under 38%/62% 17th **Both score** 36%/64% 27th

CHIEVO

Marc'Antonio Bentegodi — www.chievoverona.tv

	2014-15 H	A	Last six seasons at home P	W	D	L	OV	UN	BS	CS
Juventus	L	L	6	1	2	3	2	4	3	2
Roma	D	L	6	1	3	2	1	5	1	3
Lazio	D	D	6	0	1	5	3	3	2	1
Fiorentina	L	L	6	2	1	3	3	3	4	1
Napoli	L	W	6	3	0	3	3	3	3	3
Genoa	L	W	6	3	1	2	4	2	4	1
Sampdoria	W	L	5	2	1	2	3	2	3	1
Inter	L	L	6	2	0	4	2	4	2	0
Torino	D	L	3	0	2	1	0	3	1	1
Milan	D	L	6	0	2	4	2	4	2	2
Palermo	W	L	5	3	2	0	0	5	1	4
Sassuolo	D	L	2	0	1	1	0	2	0	1
Hellas Verona	D	W	2	0	1	1	1	1	1	0
Chievo										
Empoli	D	L	1	0	1	0	0	1	1	0
Udinese	D	D	6	1	4	1	2	4	4	1
Atalanta	D	D	5	1	3	1	0	5	2	2
Carpi			-	-	-	-	-	-	-	-
Frosinone			-	-	-	-	-	-	-	-
Bologna			5	3	1	1	1	4	1	3

Season	Division	Pos	P	W	D	L	F	A	GD	Pts
2014-15	Serie A	14	38	10	13	15	28	41	-13	43
2013-14	Serie A	16	38	10	6	22	34	54	-20	36
2012-13	Serie A	12	38	12	9	17	37	52	-15	45

Over/Under 29%/71% 20th **Both score** 37%/63% 20th

ITALIAN SERIE A

EMPOLI

| Carlo Castellani | | | www.empolicalcio.it |

	2014-15 H	A	Last six seasons at home P	W	D	L	OV	UN	BS	CS
Juventus	L	L	1	0	0	1	0	1	0	0
Roma	L	D	1	0	0	1	0	1	0	0
Lazio	W	L	1	1	0	0	1	0	1	0
Fiorentina	L	D	1	0	0	1	1	0	1	0
Napoli	W	D	1	1	0	0	1	0	1	0
Genoa	D	D	1	0	1	0	0	1	0	0
Sampdoria	D	L	2	0	1	1	1	1	2	0
Inter	D	L	1	0	1	0	0	1	0	1
Torino	D	W	4	1	3	0	0	4	1	3
Milan	D	D	1	0	1	0	1	0	1	0
Palermo	W	D	2	1	1	0	1	1	1	1
Sassuolo	W	L	5	1	2	2	2	3	3	0
Hellas Verona	D	L	3	0	2	1	1	2	2	1
Chievo	W	D	1	1	0	0	1	0	0	1
Empoli										
Udinese	L	L	1	0	0	1	1	0	1	0
Atalanta	D	D	2	1	1	0	1	1	0	2
Carpi			1	0	1	0	0	1	1	0
Frosinone			2	2	0	0	1	1	1	1
Bologna			-	-	-	-	-	-	-	-

Season	Division	Pos	P	W	D	L	F	A	GD	Pts
2014-15	Serie A	15	38	8	18	12	46	52	-6	42
2013-14	Serie B	2	42	20	12	10	59	35	+24	72
2012-13	Serie B	4	42	20	13	9	69	51	+18	73

Over/Under 45%/55% 14th **Both score** 55%/45% 13th

FIORENTINA

| Artemio Franchi | | | www.violachannel.tv |

	2014-15 H	A	Last six seasons at home P	W	D	L	OV	UN	BS	CS
Juventus	D	L	6	1	3	2	3	3	2	3
Roma	D	L	6	1	2	3	2	4	2	1
Lazio	L	L	6	1	1	4	2	4	2	2
Fiorentina										
Napoli	L	L	6	0	2	4	2	4	3	0
Genoa	D	D	6	4	2	0	3	3	2	4
Sampdoria	W	L	5	3	2	0	2	3	2	3
Inter	W	W	6	2	2	2	5	1	4	2
Torino	D	D	3	1	2	0	2	1	3	0
Milan	W	D	6	1	2	3	4	2	4	1
Palermo	W	W	5	3	1	1	2	3	2	3
Sassuolo	D	W	2	0	1	1	1	1	1	1
Hellas Verona	L	W	2	1	0	1	1	1	1	0
Chievo	W	W	6	4	0	2	4	2	3	2
Empoli	D	W	1	0	1	0	0	1	1	0
Udinese	W	D	6	6	0	0	6	0	5	1
Atalanta	W	W	5	4	1	0	3	2	3	2
Carpi			-	-	-	-	-	-	-	-
Frosinone			-	-	-	-	-	-	-	-
Bologna			5	3	1	1	2	3	2	3

Season	Division	Pos	P	W	D	L	F	A	GD	Pts
2014-15	Serie A	4	38	18	10	10	61	46	+15	64
2013-14	Serie A	4	38	19	8	11	65	44	+21	65
2012-13	Serie A	4	38	21	7	10	72	44	+28	70

Over/Under 55%/45% 6th **Both score** 53%/47% 14th

FROSINONE

| Comunale Matusa | | | www.frosinonecalcio.com |

	2014-15 H	A	Last six seasons at home P	W	D	L	OV	UN	BS	CS
Juventus			-	-	-	-	-	-	-	-
Roma			-	-	-	-	-	-	-	-
Lazio			-	-	-	-	-	-	-	-
Fiorentina			-	-	-	-	-	-	-	-
Napoli			-	-	-	-	-	-	-	-
Genoa			-	-	-	-	-	-	-	-
Sampdoria			-	-	-	-	-	-	-	-
Inter			-	-	-	-	-	-	-	-
Torino			2	1	1	0	1	1	1	1
Milan			-	-	-	-	-	-	-	-
Palermo			-	-	-	-	-	-	-	-
Sassuolo			2	0	0	2	2	0	1	0
Hellas Verona			-	-	-	-	-	-	-	-
Chievo			-	-	-	-	-	-	-	-
Empoli			2	1	0	1	2	0	2	0
Udinese			-	-	-	-	-	-	-	-
Atalanta			1	0	0	1	0	1	0	0
Carpi	W	D	1	1	0	0	0	1	0	1
Frosinone										
Bologna	W	D	1	1	0	0	1	0	1	0

Season	Division	Pos	P	W	D	L	F	A	GD	Pts
2014-15	Serie B	2	42	20	11	11	62	49	+13	71
2013-14	Lega Pro	2	32	18	8	6	53	26	+27	62
2012-13	Lega Pro	7	30	10	11	9	36	30	+6	40

Over/Under 50%/50% 8th **Both score** 57%/43% 6th

GENOA

| Luigi Ferraris | | | www.genoafc.it |

	2014-15 H	A	Last six seasons at home P	W	D	L	OV	UN	BS	CS
Juventus	W	L	6	1	2	3	2	4	2	2
Roma	L	L	6	4	0	2	4	2	4	1
Lazio	W	W	6	4	1	1	3	3	3	3
Fiorentina	D	D	6	1	3	2	3	3	5	0
Napoli	L	L	6	2	0	4	4	2	4	0
Genoa										
Sampdoria	L	D	5	2	1	2	2	3	2	1
Inter	W	L	6	2	1	3	2	4	1	2
Torino	W	L	3	1	2	0	1	2	3	0
Milan	W	W	6	2	1	3	1	5	2	2
Palermo	D	L	5	2	3	0	1	4	3	2
Sassuolo	D	L	2	1	1	0	1	1	1	1
Hellas Verona	W	D	2	2	0	0	1	1	1	1
Chievo	L	W	6	2	0	4	3	3	3	1
Empoli	D	D	1	0	1	0	0	1	1	0
Udinese	D	W	6	3	2	1	4	2	4	2
Atalanta	W	W	5	1	4	0	2	3	4	1
Carpi			-	-	-	-	-	-	-	-
Frosinone			-	-	-	-	-	-	-	-
Bologna			5	3	1	1	2	3	2	3

Season	Division	Pos	P	W	D	L	F	A	GD	Pts
2014-15	Serie A	6	38	16	11	11	62	47	+15	59
2013-14	Serie A	14	38	11	11	16	41	50	-9	44
2012-13	Serie A	17	38	11	5	22	38	52	-14	38

Over/Under 50%/50% 12th **Both score** 66%/34% 1st

HELLAS VERONA

Marcantonio Bentegodi — www.hellasverona.it

	2014-15 H	2014-15 A	Last six seasons at home P	W	D	L	OV	UN	BS	CS
Juventus	D	L	2	0	2	0	2	0	2	0
Roma	D	L	2	0	1	1	1	1	2	0
Lazio	D	L	2	1	1	0	1	1	2	0
Fiorentina	L	W	2	0	0	2	2	0	2	0
Napoli	W	L	2	1	0	1	1	1	0	1
Genoa	D	L	2	1	1	0	2	0	1	1
Sampdoria	L	D	3	1	1	1	1	2	2	1
Inter	L	D	2	0	0	2	1	1	0	0
Torino	L	W	3	0	0	3	3	0	3	0
Milan	L	D	2	1	0	1	2	0	2	0
Palermo	W	L	1	1	0	0	1	0	1	0
Sassuolo	W	L	4	4	0	0	1	3	1	3
Hellas Verona										
Chievo	L	D	2	0	0	2	0	2	0	0
Empoli	W	D	3	1	2	0	1	2	1	2
Udinese	L	W	2	0	1	1	1	1	1	0
Atalanta	W	D	2	2	0	0	1	1	1	1
Carpi			-	-	-	-	-	-	-	-
Frosinone			-	-	-	-	-	-	-	-
Bologna			1	0	1	0	0	1	0	1

Season	Division	Pos	P	W	D	L	F	A	GD	Pts
2014-15	Serie A	13	38	11	13	14	49	65	-16	46
2013-14	Serie A	10	38	16	6	16	62	68	-6	54
2012-13	Serie B	2	42	23	13	6	67	32	+35	82

Over/Under 61%/39% 2nd   **Both score** 66%/34% 1st

INTER

San Siro — www.inter.it

	2014-15 H	2014-15 A	Last six seasons at home P	W	D	L	OV	UN	BS	CS
Juventus	L	D	6	1	2	3	3	3	4	2
Roma	W	L	6	2	2	2	4	2	4	1
Lazio	D	L	6	4	1	1	5	1	5	1
Fiorentina	L	L	6	5	0	1	3	3	3	2
Napoli	D	D	6	3	2	1	5	1	4	1
Genoa	W	L	6	4	2	0	3	3	4	2
Sampdoria	W	L	5	2	3	0	1	4	3	2
Inter										
Torino	L	D	3	1	1	1	1	2	1	1
Milan	D	D	6	3	2	1	1	5	2	3
Palermo	W	D	5	4	1	0	4	1	3	2
Sassuolo	W	L	2	2	0	0	1	1	0	2
Hellas Verona	D	W	2	1	1	0	2	0	2	0
Chievo	D	W	6	4	2	0	2	4	3	3
Empoli	W	D	1	1	0	0	1	0	1	0
Udinese	L	W	6	2	1	3	4	2	4	1
Atalanta	W	W	5	2	1	2	3	2	3	2
Carpi			-	-	-	-	-	-	-	-
Frosinone			-	-	-	-	-	-	-	-
Bologna			5	2	1	2	4	1	2	1

Season	Division	Pos	P	W	D	L	F	A	GD	Pts
2014-15	Serie A	8	38	14	13	11	59	48	+11	55
2013-14	Serie A	5	38	15	15	8	62	39	+23	60
2012-13	Serie A	9	38	16	6	16	55	57	-2	54

Over/Under 55%/45% 6th   **Both score** 58%/42% 10th

JUVENTUS

Juventus Stadium — www.juventus.com

	2014-15 H	2014-15 A	Last six seasons at home P	W	D	L	OV	UN	BS	CS
Juventus										
Roma	W	D	6	4	1	1	5	1	4	2
Lazio	W	W	6	4	2	0	3	3	4	2
Fiorentina	W	D	6	4	2	0	2	4	4	2
Napoli	W	W	6	4	1	1	5	1	3	3
Genoa	W	L	6	4	2	0	3	3	4	2
Sampdoria	D	W	5	2	2	1	4	1	5	0
Inter	D	W	6	4	1	1	3	3	4	2
Torino	W	L	3	3	0	0	2	1	1	2
Milan	W	W	6	4	0	2	3	3	2	2
Palermo	W	W	5	3	0	2	2	3	1	3
Sassuolo	W	D	2	2	0	0	1	1	0	2
Hellas Verona	W	W	2	2	0	0	2	0	1	1
Chievo	W	W	6	4	2	0	2	4	3	3
Empoli	W	W	1	1	0	0	0	1	0	1
Udinese	W	D	6	5	0	1	3	3	2	4
Atalanta	W	W	5	5	0	0	4	1	3	2
Carpi			-	-	-	-	-	-	-	-
Frosinone			-	-	-	-	-	-	-	-
Bologna			5	2	2	1	1	4	3	1

Season	Division	Pos	P	W	D	L	F	A	GD	Pts
2014-15	Serie A	1	38	26	9	3	72	24	+48	87
2013-14	Serie A	1	38	33	3	2	80	23	+57	102
2012-13	Serie A	1	38	27	6	5	71	24	+47	87

Over/Under 45%/55% 14th   **Both score** 45%/55% 18th

LAZIO

Stadio Olimpico — www.sslazio.it

	2014-15 H	2014-15 A	Last six seasons at home P	W	D	L	OV	UN	BS	CS
Juventus	L	L	6	0	1	5	1	5	1	0
Roma	L	D	6	2	1	3	4	2	4	1
Lazio										
Fiorentina	W	W	6	3	2	1	1	5	1	4
Napoli	L	W	6	2	2	2	2	4	4	1
Genoa	L	L	6	2	0	4	2	4	2	1
Sampdoria	W	W	5	4	1	0	1	4	1	4
Inter	L	D	6	4	0	2	3	3	3	2
Torino	W	W	3	1	2	0	2	1	3	0
Milan	W	L	6	3	2	1	3	3	5	1
Palermo	W	W	5	3	2	0	2	3	2	3
Sassuolo	W	W	2	2	0	0	2	0	2	0
Hellas Verona	W	D	2	1	1	0	1	1	1	1
Chievo	D	D	6	1	4	1	1	5	3	2
Empoli	W	L	1	1	0	0	1	0	0	1
Udinese	L	D	6	4	1	1	5	1	4	1
Atalanta	W	D	5	4	0	1	1	4	0	4
Carpi			-	-	-	-	-	-	-	-
Frosinone			-	-	-	-	-	-	-	-
Bologna			5	3	1	1	3	2	2	3

Season	Division	Pos	P	W	D	L	F	A	GD	Pts
2014-15	Serie A	3	38	21	6	11	71	38	+33	69
2013-14	Serie A	9	38	15	11	12	54	54	0	56
2012-13	Serie A	7	38	18	7	13	51	42	+9	61

Over/Under 63%/37% 1st   **Both score** 47%/53% 17th

MILAN

San Siro   www.acmilan.com

	2014-15 H	A	Last six seasons at home P	W	D	L	OV	UN	BS	CS
Juventus	L	L	6	2	1	3	2	4	2	2
Roma	W	D	6	3	2	1	4	2	4	1
Lazio	W	L	6	2	4	0	3	3	4	2
Fiorentina	D	L	6	2	1	3	2	4	3	2
Napoli	W	L	6	2	3	1	2	4	3	3
Genoa	L	L	6	4	1	1	2	4	3	3
Sampdoria	D	D	5	3	1	1	2	3	1	3
Inter	D	D	6	2	1	3	2	4	1	2
Torino	W	D	3	2	1	0	1	2	1	2
Milan										
Palermo	L	W	5	3	0	2	2	3	1	2
Sassuolo	L	L	2	1	0	1	2	0	2	0
Hellas Verona	D	W	2	1	1	0	1	1	1	1
Chievo	W	D	6	6	0	0	4	2	2	4
Empoli	D	D	1	0	1	0	0	1	1	0
Udinese	W	L	6	4	2	0	3	3	4	2
Atalanta	L	W	5	3	0	2	2	3	1	2
Carpi			-	-	-	-	-	-	-	-
Frosinone			-	-	-	-	-	-	-	-
Bologna			5	4	1	0	1	4	2	3

Season	Division	Pos	P	W	D	L	F	A	GD	Pts
2014-15	Serie A	10	38	13	13	12	56	50	+6	52
2013-14	Serie A	8	38	16	9	13	57	49	+8	57
2012-13	Serie A	3	38	21	9	8	67	39	+28	72

Over/Under 53%/47% 10th   **Both score** 66%/34% 1st

NAPOLI

San Paolo   www.ssnapoli.it

	2014-15 H	A	Last six seasons at home P	W	D	L	OV	UN	BS	CS
Juventus	L	L	6	3	2	1	4	2	4	2
Roma	W	L	6	4	1	1	3	3	3	3
Lazio	L	W	6	3	2	1	4	2	3	3
Fiorentina	W	W	6	2	2	2	3	3	2	3
Napoli										
Genoa	W	W	6	4	2	0	2	4	3	3
Sampdoria	W	D	5	4	1	0	2	3	1	4
Inter	D	D	6	3	3	0	3	3	4	2
Torino	W	L	3	2	1	0	1	2	2	1
Milan	W	L	6	3	2	1	6	0	5	1
Palermo	D	L	5	3	2	0	2	3	1	4
Sassuolo	W	W	2	1	1	0	0	2	1	1
Hellas Verona	W	L	2	2	0	0	2	0	2	0
Chievo	L	W	6	3	1	2	1	5	2	3
Empoli	D	L	1	0	1	0	1	0	1	0
Udinese	W	L	6	3	2	1	4	2	4	2
Atalanta	D	D	5	3	1	1	2	3	3	2
Carpi			-	-	-	-	-	-	-	-
Frosinone			-	-	-	-	-	-	-	-
Bologna			5	3	1	1	4	1	4	1

Season	Division	Pos	P	W	D	L	F	A	GD	Pts
2014-15	Serie A	5	38	18	9	11	70	54	+16	63
2013-14	Serie A	3	38	23	9	6	77	39	+38	78
2012-13	Serie A	2	38	23	9	6	73	36	+37	78

Over/Under 61%/39% 2nd   **Both score** 61%/39% 7th

PALERMO

Renzo Barbera   www.palermocalcio.it

	2014-15 H	A	Last six seasons at home P	W	D	L	OV	UN	BS	CS
Juventus	L	L	5	2	0	3	1	4	1	1
Roma	D	W	5	2	2	1	2	3	3	1
Lazio	L	L	5	2	1	2	4	1	3	0
Fiorentina	L	L	5	2	0	3	4	1	2	2
Napoli	W	D	5	3	0	2	5	0	4	0
Genoa	W	D	5	3	2	0	2	3	2	3
Sampdoria	D	D	4	2	2	0	1	3	2	2
Inter	D	L	5	2	2	1	2	3	4	1
Torino	D	D	2	0	2	0	1	1	1	1
Milan	L	W	5	2	1	2	4	1	3	1
Palermo										
Sassuolo	W	D	1	1	0	0	1	0	1	0
Hellas Verona	W	L	1	1	0	0	1	0	1	0
Chievo	W	L	5	3	1	1	4	1	4	1
Empoli	D	L	2	0	1	1	1	1	1	1
Udinese	W	D	5	1	2	2	3	3	3	1
Atalanta	L	D	4	2	0	2	3	1	3	1
Carpi			1	0	0	1	1	0	1	0
Frosinone			-	-	-	-	-	-	-	-
Bologna			4	3	1	0	3	1	4	0

Season	Division	Pos	P	W	D	L	F	A	GD	Pts
2014-15	Serie A	11	38	12	13	13	53	55	-2	49
2013-14	Serie B	1	42	25	11	6	62	28	+34	86
2012-13	Serie A	18	38	6	14	18	34	54	-20	32

Over/Under 58%/42% 5th   **Both score** 63%/37% 4th

ROMA

Stadio Olimpico   www.asroma.it

	2014-15 H	A	Last six seasons at home P	W	D	L	OV	UN	BS	CS
Juventus	D	L	6	1	2	3	1	5	3	1
Roma										
Lazio	D	W	6	3	2	1	2	4	3	3
Fiorentina	W	D	6	5	0	1	5	1	5	1
Napoli	W	L	6	4	1	1	3	3	3	2
Genoa	W	W	6	6	0	0	4	2	2	4
Sampdoria	L	D	5	2	1	2	3	2	3	1
Inter	W	L	6	4	2	0	3	3	3	3
Torino	W	D	3	3	0	0	2	1	1	2
Milan	D	L	6	2	3	1	2	4	2	4
Palermo	L	D	5	3	0	2	4	1	4	1
Sassuolo	W	W	2	0	2	0	1	1	2	0
Hellas Verona	W	D	2	2	0	0	1	1	0	2
Chievo	W	D	6	5	0	1	5	0	5	5
Empoli	D	W	1	0	1	0	0	1	1	0
Udinese	W	W	6	5	0	1	5	1	5	1
Atalanta	D	W	5	4	1	0	3	2	4	1
Carpi			-	-	-	-	-	-	-	-
Frosinone			-	-	-	-	-	-	-	-
Bologna			5	2	2	1	4	1	4	1

Season	Division	Pos	P	W	D	L	F	A	GD	Pts
2014-15	Serie A	2	38	19	13	6	54	31	+23	70
2013-14	Serie A	2	38	26	7	5	72	25	+47	85
2012-13	Serie A	6	38	18	12		71	56	+15	62

Over/Under 39%/61% 18th   **Both score** 50%/50% 16th

SAMPDORIA

Luigi Ferraris — www.sampdoria.it

	2014-15 H	2014-15 A	P	W	D	L	OV	UN	BS	CS
Juventus	L	D	5	2	1	2	1	4	1	2
Roma	D	W	5	2	2	1	2	3	2	2
Lazio	L	L	5	2	1	2	1	4	2	1
Fiorentina	W	L	5	3	1	1	3	2	2	2
Napoli	D	L	5	1	1	3	2	3	3	1
Genoa	D	W	5	2	1	2	2	3	2	1
Sampdoria										
Inter	W	L	5	2	0	3	1	4	0	2
Torino	W	L	4	1	2	1	2	2	3	1
Milan	D	D	5	1	3	1	2	3	3	1
Palermo	D	D	4	0	2	2	2	2	4	0
Sassuolo	D	D	3	0	2	1	1	2	3	0
Hellas Verona	D	W	3	2	1	0	1	2	1	2
Chievo	W	L	5	4	1	0	3	2	3	2
Empoli	W	D	2	2	0	0	0	2	0	2
Udinese	D	W	5	2	2	1	3	2	2	2
Atalanta	W	W	4	3	0	1	1	3	1	3
Carpi			-	-	-	-	-	-	-	-
Frosinone			-	-	-	-	-	-	-	-
Bologna			4	3	1	0	2	2	3	1

Season	Division	Pos	P	W	D	L	F	A	GD	Pts
2014-15	Serie A	7	38	13	17	8	48	42	+6	56
2013-14	Serie A	12	38	12	9	17	48	62	-14	45
2012-13	Serie A	14	38	11	10	17	43	51	-8	42

Over/Under 34%/66% 19th **Both score** 58%/42% 10th

SASSUOLO

Alberto Braglia — www.sassuolocalcio.it

	2014-15 H	2014-15 A	P	W	D	L	OV	UN	BS	CS
Juventus	D	L	2	0	1	1	1	1	2	0
Roma	L	D	2	0	0	2	1	1	0	0
Lazio	L	D	2	0	1	1	0	2	1	0
Fiorentina	L	D	2	0	0	2	1	1	1	0
Napoli	L	L	2	0	0	2	0	2	0	0
Genoa	W	D	2	2	0	0	2	0	2	0
Sampdoria	D	D	3	0	2	1	1	2	1	2
Inter	L	L	2	1	0	1	2	0	1	0
Torino	D	W	5	0	2	3	2	3	3	1
Milan	W	W	2	2	0	0	2	0	2	0
Palermo	D	L	1	0	1	0	0	1	0	1
Sassuolo										
Hellas Verona	W	L	4	2	1	1	2	2	3	1
Chievo	W	D	2	1	0	1	0	2	0	1
Empoli	W	L	5	4	1	0	2	3	3	2
Udinese	D	W	2	0	1	1	1	1	2	0
Atalanta	D	L	3	1	1	1	0	3	0	2
Carpi			-	-	-	-	-	-	-	-
Frosinone			2	2	0	0	2	0	2	0
Bologna			1	1	0	0	1	0	1	0

Season	Division	Pos	P	W	D	L	F	A	GD	Pts
2014-15	Serie A	12	38	12	13	13	49	57	-8	49
2013-14	Serie A	17	38	9	7	22	43	72	-29	34
2012-13	Serie B	1	42	25	10	7	78	40	+38	85

Over/Under 55%/45% 6th **Both score** 63%/37% 4th

TORINO

Olimpico di Torino — www.torino.it

	2014-15 H	2014-15 A	P	W	D	L	OV	UN	BS	CS
Juventus	W	L	3	1	0	2	1	2	1	0
Roma	D	L	3	0	2	1	1	2	3	0
Lazio	L	L	3	2	0	1	0	3	0	2
Fiorentina	D	D	3	0	3	0	1	2	2	1
Napoli	W	L	3	1	0	2	1	2	1	1
Genoa	W	L	3	2	1	0	2	1	2	1
Sampdoria	W	L	4	2	1	1	2	2	2	1
Inter	D	W	3	0	2	1	1	2	1	1
Torino										
Milan	D	L	3	0	2	1	2	1	3	0
Palermo	D	D	2	0	2	0	1	1	1	1
Sassuolo	L	D	5	2	0	3	2	3	1	2
Hellas Verona	L	D	3	0	1	2	2	1	2	0
Chievo	W	D	3	3	0	0	1	2	1	2
Empoli	L	D	4	3	0	1	3	1	2	1
Udinese	W	L	3	2	1	0	0	3	0	3
Atalanta	D	W	4	2	1	1	2	2	2	2
Carpi			-	-	-	-	-	-	-	-
Frosinone			2	1	0	1	2	0	2	0
Bologna			2	1	0	1	1	1	1	1

Season	Division	Pos	P	W	D	L	F	A	GD	Pts
2014-15	Serie A	9	38	14	12	12	48	45	+3	54
2013-14	Serie A	7	38	15	12	11	58	48	+10	57
2012-13	Serie A	16	38	8	16	14	46	55	-9	39

Over/Under 45%/55% 14th **Both score** 53%/47% 14th

UDINESE

Friuli — www.udinese.it

	2014-15 H	2014-15 A	P	W	D	L	OV	UN	BS	CS
Juventus	D	L	6	1	2	3	3	3	1	3
Roma	L	L	6	2	1	3	2	4	3	1
Lazio	L	W	6	3	1	2	2	4	3	2
Fiorentina	L	L	6	4	1	1	3	3	3	2
Napoli	W	L	6	3	0	3	4	2	5	1
Genoa	L	D	6	3	1	2	1	5	1	4
Sampdoria	L	D	5	2	1	2	4	1	4	1
Inter	L	W	6	2	0	4	6	0	4	1
Torino	W	L	3	2	0	1	1	2	1	1
Milan	W	L	6	4	1	1	3	3	3	3
Palermo	L	D	5	3	1	1	3	2	4	1
Sassuolo	L	D	2	1	0	1	0	2	0	1
Hellas Verona	L	W	2	0	0	2	2	0	2	0
Chievo	D	D	6	4	2	0	3	3	3	3
Empoli	W	W	1	1	0	0	0	1	0	1
Udinese										
Atalanta	W	D	5	2	2	1	2	3	3	2
Carpi			-	-	-	-	-	-	-	-
Frosinone			-	-	-	-	-	-	-	-
Bologna			5	1	4	0	0	5	3	2

Season	Division	Pos	P	W	D	L	F	A	GD	Pts
2014-15	Serie A	16	38	10	11	17	43	56	-13	41
2013-14	Serie A	13	38	12	8	18	46	57	-11	44
2012-13	Serie A	5	38	18	12	8	59	45	+14	66

Over/Under 45%/55% 14th **Both score** 58%/42% 10th

Serie A 2014-15

Pos	H	A		P	Home W	D	L	F	A	Away W	D	L	F	A	GD	Pts
1	1	1	Juventus	38	16	3	0	45	11	10	6	3	27	13	+48	87
2	4	2	Roma	38	10	7	2	31	11	9	6	4	23	17	+23	70
3	3	3	Lazio	38	12	1	6	40	18	9	5	5	31	20	+33	69
4	5	4	Fiorentina	38	9	6	4	30	17	9	4	6	31	29	+15	64
5	2	8	Napoli	38	11	5	3	46	28	7	4	8	24	26	+16	63
6	6	6	Genoa	38	9	6	4	33	21	7	5	7	29	26	+15	59
7	9	7	Sampdoria	38	7	10	2	23	15	6	7	6	25	27	+6	56
8	12	5	Inter	38	7	7	5	33	23	7	6	6	26	25	+11	55
9	8	9	Torino	38	8	7	4	25	14	6	5	8	23	31	+3	54
10	7	11	Milan	38	9	5	5	30	19	4	8	7	26	31	+6	52
11	10	14	Palermo	38	8	6	5	30	25	4	7	8	23	30	-2	49
12	11	12	Sassuolo	38	7	8	4	25	22	5	5	9	24	35	-8	49
13	14	13	Verona	38	7	5	7	27	30	4	8	7	22	35	-16	46
14	16	10	Chievo	38	4	9	6	16	19	6	4	9	12	22	-13	43
15	13	18	Empoli	38	6	8	5	26	22	2	10	7	20	30	-6	42
16	15	17	Udinese	38	6	5	8	26	29	4	6	9	17	27	-13	41
17	18	16	Atalanta	38	4	7	8	22	33	3	9	7	16	24	-19	37
18	19	15	Cagliari	38	4	4	11	24	36	4	6	9	24	32	-20	34
19	20	19	Cesena	38	3	7	9	19	31	1	5	13	17	42	-37	24
20	17	20	Parma	38	5	4	10	19	27	1	4	14	14	48	-42	19*

*Parma deducted 7pts

Results 2014-15

	Atalanta	Cagliari	Cesena	Chievo	Empoli	Fiorentina	Genoa	Hellas Verona	Inter	Juventus	Lazio	Milan	Napoli	Palermo	Parma	Roma	Sampdoria	Sassuolo	Torino	Udinese
Atalanta		2-1	3-2	1-1	2-2	0-1	1-4	0-0	1-4	0-3	1-1	1-3	1-1	3-3	1-0	1-2	1-2	2-1	1-2	0-0
Cagliari	1-2		2-1	0-2	1-1	0-4	1-1	1-2	1-2	1-3	1-3	1-1	0-3	0-1	4-0	1-2	2-2	2-1	1-2	4-3
Cesena	2-2	0-1		0-1	2-2	1-4	0-3	1-1	0-1	2-2	2-1	1-1	1-4	0-0	1-0	0-1	1-1	2-3	2-3	1-0
Chievo	1-1	1-0	2-1		1-1	1-2	1-2	2-2	0-2	0-1	0-0	0-0	1-2	1-0	2-3	0-0	2-1	0-0	0-0	1-1
Empoli	0-0	0-4	2-0	3-0		2-3	1-1	0-0	0-0	0-2	2-1	2-2	4-2	3-0	2-2	0-1	1-1	3-1	0-0	1-2
Fiorentina	3-2	1-3	3-1	3-0	1-1		0-0	3-0	0-0	0-2	2-1	0-1	4-3	3-0	1-1	2-0	0-0	1-1	3-0	
Genoa	2-2	2-0	3-1	0-2	1-1	1-1		5-2	3-2	1-0	1-0	1-2	1-1	2-0	0-1	0-1	3-3	5-1	1-1	
Hellas Verona	1-0	1-0	3-3	0-1	2-1	1-2	2-2		0-3	2-2	1-1	1-3	2-0	2-1	3-1	1-1	1-3	3-2	1-3	0-1
Inter	2-0	1-4	1-1	0-0	4-3	0-1	3-1	2-2		1-2	2-2	0-0	2-2	3-0	1-1	2-1	1-0	7-0	0-1	1-2
Juventus	2-1	1-1	3-0	2-0	2-0	3-2	1-0	4-0	1-1		2-0	3-1	3-1	2-0	7-0	3-2	1-1	1-0	2-1	2-0
Lazio	3-0	4-2	3-0	1-1	4-0	4-0	0-1	2-0	1-2	0-3		3-1	0-1	2-1	4-0	1-2	3-0	3-2	2-1	0-1
Milan	0-1	3-1	2-0	2-0	1-1	1-1	1-3	2-2	1-1	0-1	3-1		2-0	0-2	3-1	2-1	1-1	1-2	3-0	2-0
Napoli	1-1	3-3	3-2	0-1	2-2	3-0	2-1	6-2	2-2	1-3	2-4	3-0		3-3	2-0	2-0	4-2	2-0	2-1	3-1
Palermo	2-3	5-0	2-1	1-0	0-0	2-3	2-1	2-1	1-1	0-1	0-4	1-2	3-1		2-1	1-1	1-1	2-1	2-2	1-1
Parma	0-0	0-0	1-2	0-1	0-2	1-0	1-2	2-2	2-0	1-0	1-2	4-5	2-2	1-0		1-2	0-2	1-3	0-2	1-0
Roma	1-1	2-0	2-0	3-0	1-1	2-0	2-0	2-0	4-2	1-1	2-2	0-0	1-0	1-2	0-0		0-2	2-2	3-0	2-1
Sampdoria	1-0	2-0	0-0	2-1	1-0	3-1	1-1	1-1	1-0	0-1	0-1	2-2	1-1	1-1	2-2	0-0		1-1	2-0	2-2
Sassuolo	0-0	1-1	1-1	1-0	3-1	1-3	3-1	2-1	3-1	1-1	0-3	3-2	0-1	0-0	4-1	0-3	0-0		1-1	1-1
Torino	0-0	1-1	5-0	2-0	0-1	1-1	2-1	0-1	0-0	2-1	0-2	1-1	1-0	2-2	1-0	1-1	5-1	0-1		1-0
Udinese	2-0	2-2	1-1	1-1	2-0	2-2	2-4	1-2	1-2	0-0	0-1	2-1	1-0	3-1	4-2	0-1	1-4	0-1	3-2	

Top scorers

	Team	Goals scored
M Icardi	Inter	22
L Toni	Verona	22
C Tevez	Juventus	20
G Higuain	Napoli	18
J Menez	Milan	16

Over 2.5 goals top five

	H	A	%
Lazio	14	10	63%
Cagliari	14	9	61%
Hellas Verona	12	11	61%
Napoli	14	9	61%
Palermo	12	10	58%

Both to score top five

	H	A	%
Hellas Verona	13	12	66%
Milan	11	14	66%
Genoa	11	14	66%
Cagliari	14	10	63%
Palermo	14	10	63%
Sassuolo	12	12	63%

AUGSBURG

SGL arena www.fcaugsburg.de

	2014-15		Last six seasons at home							
	H	A	P	W	D	L	OV	UN	BS	CS
B Munich	L	W	4	1	0	3	2	2	1	1
Wolfsburg	W	L	4	2	1	1	1	3	1	3
B M'gladbach	W	W	4	2	2	0	2	2	3	1
Leverkusen	D	L	4	0	1	3	4	0	4	0
Augsburg										
Schalke	D	L	4	0	3	1	1	3	2	2
Dortmund	L	W	4	0	1	3	3	1	2	1
Hoffenheim	W	L	4	3	0	1	2	2	2	1
E Frankfurt	D	W	4	2	1	0	2	1	2	1
Werder Bremen	W	L	4	3	1	0	3	1	4	0
Mainz	L	L	4	2	1	1	2	2	3	0
Cologne	D	W	2	1	1	0	1	1	1	1
Hannover	L	L	4	0	2	2	1	3	2	1
Stuttgart	W	W	4	3	0	1	4	0	3	1
Hertha	W	L	4	2	2	0	1	3	1	3
Hamburg	W	L	4	3	0	1	2	2	2	1
Ingolstadt			1	1	0	0	0	1	0	1
Darmstadt			-	-	-	-	-	-	-	-

Season	Division	Pos	P	W	D	L	F	A	GD	Pts
2014-15	Bundesliga	5	34	15	4	15	43	43	0	49
2013-14	Bundesliga	8	34	15	7	12	47	47	0	52
2012-13	Bundesliga	15	34	8	9	17	33	51	-18	33

Over/Under 50%/50% 9th   **Both score** 44%/56% 12th

BAYERN MUNICH

Allianz Arena www.fcbayern.de

	2014-15		Last six seasons at home							
	H	A	P	W	D	L	OV	UN	BS	CS
B Munich										
Wolfsburg	W	L	6	6	0	0	4	2	2	4
B M'gladbach	L	D	6	3	1	2	2	4	3	1
Leverkusen	W	L	6	4	1	1	4	2	4	2
Augsburg	L	W	4	3	0	1	3	1	1	2
Schalke	D	D	6	4	2	0	3	3	4	2
Dortmund	W	W	6	2	1	3	4	2	4	0
Hoffenheim	W	W	6	5	1	0	4	2	2	4
E Frankfurt	W	W	5	5	0	0	4	1	2	3
Werder Bremen	W	W	6	4	2	0	4	2	1	2
Mainz	W	W	6	4	1	1	4	2	3	3
Cologne	W	W	4	2	2	0	2	2	1	3
Hannover	W	W	6	6	0	0	5	1	1	5
Stuttgart	W	W	6	5	1	0	4	2	3	3
Hertha	W	W	4	4	0	0	3	1	2	2
Hamburg	W	D	6	6	0	0	5	1	2	4
Ingolstadt			-	-	-	-	-	-	-	-
Darmstadt			-	-	-	-	-	-	-	-

Season	Division	Pos	P	W	D	L	F	A	GD	Pts
2014-15	Bundesliga	1	34	25	4	5	80	18	+62	79
2013-14	Bundesliga	1	34	29	3	2	94	23	+71	90
2012-13	Bundesliga	1	34	29	4	1	98	18	+80	91

Over/Under 50%/50% 9th   **Both score** 26%/74% 18th

COLOGNE

RheinEnergieStadion www.fc-koeln.de

	2014-15		Last six seasons at home							
	H	A	P	W	D	L	OV	UN	BS	CS
B Munich	L	L	4	1	1	2	2	2	3	0
Wolfsburg	D	L	4	0	2	2	3	1	3	0
B M'gladbach	D	L	4	0	2	2	2	2	1	1
Leverkusen	D	L	4	1	1	2	0	4	1	1
Augsburg	L	D	2	1	0	1	2	0	1	1
Schalke	W	W	4	2	0	2	3	1	3	1
Dortmund	W	D	4	1	0	3	4	0	4	0
Hoffenheim	W	W	4	2	1	1	2	2	2	1
E Frankfurt	W	L	3	2	1	0	1	2	1	2
Werder Bremen	D	W	4	1	3	0	1	3	2	2
Mainz	D	L	4	2	2	0	1	3	2	2
Cologne										
Hannover	D	L	4	2	1	1	1	3	1	2
Stuttgart	D	W	4	0	2	2	2	2	3	1
Hertha	L	D	4	1	0	3	3	1	2	1
Hamburg	D	W	4	1	2	2	1	2	2	2
Ingolstadt			2	1	0	1	0	2	0	1
Darmstadt			-	-	-	-	-	-	-	-

Season	Division	Pos	P	W	D	L	F	A	GD	Pts
2014-15	Bundesliga	12	34	9	13	12	34	41	-7	40
2013-14	2.Bundesliga	1	34	19	11	4	53	20	+33	68
2012-13	2.Bundesliga	5	34	14	12	8	43	33	+10	54

Over/Under 35%/65% 18th   **Both score** 44%/56% 12th

Darmstadt narrowly escaped relegation from the third tier two years ago – now they're back in the Bundesliga

DARMSTADT

Merck-Stadion am Bollenfalltor — www.sv98.de

	2014-15 H	A	Last six seasons at home P	W	D	L	OV	UN	BS	CS
B Munich			-	-	-	-	-	-	-	-
Wolfsburg			-	-	-	-	-	-	-	-
B M'gladbach			-	-	-	-	-	-	-	-
Leverkusen			-	-	-	-	-	-	-	-
Augsburg			-	-	-	-	-	-	-	-
Schalke			-	-	-	-	-	-	-	-
Dortmund			-	-	-	-	-	-	-	-
Hoffenheim			-	-	-	-	-	-	-	-
E Frankfurt			-	-	-	-	-	-	-	-
Werder Bremen			-	-	-	-	-	-	-	-
Mainz			-	-	-	-	-	-	-	-
Cologne			-	-	-	-	-	-	-	-
Hannover			-	-	-	-	-	-	-	-
Stuttgart			-	-	-	-	-	-	-	-
Hertha			-	-	-	-	-	-	-	-
Hamburg			-	-	-	-	-	-	-	-
Ingolstadt	D	D	1	0	1	0	1	0	1	0
Darmstadt										

Season	Division	Pos	P	W	D	L	F	A	GD	Pts
2014-15	2.Bundesliga	2	34	15	14	5	44	26	+18	59
2013-14	3.Liga	3	38	21	9	8	58	29	+29	72
2012-13	3.Liga	18	38	8	14	16	32	46	-14	38

Over/Under 26%/74% 23rd **Both score** 41%/59% 18th

DORTMUND

Westfalenstadion — www.bvb.de

	2014-15 H	A	Last six seasons at home P	W	D	L	OV	UN	BS	CS
B Munich	L	L	6	2	1	3	2	4	2	2
Wolfsburg	D	L	6	3	2	1	4	2	5	1
B M'gladbach	W	L	6	5	0	1	4	2	2	4
Leverkusen	L	D	6	3	0	3	2	4	0	3
Augsburg	L	W	4	2	1	1	3	1	2	1
Schalke	W	L	6	2	2	2	4	1	4	
Dortmund										
Hoffenheim	W	D	6	3	2	1	3	3	5	1
E Frankfurt	L	L	5	4	0	1	4	1	2	3
Werder Bremen	W	L	6	6	0	0	3	3	3	3
Mainz	W	L	6	4	2	0	3	3	4	2
Cologne	D	L	4	3	1	0	1	3	0	4
Hannover	L	W	6	5	0	1	4	2	4	1
Stuttgart	D	W	6	1	5	0	3	3	5	1
Hertha	W	L	4	2	0	2	2	2	2	2
Hamburg	L	D	6	4	0	2	3	3	3	2
Ingolstadt			-	-	-	-	-	-	-	-
Darmstadt			-	-	-	-	-	-	-	-

Season	Division	Pos	P	W	D	L	F	A	GD	Pts
2014-15	Bundesliga	7	34	13	7	14	47	42	+5	46
2013-14	Bundesliga	2	34	22	5	7	80	38	+42	71
2012-13	Bundesliga	2	34	19	9	6	81	42	+39	66

Over/Under 53%/47% 6th **Both score** 47%/53% 9th

EINTRACHT FRANKFURT

Commerzbank-Arena — www.eintracht.de

	2014-15 H	A	Last six seasons at home P	W	D	L	OV	UN	BS	CS
B Munich	L	L	5	1	1	3	2	3	2	0
Wolfsburg	D	D	5	1	3	1	4	1	5	0
B M'gladbach	D	W	5	1	1	3	1	4	1	2
Leverkusen	W	D	5	3	0	2	4	1	3	0
Augsburg	L	D	3	1	1	1	1	2	2	0
Schalke	W	D	5	2	2	1	2	3	2	3
Dortmund	W	L	5	2	2	1	2	3	3	2
Hoffenheim	W	L	5	2	0	3	5	0	4	0
E Frankfurt										
Werder Bremen	W	L	5	3	2	0	2	3	3	2
Mainz	D	L	5	3	1	1	3	2	3	2
Cologne	W	L	3	1	0	2	2	1	2	0
Hannover	D	L	5	2	1	2	5	0	4	0
Stuttgart	L	L	5	1	0	4	4	1	3	0
Hertha	D	D	3	1	2	0	2	1	2	1
Hamburg	W	W	5	2	1	4	4	1	5	0
Ingolstadt			1	0	1	0	0	1	1	0
Darmstadt			-	-	-	-	-	-	-	-

Season	Division	Pos	P	W	D	L	F	A	GD	Pts
2014-15	Bundesliga	9	34	11	10	13	56	62	-6	43
2013-14	Bundesliga	13	34	9	9	16	40	57	-17	36
2012-13	Bundesliga	6	34	14	9	11	49	46	+3	51

Over/Under 68%/32% 1st **Both score** 65%/35% 2nd

HAMBURG

Volksparkstadion — www.hsv.de

	2014-15 H	A	Last six seasons at home P	W	D	L	OV	UN	BS	CS
B Munich	D	L	6	1	3	2	2	4	2	3
Wolfsburg	L	L	6	0	3	3	2	4	5	0
B M'gladbach	D	L	6	1	2	3	1	5	3	1
Leverkusen	W	L	6	2	2	2	2	4	3	2
Augsburg	W	L	4	1	1	2	1	3	2	0
Schalke	W	D	6	3	1	2	5	1	4	1
Dortmund	D	W	6	3	2	1	4	2	4	2
Hoffenheim	D	L	6	3	2	1	2	4	3	3
E Frankfurt	L	L	5	1	2	2	1	4	2	2
Werder Bremen	W	L	6	4	0	2	4	2	3	2
Mainz	W	W	6	2	1	3	3	3	3	2
Cologne	L	D	4	2	0	2	3	1	3	0
Hannover	W	L	6	4	2	0	2	4	2	4
Stuttgart	L	L	6	2	1	3	4	2	3	0
Hertha	L	L	4	1	1	2	2	2	1	1
Hamburg										
Ingolstadt			-	-	-	-	-	-	-	-
Darmstadt			-	-	-	-	-	-	-	-

Season	Division	Pos	P	W	D	L	F	A	GD	Pts
2014-15	Bundesliga	16	34	9	8	17	25	50	-25	35
2013-14	Bundesliga	16	34	7	6	21	51	75	-24	27
2012-13	Bundesliga	7	34	14	6	14	42	53	-11	48

Over/Under 41%/59% 16th **Both score** 32%/68% 17th

HANNOVER

Hannover 96

AWD-Arena — www.hannover96.de

	2014-15 H	A	Last six seasons at home P	W	D	L	OV	UN	BS	CS
B Munich	L	L	6	2	0	4	6	0	4	0
Wolfsburg	L	D	6	4	0	2	4	2	4	3
B M'gladbach	L	L	6	3	0	3	5	1	4	0
Leverkusen	L	L	6	1	4	1	3	3	4	2
Augsburg	W	W	4	3	1	0	2	2	2	2
Schalke	W	L	6	3	2	1	5	1	5	0
Dortmund	L	W	6	1	2	3	4	2	4	0
Hoffenheim	L	L	6	3	0	3	3	3	3	2
E Frankfurt	W	D	5	4	1	0	2	3	2	3
Werder Bremen	D	D	6	3	1	2	5	1	6	0
Mainz	D	D	6	2	4	0	2	4	5	1
Cologne	D	D	4	3	0	1	3	1	3	1
Hannover										
Stuttgart	D	L	6	3	3	0	2	4	3	3
Hertha	D	W	4	0	3	1	1	3	3	0
Hamburg	W	L	6	4	2	0	4	2	5	1
Ingolstadt			-	-	-	-	-	-	-	-
Darmstadt			-	-	-	-	-	-	-	-

Season	Division	Pos	P	W	D	L	F	A	GD	Pts
2014-15	Bundesliga	13	34	9	10	15	40	56	-16	37
2013-14	Bundesliga	10	34	12	6	16	46	59	-13	42
2012-13	Bundesliga	9	34	13	6	15	60	62	-2	45

Over/Under 53%/47% 6th **Both score** 59%/41% 4th

HERTHA BERLIN

Olympiastadion — www.herthabsc.de

	2014-15 H	A	Last six seasons at home P	W	D	L	OV	UN	BS	CS
B Munich	L	L	4	0	0	4	3	1	2	0
Wolfsburg	W	L	4	1	1	2	2	2	2	2
B M'gladbach	L	L	4	1	1	2	2	2	2	2
Leverkusen	L	L	4	0	2	2	2	2	2	0
Augsburg	W	L	4	2	2	0	2	2	2	2
Schalke	D	L	4	0	1	3	2	2	2	0
Dortmund	W	L	4	1	1	2	1	3	0	2
Hoffenheim	L	L	4	1	1	2	2	2	2	0
E Frankfurt	D	D	3	1	1	1	2	1	2	1
Werder Bremen	D	L	4	2	1	1	3	1	3	1
Mainz	L	W	4	1	2	1	2	2	3	1
Cologne	D	W	4	1	2	1	1	3	1	2
Hannover	L	D	4	1	0	3	1	3	0	1
Stuttgart	W	D	4	2	0	2	1	3	1	1
Hertha										
Hamburg	W	W	4	2	0	2	3	1	2	2
Ingolstadt			2	1	1	0	1	1	1	1
Darmstadt			-	-	-	-	-	-	-	-

Season	Division	Pos	P	W	D	L	F	A	GD	Pts
2014-15	Bundesliga	15	34	9	8	17	36	52	-16	35
2013-14	Bundesliga	11	34	11	8	15	40	48	-8	41
2012-13	2.Bundesliga	1	34	22	10	2	65	28	+37	76

Over/Under 44%/56% 13th **Both score** 41%/59% 16th

HOFFENHEIM

Rhein-Neckar Arena — www.achtzehn99.de

	2014-15 H	A	Last six seasons at home P	W	D	L	OV	UN	BS	CS
B Munich	L	L	6	0	2	4	2	4	3	1
Wolfsburg	D	L	6	2	1	3	5	1	6	0
B M'gladbach	L	L	6	3	2	1	4	2	4	2
Leverkusen	L	L	6	0	1	5	4	2	3	0
Augsburg	W	L	4	2	2	0	1	3	1	3
Schalke	W	L	6	3	3	0	3	3	4	2
Dortmund	D	L	6	2	2	2	3	3	4	2
Hoffenheim										
E Frankfurt	W	L	5	2	2	1	2	3	2	2
Werder Bremen	L	D	6	1	1	4	5	1	5	0
Mainz	W	D	6	1	2	3	2	4	3	2
Cologne	L	L	4	0	2	2	1	3	3	2
Hannover	W	W	6	5	1	0	5	1	4	2
Stuttgart	W	W	6	2	1	3	4	2	5	0
Hertha	W	W	4	2	1	1	3	1	4	0
Hamburg	W	D	6	4	1	1	5	1	2	4
Ingolstadt			-	-	-	-	-	-	-	-
Darmstadt			-	-	-	-	-	-	-	-

Season	Division	Pos	P	W	D	L	F	A	GD	Pts
2014-15	Bundesliga	8	34	12	8	14	49	55	-6	44
2013-14	Bundesliga	9	34	11	11	12	72	70	+2	44
2012-13	Bundesliga	16	34	8	7	19	42	67	-25	31

Over/Under 56%/44% 5th **Both score** 59%/41% 4th

GERMAN BUNDESLIGA

INGOLSTADT

Audi-Sportpark www.fcingolstadt.de

	2014-15		Last six seasons at home							
	H	A	P	W	D	L	OV	UN	BS	CS
B Munich			-	-	-	-	-	-	-	-
Wolfsburg			-	-	-	-	-	-	-	-
B M'gladbach			-	-	-	-	-	-	-	-
Leverkusen			-	-	-	-	-	-	-	-
Augsburg			1	0	0	1	1	0	1	0
Schalke			-	-	-	-	-	-	-	-
Dortmund			-	-	-	-	-	-	-	-
Hoffenheim			-	-	-	-	-	-	-	-
E Frankfurt			1	0	1	0	0	1	1	0
Werder Bremen			-	-	-	-	-	-	-	-
Mainz			-	-	-	-	-	-	-	-
Cologne			2	0	1	1	1	1	1	0
Hannover			-	-	-	-	-	-	-	-
Stuttgart			-	-	-	-	-	-	-	-
Hertha			2	0	2	0	0	2	2	0
Hamburg			-	-	-	-	-	-	-	-
Ingolstadt										
Darmstadt	D	D	1	0	1	0	1	0	1	0

Season	Division	Pos	P	W	D	L	F	A	GD	Pts
2014-15	2.Bundesliga	1	34	17	13	4	53	32	+21	64
2013-14	2.Bundesliga	10	34	11	11	12	34	33	+1	44
2012-13	2.Bundesliga	13	34	10	12	12	36	43	-7	42

Over/Under 44%/56% 14th **Both score** 56%/44% 8th

LEVERKUSEN

BayArena www.bayer04.de

	2014-15		Last six seasons at home							
	H	A	P	W	D	L	OV	UN	BS	CS
B Munich	W	L	6	2	3	1	1	5	4	2
Wolfsburg	L	L	6	4	1	1	5	1	5	1
B M'gladbach	D	L	6	2	2	2	4	2	6	0
Leverkusen										
Augsburg	W	D	4	4	0	0	3	1	3	1
Schalke	W	W	6	3	0	3	1	5	1	3
Dortmund	D	W	6	0	4	2	3	3	4	2
Hoffenheim	W	W	6	5	0	1	3	3	2	4
E Frankfurt	D	L	5	3	1	1	3	2	3	1
Werder Bremen	D	L	6	3	3	0	3	3	3	3
Mainz	D	W	6	2	2	2	3	3	3	1
Cologne	W	D	4	2	1	1	3	1	3	1
Hannover	W	W	6	6	0	0	3	3	1	5
Stuttgart	W	D	6	5	1	0	6	0	4	2
Hertha	W	W	4	2	2	0	3	1	4	0
Hamburg	W	L	6	4	2	0	5	1	4	2
Ingolstadt			-	-	-	-	-	-	-	-
Darmstadt			-	-	-	-	-	-	-	-

Season	Division	Pos	P	W	D	L	F	A	GD	Pts
2014-15	Bundesliga	4	34	17	10	7	62	37	+25	61
2013-14	Bundesliga	4	34	19	4	11	60	41	+19	61
2012-13	Bundesliga	3	34	19	8	7	65	39	+26	65

Over/Under 50%/50% 9th **Both score** 44%/56% 12th

MAINZ

Coface Arena www.mainz05.de

	2014-15		Last six seasons at home							
	H	A	P	W	D	L	OV	UN	BS	CS
B Munich	L	L	6	2	0	4	5	1	4	0
Wolfsburg	D	L	6	1	3	2	0	6	2	2
B M'gladbach	D	D	6	2	2	2	3	3	2	3
Leverkusen	L	D	6	2	1	3	3	3	3	2
Augsburg	W	W	4	3	0	1	2	2	1	2
Schalke	L		6	1	2	3	2	4	2	2
Dortmund	W	L	6	2	0	4	3	3	3	2
Hoffenheim	D	L	6	3	2	1	5	1	3	2
E Frankfurt	W	D	5	3	2	0	3	2	2	3
Werder Bremen	L	D	6	1	2	3	4	2	5	1
Mainz										
Cologne	W	D	4	4	0	0	1	3	0	4
Hannover	D	D	6	3	2	1	1	5	2	3
Stuttgart	D	L	6	4	2	0	3	3	5	1
Hertha	L	W	4	1	1	2	2	2	3	0
Hamburg	L	L	6	1	2	3	3	4	4	1
Ingolstadt			-	-	-	-	-	-	-	-
Darmstadt			-	-	-	-	-	-	-	-

Season	Division	Pos	P	W	D	L	F	A	GD	Pts
2014-15	Bundesliga	11	34	9	13	12	45	47	-2	40
2013-14	Bundesliga	7	34	16	5	13	52	54	-2	53
2012-13	Bundesliga	13	34	10	12	12	42	44	-2	42

Over/Under 50%/50% 9th **Both score** 56%/44% 6th

MONCHENGLADBACH

Borussia-Park www.borussia.de

	2014-15		Last six seasons at home							
	H	A	P	W	D	L	OV	UN	BS	CS
B Munich	D	W	6	1	3	2	3	3	4	1
Wolfsburg	W	L	6	3	2	1	3	3	3	2
B M'gladbach										
Leverkusen	W	D	6	1	3	2	4	2	4	1
Augsburg	L	L	4	1	1	2	2	2	2	2
Schalke	W	L	6	5	0	1	4	2	3	2
Dortmund	W	L	6	3	2	1	1	5	3	2
Hoffenheim	W	W	6	3	1	2	5	1	5	1
E Frankfurt	L	D	5	3	0	2	3	2	2	2
Werder Bremen	W	W	6	4	1	1	5	1	5	1
Mainz	D	D	4	1	1	2	4	3	3	3
Cologne	D	D	4	3	1	0	2	2	1	3
Hannover	W	W	6	5	0	1	4	2	3	3
Stuttgart	D	L	6	0	4	2	2	4	5	1
Hertha	W	W	4	3	1	0	3	1	2	2
Hamburg	W	D	6	3	2	1	3	4	4	2
Ingolstadt			-	-	-	-	-	-	-	-
Darmstadt			-	-	-	-	-	-	-	-

Season	Division	Pos	P	W	D	L	F	A	GD	Pts
2014-15	Bundesliga	3	34	19	9	6	53	26	+27	66
2013-14	Bundesliga	6	34	16	11	7	59	43	+16	55
2012-13	Bundesliga	8	34	12	11	11	45	49	-4	47

Over/Under 41%/59% 16th **Both score** 47%/53% 9th

SCHALKE 04

Veltins-Arena www.schalke04.de

	2014-15 H	A	Last six seasons at home P	W	D	L	OV	UN	BS	CS
B Munich	D	D	6	1	1	4	2	4	2	1
Wolfsburg	W	D	6	5	0	1	5	1	3	3
B M'gladbach	W	L	6	3	2	1	2	4	3	2
Leverkusen	L	L	6	2	2	2	2	4	3	2
Augsburg	W	D	4	4	0	0	3	1	3	1
Schalke										
Dortmund	W	L	6	3	0	3	6	0	6	0
Hoffenheim	W	L	6	5	0	1	4	2	2	3
E Frankfurt	D	L	5	3	2	0	2	3	3	2
Werder Bremen	D	W	6	4	1	1	4	2	3	2
Mainz	W	L	6	3	2	1	3	3	3	3
Cologne	L	L	4	3	0	1	3	1	2	2
Hannover	W	L	6	4	1	1	4	3	2	4
Stuttgart	W	W	6	4	1	1	6	0	5	1
Hertha	W	D	4	4	0	0	1	3	0	4
Hamburg	D	L	6	2	3	1	4	2	4	1
Ingolstadt			-	-	-	-	-	-	-	-
Darmstadt			-	-	-	-	-	-	-	-

Season	Division	Pos	P	W	D	L	F	A	GD	Pts
2014-15	Bundesliga	6	34	13	9	12	42	40	+2	48
2013-14	Bundesliga	3	34	19	7	8	63	43	+20	64
2012-13	Bundesliga	4	34	16	7	11	58	50	+8	55

Over/Under 44%/56% 13th   **Both score** 47%/53% 9th

STUTTGART

Mercedes-Benz Arena www.vfb.de

	2014-15 H	A	Last six seasons at home P	W	D	L	OV	UN	BS	CS
B Munich	L	L	6	0	1	5	3	3	3	1
Wolfsburg	L	L	6	2	1	3	4	2	4	0
B M'gladbach	L	D	6	3	0	3	3	3	1	2
Leverkusen	D	L	6	1	2	3	4	2	4	0
Augsburg	L	L	4	2	0	2	3	1	3	0
Schalke	L	L	6	4	0	2	5	1	3	2
Dortmund	L	D	6	1	1	4	5	1	6	0
Hoffenheim	L	L	6	3	1	2	3	3	3	1
E Frankfurt	W	W	5	3	1	1	4	1	5	0
Werder Bremen	W	L	6	3	1	2	4	2	4	1
Mainz	W	D	6	3	2	1	4	2	4	2
Cologne	L	D	4	0	1	3	1	3	1	0
Hannover	W	D	6	5	0	1	4	2	3	3
Stuttgart										
Hertha	D	L	4	1	2	1	2	2	2	2
Hamburg	W	W	6	3	0	3	4	2	3	2
Ingolstadt			-	-	-	-	-	-	-	-
Darmstadt			-	-	-	-	-	-	-	-

Season	Division	Pos	P	W	D	L	F	A	GD	Pts
2014-15	Bundesliga	14	34	9	9	16	42	60	-18	36
2013-14	Bundesliga	15	34	8	8	18	49	62	-13	32
2012-13	Bundesliga	12	34	12	7	15	37	55	-18	43

Over/Under 53%/47% 6th   **Both score** 53%/47% 7th

WERDER BREMEN

Weserstadion www.werder.de

	2014-15 H	A	Last six seasons at home P	W	D	L	OV	UN	BS	CS
B Munich	L	L	6	0	0	6	5	1	3	0
Wolfsburg	L	L	6	1	1	4	5	1	4	0
B M'gladbach	L	L	6	2	3	1	3	3	3	2
Leverkusen	W	D	6	2	3	1	4	2	5	1
Augsburg	W	L	4	2	1	1	1	3	2	1
Schalke	L	L	6	0	2	4	2	4	3	0
Dortmund	W	L	6	2	1	3	3	3	3	1
Hoffenheim	D	W	6	3	3	0	3	3	5	1
E Frankfurt	W	L	5	1	2	2	2	3	2	2
Werder Bremen										
Mainz	D	W	6	2	1	3	4	2	2	2
Cologne	L	D	4	3	0	1	2	2	2	1
Hannover	D	D	6	3	3	0	3	3	3	3
Stuttgart	W	L	6	2	4	0	2	4	4	2
Hertha	W	D	4	4	0	0	2	2	2	2
Hamburg	W	L	6	5	1	0	1	5	2	4
Ingolstadt			-	-	-	-	-	-	-	-
Darmstadt			-	-	-	-	-	-	-	-

Season	Division	Pos	P	W	D	L	F	A	GD	Pts
2014-15	Bundesliga	10	34	11	10	13	50	65	-15	43
2013-14	Bundesliga	12	34	10	9	15	42	66	-24	39
2012-13	Bundesliga	14	34	8	10	16	50	66	-16	34

Over/Under 59%/41% 4th   **Both score** 62%/38% 3rd

WOLFSBURG

Volkswagen Arena www.vfl-wolfsburg.de

	2014-15 H	A	Last six seasons at home P	W	D	L	OV	UN	BS	CS
B Munich	W	L	6	1	1	4	3	3	4	0
Wolfsburg										
B M'gladbach	W	L	6	5	1	0	4	2	4	2
Leverkusen	W	W	6	4	0	2	6	0	6	0
Augsburg	W	L	4	1	2	1	1	3	3	1
Schalke	D	L	6	3	2	1	5	1	5	1
Dortmund	W	D	6	2	1	3	6	0	5	0
Hoffenheim	W	D	6	3	2	1	6	0	4	2
E Frankfurt	D	D	5	2	2	1	3	2	4	0
Werder Bremen	W	W	6	3	2	1	4	2	4	2
Mainz	D	D	6	2	2	2	5	1	3	2
Cologne	W	D	4	3	0	1	3	1	3	1
Hannover	D	W	6	3	1	2	5	1	4	1
Stuttgart	W	W	6	6	0	0	2	4	2	4
Hertha	W	L	4	2	0	2	3	1	3	1
Hamburg	W	W	6	2	2	2	4	2	4	1
Ingolstadt			-	-	-	-	-	-	-	-
Darmstadt			-	-	-	-	-	-	-	-

Season	Division	Pos	P	W	D	L	F	A	GD	Pts
2014-15	Bundesliga	2	34	20	9	5	73	38	+35	69
2013-14	Bundesliga	5	34	18	6	10	63	43	+13	60
2012-13	Bundesliga	11	34	10	13	11	47	52	-5	43

Over/Under 65%/35% 3rd   **Both score** 68%/32% 1st

GERMAN BUNDESLIGA

Bundesliga 2014-15

Pos	H	A		P	Home					Away					GD	Pts
					W	D	L	F	A	W	D	L	F	A		
1	1	1	Bayern Munich	34	14	1	2	46	+7	11	3	3	34	11	+62	79
2	2	3	Wolfsburg	34	13	4	0	38	+13	7	5	5	34	25	+34	69
3	3	2	B M'gladbach	34	12	3	2	32	+14	7	6	4	21	12	+27	66
4	4	4	Leverkusen	34	10	6	1	39	+15	7	4	6	23	22	+25	61
5	7	6	Augsburg	34	9	4	4	28	+21	6	0	11	15	22	0	49
6	5	13	Schalke	34	10	5	2	26	+14	3	4	10	16	26	+2	48
7	8	8	Dortmund	34	9	3	5	26	+15	4	4	9	21	27	+5	46
8	9	12	Hoffenheim	34	9	3	5	31	+26	3	5	9	18	29	-6	44
9	6	18	E Frankfurt	34	9	5	3	36	+26	2	5	10	20	36	-6	43
10	10	11	Werder Bremen	34	8	4	5	25	+24	3	6	8	25	41	-15	43
11	11	9	Mainz	34	6	6	5	27	+19	3	7	7	18	28	-2	40
12	15	5	Cologne	34	4	9	4	18	+17	5	4	8	16	23	-6	40
13	13	10	Hannover	34	6	4	7	21	25	3	6	8	19	31	-16	37
14	17	7	Stuttgart	34	5	4	8	18	28	4	5	8	24	32	-18	36
15	14	15	Hertha Berlin	34	6	4	7	17	22	3	4	10	19	30	-16	35
16	12	17	Hamburg	34	6	5	6	16	18	3	3	11	9	32	-25	35
17	16	14	Freiburg	34	5	6	6	21	22	2	7	8	15	25	-11	34
18	18	16	Paderborn	34	4	6	7	21	31	3	4	10	10	34	-34	31

Results 2014-15

	Augsburg	Bayern Munich	Cologne	Dortmund	E Frankfurt	Freiburg	Hamburg	Hannover	Hertha Berlin	Hoffenheim	Leverkusen	Mainz	B M'gladbach	Paderborn	Schalke	Stuttgart	Werder Bremen	Wolfsburg
Augsburg		0-4	0-0	2-3	2-2	2-0	3-1	1-2	1-0	3-1	2-2	0-2	2-1	3-0	0-0	2-1	4-2	1-0
Bayern Munich	0-1		4-1	2-1	3-0	2-0	8-0	4-0	1-0	4-0	1-0	2-0	0-2	4-0	1-1	2-0	6-0	2-1
Cologne	1-2	0-2		2-1	4-2	0-1	0-0	1-1	1-2	3-2	1-1	0-0	0-0	0-0	2-0	0-0	1-1	2-2
Dortmund	0-1	0-1	0-0		2-0	3-1	0-1	0-1	2-0	1-0	0-2	4-2	1-0	3-0	3-0	2-2	3-2	2-2
E Frankfurt	0-1	0-4	3-2	2-0		1-0	2-1	2-2	4-4	3-1	2-1	2-2	0-0	4-0	1-0	4-5	5-2	1-1
Freiburg	2-0	2-1	1-0	0-3	4-1		0-0	2-2	2-2	1-1	0-0	2-3	0-0	1-2	2-0	1-4	0-1	1-2
Hamburg	3-2	0-0	0-0	1-2	1-1	2-1		1-1	1-1	0-1	1-1	0-3	2-0	0-1	2-0	0-2	0-0	0-2
Hannover	2-0	1-3	1-0	2-3	1-0	2-1	2-0		1-1	1-2	1-3	1-1	0-3	1-2	2-1	1-1	1-1	1-3
Hertha Berlin	1-0	0-1	0-0	1-0	0-0	0-2	3-0	0-2		0-5	0-1	1-3	1-2	2-0	2-2	3-2	2-2	1-0
Hoffenheim	2-0	0-2	3-4	1-1	3-2	3-3	3-0	4-3	2-1		0-1	2-0	1-4	1-0	2-1	2-1	1-2	1-1
Leverkusen	1-0	2-0	5-1	0-0	1-1	1-0	4-0	4-0	4-2	2-0		0-0	1-1	2-2	1-0	4-0	3-3	4-5
Mainz	2-1	1-2	2-0	2-0	3-1	2-2	1-2	0-0	0-2	0-0	2-3		2-2	5-0	2-0	1-1	1-2	1-1
B M'gladbach	1-3	0-0	1-0	3-1	1-3	1-0	1-0	2-0	3-2	3-1	3-0	1-1		2-0	4-1	1-1	4-1	1-0
Paderborn	2-1	0-6	0-2	2-2	3-1	1-0	0-3	2-0	3-1	0-0	0-3	2-2	1-2		1-2	1-2	2-1	3-1
Schalke	1-0	1-1	1-2	2-1	2-2	0-0	0-0	1-0	2-0	3-1	0-1	4-1	1-0	1-0		3-2	1-1	3-2
Stuttgart	0-1	0-2	0-2	2-3	3-1	2-2	2-1	1-0	0-0	0-2	3-3	2-0	0-1	0-0	0-4		3-2	0-4
Werder Bremen	3-2	0-4	0-1	2-1	1-0	1-1	1-0	3-3	2-0	1-1	2-1	0-0	0-2	4-0	0-3	2-0		3-5
Wolfsburg	1-0	4-1	2-1	2-1	2-2	3-0	2-0	2-2	2-1	3-0	4-1	3-0	1-0	1-1	1-1	3-1	2-1	

Top scorers

	Team	Goals scored
A Meier	E Frankfurt	19
R Lewandowski	B Munich	17
A Robben	B Munich	17
P Aubameyang	Dortmund	16
B Dost	Wolfsburg	16

Over 2.5 goals top five

	H	A	%
E Frankfurt	11	12	68%
Paderborn	13	10	68%
Wolfsburg	12	10	65%
Werder Bremen	8	12	59%
Hoffenheim	10	9	56%

Both to score top five

	H	A	%
Wolfsburg	11	12	68%
E Frankfurt	10	12	65%
Werder Bremen	7	14	62%
Hoffenheim	11	9	59%
Hannover	12	8	59%

ATHLETIC BILBAO

San Mames   www.athletic-club.net

	2014-15 H	A	P	W	D	L	OV	UN	BS	CS
Barcelona	L	L	6	1	3	2	4	2	5	1
Real Madrid	W	L	6	2	1	3	3	3	1	2
Atl Madrid	L	D	6	3	0	3	5	1	3	3
Valencia	D	D	6	1	2	3	3	3	4	1
Sevilla	W	L	6	5	0	1	3	3	2	3
Villarreal	W	L	5	3	1	1	2	3	2	2
Ath Bilbao										
Celta	D	W	3	2	1	0	1	2	2	1
Malaga	D	L	6	2	4	0	2	4	3	3
Espanyol	W	L	6	3	1	2	5	1	4	1
Vallecano	W	L	4	2	1	1	2	2	3	1
Sociedad	D	D	5	2	2	1	2	3	4	1
Elche	L	W	2	0	1	1	2	0	2	0
Levante	W	W	5	4	0	1	4	1	2	2
Getafe	W	W	6	3	2	1	4	2	2	4
Deportivo	D	L	4	1	2	1	1	3	3	1
Granada	L	D	4	2	0	2	1	3	0	2
Betis			3	1	0	2	3	0	3	0
Sp Gijon			3	1	1	1	2	1	2	1
Las Palmas			-	-	-	-	-	-	-	-

Season	Division	Pos	P	W	D	L	F	A	GD	Pts
2014-15	Primera Liga	7	38	15	10	13	42	41	+1	55
2013-14	Primera Liga	8	38	20	10	8	66	39	+27	70
2012-13	Primera Liga	12	38	12	9	17	44	65	-21	45

Over/Under 34%/66% 19th **Both score** 39%/61% 17th

ATLETICO MADRID

Vicente Calderon   www.clubatleticodemadrid.com

	2014-15 H	A	P	W	D	L	OV	UN	BS	CS
Barcelona	L	L	6	1	1	4	4	2	4	1
Real Madrid	W	W	6	1	1	4	6	0	5	1
Atl Madrid										
Valencia	D	L	6	2	3	1	3	3	4	2
Sevilla	W	D	6	3	3	0	4	2	3	3
Villarreal	L	W	5	3	0	2	3	2	2	2
Celta	D	L	3	2	1	0	2	1	2	1
Malaga	W	D	6	3	1	2	4	2	4	0
Espanyol	W	D	6	5	0	1	3	3	2	4
Vallecano	W	W	4	4	0	0	4	0	3	1
Sociedad	W	L	5	3	1	1	2	3	1	3
Elche	W	W	2	2	0	0	1	1	0	2
Levante	W	D	5	5	0	0	4	1	4	1
Getafe	W	W	6	5	0	1	3	3	0	5
Deportivo	W	W	4	4	0	0	2	2	0	4
Granada	W	D	4	4	0	0	1	3	0	4
Betis			3	2	0	1		2	0	2
Sp Gijon			3	3	0	0	3	0	1	2
Las Palmas			-	-	-	-	-	-	-	-

Season	Division	Pos	P	W	D	L	F	A	GD	Pts
2014-15	Primera Liga	3	38	23	9	6	67	29	+38	78
2013-14	Primera Liga	1	38	28	6	4	77	26	+51	90
2012-13	Primera Liga	3	38	23	7	8	65	31	+34	76

Over/Under 50%/50% 8th **Both score** 42%/58% 13th

BARCELONA

Camp Nou   www.fcbarcelona.cat

	2014-15 H	A	P	W	D	L	OV	UN	BS	CS
Barcelona										
Real Madrid	W	L	6	4	1	1	5	1	4	2
Atl Madrid	W	W	6	5	1	0	5	1	4	2
Valencia	W	W	6	5	0	1	4	2	3	3
Sevilla	W	D	6	5	1	0	5	1	3	3
Villarreal	W	W	5	4	1	0	4	1	4	1
Ath Bilbao	W	W	6	6	0	0	4	2	4	2
Celta	L	W	3	2	0	1	2	1	1	1
Malaga	L	D	6	5	0	1	5	1	4	1
Espanyol	W	W	6	6	0	0	3	3	1	5
Vallecano	W	W	4	4	0	0	4	0	2	2
Sociedad	W	L	5	5	0	0	4	1	3	2
Elche	W	W	2	2	0	0	2	0	0	2
Levante	W	W	5	5	0	0	4	1	1	4
Getafe	W	D	6	5	1	0	6	0	4	2
Deportivo	D	W	4	2	2	0	2	2	1	3
Granada	W	W	4	4	0	0	3	1	1	3
Betis			3	3	0	0	3	0	3	0
Sp Gijon			3	3	0	0	2	1	1	2
Las Palmas			-	-	-	-	-	-	-	-

Season	Division	Pos	P	W	D	L	F	A	GD	Pts
2014-15	Primera Liga	1	38	30	4	4	110	21	+89	94
2013-14	Primera Liga	2	38	27	6	5	100	33	+67	87
2012-13	Primera Liga	1	38	32	4	2	115	40	+75	100

Over/Under 61%/39% 2nd **Both score** 32%/68% 20th

BETIS

Benito Villamarin   www.realbetisbalompie.es

	2014-15 H	A	P	W	D	L	OV	UN	BS	CS
Barcelona			3	0	1	2	3	0	3	0
Real Madrid			3	1	0	2	2	1	1	1
Atl Madrid			3	0	1	2	2	1	2	0
Valencia			3	3	0	0	2	1	2	1
Sevilla			3	0	2	1	1	2	2	0
Villarreal			2	2	0	0	1	1	1	1
Ath Bilbao			3	1	1	1	1	2	2	0
Celta			4	1	2	1	1	3	3	1
Malaga			3	1	1	1	2	1	1	2
Espanyol			3	2	1	0	0	3	1	2
Vallecano			5	2	1	2	4	1	3	1
Sociedad			4	2	0	2	1	3	1	2
Elche			3	0	0	3	3	0	2	0
Levante			4	2	1	1	3	0	3	
Getafe			3	1	2	0	0	3	1	2
Deportivo			1	0	1	0	0	1	1	0
Granada			4	1	1	2	3	1	3	1
Betis										
Sp Gijon	L	W	2	1	0	1	1	1	0	1
Las Palmas	D	W	3	2	1	0	1	2	1	2

Season	Division	Pos	P	W	D	L	F	A	GD	Pts
2014-15	Liga Segunda	1	42	25	9	8	73	40	+33	84
2013-14	Primera Liga	20	38	6	7	25	36	78	-42	25
2012-13	Primera Liga	7	38	16	8	14	57	56	+1	56

Over/Under 57%/43% 1st **Both score** 48%/52% 15th

CELTA VIGO

Balaidos — www.celtavigo.net

	2014-15 H	A	P	W	D	L	OV	UN	BS	CS
			Last six seasons at home							
Barcelona	L	W	3	0	1	2	2	1	1	0
Real Madrid	L	L	3	1	0	2	2	1	2	1
Atl Madrid	W	D	3	1	0	2	1	2	1	1
Valencia	D	D	3	1	1	1	1	2	2	0
Sevilla	D	L	3	2	1	0	0	3	1	2
Villarreal	L	L	2	0	1	1	1	1	1	1
Ath Bilbao	L	D	3	0	2	1	1	2	2	1
Celta										
Malaga	W	L	3	1	0	2	0	3	0	1
Espanyol	W	L	3	2	1	0	2	1	2	1
Vallecano	W	L	5	1	2	2	1	4	1	2
Sociedad	D	D	4	0	3	1	2	2	3	0
Elche	D	D	5	1	2	2	3	2	4	0
Levante	W	W	4	1	2	1	1	3	2	1
Getafe	W	L	3	2	1	0	2	1	3	0
Deportivo	W	W	3	1	1	1	2	1	3	0
Granada	D	D	4	1	3	0	1	3	3	1
Betis			4	1	2	1	1	3	3	0
Sp Gijon			-	-	-	-	-	-	-	-
Las Palmas			3	2	0	1	1	2	1	2

Season	Division	Pos	P	W	D	L	F	A	GD	Pts
2014-15	Primera Liga	8	38	13	12	13	47	44	+3	51
2013-14	Primera Liga	9	38	14	7	17	49	54	-5	49
2012-13	Primera Liga	17	38	10	7	21	37	52	-15	37

Over/Under 37%/63% 18th **Both score** 53%/47% 5th

DEPORTIVO

Municipal de Riazor — www.canaldeportivo.com

	2014-15 H	A	P	W	D	L	OV	UN	BS	CS
			Last six seasons at home							
Barcelona	L	D	4	0	0	4	4	0	2	0
Real Madrid	L	L	4	0	1	3	3	1	3	1
Atl Madrid	L	L	4	1	1	2	2	2	2	1
Valencia	W	L	4	1	1	2	2	2	1	2
Sevilla	L	L	4	1	1	2	2	2	2	1
Villarreal	D	L	3	2	1	0	0	3	1	2
Ath Bilbao	W	L	4	3	1	0	2	2	3	1
Celta	L	L	3	2	0	1	2	1	2	0
Malaga	L	D	4	3	0	1	1	3	0	3
Espanyol	D	D	4	2	1	1	2	2	1	3
Vallecano	D	W	2	0	2	0	1	1	1	1
Sociedad	D	D	3	1	1	1	2	1	1	1
Elche	W	L	2	2	0	0	1	1	1	1
Levante	W	D	3	1	0	2	0	3	0	1
Getafe	L	L	4	0	2	2	3	1	4	0
Deportivo										
Granada	D	L	2	0	1	1	2	0	1	0
Betis			1	0	0	1	1	0	1	0
Sp Gijon			3	0	3	0	0	3	3	0
Las Palmas			2	1	0	1	2	0	2	0

Season	Division	Pos	P	W	D	L	F	A	GD	Pts
2014-15	Primera Liga	16	38	7	14	17	35	60	-25	35
2013-14	Liga Segunda	2	42	19	12	11	48	36	+12	69
2012-13	Primera Liga	19	38	8	11	19	47	70	-23	35

Over/Under 45%/55% 13th **Both score** 45%/55% 12th

ELCHE

Estadio Martinez Valero — www.elchecf.es

	2014-15 H	A	P	W	D	L	OV	UN	BS	CS
			Last six seasons at home							
Barcelona	L	L	2	0	1	1	1	1	0	1
Real Madrid	L	L	2	0	0	2	1	1	1	0
Atl Madrid	L	L	2	0	0	2	0	2	0	0
Valencia	L	L	2	1	0	1	2	0	1	0
Sevilla	L	L	2	0	1	1	0	1	0	1
Villarreal	D	L	3	1	1	1	1	2	1	1
Ath Bilbao	L	W	2	0	1	1	1	1	1	1
Celta	L	D	5	2	0	3	1	4	1	2
Malaga	L	W	2	0	0	2	1	1	1	0
Espanyol	W	D	2	2	0	0	2	0	2	0
Vallecano	W	W	4	2	2	0	1	3	2	2
Sociedad	W	L	3	2	1	0	1	2	2	1
Elche										
Levante	W	D	3	1	2	0	0	3	1	2
Getafe	L	D	2	1	0	1	0	2	0	1
Deportivo	W	W	2	2	0	0	2	0	1	0
Granada	D	L	3	0	2	1	0	3	1	1
Betis			3	1	1	1	1	2	0	2
Sp Gijon			1	1	0	0	1	0	1	0
Las Palmas			4	1	1	2	4	0	4	0

Season	Division	Pos	P	W	D	L	F	A	GD	Pts
2014-15	Primera Liga	13	38	11	8	19	35	62	-27	41
2013-14	Primera Liga	16	38	9	13	16	30	50	-20	40
2012-13	Liga Segunda	1	42	23	13	6	54	27	+27	82

Over/Under 47%/53% 11th **Both score** 37%/63% 19th

ESPANYOL

Cornella-El Prat — www.rcdespanyol.com

	2014-15 H	A	P	W	D	L	OV	UN	BS	CS
			Last six seasons at home							
Barcelona	L	L	6	0	2	4	1	5	2	1
Real Madrid	L	L	6	0	1	5	3	3	2	0
Atl Madrid	D	L	6	3	2	1	3	3	2	3
Valencia	L	L	6	2	2	2	4	2	5	1
Sevilla	L	L	6	1	2	3	4	2	5	1
Villarreal	D	W	5	0	3	2	1	4	2	2
Ath Bilbao	W	L	6	5	1	0	4	2	4	2
Celta	W	L	3	3	0	0	0	3	0	3
Malaga	D	W	6	2	3	1	3	3	3	3
Espanyol										
Vallecano	D	W	4	2	2	0	3	1	4	0
Sociedad	W	L	6	2	2	1	4	1	4	1
Elche	D	W	2	1	1	0	1	1	2	0
Levante	W	D	5	3	1	1	4	1	4	1
Getafe	W	L	6	3	0	3	1	5	1	2
Deportivo	D	D	3	2	1	0	0	4	0	4
Granada	W	W	4	3	1	0	2	2	1	2
Betis			3	2	1	0	0	3	0	3
Sp Gijon			3	1	1	1	1	2	0	2
Las Palmas										

Season	Division	Pos	P	W	D	L	F	A	GD	Pts
2014-15	Primera Liga	10	38	13	10	15	47	51	-4	49
2013-14	Primera Liga	14	38	11	9	18	41	51	-10	49
2012-13	Primera Liga	13	38	11	16	11	43	52	-9	44

Over/Under 53%/47% 6th **Both score** 55%/45% 2nd

GETAFE

Coliseum Alfonso Perez — www.getafecf.com

| | 2014-15 | | Last six seasons at home | | | | | | | |
	H	A	P	W	D	L	OV	UN	BS	CS
Barcelona	D	L	6	1	1	4	3	3	3	2
Real Madrid	L	L	6	1	0	5	5	1	3	0
Atl Madrid	L	L	6	2	2	2	1	5	2	2
Valencia	L	L	6	2	0	4	4	2	3	0
Sevilla	W	L	6	5	1	0	3	3	4	2
Villarreal	D	L	5	2	2	1	4	1	1	3
Ath Bilbao	L	L	6	2	2	2	2	4	2	3
Celta	W	L	3	3	0	0	2	1	2	1
Malaga	W	L	6	4	0	2	2	4	2	3
Espanyol	W	L	6	1	3	2	2	4	4	1
Vallecano	L	L	4	0	0	4	2	2	2	0
Sociedad	L	W	5	2	1	2	3	2	2	1
Elche	D	W	2	0	2	0	0	2	1	1
Levante	L	D	5	2	1	2	1	4	2	1
Getafe										
Deportivo	W	W	4	3	0	1	3	1	3	0
Granada	L	D	4	1	2	1	3	1	3	1
Betis			3	2	0	1	2	1	2	1
Sp Gijon			3	2	1	0	1	2	1	2
Las Palmas			-	-	-	-	-	-	-	-

Season	Division	Pos	P	W	D	L	F	A	GD	Pts
2014-15	Primera Liga	15	38	10	7	21	33	64	-31	37
2013-14	Primera Liga	13	38	11	9	18	35	54	-19	42
2012-13	Primera Liga	10	38	13	8	17	43	57	-14	47

Over/Under 50%/50% 8th   **Both score** 53%/47% 5th

GRANADA

Nuevo Los Carmenes — www.granadacf.es

| | 2014-15 | | Last six seasons at home | | | | | | | |
	H	A	P	W	D	L	OV	UN	BS	CS
Barcelona	L	L	4	1	0	3	2	2	2	1
Real Madrid	L	L	4	1	0	3	2	2	1	1
Atl Madrid	D	L	4	0	2	2	1	3	1	2
Valencia	D	L	4	0	1	3	1	3	2	0
Sevilla	D	L	4	0	2	2	2	2	3	0
Villarreal	D	L	3	2	1	0	0	3	0	3
Ath Bilbao	D	W	4	1	2	1	2	2	2	2
Celta	D	D	4	1	2	1	2	2	4	0
Malaga	W	L	4	4	0	0	2	2	2	2
Espanyol	L	L	4	1	1	2	2	2	2	1
Vallecano	L	L	5	1	1	3	2	3	2	1
Sociedad	D	W	4	1	2	1	2	2	3	1
Elche	W	D	3	2	1	0	1	2	1	2
Levante	L	L	4	1	1	2	3	2	0	0
Getafe	D	L	4	2	1	1	0	4	1	2
Deportivo	W	D	2	1	1	0	1	1	2	0
Granada										
Betis			4	2	0	2	2	2	1	2
Sp Gijon			1	1	0	0	1	0	1	0
Las Palmas			1	1	0	0	1	0	1	0

Season	Division	Pos	P	W	D	L	F	A	GD	Pts
2014-15	Primera Liga	17	38	7	14	17	29	64	-35	35
2013-14	Primera Liga	15	38	12	5	21	32	56	-24	41
2012-13	Primera Liga	15	38	11	9	18	37	54	-17	42

Over/Under 42%/58% 14th   **Both score** 47%/53% 10th

LAS PALMAS

Estadio Gran Canaria — www.udlaspalmas.es

| | 20 14-15 | | Last six seasons at home | | | | | | | |
	H	A	P	W	D	L	OV	UN	BS	CS
Barcelona			-	-	-	-	-	-	-	-
Real Madrid			-	-	-	-	-	-	-	-
Atl Madrid			-	-	-	-	-	-	-	-
Valencia			-	-	-	-	-	-	-	-
Sevilla			-	-	-	-	-	-	-	-
Villarreal			1	0	1	0	1	0	1	0
Ath Bilbao			-	-	-	-	-	-	-	-
Celta			3	1	2	0	1	2	3	0
Malaga			-	-	-	-	-	-	-	-
Espanyol			-	-	-	-	-	-	-	-
Vallecano			2	2	0	0	2	0	2	0
Sociedad			1	0	1	0	0	1	1	0
Elche			4	2	2	0	2	2	3	1
Levante			1	0	0	1	0	1	0	0
Getafe										
Deportivo			2	0	0	2	0	2	0	0
Granada			1	0	1	0	0	1	1	0
Betis	L	D	3	0	2	1	2	1	2	0
Sp Gijon	D	D	3	2	1	0	2	1	3	0
Las Palmas										

Season	Division	Pos	P	W	D	L	F	A	GD	Pts
2014-15	Liga Segunda	4	42	22	12	8	73	47	+26	78
2013-14	Liga Segunda	6	42	18	9	15	51	50	+1	63
2012-13	Liga Segunda	6	42	18	12	12	62	55	+7	66

Over/Under 55%/45% 3rd   **Both score** 62%/38% 1st

LEVANTE

Ciutat de Valencia — www.levanteud.com

| | 2014-15 | | Last six seasons at home | | | | | | | |
	H	A	P	W	D	L	OV	UN	BS	CS
Barcelona	L	L	5	0	2	3	3	2	3	0
Real Madrid	L	L	5	1	1	3	3	2	2	0
Atl Madrid	D	L	5	3	2	0	1	4	2	3
Valencia	W	L	5	3	0	2	1	4	1	2
Sevilla	L	D	5	2	1	2	2	3	2	3
Villarreal	L	L	4	1	0	3	2	2	1	1
Ath Bilbao	L	L	5	2	0	3	4	1	3	1
Celta	L	L	4	1	0	3	0	4	0	1
Malaga	W	L	5	4	0	1	4	1	3	2
Espanyol	D	L	5	4	1	0	4	1	3	2
Vallecano	L	L	5	1	1	3	3	2	3	1
Sociedad	D	L	6	4	2	0	3	3	4	2
Elche	D	L	3	2	1	0	1	2	1	1
Levante										
Getafe	D	W	5	1	3	1	1	4	2	3
Deportivo	D	L	3	0	1	2	2	1	1	1
Granada	W	L	4	3	0	1	3	1	3	0
Betis			4	2	1	1	2	2	3	1
Sp Gijon			2	1	1	0	1	1	0	2
Las Palmas			1	0	1	0	0	1	0	0

Season	Division	Pos	P	W	D	L	F	A	GD	Pts
2014-15	Primera Liga	14	38	9	10	19	34	67	-33	37
2013-14	Primera Liga	10	38	12	12	14	35	43	-8	48
2012-13	Primera Liga	11	38	12	10	16	40	57	+7	46

Over/Under 53%/47% 6th   **Both score** 42%/58% 13th

MALAGA

La Rosaleda — www.malagacf.es

	2014-15 H	A	Last six seasons at home P	W	D	L	OV	UN	BS	CS
Barcelona	D	W	6	0	1	5	3	3	3	1
Real Madrid	D	L	6	1	1	4	4	2	4	0
Atl Madrid	D	L	6	1	3	2	3	3	1	3
Valencia	W	L	6	3	1	2	2	4	1	4
Sevilla	L	L	6	2	1	3	5	1	5	1
Villarreal	L	L	5	3	1	1	2	3	3	2
Ath Bilbao	W	D	6	3	2	1	1	5	3	3
Celta	W	L	3	1	1	1	1	2	1	1
Malaga										
Espanyol	L	D	6	3	0	3	3	3	3	1
Vallecano	W	L	4	3	0	1	4	0	2	2
Sociedad	D	W	5	0	2	3	2	3	4	0
Elche	L	L	2	0	0	2	1	1	1	0
Levante	D	L	5	4	1	0	1	4	1	4
Getafe	W	L	6	5	1	0	4	2	4	2
Deportivo	D	W	4	1	3	0	1	3	2	2
Granada	W	L	4	4	0	0	4	0	2	2
Betis			3	2	0	1	2	1	1	1
Sp Gijon			3	2	1	0	0	3	1	2
Las Palmas			-	-	-	-	-	-	-	-

Season	Division	Pos	P	W	D	L	F	A	GD	Pts
2014-15	Primera Liga	9	38	14	8	16	42	48	-6	50
2013-14	Primera Liga	11	38	12	9	17	39	46	-7	45
2012-13	Primera Liga	6	38	16	9	13	53	50	+3	57

Over/Under 47%/53% 11th **Both score** 53%/47% 5th

REAL MADRID

Santiago Bernabeu — www.realmadrid.com

	2014-15 H	A	Last six seasons at home P	W	D	L	OV	UN	BS	CS
Barcelona	W	L	6	2	1	3	4	2	5	0
Real Madrid										
Atl Madrid	L	L	6	4	0	2	3	3	3	2
Valencia	D	L	6	2	4	0	2	4	3	3
Sevilla	W	W	6	6	0	0	5	1	4	2
Villarreal	D	W	5	4	1	0	4	1	4	1
Ath Bilbao	W	L	6	6	0	0	6	0	5	1
Celta	W	W	3	3	0	0	2	1	0	3
Malaga	W	W	6	5	1	0	3	3	3	3
Espanyol	W	W	6	5	1	0	6	0	2	4
Vallecano	W	W	4	4	0	0	3	1	2	2
Sociedad	W	L	5	5	0	0	5	0	5	0
Elche	W	W	2	2	0	0	2	0	1	1
Levante	W	W	5	5	0	0	3	2	2	3
Getafe	W	W	6	6	0	0	5	1	3	3
Deportivo	W	W	4	4	0	0	3	1	3	1
Granada	W	W	4	4	0	0	3	1	2	2
Betis			3	3	0	0	3	0	3	0
Sp Gijon			3	2	0	1	2	1	2	0
Las Palmas			-	-	-	-	-	-	-	-

Season	Division	Pos	P	W	D	L	F	A	GD	Pts
2014-15	Primera Liga	2	38	30	2	6	118	38	+80	92
2013-14	Primera Liga	3	38	27	6	5	104	38	+66	87
2012-13	Primera Liga	2	38	26	7	5	103	42	+61	85

Over/Under 79%/21% 1st **Both score** 55%/45% 2nd

SEVILLA

Ramón Sanchez Pizjuan — www.sevillafc.es

	2014-15 H	A	Last six seasons at home P	W	D	L	OV	UN	BS	CS
Barcelona	D	L	6	0	4	2	4	2	5	0
Real Madrid	L	L	6	3	0	3	5	1	5	1
Atl Madrid	D	L	6	2	2	2	3	3	4	1
Valencia	D	L	6	4	2	0	2	4	3	3
Sevilla										
Villarreal	W	W	5	3	1	1	4	1	4	1
Ath Bilbao	W	L	6	3	2	1	3	3	4	2
Celta	W	W	3	2	0	1	1	2	1	1
Malaga	W	W	6	2	3	1	3	3	3	2
Espanyol	W	W	6	3	2	1	4	2	3	3
Vallecano	W	W	4	4	0	0	3	1	3	1
Sociedad	W	W	5	4	0	1	2	3	2	3
Elche	W	W	2	2	0	0	2	0	1	1
Levante	D	W	5	1	3	1	2	3	4	1
Getafe	W	L	6	4	0	2	5	1	3	3
Deportivo	W	W	4	2	2	0	2	3	2	3
Granada	W	D	4	3	0	1	4	0	2	2
Betis			3	2	0	1	3	0	2	1
Sp Gijon			3	3	0	0	3	0	1	2
Las Palmas										

Season	Division	Pos	P	W	D	L	F	A	GD	Pts
2014-15	Primera Liga	5	38	23	7	8	71	45	+26	76
2013-14	Primera Liga	5	38	18	9	11	69	52	+17	63
2012-13	Primera Liga	9	38	14	8	16	58	54	+4	50

Over/Under 55%/45% 3rd **Both score** 58%/42% 1st

SOCIEDAD

Anoeta — www.realsociedad.com

	2014-15 H	A	Last six seasons at home P	W	D	L	OV	UN	BS	CS
Barcelona	W	L	5	4	1	0	4	1	4	1
Real Madrid	W	L	5	1	1	3	4	1	3	0
Atl Madrid	W	L	5	1	0	4	4	1	3	0
Valencia	D	L	5	3	1	1	2	3	3	2
Sevilla	W	L	5	3	1	1	3	2	4	1
Villarreal	D	L	4	1	2	1	1	3	2	2
Ath Bilbao	D	D	5	3	1	1	1	4	2	3
Celta	D	D	4	3	1	0	2	2	3	1
Malaga	L	D	5	2	1	2	3	2	2	1
Espanyol	W	L	5	3	1	1	1	4	1	3
Vallecano	L	W	5	3	0	2	3	2	1	3
Sociedad										
Elche	W	L	3	2	0	1	2	1	0	2
Levante	W	D	6	2	3	1	3	3	4	2
Getafe	L	W	5	1	3	1	1	4	3	2
Deportivo	D	D	3	1	2	0	2	1	2	1
Granada	L	D	4	1	2	1	2	2	2	1
Betis			4	2	2	0	2	2	3	1
Sp Gijon			2	2	0	0	2	0	1	0
Las Palmas			1	0	1	0	1	0	1	0

Season	Division	Pos	P	W	D	L	F	A	GD	Pts
2014-15	Primera Liga	12	38	11	13	14	44	51	-7	46
2013-14	Primera Liga	7	38	16	11	11	62	55	+7	59
2012-13	Primera Liga	4	38	18	12	8	70	49	+21	66

Over/Under 39%/61% 16th **Both score** 50%/50% 8th

SPORTING GIJON

Estadio el Molinon   www.realsporting.com/

	2014-15 H	A	Last six seasons at home P	W	D	L	OV	UN	BS	CS
Barcelona			3	0	1	2	0	3	1	0
Real Madrid			3	0	1	2	1	2	0	1
Atl Madrid			3	1	2	0	0	3	2	1
Valencia			3	0	1	2	0	3	1	0
Sevilla			3	2	0	1	0	3	0	2
Villarreal			4	2	1	1	1	3	2	2
Ath Bilbao			3	0	3	0	1	2	2	1
Celta			-	-	-	-	-	-	-	-
Malaga			3	1	1	1	3	0	3	0
Espanyol			3	2	0	1	1	2	1	2
Vallecano			1	1	0	0	1	0	1	0
Sociedad			2	0	0	2	2	0	2	0
Elche			1	0	0	1	0	1	0	0
Levante			2	1	1	0	1	1	2	0
Getafe			3	3	0	0	1	2	1	2
Deportivo			3	2	1	0	2	1	2	1
Granada			1	1	0	0	0	1	0	1
Betis	L	W	2	1	0	1	2	0	2	0
Sp Gijon										
Las Palmas	D	D	3	0	2	1	1	2	3	0

Season	Division	Pos	P	W	D	L	F	A	GD	Pts
2014-15	Liga Segunda	2	42	21	19	2	57	27	+30	82
2013-14	Liga Segunda	5	42	16	16	10	63	51	+12	64
2012-13	Liga Segunda	10	42	15	11	16	60	53	+7	56

Over/Under 36%/64% 21st   **Both score** 52%/48% 8th

VALENCIA

Mestalla   www.valenciafc.com

	2014-15 H	A	Last six seasons at home P	W	D	L	OV	UN	BS	CS
Barcelona	L	L	6	0	3	3	2	4	3	1
Real Madrid	W	D	6	1	0	5	6	0	5	0
Atl Madrid	W	D	6	3	2	1	2	4	3	2
Valencia										
Sevilla	W	D	6	4	0	2	3	3	3	2
Villarreal	D	W	5	4	1	0	3	2	2	3
Ath Bilbao	D	D	6	3	3	0	2	4	4	2
Celta	D	D	3	2	1	0	2	1	3	0
Malaga	W	L	6	6	0	0	3	3	2	4
Espanyol	W	W	6	5	1	0	5	1	5	1
Vallecano	W	D	4	3	0	1	2	2	1	2
Sociedad	W	D	5	2	0	3	3	2	2	2
Elche	W	W	2	2	0	0	2	0	2	0
Levante	W	L	5	2	3	0	2	3	2	3
Getafe	W	W	6	5	0	1	4	2	4	2
Deportivo	W	L	4	3	1	0	1	3	1	3
Granada	W	D	4	4	0	0	2	2	1	3
Betis			3	3	0	0	3	0	0	3
Sp Gijon			3	1	2	0	2	1	1	2
Las Palmas			-	-	-	-	-	-	-	-

Season	Division	Pos	P	W	D	L	F	A	GD	Pts
2014-15	Primera Liga	4	38	22	11	5	70	32	+38	77
2013-14	Primera Liga	8	38	13	10	15	51	53	-2	49
2012-13	Primera Liga	5	38	19	8	11	67	54	+13	65

Over/Under 55%/45% 3rd   **Both score** 55%/45% 2nd

VALLECANO

Campo de Vallecas   www.rayovallecano.es

	2014-15 H	A	Last six seasons at home P	W	D	L	OV	UN	BS	CS
Barcelona	L	L	4	0	0	4	3	1	0	0
Real Madrid	L	L	4	0	0	4	1	3	1	0
Atl Madrid	D	L	4	1	1	2	2	2	2	1
Valencia	D	L	4	1	1	2	2	2	2	1
Sevilla	L	L	4	1	1	2	1	3	1	1
Villarreal	W	L	3	1	0	2	1	2	1	1
Ath Bilbao	W	L	4	1	1	2	4	0	3	0
Celta	W	L	5	3	0	2	4	1	3	2
Malaga	W	L	4	3	0	1	2	2	2	2
Espanyol	L	D	4	1	0	3	2	2	2	1
Vallecano										
Sociedad	L	W	5	2	1	2	3	2	2	2
Elche	L	L	4	1	0	3	3	1	2	1
Levante	W	W	5	2	1	2	4	1	3	2
Getafe	W	W	4	3	0	1	2	2	2	2
Deportivo	L	D	4	1	2	1	2	0	2	0
Granada	W	W	5	3	1	1	4	2	2	2
Betis			5	4	1	0	4	1	2	3
Sp Gijon			1	0	0	1	1	0	1	0
Las Palmas			2	2	0	0	1	1	1	1

Season	Division	Pos	P	W	D	L	F	A	GD	Pts
2014-15	Primera Liga	11	38	15	4	19	46	68	-22	49
2013-14	Primera Liga	12	38	13	4	21	46	80	-34	43
2012-13	Primera Liga	8	38	16	5	17	50	66	-16	53

Over/Under 50%/50% 8th   **Both score** 50%/50% 8th

VILLARREAL

El Madrigal   www.villarrealcf.es

	2014-15 H	A	Last six seasons at home P	W	D	L	OV	UN	BS	CS
Barcelona	L	L	5	0	1	4	2	3	2	1
Real Madrid	L	D	5	0	3	2	3	3	3	0
Atl Madrid	L	W	5	2	1	2	1	4	2	1
Valencia	L	L	5	2	2	1	3	2	4	1
Sevilla	L	L	5	2	1	2	3	2	2	2
Villarreal										
Ath Bilbao	W	L	5	3	2	0	3	2	4	1
Celta	W	W	2	1	0	1	1	1	1	0
Malaga	W	D	5	3	2	0	3	2	5	0
Espanyol	L	D	5	2	2	1	3	2	1	3
Vallecano	W	L	3	3	0	0	2	1	1	2
Sociedad	W	D	4	3	1	0	3	1	3	1
Elche	W	D	3	1	1	1	1	2	2	1
Levante	W	W	4	2	0	2	1	3	0	2
Getafe	W	D	5	3	0	2	4	1	4	0
Deportivo	W	D	3	3	0	0	1	2	0	3
Granada	W	D	3	3	0	0	2	1	1	2
Betis			2	1	1	0	0	2	1	1
Sp Gijon			4	3	1	0	2	2	2	2
Las Palmas			1	0	1	0	0	1	1	0

Season	Division	Pos	P	W	D	L	F	A	GD	Pts
2014-15	Primera Liga	6	38	16	12	10	48	37	+11	60
2013-14	Primera Liga	6	38	17	8	13	60	44	+16	59
2012-13	Liga Segunda	2	42	21	14	7	68	38	+30	77

Over/Under 34%/66% 19th   **Both score** 39%/61% 17th

Primera Liga 2014-15

Pos	H	A		P	W	D	L	F	A	W	D	L	F	A	GD	Pts
					Home					**Away**						
1	2	1	Barcelona	38	16	1	2	64	11	14	3	2	46	10	+89	94
2	1	2	Real Madrid	38	16	2	1	65	15	14	0	5	53	23	+80	92
3	4	3	Atletico Madrid	38	14	3	2	42	11	9	6	4	25	18	+38	78
4	3	5	Valencia	38	15	3	1	42	10	7	8	4	28	22	+38	77
5	5	4	Seville	38	13	5	1	38	13	10	2	7	33	32	+26	76
6	6	7	Villarreal	38	12	1	6	29	17	4	11	4	19	20	+11	60
7	8	6	Athletic Bilbao	38	8	6	5	28	20	7	4	8	14	21	+1	55
8	11	9	Celta Vigo	38	8	5	6	30	22	5	7	7	17	22	+3	51
9	9	10	Malaga	38	8	6	5	26	20	6	2	11	16	28	-6	50
10	10	12	Espanyol	38	8	6	5	23	19	5	4	10	24	32	-4	49
11	12	8	Rayo Vallecano	38	8	2	9	26	26	7	2	10	20	42	-22	49
12	7	15	Sociedad	38	9	5	5	29	21	2	8	9	15	30	-7	46
13	17	11	Elche	38	6	3	10	19	31	5	5	9	16	31	-27	41
14	13	18	Levante	38	6	6	7	20	30	3	4	12	14	37	-33	37
15	14	17	Getafe	38	6	5	8	16	22	4	2	13	17	42	-31	37
16	16	16	Deportivo	38	5	6	8	22	30	2	8	9	13	30	-25	35
17	15	19	Granada	38	4	10	5	13	17	3	4	12	16	47	-35	35
18	18	13	Eibar	38	5	3	11	20	29	4	5	10	14	26	-21	35
19	19	14	Almeria	38	3	7	9	20	28	5	1	13	15	36	-29	29
20	20	20	Cordoba	38	1	6	12	12	33	2	5	12	10	35	-46	20

*Almeria deducted 3pts

Results 2014-15

	Almeria	Athletic Bilbao	Atletico Madrid	Barcelona	Celta	Cordoba	Deportivo	Eibar	Elche	Espanyol	Getafe	Granada	Levante	Malaga	Real Madrid	Seville	Sociedad	Valencia	Vallecano	Villarreal
Almeria		0-1	0-1	1-2	2-2	1-1	0-0	2-0	2-2	1-1	1-0	3-0	1-4	1-2	1-4	0-2	2-2	2-3	0-1	0-0
Athletic Bilbao	2-1		1-4	2-5	1-1	0-1	1-1	0-0	1-2	3-1	4-0	0-1	3-0	1-1	1-0	1-0	1-1	1-1	1-0	4-0
Atletico Madrid	3-0	0-0		0-1	2-2	4-2	2-0	2-1	3-0	2-0	2-0	2-0	3-1	3-1	4-0	4-0	2-0	1-1	3-1	0-1
Barcelona	4-0	2-0	3-1		0-1	5-0	2-2	3-0	3-0	5-1	6-0	6-0	5-0	0-1	2-1	5-1	2-0	2-0	6-1	3-2
Celta	0-1	1-2	2-0	0-1		1-0	2-1	0-1	1-1	3-2	3-1	0-0	3-0	1-0	2-4	1-1	2-2	1-1	6-1	1-3
Cordoba	1-2	0-1	0-2	0-8	1-1		0-0	1-1	0-2	0-0	1-2	2-0	0-0	1-2	1-2	1-3	1-1	1-2	1-2	0-2
Deportivo	0-1	1-0	1-2	0-4	0-2	1-1		2-0	1-0	0-0	1-2	2-2	2-0	0-1	2-8	3-4	0-0	3-0	2-2	1-1
Eibar	5-2	0-1	1-3	0-2	0-1	3-0	0-1		0-1	0-2	2-1	1-1	3-3	1-0	0-4	1-3	1-0	0-1	1-2	1-1
Elche	1-0	2-3	0-2	0-6	0-1	2-2	4-0	0-2		2-1	0-1	1-1	1-0	1-2	0-2	0-2	1-0	0-4	2-0	2-2
Espanyol	3-0	1-0	0-0	0-2	1-0	1-0	0-0	1-2	1-1		2-0	2-1	2-1	2-2	1-4	1-2	2-0	1-2	1-1	1-1
Getafe	1-0	1-2	0-1	0-0	2-1	1-1	2-1	1-1	0-0	2-1		1-2	0-1	1-0	0-3	2-1	0-1	0-3	1-2	1-1
Granada	0-0	0-0	0-0	1-3	1-1	2-0	2-1	0-0	1-0	1-2	1-1		0-1	1-0	0-4	1-1	1-1	1-1	0-1	0-0
Levante	2-1	0-2	2-2	0-5	0-1	1-0	0-0	2-1	0-0	2-2	1-1	2-1		4-1	0-5	1-2	1-1	2-1	0-2	0-2
Malaga	1-2	1-0	2-2	0-0	1-0	2-0	1-1	2-1	1-2	0-2	3-2	2-1	0-0		1-2	2-3	1-1	1-0	4-0	1-1
Real Madrid	3-0	5-0	1-2	3-1	3-0	2-0	2-0	3-0	5-1	3-0	7-3	9-1	2-0	3-1		2-1	4-1	2-2	5-1	1-1
Seville	2-1	2-0	0-0	2-2	1-0	3-0	4-1	0-0	3-0	3-2	2-0	5-1	1-1	2-0	2-3		1-0	1-1	2-0	2-1
Sociedad	1-2	1-1	2-1	1-0	1-1	3-1	2-2	1-0	3-0	1-0	1-2	0-3	3-0	1-0	4-2	4-3		1-1	0-1	0-0
Valencia	3-2	0-0	3-1	0-1	1-1	3-0	2-0	3-1	3-1	3-1	1-0	4-0	3-0	3-0	2-1	3-1	2-0		3-0	0-0
Vallecano	2-0	2-1	0-0	0-2	1-0	0-1	1-2	2-3	2-3	1-3	2-0	3-1	4-2	1-0	0-2	0-1	2-4	1-1		2-0
Villarreal	2-0	2-0	0-1	0-1	4-1	0-0	3-0	1-0	1-0	0-3	2-1	2-0	1-0	2-1	0-2	0-2	4-0	1-3	4-2	

Top scorers

	Team	Goals scored
C Ronaldo	Real Madrid	48
L Messi	Barcelona	43
A Griezmann	Atl Madrid	22
Neymar	Barcelona	22
C Bacca	Seville	20

Over 2.5 goals top five

	H	A	%
Real Madrid	15	15	79%
Barcelona	14	9	61%
Almeria	9	12	55%
Sevilla	9	12	55%
Valencia	12	9	55%

Both to score top five

	H	A	%
Sevilla	9	13	58%
Real Madrid	11	10	55%
Valencia	8	13	55%
Espanyol, Getafe			53%
Malaga, Celta			

ANGERS

Stade Jean Bouin — www.angers-sco.fr

	2014-15 H	A	P	W	D	L	OV	UN	BS	CS
						Last six seasons at home				
Paris SG			-	-	-	-	-	-	-	-
Lyon			-	-	-	-	-	-	-	-
Monaco			2	0	0	2	2	0	2	0
Marseille			-	-	-	-	-	-	-	-
St-Etienne			-	-	-	-	-	-	-	-
Bordeaux			-	-	-	-	-	-	-	-
Montpellier			-	-	-	-	-	-	-	-
Lille			-	-	-	-	-	-	-	-
Rennes			-	-	-	-	-	-	-	-
Guingamp			3	2	0	1	1	2	1	2
Nice			-	-	-	-	-	-	-	-
Bastia			2	1	1	0	0	2	1	1
Caen			3	0	2	1	2	1	3	0
Nantes			4	3	1	0	0	4	1	3
Reims			2	0	1	1	0	2	0	1
Lorient			-	-	-	-	-	-	-	-
Toulouse			-	-	-	-	-	-	-	-
Troyes	L	L	4	1	1	2	3	1	2	1
GFC Ajaccio	W	L	2	2	0	0	0	2	0	2
Angers										

Season	Division	Pos	P	W	D	L	F	A	GD	Pts
2014-15	Ligue 2	3	38	18	10	10	47	30	+17	64
2013-14	Ligue 2	9	38	14	13	11	46	45	+1	55
2012-13	Ligue 2	5	38	17	10	11	52	39	+13	61

Over/Under 37%/63% 12th **Both score** 37%/63% 22nd

BASTIA

Stade Armand Cesari — www.sc-bastia.net

	2014-15 H	A	P	W	D	L	OV	UN	BS	CS
						Last six seasons at home				
Paris SG	W	L	3	1	0	2	3	0	1	0
Lyon	D	L	3	1	1	1	2	1	2	1
Monaco	L	L	3	0	1	2	1	2	2	0
Marseille	D	L	3	0	2	1	2	1	2	1
St-Etienne	W	L	3	1	0	2	1	2	0	1
Bordeaux	D	D	3	2	1	0	1	2	1	2
Montpellier	W	L	3	2	1	0	1	2	1	2
Lille	W	L	3	1	1	1	2	1	3	0
Rennes	W	W	3	2	0	1	0	3	0	2
Guingamp	D	L	4	2	2	0	2	2	2	2
Nice	W	W	3	2	0	1	1	2	1	1
Bastia										
Caen	D	D	2	0	1	1	1	1	2	0
Nantes	D	W	4	1	3	0	1	3	2	2
Reims	L	W	4	3	0	1	2	1	2	0
Lorient	L	L	3	2	0	1	2	1	2	0
Toulouse	W	D	3	2	1	0	1	2	1	2
Troyes			2	2	0	0	2	0	2	0
GFC Ajaccio			-	-	-	-	-	-	-	-
Angers			2	2	0	0	2	0	2	0

Season	Division	Pos	P	W	D	L	F	A	GD	Pts
2014-15	Ligue 1	12	38	12	11	15	37	46	-9	47
2013-14	Ligue 1	10	38	13	15	10	42	56	-14	49
2012-13	Ligue 1	12	38	13	8	17	50	66	-16	47

Over/Under 34%/66% 16th **Both score** 45%/55% 10th

BORDEAUX

Stade Chaban-Delmas — www.girondins.com

	2014-15 H	A	P	W	D	L	OV	UN	BS	CS
						Last six seasons at home				
Paris SG	W	L	6	3	1	2	1	5	2	2
Lyon	L	D	6	2	1	3	4	2	2	2
Monaco	W	D	4	2	0	2	1	3	1	1
Marseille	W	L	6	3	3	0	1	5	4	2
St-Etienne	W	D	6	4	1	1	2	4	2	4
Bordeaux										
Montpellier	W	W	6	4	2	0	3	3	4	2
Lille	W	L	6	3	3	0	1	5	4	2
Rennes	W	D	6	2	2	0	2	4	2	4
Guingamp	D	L	2	1	1	0	1	1	2	0
Nice	L	W	6	2	2	2	3	3	4	2
Bastia	D	D	3	2	1	0	0	3	1	2
Caen	D	W	2	1	1	1	1	2	2	1
Nantes	W	L	2	1	0	1	2	0	1	0
Reims	D	L	3	0	3	0	0	3	1	2
Lorient	W	D	6	5	1	0	3	3	4	2
Toulouse	W	L	6	4	0	2	2	4	2	3
Troyes			1	0	1	0	0	1	0	1
GFC Ajaccio			-	-	-	-	-	-	-	-
Angers			-	-	-	-	-	-	-	-

Season	Division	Pos	P	W	D	L	F	A	GD	Pts
2014-15	Ligue 1	6	38	17	12	9	47	44	+3	63
2013-14	Ligue 1	7	38	13	14	11	49	43	+6	53
2012-13	Ligue 1	7	38	13	16	9	40	34	+6	55

Over/Under 50%/50% 7th **Both score** 66%/34% 1st

CAEN

Stade Michel D'Ornano — www.smcaen.fr

	2014-15 H	A	P	W	D	L	OV	UN	BS	CS
						Last six seasons at home				
Paris SG	L	D	3	0	1	2	2	1	2	0
Lyon	W	L	3	3	0	0	1	1	1	2
Monaco	L	D	3	1	1	1	2	1	0	2
Marseille	L	W	3	0	1	2	3	0	3	0
St-Etienne	W	L	3	2	0	1	1	2	1	2
Bordeaux	L	D	3	1	1	1	2	1	1	2
Montpellier	D	L	3	1	1	1	1	2	2	1
Lille	L	L	3	0	0	3	2	1	2	0
Rennes	L	L	3	1	0	2	0	3	0	1
Guingamp	L	L	3	1	0	2	1	1	1	1
Nice	L	D	3	0	2	1	1	2	2	1
Bastia	D	D	2	1	1	0	0	2	1	1
Caen										
Nantes	L	W	3	1	0	2	1	2	1	1
Reims	W	W	1	1	0	0	1	0	1	0
Lorient	W	L	3	2	0	1	1	2	1	1
Toulouse	W	L	3	1	1	1	0	3	1	1
Troyes			1	0	1	0	0	1	1	0
GFC Ajaccio			1	1	0	0	1	0	1	0
Angers			3	2	1	0	1	2	2	1

Season	Division	Pos	P	W	D	L	F	A	GD	Pts
2014-15	Ligue 1	13	38	12	10	16	54	55	-1	46
2013-14	Ligue 2	3	38	18	10	10	65	44	+21	64
2012-13	Ligue 2	4	38	17	12	9	48	28	+20	63

Over/Under 55%/45% 3rd **Both score** 58%/42% 4th

GFC AJACCIO

Stade Ange Casanova www.gfca-foot.com

	2014-15 H	A	Last six seasons at home P	W	D	L	OV	UN	BS	CS
Paris SG			-	-	-	-	-	-	-	-
Lyon			-	-	-	-	-	-	-	-
Monaco			1	0	0	1	0	1	0	0
Marseille			-	-	-	-	-	-	-	-
St-Etienne			-	-	-	-	-	-	-	-
Bordeaux			-	-	-	-	-	-	-	-
Montpellier			-	-	-	-	-	-	-	-
Lille			-	-	-	-	-	-	-	-
Rennes			-	-	-	-	-	-	-	-
Guingamp			1	0	0	1	0	1	0	0
Nice			-	-	-	-	-	-	-	-
Bastia			-	-	-	-	-	-	-	-
Caen			1	0	1	0	0	1	0	1
Nantes			1	1	0	0	1	0	1	0
Reims			-	-	-	-	-	-	-	-
Lorient			-	-	-	-	-	-	-	-
Toulouse			-	-	-	-	-	-	-	-
Troyes	L	D	1	0	0	1	1	0	0	0
GFC Ajaccio										
Angers	W	L	2	1	0	1	0	2	0	1

Season	Division	Pos	P	W	D	L	F	A	GD	Pts
2014-15	Ligue 2	2	38	18	11	9	49	37	+12	65
2012-13	Ligue 2	20	38	6	10	22	34	54	-20	25
2011-12	National	3	38	20	8	10	57	32	+25	66

Over/Under 29%/71% 21st **Both score** 42%/58% 18th

GUINGAMP

Municipal du Roudourou www.eaguingamp.com

	2014-15 H	A	Last six seasons at home P	W	D	L	OV	UN	BS	CS
Paris SG	W	L	2	1	1	0	0	2	1	1
Lyon	L	L	2	0	0	2	1	1	1	0
Monaco	W	L	4	2	0	2	2	2	1	0
Marseille	L	L	2	0	0	2	1	1	1	0
St-Etienne	L	L	2	0	1	1	0	2	0	1
Bordeaux	W	D	2	1	0	1	1	1	1	0
Montpellier	L	L	2	0	0	2	1	1	1	0
Lille	L	W	2	0	1	1	0	2	0	1
Rennes	L	L	2	1	0	1	0	2	0	1
Guingamp										
Nice	L	W	2	1	0	1	1	1	1	1
Bastia	W	D	4	1	3	0	0	4	3	1
Caen	W	W	3	2	1	0	1	2	1	2
Nantes	L	L	5	4	0	1	1	4	1	3
Reims	W	W	3	1	0	2	2	1	2	1
Lorient	W	L	2	2	0	0	1	1	1	1
Toulouse	W	D	2	2	0	0	1	1	1	1
Troyes			1	0	1	0	0	1	0	1
GFC Ajaccio			1	0	1	0	0	1	0	1
Angers			3	2	1	0	1	2	1	2

Season	Division	Pos	P	W	D	L	F	A	GD	Pts
2014-15	Ligue 1	10	38	15	4	19	41	55	-14	49
2013-14	Ligue 1	16	38	11	9	18	34	42	-8	42
2012-13	Ligue 2	2	38	20	10	8	63	38	+25	70

Over/Under 39%/61% 12th **Both score** 42%/58% 12th

LILLE

Grand Stade Lille Metropole www.losc.fr

	2014-15 H	A	Last six seasons at home P	W	D	L	OV	UN	BS	CS
Paris SG	D	L	6	2	2	2	4	2	5	1
Lyon	W	L	6	3	3	0	3	3	5	1
Monaco	L	D	4	3	0	1	2	2	1	2
Marseille	L	L	6	3	1	2	4	2	3	2
St-Etienne	D	L	6	3	0	2	4	3	3	3
Bordeaux	W	L	6	4	1	1	3	3	4	2
Montpellier	D	W	6	4	1	1	3	3	3	2
Lille										
Rennes	W	L	6	4	2	0	2	4	2	4
Guingamp	L	W	2	1	0	1	1	1	1	1
Nice	D	L	6	0	4	2	1	5	3	1
Bastia	W	L	3	2	1	0	1	2	1	2
Caen	W	W	3	3	0	0	2	1	1	2
Nantes	W	D	2	1	1	0	0	2	0	2
Reims	W	L	3	2	0	1	3	0	2	1
Lorient	W	L	6	4	1	1	3	3	3	3
Toulouse	W	L	6	5	1	0	2	4	2	4
Troyes			1	0	1	0	0	1	1	0
GFC Ajaccio			-	-	-	-	-	-	-	-
Angers			-	-	-	-	-	-	-	-

Season	Division	Pos	P	W	D	L	F	A	GD	Pts
2014-15	Ligue 1	8	38	16	8	14	43	42	+1	56
2013-14	Ligue 1	3	38	20	11	7	46	26	+20	71
2012-13	Ligue 1	6	38	16	14	8	59	40	+19	62

Over/Under 37%/63% 14th **Both score** 39%/61% 15th

LORIENT

Stade du Moustoir www.fclweb.fr

	2014-15 H	A	Last six seasons at home P	W	D	L	OV	UN	BS	CS
Paris SG	L	L	6	0	4	2	3	3	5	0
Lyon	D	L	6	1	3	2	2	4	4	1
Monaco	L	W	4	1	2	1	3	1	3	0
Marseille	D	L	6	1	2	3	3	3	4	0
St-Etienne	L	L	6	4	1	1	3	3	1	4
Bordeaux	D	L	6	2	3	1	3	3	3	2
Montpellier	D	L	6	2	4	0	4	2	4	2
Lille	W	L	6	3	1	2	2	4	3	2
Rennes	L	L	6	2	2	2	2	4	2	2
Guingamp	W	L	2	2	0	0	1	1	0	2
Nice	D	L	6	3	2	1	3	3	3	3
Bastia	W	W	3	2	1	0	1	2	2	1
Caen	W	L	3	1	1	1	2	1	1	1
Nantes	L	D	2	1	0	1	2	0	2	0
Reims	L	W	3	0	2	1	1	2	1	1
Lorient										
Toulouse	L	W	6	1	3	2	1	5	2	3
Troyes			1	1	0	0	1	0	1	0
GFC Ajaccio			-	-	-	-	-	-	-	-
Angers			-	-	-	-	-	-	-	-

Season	Division	Pos	P	W	D	L	F	A	GD	Pts
2014-15	Ligue 1	16	38	12	7	19	44	50	-6	43
2013-14	Ligue 1	8	38	13	10	15	48	53	-5	49
2012-13	Ligue 1	8	38	14	11	13	57	58	-1	53

Over/Under 45%/55% 10th **Both score** 42%/58% 12th

LYON

Stade de Gerland — www.olweb.fr

	2014-15 H	A	Last six seasons at home P	W	D	L	OV	UN	BS	CS
Paris SG	D	D	6	2	3	1	3	3	4	1
Lyon										
Monaco	W	D	4	2	1	1	3	1	2	2
Marseille	W	D	6	3	3	0	3	3	3	3
St-Etienne	D	L	6	1	3	2	2	4	4	1
Bordeaux	D	W	6	1	3	2	1	5	3	1
Montpellier	W	W	6	4	1	1	4	2	4	2
Lille	W	L	6	3	2	1	4	2	4	2
Rennes	W	W	6	2	3	1	1	5	3	3
Guingamp	W	W	2	2	0	0	1	1	1	1
Nice	L	W	6	4	0	2	4	2	2	4
Bastia	W	D	3	3	0	0	2	1	2	1
Caen	W	L	3	1	1	1	2	1	1	2
Nantes	W	D	2	2	0	0	1	1	1	1
Reims	W	W	3	2	0	1	2	1	1	1
Lorient	W	D	6	5	0	1	4	2	2	3
Toulouse	W	L	6	5	1	0	4	2	4	2
Troyes			1	1	0	0	1	0	1	0
GFC Ajaccio			-	-	-	-	-	-	-	-
Angers			-	-	-	-	-	-	-	-

Season	Division	Pos	P	W	D	L	F	A	GD	Pts
2014-15	Ligue 1	2	38	22	9	7	72	33	+39	75
2013-14	Ligue 1	5	38	17	10	11	56	44	+12	61
2012-13	Ligue 1	3	38	19	10	9	61	38	+23	67

Over/Under 55%/45% 3rd   **Both score** 50%/50% 8th

MARSEILLE

Stade Velodrome — www.om.net

	2014-15 H	A	Last six seasons at home P	W	D	L	OV	UN	BS	CS
Paris SG	L	L	6	3	1	2	5	1	4	2
Lyon	D	L	6	2	3	1	4	2	5	1
Monaco	W	L	4	1	1	2	4	0	4	0
Marseille										
St-Etienne	W	D	6	5	1	0	3	3	3	3
Bordeaux	W	L	6	3	3	0	3	3	3	3
Montpellier	L	W	6	4	0	2	4	2	3	2
Lille	W	W	6	4	1	1	2	4	2	4
Rennes	W	D	6	3	1	2	3	3	2	2
Guingamp	W	W	2	2	0	0	1	1	1	1
Nice	W	L	6	4	1	1	4	2	3	2
Bastia	W	D	3	3	0	0	3	0	1	2
Caen	L	W	3	0	1	2	2	1	3	0
Nantes	W	W	2	1	0	1	0	2	0	1
Reims	D	W	3	0	2	1	2	1	2	1
Lorient	L	D	6	3	1	2	3	3	3	2
Toulouse	W	W	6	2	3	1	3	3	4	1
Troyes			1	1	0	0	1	0	1	0
GFC Ajaccio			-	-	-	-	-	-	-	-
Angers			-	-	-	-	-	-	-	-

Season	Division	Pos	P	W	D	L	F	A	GD	Pts
2014-15	Ligue 1	4	38	21	6	11	76	42	+34	69
2013-14	Ligue 1	6	38	16	12	10	53	40	+13	60
2012-13	Ligue 1	2	38	21	8	9	42	36	+6	71

Over/Under 63%/37% 1st   **Both score** 53%/47% 6th

MONACO

Stade Louis II — www.asm-fc.com

	2014-15 H	A	Last six seasons at home P	W	D	L	OV	UN	BS	CS
Paris SG	D	D	4	1	3	0	0	4	2	2
Lyon	D	L	4	1	2	1	1	3	2	1
Monaco										
Marseille	W	L	4	2	1	1	1	3	1	3
St-Etienne	D	D	4	1	1	2	2	2	3	0
Bordeaux	D	L	4	0	4	0	1	3	2	2
Montpellier	D	W	4	2	2	0	2	2	1	3
Lille	D	W	4	1	2	1	1	3	2	1
Rennes	D	L	4	3	1	0	0	4	1	3
Guingamp	W	L	4	2	2	0	1	3	2	2
Nice	L	W	4	2	1	1	1	3	2	1
Bastia	W	W	3	2	0	1	2	1	0	2
Caen	D	W	3	0	2	1	2	1	2	0
Nantes	W	W	4	3	0	1	2	2	2	1
Reims	D	W	3	1	1	1	2	1	3	0
Lorient	L	W	4	2	0	2	2	2	2	2
Toulouse	W	W	4	2	2	0	1	3	1	3
Troyes			1	0	0	1	0	1	0	0
GFC Ajaccio			1	0	1	0	1	0	1	0
Angers			2	0	1	1	2	0	2	0

Season	Division	Pos	P	W	D	L	F	A	GD	Pts
2014-15	Ligue 1	3	38	20	11	7	51	26	+25	71
2013-14	Ligue 1	2	38	23	11	4	63	31	+32	80
2012-13	Ligue 2	1	38	21	13	4	64	33	+31	76

Over/Under 32%/68% 18th   **Both score** 39%/61% 15th

MONTPELLIER

Stade de la Mosson — www.mhscfoot.com

	2014-15 H	A	Last six seasons at home P	W	D	L	OV	UN	BS	CS
Paris SG	L	D	6	0	4	2	2	4	5	0
Lyon	L	L	6	2	0	4	2	4	5	0
Monaco	L	D	4	0	2	2	0	4	1	1
Marseille	W	W	6	3	0	3	3	3	3	2
St-Etienne	L	L	6	2	1	3	2	4	3	1
Bordeaux	L	L	6	3	1	2	0	6	1	3
Montpellier										
Lille	L	D	6	3	1	2	1	5	1	4
Rennes	D	W	6	3	2	1	2	4	1	4
Guingamp	W	W	2	1	1	0	1	1	2	0
Nice	W	D	6	5	1	0	3	3	4	2
Bastia	W	L	3	2	0	1	2	1	1	1
Caen	D	D	3	2	1	0	2	0	0	3
Nantes	W	L	2	1	1	0	1	1	1	1
Reims	W	L	3	2	1	0	2	1	2	1
Lorient	W	D	6	5	0	1	3	3	2	3
Toulouse	W	L	6	3	0	3	1	5	4	2
Troyes			1	0	1	0	0	1	1	0
GFC Ajaccio			-	-	-	-	-	-	-	-
Angers			-	-	-	-	-	-	-	-

Season	Division	Pos	P	W	D	L	F	A	GD	Pts
2014-15	Ligue 1	7	38	16	8	14	46	39	+7	56
2013-14	Ligue 1	15	38	8	18	12	45	53	-8	42
2012-13	Ligue 1	9	38	16	14	8	54	51	+3	52

Over/Under 37%/63% 14th   **Both score** 37%/63% 18th

NANTES

Beaujoire-Louis Fonteneau — www.fcnantes.com

	2014-15 H	2014-15 A	Last six seasons at home P	W	D	L	OV	UN	BS	CS
Paris SG	L	L	2	0	0	2	1	1	1	0
Lyon	D	L	2	0	1	1	1	1	2	0
Monaco	L	L	4	1	1	2	1	3	1	1
Marseille	W	L	2	1	1	0	0	2	1	1
St-Etienne	D	L	2	0	1	1	1	1	1	1
Bordeaux	W	L	2	1	1	0	1	1	1	1
Montpellier	W	L	2	2	0	0	1	1	1	1
Lille	D	L	2	0	1	1	0	2	1	0
Rennes	D	D	2	0	1	1	1	1	1	0
Guingamp	W	W	5	3	1	1	1	4	1	3
Nice	W	D	2	2	0	0	1	1	1	1
Bastia	L	D	4	2	0	2	1	3	1	1
Caen	L	W	3	1	0	2	3	0	3	0
Nantes										
Reims	D	L	4	1	3	0	0	4	2	2
Lorient	D	W	2	1	1	0	0	2	1	1
Toulouse	L	D	2	0	0	2	2	0	2	0
Troyes			2	0	1	1	0	2	1	0
GFC Ajaccio			1	1	0	0	1	0	1	0
Angers			4	3	0	1	2	2	2	2

Season	Division	Pos	P	W	D	L	F	A	GD	Pts
2014-15	Ligue 1	14	38	11	12	15	29	40	-11	45
2013-14	Ligue 1	13	38	12	10	16	38	43	-5	46
2012-13	Ligue 2	3	38	19	12	7	54	29	+25	69

Over/Under 29%/71% 20th **Both score** 45%/55% 10th

NICE

Stade du Ray — www.ogcnice.com

	2014-15 H	2014-15 A	Last six seasons at home P	W	D	L	OV	UN	BS	CS
Paris SG	L	L	6	2	1	3	3	3	2	2
Lyon	L	W	6	1	2	3	4	2	5	0
Monaco	L	W	4	1	0	3	3	1	2	0
Marseille	W	L	6	3	1	2	2	4	3	2
St-Etienne	D	L	6	1	3	2	1	5	3	1
Bordeaux	L	W	6	2	1	3	4	2	4	1
Montpellier	D	L	6	1	2	3	2	4	2	1
Lille	W	D	6	2	2	2	1	5	2	2
Rennes	L	L	6	3	1	2	3	3	4	2
Guingamp	L	W	2	1	0	1	1	1	1	1
Nice										
Bastia	L	L	3	1	1	1	1	2	1	1
Caen	D	W	3	1	1	1	1	2	1	1
Nantes	D	L	2	0	2	0	0	2	0	2
Reims	D	W	3	2	1	0	0	3	0	3
Lorient	W	D	6	4	1	1	2	4	3	3
Toulouse	W	W	6	4	1	1	1	5	2	3
Troyes			1	1	0	0	1	0	1	0
GFC Ajaccio			-	-	-	-	-	-	-	-
Angers			-	-	-	-	-	-	-	-

Season	Division	Pos	P	W	D	L	F	A	GD	Pts
2014-15	Ligue 1	11	38	13	9	16	44	53	-9	48
2013-14	Ligue 1	17	38	12	6	20	30	44	-14	42
2012-13	Ligue 1	4	38	18	10	10	57	46	+11	64

Over/Under 55%/45% 3rd **Both score** 55%/45% 5th

PARIS SAINT-GERMAIN

Parc des Princes — www.psg.fr

	2014-15 H	2014-15 A	Last six seasons at home P	W	D	L	OV	UN	BS	CS
Paris SG										
Lyon	D	D	6	4	2	0	1	5	2	4
Monaco	D	D	4	0	3	1	1	3	3	0
Marseille	W	W	6	5	0	1	3	3	2	3
St-Etienne	W	W	6	5	0	1	4	2	2	4
Bordeaux	W	L	6	3	2	1	3	3	3	3
Montpellier	D	W	6	2	3	1	4	2	3	3
Lille	W	D	6	3	3	0	4	2	3	3
Rennes	W	D	6	2	2	2	3	3	3	3
Guingamp	W	L	2	2	0	0	1	1	0	2
Nice	W	W	6	4	1	1	3	3	2	3
Bastia	W	L	3	3	0	0	2	1	1	2
Caen	D	W	3	2	1	0	0	3	0	3
Nantes	W	W	2	2	0	0	2	0	1	1
Reims	W	D	3	3	0	0	2	1	1	2
Lorient	W	W	6	2	2	2	4	2	2	2
Toulouse	W	D	6	6	0	0	3	3	3	3
Troyes			1	1	0	0	1	0	0	1
GFC Ajaccio			-	-	-	-	-	-	-	-
Angers			-	-	-	-	-	-	-	-

Season	Division	Pos	P	W	D	L	F	A	GD	Pts
2014-15	Ligue 1	1	38	24	11	3	83	36	+47	83
2013-14	Ligue 1	1	38	27	8	3	84	23	+61	89
2012-13	Ligue 1	1	38	25	8	5	69	23	+46	83

Over/Under 55%/45% 3rd **Both score** 63%/37% 2nd

REIMS

Auguste-Delaune II — www.stade-de-reims.com

	2014-15 H	2014-15 A	Last six seasons at home P	W	D	L	OV	UN	BS	CS
Paris SG	D	L	3	1	1	1	2	1	1	1
Lyon	L	L	3	1	0	2	1	2	1	1
Monaco	L	D	3	1	1	1	1	2	2	1
Marseille	L	L	3	0	1	2	1	2	1	0
St-Etienne	L	L	3	0	2	1	2	1	3	0
Bordeaux	W	D	3	2	1	0	0	3	0	3
Montpellier	W	L	3	2	0	1	2	1	2	1
Lille	W	L	3	2	1	0	1	2	2	1
Rennes	W	L	3	2	0	1	1	2	1	2
Guingamp	L	L	3	1	1	1	2	1	3	0
Nice	L	D	3	2	0	1	1	2	1	1
Bastia	W	L	4	3	0	1	3	1	3	1
Caen	L	L	1	0	0	1	0	1	0	0
Nantes	W	D	4	3	1	0	3	1	3	1
Reims										
Lorient	L	W	3	1	1	1	1	2	2	1
Toulouse	W	L	3	1	1	1	1	2	2	1
Troyes			3	1	1	1	0	3	1	1
GFC Ajaccio			-	-	-	-	-	-	-	-
Angers			2	2	0	0	1	1	0	2

Season	Division	Pos	P	W	D	L	F	A	GD	Pts
2014-15	Ligue 1	15	38	12	8	18	47	66	-19	44
2013-14	Ligue 1	11	38	12	12	14	44	52	-8	48
2012-13	Ligue 1	14	38	10	13	15	33	42	-9	43

Over/Under 58%/42% 2nd **Both score** 61%/39% 3rd

RENNES

Stade Route de Lorient www.staderennais.com

	2014-15		Last six seasons at home							
	H	A	P	W	D	L	OV	UN	BS	CS
Paris SG	D	L	6	2	2	2	1	5	3	2
Lyon	L	L	6	1	2	3	1	5	3	1
Monaco	W	D	4	3	0	1	0	4	0	3
Marseille	D	L	6	0	4	2	2	4	5	0
St-Etienne	D	D	6	2	4	0	2	4	3	3
Bordeaux	D	L	6	2	3	1	1	5	3	2
Montpellier	L	D	6	2	1	3	4	2	2	1
Lille	W	L	6	2	3	1	1	5	3	3
Rennes										
Guingamp	W	W	2	1	0	1	0	2	0	1
Nice	W	W	6	3	2	1	4	2	3	2
Bastia	L	L	3	2	0	1	2	1	1	1
Caen	L	W	3	1	1	1	2	1	3	0
Nantes	D	D	2	0	1	1	1	1	1	1
Reims	L	L	3	2	0	1	2	1	2	1
Lorient	W	W	6	3	1	2	2	4	3	3
Toulouse	L	L	6	3	0	3	4	2	3	1
Troyes			1	0	0	1	1	0	1	0
GFC Ajaccio	-	-	-	-	-	-	-	-	-	-
Angers	-	-	-	-	-	-	-	-	-	-

Season	Division	Pos	P	W	D	L	F	A	GD	Pts
2014-15	Ligue 1	9	38	13	11	14	35	42	-7	50
2013-14	Ligue 1	12	38	11	13	14	47	45	+2	46
2012-13	Ligue 1	13	38	13	7	18	48	59	-11	46

Over/Under 32%/68% 18th **Both score** 34%/66% 20th

SAINT-ETIENNE

Stade Geoffroy-Guichard www.asse.fr

	2014-15		Last six seasons at home							
	H	A	P	W	D	L	OV	UN	BS	CS
Paris SG	L	L	6	0	4	2	2	4	3	1
Lyon	W	D	6	1	0	5	3	3	2	1
Monaco	D	D	4	2	2	0	1	3	2	2
Marseille	D	L	6	1	5	0	1	5	3	3
St-Etienne										
Bordeaux	D	L	6	2	3	1	4	2	5	1
Montpellier	W	W	6	5	1	0	2	4	2	4
Lille	W	D	6	2	1	3	3	3	4	2
Rennes	D	D	6	2	3	1	2	4	1	5
Guingamp	W	W	2	2	0	0	1	1	1	1
Nice	W	W	6	2	1	3	3	3	2	2
Bastia	W	L	3	2	1	0	0	3	1	2
Caen	W	L	3	2	1	0	0	3	1	2
Nantes	W	D	2	2	0	0	0	2	0	2
Reims	W	W	3	2	1	0	2	1	1	2
Lorient	W	W	6	3	0	3	3	3	3	1
Toulouse	L	D	6	1	2	3	3	3	4	0
Troyes	W		1	1	0	0	0	1	0	1
GFC Ajaccio	-	-	-	-	-	-	-	-	-	-
Angers	-	-	-	-	-	-	-	-	-	-

Season	Division	Pos	P	W	D	L	F	A	GD	Pts
2014-15	Ligue 1	5	38	19	12	7	51	30	+21	69
2013-14	Ligue 1	4	38	20	9	9	56	34	+22	69
2012-13	Ligue 1	5	38	16	15	7	60	32	+28	63

Over/Under 34%/66% 16th **Both score** 37%/63% 18th

TOULOUSE

Stadium Municipal www.tfc.info

	2014-15		Last six seasons at home							
	H	A	P	W	D	L	OV	UN	BS	CS
Paris SG	D	L	6	1	1	4	3	3	3	1
Lyon	W	L	6	4	2	0	3	3	1	5
Monaco	L	L	4	1	1	2	0	4	0	2
Marseille	L	L	6	0	3	3	1	5	3	1
St-Etienne	D	W	6	2	2	2	2	4	3	1
Bordeaux	W	L	6	3	1	3	3	3	4	2
Montpellier	W	L	6	2	1	3	0	6	1	2
Lille	W	L	6	2	2	2	3	3	4	1
Rennes	W	W	6	3	1	2	5	1	4	1
Guingamp	D	L	2	0	2	0	0	2	1	1
Nice	L	L	6	1	2	3	2	4	3	2
Bastia	D	L	3	0	2	1	1	2	2	1
Caen	D	L	3	2	1	0	1	2	1	2
Nantes	D	W	2	0	2	0	0	2	2	0
Reims	W	L	3	2	1	0	1	2	2	1
Lorient	L	W	6	2	1	3	2	4	2	2
Toulouse										
Troyes			1	0	1	0	1	0	1	0
GFC Ajaccio	-	-	-	-	-	-	-	-	-	-
Angers	-	-	-	-	-	-	-	-	-	-

Season	Division	Pos	P	W	D	L	F	A	GD	Pts
2014-15	Ligue 1	17	38	12	6	20	43	64	-21	42
2013-14	Ligue 1	9	38	12	13	13	46	53	-7	49
2012-13	Ligue 1	10	38	13	12	13	49	47	+2	51

Over/Under 50%/50% 7th **Both score** 53%/47% 6th

TROYES

Stade de l'Aube www.estac.fr

	2014-15		Last six seasons at home							
	H	A	P	W	D	L	OV	UN	BS	CS
Paris SG			1	0	0	1	0	1	0	0
Lyon			1	0	0	1	0	1	0	0
Monaco			1	0	1	0	0	1	1	0
Marseille			1	1	0	0	0	1	0	1
St-Etienne			1	0	1	0	1	0	1	0
Bordeaux			1	1	0	0	0	1	0	1
Montpellier			1	0	1	0	0	1	1	0
Lille			1	0	1	0	0	1	1	0
Rennes			1	0	0	1	1	0	1	0
Guingamp			1	0	1	0	0	1	1	0
Nice			1	0	1	0	0	1	1	0
Bastia			2	1	1	0	0	2	0	2
Caen			1	1	0	0	0	1	0	1
Nantes			2	1	0	1	0	2	0	1
Reims			3	3	0	0	2	1	2	1
Lorient			1	0	1	0	1	0	1	0
Toulouse			1	0	0	1	0	1	0	0
Troyes										
GFC Ajaccio	D	W	1	0	1	0	0	1	1	0
Angers	W	W	4	2	1	1	4	0	4	0

Season	Division	Pos	P	W	D	L	F	A	GD	Pts
2014-15	Ligue 2	1	38	24	6	8	61	24	+37	78
2013-14	Ligue 2	10	38	15	7	16	56	44	+12	52
2012-13	Ligue 1	19	38	8	13	17	43	61	-18	37

Over/Under 37%/63% 12th **Both score** 34%/66% 24th

FRENCH LIGUE 1

Ligue 1 2014-15

Pos	H	A		P	Home W	D	L	F	A	Away W	D	L	F	A	GD	Pts
1	1	2	Paris St-Germain	38	15	4	0	52	14	9	7	3	31	22	+47	83
2	2	3	Lyon	38	14	3	2	40	11	8	6	5	32	22	+39	75
3	8	1	Monaco	38	8	9	2	23	10	12	2	5	28	16	+25	71
4	4	4	Marseille	38	13	2	4	40	22	8	4	7	36	20	+34	69
5	3	5	St Etienne	38	12	5	2	32	11	7	7	5	19	19	+21	69
6	5	8	Bordeaux	38	12	5	2	31	23	5	7	7	16	21	+3	63
7	7	9	Montpellier	38	11	2	6	30	21	5	6	8	16	18	+7	56
8	6	13	Lille	38	11	5	3	26	12	5	3	11	17	30	+1	56
9	11	10	Rennes	38	8	5	6	22	22	5	6	8	13	20	-7	50
10	13	11	Guingamp	38	9	1	9	23	25	6	3	10	18	30	-14	49
11	16	6	Nice	38	6	6	7	21	24	7	3	9	23	29	-9	48
12	9	16	Bastia	38	8	7	4	24	18	4	4	11	13	28	-9	47
13	15	7	Caen	38	7	3	9	26	25	5	7	7	28	30	-1	46
14	12	14	Nantes	38	7	7	5	17	17	4	5	10	12	23	-11	45
15	14	15	Reims	38	8	3	8	24	29	4	5	10	23	37	-19	44
16	17	12	Lorient	38	6	5	8	17	17	6	2	11	27	33	-6	43
17	10	18	Toulouse	38	8	6	5	28	29	4	0	15	15	35	-21	42
18	18	17	Evian TG	38	7	2	10	20	25	4	2	13	21	37	-21	37
19	19	20	Metz	38	6	4	9	26	32	1	5	13	5	29	-30	30
20	20	19	Lens	38	5	4	10	14	24	2	4	13	18	37	-29	29

Results 2014-15

	Bastia	Bordeaux	Caen	Evian TG	Guingamp	Lens	Lille	Lorient	Lyon	Marseille	Metz	Monaco	Montpellier	Nantes	Nice	Paris SG	Reims	Rennes	St Etienne	Toulouse
Bastia		0-0	1-1	1-2	0-0	1-1	2-1	0-2	0-0	3-3	2-0	1-3	2-0	0-0	2-1	4-2	1-2	2-0	1-0	1-0
Bordeaux	1-1		1-1	2-1	1-1	2-1	1-0	3-2	0-5	1-0	1-1	4-1	2-1	2-1	1-2	3-2	1-1	2-1	1-0	2-1
Caen	1-1	1-2		3-2	0-2	4-1	0-1	2-1	3-0	1-2	0-0	0-3	1-1	1-2	2-3	0-2	4-1	0-1	1-0	2-0
Evian TG	1-2	0-1	0-3		2-0	2-1	0-1	1-0	2-3	1-3	3-0	1-3	1-0	0-2	1-0	0-0	2-3	1-1	1-2	1-0
Guingamp	1-0	2-1	5-1	1-1		2-0	0-1	3-2	1-3	0-1	0-1	1-0	0-2	0-1	2-7	1-0	2-0	0-1	0-2	2-1
Lens	1-1	1-2	0-0	0-2	0-1		1-1	0-0	0-2	0-4	2-0	0-3	0-1	1-0	2-0	1-3	4-2	0-1	0-1	1-0
Lille	1-0	2-0	1-0	1-0	1-2	3-1		2-0	2-1	0-4	0-0	0-1	0-0	2-0	0-0	1-1	3-1	3-0	1-1	3-0
Lorient	2-0	0-0	2-1	0-2	4-0	1-0	1-0		1-1	1-1	3-1	0-1	0-0	1-2	0-0	1-2	0-1	0-3	0-1	0-1
Lyon	2-0	1-1	3-0	2-0	3-1	0-1	3-0	4-0		1-0	2-0	2-1	5-1	1-0	1-2	1-1	2-1	2-0	2-2	3-0
Marseille	3-0	3-1	2-3	1-0	2-1	2-1	2-1	3-5	0-0		3-1	2-1	0-2	2-0	4-0	2-3	2-2	3-0	2-1	2-0
Metz	3-1	0-0	3-2	1-2	0-2	3-1	1-4	0-4	2-1	0-2		0-1	2-3	1-1	0-0	2-3	3-0	0-0	2-3	3-2
Monaco	3-0	0-0	2-2	2-0	1-0	2-0	1-1	1-2	0-0	1-0	2-0		0-0	0-1	0-0	1-1	1-1	1-1	1-1	4-1
Montpellier	3-1	0-1	1-0	2-0	2-1	3-3	1-2	1-0	1-5	2-1	2-0	0-1		4-0	2-1	1-2	3-1	0-0	0-2	2-0
Nantes	0-2	2-1	1-2	2-1	1-0	1-0	1-1	1-1	1-1	1-0	0-0	0-1	1-0		2-1	0-2	1-1	1-1	0-0	1-2
Nice	0-1	1-3	1-1	2-2	1-2	2-1	1-0	3-1	1-3	2-1	1-0	0-1	1-1	0-0		1-3	0-0	1-2	0-0	3-2
Paris St-Germain	2-0	3-0	2-2	4-2	6-0	4-1	6-1	3-1	1-1	2-0	3-1	1-1	0-0	2-1	1-0		3-2	1-0	5-0	3-1
Reims	2-1	1-0	0-2	3-2	2-3	0-0	2-0	1-3	2-4	0-5	0-0	1-3	1-0	3-1	0-1	2-2		1-0	1-2	2-0
Rennes	0-1	1-1	1-4	6-2	1-0	2-0	2-0	1-0	0-1	1-1	1-0	2-0	0-4	0-0	2-1	1-1	1-3		0-0	0-3
St Etienne	1-0	1-1	1-0	3-0	2-1	3-3	2-0	2-0	3-0	2-2	1-1	1-0	1-0	5-0	1-0	3-1	0-0			0-1
Toulouse	1-1	2-1	3-3	1-0	1-1	0-2	3-2	2-3	2-1	1-6	3-0	0-2	1-0	1-1	2-3	1-1	1-0	2-1	1-1	

Top scorers

	Team	Goals scored	
A Lacazette	Lyon	27	▩▩▩▩▩▩▩▩▩▩▩▩▩▩▩▩▩▩▩▩▩▩▩▩▩▩▩
A-P Gignac	Marseille	21	▩▩▩▩▩▩▩▩▩▩▩▩▩▩▩▩▩▩▩▩▩
Z Ibrahimovic	Paris SG	19	▩▩▩▩▩▩▩▩▩▩▩▩▩▩▩▩▩▩▩
E Cavani	Paris SG	18	▩▩▩▩▩▩▩▩▩▩▩▩▩▩▩▩▩▩
C Beauvue	Guingamp	17	▩▩▩▩▩▩▩▩▩▩▩▩▩▩▩▩▩
M Gradel	St-Etienne	17	▩▩▩▩▩▩▩▩▩▩▩▩▩▩▩▩▩

Over 2.5 goals top five

	H	A	%
Marseille	14	10	63%
Reims	10	12	58%
Paris SG	12	9	55%
Caen	10	11	55%
Nice	10	11	55%
Lyon	10	11	55%

Both to score top five

	H	A	%
Bordeaux	15	10	66%
Paris SG	11	13	63%
Reims	9	14	61%
Caen	10	12	58%
Nice	12	9	55%

Uefa Association Coefficients 2014-15

Pos	Change	Country	10-11	11-12	12-13	13-14	14-15	Pts	Change
1	=	Spain	18.214	20.857	17.714	23	19.642	**99.427**	+1.714
2	=	England	18.357	15.25	16.428	16.785	13.571	**80.391**	-4.357
3	=	Germany	15.666	15.25	17.928	14.714	15.857	**79.415**	-2.226
4	=	Italy	11.571	11.357	14.416	14.166	19	**70.51**	+3.572
5	=	Portugal	18.8	11.833	11.75	9.916	9.083	**61.382**	-0.917
6	=	France	10.75	10.5	11.75	8.5	10.916	**52.416**	-4.084
7	=	Russia	10.916	9.75	9.75	10.416	9.666	**50.498**	+3.500
8	+1	Ukraine	10.083	7.75	9.5	7.833	10	**45.166**	+4.200
9	-1	Holland	11.166	13.6	4.214	5.916	6.083	**40.979**	-3.333
10	=	Belgium	4.6	10.1	6.5	6.4	9.6	**37.2**	+0.900
11	+2	Switzerland	5.9	6	8.375	7.2	6.9	**34.375**	+1.150
12	-1	Turkey	4.6	5.1	10.2	6.7	6	**32.6**	-1.600
13	-1	Greece	7.6	7.6	4.4	6.1	6.2	**31.9**	-1.700
14	+1	Czech Rep	3.5	5.25	8.5	8	3.875	**29.125**	-0.225
15	+1	Romania	3.166	4.333	6.8	6.875	5.125	**26.299**	-0.958
16	-2	Austria	4.375	7.125	2.25	7.8	4.125	**25.675**	-5.250
17	+3	Croatia	4.125	3.75	4.375	4.375	6.875	**23.5**	+3.875
18	=	Cyprus	3.125	9.125	4	2.75	3.3	**22.3**	-0.950
19	+2	Poland	4.5	6.625	2.5	3.125	4.75	**21.5**	+2.625
20	-3	Israel	4.625	6	3.25	5.75	1.375	**21**	-5.875
21	+1	Belarus	5.875	3.125	4.5	1.75	5.5	**20.75**	+2.125
22	-3	Denmark	6.7	3.1	3.3	3.8	2.9	**19.8**	-1.500
23	=	Scotland	3.6	2.75	4.3	3.25	4	**17.9**	+1.334
24	=	Sweden	2.6	2.9	5.125	3.2	3.9	**17.725**	+1.400
25	=	Bulgaria	4.625	1.5	0.75	5.625	4.25	**16.75**	+1.125
26	=	Norway	2.375	2.3	4.9	2.6	2.2	**14.375**	+0.100
27	=	Serbia	3.5	2.125	3	2.5	2.75	**13.875**	-0.250
28	+1	Slovenia	1.5	2.25	3.25	2.625	4	**13.625**	+2.625
29	+3	Azerbaijan	2	1.375	3	2.5	3.625	**12.5**	+2.125
30	=	Slovakia	3	2.375	1.5	1.625	2.75	**11.25**	+0.250
31	-3	Hungary	2.75	2.25	3	0.875	2.125	**11**	-0.625
32	+2	Kazakhstan	0.875	1.625	1.375	3.125	3.375	**10.375**	+2.125
33	-2	Moldova	2.125	0.5	2.25	3.375	1.75	**10**	-0.375
34	-1	Georgia	1.875	2.875	1.5	1.875	1.25	**9.375**	-0.500
35	+1	Finland	1.8	1.5	2	0.5	2.4	**8.2**	+1.025
36	+1	Iceland	0.375	1.375	1.25	2.5	2.5	**8**	+1.250
37	-2	Bosnia-Hz	1.875	1.125	1.25	1.5	1.75	**7.5**	=
38	+8	Liechtenstein	0.5	2	0	1	2.5	**6**	+1.500
39	+3	Macedonia	1.375	1.625	1.25	0.5	1.125	**5.875**	+0.625
40	+3	Ireland	1	1.5	1	0.25	2	**5.75**	+0.625
41	-2	Montenegro	1.75	0.5	1.375	1.25	0.75	**5.625**	-0.375
42	-2	Albania	0.875	0.875	0.75	2	0.875	**5.375**	-0.125
43	+1	Luxembourg	0.625	1.125	1.375	1.5	0.5	**5.125**	+0.250
44	+3	N Ireland	1.125	0.5	1	0.875	1.375	**4.875**	+1.250
45	-4	Lithuania	0.625	1	1.125	1.25	0.5	**4.5**	-0.750
46	-8	Latvia	0.5	0.625	1.25	1.625	0.25	**4.25**	-2.000
47	-2	Malta	1.5	0.833	0.875	0.875	0.125	**4.208**	-0.625
48	+2	Estonia	0.25	0.375	0.375	1	1.5	**3.5**	+0.625
49	+2	Faroe Islands	0.25	0.5	0.5	0.875	1.375	**3.5**	+1.375
50	-2	Wales	0.875	0.625	0.5	0.75	0.125	**2.875**	-0.125
51	-2	Armenia	0.25	0.125	0.875	1.125	0.375	**2.75**	-0.125
52	+1	Andorra	0	0	0	0.333	0.5	**0.833**	=
53	-1	San Marino	0.166	0	0	0.333	0	**0.499**	-0.500
54	-	Gibraltar	0	0	0	0	0.25	**0.25**	+0.250

Uefa's country coefficients are calculated from performances of each FA's clubs in the last five Europa League and Champions League seasons. They are used to allocate places in Uefa's club competitions and determine seedings with the top 12, shown on the facing page, receiving at least one place in the Champions League group stage.

Two points are awarded for a win and one for a draw, and half that in qualifying matches. An extra point is awarded for every round from the last 16 of the Champions League and the quarter-finals of the Europa League. Four extra points are given for reaching the group stage of the Champions League and four more for the knockout rounds.

The country coefficient is the sum of the average points for each nation in each of the last five seasons. England's clubs have averaged 18.357, 15.25, 16.428, 16.785 and 13.571 over the last five campaigns – add them together and you get 80.391, England's country coefficient.

Portugal

		P	W	D	L	F	A	GD	Pts
1	Benfica	34	27	4	3	86	16	+70	85
2	Porto	34	25	7	2	74	13	+61	82
3	Sporting	34	22	10	2	67	29	+38	76
4	Sp Braga	34	17	7	10	55	28	+27	58
5	Vit Guimaraes	34	15	10	9	50	35	+15	55
6	Belenenses	34	12	12	10	34	35	-1	48
7	Nacional	34	13	8	13	45	46	-1	47
8	Pacos Ferreira	34	12	11	11	40	45	-5	47
9	Maritimo	34	12	8	14	46	45	+1	44
10	Rio Ave	34	10	13	11	38	42	-4	43
11	Moreirense	34	11	10	13	33	42	-9	43
12	Estoril	34	9	13	12	38	56	-18	40
13	Boavista	34	9	7	18	27	50	-23	34
14	Vitoria Setubal	34	7	8	19	24	56	-32	29
15	Academica	34	4	17	13	26	46	-20	29
16	Arouca	34	7	7	20	26	50	-24	28
17	Gil Vicente	34	4	11	19	25	60	-35	23
18	Penafiel	34	5	7	22	29	69	-40	22

Russia

		P	W	D	L	F	A	GD	Pts
1	Zenit	30	20	7	3	58	17	+41	67
2	CSKA Moscow	30	19	3	8	67	27	+40	60
3	Krasnodar	30	17	9	4	52	27	+25	60
4	Din Moscow	30	14	8	8	53	36	+17	50
5	Rubin Kazan	30	13	9	8	39	33	+6	48
6	Spartak Moscow	30	12	8	10	42	42	0	44
7	Lok Moscow	30	11	10	9	31	25	+6	43
8	Mordovia	30	11	5	14	22	43	-21	38
9	Terek Grozny	30	10	7	13	30	30	0	37
10	Kuban	30	8	12	10	32	36	-4	36
11	Amkar Perm	30	8	8	14	25	42	-17	32
12	Ufa	30	7	10	13	26	39	-13	31
13	Ural	30	9	3	18	31	44	-13	30
14	Rostov	30	7	8	15	27	51	-24	29
15	Torp Moscow	30	6	11	13	28	45	-17	29
16	Arsenal Tula	30	7	4	19	20	46	-26	25

Ukraine

		P	W	D	L	F	A	GD	Pts
1	Dynamo Kiev	26	20	6	0	65	12	+53	66
2	Shakhtar	26	17	5	4	71	21	+50	56
3	Dnipro	26	16	6	4	47	17	+30	54
4	Zorya	26	13	6	7	40	31	+9	45
5	Vorskla	26	11	9	6	35	22	+13	42
6	Metalist	25	8	11	6	34	32	+2	35
7	Volyn	26	9	7	10	38	44	-6	34
8	Met Donetsk	26	6	10	10	27	38	-11	28
9	Met Zaporizhya	26	6	8	12	20	40	-20	26
10	Olimpik Donetsk	26	7	5	14	24	64	-40	26
11	Chornomorets	25	3	11	11	15	31	-16	20
12	Hoverla	26	3	10	13	22	47	-25	19
13	Karpaty	26	5	9	12	22	31	-9	15
14	Illichivets	26	3	5	18	25	55	-30	14

Holland

		P	W	D	L	F	A	GD	Pts
1	PSV	34	29	1	4	92	31	+61	88
2	Ajax	34	21	8	5	69	29	+40	71
3	AZ	34	19	5	10	63	56	+7	62
4	Feyenoord	34	17	8	9	56	39	+17	59
5	Vitesse	34	16	10	8	66	43	+23	58
6	PEC Zwolle	34	16	5	13	59	43	+16	53
7	Heerenveen	34	13	11	10	53	46	+7	50
8	Groningen	34	11	13	10	49	53	-4	46
9	Willem II	34	13	7	14	46	50	-4	46
10	Twente	34	13	10	11	56	51	+5	43
11	Utrecht	34	11	8	15	60	62	-2	41
12	Cambuur	34	11	8	15	46	56	-10	41
13	ADO Den Haag	34	9	10	15	44	53	-9	37
14	Heracles	34	11	4	19	47	64	-17	37
15	Excelsior	34	6	14	14	47	63	-16	32
16	NAC Breda	34	6	10	18	36	68	-32	28
17	Go Ahead Eagles	34	7	6	21	29	59	-30	27
18	Dordrecht	34	4	8	22	24	76	-52	20

Belgium (Championship playoff)

		P	W	D	L	F	A	GD	Pts
1	Gent	10	6	2	2	18	11	7	49
2	Club Brugge	10	5	1	4	16	16	0	47
3	Anderlecht	10	5	2	3	18	13	5	46
4	Standard Liege	10	4	1	5	14	13	1	40
5	Charleroi	10	3	2	5	13	15	-2	36
6	Kortrijk	10	2	2	6	11	22	-11	34

Points from regular season are halved, rounded up and carried over into round-robin championship playoff

Switzerland

		P	W	D	L	F	A	GD	Pts
1	Basel	36	24	6	6	84	41	+43	78
2	Young Boys	36	19	9	8	64	45	+19	66
3	Zurich	36	15	8	13	55	48	+7	53
4	Thun	36	13	13	10	47	45	+2	52
5	Luzern	36	12	11	13	54	46	+8	47
6	St Gallen	36	13	8	15	57	65	-8	47
7	Sion	36	12	9	15	47	48	-1	45
8	Grasshoppers	36	11	10	15	50	56	-6	43
9	Vaduz	36	7	10	19	28	59	-31	31
10	Aarau	36	6	12	18	31	64	-33	30

Turkey

		P	W	D	L	F	A	GD	Pts
1	Galatasaray	34	24	5	5	60	35	+25	77
2	Fenerbahce	34	22	8	4	60	29	+31	74
3	Besiktas	34	21	6	7	55	32	+23	69
4	Basaksehir	34	15	14	5	49	30	+19	59
5	Trabzonspor	34	15	12	7	58	48	+10	57
6	Bursaspor	34	16	9	9	69	44	+25	57
7	Mersin	34	13	8	13	54	48	+6	47
8	Konyaspor	34	12	10	12	30	39	-9	46
9	Genclerbirligi	34	10	10	14	46	44	+2	40
10	Gaziantepspor	34	11	7	16	31	48	-17	40
11	Eskisehirspor	34	9	12	13	45	52	-7	39
12	Akhisar Belediye	34	9	11	14	41	51	-10	38
13	Kasimpasa	34	9	10	15	56	73	-17	37
14	Sivasspor	34	9	9	16	43	50	-7	36
15	Rizespor	34	9	9	16	41	55	-14	36
16	Karabukspor	34	7	7	20	44	64	-20	28
17	Erciyesspor	34	5	12	17	43	62	-19	27
18	Balikesirspor	34	6	9	19	48	69	-21	27

YOUR BUNDESLIGA BUDDY

SOCCERBASE.COM
BET SMARTER THIS SEASON

First qualifying round

Tuesday July 1, 2014
Jeunesse Esch.(0) 0-2 (0)..........Dundalk
Shkendija........(1) 2-1 (0).......FC Zimbru
Sliema W. ....(1) 1-1 (0)..... Ferencvaros

Thursday July 3, 2014
Aberdeen........(1) 5-0 (0).Daugava Riga
Airbus UK ......(1) 1-1 (1).....Haugesund
B36 Torshavn..(0) 1-2 (1)...........Linfield
Banga.............(0) 0-0 (0)....Sligo Rovers
Botev Plovdiv..(1) 4-0 (0).........Libertas
Celik Zenica ....(0) 0-5 (2).............Koper
Crusaders ....(2) 3-1 (0)...........Ekranas
Cukaricki.........(1) 4-0 (0)...UE Sant Julia
Derry City ....(2) 4-0 (0)...Aberystwyth
Differdange.....(0) 1-0 (0)..........Atlantas
Diosgyor.........(1) 2-1 (1).......Birkirkara
FC Tiraspol......(0) 2-3 (2)....... Inter Baku
Folgore ....(0) 1-2 (2)... Buducnost P.
Fram Reykjavik(0) 0-1 (0)..Nomme Kalju
Hafnarfjordur..(0) 3-0 (0)........Glenavon
Hibernians .....(0) 2-4 (3)Spartak Trnava
IFK Goth'burg .(0) 0-0 (0)........ Fola Esch
Kairat Almaty..(0) 0-0 (0)............Kukes
Kalev Sillamae (1) 2-1 (0).............Honka
MyPa-47 ....(0) 1-0 (0) IF Fuglafjordur
NK Split ....(1) 2-0 (0)..........FC Mika
Pyunik Yerevan(0) 1-4 (1)...........Astana
Qabala............(0) 0-2 (0)NK Siroki Brijeg
Rosenborg ......(2) 4-0 (0)...........Jelgava
Rudar Velenje .(1) 1-1 (0)..........KF Laci
Shirak Gumri...(0) 1-2 (0)... S Karagandy
Sioni ....(2) 2-3 (1).......Flamurtari
Stjarnan..........(2) 4-0 (0).....Bangor City
Tartu FC Santos(0) 0-7 (4)...........Tromso
Turnovo ....(0) 0-1 (1) Chikhura Sach.
UE Santa.........(0) 0-3 (2).....Metalurg S.
VPS Vaasa.......(0) 2-1 (1).Brommapojkarna
Vaduz ....(2) 3-0 (0)College Europa
Veris ....(0) 0-0 (0).............. Litex
Vikingur..........(1) 2-1 (0) ... FC Daugava
Zeljeznicar ......(0) 0-0 (0)...........Lovcen

Second legs

Tuesday July 8, 2014
Linfield ....(1) 1-1 (0)..B36 Torshavn
Aggregate: 3-2

Thursday July 10, 2014
Aberystwyth ...(0) 0-5 (0)....... Derry City
Aggregate: 0-9
Astana ....(1) 2-0 (0)Pyunik Yerevan
Aggregate: 6-1
Atlantas..........(1) 3-1 (0).....Differdange
Aggregate: 3-2
Bangor City.....(0) 0-4 (0)..........Stjarnan
Aggregate: 0-8
Birkirkara ....(1) 1-4 (1).........Diosgyor
Aggregate: 2-6

The draw for the first qualifying round of the Europa League

Brommapojkarna.(0) 2-0 (0).......VPS Vaasa
Aggregate: 3-2
Buducnost P. ...(1) 3-0 (0)...........Folgore
Aggregate: 5-1
Chikhura Sach. (1) 3-1 (1)..........Turnovo
Aggregate: 4-1
College Europa(0) 0-1 (0)............. Vaduz
Aggregate: 0-4
Daugava Riga .(0) 0-3 (3)..........Aberdeen
Aggregate: 0-8
Dundalk..........(3) 3-1 (0).Jeunesse Esch
Aggregate: 5-1
Ekranas...........(0) 1-2 (0)....... Crusaders
Aggregate: 2-5
FC Daugava ....(0) 1-1 (0)..........Vikingur
Aggregate: 2-3
FC Mika ....(1) 1-1 (0).......... NK Split
Aggregate: 1-3
FC Zimbru ....(1) 2-0 (0)........Shkendija
Aggregate: 3-2
Ferencvaros ....(1) 2-1 (0)..... Sliema W.
Aggregate: 3-2
Flamurtari ....(0) 1-2 (0) .... Sioni
Aggregate: 4-4, Flamurtari won on away goals
Fola Esch ....(0) 0-2 (0). IFK Goth'burg
Aggregate: 0-2
Glenavon ....(0) 2-3 (2)..Hafnarfjordur
Aggregate: 2-6
Haugesund .....(1) 2-1 (1)...... Airbus UK
Aggregate: 3-2
Honka.............(1) 3-2 (1) Kalev Sillamae
AET 2-1 after 90 mins, aggregate: 4-4
Kalev Sillamae won on away goals
IF Fuglafjordur (0) 0-0 (0).........MyPa-47
Aggregate: 0-1
Inter Baku ....(0) 3-1 (1)......FC Tiraspol
Aggregate: 6-3
Jelgava ....(0) 0-2 (1)......Rosenborg
Aggregate: 0-6
KF Laci ....(0) 1-1 (0). Rudar Velenje
AET 1-1 after 90 mins, aggregate 2-2
KF Laci won 3-2 on pens

Koper..............(2) 4-0 (0)....Celik Zenica
Aggregate: 9-0
Kukes..............(0) 0-0 (0)..Kairat Almaty
Aggregate: 0-1
Libertas...........(0) 0-2 (0)..Botev Plovdiv
Aggregate: 0-6
Lovcen ....(0) 0-1 (0)...... Zeljeznicar
Aggregate: 0-1
Metalurg S......(2) 2-0 (0)........UE Santa
Aggregate: 5-0
NK Siroki Brijeg(2) 3-0 (0)............Qabala
Aggregate: 5-0
Nomme Kalju..(1) 2-2 (1) Fram Reykjavik
Aggregate: 3-2
S Karagandy ...(3) 4-0 (0)...Shirak Gumri
Aggregate: 6-1
Sligo Rovers....(1) 4-0 (0)............Banga
Aggregate: 4-0
Spartak Trnava (3) 5-0 (0)...... Hibernians
Aggregate: 9-2
Tromso............(3) 6-1 (1)Tartu FC Santos
Aggregate: 13-1
UE Sant Julia...(0) 0-0 (0).......Cukaricki
Aggregate: 0-4

Friday July 11, 2014
Litex ....(1) 3-0 (0).............. Veris
Aggregate: 3-0

Second qualifying round

Thursday July 17, 2014
Aberdeen........(0) 0-0 (0)..FC Groningen
Astana ....(1) 3-0 (0)...... H Tel Aviv
Atlantas..........(0) 0-0 (0) ... S Karagandy
Botev Plovdiv..(1) 2-1 (0) .... St Polten
Brommapojkarna.(2) 4-0 (0)....... Crusaders
Buducnost P. ...(0) 0-2 (1)Omonia Nicosia
Bursaspor........(0) 0-0 (0) Chikhura Sach.
CFR Cluj..........(0) 0-0 (0).........Jagodina
CSKA Sofia......(1) 1-1 (1).......FC Zimbru
Cukaricki.........(0) 0-4 (1)....... SV Grodig

Derry City .... (0) 0-1 (1) .... Shakhtyor
Dinamo Minsk (1) 3-0 (0) MyPa-47
Dundalk......... (0) 0-2 (1) .... Hajduk Split
Elfsborg .... (0) 0-1 (1) .... Inter Baku
FC Kosice .... (0) 0-1 (0) Slovan Liberec
Gyori ETO .... (0) 0-3 (1) . IFK Goth'burg
KF Laci .... (0) 0-3 (1) .... Zorya
Kairat Almaty.. (0) 1-1 (0) .... Esbjerg
Kalev Sillamae (0) 0-4 (2) .. FK Krasnodar
Linfield .... (0) 1-0 (0) .... AIK Solna
Litex .... (0) 0-2 (0) .... Diosgyor
Lucerne........... (1) 1-1 (0) ... St Johnstone
Metalurg S...... (0) 0-0 (0) ...... Zeljeznicar
Mlada Boleslav(0) 2-1 (0)NK Siroki Brijeg
Molde............. (3) 4-1 (0).ND HIT Gorica
Motherwell..... (2) 2-2 (1) .... Stjarnan
NK Split .... (0) 2-1 (1) . H. Beer Sheva
Neftchi Baku... (1) 1-2 (2) .... Koper
Neman Grodno(0) 1-1 (0)..Hafnarfjordur
Nomme Kalju... (1) 0-0 (0) ....Lech Poznan
Odu Trencin ... (1) 4-0 (0).. Vojvodina NS
Petrolul Ploiesti(0) 2-0 (0) .... Flamurtari
Rijeka .... (0) 1-0 (0) .... Ferencvaros
RoPS............... (1) 1-1 (1) .... Asteras T.
Rosenborg ...... (0) 1-2 (0) .... Sligo Rovers
Ruch Chorzow (2) 3-2 (1) .... Vaduz
Sarajevo .... (0) 0-1 (0) ..... Haugesund
Vikingur.......... (0) 0-0 (0) .... Tromso
Waregem......... (2) 2-1 (1) ....Z Bydgoszcz
Zestafoni......... (0) 0-0 (0) Spartak Trnava

Second legs
Tuesday July 22, 2014
Zeljeznicar ...... (1) 2-2 (0) .....Metalurg S.
Aggregate: 2-2, Metalurg S. won on away goals

Thursday July 24, 2014
AIK Solna........ (0) 2-0 (0) .... Linfield
Aggregate: 2-1
Asteras T. .... (2) 4-2 (0) .... RoPS
Aggregate: 5-3
Chikhura Sach. (0) 0-0 (0) ...... Bursaspor
AET 0-0 after 90 mins, Chikhura won 4-1 on pens
Crusaders .... (1) 1-1 (1) .Brommapojkarna
Aggregate: 1-5
Diosgyor......... (1) 1-2 (0) .... Litex
Aggregate: 3-2
Esbjerg .... (1) 1-0 (0)..Kairat Almaty
Aggregate: 2-1
FC Groningen.. (1) 1-2 (2) ....Aberdeen
Aggregate: 1-2
FC Zimbru ...... (0) 0-0 (0) ......CSKA Sofia
AET 0-0 after 90 mins, aggregate: 1-1
FC Zimbru won on away goals
FK Krasnodar .. (1) 5-0 (0) Kalev Sillamae
Aggregate: 9-0
Ferencvaros .... (0) 1-2 (2) .... Rijeka
Aggregate: 1-3
Flamurtari ...... (1) 1-3 (1)Petrolul Ploiesti
Aggregate: 1-5
H Tel Aviv .... (0) 1-0 (0) ....Astana
Aggregate: 1-3
H. Beer Sheva . (0) 0-0 (0) .... NK Split
Aggregate: 1-2
Hafnarfjordur.. (1) 2-0 (0)Neman Grodno
Aggregate: 3-1

Hajduk Split .... (1) 1-2 (0) ....Dundalk
Aggregate: 3-2
Haugesund ..... (0) 1-3 (2) .... Sarajevo
Aggregate: 2-3
IFK Goth'burg . (0) 0-1 (0) .... Gyori ETO
Aggregate: 3-1
Inter Baku....... (0) 0-1 (1) .... Elfsborg
AET 0-1 after 90 mins, aggregate: 1-1
Elfsborg won 4-3 on pens
Jagodina......... (0) 0-1 (0) .... CFR Cluj
Aggregate: 0-1
Koper.............. (0) 0-2 (1) ... Neftchi Baku
Aggregate: 2-3
Lech Poznan.... (2) 3-0 (0) ..Nomme Kalju
Aggregate: 3-1
MyPa-47 .... (0) 0-0 (0) Dinamo Minsk
Aggregate: 0-3
ND HIT Gorica . (0) 1-1 (0) ....Molde
Aggregate: 2-5
NK Siroki Brijeg(0) 0-4 (1)Mlada Boleslav
Aggregate: 1-6
Omonia Nicosia(0) 0-0 (0) ... Buducnost P.
Aggregate: 2-0
S Karagandy ... (0) 3-0 (0) ....Atlantas
Aggregate: 3-0
SV Grodig .... (1) 1-2 (0) ....Cukaricki
Aggregate: 5-2
Shakhtyor .... (2) 5-1 (1) .... Derry City
Aggregate: 6-1
Sligo Rovers.... (1) 1-3 (1) ...... Rosenborg
Aggregate: 3-4
Slovan Liberec (1) 3-0 (0) .... FC Kosice
Aggregate: 4-0
Spartak Trnava (2) 3-0 (0) ....Zestafoni
Aggregate: 3-0
St Johnstone ... (1) 1-1 (0) ....Lucerne
AET 1-1 after 90 mins, aggregate: 2-2
St Johnstone won 5-4 on pens
St Polten .... (1) 2-0 (0)..Botev Plovdiv
Aggregate: 3-2
Stjarnan .... (1) 3-2 (1) .....Motherwell
AET 2-2 after 90 mins, aggregate: 5-4
Tromso............ (0) 1-2 (0) .... Vikingur
Aggregate: 1-2

Vaduz .... (0) 0-0 (0) Ruch Chorzow
Aggregate: 2-3
Vojvodina NS .. (1) 3-0 (0) .... Odu Trencin
Aggregate: 3-4
Z Bydgoszcz .... (0) 1-3 (1) ....Waregem
Aggregate: 2-5
Zorya .... (0) 2-1 (0) .... KF Laci
Aggregate: 5-1

Third qualifying round
Thursday July 31, 2014
Astana .... (1) 1-1 (1) .... AIK Solna
Astra Giurgiu .. (1) 3-0 (0) Slovan Liberec
Din. Moscow .. (0) 1-1 (0) ...Ironi Kiryat S
Dinamo Minsk (0) 1-0 (0) ....CFR Cluj
Diosgyor......... (0) 1-5 (2) .. FK Krasnodar
Elfsborg .... (0) 4-1 (0) ..Hafnarfjordur
FC Bruges .... (2) 3-0 (0) ....Brondby
Brommapojkarna. (0) 0-3 (1) .... Torino
IFK Goth'burg . (0) 0-1 (1) ....Rio Ave
Kardemir......... (0) 0-0 (0) ...... Rosenborg
Mainz .... (1) 1-0 (0) .... Asteras T.
Mlada Boleslav(0) 1-4 (2) .... Lyon
NK Split .... (1) 2-0 (0) .... Ch. Odessa
Neftchi Baku... (0) 0-0 (0) Chikhura Sach.
Odu Trencin ... (0) 0-0 (0) .... Hull
Omonia Nicosia(2) 3-0 (0) .....Metalurg S.
PSV Eindhoven (1) 1-0 (0) .... St Polten
Petrolul Ploiesti(0) 1-1 (0)..Viktoria Plzen
Ruch Chorzow (0) 0-0 (0) .... Esbjerg
S Karagandy ... (2) 4-2 (1) .... Hajduk Split
SV Grodig .... (0) 1-2 (1) .... FC Zimbru
Sarajevo .... (1) 1-2 (1) .... Atromitos
Sociedad......... (0) 2-0 (0) .... Aberdeen
St Johnstone ... (0) 1-2 (1) Spartak Trnava
Stjarnan .... (0) 1-0 (0) ....Lech Poznan
Vikingur.......... (1) 1-5 (2) .... Rijeka
Waregem......... (1) 2-5 (3) .... Shakhtyor
Young Boys..... (0) 1-0 (0) .... Ermis
Zorya .... (0) 1-1 (0) ....Molde

Aberdeen lost out to Real Sociedad in the third qualifying round

Second legs

Thursday August 1, 2014

AIK Solna .... (0) 0-3 (1) .... Astana
    Aggregate: 1-4
Aberdeen .... (1) 2-3 (1) .... Sociedad
    Aggregate: 2-5
Asteras T. .... (1) 3-1 (1) .... Mainz
    Aggregate: 3-2
Atromitos .... (0) 1-3 (1) .... Sarajevo
    AET 1-2 after 90 mins, aggregate: 3-4
Brondby .... (0) 0-2 (2) .... FC Bruges
    Aggregate: 0-5
CFR Cluj .... (0) 0-2 (0) Dinamo Minsk
    Aggregate: 0-3
Ch. Odessa ...... (0) 0-0 (0) .... NK Split
    Aggregate: 0-2
Chikhura Sach. (1) 2-3 (3) ... Neftchi Baku
    Aggregate: 2-3
Ermis .... (0) 0-2 (1) ..... Young Boys
    Aggregate: 0-3
Esbjerg .... (1) 2-2 (1) Ruch Chorzow
    Aggregate: 2-2. Ruch Chorzow
    won on away goals
FC Zimbru .... (0) 0-1 (0) .... SV Grodig
Aggregate: 2-2, FC Zimbru won on away goals
FK Krasnodar .. (1) 3-0 (0) .... Diosgyor
    Aggregate: 8-1
Hafnarfjordur.. (1) 2-1 (0) .... Elfsborg
    Aggregate: 3-5
Hajduk Split .... (2) 3-0 (0) ... S Karagandy
    Aggregate: 5-4
Hull .... (1) 2-1 (1) .... Odu Trencin
    Aggregate: 2-1
Ironi Kiryat S... (1) 1-2 (2) .. Din. Moscow
    Aggregate: 2-3
Lech Poznan.... (0) 0-0 (0) .... Stjarnan
    Aggregate: 0-1
Lyon .... (0) 2-1 (0)Mlada Boleslav
    Aggregate: 6-2
Metalurg S...... (0) 0-1 (0)Omonia Nicosia
    Aggregate: 0-4
Molde............. (1) 1-2 (1) .... Zorya
    Aggregate: 2-3
Rijeka .... (1) 4-0 (0) .... Vikingur
    Aggregate: 9-1
Rio Ave........... (0) 0-0 (0) . IFK Goth'burg
    Aggregate: 1-0
Rosenborg ...... (1) 1-1 (1) .... Kardemir
Aggregate: 1-1, Kardemir won on away goals
Shakhtyor .... (2) 2-2 (1) .... Waregem
    Aggregate: 7-4
Slovan Liberec (2) 2-3 (1) .. Astra Giurgiu
    Aggregate: 2-6
Spartak Trnava (0) 1-1 (1) ... St Johnstone
    Aggregate: 3-2
St Polten .... (0) 2-3 (1) PSV Eindhoven
    Aggregate: 2-4
Torino .... (2) 4-0 (0) .Brommapojkarna
    Aggregate: 7-0
Viktoria Plzen.. (1) 1-4 (3)Petrolul Ploiesti
    Aggregate: 2-5

Play-offs

Wednesday August 20, 2014

Dnipro .... (0) 2-1 (0) .... Hajduk Split
Stjarnan .... (0) 0-3 (1) .... Inter

Thursday August 21, 2014

AEL Limassol... (1) 1-2 (0) ...... Tottenham
Aktobe............ (0) 0-1 (0) . Legia Warsaw

Hull's Europa League bid ended in the playoff round

Ap Limassol .... (0) 1-1 (1) .. Lok. Moscow
Astana .... (0) 0-3 (1) .... Villarreal
Asteras T. .... (1) 2-0 (0) ....M. Tel Aviv
Din. Moscow .. (1) 2-2 (1)Omonia Nicosia
Dinamo Minsk (1) 2-0 (0) .... Nacional
Elfsborg .... (2) 2-1 (0) .... Rio Ave
FC Zimbru .... (0) 1-0 (0) PAOK Salonika
FK Qarabag..... (0) 0-0 (0) ....FC Twente
Grasshoppers.. (1) 1-2 (2) ...... FC Bruges
HJK Helsinki .... (0) 2-1 (0) .. Rapid Vienna
Kardemir......... (0) 1-0 (0) .... St-Etienne
Lokeren .... (0) 1-0 (0) .... Hull
Lyon .... (1) 1-2 (0) .. Astra Giurgiu
NK Split .... (0) 0-0 (0) .... Torino
PEC Zwolle ...... (0) 1-0 (0) . Sparta Prague
PSV Eindhoven (0) 1-0 (0) .... Shakhtyor
Panathinaikos . (3) 4-1 (1) .... Midtjylland
Partizan .... (2) 3-2 (2) ...Neftchi Baku
Petrolul Ploiesti(1) 1-3 (1) ....Dyn. Zagreb
Rijeka .... (0) 1-0 (0) .... FC Sheriff
Ruch Chorzow (0) 0-0 (0) .... Metalist
Sarajevo .... (1) 2-3 (2) .... Mgladbach
Sociedad......... (0) 1-0 (0) .. FK Krasnodar
Spartak Trnava (1) 1-3 (2) .... FC Zurich
Trabzonspor.... (1) 2-0 (0) ...... R. Rostov
Young Boys..... (1) 3-1 (1) .... Debrecen
Zorya............. (1) 1-1 (1) ...... Feyenoord

Second legs

Thursday August 28, 2014

Astra Giurgiu .. (0) 0-1 (1) .... Lyon
    Aggregate: 2-2, Astra Giurgiu
    won on away goals
Debrecen .... (0) 0-0 (0) ..... Young Boys
    Aggregate: 1-3
Dyn. Zagreb.... (1) 2-1 (0)Petrolul Ploiesti
    Aggregate: 5-2
FC Bruges .... (0) 1-0 (0) ..Grasshoppers
    Aggregate: 3-1
FC Sheriff .... (0) 0-3 (2) .... Rijeka
    Aggregate: 0-4
FC Twente....... (1) 1-1 (0) .....FK Qarabag
    Aggregate: 1-1, FK Qarabag
    won on away goals

FC Zurich .... (0) 1-1 (0) Spartak Trnava
    Aggregate: 4-2
FK Krasnodar .. (0) 3-0 (0) ....Sociedad
    Aggregate: 3-1
Feyenoord ...... (2) 4-3 (0) ....Zorya
    Aggregate: 5-4
Hajduk Split .... (0) 0-0 (0) .... Dnipro
    Aggregate: 1-2
Hull .... (1) 2-1 (0) .... Lokeren
Aggregate: 2-2, Lokeren won on away goals
Inter .... (2) 6-0 (0) .... Stjarnan
    Aggregate: 9-0
Legia Warsaw . (1) 2-0 (0) ....Aktobe
    Aggregate: 3-0
Lok. Moscow .. (1) 1-4 (1) .... Ap Limassol
    Aggregate: 2-5
M. Tel Aviv...... (1) 3-1 (1) .... Asteras T.
    Aggregate: 3-3, Asteras won on away goals
Metalist .... (0) 1-0 (0) Ruch Chorzow
    AET 0-0 after 90 mins
Mgladbach ..... (3) 7-0 (0) .... Sarajevo
    Aggregate: 10-2
Midtjylland ..... (0) 1-2 (0) . Panathinaikos
    Aggregate: 2-6
Nacional .... (1) 2-3 (2) Dinamo Minsk
    Aggregate: 2-5
Neftchi Baku... (0) 1-2 (1) .... Partizan
    Aggregate: 3-5
Omonia Nicosia(1) 1-2 (1) .. Din. Moscow
    Aggregate: 3-4
PAOK Salonika (2) 4-0 (0) .... FC Zimbru
    Aggregate: 4-1
R. Rostov .... (0) 0-0 (0) ....Trabzonspor
    Aggregate: 0-2
Rapid Vienna .. (2) 3-3 (1) .... HJK Helsinki
    Aggregate: 4-5
Rio Ave........... (0) 1-0 (0) .... Elfsborg
Aggregate: 2-2, Rio Ave won on away goals
Shakhtyor .... (0) 0-2 (0)PSV Eindhoven
    Aggregate: 0-3
Sparta Prague . (2) 3-1 (0) ..... PEC Zwolle
    Aggregate: 4-2
St-Etienne....... (1) 1-0 (0) ....Kardemir
    AET 1-0 after 90 mins, aggregate: 1-1
    St-Etienne won 4-3 on pens
Torino .... (1) 1-0 (0) .... NK Split
    Aggregate: 1-0

Tottenham ...... (1) 3-0 (0) ...AEL Limassol
Aggregate: 5-1
Villarreal .... (1) 4-0 (0) ....Astana
Aggregate: 7-0

Group stage

Group A

	P	W	D	L	F	A	GD	Pts
Mgladbach	6	3	3	0	14	4	+10	12
Villarreal	6	3	2	1	15	7	+8	11
FC Zurich	6	2	1	3	10	14	-4	7
Ap Limassol	6	1	0	5	4	18	-14	3

Thursday September 18, 2014
Ap Limassol .... (2) 3-2 (0) .... FC Zurich
Mgladbach ..... (1) 1-1 (0) .... Villarreal

Thursday October 2, 2014
FC Zurich .... (1) 1-1 (1) ..... Mgladbach
Villarreal .... (2) 4-0 (0) .... Ap Limassol

Thursday October 23, 2014
Mgladbach ...... (1) 5-0 (0) .... Ap Limassol
Villarreal .... (1) 4-1 (1) .... FC Zurich

Thursday November 6, 2014
Ap Limassol .... (0) 0-2 (0) ...... Mgladbach
FC Zurich .... (3) 3-2 (2) .... Villarreal

Thursday November 27, 2014
FC Zurich .... (2) 3-1 (1) .... Ap Limassol
Villarreal .... (1) 2-2 (0) ..... Mgladbach

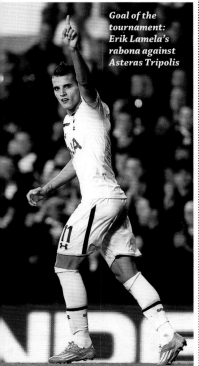

Goal of the tournament: Erik Lamela's rabona against Asteras Tripolis

Thursday December 11, 2014
Ap Limassol .... (0) 0-2 (2) .... Villarreal
Mgladbach ..... (1) 3-0 (0) .... FC Zurich

Group B

	P	W	D	L	F	A	GD	Pts
FC Bruges	6	3	3	0	10	2	+8	12
Torino	6	3	2	1	9	3	+6	11
HJK Helsinki	6	2	0	4	5	11	-6	6
FC Copenhagen	6	1	1	4	5	13	-8	4

Thursday September 18, 2014
FC Bruges .... (0) 0-0 (0) .... Torino
FC Copenhagen(0) 2-0 (0) .... HJK Helsinki

Thursday October 2, 2014
HJK Helsinki .... (0) 0-3 (1) .... FC Bruges
Torino .... (0) 1-0 (0)FC Copenhagen

Thursday October 23, 2014
FC Bruges .... (0) 1-1 (0)FC Copenhagen
Torino .... (1) 2-0 (0) .... HJK Helsinki

Thursday November 6, 2014
FC Copenhagen(0) 0-4 (3) .... FC Bruges
HJK Helsinki .... (0) 2-1 (0) .... Torino

Thursday November 27, 2014
HJK Helsinki .... (1) 1-0 (0)FC Copenhagen
Torino .... (0) 0-0 (0) .... FC Bruges

Thursday December 11, 2014
FC Bruges .... (1) 2-1 (0) ... HJK Helsinki
FC Copenhagen(1) 1-5 (2) .... Torino

Group C

	P	W	D	L	F	A	GD	Pts
Besiktas	6	3	3	0	11	5	+6	12
Tottenham	6	3	2	1	9	4	+5	11
Asteras T	6	1	3	2	7	10	-3	6
Partizan	6	0	2	4	1	9	-8	2

Thursday September 18, 2014
Besiktas .... (1) 1-1 (0) .... Asteras T.
Partizan .... (0) 0-0 (0) ...... Tottenham

Thursday October 2, 2014
Asteras T. .... (1) 2-0 (0) .... Partizan
Tottenham ...... (1) 1-1 (0) .... Besiktas

Thursday October 23, 2014
Partizan .... (0) 0-4 (2) .... Besiktas
Tottenham ...... (2) 5-1 (0) .... Asteras T.

Thursday November 6, 2014
Asteras T. .... (0) 1-2 (2) ...... Tottenham
Besiktas .... (0) 2-1 (0) .... Partizan

Thursday November 27, 2014
Asteras T. .... (0) 2-2 (1) .... Besiktas
Tottenham ...... (0) 1-0 (0) .... Partizan

Thursday December 11, 2014
Besiktas .... (0) 1-0 (0) ...... Tottenham
Partizan .... (0) 0-0 (0) .... Asteras T.

Group D

	P	W	D	L	F	A	GD	Pts
RB Salzburg	6	5	1	0	21	8	+13	16
Celtic	6	2	2	2	10	11	-1	8
Dyn. Zagreb	6	2	0	4	12	15	-3	6
Astra Giurgiu	6	1	1	4	6	15	-9	4

Thursday September 18, 2014
Dyn. Zagreb .... (3) 5-1 (0) .. Astra Giurgiu
RB Salzburg .... (1) 2-2 (1) .... Celtic

Thursday October 2, 2014
Astra Giurgiu .. (1) 1-2 (2) .... RB Salzburg
Celtic .... (1) 1-0 (0) ....Dyn. Zagreb

Thursday October 23, 2014
Celtic .... (0) 2-1 (0) .. Astra Giurgiu
RB Salzburg .... (2) 4-2 (0) ....Dyn. Zagreb

Thursday November 6, 2014
Astra Giurgiu .. (0) 1-1 (1) .... Celtic
Dyn. Zagreb.... (0) 1-5 (1) .... RB Salzburg

Thursday November 27, 2014
Astra Giurgiu .. (0) 1-0 (0) ...Dyn. Zagreb
Celtic .... (1) 1-3 (2) .... RB Salzburg

Thursday December 11, 2014
Dyn. Zagreb .... (2) 4-3 (2) .... Celtic
RB Salzburg .... (2) 5-1 (0) .. Astra Giurgiu

Group E

	P	W	D	L	F	A	GD	Pts
Din. Moscow	6	6	0	0	9	3	+6	18
PSV Eindhoven	6	2	2	2	8	8	0	8
Estoril	6	1	2	3	7	8	-1	5
Panathinaikos	6	0	2	4	6	11	-5	2

Thursday September 18, 2014
PSV Eindhoven(1) 1-0 (0) .... Estoril
Panathinaikos . (0) 1-2 (1) .. Din. Moscow

Thursday October 2, 2014
Din. Moscow .. (0) 1-0 (0)PSV Eindhoven
Estoril .... (0) 2-0 (0) . Panathinaikos

Thursday October 23, 2014
Estoril .... (0) 1-2 (0) .. Din. Moscow
PSV Eindhoven(1) 1-1 (0) . Panathinaikos

Thursday November 6, 2014
Din. Moscow .. (0) 1-0 (0) .... Estoril
Panathinaikos . (2) 2-3 (1)PSV Eindhoven

Thursday November 27, 2014
Din. Moscow .. (0) 2-1 (1) . Panathinaikos

Friday November 28, 2014
Estoril .... (3) 3-3 (2)PSV Eindhoven

Thursday December 11, 2014
PSV Eindhoven(0) 0-1 (1) .. Din. Moscow
Panathinaikos . (0) 1-1 (0) .... Estoril

Group F

	P	W	D	L	F	A	GD	Pts
Inter	6	3	3	0	6	2	+4	12
Dnipro	6	2	1	3	4	5	-1	7
FK Qarabag	6	1	3	2	3	5	-2	6
St-Etienne	6	0	5	1	2	3	-1	5

Thursday September 18, 2014
Dnipro .... (0) 0-1 (0) .... Inter
FK Qarabag.... (0) 0-0 (0) .... St-Etienne

Thursday October 2, 2014
Inter .... (1) 2-0 (0) ....FK Qarabag
St-Etienne .... (0) 0-0 (0) .... Dnipro

Thursday October 23, 2014
Dnipro .... (0) 0-1 (1) .....FK Qarabag
Inter .... (0) 0-0 (0) .... St-Etienne

Thursday November 6, 2014
FK Qarabag.....(1) 1-2 (1)............Dnipro
St-Etienne.......(0) 1-1 (1)...............Inter

Thursday November 27, 2014
Inter...............(1) 2-1 (1)............Dnipro
St-Etienne.......(1) 1-1 (1).....FK Qarabag

Thursday December 11, 2014
Dnipro............(0) 1-0 (0).......St-Etienne
FK Qarabag....(0) 0-0 (0)...............Inter

Group G

	P	W	D	L	F	A	GD	Pts
Feyenoord	6	4	0	2	10	6	+4	12
Seville	6	3	2	1	8	5	+3	11
Rijeka	6	2	1	3	7	8	-1	7
Standard Liege	6	1	1	4	4	10	-6	4

Thursday September 18, 2014
Seville.............(2) 2-0 (0)......Feyenoord
Standard Liege(0) 2-0 (0)..............Rijeka

Thursday October 2, 2014
Feyenoord......(0) 2-1 (0)Standard Liege
Rijeka.............(0) 2-2 (1)..............Seville

Thursday October 23, 2014
Rijeka.............(0) 3-1 (0)......Feyenoord
Standard Liege(0) 0-0 (0)..............Seville

Thursday November 6, 2014
Feyenoord......(2) 2-0 (0)..............Rijeka
Seville.............(2) 3-1 (1)Standard Liege

Thursday November 27, 2014
Feyenoord......(0) 2-0 (0)..............Seville
Rijeka.............(2) 2-0 (0)Standard Liege

Thursday December 11, 2014
Seville.............(1) 1-0 (0)..............Rijeka
Standard Liege(0) 0-3 (1)......Feyenoord

Group H

	P	W	D	L	F	A	GD	Pts
Everton	6	3	2	1	10	3	+7	11
Wolfsburg	6	3	1	2	14	10	+4	10
FK Krasnodar	6	1	3	2	7	12	-5	6
Lille	6	0	4	2	3	9	-6	4

Thursday September 18, 2014
Everton...........(2) 4-1 (0).......Wolfsburg
Lille.................(0) 1-1 (1)..FK Krasnodar

Thursday October 2, 2014
FK Krasnodar..(1) 1-1 (0)...........Everton
Wolfsburg.......(0) 1-1 (0)...............Lille

Thursday October 23, 2014
FK Krasnodar..(0) 2-4 (1).......Wolfsburg
Lille.................(0) 0-0 (0)...........Everton

Thursday November 6, 2014
Everton...........(2) 3-0 (0)................Lille
Wolfsburg.......(0) 5-1 (0)..FK Krasnodar

Thursday November 27, 2014
FK Krasnodar..(1) 1-1 (0)................Lille
Wolfsburg.......(0) 0-2 (1)...........Everton

Thursday December 11, 2014
Everton...........(0) 0-1 (1)..FK Krasnodar
Lille.................(0) 0-3 (1).......Wolfsburg

Group I

	P	W	D	L	F	A	GD	Pts
Napoli	6	4	1	1	11	3	+8	13
Young Boys	6	4	0	2	13	7	+6	12
Sparta Prague	6	3	1	2	11	6	+5	10
S. Bratislava	6	0	0	6	1	20	-19	0

Thursday September 18, 2014
Napoli.............(1) 3-1 (1). Sparta Prague
Young Boys.....(2) 5-0 (0)....S. Bratislava

Thursday October 2, 2014
S. Bratislava....(0) 0-2 (1)............Napoli
Sparta Prague.(2) 3-1 (0)....Young Boys

Thursday October 23, 2014
S. Bratislava....(0) 0-3 (0). Sparta Prague
Young Boys.....(0) 2-0 (0)............Napoli

Thursday November 6, 2014
Napoli.............(1) 3-0 (0).....Young Boys
Sparta Prague.(2) 4-0 (0)....S. Bratislava

Thursday November 27, 2014
S. Bratislava....(1) 1-3 (2)....Young Boys
Sparta Prague.(0) 0-0 (0)............Napoli

Thursday December 11, 2014
Napoli.............(2) 3-0 (0)....S. Bratislava
Young Boys.....(0) 2-0 (0). Sparta Prague

Group J

	P	W	D	L	F	A	GD	Pts
Dynamo Kiev	6	5	0	1	12	4	+8	15
Aalborg	6	3	0	3	5	10	-5	9
Steaua	6	2	1	3	11	9	+2	7
Rio Ave	6	1	1	4	5	10	-5	4

Thursday September 18, 2014
Rio Ave...........(0) 0-3 (2)..Dynamo Kiev
Steaua.............(0) 6-0 (0)...........Aalborg

Thursday October 2, 2014
Aalborg...........(0) 1-0 (0)...........Rio Ave
Dynamo Kiev..(1) 3-1 (0)............Steaua

Thursday October 23, 2014
Aalborg...........(2) 3-0 (0)..Dynamo Kiev
Steaua.............(2) 2-1 (0)...........Rio Ave

Thursday November 6, 2014
Dynamo Kiev..(0) 2-0 (0)..........Aalborg
Rio Ave...........(1) 2-2 (0)............Steaua

Thursday November 27, 2014
Aalborg...........(0) 1-0 (0)............Steaua
Dynamo Kiev..(0) 2-0 (0)...........Rio Ave

Thursday December 11, 2014
Rio Ave...........(0) 2-0 (0)..........Aalborg
Steaua.............(0) 0-2 (1)..Dynamo Kiev

Carlos Bacca bags the first of his two goals in the final as Seville retain the trophy

Group K

	P	W	D	L	F	A	GD	Pts
Fiorentina	6	4	1	1	11	4	+7	13
Guingamp	6	3	1	2	7	6	+1	10
PAOK Salonika	6	2	1	3	10	7	+3	7
Dinamo Minsk	6	1	1	4	3	14	-11	4

Thursday September 18, 2014
Fiorentina.......(1) 3-0 (0).......Guingamp
PAOK Salonika (4) 6-1 (0) Dinamo Minsk

Thursday October 2, 2014
Dinamo Minsk (0) 0-3 (1)....... Fiorentina
Guingamp.......(0) 2-0 (0) PAOK Salonika

Thursday October 23, 2014
Dinamo Minsk (0) 0-0 (0).......Guingamp
PAOK Salonika (0) 0-1 (1)....... Fiorentina

Thursday November 6, 2014
Fiorentina.......(0) 1-1 (0) PAOK Salonika
Guingamp.......(1) 2-0 (0) Dinamo Minsk

Thursday November 27, 2014
Dinamo Minsk (0) 0-2 (0) PAOK Salonika
Guingamp.......(1) 1-2 (2)....... Fiorentina

Joint-top scorers: Alan of Red Bull Salzburg (above) and Everton's Romelu Lukaku

Thursday December 11, 2014
Fiorentina .... (0) 1-2 (1) Dinamo Minsk
PAOK Salonika (1) 1-2 (1) .... Guingamp

Group L

	P	W	D	L	F	A	GD	Pts
Legia Warsaw	6	5	0	1	7	2	+5	15
Trabzonspor	6	3	1	2	8	6	+2	10
Lokeren	6	3	1	2	4	4	0	10
Metalist	6	0	0	6	3	10	-7	0

Thursday September 18, 2014
Legia Warsaw . (0) 1-0 (0) .... Lokeren
Metalist .... (0) 1-2 (1) .... Trabzonspor

Thursday October 2, 2014
Lokeren .... (0) 1-0 (0) .... Metalist
Trabzonspor.... (0) 0-1 (1) . Legia Warsaw

Wednesday October 22, 2014
Metalist .... (0) 0-1 (1) . Legia Warsaw

Thursday October 23, 2014
Trabzonspor.... (0) 2-0 (0) .... Lokeren

Thursday November 6, 2014
Legia Warsaw . (1) 2-1 (1) .... Metalist
Lokeren .... (1) 1-1 (1) .... Trabzonspor

Thursday November 27, 2014
Lokeren .... (1) 1-0 (0) . Legia Warsaw
Trabzonspor.... (1) 3-1 (1) .... Metalist

Thursday December 11, 2014
Legia Warsaw . (1) 2-0 (0) .... Trabzonspor
Metalist .... (0) 0-1 (1) .... Lokeren

Round of 32

Thursday February 19, 2015
Aalborg .... (0) 1-3 (2) .... FC Bruges
Ajax................ (1) 1-0 (0) . Legia Warsaw
Anderlecht...... (0) 0-0 (0) .. Din. Moscow
Celtic .... (2) 3-3 (3) .... Inter
Dnipro .... (0) 2-0 (0) ..... Olympiakos
Guingamp....... (0) 2-1 (1) .. Dynamo Kiev
Liverpool .... (0) 1-0 (0) .... Besiktas
PSV Eindhoven(0) 0-1 (0) .... Zenit
Roma.............. (1) 1-1 (0)...... Feyenoord
Seville............. (0) 1-0 (0) ..... Mgladbach
Torino .... (2) 2-2 (1) ...... Ath Bilbao
Tottenham ...... (1) 1-1 (1) ...... Fiorentina
Trabzonspor.... (0) 0-4 (3) .... Napoli
Villarreal .... (1) 2-1 (0) .... RB Salzburg
Wolfsburg....... (0) 2-0 (0)Sporting Lisbon
Young Boys..... (1) 1-4 (3) .... Everton

Second legs

Thursday February 26, 2015
Ath Bilbao ...... (1) 2-3 (2) .... Torino
Aggregate: 4-5
Besiktas .... (0) 1-0 (0) .... Liverpool
AET 1-0 after 90 mins, aggregate: 1-1
Besiktas won 5-4 on pens
Din. Moscow .. (0) 3-1 (1) ...... Anderlecht
Aggregate: 3-1
Dynamo Kiev .. (1) 3-1 (0) .... Guingamp
Aggregate: 4-3
Everton .... (3) 3-1 (1) ..... Young Boys
Aggregate: 7-2
FC Bruges .... (1) 3-0 (0) .... Aalborg
Aggregate: 6-1
Feyenoord ...... (0) 1-2 (1) .... Roma
Aggregate: 2-3
Fiorentina .... (0) 2-0 (0) ...... Tottenham
Aggregate: 3-1
Inter .... (0) 1-0 (0) .... Celtic
Aggregate: 4-3
Legia Warsaw.(0) 0-3 (3) .... Ajax
Aggregate: 0-4
Mgladbach ..... (2) 2-3 (2) .... Seville
Aggregate: 2-4
Napoli .... (1) 1-0 (0) .... Trabzonspor
Aggregate: 5-0
Olympiakos..... (1) 2-2 (1) .... Dnipro
Aggregate: 2-4
RB Salzburg .... (1) 1-3 (1) .... Villarreal
Aggregate: 2-5
Sporting Lisbon(0) 0-0 (0) .... Wolfsburg
Aggregate: 0-2

Zenit.............. (1) 3-0 (0) PSV Eindhoven
Aggregate: 4-0

Round of 16

Thursday March 12, 2015
Dnipro .... (1) 1-0 (0) .... Ajax
Everton........... (1) 2-1 (1) .. Dynamo Kiev
FC Bruges .... (0) 2-1 (0) .... Besiktas
Fiorentina .... (1) 1-1 (0) .... Roma
Napoli .... (2) 3-1 (1) .. Din. Moscow
Villarreal .... (0) 1-3 (2) .... Seville
Wolfsburg....... (1) 3-1 (1) .... Inter
Zenit.............. (1) 2-0 (0) .... Torino

Second legs

Thursday March 19, 2015
Ajax................ (0) 2-1 (0) .... Dnipro
AET 1-0 after 90 mins, aggregate 2-2
Dnipro won on away goals
Besiktas .... (0) 1-3 (0) .... FC Bruges
Aggregate: 2-5
Din. Moscow .. (0) 0-0 (0) .... Napoli
Aggregate: 1-3
Dynamo Kiev .. (3) 5-2 (1) .... Everton
Aggregate: 6-4
Inter .... (0) 1-2 (1) ...... Wolfsburg
Aggregate: 2-5
Roma.............. (0) 0-3 (3) .... Fiorentina
Aggregate: 1-4
Seville............. (0) 2-1 (0) .... Villarreal
Aggregate: 5-2
Torino .... (0) 1-0 (0) .... Zenit
Aggregate: 1-2

Quarter-finals

Thursday April 16, 2015
Dynamo Kiev .. (1) 1-1 (0) .... Fiorentina
FC Bruges .... (0) 0-0 (0) .... Dnipro
Seville............. (0) 2-1 (1) .... Zenit
Wolfsburg....... (0) 1-4 (2) .... Napoli

Second legs

Thursday April 23, 2015
Dnipro .... (0) 1-0 (0) .... FC Bruges
Aggregate: 1-0
Fiorentina .... (1) 2-0 (0) .. Dynamo Kiev
Aggregate: 3-1
Napoli .... (0) 2-2 (0) ...... Wolfsburg
Aggregate: 6-3
Zenit.............. (0) 2-2 (1) .... Seville
Aggregate: 3-4

Semi-finals

Thursday May 7, 2015
Napoli .... (0) 1-1 (0) .... Dnipro
Seville............. (1) 3-0 (0) .... Fiorentina

Second legs

Thursday May 14, 2015
Dnipro .... (0) 1-0 (0) .... Napoli
Aggregate: 2-1
Fiorentina .... (0) 0-2 (2) .... Seville
Aggregate: 0-5

Final

Thursday May 27, 2015
Dnipro .... (2) 2-3 (2) .... Seville

CHAMPIONS LEAGUE

First qualifying round

Tuesday July 1, 2014
FC Santa Coloma(1) 1-0 (0) .... Banants
La Fiorita .... (0) 0-1 (0) Levadia Tallinn

Wednesday July 2, 2014
Lincoln R I ...... (1) 1-1 (0) ....HB Torshavn

Second legs

Tuesday July 8, 2014
Banants .... (1) 3-2 (1) .... FC Santa Coloma
AET 3-3 after 90 mins, aggregate: 3-3
FC Santa Coloma won on away goals
HB Torshavn.... (3) 5-2 (0) .... Lincoln R I
Aggregate: 6-3
Levadia Tallinn (2) 7-0 (0) .... La Fiorita
Aggregate: 8-0

Second qualifying round

Tuesday July 15, 2014
BATE Borisov .. (0) 0-0 (0) .... Skenderbeu
Cliftonville ...... (0) 0-0 (0) .... Debrecen
Dyn. Zagreb .... (0) 2-0 (0) Zalgiris Vilnius
FC Santa Coloma(0)0-1 (0) ......M. Tel Aviv
FC Sheriff .... (0) 2-0 (0) .... Sutjeska
KR Reykjavik ... (0) 0-1 (0) .... Celtic
Partizan .... (1) 3-0 (0) ....HB Torshavn
Rabotnicki....... (0) 0-0 (0) .... HJK Helsinki
S. Bratislava.... (0) 1-0 (0)The New Saints
Sparta Prague . (3) 7-0 (0) Levadia Tallinn
Valletta .... (0) 0-1 (1) ....FK Qarabag
Zrinjski Mostar (0) 0-0 (0) ....NK Maribor

Wednesday July 16, 2014
Dinamo Tbilisi. (0) 0-1 (0) ....Aktobe
Legia Warsaw.. (1) 1-1 (1) ...... St Patrick's
Ludogorets ..... (2) 4-0 (0)F91 Dudelange
Malmo............ (0) 0-0 (0) .... Ventspils
Stromsgodset.. (0) 0-1 (0) .... Steaua

Second legs

Tuesday July 22, 2014
Celtic .... (3) 4-0 (0) ... KR Reykjavik
Aggregate: 5-0
Debrecen .... (0) 2-0 (0) ...... Cliftonville
Aggregate: 2-0
F91 Dudelange(0) 1-1 (0) ..... Ludogorets
Aggregate: 1-5
FK Qarabag..... (1) 4-0 (0) .... Valletta
Aggregate: 5-0
HB Torshavn.... (1) 1-3 (0) .... Partizan
Aggregate: 1-6
Levadia Tallinn (1) 1-1 (1). Sparta Prague
Aggregate: 1-8
M. Tel Aviv...... (0) 2-0 (0) .... FC Santa Coloma
Aggregate: 3-0
Skenderbeu .... (0) 1-1 (1) .. BATE Borisov
AET 1-1 after 90 mins, aggregate: 1-1
BATE won on away goals
Sutjeska.......... (0) 0-3 (2) .... FC Sheriff
Aggregate: 0-5
The New Saints(0) 0-2 (0) ....S. Bratislava
Aggregate: 0-3

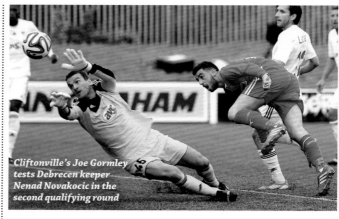

Cliftonville's Joe Gormley tests Debrecen keeper Nenad Novakocic in the second qualifying round

Zalgiris Vilnius (0) 0-2 (0) ....Dyn. Zagreb
Aggregate: 0-4

Wednesday July 23, 2014
Aktobe............ (0) 3-0 (0).Dinamo Tbilisi
Aggregate: 4-0
HJK Helsinki .... (2) 2-1 (0) ....Rabotnicki
Aggregate: 2-1
NK Maribor..... (1) 2-0 (0) Zrinjski Mostar
Aggregate: 2-0
St Patrick's ...... (0) 0-5 (1) .Legia Warsaw
Aggregate: 1-6
Steaua .... (0) 2-0 (0) ..Stromsgodset
Aggregate: 3-0
Ventspils......... (0) 0-1 (1) ....Malmo
Aggregate: 0-1

Third qualifying round

Tuesday July 29, 2014
Debrecen .... (0) 1-0 (0) .. BATE Borisov
S. Bratislava.... (1) 2-1 (0) .... FC Sheriff
Sparta Prague . (1) 4-2 (2) ....Malmo

Wednesday July 30, 2014
AEL Limassol... (0) 1-0 (0) ....Zenit
Aalborg .... (0) 0-1 (0) ....Dyn. Zagreb
Aktobe............ (0) 2-2 (1) .... Steaua
Dnipro .... (0) 0-0 (0)FC Copenhagen
FK Qarabag..... (1) 2-1 (0) ... RB Salzburg
Feyenoord ...... (0) 1-2 (1) .... Besiktas
Grasshoppers.. (0) 0-2 (1) .... Lille
HJK Helsinki .... (2) 2-2 (0) . Apoel Nicosia
Legia Warsaw. (2) 4-1 (1) .... Celtic
Ludogorets ..... (0) 0-0 (0) .... Partizan
NK Maribor..... (0) 1-0 (0) ......M. Tel Aviv
Standard Liege (0) 0-0 (0) . Panathinaikos

Second legs

Tuesday August 5, 2014
BATE Borisov .. (1) 3-1 (1) .... Debrecen
Aggregate: 3-2
Lille .... (1) 1-1 (1) ..Grasshoppers
Aggregate: 3-1
M. Tel Aviv...... (1) 2-2 (1) ......NK Maribor
Aggregate: 2-3
Panathinaikos . (1) 1-2 (2) Standard Liege
Aggregate: 1-2

Wednesday August 6, 2014
Apoel Nicosia . (2) 2-0 (0) ....HJK Helsinki
Aggregate: 4-2
Besiktas .... (1) 3-1 (0) ...... Feyenoord
Aggregate: 5-2
Celtic .... (0) 0-2 (1) . Legia Warsaw
Aggregate: 4-4, Celtic won on away goals
The match was completed as detailed
above, but Legia forfeited the match 3-0
after fielding a suspended player
Dyn. Zagreb.... (0) 0-2 (1) .... Aalborg
Aggregate: 1-2
FC Copenhagen(1) 2-0 (0) .... Dnipro
Aggregate: 2-0
FC Sheriff .... (0) 0-0 (0) ...S. Bratislava
Aggregate: 1-2
Malmo............ (1) 2-0 (0). Sparta Prague
AET 2-0 after 90 mins, aggregate: 4-4
Malmo won on away goals
Partizan .... (2) 2-2 (2) ..... Ludogorets
AET 2-2 after 90 mins, aggregate: 2-2
Ludogorets won on away goals
RB Salzburg .... (2) 2-0 (0) .....FK Qarabag
Aggregate: 3-2
Steaua .... (2) 2-1 (0) ....Aktobe
Aggregate: 4-3
Zenit.............. (0) 3-0 (0) ...AEL Limassol
Aggregate: 3-1

Playoffs

Tuesday August 19, 2014
Besiktas .... (0) 0-0 (0) .... Arsenal
FC Copenhagen(2) 2-3 (3) .. B Leverkusen
Napoli .... (0) 1-1 (0) .... Ath Bilbao
RB Salzburg .... (1) 2-1 (0) ....Malmo
Steaua .... (0) 1-0 (0) .... Ludogorets

Wednesday August 20, 2014
Aalborg .... (1) 1-1 (0) . Apoel Nicosia
Lille .... (0) 0-1 (0) ....Porto
NK Maribor..... (1) 1-1 (1) .... Celtic
S. Bratislava.... (0) 1-1 (1) .. BATE Borisov
Standard Liege (0) 1-1 (1) ....Zenit

Second legs

Tuesday August 26, 2014
Apoel Nicosia . (2) 4-0 (0) .... Aalborg
Aggregate: 5-1

BATE Borisov ..(1) 3-0 (0) ....S. Bratislava
          Aggregate: 4-1
Celtic ....(0) 0-1 (0) .....NK Maribor
          Aggregate: 1-2
Porto...............(0) 2-0 (0) .... Lille
          Aggregate: 3-0
Zenit...............(1) 3-0 (0) Standard Liege
          Aggregate: 4-0

Wednesday August 27, 2014
Arsenal ....(1) 1-0 (0) .... Besiktas
          Aggregate: 1-0
Ath Bilbao ......(0) 3-1 (0) .... Napoli
          Aggregate: 4-2
B Leverkusen ..(3) 4-0 (0)FC Copenhagen
          Aggregate: 7-2
Ludogorets .....(0) 1-0 (0) .... Steaua
     AET 1-0 after 90 mins, aggregate: 1-1
          Ludogorets won 6-5 on pens
Malmo............(2) 3-0 (0) .... RB Salzburg
          Aggregate: 4-2

Group stage

Group A

	P	W	D	L	F	A	GD	Pts
Atl Madrid	6	4	1	1	14	3	+11	13
Juventus	6	3	1	2	7	4	+3	10
Olympiakos	6	3	0	3	10	13	-3	9
Malmo	6	1	0	5	4	15	-11	3

Tuesday September 16, 2014
Juventus ....(0) 2-0 (0) ....Malmo
Olympiakos.....(2) 3-2 (1) .....Atl Madrid

Wednesday October 1, 2014
Atl Madrid ......(0) 1-0 (0) .... Juventus
Malmo............(1) 2-0 (0) .....Olympiakos

Wednesday October 22, 2014
Atl Madrid ......(0) 5-0 (0) ....Malmo
Olympiakos.....(1) 1-0 (0) .... Juventus

Tuesday November 4, 2014
Juventus ....(1) 3-2 (1) .....Olympiakos
Malmo............(0) 0-2 (1) ......Atl Madrid

Wednesday November 26, 2014
Atl Madrid ......(2) 4-0 (0) ....Olympiakos
Malmo............(0) 0-2 (0) .... Juventus

Tuesday December 9, 2014
Juventus ....(0) 0-0 (0) ......Atl Madrid
Olympiakos.....(1) 4-2 (0) ....Malmo

Group B

	P	W	D	L	F	A	GD	Pts
Real Madrid	6	6	0	0	16	2	+14	18
Basel	6	2	1	3	7	8	-1	7
Liverpool	6	1	2	3	5	9	-4	5
Ludogorets	6	1	1	4	5	14	-9	4

Tuesday September 16, 2014
Liverpool ....(0) 2-1 (0) ..... Ludogorets
Real Madrid ....(4) 5-1 (1) .... Basel

Wednesday October 1, 2014
Basel ....(0) 1-0 (0) .... Liverpool
Ludogorets .....(1) 1-2 (1) ....Real Madrid

Wednesday October 22, 2014
Liverpool ....(0) 0-3 (3) ....Real Madrid
Ludogorets .....(0) 1-0 (0) .... Basel

Tuesday November 4, 2014
Basel ....(2) 4-0 (0) ..... Ludogorets
Real Madrid....(1) 1-0 (0) .... Liverpool

Wednesday November 26, 2014
Basel ....(0) 0-1 (1) ....Real Madrid
Ludogorets .....(1) 2-2 (2) .... Liverpool

Tuesday December 9, 2014
Liverpool ....(0) 1-1 (1) .... Basel
Real Madrid....(2) 4-0 (0) ..... Ludogorets

Group C

	P	W	D	L	F	A	GD	Pts
Monaco	6	3	2	1	4	1	+3	11
Leverkusen	6	3	1	2	7	4	+3	10
Zenit	6	2	1	3	4	6	-2	7
Benfica	6	1	2	3	2	6	-4	5

Tuesday September 16, 2014
Benfica ....(0) 0-2 (2) ....Zenit
Monaco ....(0) 1-0 (0).. B Leverkusen

Wednesday October 1, 2014
B Leverkusen ..(2) 3-1 (0) .... Benfica
Zenit...............(0) 3-0 (0) .... Monaco

Wednesday October 22, 2014
B Leverkusen ..(0) 2-0 (0) ....Zenit
Monaco ....(0) 0-0 (0) .... Benfica

A bad year for the Premier League (clockwise from above): Barcelona were too good for Manchester City, former Monaco boss Arsene Wenger's return to Stade Louis II was an unhappy one, Liverpool didn't get out of the group stage and Chelsea old boy David Luiz scored against the Blues as they went out to PSG

Tuesday November 4, 2014

Benfica .... (0) 1-0 (0) .... Monaco
Zenit .... (0) 1-2 (0) .. B Leverkusen

Wednesday November 26, 2014

B Leverkusen .. (0) 0-1 (0) .... Monaco
Zenit .... (0) 1-0 (0) .... Benfica

Tuesday December 9, 2014

Benfica .... (0) 0-0 (0) .. B Leverkusen
Monaco .... (0) 2-0 (0) .... Zenit

Group D

	P	W	D	L	F	A	GD	Pts
Dortmund	6	4	1	1	14	4	+10	13
Arsenal	6	4	1	1	15	8	+7	13
Anderlecht	6	1	3	2	8	10	-2	6
Galatasaray	6	0	1	5	4	19	-15	1

Tuesday September 16, 2014

B Dortmund .... (1) 2-0 (0) .... Arsenal
Galatasaray .... (0) 1-1 (0) ...... Anderlecht

Wednesday October 1, 2014

Anderlecht ...... (0) 0-3 (1) .... B Dortmund
Arsenal .... (3) 4-1 (0) .... Galatasaray

Wednesday October 22, 2014

Anderlecht ...... (0) 1-2 (0) .... Arsenal
Galatasaray .... (0) 0-4 (3) .... B Dortmund

Tuesday November 4, 2014

Arsenal .... (2) 3-3 (0) ...... Anderlecht
B Dortmund .... (1) 4-1 (0) .... Galatasaray

Wednesday November 26, 2014

Anderlecht ...... (1) 2-0 (0) .... Galatasaray
Arsenal .... (1) 2-0 (0) .... B Dortmund

Tuesday December 9, 2014

B Dortmund .... (0) 1-1 (0) ...... Anderlecht
Galatasaray .... (0) 1-4 (3) .... Arsenal

Group E

	P	W	D	L	F	A	GD	Pts
B Munich	6	5	0	1	16	4	+12	15
Man City	6	2	2	2	9	8	+1	8
Roma	6	1	2	3	8	14	-6	5
CSKA Moscow	6	1	2	3	6	13	-7	5

Wednesday September 17, 2014

B Munich .... (0) 1-0 (0) .... Man City
Roma .... (4) 5-1 (0) .... CSKA Mosc.

Tuesday September 30, 2014

CSKA Mosc. ..... (0) 0-1 (1) .... B Munich
Man City .... (1) 1-1 (1) .... Roma

Tuesday October 21, 2014

CSKA Mosc. ..... (0) 2-2 (2) .... Man City
Roma .... (0) 1-7 (5) .... B Munich

Wednesday November 5, 2014

B Munich .... (1) 2-0 (0) .... Roma
Man City .... (1) 1-2 (2) .... CSKA Mosc.

Tuesday November 25, 2014

CSKA Mosc. ..... (0) 1-1 (1) .... Roma
Man City .... (1) 3-2 (2) .... B Munich

Wednesday December 10, 2014

B Munich .... (1) 3-0 (0) .... CSKA Mosc.
Roma .... (0) 0-2 (0) .... Man City

Group F

	P	W	D	L	F	A	GD	Pts
Barcelona	6	5	0	1	15	5	+10	15
Paris St-G	6	4	1	1	10	7	+3	13
Ajax	6	1	2	3	8	10	-2	5
Apoel Nicosia	6	0	1	5	1	12	-11	1

Wednesday September 17, 2014

Ajax .... (0) 1-1 (1) .... Paris St-G.
Barcelona .... (1) 1-0 (0) . Apoel Nicosia

Tuesday September 30, 2014

Apoel Nicosia . (1) 1-1 (1) .... Ajax
Paris St-G. .... (2) 3-2 (1) ...... Barcelona

Tuesday October 21, 2014
Apoel Nicosia . (0) 0-1 (0) .... Paris St-G.
Barcelona .... (2) 3-1 (0) .... Ajax

Wednesday November 5, 2014
Ajax .... (0) 0-2 (1) ...... Barcelona
Paris St-G. .... (1) 1-0 (0) . Apoel Nicosia

Tuesday November 25, 2014
Apoel Nicosia . (0) 0-4 (2) ...... Barcelona
Paris St-G. .... (1) 3-1 (0) .... Ajax

Wednesday December 10, 2014
Ajax .... (1) 4-0 (0) . Apoel Nicosia
Barcelona .... (2) 3-1 (1) .... Paris St-G.

Group G

	P	W	D	L	F	A	GD	Pts
Chelsea	6	4	2	0	17	3	+14	14
Schalke	6	2	2	2	9	14	-5	8
Sporting Lisbon	6	2	1	3	12	12	0	7
NK Maribor	6	0	3	3	4	13	-9	3

Wednesday September 17, 2014
Chelsea .... (1) 1-1 (0) .... Schalke
NK Maribor ..... (0) 1-1 (0)Sporting Lisbon

Tuesday September 30, 2014
Schalke .... (0) 1-1 (1) ..... NK Maribor
Sporting Lisbon(0) 0-1 (1) .... Chelsea

Tuesday October 21, 2014
Chelsea .... (3) 6-0 (0) ..... NK Maribor
Schalke .... (1) 4-3 (1)Sporting Lisbon

Wednesday November 5, 2014
NK Maribor ..... (0) 1-1 (0) .... Chelsea
Sporting Lisbon(1) 4-2 (1) .... Schalke

Tuesday November 25, 2014
Schalke .... (0) 0-5 (3) .... Chelsea
Sporting Lisbon(2) 3-1 (1) ..... NK Maribor

Wednesday December 10, 2014
Chelsea .... (2) 3-1 (0)Sporting Lisbon
NK Maribor ..... (0) 0-1 (0) .... Schalke

Group H

	P	W	D	L	F	A	GD	Pts
Porto	6	4	2	0	16	4	+12	14
Shakhtar	6	2	3	1	15	4	+11	9
Ath Bilbao	6	2	1	3	5	6	-1	7
BATE	6	1	0	5	2	24	-22	3

Wednesday September 17, 2014
Ath Bilbao ...... (0) 0-0 (0) .... Shakhtar
Porto .... (3) 6-0 (0) .. BATE Borisov

Tuesday September 30, 2014
BATE Borisov .. (2) 2-1 (1) ...... Ath Bilbao
Shakhtar .... (0) 2-2 (0) ....Porto

Tuesday October 21, 2014
BATE Borisov .. (0) 0-7 (6) .... Shakhtar
Porto .... (1) 2-1 (0) ...... Ath Bilbao

Wednesday November 5, 2014
Ath Bilbao ...... (0) 0-2 (0) ....Porto
Shakhtar .... (1) 5-0 (0) .. BATE Borisov

Tuesday November 25, 2014
BATE Borisov .. (0) 0-3 (0) ....Porto
Shakhtar .... (0) 0-1 (0) ...... Ath Bilbao

Wednesday December 10, 2014
Ath Bilbao ...... (0) 2-0 (0) .. BATE Borisov
Porto .... (0) 1-1 (0) .... Shakhtar

Round of 16

Tuesday February 17, 2015
Paris St-G. .... (0) 1-1 (1) ....Chelsea
Shakhtar .... (0) 0-0 (0) .... B Munich

Wednesday February 18, 2015
Basel .... (1) 1-1 (0) ....Porto
Schalke .... (0) 0-2 (1) .... Real Madrid

Tuesday February 24, 2015
Juventus .... (2) 2-1 (1) ... B Dortmund
Man City .... (0) 1-2 (2) .... Barcelona

Wednesday February 25, 2015
Arsenal .... (0) 1-3 (1) .... Monaco
B Leverkusen .. (0) 1-0 (0) ...... Atl Madrid

Second legs

Tuesday March 10, 2015
Porto .... (1) 4-0 (0) .... Basel
Aggregate: 5-1
Real Madrid .... (2) 3-4 (2) .... Schalke
Aggregate: 5-4

Wednesday March 11, 2015
B Munich .... (2) 7-0 (0) .... Shakhtar
Aggregate: 7-0
Chelsea .... (0) 2-2 (0) .... Paris St-G.
AET 1-1 after 90 mins, aggregate: 3-3
Paris St-G. won on away goals

Tuesday March 17, 2015
Atl Madrid ...... (1) 1-0 (0) .. B Leverkusen
AET 1-0 after 90 mins, aggregate: 1-1
Atl Madrid won 3-2 on pens
Monaco .... (0) 0-2 (1) .... Arsenal
Aggregate: 3-3, Monaco won on away goals

Wednesday March 18, 2015

B Dortmund .... (0) 0-3 (1) .... Juventus
Aggregate: 1-5

Barcelona .... (1) 1-0 (0) .... Man City
Aggregate: 3-1

Quarter-finals

Tuesday April 15, 2015

Atl Madrid ...... (0) 0-0 (0) .... Real Madrid

Juventus .... (0) 1-0 (0) .... Monaco

Wednesday April 16, 2015

Paris St-G. .... (0) 1-3 (1) .... Barcelona

Porto .... (2) 3-1 (1) .... B Munich

Second legs

Tuesday April 21, 2015

B Munich .... (5) 6-1 (0) .... Porto
Aggregate: 7-4

Barcelona .... (2) 2-0 (0) .... Paris St-G.
Aggregate: 5-1

Wednesday April 22, 2015

Monaco .... (0) 0-0 (0) .... Juventus
Aggregate: 0-1

Real Madrid .... (0) 1-0 (0) ...... Atl Madrid
Aggregate: 1-0

Semi-finals

Tuesday May 5, 2015

Juventus .... (1) 2-1 (1) .... Real Madrid

Wednesday May 6, 2015

Barcelona .... (0) 3-0 (0) .... B Munich

Second legs

Tuesday May 13, 2015

B Munich .... (1) 3-2 (2) .... Barcelona
Aggregate: 3-5

Wednesday May 14, 2015

Real Madrid .... (1) 1-1 (0) .... Juventus
Aggregate: 2-3

Final

Saturday June 6, 2015

Juventus .... (0) 1-3 (1) .... Barcelona

Below: Neymar grabs Barcelona's third goal with the last kick of the Champions League final to finish in a dead heat with Lionel Messi and Cristiano Ronaldo at the top of the scoring table

Qualifying format

Nine group winners, nine runners-up and best third-placed side qualify for Euro 2016 finals. Eight remaining third-placed teams contest home and away two-legged playoffs to decide final four qualifiers.

If two or more teams are level on points, positions are decided by points won in group matches between the teams in question, then goal difference from those games, goals scored, away goals scored, goal difference in all group matches, goals scored in all group matches, away goals scored in all group matches, fair play, Uefa national team coefficient.

The best third-placed team is decided as follows, discarding results against teams finishing in sixth place: points, goal difference, goals scored, away goals scored, fair play, Uefa national team coefficient.

Key dates

12-14 November
Playoff first legs

15-17 November
Playoff second legs

12 December
Final tournament draw

Dec 2015-Jan 2016
Tickets for specific team matches go on sale

10 June 2016
Euro 2016 begins (France)

10 July 2016
Euro 2016 final (Paris)

Group A

	P	W	D	L	F	A	GD	Pts
Iceland	6	5	0	1	14	3	+11	15
Czech Rep	6	4	1	1	12	8	+4	13
Holland	6	3	1	2	13	6	+7	10
Turkey	6	2	2	2	7	8	-1	8
Latvia	6	0	3	3	2	13	-11	3
Kazakhstan	6	0	1	5	4	14	-10	1

September 9, 2014
Czech Rep ...... (1) 2-1 (0) ....Holland
Iceland .... (1) 3-0 (0) ....Turkey
Kazakhstan .... (0) 0-0 (0) .... Latvia

October 10, 2014
Holland .... (0) 3-1 (1).....Kazakhstan
Latvia.............. (0) 0-3 (0) ....Iceland
Turkey .... (1) 1-2 (1).......Czech Rep

October 13, 2014
Iceland .... (2) 2-0 (0) ....Holland
Kazakhstan .... (0) 2-4 (2) ....Czech Rep
Latvia.............. (0) 1-1 (0) ....Turkey

November 16, 2014
Czech Rep ...... (1) 2-1 (1)............Iceland
Holland .... (3) 6-0 (0) .... Latvia
Turkey ....(2) 3-1 (0) .....Kazakhstan

March 28, 2015
Czech Rep ...... (0) 1-1 (1).............. Latvia
Holland .... (0) 1-1 (1)............Turkey
Kazakhstan .... (0) 0-3 (2) ....Iceland

Friday June 12
Iceland .... (0) 2-1 (0) ....Czech Rep
Kazakhstan .... (0) 0-1 (0) ....Turkey
Latvia.............. (0) 0-2 (0) ....Holland

Thursday September 3
Czech Rep v Kazakhstan, Holland v Iceland, Turkey v Latvia

Sunday September 6
Iceland v Kazakhstan, Latvia v Czech Rep, Turkey v Holland

Saturday October 10
Czech Rep v Turkey, Iceland v Latvia, Kazakhstan v Holland

Tuesday October 13
Latvia v Kazakhstan, Holland v Czech Rep, Turkey v Iceland

Group B

	P	W	D	L	F	A	GD	Pts
Wales	6	4	2	0	8	2	+6	14
Belgium	6	3	2	1	13	2	+11	11
Israel	6	3	0	3	10	9	+1	9
Cyprus	6	3	0	3	12	11	+1	9
Bosnia-Hz	6	2	2	2	8	7	+1	8
Andorra	6	0	0	6	3	23	-20	0

September 9, 2014
Andorra.......... (1) 1-2 (1).............. Wales
Bosnia-Hz....... (1) 1-2 (1)............. Cyprus

Octobe r 10, 2014
Belgium.......... (3) 6-0 (0) .... Andorra
Cyprus............. (0) 1-2 (2) .... Israel
Wales.............. (0) 0-0 (0) ..... Bosnia-Hz.

October 13, 2014
Andorra.......... (1) 1-4 (2) .... Israel
Bosnia-Hz....... (1) 1-1 (0) .... Belgium
Wales.............. (2) 2-1 (1)............. Cyprus

November 16, 2014
Belgium.......... (0) 0-0 (0) .... Wales
Cyprus............. (3) 5-0 (0) .... Andorra
Israel.............. (2) 3-0 (0) ..... Bosnia-Hz.

March 28, 2015
Andorra.......... (0) 0-3 (1)...... Bosnia-Hz.
Belgium.......... (2) 5-0 (0) .... Cyprus
Israel.............. (0) 0-3 (1).............. Wales

March 31, 2015
Israel.............. (0) 0-1 (1).......... Belgium

Friday June 12
Andorra.......... (1) 1-3 (2) .... Cyprus
Bosnia-Hz....... (2) 3-1 (1).............. Israel
Wales.............. (1) 1-0 (0) .... Belgium

Thursday September 3
Belgium v Bosnia-Hz, Cyprus v Wales, Israel v Andorra

Sunday September 6
Bosnia-Hz v Andorra, Cyprus v Belgium, Wales v Israel

Saturday October 10
Andorra v Belgium, Bosnia-Hz v Wales, Israel v Cyprus

Tuesday October 13
Belgium v Israel, Cyprus v Bosnia-Hz, Wales v Andorra

Group C

	P	W	D	L	F	A	GD	Pts
Slovakia	6	6	0	0	13	3	+10	18
Spain	6	5	0	1	15	3	+12	15
Ukraine	6	4	0	2	9	2	+7	12
Belarus	6	1	1	4	4	11	-7	4
Macedonia	6	1	0	5	6	14	-8	3
Luxembourg	6	0	1	5	3	17	-14	1

September 8, 2014
Luxembourg... (1) 1-1 (0) .... Belarus
Spain.............. (3) 5-1 (1)...... Macedonia
Ukraine .... (0) 0-1 (1)..........Slovakia

October 9, 2014
Belarus........... (0) 0-2 (0) ....Ukraine
Macedonia..... (1) 3-2 (2) ... Luxembourg
Slovakia .... (1) 2-1 (0) .... Spain

October 12, 2014
Belarus........... (0) 1-3 (0) ....Slovakia
Luxembourg... (0) 0-4 (2) .... Spain
Ukraine .... (1) 1-0 (0) ..... Macedonia

November 15, 2014
Luxembourg... (0) 0-3 (1)...........Ukraine
Macedonia..... (0) 0-2 (2) ....Slovakia
Spain.............. (2) 3-0 (0) .... Belarus

March 27, 2015
Macedonia..... (1) 1-2 (1)......... Belarus
Slovakia .... (3) 3-0 (0) ... Luxembourg
Spain.............. (1) 1-0 (0) ....Ukraine

Sunday June 14
Belarus........... (0) 0-1 (1)............. Spain
Slovakia .... (2) 2-1 (0) .... Macedonia
Ukraine .... (0) 3-0 (0) ... Luxembourg

Saturday September 5
Luxembourg v Macedonia, Spain v Slovakia, Ukraine v Belarus

Gibraltar were drawn against World Cup winners Germany

Tuesday September 8
Belarus v Luxembourg, Macedonia v Spain, Slovakia v Ukraine

Friday October 9
Macedonia v Ukraine, Slovakia v Belarus, Spain v Luxembourg

Monday October 12
Belarus v Macedonia, Luxembourg v Slovakia, Ukraine v Spain

Group D

	P	W	D	L	F	A	GD	Pts
Poland	6	4	2	0	20	3	+17	14
Germany	6	4	1	1	16	4	+12	13
Scotland	6	3	2	1	12	6	+6	11
Ireland	6	2	3	1	12	5	+7	9
Georgia	6	1	0	5	4	13	-9	3
Gibraltar	6	0	0	6	1	34	-33	0

September 7, 2014
Georgia .... (1) 1-2 (1)..Rep of Ireland
Germany .... (1) 2-1 (0) .... Scotland
Gibraltar......... (0) 0-7 (1)............. Poland

October 11, 2014
Rep of Ireland (3) 7-0 (0) .... Gibraltar
Poland............ (0) 2-0 (0) ....Germany
Scotland......... (1) 1-0 (0) .... Georgia

October 14, 2014
Germany .... (0) 1-1 (0) .Rep of Ireland
Gibraltar......... (0) 0-3 (2) .... Georgia
Poland............ (1) 2-2 (1).......... Scotland

November 14, 2014
Georgia .... (0) 0-4 (0) .... Poland
Germany .... (3) 4-0 (0) .... Gibraltar
Scotland......... (0) 1-0 (0) .Rep of Ireland

March 29, 2015
Georgia .... (0) 0-2 (2) ....Germany
Rep of Ireland (0) 1-1 (1)............. Poland
Scotland......... (4) 6-1 (1).......... Gibraltar

Saturday June 13
Gibraltar......... (0) 0-7 (1).........Germany
Poland............ (0) 4-0 (0) .... Georgia
Rep of Ireland (1) 1-1 (0) .... Scotland

Friday September 4
Georgia v Scotland, Germany v Poland, Gibraltar v Rep of Ireland

Monday September 7
Poland v Gibraltar, Rep of Ireland v Georgia, Scotland v Germany

Thursday October 8
Georgia v Gibraltar, Rep of Ireland v Germany, Scotland v Poland

Sunday October 11
Germany v Georgia, Gibraltar v Scotland, Poland v Rep of Ireland

Group E

	P	W	D	L	F	A	GD	Pts
England	6	6	0	0	18	3	+15	18
Switzerland	6	4	0	2	13	4	+9	12
Slovenia	6	3	0	3	12	7	+5	9
Estonia	6	2	1	3	3	5	-2	7
Lithuania	6	2	0	4	4	12	-8	6
San Marino	6	0	1	5	0	19	-19	1

September 8, 2014
Estonia........... (0) 1-0 (0) ....Slovenia
San Marino .... (0) 0-2 (2) .... Lithuania
Switzerland.... (0) 0-2 (0) .... England

October 9, 2014
England.......... (2) 5-0 (0) .....San Marino
Lithuania........ (0) 1-0 (0) .... Estonia
Slovenia .... (0) 1-0 (0) .... Switzerland

October 12, 2014
Estonia........... (0) 0-1 (0) .... England
Lithuania........ (0) 0-2 (2) ....Slovenia

October 14, 2014
San Marino .... (0) 0-4 (3) .... Switzerland

November 15, 2014
England.......... (0) 3-1 (0) ....Slovenia
San Marino .... (0) 0-0 (0) .... Estonia
Switzerland.... (0) 4-0 (0) .... Lithuania

March 27, 2015
England.......... (2) 4-0 (0) .... Lithuania
Slovenia .... (1) 6-0 (0) .....San Marino
Switzerland.... (2) 3-0 (0) .... Estonia

Sunday June 14
Estonia........... (1) 2-0 (0) .....San Marino
Lithuania........ (0) 1-2 (0) .... Switzerland
Slovenia .... (1) 2-3 (0) .... England

Saturday September 5
Estonia v Lithuania, San Marino v England, Switzerland v Slovenia

Tuesday September 8
England v Switzerland, Lithuania v San Marino, Slovenia v Estonia

Friday October 9
England v Estonia, Slovenia v Lithuania, Switzerland v San Marino

Monday October 12
Estonia v Switzerland, Lithuania v England, San Marino v Slovenia

Harry Kane scores against Lithuania on his England debut

Group F

	P	W	D	L	F	A	GD	Pts
Romania	6	4	2	0	7	1	+6	14
N Ireland	6	4	1	1	8	4	+4	13
Hungary	6	3	2	1	5	3	+2	11
Faroe Islands	6	2	0	4	4	8	-4	6
Finland	6	1	1	4	5	8	-3	4
Greece	6	0	2	4	2	7	-5	2

September 7, 2014
Faroe Islands.. (1) 1-3 (0) .... Finland
Greece............ (0) 0-1 (1).......... Romania
Hungary .... (0) 1-2 (0) .... N Ireland

October 11, 2014
Finland .... (0) 1-1 (1)............. Greece
N Ireland........ (2) 2-0 (0) .. Faroe Islands
Romania .... (1) 1-1 (0) ....Hungary

October 14, 2014
Faroe Islands.. (0) 0-1 (1)..........Hungary
Finland .... (0) 0-2 (0) .... Romania
Greece............ (0) 0-2 (1)......... N Ireland

November 14, 2014
Greece............ (0) 0-1 (0) .. Faroe Islands
Hungary .... (0) 1-0 (0) .... Finland
Romania .... (0) 2-0 (0) .... N Ireland

March 29, 2015
Hungary .... (0) 0-0 (0) .... Greece
N Ireland........ (2) 2-1 (0) .... Finland
Romania .... (1) 1-0 (0) .. Faroe Islands

Saturday June 13
Faroe Islands.. (1) 2-1 (0) .... Greece
Finland .... (0) 0-1 (0) ....Hungary
N Ireland........ (0) 0-0 (0) .... Romania

Friday September 4
Faroe Islands v N Ireland, Greece v
Finland, Hungary v Romania

Monday September 7
Finland v Faroe Islands, N Ireland v
Hungary, Romania v Greece

Thursday October 8
Hungary v Faroe Islands, N Ireland v
Greece, Romania v Finland

Sunday October 11
Faroe Islands v Romania, Finland v
N Ireland, Greece v Hungary

Group G

	P	W	D	L	F	A	GD	Pts
Austria	6	5	1	0	11	2	+9	16
Sweden	6	3	3	0	10	4	+6	12
Russia	6	2	2	2	9	4	+5	8
Montenegro	6	1	2	3	4	8	-4	5
Liechtenstein	6	1	2	3	2	12	-10	5
Moldova	6	0	2	4	3	9	-6	2

September 8, 2014
Austria .... (1) 1-1 (1)...........Sweden
Montenegro... (1) 2-0 (0) .... Moldova
Russia .... (1) 4-0 (0) .. Liechtenstein

October 9, 2014
Liechtenstein . (0) 0-0 (0) ... Montenegro
Moldova......... (1) 1-2 (1)...........Austria
Sweden.......... (0) 1-1 (1)............. Russia

October 12, 2014
Austria .... (1) 1-0 (0) ... Montenegro
Russia .... (0) 1-1 (0) .... Moldova
Sweden .... (1) 2-0 (0) .. Liechtenstein

November 15, 2014
Austria .... (0) 1-0 (0) .... Russia
Moldova......... (0) 0-1 (0) .. Liechtenstein
Montenegro... (0) 1-1 (1)...........Sweden

March 27, 2015
Liechtenstein . (0) 0-5 (2) ....Austria
Moldova......... (0) 0-t2(0) ....Sweden
Montenegro..... 0-3 ....Russia
MATCH FORFEITED
Abandoned with the score at 0-0

Sunday June 14
Liechtenstein . (1) 1-1 (1).........Moldova
Russia .... (0) 0-1 (1)............Austria
Sweden .... (3) 3-1 (0) ... Montenegro

Saturday September 5
Austria v Moldova, Montenegro v
Liechtenstein, Russia v Sweden

Tuesday September 8
Liechtenstein v Russia, Moldova v
Montenegro, Sweden v Austria

Friday October 9
Liechtenstein v Sweden, Moldova v
Russia, Montenegro v Austria

Monday October 12
Austria v Liechtenstein, Russia v
Montenegro, Sweden v Moldova

Group H

	P	W	D	L	F	A	GD	Pts
Croatia	6	4	2	0	16	3	+13	14
Italy	6	3	3	0	9	5	+4	12
Norway	6	3	1	2	7	8	-1	10
Bulgaria	6	2	2	2	7	7	0	8
Azerbaijan	6	1	1	4	4	11	-7	4
Malta	6	0	1	5	1	10	-9	1

September 9, 2014
Azerbaijan...... (0) 1-2 (1)...........Bulgaria
Croatia .... (0) 2-0 (0) ....Malta
Norway .... (0) 0-2 (1)................Italy

October 10, 2014
Bulgaria .... (0) 0-1 (1)...........Croatia
Italy................ (1) 2-1 (0) ......Azerbaijan
Malta .... (0) 0-3 (2) ....Norway

October 13, 2014
Croatia .... (4) 6-0 (0) ......Azerbaijan
Malta .... (0) 0-1 (1)................Italy
Norway .... (1) 2-1 (1)........Bulgaria

November 16, 2014
Azerbaijan...... (0) 0-1 (1)...........Norway
Bulgaria .... (1) 1-1 (0) ....Malta
Italy................ (1) 1-1 (1)............Croatia

March 28, 2015
Azerbaijan...... (1) 2-0 (0) ....Malta
Bulgaria .... (2) 2-2 (1)................Italy
Croatia .... (1) 5-1 (0) ....Norway

Friday June 12
Croatia .... (1) 1-1 (1)................Italy
Malta .... (0) 0-1 (0) ....Bulgaria
Norway .... (0) 0-0 (0) ......Azerbaijan

Thursday September 3
Azerbaijan v Croatia, Bulgaria v
Norway, Italy v Malta

Sunday September 6
Italy v Bulgaria, Malta v Azerbaijan,
Norway v Croatia

Saturday October 10
Azerbaijan v Italy, Croatia v Bulgaria,
Norway v Malta

Tuesday October 13
Bulgaria v Azerbaijan, Italy v Norway,
Malta v Croatia

Group I

	P	W	D	L	F	A	GD	Pts
Portugal	5	4	0	1	7	4	+3	12
Denmark	5	3	1	1	8	4	+4	10
Albania	4	2	1	1	4	5	-1	7
Serbia	5	1	1	3	6	8	-2	1
Armenia	5	0	1	4	5	9	-4	1

September 7, 2014
Denmark .... (0) 2-1 (0) ....Armenia
Portugal .... (0) 0-1 (0) ....Albania

October 11, 2014
Albania .... (1) 1-1 (0) ....Denmark
Armenia .... (1) 1-1 (0) .... Serbia

October 14, 2014
Denmark .... (0) 0-1 (0) .... Portugal
Serbia............. (0) 3-0 (0) ....Albania
MATCH FORFEITED
Abandoned with the score at 0-0

November 14, 2014
Portugal .... (0) 1-0 (0) ....Armenia
Serbia............. (1) 1-3 (0) ....Denmark

March 29, 2015
Albania .... (0) 2-1 (1)...........Armenia
Portugal .... (1) 2-1 (0) .... Serbia

Saturday June 13
Armenia .... (1) 2-3 (1)......... Portugal
Denmark .... (1) 2-0 (0) .... Serbia

Friday September 4
Denmark v Albania, Serbia v Armenia

Monday September 7
Albania v Portugal, Armenia v
Denmark

Thursday October 8
Albania v Serbia, Portugal v Denmark

Sunday October 11
Armenia v Albania, Serbia v Portugal

Euro 2016 – winner

	b365	BFred	Coral	Hills	Lads	Power
Germany	10-3	3	10-3	3	10-3	16-5
France	4	4	4	7-2	6	4
Spain	11-2	13-2	6	6	10-3	6
Belgium	10	12	12	10	12	12
England	11	11	12	10	12	12
Italy	14	16	12	14	11	16
Holland	20	16	18	14	10	14
Portugal	20	20	20	20	12	25
Croatia	20	25	33	25	33	25
Switzerland	66	66	50	66	50	66
Russia	66	66	80	66	20	66
Denmark	80	66	66	50	50	66
Sweden	66	80	80	66	66	66
Czech Rep	50	80	80	66	66	80
Poland	66	66	80	50	100	66
Austria	100	100	66	66	80	80
Bosnia-Hz	150	125	100	100	100	80
Romania	100	125	80	100	125	100
Ukraine	150	100	150	100	100	175
Scotland	200	150	200	125	150	150
Iceland	80	150	200	125	125	125
Slovakia	100	150	150	100	100	175
Turkey	250	125	125	100	66	100
Wales	80	80	125	100	150	125
Rep of Ireland	500	250	400	200	150	400
Norway	350	200	250	150	100	175
Hungary	350	250	300	300	150	375
N Ireland	500	750	750	500	300	250

Others available. Win or each-way. See bookmakers for terms

Euro 2016 qualifying Group A – winner

	b365	BFred	Coral	Hills	Lads	Power
Holland	13-8	11-8	11-8	11-8	11-8	7-5
Iceland	2	2	2	2	11-5	2
Czech Rep	7-4	9-4	9-4	9-4	9-5	21-10

Euro 2016 qualifying Group B – winner

	b365	BFred	Coral	Hills	Lads	Power
Belgium	4-5	4-5	10-11	5-6	5-6	10-11
Wales	Evs	11/10	11/10	21/20	Evs	Evs
Bosnia-Hz	33	16	16	16	25	14

Euro 2016 qualifying Group C – winner

	b365	BFred	Coral	Hills	Lads	Power
Spain	1-9	1-8	1-8	1-8	1-9	1-12
Slovakia	6	9-2	9-2	9-2	9-2	11-2
Ukraine	33	20	22	20	22	25

Euro 2016 qualifying Group D – winner

	b365	BFred	Coral	Hills	Lads	Power
Germany	1-6	1-7	1-7	1-7	1-7	1-7
Poland	4	6	11-2	5	9-2	6
Scotland	40	16	20	20	20	12

Euro 2016 qualifying Group F – winner

	b365	BFred	Coral	Hills	Lads	Power
Romania	2-9	2-7	3-10	2-7	2-7	1-4
N Ireland	5	7-2	4	7-2	7-2	7-2
Hungary	8	10	13-2	8	8	15-2

Euro 2016 qualifying GroupG – winner

	b365	BFred	Coral	Hills	Lads	Power
Austria	1-3	1-3	2-7	1-3	2-7	1-4
Sweden	9-4	9-4	9-4	9-4	9-4	5-2

Euro 2016 qualifying Group H – winner

	b365	BFred	Coral	Hills	Lads	Power
Italy	4-5	4-5	10-11	4-5	4-5	10-11
Croatia	10-11	10-11	10-11	10-11	10-11	8-11

Euro 2016 qualifying Group I – winner

	b365	BFred	Coral	Hills	Lads	Power
Portugal	1-4	1-4	1-4	1-4	1-4	1-4
Denmark	11-4	11-4	11-4	11-4	11-4	11-4
Albania	33	33	33	25	25	33

Gareth Bale celebrates his winner for Wales against Belgium

FIXTURE LIST 2015-16

To the right of each fixture are results for the corresponding league match in each of the last six seasons. The most recent result – 2014-15 – is on the right. The results cover matches in the Premier League, Championship, League 1, League 2, National League, Scottish Premiership, Scottish Championship, Scottish League One and Scottish League Two.

Where Scottish clubs have met more than once at the same venue in the same season, results are separated by an oblique stroke with the most recent to the right. The Scottish Premiership will split into top- and bottom-six sections later in the season. These fixtures cover the period until the split.

Please note that TV coverage and postponements will cause alterations to the fixture list.

	2009-10	2010-11	2011-12	2012-13	2013-14	2014-15
Saturday August 1st, 2015						
Ladbrokes Premiership						
Celtic v Ross County	-	-	-	4-0	2-1/1-1	0-0
Hamilton v Partick	-	-	1-0/2-2	1-0/0-2	-	3-3/1-1
Inverness CT v Motherwell	-	1-2/3-0	2-3	1-5/4-3	2-0/1-2	3-1
Kilmarnock v Dundee	-	-	-	0-0/1-2	-	1-3
Sunday August 2nd, 2015						
Ladbrokes Premiership						
Dundee United v Aberdeen	0-1	3-1/3-1	1-2	1-1/1-0	1-2/1-3	0-2/1-0
Hearts v St Johnstone	1-2	1-1/1-0	1-2/2-0	2-0/2-0	0-2	-
Friday August 7th, 2015						
Championship						
Brighton v Nottm Forest	-	-	1-0	0-0	1-3	2-3
Saturday August 8th, 2015						
Premier League						
Bournemouth v Aston Villa	-	-	-	-	-	-
Chelsea v Swansea	-	-	4-1	2-0	1-0	4-2 Everton
v Watford	-	-	-	-	-	-
Leicester v Sunderland	-	-	-	-	-	0-0
Man United v Tottenham	3-1	2-0	3-0	2-3	1-2	3-0
Norwich v Crystal Palace	-	1-2	-	-	1-0	-
Championship						
Birmingham v Reading	-	-	2-0	-	1-2	6-1
Blackburn v Wolves	3-1	3-0	1-2	0-1	-	0-1
Bolton v Derby	-	-	-	2-0	2-2	0-2
Brentford v Ipswich	-	-	-	-	-	2-4
Cardiff v Fulham	-	-	-	-	3-1	1-0
Charlton v QPR	-	-	-	-	1-0	-
Hull v Huddersfield	-	-	-	2-0	-	-
Leeds v Burnley	-	1-0	2-1	1-0	1-2	-
Rotherham v MK Dons	-	-	-	-	2-2	-
Sheffield Weds v Bristol City	0-1	-	-	2-3	-	-
League One						
Burton v Scunthorpe	-	-	-	-	2-2	-
Chesterfield v Barnsley	-	-	-	-	-	2-1
Colchester v Blackpool	-	-	-	-	-	-
Coventry v Wigan	-	-	-	-	-	-
Crewe v Port Vale	1-2	2-1	1-1	-	1-2	2-1
Doncaster v Bury	-	-	-	2-1	-	-
Fleetwood Town v Southend	-	-	-	0-0	1-1	-
Gillingham v Sheffield United	-	-	-	-	0-1	2-0

Results cover matches from Premier League to National League and Scottish Premiership to League Two

	2009-10	2010-11	2011-12	2012-13	2013-14	2014-15
Rochdale v Peterborough	-	2-2	-	-	-	0-1
Shrewsbury v Millwall	-	-	-	-	-	-
Swindon v Bradford	-	-	0-0	-	1-0	2-1
Walsall v Oldham	3-0	1-1	0-1	3-1	1-0	2-0
League Two						
Accrington v Luton	-	-	-	-	-	2-2
AFC Wimbledon v Plymouth	-	-	1-2	1-1	1-1	0-0
Bristol Rovers v Northampton	-	-	2-1	3-1	1-0	-
Cambridge U v Newport County	-	0-1	1-1	0-0	-	4-0
Exeter v Yeovil	1-1	2-3	1-1	-	-	-
Hartlepool v Morecambe	-	-	-	-	2-1	0-2
Leyton Orient v Barnet	-	-	-	-	-	-
Mansfield v Carlisle	-	-	-	-	-	3-2
Oxford v Crawley Town	3-1	-	1-1	-	-	-
Portsmouth v Dag & Red	-	-	-	-	1-0	3-0
Stevenage v Notts County	-	-	0-2	2-0	0-1	-
Wycombe v York	-	-	-	4-0	1-1	1-0
National League						
Aldershot v Gateshead	-	-	-	-	1-2	1-2
Altrincham v Forest Green	2-2	2-1	-	-	-	2-2
Barrow v Dover	-	-	-	-	-	-
Boreham W v Halifax	-	-	-	-	-	-
Bromley v Wrexham	-	-	-	-	-	-
Chester v Braintree	-	-	-	-	0-2	2-3
Kidderminster v Grimsby	-	3-2	1-1	0-0	0-1	0-1
Lincoln v Cheltenham	1-1	0-2	-	-	-	-
Southport v Eastleigh	-	-	-	-	-	1-2
Torquay v Macclesfield	1-0	1-3	3-0	-	-	1-1
Tranmere v Woking	-	-	-	-	-	-
Welling v Guiseley	-	-	-	-	-	-
Ladbrokes Premiership						
Aberdeen v Kilmarnock	1-0/1-2	0-1/5-0	2-2/0-0	0-2/1-0	2-1/2-1	1-0
Dundee v Hearts	-	-	-	1-0/1-0	-	-
Motherwell v Dundee United	2-2/2-3	2-1/2-1	0-0/0-2	0-1/0-1	0-4	1-0
Partick v Celtic	-	-	-	-	1-2/1-5	0-3
Ross County v Hamilton	-	-	1-0/5-1	-	-	0-1/2-1
St Johnstone v Inverness CT	-	1-0/0-3	2-0/0-0	0-0/1-0	4-0/0-1	1-0/1-1
Ladbrokes Championship						
Dumbarton v Hibernian	-	-	-	-	-	3-6/1-2
Morton v Falkirk	-	0-0/2-2	3-2/0-0	1-2/2-0	0-2/1-1	-
Queen of Sth v Alloa	-	-	-	1-0/0-0	0-0/3-1	2-0/1-0
Raith v Livingston	-	-	0-1/0-3	0-0/0-2	1-0/2-4	1-5/0-4
Rangers v St Mirren	2-1/3-1	2-1	1-1/3-1	-	-	-
Ladbrokes League One						
Airdrieonians v Forfar	-	2-0/3-1	4-4/3-0	-	0-2/5-1	1-2/3-1
Albion v Ayr	-	-	-	2-0/1-3	-	-
Brechin v Dunfermline	-	-	-	-	1-1/3-2	1-1/3-0
Cowdenbeath v Stranraer	-	-	-	-	-	-
Peterhead v Stenhousemuir	2-2/0-1	2-2/0-3	-	-	-	1-0/2-0
Ladbrokes League Two						
Arbroath v Elgin	-	2-0/3-5	-	-	-	1-0/3-3
Berwick v Montrose	2-0/0-2	1-0/0-1	1-2/2-2	1-4/4-0	1-1/5-0	2-2/3-3
East Stirling v East Fife	-	-	-	-	-	1-1/2-0
Queens Park v Annan	0-0/3-2	3-0/0-1	0-0/2-0	2-2/2-2	2-5/0-1	0-0/2-0
Stirling v Clyde	1-1/1-0	-	-	0-1/2-0	1-1/4-1	-

Results cover matches from Premier League to National League and Scottish Premiership to League Two

Sunday August 9th, 2015

Premier League

	2009-10	2010-11	2011-12	2012-13	2013-14	2014-15
Arsenal v West Ham	2-0	1-0	-	5-1	3-1	3-0
Newcastle v Southampton	-	-	-	4-2	1-1	1-2
Stoke v Liverpool	1-1	2-0	1-0	3-1	3-5	6-1

Championship

Preston v Middlesbrough	2-2	1-3	-	-	-	-

Monday August 10th, 2015

Premier League

West Brom v Man City	-	0-2	0-0	1-2	2-3	1-3

Tuesday August 11th, 2015

National League

Braintree v Lincoln	-	-	1-0	0-3	0-2	1-3
Cheltenham v Aldershot	1-2	1-2	2-0	1-1	-	-
Dover v Kidderminster	-	-	-	-	-	0-1
Eastleigh v Boreham W	-	-	-	-	0-1	-
Forest Green v Welling	-	-	-	-	0-0	4-1
Gateshead v Tranmere	-	-	-	-	-	-
Grimsby v Barrow	-	1-1	5-2	0-0	-	-
Guiseley v Altrincham	-	-	-	-	2-2	-
Halifax v Chester	-	-	-	-	2-1	0-2
Macclesfield v Southport	-	-	-	2-2	2-2	3-0
Woking v Bromley	-	-	-	-	-	-
Wrexham v Torquay	-	-	-	-	-	0-0

Wednesday August 12th, 2015

Ladbrokes Premiership

Aberdeen v Hamilton	1-2/1-3	4-0/1-0	-	-	-	3-0
Dundee United v Dundee	-	-	-	3-0/1-1	-	6-2/3-0
Hearts v Motherwell	1-0/0-2	0-2/0-0/3-3	2-0/0-1	1-0/1-2	0-1	-
Inverness CT v Partick	2-3/2-1	-	-	-	1-2/1-0	0-4
Kilmarnock v Celtic	1-0	1-2/0-4/0-2	3-3/0-6	1-3	2-5/0-3	0-2
St Johnstone v Ross County	-	-	-	1-1/2-2	4-0/0-1	2-1

Friday August 14th, 2015

Premier League

Aston Villa v Man United	1-1	2-2	0-1	2-3	0-3	1-1

League Two

Notts County v Mansfield	-	-	-	-	-	-

Saturday August 15th, 2015

Premier League

Southampton v Everton	-	-	-	0-0	2-0	3-0
Sunderland v Norwich	-	-	3-0	1-1	0-0	-
Swansea v Newcastle	1-1	-	0-2	1-0	3-0	2-2
Tottenham v Stoke	0-1	3-2	1-1	0-0	3-0	1-2
Watford v West Brom	1-1	-	-	-	-	-
West Ham v Leicester	-	-	3-2	-	-	2-0

Championship

Bristol City v Brentford	-	-	-	-	1-2	-
Burnley v Birmingham	2-1	-	1-3	1-2	3-0	-
Derby v Charlton	-	-	-	3-2	3-0	2-0
Fulham v Brighton	-	-	-	-	-	0-2
Huddersfield v Blackburn	-	-	-	2-2	2-4	2-2
Ipswich v Sheffield Weds	0-0	-	-	0-3	2-1	2-1

Results cover matches from Premier League to National League and Scottish Premiership to League Two

	2009-10	2010-11	2011-12	2012-13	2013-14	2014-15
Middlesbrough v Bolton	-	-	-	2-1	1-0	1-0
MK Dons v Preston	-	-	0-1	1-1	0-0	0-2
Nottm Forest v Rotherham	-	-	-	-	-	2-0
QPR v Cardiff	0-1	2-1	-	-	-	-
League One						
Barnsley v Burton	-	-	-	-	-	-
Blackpool v Rochdale	-	-	-	-	-	-
Bradford v Shrewsbury	1-3	1-2	3-1	-	2-1	-
Bury v Swindon	-	-	-	0-1	-	-
Millwall v Coventry	-	3-1	3-0	-	-	-
Oldham v Fleetwood Town	-	-	-	-	-	1-0
Peterborough v Colchester	-	1-1	-	-	2-0	0-2
Port Vale v Gillingham	-	0-0	2-1	0-2	2-1	2-1
Scunthorpe v Crewe	-	-	-	1-2	-	2-1
Sheffield United v Chesterfield	-	-	4-1	-	-	1-1
Southend v Walsall	3-0	-	-	-	-	-
League Two						
Barnet v Wycombe	-	0-1	-	1-0	-	-
Carlisle v Cambridge U	-	-	-	-	-	0-1
Crawley Town v AFC Wimbledon	2-1	3-1	1-1	-	-	-
Dag & Red v Leyton Orient	-	2-0	-	-	-	-
Luton v Oxford	2-1	-	-	-	-	2-0
Morecambe v Accrington	1-2	1-2	1-2	0-0	1-2	1-1
Newport County v Stevenage	-	-	-	-	-	2-0
Northampton v Exeter	-	-	-	3-0	1-2	1-0
Plymouth v Portsmouth	-	-	-	-	1-1	3-0
Yeovil v Bristol Rovers	0-3	0-1	-	-	-	-
York v Hartlepool	-	-	-	-	0-0	1-0
National League						
Braintree v Tranmere	-	-	-	-	-	-
Cheltenham v Southport	-	-	-	-	-	-
Dover v Chester	-	-	-	-	-	2-0
Eastleigh v Lincoln	-	-	-	-	-	4-0
Forest Green v Barrow	1-0	2-3	3-0	1-1	-	-
Gateshead v Boreham W	-	-	-	-	-	-
Grimsby v Bromley	-	-	-	-	-	-
Guiseley v Kidderminster	-	-	-	-	-	-
Halifax v Torquay	-	-	-	-	-	0-2
Macclesfield v Welling	-	-	-	-	2-1	3-2
Woking v Altrincham	-	-	-	-	-	2-0
Wrexham v Aldershot	-	-	-	-	2-1	3-1
Ladbrokes Premiership						
Celtic v Inverness CT	-	2-2	2-0/1-0	0-1/4-1	2-2/5-0/6-0	1-0/5-0
Dundee v St Johnstone	-	-	-	1-3/2-2	-	1-1/0-2
Hamilton v Dundee United	0-1	0-1/1-1	-	-	-	2-3
Motherwell v Aberdeen	1-1	1-1/2-1	1-0/1-0	4-1	1-3/2-2	0-2
Partick v Kilmarnock	-	-	-	-	1-1/1-1	1-1/1-4
Ross County v Hearts	-	-	-	2-2	2-1/1-2	-
Ladbrokes Championship						
Alloa v Rangers	-	-	-	-	-	1-1/0-1
Falkirk v Raith	-	0-0/2-1	2-0/2-3	0-2/1-1	3-1/2-1	0-1/1-0
Hibernian v Morton	-	-	-	-	-	-
Livingston v Queen of Sth	-	-	2-2/2-2	-	3-3/1-2	2-2/1-0
St Mirren v Dumbarton	-	-	-	-	-	-

Results cover matches from Premier League to National League and Scottish Premiership to League Two

	2009-10	2010-11	2011-12	2012-13	2013-14	2014-15
Ladbrokes League One						
Ayr v Brechin	-	0-2/2-0	-	3-0/1-2	2-2/1-3	0-2/2-2
Dunfermline v Cowdenbeath	-	2-1/5-0	-	3-0/1-0	-	-
Forfar v Albion	2-2/1-1	-	0-2/4-0	4-2/4-2	-	-
Stenhousemuir v Airdrieonians	-	1-3/1-0	1-1/0-3	-	1-1/1-2	1-0/0-2
Stranraer v Peterhead	-	-	2-1/0-3	-	-	5-0/2-0
Ladbrokes League Two						
Annan v Stirling	-	-	-	5-2/0-1	4-4/1-2	-
Clyde v Queens Park	-	2-3/0-2	0-2/1-2	0-3/2-3	3-0/1-2	0-2/2-0
East Fife v Berwick	-	-	-	-	-	2-3/1-4
Elgin v East Stirling	1-2/0-1	0-2/2-0	2-0/3-1	3-4/3-2	0-1/5-0	1-2/0-0
Montrose v Arbroath	-	3-0/0-5	-	-	-	1-5/3-0

Sunday August 16th, 2015

	2009-10	2010-11	2011-12	2012-13	2013-14	2014-15
Premier League						
Crystal Palace v Arsenal	-	-	-	-	0-2	1-2
Man City v Chelsea	2-1	1-0	2-1	2-0	0-1	1-1
Championship						
Reading v Leeds	-	0-0	2-0	-	1-0	0-2
Wolves v Hull	1-1	-	-	1-0	-	-
League One						
Wigan v Doncaster	-	-	-	-	2-2	-

Monday August 17th, 2015

	2009-10	2010-11	2011-12	2012-13	2013-14	2014-15
Premier League						
Liverpool v Bournemouth	-	-	-	-	-	-

Tuesday August 18th, 2015

	2009-10	2010-11	2011-12	2012-13	2013-14	2014-15
Championship						
Blackburn v Cardiff	-	-	-	1-4	-	1-1
Brentford v Birmingham	-	-	-	-	-	1-1
Derby v Middlesbrough	2-2	3-1	0-1	3-1	2-1	0-1
Huddersfield v Brighton	7-1	2-1	-	1-2	1-1	1-1
Ipswich v Burnley	-	1-1	1-0	2-1	0-1	-
MK Dons v Bolton	-	-	-	-	-	-
Nottm Forest v Charlton	-	-	-	2-1	0-1	1-1
Rotherham v Preston	-	-	-	-	0-0	-
League One						
Blackpool v Burton	-	-	-	-	-	-
Bradford v Gillingham	-	1-0	2-2	0-1	1-1	1-1
Bury v Fleetwood Town	-	-	-	-	2-2	-
Colchester v Oldham	1-0	1-0	4-1	0-2	0-1	2-2
Coventry v Crewe	-	-	-	1-2	2-2	1-3
Millwall v Barnsley	-	2-0	0-0	1-2	1-0	-
Peterborough v Sheffield United	1-0	-	-	-	0-0	1-2
Rochdale v Walsall	-	3-2	3-3	-	-	4-0
Shrewsbury v Chesterfield	1-1	0-0	-	-	-	-
Swindon v Port Vale	-	-	5-0	-	5-2	1-0
League Two						
Accrington v Mansfield	-	-	-	-	1-1	2-1
AFC Wimbledon v Cambridge U	0-0	3-0	-	-	-	1-2
Barnet v Northampton	0-0	4-1	1-2	4-0	-	-
Crawley Town v Portsmouth	-	-	-	0-3	-	-
Dag & Red v Exeter	-	1-1	-	1-1	1-1	1-2
Hartlepool v Newport County	-	-	-	-	3-0	2-2
Leyton Orient v Stevenage	-	-	0-0	0-1	2-0	-

Results cover matches from Premier League to National League and Scottish Premiership to League Two

	2009-10	2010-11	2011-12	2012-13	2013-14	2014-15
Luton v Bristol Rovers	-	-	-	-	-	-
Morecambe v Wycombe	-	0-3	-	0-1	1-1	1-3
Oxford v Notts County	-	-	-	-	-	-
Plymouth v Carlisle	-	1-1	-	-	-	1-0
York v Yeovil	-	-	-	-	-	-
National League						
Aldershot v Dover	-	-	-	-	-	3-1
Altrincham v Grimsby	-	2-2	-	-	-	1-1
Barrow v Guiseley	-	-	-	-	1-0	1-0
Boreham W v Forest Green	-	-	-	-	-	-
Bromley v Braintree	-	-	-	-	-	-
Chester v Cheltenham	-	-	-	-	-	-
Kidderminster v Wrexham	2-0	1-0	0-1	2-0	3-1	1-1
Lincoln v Macclesfield	0-0	2-1	-	2-3	1-0	2-0
Southport v Gateshead	-	5-1	1-3	2-1	2-1	0-1
Torquay v Woking	-	-	-	-	-	1-0
Tranmere v Halifax	-	-	-	-	-	-
Welling v Eastleigh	-	-	-	-	-	1-2

Wednesday August 19th, 2015

Championship						
Bristol City v Leeds	-	0-2	0-3	2-3	-	-
Hull v Fulham	2-0	-	-	-	6-0	-
Sheffield Weds v Reading	0-2	-	-	-	5-2	1-0
Wolves v QPR	-	-	0-3	-	-	-
League One						
Doncaster v Southend	-	-	-	-	-	-
Wigan v Scunthorpe	-	-	-	-	-	-

Friday August 21st, 2015

Championship						
Birmingham v Derby	-	-	2-2	3-1	3-3	0-4

Saturday August 22nd, 2015

Premier League						
Crystal Palace v Aston Villa	-	-	-	-	1-0	0-1
Leicester v Tottenham	-	-	-	-	-	1-2
Man United v Newcastle	-	3-0	1-1	4-3	0-1	3-1
Norwich v Stoke	-	-	1-1	1-0	1-1	-
Sunderland v Swansea	-	-	2-0	0-0	1-3	0-0
West Ham v Bournemouth	-	-	-	-	-	-
Championship						
Bolton v Nottm Forest	-	-	-	2-2	1-1	2-2
Brighton v Blackburn	-	-	-	1-1	3-0	1-1
Burnley v Brentford	-	-	-	-	-	-
Cardiff v Wolves	-	-	-	3-1	-	0-1
Charlton v Hull	-	-	-	0-0	-	-
Fulham v Huddersfield	-	-	-	-	-	3-1
Leeds v Sheffield Weds	-	-	-	2-1	1-1	1-1
Middlesbrough v Bristol City	0-0	1-2	1-1	1-3	-	-
Preston v Ipswich	2-0	1-0	-	-	-	-
QPR v Rotherham	-	-	-	-	-	-
Reading v MK Dons	-	-	-	-	-	-
League One						
Barnsley v Bradford	-	-	-	-	-	3-1
Burton v Peterborough	-	-	-	-	-	-
Chesterfield v Rochdale	2-0	-	2-1	1-1	2-2	2-1

Results cover matches from Premier League to National League and Scottish Premiership to League Two

	2009-10	2010-11	2011-12	2012-13	2013-14	2014-15
Crewe v Bury	2-3	3-0	-	1-0	-	-
Fleetwood Town v Colchester	-	-	-	-	-	2-3
Gillingham v Wigan	-	-	-	-	-	-
Oldham v Shrewsbury	-	-	-	1-0	1-2	-
Port Vale v Doncaster	-	-	-	-	-	3-0
Scunthorpe v Millwall	-	1-2	-	-	-	-
Sheffield United v Blackpool	3-0	-	-	-	-	-
Southend v Swindon	2-2	-	1-4	-	-	-
Walsall v Coventry	-	-	-	4-0	0-1	0-2
League Two						
Bristol Rovers v Barnet	-	-	0-2	2-1	-	2-1
Cambridge U v Crawley Town	0-1	2-2	-	-	-	-
Carlisle v AFC Wimbledon	-	-	-	-	-	4-4
Exeter v York	-	-	-	1-1	2-1	1-1
Mansfield v Oxford	2-1	-	-	-	1-3	2-1
Newport County v Leyton Orient	-	-	-	-	-	-
Northampton v Plymouth	-	-	0-0	1-0	0-2	2-3
Notts County v Accrington	1-2	-	-	-	-	-
Portsmouth v Morecambe	-	-	-	-	3-0	3-0
Stevenage v Hartlepool	-	-	2-2	1-0	-	1-0
Wycombe v Dag & Red	-	-	-	1-0	2-0	1-1
Yeovil v Luton	-	-	-	-	-	-
National League						
Braintree v Southport	-	-	0-0	1-3	1-0	0-2
Cheltenham v Barrow	-	-	-	-	-	-
Dover v Altrincham	-	-	-	-	-	2-1
Eastleigh v Macclesfield	-	-	-	-	-	4-0
Forest Green v Lincoln	-	-	0-2	3-0	4-1	3-3
Gateshead v Kidderminster	0-2	2-2	2-1	2-0	3-1	2-0
Grimsby v Torquay	0-3	-	-	-	-	0-2
Guiseley v Aldershot	-	-	-	-	-	-
Halifax v Bromley	-	-	-	-	-	-
Tranmere v Boreham W	-	-	-	-	-	-
Woking v Chester	-	-	-	-	0-1	1-0
Wrexham v Welling	-	-	-	-	2-1	2-1
Ladbrokes Premiership						
Aberdeen v Dundee	-	-	-	2-0/1-0	-	3-3
Dundee United v Celtic	2-1/0-2	1-2/1-3	0-1/1-0	2-2/0-4	0-1/0-2	2-1/0-3
Hearts v Partick	-	-	-	-	0-2/2-4	-
Inverness CT v Hamilton	-	0-1/1-1	-	-	-	4-2
Kilmarnock v Ross County	-	-	-	3-0	2-0/2-2	0-3/1-2
St Johnstone v Motherwell	2-2/1-2	0-2/1-0	0-3	1-3/2-0	2-0/3-0	2-1
Ladbrokes Championship						
Dumbarton v Queen of Sth	-	-	-	-	0-1/0-3	0-4/0-0
Livingston v Falkirk	-	-	1-1/1-2	2-1/1-2	0-3/0-1	0-1/2-1
Morton v St Mirren	-	-	-	-	-	-
Raith v Alloa	-	-	-	-	4-2/1-1	1-1/2-1
Rangers v Hibernian	1-1/3-0	0-3	1-0/4-0	-	-	1-3/0-2
Ladbrokes League One						
Brechin v Airdrieonians	-	3-1/1-2	1-1/1-1	-	4-3/1-1	1-1/0-0
Cowdenbeath v Albion	-	-	2-1/3-0	-	-	-
Forfar v Stenhousemuir	-	1-1/2-0	2-3/1-2	3-2/3-3	1-2/3-0	3-0/1-0
Peterhead v Dunfermline	-	-	-	-	-	1-1/1-1
Stranraer v Ayr	-	-	-	2-0/0-1	1-1/4-0	3-1/1-0

Results cover matches from Premier League to National League and Scottish Premiership to League Two

	2009-10	2010-11	2011-12	2012-13	2013-14	2014-15
Ladbrokes League Two						
Arbroath v Queens Park	-	1-0/2-2	-	-	-	1-2/1-1
East Fife v Elgin	-	-	-	-	-	1-1/3-1
East Stirling v Annan	1-3/3-1	1-5/2-0	1-0/0-4	2-2/1-2	1-1/2-1	0-1/1-3
Montrose v Clyde	-	8-1/3-1	4-0/5-0	2-3/1-1	0-2/0-2	0-3/0-1
Stirling v Berwick	-	-	-	6-3/1-0	3-1/2-1	-

Sunday August 23rd, 2015

	2009-10	2010-11	2011-12	2012-13	2013-14	2014-15
Premier League						
Everton v Man City	2-0	2-1	1-0	2-0	2-3	1-1
Watford v Southampton	-	-	0-3	-	-	-
West Brom v Chelsea	-	1-3	1-0	2-1	1-1	3-0

Monday August 24th, 2015

	2009-10	2010-11	2011-12	2012-13	2013-14	2014-15
Premier League						
Arsenal v Liverpool	1-0	1-1	0-2	2-2	2-0	4-1

Friday August 28th, 2015

	2009-10	2010-11	2011-12	2012-13	2013-14	2014-15
Championship						
Blackburn v Bolton	3-0	1-0	1-2	1-2	4-1	1-0

Saturday August 29th, 2015

	2009-10	2010-11	2011-12	2012-13	2013-14	2014-15
Premier League						
Aston Villa v Sunderland	1-1	0-1	0-0	6-1	0-0	0-0
Bournemouth v Leicester	-	-	-	-	0-1	-
Chelsea v Crystal Palace	-	-	-	-	2-1	1-0
Liverpool v West Ham	3-0	3-0	-	0-0	4-1	2-0
Man City v Watford	-	-	-	-	-	-
Newcastle v Arsenal	-	4-4	0-0	0-1	0-1	1-2
Stoke v West Brom	-	1-1	1-2	0-0	0-0	2-0
Tottenham v Everton	2-1	1-1	2-0	2-2	1-0	2-1
Championship						
Brentford v Reading	-	-	-	-	-	3-1
Bristol City v Burnley	-	2-0	3-1	3-4	-	-
Derby v Leeds	-	2-1	1-0	3-1	3-1	2-0
Huddersfield v QPR	-	-	-	-	1-1	-
Hull v Preston	-	1-0	-	-	-	-
Ipswich v Brighton	-	-	3-1	0-3	2-0	2-0
MK Dons v Birmingham	-	-	-	-	-	-
Nottm Forest v Cardiff	0-0	2-1	0-1	3-1	-	1-2
Rotherham v Fulham	-	-	-	-	-	3-3
Sheffield Weds v Middlesbrough	1-3	-	-	2-0	1-0	2-0
Wolves v Charlton	-	-	-	1-1	-	0-0
League One						
Blackpool v Walsall	-	-	-	-	-	-
Bradford v Port Vale	0-0	0-2	1-1	0-1	1-0	1-1
Bury v Oldham	-	-	0-0	0-1	-	-
Colchester v Scunthorpe	-	-	1-1	1-2	-	2-2
Coventry v Southend	-	-	-	-	-	-
Doncaster v Fleetwood Town	-	-	-	-	-	0-0
Millwall v Chesterfield	-	-	-	-	-	-
Peterborough v Gillingham	-	-	-	-	2-0	1-2
Rochdale v Barnsley	-	-	-	-	-	0-1
Shrewsbury v Burton	3-1	3-0	1-0	-	-	1-0
Swindon v Sheffield United	-	-	-	0-0	2-1	5-2
Wigan v Crewe	-	-	-	-	-	-

Results cover matches from Premier League to National League and Scottish Premiership to League Two

	2009-10	2010-11	2011-12	2012-13	2013-14	2014-15
League Two						
Accrington v Northampton	0-3	3-1	2-1	2-4	0-1	1-5
AFC Wimbledon v Exeter	-	-	-	2-2	2-1	4-1
Barnet v Cambridge U	-	-	-	-	2-2	-
Crawley Town v Wycombe	-	-	-	-	-	-
Dag & Red v Stevenage	-	-	-	-	-	0-2
Hartlepool v Carlisle	4-1	0-4	4-0	1-2	-	0-3
Leyton Orient v Bristol Rovers	5-0	4-1	-	-	-	-
Luton v Portsmouth	-	-	-	-	-	1-1
Morecambe v Notts County	2-1	-	-	-	-	-
Oxford v Yeovil	-	-	-	-	-	-
Plymouth v Newport County	-	-	-	-	0-0	0-0
York v Mansfield	3-0	2-1	2-2	-	1-2	1-1
National League						
Aldershot v Eastleigh	-	-	-	-	-	0-2
Altrincham v Tranmere	-	-	-	-	-	-
Barrow v Southport	-	1-1	2-2	3-2	-	-
Boreham W v Woking	-	-	-	-	-	-
Bromley v Dover	-	-	-	-	0-4	-
Guiseley v Gateshead	-	-	-	-	-	-
Kidderminster v Forest Green	2-1	1-0	1-0	0-1	4-1	2-4
Lincoln v Grimsby	0-0	-	1-2	1-4	0-2	3-2
Macclesfield v Chester	-	-	-	-	3-2	3-1
Torquay v Cheltenham	3-0	2-1	2-2	2-2	4-2	-
Welling v Braintree	-	-	-	-	0-2	2-1
Wrexham v Halifax	-	-	-	-	0-0	0-0
Ladbrokes Premiership						
Celtic v St Johnstone	5-2/3-0	2-0	0-1/2-0/1-0	1-1/4-0	2-1/3-0	0-1
Dundee v Inverness CT	2-2/2-2	-	-	1-4/1-1	-	1-2/0-1
Hamilton v Hearts	2-1	0-4/0-2	-	-	-	-
Motherwell v Kilmarnock	3-1/1-0	0-1/1-1	0-0	2-2	2-1/1-2	1-1/3-1
Partick v Aberdeen	-	-	-	-	0-3/3-1	0-1
Ross County v Dundee United	-	-	-	1-2/1-0	2-4/3-0	2-3
Ladbrokes Championship						
Alloa v Morton	-	-	-	-	2-0/2-0	-
Falkirk v Dumbarton	-	-	-	3-4/1-3	1-2/2-0	1-1/3-3
Hibernian v Raith	-	-	-	-	-	1-1/1-1
Queen of Sth v Rangers	-	-	-	-	-	2-0/3-0
St Mirren v Livingston	-	-	-	-	-	-
Ladbrokes League One						
Airdrieonians v Peterhead	-	2-2/1-0	-	-	-	0-2/1-3
Albion v Brechin	-	-	1-2/0-1	1-2/3-1	-	-
Ayr v Forfar	-	0-1/3-1	-	2-3/2-1	2-0/2-3	2-0/1-0
Dunfermline v Stranraer	-	-	-	-	3-1/3-2	0-1/1-0
Stenhousemuir v Cowdenbeath	0-2/0-0	-	3-1/0-2	-	-	-
Ladbrokes League Two						
Annan v Montrose	2-0/0-0	2-2/2-1	2-1/1-2	2-1/1-1	2-1/1-0	2-2/4-3
Berwick v Arbroath	-	4-1/0-4	-	-	-	1-2/3-1
Clyde v East Stirling	-	1-2/2-0	7-1/3-0	2-1/2-0	1-2/1-0	0-1/1-1
Elgin v Stirling	-	-	-	3-1/1-2	4-0/2-3	-
Queens Park v East Fife	-	-	-	-	-	3-0/1-0

Sunday August 30th, 2015

	2009-10	2010-11	2011-12	2012-13	2013-14	2014-15
Premier League						
Southampton v Norwich	2-2	-	-	1-1	4-2	-
Swansea v Man United	-	-	0-1	1-1	1-4	2-1

Results cover matches from Premier League to National League and Scottish Premiership to League Two

Monday August 31st, 2015

National League

Braintree v Aldershot	-	-	-	-	1-0	1-1
Cheltenham v Wrexham	-	-	-	-	-	-
Chester v Guiseley	-	-	-	-	-	-
Dover v Boreham W	-	-	-	-	0-0	-
Eastleigh v Torquay	-	-	-	-	-	1-2
Forest Green v Bromley	-	-	-	-	-	-
Gateshead v Lincoln	-	-	3-3	1-1	3-1	3-3
Grimsby v Macclesfield	1-1	-	-	0-1	2-3	1-2
Halifax v Barrow	-	-	-	-	-	-
Southport v Altrincham	-	1-0	-	-	-	2-1
Tranmere v Kidderminster	-	-	-	-	-	-
Woking v Welling	-	-	-	-	2-4	2-2

Saturday September 5th, 2015

League One

Barnsley v Shrewsbury	-	-	-	-	-	-
Chesterfield v Wigan	-	-	-	-	-	-
Crewe v Swindon	-	-	2-0	2-1	1-1	0-0
Fleetwood Town v Rochdale	-	-	-	0-3	0-0	1-0
Gillingham v Doncaster	-	-	-	-	-	1-1
Oldham v Bradford	-	-	-	-	1-1	2-1
Port Vale v Millwall	-	-	-	-	-	-
Scunthorpe v Blackpool	2-4	-	-	-	-	-
Sheffield United v Colchester	-	-	3-0	3-0	1-1	4-1
Southend v Peterborough	-	-	-	-	-	-
Walsall v Bury	-	-	2-4	1-1	-	-

League Two

Cambridge U v Luton	3-4	0-0	1-1	2-2	1-1	0-1
Carlisle v Barnet	-	-	-	-	-	-
Exeter v Leyton Orient	0-0	2-1	3-0	-	-	-
Mansfield v AFC Wimbledon	0-1	2-5	-	-	1-0	2-1
Newport County v York	-	4-0	2-1	-	3-0	3-1
Northampton v Dag & Red	1-0	-	2-1	3-1	2-2	1-0
Notts County v Crawley Town	-	-	-	1-1	1-0	5-3
Portsmouth v Accrington	-	-	-	-	1-0	2-3
Stevenage v Plymouth	-	-	-	-	-	1-0
Wycombe v Hartlepool	2-0	-	5-0	-	2-1	1-0
Yeovil v Morecambe	-	-	-	-	-	-

National League

Aldershot v Halifax	-	-	-	-	2-2	1-1
Altrincham v Cheltenham	-	-	-	-	-	-
Barrow v Eastleigh	-	-	-	-	-	-
Boreham W v Grimsby	-	-	-	-	-	-
Bromley v Gateshead	-	-	-	-	-	-
Chester v Forest Green	-	-	-	-	1-2	1-4
Kidderminster v Braintree	-	-	5-4	2-1	2-2	3-1
Lincoln v Wrexham	-	-	1-2	1-2	2-0	1-1
Macclesfield v Woking	-	-	-	0-0	3-2	2-1
Southport v Dover	-	-	-	-	-	2-2
Torquay v Guiseley	-	-	-	-	-	-
Welling v Tranmere	-	-	-	-	-	-

Ladbrokes Championship

Dumbarton v Alloa	1-3/3-1	4-1/2-2	-	-	1-1/4-1	3-1/1-0
Falkirk v Hibernian	1-3/1-3	-	-	-	-	1-0/0-3
Livingston v Morton	-	-	1-1/0-0	2-2/0-2	2-2/0-1	-

Results cover matches from Premier League to National League and Scottish Premiership to League Two

	2009-10	2010-11	2011-12	2012-13	2013-14	2014-15
Queen of Sth v St Mirren	-	-	-	-	-	-
Rangers v Raith	-	-	-	-	-	6-1/4-0
Ladbrokes League One						
Airdrieonians v Cowdenbeath	-	-	1-5/1-1	0-3/1-1	-	-
Ayr v Stenhousemuir	-	2-0/4-3	-	1-1/1-2	4-3/2-3	2-3/0-0
Forfar v Dunfermline	-	-	-	-	4-0/2-4	2-0/1-0
Peterhead v Albion	-	-	-	-	1-1/2-0	-
Stranraer v Brechin	-	-	-	0-2/3-2	3-0/1-2	2-2/0-2
Ladbrokes League Two						
Annan v East Fife	-	-	-	-	-	2-1/2-1
Arbroath v Clyde	0-3/2-0	3-2/2-0	-	-	-	4-0/3-1
Berwick v Queens Park	1-0/1-1	1-1/3-1	2-0/1-4	2-0/4-1	4-0/1-0	0-0/1-1
East Stirling v Stirling	-	-	-	3-1/1-1	2-2/1-0	-
Montrose v Elgin	1-1/0-4	0-1/1-0	3-0/2-3	2-2/4-1	3-3/0-3	2-3/2-1

Sunday September 6th, 2015

League One						
Burton v Coventry	-	-	-	-	-	-

League Two						
Bristol Rovers v Oxford	-	-	0-0	0-2	1-1	-

Friday September 11th, 2015

Championship						
Reading v Ipswich	1-1	1-0	1-0	-	2-1	1-0

Saturday September 12th, 2015

Premier League						
Arsenal v Stoke	2-0	1-0	3-1	1-0	3-1	3-0
Crystal Palace v Man City	-	-	-	-	0-2	2-1
Everton v Chelsea	2-1	1-0	2-0	1-2	1-0	3-6
Man United v Liverpool	2-1	3-2	2-1	2-1	0-3	3-0
Norwich v Bournemouth	-	-	-	-	-	1-1
Watford v Swansea	0-1	2-3	-	-	-	-
West Brom v Southampton	-	-	-	2-0	0-1	1-0
Championship						
Birmingham v Bristol City	-	-	2-2	2-0	-	-
Bolton v Wolves	1-0	1-0	1-1	2-0	-	2-2
Brighton v Hull	-	-	0-0	1-0	-	-
Burnley v Sheffield Weds	-	-	-	3-3	1-1	-
Cardiff v Huddersfield	-	-	-	1-0	-	3-1
Charlton v Rotherham	-	-	-	-	-	1-1
Fulham v Blackburn	3-0	3-2	1-1	-	-	0-1
Leeds v Brentford	1-1	-	-	-	-	0-1
Middlesbrough v MK Dons	-	-	-	-	-	-
Preston v Derby	0-0	1-2	-	-	-	-
QPR v Nottm Forest	1-1	1-1	-	-	5-2	-
League One						
Barnsley v Swindon	-	-	-	-	-	0-3
Burton v Rochdale	1-0	-	-	3-2	1-0	-
Chesterfield v Colchester	-	-	0-1	-	-	6-0
Crewe v Millwall	-	-	-	-	-	-
Fleetwood Town v Bradford	-	-	-	2-2	-	0-2
Gillingham v Blackpool	-	-	-	-	-	-
Oldham v Peterborough	-	0-5	-	-	5-4	1-1
Port Vale v Wigan	-	-	-	-	-	-
Scunthorpe v Coventry	1-0	0-2	-	1-2	-	2-1

Results cover matches from Premier League to National League and Scottish Premiership to League Two

	2009-10	2010-11	2011-12	2012-13	2013-14	2014-15
Sheffield United v Bury	-	-	4-0	1-1	-	-
Southend v Shrewsbury	-	0-2	3-0	-	-	1-0
Walsall v Doncaster	-	-	-	0-3	-	3-0
League Two						
Bristol Rovers v Accrington	-	-	5-1	0-1	0-1	-
Cambridge U v Leyton Orient	-	-	-	-	-	-
Carlisle v Dag & Red	-	0-2	-	-	-	1-0
Exeter v Hartlepool	3-1	1-2	0-0	-	0-3	1-2
Mansfield v Crawley Town	4-0	1-4	-	-	-	-
Newport County v Morecambe	-	-	-	-	2-3	0-1
Northampton v Oxford	-	2-1	2-1	1-0	3-1	1-3
Notts County v Luton	-	-	-	-	-	-
Portsmouth v Barnet	-	-	-	-	-	-
Stevenage v York	1-0	-	-	-	-	2-3
Wycombe v Plymouth	-	-	-	1-1	0-1	0-2
Yeovil v AFC Wimbledon	-	-	-	-	-	-
National League						
Braintree v Barrow	-	-	1-0	2-3	-	-
Bromley v Macclesfield	-	-	-	-	-	-
Cheltenham v Dover	-	-	-	-	-	-
Eastleigh v Gateshead	-	-	-	-	-	2-2
Forest Green v Southport	-	0-0	2-3	0-1	3-1	5-3
Grimsby v Aldershot	1-2	-	-	-	1-1	3-1
Guiseley v Woking	-	-	-	-	-	-
Halifax v Kidderminster	-	-	-	-	1-1	2-0
Lincoln v Boreham W	-	-	-	-	-	-
Tranmere v Chester	-	-	-	-	-	-
Welling v Torquay	-	-	-	-	-	0-0
Wrexham v Altrincham	1-1	2-1	-	-	-	2-3
Ladbrokes Premiership						
Aberdeen v Celtic	1-3/4-4	0-3	0-1/1-1	0-2	0-2/2-1	1-2/0-1
Dundee United v Kilmarnock	0-0	1-1/4-2	1-1/4-0	3-3	1-0/3-2	3-1
Inverness CT v Hearts	-	1-3/1-1	1-1/1-0	1-1	2-0/0-0	-
Motherwell v Ross County	-	-	-	3-2/2-0	3-1/2-1	2-2/1-1
Partick v Dundee	0-2/0-1	1-0/0-0	0-1/0-0	-	-	1-1
St Johnstone v Hamilton	1-1/2-3	2-0/1-0	-	-	-	0-1
Ladbrokes Championship						
Hibernian v Alloa	-	-	-	-	-	2-0/4-1
Morton v Dumbarton	-	-	-	3-0/0-3	2-0/3-0	-
Raith v Queen of Sth	1-0/0-0	0-1/0-1	0-2/3-1	-	2-1/3-2	3-4/3-0
Rangers v Livingston	-	-	-	-	-	2-0/1-1
St Mirren v Falkirk	1-1	-	-	-	-	-
Ladbrokes League One						
Albion v Airdrieonians	-	-	7-2/0-1	-	-	-
Brechin v Forfar	-	0-0/0-1	0-1/2-1	4-1/3-4	2-1/1-5	3-3/2-3
Cowdenbeath v Peterhead	5-0/1-3	-	-	-	-	-
Dunfermline v Ayr	3-1/0-1	-	-	-	5-1/3-0	4-2/2-1
Stenhousemuir v Stranraer	-	-	-	0-0/1-2	1-0/1-1	2-2/1-0
Ladbrokes League Two						
Clyde v Annan	-	0-2/0-2	0-0/1-1	2-1/2-3	2-1/0-3	1-1/1-0
East Fife v Arbroath	1-1/3-1	-	2-2/1-3	2-1/0-1	2-1/1-0	1-5/2-0
Elgin v Berwick	3-3/1-5	1-2/3-2	4-1/4-0	3-1/1-2	2-0/1-3	2-1/3-3
Queens Park v East Stirling	1-0/2-0	2-0/2-0	2-0/5-1	1-2/5-1	1-3/0-0	3-0/1-1
Stirling v Montrose	-	-	-	1-3/3-1	3-1/2-2	-

Results cover matches from Premier League to National League and Scottish Premiership to League Two

Sunday September 13th, 2015

Premier League

	2009-10	2010-11	2011-12	2012-13	2013-14	2014-15
Leicester v Aston Villa	-	-	-	-	-	1-0
Sunderland v Tottenham	3-1	1-2	0-0	1-2	1-2	2-2

Monday September 14th, 2015

Premier League

	2009-10	2010-11	2011-12	2012-13	2013-14	2014-15
West Ham v Newcastle	-	1-2	-	0-0	1-3	1-0

Tuesday September 15th, 2015

Championship

	2009-10	2010-11	2011-12	2012-13	2013-14	2014-15
Birmingham v Nottm Forest	-	-	1-2	2-1	0-0	2-1
Bolton v Sheffield Weds	-	-	-	0-1	1-1	0-0
Brighton v Rotherham	-	-	-	-	-	1-1
Burnley v MK Dons	-	-	-	-	-	-
Cardiff v Hull	-	2-0	0-3	2-1	0-4	-
Charlton v Huddersfield	2-1	0-1	2-0	1-1	0-0	3-0
Fulham v Wolves	0-0	2-1	5-0	-	-	0-1
Leeds v Ipswich	-	0-0	3-1	2-0	1-1	2-1
Middlesbrough v Brentford	-	-	-	-	-	4-0
Preston v Bristol City	2-2	0-4	-	-	1-0	1-1
QPR v Blackburn	-	-	1-1	-	0-0	-
Reading v Derby	4-1	2-1	2-2	-	0-0	0-3

National League

	2009-10	2010-11	2011-12	2012-13	2013-14	2014-15
Aldershot v Welling	-	-	-	-	3-1	2-1
Altrincham v Eastleigh	-	-	-	-	-	3-3
Barrow v Lincoln	-	-	1-0	1-2	-	-
Boreham W v Bromley	-	-	-	-	1-1	1-1
Cheltenham v Macclesfield	1-2	0-1	2-0	-	-	-
Chester v Grimsby	-	-	-	-	0-0	2-2
Dover v Braintree	-	-	-	-	-	1-0
Gateshead v Wrexham	1-0	0-1	1-4	0-1	0-3	3-1
Guiseley v Halifax	-	-	-	-	-	-
Kidderminster v Torquay	-	-	-	-	-	2-1
Southport v Tranmere	-	-	-	-	-	-
Woking v Forest Green	-	-	-	2-0	2-1	1-0

Saturday September 19th, 2015

Premier League

	2009-10	2010-11	2011-12	2012-13	2013-14	2014-15
Aston Villa v West Brom	-	2-1	1-2	1-1	4-3	2-1
Bournemouth v Sunderland	-	-	-	-	-	-
Chelsea v Arsenal	2-0	2-0	3-5	2-1	6-0	2-0
Man City v West Ham	3-1	2-1	-	2-1	2-0	2-0
Newcastle v Watford	2-0	-	-	-	-	-
Stoke v Leicester	-	-	-	-	-	0-1
Swansea v Everton	-	-	0-2	0-3	1-2	1-1

Championship

	2009-10	2010-11	2011-12	2012-13	2013-14	2014-15
Blackburn v Charlton	-	-	-	1-2	0-1	2-0
Brentford v Preston	-	-	1-3	1-0	1-0	-
Bristol City v Reading	1-1	1-0	2-3	-	-	-
Derby v Burnley	-	2-4	1-2	1-2	0-3	-
Huddersfield v Bolton	-	-	-	2-2	0-1	2-1
Hull v QPR	-	0-0	-	-	-	2-1
Ipswich v Birmingham	-	-	1-1	3-1	1-0	4-2
MK Dons v Leeds	0-1	-	-	-	-	-
Nottm Forest v Middlesbrough	1-0	1-0	2-0	0-0	2-2	2-1
Rotherham v Cardiff	-	-	-	-	-	1-3
Sheffield Weds v Fulham	-	-	-	-	-	1-1
Wolves v Brighton	-	-	-	3-3	-	1-1

Results cover matches from Premier League to National League and Scottish Premiership to League Two

League One						
Blackpool v Barnsley	1-2	-	1-1	1-2	1-0	-
Bradford v Sheffield United	-	-	-	-	2-0	0-2
Bury v Port Vale	1-1	0-1	-	-	-	-
Colchester v Gillingham	2-1	-	-	-	3-0	1-2
Coventry v Chesterfield	-	-	-	-	-	0-0
Doncaster v Oldham	-	-	-	1-0	-	0-2
Millwall v Southend	2-0	-	-	-	-	-
Peterborough v Walsall	-	4-1	-	-	0-0	0-0
Rochdale v Scunthorpe	-	-	1-0	-	0-4	3-1
Shrewsbury v Crewe	2-0	0-1	2-0	1-0	1-3	-
Swindon v Burton	-	-	2-0	-	-	-
Wigan v Fleetwood Town	-	-	-	-	-	-

League Two						
Accrington v Exeter	-	-	-	0-3	2-3	2-3
AFC Wimbledon v Notts County	-	-	-	-	-	-
Barnet v Stevenage	-	0-3	-	-	-	-
Crawley Town v Yeovil	-	-	-	0-1	-	2-0
Dag & Red v Newport County	-	-	-	-	1-1	0-1
Hartlepool v Cambridge U	-	-	-	-	-	2-1
Leyton Orient v Wycombe	2-0	-	1-3	-	-	-
Luton v Mansfield	4-1	2-0	0-0	2-3	-	3-0
Morecambe v Northampton	2-4	1-2	1-2	1-1	1-1	0-1
Oxford v Portsmouth	-	-	-	-	0-0	0-1
Plymouth v Bristol Rovers	-	3-1	1-1	1-1	1-0	-
York v Carlisle	-	-	-	-	-	0-0

National League						
Altrincham v Braintree	-	-	-	-	-	1-0
Barrow v Aldershot	-	-	-	-	-	-
Boreham W v Wrexham	-	-	-	-	-	-
Chester v Eastleigh	-	-	-	-	-	0-1
Dover v Guiseley	-	-	-	-	-	-
Gateshead v Welling	-	-	-	-	1-1	1-1
Grimsby v Tranmere	-	-	-	-	-	-
Halifax v Southport	-	-	-	-	1-0	3-1
Kidderminster v Lincoln	-	-	1-1	3-0	4-1	2-1
Macclesfield v Forest Green	-	-	-	1-2	1-2	2-2
Torquay v Bromley	-	-	-	-	-	-
Woking v Cheltenham	-	-	-	-	-	-

Ladbrokes Premiership						
Celtic v Dundee	-	-	-	2-0/5-0	-	2-1/5-0
Dundee United v Inverness CT	-	0-4/1-0	3-1/3-0	4-4	0-1/2-1	1-1
Hamilton v Motherwell	2-2/0-0	0-0	-	-	-	5-0/2-0
Hearts v Aberdeen	0-3	5-0	3-0/3-0	2-0	2-1/1-1	-
Kilmarnock v St Johnstone	2-1/3-2/1-2	1-1	1-2/0-0	1-2	0-0/1-2	0-1
Ross County v Partick	2-2/1-2	0-2/0-0	2-2/3-0	-	1-3/1-1	1-0/1-2

Ladbrokes Championship						
Alloa v Falkirk	-	-	-	-	0-0/3-0	2-3/1-3
Dumbarton v Rangers	-	-	-	-	-	0-3/1-3
Livingston v Hibernian	-	-	-	-	-	0-4/1-3
Queen of Sth v Morton	2-3/1-2	2-0/1-4	4-1/2-1	-	2-0/3-0	-
St Mirren v Raith	-	-	-	-	-	-

Ladbrokes League One						
Airdrieonians v Ayr	3-1/1-1	2-2/0-5	-	-	0-1/3-0	3-0/2-0
Cowdenbeath v Forfar	-	-	3-1/2-0	-	-	-

Results cover matches from Premier League to National League and Scottish Premiership to League Two

	2009-10	2010-11	2011-12	2012-13	2013-14	2014-15
Peterhead v Brechin	1-0/0-3	0-5/1-1	-	-	-	1-1/3-0
Stenhousemuir v Dunfermline	-	-	-	-	4-5/1-2	1-0/0-1
Stranraer v Albion	1-1/2-1	3-2/1-3	-	1-1/3-2	-	-

Ladbrokes League Two						
Arbroath v Stirling	3-4/2-4	-	4-2/2-0	-	-	-
Berwick v Annan	2-1/0-2	2-2/2-3	0-1/1-3	3-1/0-2	4-2/1-4	2-0/2-2
East Fife v Clyde	1-0/1-1	-	-	-	-	0-1/1-1
Montrose v East Stirling	0-3/0-1	0-2/3-0	2-1/3-1	3-1/2-2	2-0/2-0	4-1/0-1
Queens Park v Elgin	0-3/0-1	1-1/1-0	6-0/1-3	1-1/0-1	3-3/2-0	2-1/1-1

Sunday September 20th, 2015

Premier League						
Liverpool v Norwich	-	-	1-1	5-0	5-1	-
Southampton v Man United	-	-	-	2-3	1-1	1-2
Tottenham v Crystal Palace	-	-	-	-	2-0	0-0

Tuesday September 22nd, 2015

National League						
Braintree v Woking	-	-	-	1-1	2-0	0-0
Bromley v Kidderminster	-	-	-	-	-	-
Eastleigh v Dover	-	-	-	-	1-0	0-1
Forest Green v Cheltenham	-	-	-	-	-	-
Guiseley v Southport	-	-	-	-	-	-
Halifax v Gateshead	-	-	-	-	3-3	2-2
Lincoln v Altrincham	-	-	-	-	-	1-2
Macclesfield v Barrow	-	-	-	2-0	-	-
Torquay v Boreham W	-	-	-	-	-	-
Tranmere v Aldershot	-	-	-	-	-	-
Welling v Chester	-	-	-	-	2-0	1-3
Wrexham v Grimsby	-	2-0	2-2	0-0	0-1	0-1

Friday September 25th, 2015

Championship						
Fulham v QPR	-	-	6-0	3-2	-	-

Saturday September 26th, 2015

Premier League						
Leicester v Arsenal	-	-	-	-	-	1-1
Liverpool v Aston Villa	1-3	3-0	1-1	1-3	2-2	0-1
Man United v Sunderland	2-2	2-0	1-0	3-1	0-1	2-0
Newcastle v Chelsea	-	1-1	0-3	3-2	2-0	2-1
Southampton v Swansea	-	-	-	1-1	2-0	0-1
Stoke v Bournemouth	-	-	-	-	-	-
Tottenham v Man City	3-0	0-0	1-5	3-1	1-5	0-1
West Ham v Norwich	-	-	-	2-1	2-0	-

Championship						
Birmingham v Rotherham	-	-	-	-	-	2-1
Bolton v Brighton	-	-	-	1-0	0-2	1-0
Brentford v Sheffield Weds	-	1-0	1-2	-	-	0-0
Burnley v Reading	-	0-4	0-1	-	2-1	-
Cardiff v Charlton	-	-	-	0-0	-	1-2
Huddersfield v Nottm Forest	-	-	-	1-1	0-3	3-0
Hull v Blackburn	0-0	-	-	2-0	-	-
Ipswich v Bristol City	0-0	2-0	3-0	1-1	-	-
Middlesbrough v Leeds	-	1-2	0-2	1-0	0-0	0-1
MK Dons v Derby	-	-	-	-	-	-
Preston v Wolves	-	-	-	-	0-0	-

Results cover matches from Premier League to National League and Scottish Premiership to League Two

	2009-10	2010-11	2011-12	2012-13	2013-14	2014-15
League One						
Barnsley v Gillingham	-	-	-	-	-	4-1
Bradford v Peterborough	-	-	-	-	1-0	0-1
Bury v Coventry	-	-	-	0-2	-	-
Chesterfield v Burton	5-2	1-2	-	1-1	0-2	-
Fleetwood Town v Port Vale	-	-	-	2-5	-	1-0
Millwall v Rochdale	-	-	-	-	-	-
Oldham v Wigan	-	-	-	-	-	-
Sheffield United v Doncaster	1-1	2-2	-	0-0	-	3-2
Shrewsbury v Blackpool	-	-	-	-	-	-
Southend v Scunthorpe	-	-	-	-	0-1	-
Swindon v Colchester	1-1	2-1	-	0-1	0-0	2-2
Walsall v Crewe	-	-	-	2-2	1-1	0-1
League Two						
Barnet v Dag & Red	2-0	-	2-2	0-0	-	-
Bristol Rovers v Portsmouth	-	-	-	-	2-0	-
Cambridge U v Stevenage	1-3	-	-	-	-	1-1
Carlisle v Newport County	-	-	-	-	-	2-3
Crawley Town v Accrington	-	-	1-1	-	-	-
Exeter v Wycombe	1-1	-	1-3	3-2	0-1	2-1
Luton v AFC Wimbledon	1-2	3-0	-	-	-	0-1
Mansfield v Plymouth	-	-	-	-	0-1	1-0
Northampton v Leyton Orient	-	-	-	-	-	-
Notts County v York	-	-	-	-	-	-
Oxford v Morecambe	-	4-0	1-2	1-1	3-0	1-1
Yeovil v Hartlepool	4-0	0-2	0-1	1-0	-	-
National League						
Aldershot v Macclesfield	0-0	0-0	1-2	-	1-0	0-1
Barrow v Kidderminster	1-0	2-1	3-1	1-1	-	-
Boreham W v Altrincham	-	-	-	-	-	-
Braintree v Guiseley	-	-	-	-	-	-
Bromley v Chester	-	-	-	-	-	-
Cheltenham v Tranmere	-	-	-	-	-	2-0
Dover v Woking	-	-	-	-	-	2-1
Forest Green v Gateshead	1-0	1-1	2-1	1-0	1-0	1-1
Lincoln v Torquay	0-0	0-2	-	-	-	1-3
Southport v Grimsby	-	2-2	1-2	1-1	2-1	2-2
Welling v Halifax	-	-	-	-	0-1	2-1
Wrexham v Eastleigh	-	-	-	-	-	3-0
Ladbrokes Premiership						
Celtic v Hearts	2-1/2-0	3-0/4-0	1-0/5-0	1-0/4-1	2-0	-
Dundee v Ross County	2-0/0-1	0-0/2-0	1-2/1-1	0-1/0-2	-	1-1
Inverness CT v Aberdeen	-	2-0/0-2	2-1/0-2	1-1/3-0	3-4/0-0	0-1/1-2
Kilmarnock v Hamilton	3-0/1-2	3-0	-	-	-	1-0/2-3
Motherwell v Partick	-	-	-	-	1-0/4-3	1-0/0-0
St Johnstone v Dundee United	2-3/0-1	0-0	3-3/1-5/0-2	0-0/1-1	3-0/2-0	2-1/1-1
Ladbrokes Championship						
Alloa v Livingston	-	2-2/1-3	-	-	1-0/0-3	1-0/2-2
Falkirk v Queen of Sth	-	3-1/0-3	1-0/3-0	-	2-1/1-0	1-1/1-1
Hibernian v St Mirren	2-1/2-1	2-0/1-1	1-2/0-0	2-1/3-3	2-0/2-3	-
Morton v Rangers	-	-	-	-	-	-
Raith v Dumbarton	-	-	-	2-2/3-2	2-1/1-3	3-1/2-1
Ladbrokes League One						
Albion v Stenhousemuir	-	-	1-1/1-0	4-4/4-3	-	-
Ayr v Peterhead	-	1-1/2-2	-	-	-	3-3/2-4

Results cover matches from Premier League to National League and Scottish Premiership to League Two

	2009-10	2010-11	2011-12	2012-13	2013-14	2014-15
Brechin v Cowdenbeath	3-1/3-3	-	1-0/2-2	-	-	-
Dunfermline v Airdrieonians	2-0/2-0	-	-	1-3/1-2	2-1/0-1	3-0/2-2
Forfar v Stranraer	1-0/2-0	-	-	4-0/3-1	1-2/1-0	1-1/1-0

Ladbrokes League Two

Annan v Elgin	0-2/3-3	0-1/2-2	1-1/1-1	2-0/2-2	2-1/2-0	3-3/2-3
Clyde v Berwick	-	1-4/2-0	1-4/2-2	2-1/2-1	1-0/3-3	3-0/0-3
East Stirling v Arbroath	-	1-3/2-5	-	-	-	2-3/1-0
Montrose v East Fife	-	-	-	-	-	0-4/0-3
Stirling v Queens Park	-	-	-	1-2/2-3	3-0/2-2	-

Sunday September 27th, 2015

Premier League

Watford v Crystal Palace	1-3	1-1	0-2	2-2	-	-

Monday September 28th, 2015

Premier League

West Brom v Everton	-	1-0	0-1	2-0	1-1	0-2

Tuesday September 29th, 2015

League One

Blackpool v Chesterfield	-	-	-	-	-	-
Burton v Sheffield United	-	-	-	-	-	-
Colchester v Bradford	-	-	-	-	0-2	0-0
Coventry v Barnsley	3-1	3-0	1-0	-	-	2-2
Crewe v Southend	-	1-0	1-3	-	-	-
Doncaster v Swindon	-	-	-	1-0	-	1-2
Gillingham v Fleetwood Town	-	-	-	2-2	-	0-1
Peterborough v Bury	-	-	-	-	-	-
Port Vale v Oldham	-	-	-	-	1-0	0-1
Rochdale v Shrewsbury	4-0	-	-	-	-	-
Scunthorpe v Walsall	-	-	0-1	1-1	-	2-1
Wigan v Millwall	-	-	-	-	0-1	0-0

League Two

Accrington v Yeovil	-	-	-	-	-	-
AFC Wimbledon v Northampton	-	-	0-3	1-1	0-2	2-2
Dag & Red v Notts County	0-3	3-1	-	-	-	-
Hartlepool v Bristol Rovers	1-2	2-2	-	-	4-0	-
Leyton Orient v Carlisle	2-2	0-0	1-2	4-1	4-0	-
Morecambe v Luton	-	-	-	-	-	3-0
Newport County v Crawley Town	-	0-1	-	-	-	-
Plymouth v Barnet	-	-	0-0	2-1	-	-
Portsmouth v Exeter	-	-	-	-	3-2	1-0
Stevenage v Mansfield	3-1	-	-	-	-	3-0
Wycombe v Cambridge U	-	-	-	-	-	1-0
York v Oxford	1-1	-	-	3-1	0-0	0-1

Friday October 2nd, 2015

Championship

Rotherham v Burnley	-	-	-	-	-	-

Saturday October 3rd, 2015

Premier League

Arsenal v Man United	1-3	1-0	1-2	1-1	0-0	1-2
Aston Villa v Stoke	1-0	1-1	1-1	0-0	1-4	1-2
Bournemouth v Watford	-	-	-	-	1-1	2-0
Chelsea v Southampton	-	-	-	2-2	3-1	1-1
Crystal Palace v West Brom	1-1	-	-	-	3-1	0-2
Everton v Liverpool	0-2	2-0	0-2	2-2	3-3	0-0

Results cover matches from Premier League to National League and Scottish Premiership to League Two

	2009-10	2010-11	2011-12	2012-13	2013-14	2014-15
Man City v Newcastle	-	2-1	3-1	4-0	4-0	5-0
Norwich v Leicester	-	4-3	-	-	-	-
Sunderland v West Ham	2-2	1-0	-	3-0	1-2	1-1
Swansea v Tottenham	-	-	1-1	1-2	1-3	1-2
Championship						
Blackburn v Ipswich	-	-	-	1-0	2-0	3-2
Brighton v Cardiff	-	-	2-2	0-0	-	1-1
Bristol City v MK Dons	-	-	-	-	2-2	3-2
Charlton v Fulham	-	-	-	-	-	1-1
Derby v Brentford	-	-	-	-	-	1-1
Leeds v Birmingham	-	-	1-4	0-1	4-0	1-1
Nottm Forest v Hull	-	0-1	0-1	1-2	-	-
QPR v Bolton	-	-	0-4	-	2-1	-
Reading v Middlesbrough	0-2	5-2	0-0	-	2-0	0-0
Sheffield Weds v Preston	1-2	-	2-0	-	-	-
Wolves v Huddersfield	-	-	-	1-3	-	1-3
League One						
Blackpool v Swindon	-	-	-	-	-	-
Burton v Southend	-	3-1	0-2	2-0	0-1	2-1
Colchester v Bury	-	-	4-1	2-0	-	-
Coventry v Shrewsbury	-	-	-	0-1	0-0	-
Crewe v Chesterfield	0-1	2-0	-	-	-	0-0
Doncaster v Barnsley	0-1	0-2	2-0	-	2-2	1-0
Gillingham v Oldham	1-0	-	-	-	0-1	3-2
Peterborough v Millwall	-	-	0-3	1-2	-	-
Port Vale v Sheffield United	-	-	-	-	1-2	2-1
Rochdale v Bradford	1-3	-	-	0-0	-	0-2
Scunthorpe v Fleetwood Town	-	-	-	-	0-0	0-2
Wigan v Walsall	-	-	-	-	-	-
League Two						
Accrington v Oxford	-	0-0	0-2	0-3	0-0	1-0
AFC Wimbledon v Barnet	-	-	1-1	0-1	-	-
Dag & Red v Mansfield	-	-	-	-	0-0	2-0
Hartlepool v Luton	-	-	-	-	-	1-2
Leyton Orient v Notts County	-	2-0	0-3	2-1	5-1	0-1
Morecambe v Bristol Rovers	-	-	2-3	1-1	2-1	-
Newport County v Exeter	-	-	-	-	1-1	2-2
Plymouth v Crawley Town	-	-	1-1	-	-	-
Portsmouth v Yeovil	-	-	-	1-2	-	-
Stevenage v Carlisle	-	-	1-0	1-1	1-3	1-0
Wycombe v Northampton	-	2-2	-	0-0	1-1	1-1
York v Cambridge U	2-2	0-0	2-2	-	-	2-2
National League						
Altrincham v Barrow	0-1	2-0	-	-	2-1	-
Chester v Wrexham	-	-	-	-	0-0	2-1
Eastleigh v Braintree	-	-	-	-	-	1-0
Gateshead v Dover	-	-	-	-	-	1-2
Grimsby v Forest Green	-	1-1	2-1	1-0	3-1	2-1
Guiseley v Lincoln	-	-	-	-	-	-
Halifax v Cheltenham	-	-	-	-	-	-
Kidderminster v Welling	-	-	-	-	2-0	2-1
Macclesfield v Boreham W	-	-	-	-	-	-
Torquay v Aldershot	1-1	0-1	1-0	4-3	-	1-1
Tranmere v Bromley	-	-	-	-	-	-
Woking v Southport	-	-	-	2-3	2-0	1-2

Results cover matches from Premier League to National League and Scottish Premiership to League Two

	2009-10	2010-11	2011-12	2012-13	2013-14	2014-15
Ladbrokes Premiership						
Aberdeen v St Johnstone	2-1/1-3	0-1/0-2	0-0/0-0	2-0	0-0/1-0/1-1	2-0/0-1
Dundee v Motherwell	-	-	-	1-2/0-3	-	4-1
Hamilton v Celtic	1-2/0-1	1-1	-	-	-	0-2
Hearts v Kilmarnock	1-0/1-0	0-3/0-2	0-1	1-3/0-3	0-4/5-0	-
Partick v Dundee United	-	-	-	-	0-0/1-1	2-2
Ross County v Inverness CT	2-1/0-0	-	-	0-0/1-0	0-3/1-2	1-3
Ladbrokes Championship						
Dumbarton v Livingston	-	1-2/0-3	-	3-4/0-3	1-2/2-2	1-0/1-5
Queen of Sth v Hibernian	-	-	-	-	-	1-0/0-2
Raith v Morton	3-0/1-2	1-0/2-2	1-1/5-0	3-3/2-1	2-1/2-1	-
Rangers v Falkirk	4-1/3-0	-	-	-	-	4-0/2-2
St Mirren v Alloa	-	-	-	-	-	-
Ladbrokes League One						
Airdrieonians v Stranraer	-	-	-	-	3-2/1-1	3-3/1-1
Ayr v Cowdenbeath	-	-	-	-	-	-
Dunfermline v Albion	-	-	-	-	-	-
Peterhead v Forfar	-	1-2/1-1	-	-	-	3-2/1-0
Stenhousemuir v Brechin	1-1/1-2	0-0/1-3	1-1/2-1	3-1/3-3	3-2/4-2	0-2/2-2
Ladbrokes League Two						
Arbroath v Annan	-	0-2/2-1	-	-	-	3-2/1-1
Berwick v East Stirling	0-1/2-2	3-0/1-1	4-2/0-2	3-0/2-0	2-0/1-0	5-0/3-0
East Fife v Stirling	1-2/0-3	-	1-0/1-0	-	-	-
Elgin v Clyde	-	0-1/0-1	0-3/1-1	2-1/4-2	1-0/3-1	1-0/2-0
Queens Park v Montrose	3-2/3-0	1-0/4-1	3-1/5-0	2-2/1-2	0-1/1-1	2-0/4-1

Tuesday October 6th, 2015

	2009-10	2010-11	2011-12	2012-13	2013-14	2014-15
National League						
Aldershot v Forest Green	-	-	-	-	2-2	1-1
Altrincham v Halifax	-	-	-	-	-	0-0
Barrow v Chester	-	-	-	-	-	-
Cheltenham v Braintree	-	-	-	-	-	-
Grimsby v Gateshead	-	2-2	2-0	3-0	2-2	2-2
Guiseley v Macclesfield	-	-	-	-	-	-
Kidderminster v Boreham W	-	-	-	-	-	-
Torquay v Dover	-	-	-	-	-	2-0
Welling v Bromley	-	-	-	-	-	-
Wrexham v Tranmere	-	-	-	-	-	-

Saturday October 10th, 2015

	2009-10	2010-11	2011-12	2012-13	2013-14	2014-15
League One						
Barnsley v Crewe	-	-	-	-	-	2-0
Bradford v Blackpool	-	-	-	-	-	-
Bury v Wigan	-	-	-	-	-	-
Chesterfield v Gillingham	-	3-1	-	0-1	-	3-0
Fleetwood Town v Coventry	-	-	-	-	-	0-2
Millwall v Doncaster	-	1-0	3-2	-	0-0	-
Oldham v Scunthorpe	-	-	1-2	1-1	-	3-2
Sheffield United v Rochdale	-	-	3-0	-	-	1-0
Shrewsbury v Colchester	-	-	-	2-2	1-1	-
Southend v Port Vale	-	1-3	3-0	0-0	-	-
Swindon v Peterborough	-	1-1	-	-	2-1	1-0
Walsall v Burton	-	-	-	-	-	-
League Two						
Barnet v Accrington	1-2	2-0	0-0	1-1	-	-
Bristol Rovers v Wycombe	2-3	-	-	1-0	0-1	-
Cambridge U v Portsmouth	-	-	-	-	-	2-6

Results cover matches from Premier League to National League and Scottish Premiership to League Two

	2009-10	2010-11	2011-12	2012-13	2013-14	2014-15
Carlisle v Morecambe	-	-	-	-	-	1-1
Crawley Town v Leyton Orient	-	-	-	1-0	2-1	1-0
Exeter v Stevenage	-	-	1-1	-	-	0-0
Luton v York	1-1	5-0	1-2	-	-	2-2
Mansfield v Newport County	-	3-3	5-0	3-4	2-1	1-0
Northampton v Hartlepool	-	-	-	-	2-0	5-1
Notts County v Plymouth	-	2-0	-	-	-	-
Oxford v AFC Wimbledon	2-0	-	1-0	3-2	2-1	0-0
Yeovil v Dag & Red	-	1-3	-	-	-	-

National League

	2009-10	2010-11	2011-12	2012-13	2013-14	2014-15
Aldershot v Altrincham	-	-	-	-	-	3-1
Boreham W v Welling	-	-	-	-	-	-
Braintree v Grimsby	-	-	5-0	2-0	0-0	0-1
Bromley v Barrow	-	-	-	-	-	-
Chester v Lincoln	-	-	-	-	3-3	4-0
Dover v Wrexham	-	-	-	-	-	2-0
Forest Green v Guiseley	-	-	-	-	-	-
Gateshead v Cheltenham	-	-	-	-	-	-
Halifax v Woking	-	-	-	-	3-4	1-3
Macclesfield v Kidderminster	-	-	-	1-0	1-1	0-0
Southport v Torquay	-	-	-	-	-	2-1
Tranmere v Eastleigh	-	-	-	-	-	-

Tuesday October 13th, 2015

National League

	2009-10	2010-11	2011-12	2012-13	2013-14	2014-15
Altrincham v Kidderminster	3-2	1-2	-	-	-	2-1
Boreham W v Aldershot	-	-	-	-	-	-
Braintree v Dover	-	-	-	-	-	3-0
Bromley v Cheltenham	-	-	-	-	-	-
Eastleigh v Forest Green	-	-	-	-	-	2-2
Grimsby v Halifax	-	-	-	-	0-1	1-0
Macclesfield v Gateshead	-	-	-	0-4	0-2	1-1
Southport v Chester	-	-	-	-	0-0	0-0
Tranmere v Barrow	-	-	-	-	-	-
Welling v Lincoln	-	-	-	-	1-0	2-0
Woking v Torquay	-	-	-	-	-	3-2
Wrexham v Guiseley	-	-	-	-	-	-

Saturday October 17th, 2015

Premier League

	2009-10	2010-11	2011-12	2012-13	2013-14	2014-15
Chelsea v Aston Villa	7-1	3-3	1-3	8-0	2-1	3-0
Crystal Palace v West Ham	-	-	2-2	-	1-0	1-3
Everton v Man United	3-1	3-3	0-1	1-0	2-0	3-0
Man City v Bournemouth	-	-	-	-	-	-
Newcastle v Norwich	-	-	1-0	1-0	2-1	-
Southampton v Leicester	-	-	0-2	-	-	2-0
Swansea v Stoke	-	-	2-0	3-1	3-3	2-0
Tottenham v Liverpool	2-1	2-1	4-0	2-1	0-5	0-3
Watford v Arsenal	-	-	-	-	-	-
West Brom v Sunderland	-	1-0	4-0	2-1	3-0	2-2

Championship

	2009-10	2010-11	2011-12	2012-13	2013-14	2014-15
Birmingham v QPR	-	-	-	-	0-2	-
Brentford v Rotherham	-	-	-	-	0-1	1-0
Bristol City v Nottm Forest	1-1	2-3	0-0	2-0	-	-
Burnley v Bolton	1-1	-	-	2-0	1-1	-
Derby v Wolves	-	-	-	0-0	-	5-0
Ipswich v Huddersfield	-	-	-	2-2	2-1	2-2
Leeds v Brighton	1-1	-	1-2	1-2	2-1	0-2

Results cover matches from Premier League to National League and Scottish Premiership to League Two

	2009-10	2010-11	2011-12	2012-13	2013-14	2014-15
Middlesbrough v Fulham	-	-	-	-	-	2-0
MK Dons v Blackburn	-	-	-	-	-	-
Preston v Cardiff	3-0	0-1	-	-	-	-
Reading v Charlton	-	-	-	-	1-0	0-1
Sheffield Weds v Hull	-	-	-	0-1	-	-

League One						
Bury v Rochdale	1-0	-	2-4	-	0-0	-
Coventry v Blackpool	1-1	-	2-2	-	-	-
Crewe v Gillingham	-	1-1	1-2	-	0-3	3-1
Doncaster v Bradford	-	-	-	-	-	0-3
Fleetwood Town v Burton	-	-	-	0-4	2-3	-
Millwall v Swindon	3-2	-	-	-	-	-
Oldham v Sheffield United	-	-	0-2	0-2	1-1	2-2
Port Vale v Peterborough	-	-	-	-	0-1	2-1
Scunthorpe v Shrewsbury	-	-	-	0-0	-	-
Southend v Barnsley	-	-	-	-	-	-
Walsall v Chesterfield	-	-	3-2	-	-	1-0
Wigan v Colchester	-	-	-	-	-	-

League Two						
AFC Wimbledon v Morecambe	-	-	1-1	2-0	0-3	1-0
Barnet v York	-	-	-	1-3	-	-
Cambridge U v Northampton	-	-	-	-	-	2-1
Carlisle v Exeter	0-1	2-2	4-1	-	-	1-3
Crawley Town v Luton	2-1	1-1	-	-	-	-
Dag & Red v Hartlepool	-	1-1	-	-	0-2	2-0
Leyton Orient v Oxford	-	-	-	-	-	-
Mansfield v Bristol Rovers	-	-	-	-	1-1	-
Newport County v Portsmouth	-	-	-	-	1-2	1-0
Notts County v Yeovil	-	4-0	3-1	1-2	-	1-2
Plymouth v Accrington	-	-	2-2	0-0	0-0	1-0
Stevenage v Wycombe	-	0-2	1-1	-	-	1-3

National League						
Aldershot v Bromley	-	-	-	-	-	-
Barrow v Welling	-	-	-	-	-	-
Cheltenham v Eastleigh	-	-	-	-	-	-
Chester v Halifax	-	-	-	-	2-1	0-3
Dover v Macclesfield	-	-	-	-	-	0-1
Forest Green v Tranmere	-	-	-	-	-	-
Gateshead v Altrincham	1-0	2-0	-	-	-	1-0
Guiseley v Boreham W	-	-	-	-	-	-
Kidderminster v Southport	-	3-4	2-0	2-2	1-1	0-1
Lincoln v Braintree	-	-	3-3	3-0	2-0	3-2
Torquay v Grimsby	0-2	-	-	-	-	2-3
Woking v Wrexham	-	-	-	2-0	2-1	1-1

Ladbrokes Premiership						
Dundee United v Hearts	2-0/1-0	2-0/2-1	1-0/2-2	0-3/3-1	4-1	-
Hamilton v Dundee	-	-	1-6/3-1	-	0-3/1-1	2-1
Kilmarnock v Inverness CT	-	1-2/1-1	3-6/4-3	1-2	1-2/2-0	1-2
Motherwell v Celtic	2-3	0-1/2-0	1-2/0-3	0-2/2-1/3-1	0-5/3-3	0-1
Ross County v Aberdeen	-	-	-	2-1	1-0/1-1	0-1
St Johnstone v Partick	-	-	-	-	1-1/1-1	2-0

Ladbrokes Championship						
Alloa v Raith	-	-	-	-	1-0/0-1	0-1/0-0
Falkirk v Morton	-	2-1/1-0	1-0/0-2	0-1/4-1	3-1/1-1	-
Hibernian v Dumbarton	-	-	-	-	-	0-0/3-0
Livingston v St Mirren	-	-	-	-	-	-
Rangers v Queen of Sth	-	-	-	-	-	4-2/1-1

Results cover matches from Premier League to National League and Scottish Premiership to League Two

Ladbrokes League One						
Airdrieonians v Brechin	-	1-1/2-2	2-3/4-1	-	3-1/2-1	4-0/1-1
Albion v Peterhead	-	-	-	-	1-2/0-0	-
Cowdenbeath v Stenhousemuir	2-1/1-0	-	2-0/0-0	-	-	-
Forfar v Ayr	-	4-1/3-2	-	2-1/2-1	0-1/4-2	2-0/1-3
Stranraer v Dunfermline	-	-	-	-	1-2/3-1	1-2/5-1
Ladbrokes League Two						
Annan v Queens Park	3-1/0-2	2-1/1-2	5-2/2-3	2-3/2-0	3-2/1-1	0-1/2-0
Arbroath v Montrose	-	4-0/4-1	-	-	-	3-1/2-2
Berwick v East Fife	-	-	-	-	-	2-3/0-3
Clyde v Stirling	0-1/1-2	-	-	2-1/1-2	2-1/1-0	-
East Stirling v Elgin	1-1/2-0	0-2/2-1	1-1/2-2	1-4/3-2	3-0/3-0	2-1/1-0

Tuesday October 20th, 2015

Championship						
Blackburn v Derby	-	-	-	2-0	1-1	2-3
Bolton v Birmingham	2-1	2-2	-	3-1	2-2	0-1
Brighton v Bristol City	-	-	2-0	2-0	-	-
Cardiff v Middlesbrough	1-0	0-3	2-3	1-0	-	0-1
Charlton v Preston	-	-	5-2	-	-	-
Huddersfield v MK Dons	1-0	4-1	1-1	-	-	-
Hull v Ipswich	-	1-0	2-2	2-1	-	-
Nottm Forest v Burnley	-	2-0	0-2	2-0	1-1	-
QPR v Sheffield Weds	1-1	-	-	-	2-1	-
Rotherham v Reading	-	-	-	-	-	2-1
Wolves v Brentford	-	-	-	-	0-0	2-1
League One						
Barnsley v Walsall	-	-	-	-	-	3-0
Blackpool v Millwall	-	-	1-0	2-1	1-0	1-0
Bradford v Bury	0-1	1-0	-	-	-	-
Burton v Crewe	1-2	1-1	1-0	-	-	-
Chesterfield v Southend	-	2-1	-	0-1	2-1	-
Colchester v Port Vale	-	-	-	-	1-0	1-2
Gillingham v Scunthorpe	-	-	-	-	-	0-3
Peterborough v Wigan	-	-	-	-	-	-
Rochdale v Coventry	-	-	-	-	-	1-0
Sheffield United v Fleetwood Town	-	-	-	-	-	1-2
Shrewsbury v Doncaster	-	-	-	1-2	-	-
Swindon v Oldham	4-2	0-2	-	1-1	0-1	2-2
League Two						
Accrington v AFC Wimbledon	-	-	2-1	4-0	3-2	1-0
Bristol Rovers v Notts County	-	2-1	-	-	-	-
Hartlepool v Barnet	-	-	-	-	-	-
Luton v Leyton Orient	-	-	-	-	-	-
Morecambe v Crawley Town	-	-	6-0	-	-	-
Northampton v Carlisle	-	-	-	-	-	0-2
Oxford v Plymouth	-	-	5-1	2-1	2-3	0-0
Portsmouth v Stevenage	-	-	-	0-0	-	3-2
Wycombe v Newport County	-	-	-	-	0-1	1-2
Yeovil v Mansfield	-	-	-	-	-	-
York v Dag & Red	-	-	-	3-2	3-1	0-2

Wednesday October 21st, 2015

Championship						
Fulham v Leeds	-	-	-	-	-	0-3
League Two						
Exeter v Cambridge U	-	-	-	-	-	2-2

Results cover matches from Premier League to National League and Scottish Premiership to League Two

Saturday October 24th, 2015

Premier League

	2009-10	2010-11	2011-12	2012-13	2013-14	2014-15
Arsenal v Everton	2-2	2-1	1-0	0-0	1-1	2-0
Aston Villa v Swansea	-	-	0-2	2-0	1-1	0-1
Bournemouth v Tottenham	-	-	-	-	-	-
Leicester v Crystal Palace	2-0	1-1	3-0	1-2	-	0-1
Liverpool v Southampton	-	-	-	1-0	0-1	2-1
Man United v Man City	4-3	2-1	1-6	1-2	0-3	4-2
Norwich v West Brom	-	-	0-1	4-0	0-1	-
Stoke v Watford	-	-	-	-	-	-
Sunderland v Newcastle	-	1-1	0-1	1-1	2-1	1-0
West Ham v Chelsea	1-1	1-3	-	3-1	0-3	0-1

Championship

	2009-10	2010-11	2011-12	2012-13	2013-14	2014-15
Blackburn v Burnley	3-2	-	-	1-1	1-2	-
Bolton v Leeds	-	-	-	2-2	0-1	1-1
Brighton v Preston	-	-	-	-	-	-
Cardiff v Bristol City	3-0	3-2	3-1	2-1	-	-
Charlton v Brentford	2-0	0-1	2-0	-	-	3-0
Fulham v Reading	-	-	-	2-4	-	2-1
Huddersfield v Derby	-	-	-	1-0	1-1	4-4
Hull v Birmingham	0-1	-	2-1	5-2	-	-
Nottm Forest v Ipswich	3-0	2-0	3-2	1-0	0-0	2-2
QPR v MK Dons	-	-	-	-	-	-
Rotherham v Sheffield Weds	-	-	-	-	-	2-3
Wolves v Middlesbrough	-	-	-	3-2	-	2-0

League One

	2009-10	2010-11	2011-12	2012-13	2013-14	2014-15
Barnsley v Fleetwood Town	-	-	-	-	-	1-2
Blackpool v Crewe	-	-	-	-	-	-
Bradford v Wigan	-	-	-	-	-	-
Burton v Port Vale	1-0	0-0	1-1	1-1	-	-
Chesterfield v Scunthorpe	-	-	1-4	-	1-1	4-1
Colchester v Walsall	2-1	2-0	1-0	2-0	1-1	0-2
Gillingham v Southend	3-0	0-0	1-2	1-0	-	-
Peterborough v Doncaster	1-2	-	1-2	-	-	0-0
Rochdale v Oldham	-	1-1	3-2	-	-	0-3
Sheffield United v Millwall	-	1-1	-	-	-	-
Shrewsbury v Bury	1-1	0-3	-	0-0	-	5-0
Swindon v Coventry	-	-	-	2-2	2-1	1-1

League Two

	2009-10	2010-11	2011-12	2012-13	2013-14	2014-15
Accrington v Dag & Red	0-1	-	3-0	0-2	1-2	1-2
Bristol Rovers v Newport County	-	-	-	-	3-1	-
Exeter v Notts County	-	3-1	1-1	-	-	-
Hartlepool v Crawley Town	-	-	-	0-1	-	-
Luton v Plymouth	-	-	-	-	-	0-1
Morecambe v Leyton Orient	-	-	-	-	-	-
Northampton v Stevenage	-	2-0	-	-	-	1-0
Oxford v Barnet	-	2-1	2-1	1-0	-	-
Portsmouth v Mansfield	-	-	-	-	1-1	1-1
Wycombe v Carlisle	0-0	-	1-1	-	-	3-1
Yeovil v Cambridge U	-	-	-	-	-	-
York v AFC Wimbledon	5-0	4-1	-	0-3	0-2	2-3

Ladbrokes Premiership

	2009-10	2010-11	2011-12	2012-13	2013-14	2014-15
Aberdeen v Motherwell	0-0/0-3	1-2	1-2	3-3/0-0	0-1/0-1	1-0/2-1
Celtic v Dundee United	1-1/1-0	1-1/4-1	5-1/2-1	4-0/6-2	1-1/3-1	6-1/3-0
Dundee v Kilmarnock	-	-	-	0-0/2-3	-	1-1/1-0
Hearts v Ross County	-	-	-	2-2/4-2	2-2/2-0	-

Results cover matches from Premier League to National League and Scottish Premiership to League Two

	2009-10	2010-11	2011-12	2012-13	2013-14	2014-15
Inverness CT v St Johnstone	-	1-1/2-0	0-1	1-1/0-0	1-0/2-0	2-1/2-0
Partick v Hamilton	-	-	1-1/2-0	4-0/1-0	-	1-2/5-0

Ladbrokes Championship						
Dumbarton v Falkirk	-	-	-	0-2/0-2	1-1/2-1	0-3/1-0
Morton v Alloa	-	-	-	-	0-2/0-1	-
Queen of Sth v Livingston	-	-	0-2/0-4	-	2-2/2-0	1-1/3-1
Raith v Hibernian	-	-	-	-	-	1-3/2-1
St Mirren v Rangers	0-2	1-3/0-1	2-1	-	-	-

Ladbrokes League One						
Brechin v Albion	-	-	1-4/2-1	1-0/2-0	-	-
Dunfermline v Forfar	-	-	-	-	1-1/0-0	0-0/1-3
Peterhead v Airdrieonians	-	5-1/2-4	-	-	-	1-1/0-1
Stenhousemuir v Ayr	-	3-1/2-1	-	1-1/4-0	1-1/1-1	1-1/1-1
Stranraer v Cowdenbeath	-	-	-	-	-	-

Saturday October 31st, 2015

Premier League						
Chelsea v Liverpool	2-0	0-1	1-2	1-1	2-1	1-1
Crystal Palace v Man United	-	-	-	-	0-2	1-2
Everton v Sunderland	2-0	2-0	4-0	2-1	0-1	0-2
Man City v Norwich	-	-	5-1	2-3	7-0	-
Newcastle v Stoke	-	1-2	3-0	2-1	5-1	1-1
Southampton v Bournemouth	-	2-0	-	-	-	-
Swansea v Arsenal	-	-	3-2	0-2	1-2	2-1
Tottenham v Aston Villa	0-0	2-1	2-0	2-0	3-0	0-1
Watford v West Ham	-	-	0-4	-	-	-
West Brom v Leicester	3-0	-	-	-	-	2-3

Championship						
Birmingham v Wolves	2-1	1-1	-	2-3	-	2-1
Brentford v QPR	-	-	-	-	-	-
Bristol City v Fulham	-	-	-	-	-	-
Burnley v Huddersfield	-	-	-	0-1	3-2	-
Derby v Rotherham	-	-	-	-	-	1-0
Ipswich v Cardiff	2-0	2-0	3-0	1-2	-	3-1
Leeds v Blackburn	-	-	-	3-3	1-2	0-3
Middlesbrough v Charlton	-	-	-	2-2	1-0	3-1
MK Dons v Hull	-	-	-	-	-	-
Preston v Bolton	-	-	-	-	-	-
Reading v Brighton	-	-	3-0	-	0-0	2-1
Sheffield Weds v Nottm Forest	1-1	-	-	0-1	0-1	0-1

League One						
Bury v Blackpool	-	-	-	-	-	-
Coventry v Peterborough	3-2	-	2-2	-	4-2	3-2
Crewe v Sheffield United	-	-	-	1-0	3-0	0-1
Doncaster v Colchester	-	-	-	1-0	-	2-0
Fleetwood Town v Chesterfield	-	-	-	1-3	1-1	0-0
Millwall v Bradford	-	-	-	-	-	-
Oldham v Burton	-	-	-	-	-	-
Port Vale v Shrewsbury	1-1	1-0	2-3	-	3-1	-
Scunthorpe v Barnsley	2-1	0-0	-	-	-	0-1
Southend v Rochdale	-	-	-	3-1	1-1	-
Walsall v Gillingham	0-0	-	-	-	1-1	1-1
Wigan v Swindon	-	-	-	-	-	-

League Two						
AFC Wimbledon v Hartlepool	-	-	-	-	2-1	1-2
Barnet v Exeter	-	-	-	1-2	-	-

Results cover matches from Premier League to National League and Scottish Premiership to League Two

	2009-10	2010-11	2011-12	2012-13	2013-14	2014-15
Cambridge U v Bristol Rovers	-	-	-	-	-	-
Carlisle v Yeovil	1-0	0-2	3-2	3-3	-	-
Crawley Town v York	3-1	1-1	-	-	-	-
Dag & Red v Luton	-	-	-	-	-	0-0
Leyton Orient v Accrington	-	-	-	-	-	-
Mansfield v Wycombe	-	-	-	-	2-2	0-0
Newport County v Northampton	-	-	-	-	1-2	3-2
Notts County v Portsmouth	-	-	-	3-0	-	-
Plymouth v Morecambe	-	-	1-1	2-1	5-0	1-1
Stevenage v Oxford	1-0	0-0	-	-	-	0-2

National League

	2009-10	2010-11	2011-12	2012-13	2013-14	2014-15
Altrincham v Torquay	-	-	-	-	-	2-1
Boreham W v Gateshead	-	-	-	-	-	-
Braintree v Macclesfield	-	-	-	0-3	0-1	0-1
Eastleigh v Halifax	-	-	-	-	-	4-1
Forest Green v Chester	-	-	-	-	3-0	2-1
Grimsby v Cheltenham	0-0	-	-	-	-	-
Guiseley v Welling	-	-	-	-	-	-
Kidderminster v Woking	-	-	-	2-2	2-0	1-1
Lincoln v Bromley	-	-	-	-	-	-
Southport v Aldershot	-	-	-	-	1-0	1-3
Tranmere v Dover	-	-	-	-	-	-
Wrexham v Barrow	0-0	1-1	2-0	3-0	-	-

Ladbrokes Premiership

	2009-10	2010-11	2011-12	2012-13	2013-14	2014-15
Celtic v Aberdeen	3-0	9-0/1-0	2-1	1-0/4-3	3-1/5-2	2-1/4-0
Dundee United v Ross County	-	-	-	0-0/1-1	1-0	2-1/1-2
Hamilton v St Johnstone	0-2/1-0	1-2/0-0	-	-	-	1-0/1-1
Inverness CT v Dundee	1-1/1-0	-	-	4-1	-	0-0/1-1
Kilmarnock v Motherwell	0-3	0-1/3-1	0-0/2-0	1-2/2-0	0-2	2-0/1-2
Partick v Hearts	-	-	-	-	1-1/2-4	-

Ladbrokes Championship

	2009-10	2010-11	2011-12	2012-13	2013-14	2014-15
Alloa v Queen of Sth	-	-	-	1-0/1-2	0-3/0-1	1-1/2-2
Dumbarton v Morton	-	-	-	1-5/0-3	3-1/2-0	-
Falkirk v St Mirren	1-3/2-1/1-1	-	-	-	-	-
Hibernian v Rangers	1-4/0-1	0-3/0-2	0-2	-	-	4-0/0-2
Livingston v Raith	-	-	1-1/4-0	2-1/2-3	3-0/2-0	0-1/0-2

Ladbrokes League One

	2009-10	2010-11	2011-12	2012-13	2013-14	2014-15
Airdrieonians v Albion	-	-	4-0/1-0	-	-	-
Ayr v Stranraer	-	-	-	2-1/2-1	3-6/5-0	0-2/0-2
Cowdenbeath v Dunfermline	-	0-4/0-1	-	0-4/4-2	-	-
Forfar v Brechin	-	1-1/2-1	0-0/4-1	1-0/1-4	2-0/1-1	3-1/0-2
Stenhousemuir v Peterhead	2-0/1-1	3-1/4-2	-	-	-	1-2/2-1

Ladbrokes League Two

	2009-10	2010-11	2011-12	2012-13	2013-14	2014-15
East Fife v Annan	-	-	-	-	-	1-1/2-1
Elgin v Arbroath	-	3-5/3-2	-	-	-	1-1/2-1
Montrose v Berwick	1-3/1-1	1-1/1-1	3-5/1-1	3-1/1-3	1-1/0-0	2-1/0-2
Queens Park v Clyde	-	0-1/4-0	3-0/3-0	1-0/4-1	1-1/1-3	1-2/1-1
Stirling v East Stirling	-	-	-	1-1/9-1	1-3/2-1	-

Tuesday November 3rd, 2015

Championship

	2009-10	2010-11	2011-12	2012-13	2013-14	2014-15
Birmingham v Blackburn	2-1	2-1	-	1-1	2-4	2-2
Brentford v Hull	-	-	-	-	-	-
Bristol City v Wolves	-	-	-	1-4	1-2	-
Burnley v Fulham	1-1	-	-	-	-	-
Derby v QPR	2-4	2-2	-	-	1-0	-
Ipswich v Bolton	-	-	-	1-0	1-0	1-0

Results cover matches from Premier League to National League and Scottish Premiership to League Two

	2009-10	2010-11	2011-12	2012-13	2013-14	2014-15
Leeds v Cardiff	-	0-4	1-1	0-1	-	1-2
Middlesbrough v Rotherham	-	-	-	-	-	2-0
MK Dons v Charlton	0-1	2-0	1-1	-	-	-
Preston v Nottm Forest	3-2	1-2	-	-	-	-
Reading v Huddersfield	-	-	-	-	1-1	1-2
Sheffield Weds v Brighton	-	1-0	-	3-1	1-0	0-0

Saturday November 7th, 2015

Premier League

	2009-10	2010-11	2011-12	2012-13	2013-14	2014-15
Arsenal v Tottenham	3-0	2-3	5-2	5-2	1-0	1-1
Aston Villa v Man City	1-1	1-0	0-1	0-1	3-2	0-2
Bournemouth v Newcastle	-	-	-	-	-	-
Leicester v Watford	4-1	4-2	2-0	1-2	2-2	-
Liverpool v Crystal Palace	-	-	-	-	3-1	1-3
Man United v West Brom	-	2-2	2-0	2-0	1-2	0-1
Norwich v Swansea	-	2-0	3-1	2-2	1-1	-
Stoke v Chelsea	1-2	1-1	0-0	0-4	3-2	0-2
Sunderland v Southampton	-	-	-	1-1	2-2	2-1
West Ham v Everton	1-2	1-1	-	1-2	2-3	1-2

Championship

	2009-10	2010-11	2011-12	2012-13	2013-14	2014-15
Blackburn v Brentford	-	-	-	-	-	2-3
Bolton v Bristol City	-	-	-	3-2	-	-
Brighton v MK Dons	0-1	2-0	-	-	-	-
Cardiff v Reading	0-0	2-2	3-1	-	-	2-1
Charlton v Sheffield Weds	-	1-0	1-1	1-2	1-1	1-1
Fulham v Birmingham	2-1	1-1	-	-	-	1-1
Huddersfield v Leeds	2-2	-	-	2-4	3-2	1-2
Hull v Middlesbrough	-	2-4	2-1	1-0	-	-
Nottm Forest v Derby	3-2	5-2	1-2	0-1	1-0	1-1
QPR v Preston	4-0	3-1	-	-	-	-
Rotherham v Ipswich	-	-	-	-	-	2-0
Wolves v Burnley	2-0	-	-	1-2	-	-

Ladbrokes Premiership

	2009-10	2010-11	2011-12	2012-13	2013-14	2014-15
Aberdeen v Dundee United	0-2/2-2	1-1	3-1/3-1	2-2	1-0/1-1	0-3/1-0
Dundee v Partick	2-0/1-0	2-1/3-2	0-1/0-3	-	-	1-1/1-0
Hearts v Hamilton	2-1/2-0	2-0	-	-	-	-
Motherwell v Inverness CT	-	0-0	3-0/0-1	4-1/3-0	2-0/2-1	0-2/2-1
Ross County v Celtic	-	-	-	1-1/3-2/1-1	1-4	0-5/0-1
St Johnstone v Kilmarnock	0-1	0-3/0-0	2-0	2-1/2-0	3-1	1-2/0-0

Ladbrokes Championship

	2009-10	2010-11	2011-12	2012-13	2013-14	2014-15
Morton v Livingston	-	-	2-1/1-3	2-2/2-1	1-5/2-0	-
Queen of Sth v Dumbarton	-	-	-	-	1-2/3-1	3-0/2-1
Raith v Falkirk	-	2-1/1-2	1-0/2-2	2-1/0-0	1-1/2-4	0-0/2-2
Rangers v Alloa	-	-	-	-	-	1-1/2-2
St Mirren v Hibernian	1-1	1-0/0-1	2-3/1-0	1-2/0-1	0-0/2-0	-

Ladbrokes League One

	2009-10	2010-11	2011-12	2012-13	2013-14	2014-15
Albion v Cowdenbeath	-	-	3-3/1-0	-	-	-
Brechin v Ayr	-	0-3/1-0	-	2-1/2-1	1-1/2-1	2-4/2-1
Dunfermline v Peterhead	-	-	-	-	-	3-0/1-1
Forfar v Airdrieonians	-	1-2/1-2	3-2/2-3	-	3-3/1-1	1-1/2-0
Stranraer v Stenhousemuir	-	-	-	1-1/1-1	1-0/1-1	0-2/3-2

Ladbrokes League Two

	2009-10	2010-11	2011-12	2012-13	2013-14	2014-15
Arbroath v East Fife	0-1/2-2	-	3-0/2-2	2-0/1-0	2-2/2-1	0-2/1-1
Berwick v Stirling	-	-	-	4-1/1-0	1-1/4-0	-
Clyde v Montrose	-	2-0/1-1	1-0/1-2	1-2/1-0	0-3/1-1	1-2/2-0
East Stirling v Queens Park	1-0/0-3	0-1/3-2	1-3/1-2	0-2/0-2	1-1/1-4	1-3/3-1
Elgin v Annan	1-1/1-0	2-0/2-3	3-0/1-2	2-2/3-1	2-3/2-3	0-0/4-5

Results cover matches from Premier League to National League and Scottish Premiership to League Two

Tuesday November 10th, 2015

National League

	2009-10	2010-11	2011-12	2012-13	2013-14	2014-15
Aldershot v Lincoln	3-1	2-2	-	-	2-3	1-0
Barrow v Grimsby	-	0-2	2-2	2-2	-	-
Bromley v Boreham W	-	-	-	-	2-1	2-1
Cheltenham v Guiseley	-	-	-	-	-	-
Chester v Kidderminster	-	-	-	-	0-0	1-0
Dover v Eastleigh	-	-	-	-	1-2	2-1
Gateshead v Southport	-	1-0	2-3	2-2	2-2	1-1
Macclesfield v Altrincham	-	-	-	-	-	2-1
Torquay v Wrexham	-	-	-	-	-	2-1
Welling v Forest Green	-	-	-	-	5-2	1-1
Woking v Braintree	-	-	-	1-4	1-0	1-0

Saturday November 14th, 2015

League One

	2009-10	2010-11	2011-12	2012-13	2013-14	2014-15
Barnsley v Port Vale	-	-	-	-	-	2-1
Blackpool v Doncaster	2-0	-	2-1	-	1-1	-
Bradford v Crewe	2-3	1-5	3-0	-	3-3	2-0
Burton v Millwall	-	-	-	-	-	-
Chesterfield v Oldham	-	-	1-1	-	-	1-1
Colchester v Coventry	-	-	-	1-3	2-1	0-1
Gillingham v Bury	-	1-1	-	-	-	-
Peterborough v Fleetwood Town	-	-	-	-	-	1-0
Rochdale v Wigan	-	-	-	-	-	-
Sheffield United v Southend	-	-	-	-	-	-
Shrewsbury v Walsall	-	-	-	1-0	0-1	-
Swindon v Scunthorpe	-	-	-	1-1	-	3-1

League Two

	2009-10	2010-11	2011-12	2012-13	2013-14	2014-15
Accrington v Newport County	-	-	-	-	3-3	0-2
Bristol Rovers v Carlisle	3-2	1-1	-	-	-	-
Exeter v Crawley Town	-	-	-	-	-	-
Hartlepool v Leyton Orient	1-0	0-1	2-1	2-1	-	-
Luton v Barnet	-	-	-	-	2-1	-
Morecambe v Dag & Red	1-0	-	1-2	2-1	2-2	2-3
Northampton v Mansfield	-	-	-	-	1-1	1-0
Oxford v Cambridge U	0-0	-	-	-	-	2-0
Portsmouth v AFC Wimbledon	-	-	-	-	1-0	0-2
Wycombe v Notts County	-	-	3-4	-	-	-
Yeovil v Stevenage	-	-	0-6	1-3	-	-
York v Plymouth	-	-	-	2-0	1-1	0-0

National League

	2009-10	2010-11	2011-12	2012-13	2013-14	2014-15
Barrow v Torquay	-	-	-	-	-	-
Boreham W v Chester	-	-	-	-	-	-
Bromley v Altrincham	-	-	-	-	-	-
Forest Green v Dover	-	-	-	-	-	0-0
Grimsby v Welling	-	-	-	-	1-1	2-0
Guiseley v Eastleigh	-	-	-	-	-	-
Halifax v Braintree	-	-	-	-	0-0	1-0
Kidderminster v Aldershot	-	-	-	-	0-0	0-2
Lincoln v Tranmere	-	-	-	-	-	-
Southport v Cheltenham	-	-	-	-	-	-
Woking v Macclesfield	-	-	-	5-4	3-2	0-0
Wrexham v Gateshead	0-0	2-7	2-1	1-1	3-2	0-3

Ladbrokes Championship

	2009-10	2010-11	2011-12	2012-13	2013-14	2014-15
Falkirk v Alloa	-	-	-	-	0-0/3-1	2-1/1-0
Hibernian v Livingston	-	-	-	-	-	2-1/2-1
Morton v Queen of Sth	1-2/3-3	2-0/0-4	2-2/2-2	-	0-2/1-1	-

Results cover matches from Premier League to National League and Scottish Premiership to League Two

	2009-10	2010-11	2011-12	2012-13	2013-14	2014-15
Raith v St Mirren	-	-	-	-	-	-
Rangers v Dumbarton	-	-	-	-	-	4-1/3-1

Ladbrokes League One						
Airdrieonians v Dunfermline	1-1/0-1	-	-	1-2/3-3	0-3/2-0	3-1/3-2
Ayr v Albion	-	-	-	2-1/5-2	-	-
Cowdenbeath v Brechin	0-0/4-0	-	3-1/1-0	-	-	-
Peterhead v Stranraer	-	-	1-3/1-1	-	-	1-4/1-2
Stenhousemuir v Forfar	-	3-0/0-1	2-3/1-2	0-4/2-0	1-1/4-1	0-2/1-3

Ladbrokes League Two						
Annan v Berwick	1-1/0-1	1-1/2-3	2-2/1-1	3-2/2-2	3-2/4-0	2-0/4-2
Clyde v Elgin	-	1-1/3-3	1-2/0-2	2-2/1-1	2-1/4-0	2-1/0-2
East Fife v East Stirling	-	-	-	-	-	3-1/2-1
Montrose v Queens Park	1-2/1-2	1-2/0-2	0-1/3-1	1-1/1-2	1-2/1-0	1-2/2-2
Stirling v Arbroath	2-2/2-2	-	0-1/1-1	-	-	-

Saturday November 21st, 2015

Premier League						
Chelsea v Norwich	-	-	3-1	4-1	0-0	-
Crystal Palace v Sunderland	-	-	-	-	3-1	1-3
Everton v Aston Villa	1-1	2-2	2-2	3-3	2-1	3-0
Man City v Liverpool	0-0	3-0	3-0	2-2	2-1	3-1
Newcastle v Leicester	1-0	-	-	-	-	1-0
Southampton v Stoke	-	-	-	1-1	2-2	1-0
Swansea v Bournemouth	-	-	-	-	-	-
Tottenham v West Ham	2-0	0-0	-	3-1	0-3	2-2
Watford v Man United	-	-	-	-	-	-
West Brom v Arsenal	-	2-2	2-3	1-2	1-1	0-1

Championship						
Birmingham v Charlton	-	-	-	1-1	0-1	1-0
Brentford v Nottm Forest	-	-	-	-	-	2-2
Bristol City v Hull	-	3-0	1-1	1-2	-	-
Burnley v Brighton	-	-	1-0	1-3	0-0	-
Derby v Cardiff	2-0	1-2	0-3	1-1	-	2-2
Ipswich v Wolves	-	-	-	0-2	-	2-1
Leeds v Rotherham	-	-	-	-	-	0-0
Middlesbrough v QPR	2-0	0-3	-	-	1-3	-
MK Dons v Fulham	-	-	-	-	-	-
Preston v Blackburn	-	-	-	-	-	-
Reading v Bolton	-	-	-	-	7-1	0-0
Sheffield Weds v Huddersfield	-	0-2	4-4	1-3	1-2	1-1

League One						
Bury v Burton	3-0	1-0	-	-	0-0	3-1
Coventry v Gillingham	-	-	-	-	2-1	1-0
Crewe v Peterborough	-	-	-	-	2-2	1-0
Doncaster v Rochdale	-	-	-	-	-	1-1
Fleetwood Town v Swindon	-	-	-	-	-	2-2
Millwall v Colchester	2-1	-	-	-	-	-
Oldham v Barnsley	-	-	-	-	-	1-3
Port Vale v Chesterfield	1-2	1-1	-	0-2	-	1-2
Scunthorpe v Bradford	-	-	-	-	-	1-1
Southend v Blackpool	-	-	-	-	-	-
Walsall v Sheffield United	-	-	3-2	1-1	2-1	1-1
Wigan v Shrewsbury	-	-	-	-	-	-

League Two						
AFC Wimbledon v Wycombe	-	-	-	2-2	1-0	0-0
Barnet v Morecambe	2-0	1-2	0-2	4-1	-	-

Results cover matches from Premier League to National League and Scottish Premiership to League Two

	2009-10	2010-11	2011-12	2012-13	2013-14	2014-15
Cambridge U v Accrington	-	-	-	-	-	2-2
Carlisle v Portsmouth	-	-	-	4-2	-	2-2
Crawley Town v Bristol Rovers	-	-	4-1	-	-	-
Dag & Red v Oxford	-	-	0-1	0-1	1-0	0-0
Leyton Orient v York	-	-	-	-	-	-
Mansfield v Hartlepool	-	-	-	-	1-4	1-1
Newport County v Yeovil	-	-	-	-	-	-
Notts County v Northampton	5-2	-	-	-	-	-
Plymouth v Exeter	-	2-0	-	1-0	1-2	3-0
Stevenage v Luton	0-1	-	-	-	-	1-2

National League

	2009-10	2010-11	2011-12	2012-13	2013-14	2014-15
Aldershot v Wrexham	-	-	-	-	2-0	1-1
Altrincham v Boreham W	-	-	-	-	-	-
Braintree v Kidderminster	-	-	1-4	1-1	0-1	2-0
Cheltenham v Forest Green	-	-	-	-	-	-
Chester v Woking	-	-	-	-	0-2	2-3
Dover v Barrow	-	-	-	-	-	-
Eastleigh v Grimsby	-	-	-	-	-	0-1
Gateshead v Halifax	-	-	-	-	1-1	2-2
Macclesfield v Bromley	-	-	-	-	-	-
Torquay v Lincoln	2-3	2-0	-	-	-	1-0
Tranmere v Guiseley	-	-	-	-	-	-
Welling v Southport	-	-	-	-	4-3	0-1

Ladbrokes Premiership

	2009-10	2010-11	2011-12	2012-13	2013-14	2014-15
Celtic v Kilmarnock	3-0/3-1	1-1	2-1	0-2/4-1	4-0	2-0/4-1
Dundee United v St Johnstone	3-3	1-0/2-0	0-0	1-1/0-1	4-0/0-1	2-0/0-2
Hamilton v Aberdeen	0-3/1-1	0-1/1-1	-	-	-	3-0/0-3
Hearts v Dundee	-	-	-	0-1/1-0	-	-
Partick v Inverness CT	2-1/0-1	-	-	-	0-0	3-1/1-0
Ross County v Motherwell	-	-	-	0-0/3-0	1-2	1-2/3-2

Ladbrokes Championship

	2009-10	2010-11	2011-12	2012-13	2013-14	2014-15
Alloa v Hibernian	-	-	-	-	-	2-1/0-1
Dumbarton v Raith	-	-	-	4-2/1-2	2-4/3-3	2-1/2-2
Livingston v Rangers	-	-	-	-	-	0-1/1-1
Queen of Sth v Falkirk	-	1-5/0-1	1-5/0-0	-	2-0/1-2	3-0/1-0
St Mirren v Morton	-	-	-	-	-	-

Ladbrokes League One

	2009-10	2010-11	2011-12	2012-13	2013-14	2014-15
Albion v Dunfermline	-	-	-	-	-	-
Ayr v Airdrieonians	1-1/1-4	1-0/3-1	-	-	2-2/3-0	2-3/0-1
Brechin v Stenhousemuir	1-0/2-2	0-0/3-1	2-0/1-0	7-2/1-2	0-1/1-3	1-0/2-1
Peterhead v Cowdenbeath	0-2/1-0	-	-	-	-	-
Stranraer v Forfar	1-0/2-0	-	-	4-1/0-3	0-4/3-1	1-1/4-2

Ladbrokes League Two

	2009-10	2010-11	2011-12	2012-13	2013-14	2014-15
Annan v Arbroath	-	1-2/3-0	-	-	-	0-1/2-0
Berwick v Clyde	-	2-1/1-1	0-2/3-0	2-1/3-3	0-1/3-0	4-0/0-0
East Stirling v Montrose	1-0/2-3	2-1/1-2	1-0/3-1	2-2/1-2	2-2/1-2	4-0/0-1
Elgin v East Fife	-	-	-	-	-	1-0/3-5
Queens Park v Stirling	-	-	-	2-1/2-2	0-2/0-1	-

Tuesday November 24th, 2015

League One

	2009-10	2010-11	2011-12	2012-13	2013-14	2014-15
Bradford v Coventry	-	-	-	-	3-3	3-2
Bury v Scunthorpe	-	-	0-0	2-1	2-2	-
Colchester v Crewe	-	-	-	1-2	1-2	2-3
Doncaster v Chesterfield	-	-	-	-	-	3-2
Fleetwood Town v Millwall	-	-	-	-	-	-

Results cover matches from Premier League to National League and Scottish Premiership to League Two

	2009-10	2010-11	2011-12	2012-13	2013-14	2014-15
Gillingham v Rochdale	-	-	-	1-2	-	1-0
Oldham v Southend	2-2	-	-	-	-	-
Peterborough v Barnsley	1-2	-	3-4	2-1	-	2-1
Port Vale v Blackpool	-	-	-	-	-	-
Sheffield United v Shrewsbury	-	-	-	1-0	2-0	-
Swindon v Walsall	1-1	0-0	-	2-2	1-3	3-3
Wigan v Burton	-	-	-	-	-	-

League Two						
Accrington v Hartlepool	-	-	-	-	0-0	3-1
AFC Wimbledon v Dag & Red	-	-	2-1	2-2	1-1	1-0
Bristol Rovers v Stevenage	-	-	-	-	-	-
Crawley Town v Northampton	-	-	3-1	-	-	-
Luton v Carlisle	-	-	-	-	-	1-0
Mansfield v Exeter	-	-	-	-	0-0	2-3
Morecambe v Cambridge U	-	-	-	-	-	0-2
Notts County v Barnet	2-0	-	-	-	-	-
Oxford v Newport County	-	-	-	-	0-0	1-0
Plymouth v Leyton Orient	-	1-4	-	-	-	-
Portsmouth v York	-	-	-	-	0-1	1-1
Yeovil v Wycombe	4-0	-	1-0	-	-	-

National League						
Boreham W v Lincoln	-	-	-	-	-	-
Chester v Dover	-	-	-	-	-	3-1
Guiseley v Barrow	-	-	-	-	2-1	2-3
Woking v Tranmere	-	-	-	-	-	-

Saturday November 28th, 2015

Premier League						
Aston Villa v Watford	-	-	-	-	-	-
Bournemouth v Everton	-	-	-	-	-	-
Crystal Palace v Newcastle	0-2	-	-	-	0-3	1-1
Leicester v Man United	-	-	-	-	-	5-3
Liverpool v Swansea	-	-	0-0	5-0	4-3	4-1
Man City v Southampton	-	-	-	3-2	4-1	2-0
Norwich v Arsenal	-	-	1-2	1-0	0-2	-
Sunderland v Stoke	0-0	2-0	4-0	1-1	1-0	3-1
Tottenham v Chelsea	2-1	1-1	1-1	2-4	1-1	5-3
West Ham v West Brom	-	2-2	-	3-1	3-3	1-1

Championship						
Blackburn v Sheffield Weds	-	-	-	1-0	0-0	1-2
Bolton v Brentford	-	-	-	-	-	3-1
Brighton v Birmingham	-	-	1-1	0-1	1-0	4-3
Cardiff v Burnley	-	1-1	0-0	4-0	-	-
Charlton v Ipswich	-	-	-	1-2	0-1	0-1
Fulham v Preston	-	-	-	-	-	-
Huddersfield v Middlesbrough	-	-	-	2-1	2-2	1-2
Hull v Derby	-	2-0	0-1	2-1	-	-
Nottm Forest v Reading	2-1	3-4	1-0	-	2-3	4-0
QPR v Leeds	-	1-2	-	-	1-1	-
Rotherham v Bristol City	-	-	-	-	2-1	-
Wolves v MK Dons	-	-	-	-	0-2	-

League One						
Barnsley v Sheffield United	2-2	1-0	-	-	-	0-2
Blackpool v Fleetwood Town	-	-	-	-	-	-
Burton v Colchester	-	-	-	-	-	-
Chesterfield v Swindon	-	-	-	-	-	0-3
Coventry v Doncaster	1-0	2-1	0-2	1-0	-	1-3

Results cover matches from Premier League to National League and Scottish Premiership to League Two

	2009-10	2010-11	2011-12	2012-13	2013-14	2014-15
Crewe v Oldham	-	-	-	0-2	1-1	0-1
Millwall v Bury	-	-	-	-	-	-
Rochdale v Port Vale	0-0	-	-	2-2	-	1-0
Scunthorpe v Peterborough	4-0	-	-	-	-	2-0
Shrewsbury v Gillingham	-	0-0	2-0	-	2-0	-
Southend v Wigan	-	-	-	-	-	-
Walsall v Bradford	-	-	-	-	0-2	0-0

League Two

	2009-10	2010-11	2011-12	2012-13	2013-14	2014-15
Barnet v Mansfield	-	-	-	-	-	-
Cambridge U v Notts County	-	-	-	-	-	-
Carlisle v Crawley Town	-	-	-	0-2	1-1	-
Dag & Red v Plymouth	-	0-1	2-3	0-0	1-2	2-0
Exeter v Bristol Rovers	1-0	2-2	-	1-2	2-1	-
Hartlepool v Oxford	-	-	-	-	1-3	1-1
Leyton Orient v AFC Wimbledon	-	-	-	-	-	-
Newport County v Luton	-	1-1	0-1	5-2	-	1-0
Northampton v Yeovil	-	-	-	-	-	-
Stevenage v Morecambe	-	2-0	-	-	-	1-1
Wycombe v Portsmouth	-	-	-	-	0-1	0-0
York v Accrington	-	-	-	1-1	1-1	1-0

National League

	2009-10	2010-11	2011-12	2012-13	2013-14	2014-15
Aldershot v Cheltenham	4-1	0-2	1-0	0-1	-	-
Barrow v Woking	-	-	-	2-0	-	-
Boreham W v Tranmere	-	-	-	-	-	-
Braintree v Torquay	-	-	-	-	-	2-0
Eastleigh v Southport	-	-	-	-	-	2-1
Forest Green v Altrincham	4-3	1-0	-	-	-	1-1
Gateshead v Chester	-	-	-	-	3-2	2-1
Grimsby v Kidderminster	-	3-3	1-2	1-3	3-1	0-2
Guiseley v Bromley	-	-	-	-	-	-
Halifax v Dover	-	-	-	-	-	3-2
Lincoln v Welling	-	-	-	-	1-2	0-2
Wrexham v Macclesfield	-	-	-	0-0	1-0	2-2

Ladbrokes Premiership

	2009-10	2010-11	2011-12	2012-13	2013-14	2014-15
Aberdeen v Ross County	-	-	-	0-0/0-1	1-0	3-0/4-0
Dundee United v Hamilton	1-1/0-2	2-1	-	-	-	2-2/1-0
Inverness CT v Celtic	-	0-1/3-2	0-2	2-4/1-3	0-1	1-0/1-1
Kilmarnock v Partick	-	-	-	-	2-1/1-2	3-0/2-2
Motherwell v Hearts	1-0/3-1	1-2	1-0/3-0	0-0	2-1/4-1	-
St Johnstone v Dundee	-	-	-	1-0	-	0-1/1-0

Saturday December 5th, 2015

Premier League

	2009-10	2010-11	2011-12	2012-13	2013-14	2014-15
Arsenal v Sunderland	2-0	0-0	2-1	0-0	4-1	0-0
Chelsea v Bournemouth	-	-	-	-	-	-
Everton v Crystal Palace	-	-	-	-	2-3	2-3
Man United v West Ham	3-0	3-0	-	1-0	3-1	2-1
Newcastle v Liverpool	-	3-1	2-0	0-6	2-2	1-0
Southampton v Aston Villa	-	-	-	4-1	2-3	6-1
Stoke v Man City	1-1	1-1	1-1	1-1	0-0	1-4
Swansea v Leicester	1-0	2-0	-	-	-	2-0
Watford v Norwich	-	2-2	-	-	-	0-3
West Brom v Tottenham	-	1-1	1-3	0-1	3-3	0-3

Championship

	2009-10	2010-11	2011-12	2012-13	2013-14	2014-15
Birmingham v Huddersfield	-	-	-	0-1	1-2	1-1
Bolton v Cardiff	-	-	-	2-1	-	3-0
Brentford v MK Dons	3-3	0-2	3-3	3-2	3-1	-

Results cover matches from Premier League to National League and Scottish Premiership to League Two

	2009-10	2010-11	2011-12	2012-13	2013-14	2014-15
Brighton v Charlton	0-2	1-1	-	0-0	3-0	2-2
Bristol City v Blackburn	-	-	-	3-5	-	-
Burnley v Preston	-	4-3	-	-	-	-
Ipswich v Middlesbrough	1-1	3-3	1-1	4-0	3-1	2-0
Leeds v Hull	-	2-2	4-1	2-3	-	-
Nottm Forest v Fulham	-	-	-	-	-	5-3
Reading v QPR	1-0	0-1	-	0-0	1-1	-
Rotherham v Wolves	-	-	-	-	3-3	1-0
Sheffield Weds v Derby	0-0	-	-	2-2	0-1	0-0
National League						
Altrincham v Wrexham	1-3	0-0	-	-	-	1-4
Barrow v Boreham W	-	-	-	-	-	-
Bromley v Grimsby	-	-	-	-	-	-
Cheltenham v Chester	-	-	-	-	-	-
Dover v Aldershot	-	-	-	-	-	3-0
Halifax v Guiseley	-	-	-	-	-	-
Kidderminster v Gateshead	3-2	2-1	2-3	1-1	3-1	2-1
Macclesfield v Eastleigh	-	-	-	-	-	2-0
Southport v Forest Green	-	4-0	1-3	1-2	2-0	0-1
Torquay v Welling	-	-	-	-	-	3-0
Tranmere v Braintree	-	-	-	-	-	-
Woking v Lincoln	-	-	-	1-1	0-0	3-1
Ladbrokes Premiership						
Celtic v Hamilton	2-0	3-1/2-0	-	-	-	0-1/4-0
Dundee v Aberdeen	-	-	-	1-3/1-1	-	2-3/1-1/1-1
Hearts v Inverness CT	-	1-1	2-1	2-2/2-3	0-2	-
Kilmarnock v Dundee United	0-2/4-4	1-2/1-1	1-1	3-1/2-3	1-4	2-0/3-2
Partick v Motherwell	-	-	-	-	1-5	3-1/2-0
Ross County v St Johnstone	-	-	-	1-2/1-0	1-0	1-2/1-0
Ladbrokes Championship						
Alloa v Dumbarton	1-3/1-2	0-0/2-3	-	-	1-2/1-5	0-1/3-0
Falkirk v Livingston	-	-	4-3/2-5	1-2/2-0	4-1/1-1	0-0/2-0
Morton v Hibernian	-	-	-	-	-	-
Raith v Rangers	-	-	-	-	-	0-4/1-2
St Mirren v Queen of Sth	-	-	-	-	-	-
Ladbrokes League One						
Airdrieonians v Stenhousemuir	-	1-0/2-2	5-2/0-3	-	0-1/1-1	2-0/2-1
Albion v Stranraer	3-1/0-0	1-2/1-0	-	2-1/2-3	-	-
Cowdenbeath v Ayr	-	-	-	-	-	-
Dunfermline v Brechin	-	-	-	-	3-1/2-1	0-0/0-1
Forfar v Peterhead	-	1-1/2-1	-	-	-	1-0/3-1
Ladbrokes League Two						
Arbroath v Berwick	-	3-2/2-1	-	-	-	2-0/5-0
East Fife v Queens Park	-	-	-	-	-	2-2/0-0
East Stirling v Clyde	-	0-0/2-0	1-1/0-1	3-0/3-0	0-1/2-4	1-0/1-2
Montrose v Annan	0-0/1-2	1-1/0-1	2-3/1-1	0-0/5-1	0-2/2-1	2-0/2-1
Stirling v Elgin	-	-	-	1-4/1-1	1-1/2-2	-

Saturday December 12th, 2015

Premier League						
Aston Villa v Arsenal	0-0	2-4	1-2	0-0	1-2	0-3
Bournemouth v Man United	-	-	-	-	-	-
Crystal Palace v Southampton	-	-	0-2	-	0-1	1-3
Leicester v Chelsea	-	-	-	-	-	1-3
Liverpool v West Brom	-	1-0	0-1	0-2	4-1	2-1
Man City v Swansea	-	-	4-0	1-0	3-0	2-1

Results cover matches from Premier League to National League and Scottish Premiership to League Two

	2009-10	2010-11	2011-12	2012-13	2013-14	2014-15
Norwich v Everton	-	-	2-2	2-1	2-2	-
Sunderland v Watford	-	-	-	-	-	-
Tottenham v Newcastle	-	2-0	5-0	2-1	0-1	1-2
West Ham v Stoke	0-1	3-0	-	1-1	0-1	1-1

Championship

	2009-10	2010-11	2011-12	2012-13	2013-14	2014-15
Blackburn v Rotherham	-	-	-	-	-	2-1
Cardiff v Sheffield Weds	3-2	-	-	1-0	-	2-1
Charlton v Leeds	1-0	-	-	2-1	2-4	2-1
Derby v Brighton	-	-	0-1	0-0	1-0	3-0
Fulham v Brentford	-	-	-	-	-	1-4
Huddersfield v Bristol City	-	-	-	1-0	-	-
Hull v Bolton	1-0	-	-	3-1	-	-
Middlesbrough v Birmingham	-	-	3-1	0-1	3-1	2-0
MK Dons v Ipswich	-	-	-	-	-	-
Preston v Reading	1-2	1-1	-	-	-	-
QPR v Burnley	-	1-1	-	-	3-3	2-0
Wolves v Nottm Forest	-	-	-	1-2	-	0-3

League One

	2009-10	2010-11	2011-12	2012-13	2013-14	2014-15
Bradford v Southend	-	0-2	2-0	2-2	-	-
Bury v Chesterfield	2-1	1-1	1-1	-	0-2	-
Colchester v Barnsley	-	-	-	-	-	3-1
Doncaster v Crewe	-	-	-	0-2	-	2-1
Fleetwood Town v Walsall	-	-	-	-	-	0-1
Gillingham v Burton	-	1-0	3-1	4-1	-	-
Oldham v Millwall	0-1	-	-	-	-	-
Peterborough v Shrewsbury	-	-	-	-	1-0	-
Port Vale v Scunthorpe	-	-	-	-	-	2-2
Sheffield United v Coventry	1-0	0-1	-	1-2	2-1	2-2
Swindon v Rochdale	-	1-1	-	-	-	2-3
Wigan v Blackpool	-	0-4	-	-	0-2	1-0

League Two

	2009-10	2010-11	2011-12	2012-13	2013-14	2014-15
Accrington v Wycombe	-	1-1	-	0-2	1-1	1-1
AFC Wimbledon v Stevenage	0-3	-	-	-	-	2-3
Bristol Rovers v York	-	-	-	0-0	3-2	-
Crawley Town v Dag & Red	-	-	3-1	-	-	-
Luton v Northampton	-	-	-	-	-	1-0
Mansfield v Leyton Orient	-	-	-	-	-	-
Morecambe v Exeter	-	-	-	0-3	2-0	0-2
Notts County v Newport County	-	-	-	-	-	-
Oxford v Carlisle	-	-	-	-	-	2-1
Plymouth v Cambridge U	-	-	-	-	-	2-0
Portsmouth v Hartlepool	-	-	-	1-3	1-0	1-0
Yeovil v Barnet	-	-	-	-	-	-

Ladbrokes Premiership

	2009-10	2010-11	2011-12	2012-13	2013-14	2014-15
Aberdeen v Hearts	1-1/0-1	0-1/0-0	0-0	0-0/2-0/1-1	1-3	-
Dundee United v Partick	-	-	-	-	4-1	1-0/0-2
Hamilton v Ross County	-	-	5-1/0-2	-	-	4-0/2-2
Inverness CT v Kilmarnock	-	1-3	2-1/1-1	1-1/1-1	2-1	2-0/3-3
Motherwell v Dundee	-	-	-	1-1	-	1-3/0-1
St Johnstone v Celtic	1-4	0-3/0-1	0-2	2-1/1-1	0-1/3-3	0-3/1-2/0-0

Ladbrokes Championship

	2009-10	2010-11	2011-12	2012-13	2013-14	2014-15
Dumbarton v St Mirren	-	-	-	-	-	-
Hibernian v Falkirk	2-0	-	-	-	-	0-1/3-3
Livingston v Alloa	-	3-3/4-0	-	-	3-2/2-0	4-0/0-0
Queen of Sth v Raith	1-1/3-0	1-3/0-2	1-3/1-0	-	0-1/1-0	2-0/2-1
Rangers v Morton	-	-	-	-	-	-

Results cover matches from Premier League to National League and Scottish Premiership to League Two

	2009-10	2010-11	2011-12	2012-13	2013-14	2014-15
Ladbrokes League One						
Ayr v Dunfermline	1-0/1-2	-	-	-	2-4/1-1	0-1/0-2
Brechin v Peterhead	3-0/1-2	4-2/3-1	-	-	-	1-1/2-2
Forfar v Cowdenbeath	-	-	2-2/1-0	-	-	-
Stenhousemuir v Albion	-	-	3-0/1-2	1-0/0-1	-	-
Stranraer v Airdrieonians	-	-	-	-	3-1/1-1	1-0/1-0
Ladbrokes League Two						
Annan v East Stirling	0-1/1-0	3-1/2-1	3-0/2-2	5-2/1-2	1-2/2-3	4-3/3-2
Berwick v Elgin	2-0/2-1	6-2/4-0	1-1/3-3	0-0/2-1	2-3/2-3	1-1/0-2
Clyde v East Fife	1-3/2-1	-	-	-	-	3-1/1-0
Montrose v Stirling	-	-	-	3-2/2-2	1-2/0-0	-
Queens Park v Arbroath	-	5-2/1-1	-	-	-	0-2/2-1

Tuesday December 15th, 2015

Championship						
Blackburn v Nottm Forest	-	-	-	3-0	0-1	3-3
Cardiff v Brentford	-	-	-	-	-	2-3
Charlton v Bolton	-	-	-	3-2	0-0	2-1
Derby v Bristol City	1-0	0-2	2-1	3-0	-	-
Fulham v Ipswich	-	-	-	-	-	1-2
Huddersfield v Rotherham	-	-	-	-	-	0-2
Hull v Reading	-	1-1	1-0	-	-	-
Middlesbrough v Burnley	-	2-1	0-2	3-2	1-0	-
MK Dons v Sheffield Weds	-	1-4	1-1	-	-	-
Preston v Birmingham	-	-	-	-	-	-
QPR v Brighton	-	-	-	-	0-0	-
Wolves v Leeds	-	-	-	2-2	-	4-3

Friday December 18th, 2015

League One						
Southend v Bury	-	1-1	-	-	0-0	1-1

Saturday December 19th, 2015

Premier League						
Arsenal v Man City	0-0	0-0	1-0	0-2	1-1	2-2
Chelsea v Sunderland	7-2	0-3	1-0	2-1	1-2	3-1
Everton v Leicester	-	-	-	-	-	2-2
Man United v Norwich	-	-	2-0	4-0	4-0	-
Newcastle v Aston Villa	-	6-0	2-1	1-1	1-0	1-0
Southampton v Tottenham	-	-	-	1-2	2-3	2-2
Stoke v Crystal Palace	-	-	-	-	2-1	1-2
Swansea v West Ham	-	-	-	3-0	0-0	1-1
Watford v Liverpool	-	-	-	-	-	-
West Brom v Bournemouth	-	-	-	-	-	-

Championship						
Birmingham v Cardiff	-	-	1-1	0-1	-	0-0
Bolton v Fulham	0-0	0-0	0-3	-	-	3-1
Brentford v Huddersfield	3-0	0-1	0-4	-	-	4-1
Brighton v Middlesbrough	-	-	1-1	0-1	0-2	1-2
Bristol City v QPR	1-0	1-1	-	-	-	-
Burnley v Charlton	-	-	-	0-1	3-0	-
Ipswich v Derby	1-0	0-2	1-0	1-2	2-1	0-1
Leeds v Preston	-	4-6	-	-	-	-
Nottm Forest v MK Dons	-	-	-	-	-	-
Reading v Blackburn	-	-	-	-	0-1	0-0
Rotherham v Hull	-	-	-	-	-	-
Sheffield Weds v Wolves	-	-	-	0-0	-	0-1

Results cover matches from Premier League to National League and Scottish Premiership to League Two

	2009-10	2010-11	2011-12	2012-13	2013-14	2014-15
League One						
Barnsley v Wigan	-	-	-	-	0-4	-
Blackpool v Peterborough	2-0	-	2-1	0-1	-	-
Burton v Doncaster	-	-	-	-	-	-
Chesterfield v Bradford	1-1	2-2	-	2-2	-	0-1
Coventry v Oldham	-	-	-	2-1	1-1	1-1
Crewe v Fleetwood Town	-	-	-	-	-	2-0
Millwall v Gillingham	4-0	-	-	-	-	-
Rochdale v Colchester	-	1-2	2-2	-	-	2-1
Scunthorpe v Sheffield United	3-1	3-2	1-1	1-1	-	1-1
Shrewsbury v Swindon	-	-	2-1	0-1	2-0	-
Walsall v Port Vale	-	-	-	-	0-2	0-1
League Two						
Barnet v Crawley Town	-	-	1-2	-	-	-
Cambridge U v Mansfield	3-2	1-5	1-2	4-1	-	3-1
Carlisle v Notts County	-	1-0	0-3	0-4	2-1	-
Dag & Red v Bristol Rovers	-	0-3	4-0	2-4	2-0	-
Exeter v Luton	-	-	-	-	-	1-1
Hartlepool v Plymouth	-	2-0	-	-	1-0	3-2
Leyton Orient v Yeovil	2-0	1-5	2-2	4-1	-	3-0
Newport County v AFC Wimbledon	-	3-3	-	-	1-2	4-1
Northampton v Portsmouth	-	-	-	-	0-1	1-0
Stevenage v Accrington	-	2-2	-	-	-	2-1
Wycombe v Oxford	-	0-0	-	1-3	0-1	2-3
York v Morecambe	-	-	-	1-4	1-0	2-1
National League						
Aldershot v Guiseley	-	-	-	-	-	-
Braintree v Wrexham	-	-	0-0	1-5	3-0	1-0
Cheltenham v Altrincham	-	-	-	-	-	-
Chester v Torquay	-	-	-	-	-	0-2
Eastleigh v Kidderminster	-	-	-	-	-	2-1
Forest Green v Boreham W	-	-	-	-	-	-
Gateshead v Woking	-	-	-	2-1	0-2	0-0
Grimsby v Dover	-	-	-	-	-	1-1
Halifax v Tranmere	-	-	-	-	-	-
Lincoln v Barrow	-	-	2-1	0-0	-	-
Southport v Bromley	-	-	-	-	-	-
Welling v Macclesfield	-	-	-	-	1-0	0-0
Ladbrokes Premiership						
Celtic v Motherwell	0-0/2-1/4-0	1-0/4-0	4-0/1-0	1-0	2-0/3-0	1-1/4-0
Dundee v Hamilton	-	-	0-1/2-2	-	0-0/1-0	2-0/1-1
Inverness CT v Dundee United	-	0-2	2-3	4-0/0-0/1-2	1-1/1-1	1-0/2-1/3-0
Kilmarnock v Aberdeen	1-1/2-0	2-0	2-0/1-1	1-3/1-1	0-1	0-2/1-2
Partick v Ross County	0-0/2-1	1-1/1-1	0-1/0-1	-	3-3/2-3	4-0/1-3
St Johnstone v Hearts	2-2/1-0	0-2	2-0/2-1	2-2	1-0/3-3	-
Ladbrokes Championship						
Alloa v St Mirren	-	-	-	-	-	-
Falkirk v Rangers	1-3	-	-	-	-	0-2/1-1
Hibernian v Queen of Sth	-	-	-	-	-	0-0/0-1
Livingston v Dumbarton	-	2-0/1-1	-	5-0/2-3	1-3/1-2	1-2/1-2
Morton v Raith	5-0/1-1	0-1/0-0	1-1/1-3	1-0/1-0	1-1/0-0	-
Ladbrokes League One						
Albion v Forfar	1-1/0-1	-	1-0/2-2	2-3/1-2	-	-
Brechin v Stranraer	-	-	-	3-0/2-2	1-1/1-3	1-2/1-3
Cowdenbeath v Airdrieonians	-	-	2-0/0-0	1-1/3-2	-	-
Dunfermline v Stenhousemuir	-	-	-	-	3-2/0-0	2-0/3-2
Peterhead v Ayr	-	2-4/1-2	-	-	-	2-0/2-0

Results cover matches from Premier League to National League and Scottish Premiership to League Two

Ladbrokes League Two

	2009-10	2010-11	2011-12	2012-13	2013-14	2014-15
Clyde v Arbroath	1-0/0-2	1-1/0-3	-	-	-	2-5/1-1
East Fife v Montrose	-	-	-	-	-	3-0/3-0
East Stirling v Berwick	1-0/3-2	0-0/1-0	1-3/2-1	0-1/0-3	1-0/1-1	0-2/0-4
Elgin v Queens Park	0-1/0-1	4-2/0-1	2-0/1-1	0-4/3-5	3-2/1-1	1-4/1-2
Stirling v Annan	-	-	-	5-1/2-1	0-2/1-1	-

Saturday December 26th, 2015

Premier League

	2009-10	2010-11	2011-12	2012-13	2013-14	2014-15
Aston Villa v West Ham	0-0	3-0	-	2-1	0-2	1-0
Bournemouth v Crystal Palace	-	-	-	-	-	-
Chelsea v Watford	-	-	-	-	-	-
Liverpool v Leicester	-	-	-	-	-	2-2
Man City v Sunderland	4-3	5-0	3-3	3-0	2-2	3-2
Newcastle v Everton	-	1-2	2-1	1-2	0-3	3-2
Southampton v Arsenal	-	-	-	1-1	2-2	2-0
Stoke v Man United	0-2	1-2	1-1	0-2	2-1	1-1
Swansea v West Brom	0-2	-	3-0	3-1	1-2	3-0
Tottenham v Norwich	-	-	1-2	1-1	2-0	-

Championship

	2009-10	2010-11	2011-12	2012-13	2013-14	2014-15
Blackburn v Middlesbrough	-	-	-	1-2	1-0	0-0
Brentford v Brighton	0-0	0-1	-	-	-	3-2
Bristol City v Charlton	-	-	-	0-2	-	-
Derby v Fulham	-	-	-	-	-	5-1
Huddersfield v Preston	-	-	3-1	-	-	-
Hull v Burnley	1-4	0-1	2-3	0-1	-	0-1
Ipswich v QPR	3-0	0-3	-	-	1-3	-
MK Dons v Cardiff	-	-	-	-	-	-
Nottm Forest v Leeds	-	1-1	0-4	4-2	2-1	1-1
Rotherham v Bolton	-	-	-	-	-	4-2
Sheffield Weds v Birmingham	-	-	-	3-2	4-1	0-0
Wolves v Reading	-	-	-	-	-	1-2

League One

	2009-10	2010-11	2011-12	2012-13	2013-14	2014-15
Blackpool v Oldham	-	-	-	-	-	-
Bradford v Burton	1-1	1-1	1-1	1-0	-	-
Bury v Barnsley	-	-	-	-	-	-
Colchester v Southend	2-0	-	-	-	-	-
Coventry v Port Vale	-	-	-	-	2-2	2-3
Doncaster v Scunthorpe	4-3	3-0	-	4-0	-	5-2
Millwall v Walsall	2-1	-	-	-	-	-
Peterborough v Chesterfield	-	-	-	-	-	1-0
Rochdale v Crewe	2-0	-	-	-	-	4-0
Shrewsbury v Fleetwood Town	-	-	-	-	-	-
Swindon v Gillingham	3-1	-	2-0	-	2-2	0-3
Wigan v Sheffield United	-	-	-	-	-	-

League Two

	2009-10	2010-11	2011-12	2012-13	2013-14	2014-15
Accrington v Carlisle	-	-	-	-	-	3-1
AFC Wimbledon v Bristol Rovers	-	-	2-3	3-1	0-0	-
Barnet v Newport County	-	-	-	-	-	-
Crawley Town v Stevenage	0-3	-	-	1-1	1-1	-
Dag & Red v Cambridge U	-	-	-	-	-	2-3
Hartlepool v Notts County	-	1-1	3-0	2-1	-	-
Leyton Orient v Portsmouth	-	-	-	1-0	-	-
Luton v Wycombe	-	-	-	-	-	2-3
Morecambe v Mansfield	-	-	-	-	0-1	2-1
Oxford v Exeter	-	-	-	2-4	0-0	2-2
Plymouth v Yeovil	-	0-0	-	-	-	-
York v Northampton	-	-	-	1-1	1-0	1-1

Results cover matches from Premier League to National League and Scottish Premiership to League Two

	2009-10	2010-11	2011-12	2012-13	2013-14	2014-15
National League						
Aldershot v Woking	-	-	-	-	2-1	0-1
Altrincham v Chester	-	-	-	-	-	4-1
Barrow v Gateshead	3-3	1-3	1-2	0-2	-	-
Boreham W v Braintree	-	-	-	-	-	-
Bromley v Eastleigh	-	-	-	-	1-2	-
Guiseley v Grimsby	-	-	-	-	-	-
Kidderminster v Cheltenham	-	-	-	-	-	-
Lincoln v Halifax	-	-	-	-	3-1	1-1
Macclesfield v Tranmere	-	-	-	-	-	-
Torquay v Forest Green	-	-	-	-	-	3-3
Welling v Dover	-	-	-	-	-	0-2
Wrexham v Southport	-	2-1	2-0	2-2	1-0	0-0
Ladbrokes Premiership						
Aberdeen v Inverness CT	-	1-2/1-0	2-1/0-1	2-3	1-0/0-1	3-2/1-0
Dundee United v Motherwell	0-1/3-0	2-0/4-0	1-3/1-1	1-2/1-3	2-2/3-1/5-1	1-0/3-1
Hamilton v Kilmarnock	0-0/3-0	2-2/1-1				0-0/0-0
Hearts v Celtic	2-1/1-2	2-0/0-3	2-0/0-4	0-4	1-3/0-2	-
Partick v St Johnstone	-	-	-	-	0-1	0-0/3-0
Ross County v Dundee	0-1/1-1	0-3/0-1	1-1/3-0	1-1	-	2-1/1-0
Ladbrokes Championship						
Falkirk v Dumbarton	-	-	-	3-4/1-3	1-2/2-0	1-1/3-3
Queen of Sth v Morton	2-3/1-2	2-0/1-4	4-1/2-1	-	2-0/3-0	-
Raith v Alloa	-	-	-	-	4-2/1-1	1-1/2-1
Rangers v Hibernian	1-1/3-0	0-3	1-0/4-0	-	-	1-3/0-2
St Mirren v Livingston	-	-	-	-	-	-
Ladbrokes League One						
Airdrieonians v Peterhead	-	2-2/1-0	-	-	-	0-2/1-3
Ayr v Brechin	-	0-2/2-0	-	3-0/1-2	2-2/1-3	0-2/2-2
Cowdenbeath v Albion	-	-	2-1/3-0	-	-	-
Forfar v Dunfermline	-	-	-	-	4-0/2-4	2-0/1-0
Stenhousemuir v Stranraer	-	-	-	0-0/1-2	1-0/1-1	2-2/1-0
Ladbrokes League Two						
Annan v Clyde	-	0-2/1-0	1-0/1-0	1-3/0-1	1-2/0-1	2-1/0-1
Arbroath v East Stirling	-	2-0/3-5	-	-	-	4-0/0-1
Elgin v Montrose	0-1/5-2	3-2/1-0	3-1/2-1	3-1/2-0	3-3/2-3	0-1/4-0
Queens Park v Berwick	2-0/2-3	0-2/1-0	1-1/2-2	1-1/2-1	0-4/1-3	2-0/2-1
Stirling v East Fife	3-0/3-3	-	1-0/0-1	-	-	-

Monday December 28th, 2015

	2009-10	2010-11	2011-12	2012-13	2013-14	2014-15
Premier League						
Arsenal v Bournemouth	-	-	-	-	-	-
Crystal Palace v Swansea	0-1	0-3	-	-	0-2	1-0
Everton v Stoke	1-1	1-0	0-1	1-0	4-0	0-1
Leicester v Man City	-	-	-	-	-	0-1
Man United v Chelsea	1-2	2-1	3-1	0-1	0-0	1-1
Norwich v Aston Villa	-	-	2-0	1-2	0-1	-
Sunderland v Liverpool	1-0	0-2	1-0	1-1	1-3	0-1
Watford v Tottenham	-	-	-	-	-	-
West Brom v Newcastle	1-1	3-1	1-3	1-1	1-0	0-2
West Ham v Southampton	-	-	1-1	4-1	3-1	1-3
Championship						
Birmingham v MK Dons	-	-	-	-	-	-
Bolton v Blackburn	0-2	2-1	2-1	1-0	4-0	2-1
Burnley v Bristol City	-	0-0	1-1	3-1	-	-
Cardiff v Nottm Forest	1-1	0-2	1-0	3-0	-	2-1

Results cover matches from Premier League to National League and Scottish Premiership to League Two

	2009-10	2010-11	2011-12	2012-13	2013-14	2014-15
Charlton v Wolves	-	-	-	2-1	-	1-1
Leeds v Derby	-	1-2	0-2	1-2	1-1	2-0
Middlesbrough v Sheffield Weds	1-0	-	-	3-1	1-1	2-3
Preston v Hull	-	0-2	-	-	-	-
QPR v Huddersfield	-	-	-	-	2-1	-
Reading v Brentford	-	-	-	-	-	0-2

League One						
Barnsley v Blackpool	1-0	-	1-3	1-1	2-0	-
Burton v Swindon	-	-	2-0	-	-	-
Chesterfield v Coventry	-	-	-	-	-	2-3
Crewe v Shrewsbury	0-3	1-2	1-1	1-1	1-1	-
Fleetwood Town v Wigan	-	-	-	-	-	-
Gillingham v Colchester	0-0	-	-	-	0-1	2-2
Oldham v Doncaster	-	-	-	1-2	-	2-2
Port Vale v Bury	0-1	0-0	-	-	-	-
Scunthorpe v Rochdale	-	-	1-0	-	3-0	2-1
Sheffield United v Bradford	-	-	-	-	2-2	1-1
Southend v Millwall	0-0	-	-	-	-	-
Walsall v Peterborough	-	1-3	-	-	2-0	0-0

League Two						
Bristol Rovers v Leyton Orient	1-2	0-3	-	-	-	-
Cambridge U v Barnet	-	-	-	-	1-1	-
Carlisle v Hartlepool	3-2	1-0	1-2	3-0	-	3-3
Exeter v AFC Wimbledon	-	-	-	2-0	2-0	3-2
Mansfield v York	0-1	5-0	1-1	-	0-1	1-4
Newport County v Plymouth	-	-	-	-	1-2	2-0
Northampton v Accrington	4-0	0-0	0-0	2-0	1-0	4-5
Notts County v Morecambe	4-1	-	-	-	-	-
Portsmouth v Luton	-	-	-	-	-	2-0
Stevenage v Dag & Red	-	-	-	-	-	0-1
Wycombe v Crawley Town	-	-	-	-	-	-
Yeovil v Oxford	-	-	-	-	-	-

National League						
Braintree v Welling	-	-	-	-	2-3	0-1
Cheltenham v Torquay	1-1	2-2	0-1	2-1	1-0	-
Chester v Macclesfield	-	-	-	-	2-1	1-0
Dover v Bromley	-	-	-	-	0-2	-
Eastleigh v Aldershot	-	-	-	-	-	1-0
Forest Green v Kidderminster	1-1	1-1	1-1	0-1	1-1	2-3
Gateshead v Guiseley	-	-	-	-	-	-
Grimsby v Lincoln	2-2	-	3-1	1-1	1-1	1-3
Halifax v Wrexham	-	-	-	-	3-2	2-2
Southport v Barrow	-	2-4	2-1	5-2	-	-
Tranmere v Altrincham	-	-	-	-	-	-
Woking v Boreham W	-	-	-	-	-	-

Tuesday December 29th, 2015

Championship						
Brighton v Ipswich	-	-	3-0	1-1	0-2	3-2
Fulham v Rotherham	-	-	-	-	-	1-1

Wednesday December 30th, 2015

Ladbrokes Premiership						
Aberdeen v Partick	-	-	-	-	4-0	2-0/0-0
Dundee v Celtic	-	-	-	0-2	-	1-1/1-2
Hamilton v Inverness CT	-	1-3/1-2	-	-	-	0-2/0-2
Hearts v Dundee United	0-0/0-0	1-1/2-1	0-1/0-2	2-1	0-0/1-2	-

Results cover matches from Premier League to National League and Scottish Premiership to League Two

	2009-10	2010-11	2011-12	2012-13	2013-14	2014-15
Motherwell v St Johnstone	1-3	4-0	0-3/3-2/5-1	1-1/3-2	4-0/2-1	0-1/1-1
Ross County v Kilmarnock	-	-	-	0-0/0-1	1-2/2-1	1-2/2-1

Saturday January 2nd, 2016

Premier League

	2009-10	2010-11	2011-12	2012-13	2013-14	2014-15
Arsenal v Newcastle	-	0-1	2-1	7-3	3-0	4-1
Crystal Palace v Chelsea	-	-	-	-	1-0	1-2
Everton v Tottenham	2-2	2-1	1-0	2-1	0-0	0-1
Leicester v Bournemouth	-	-	-	-	2-1	-
Man United v Swansea	-	-	2-0	2-1	2-0	1-2
Norwich v Southampton	0-2	-	-	0-0	1-0	-
Sunderland v Aston Villa	0-2	1-0	2-2	0-1	0-1	0-4
Watford v Man City	-	-	-	-	-	-
West Brom v Stoke	-	0-3	0-1	0-1	1-2	1-0
West Ham v Liverpool	2-3	3-1	-	2-3	1-2	3-1

Championship

	2009-10	2010-11	2011-12	2012-13	2013-14	2014-15
Birmingham v Brentford	-	-	-	-	-	1-0
Bolton v Huddersfield	-	-	-	1-0	0-1	1-0
Brighton v Wolves	-	-	-	2-0	-	1-1
Burnley v Ipswich	-	1-2	4-0	2-0	1-0	-
Cardiff v Blackburn	-	-	-	3-0	-	1-1
Charlton v Nottm Forest	-	-	-	0-2	1-1	2-1
Fulham v Sheffield Weds	-	-	-	-	-	4-0
Leeds v MK Dons	4-1	-	-	-	-	-
Middlesbrough v Derby	2-0	2-1	2-0	2-2	1-0	2-0
Preston v Rotherham	-	-	-	-	3-3	-
QPR v Hull	-	1-1	-	-	-	0-1
Reading v Bristol City	2-0	4-1	1-0	-	-	-

League One

	2009-10	2010-11	2011-12	2012-13	2013-14	2014-15
Barnsley v Millwall	-	1-0	1-3	2-0	1-0	-
Burton v Blackpool	-	-	-	-	-	-
Chesterfield v Shrewsbury	0-1	4-3	-	-	-	-
Crewe v Coventry	-	-	-	1-0	1-2	2-1
Fleetwood Town v Bury	-	-	-	-	2-1	-
Gillingham v Bradford	-	2-0	0-0	3-1	0-1	1-0
Oldham v Colchester	2-2	0-0	1-1	1-1	0-2	0-1
Port Vale v Swindon	-	-	0-2	-	2-3	0-1
Scunthorpe v Wigan	-	-	-	-	-	-
Sheffield United v Peterborough	1-0	-	-	-	2-0	1-2
Southend v Doncaster	-	-	-	-	-	-
Walsall v Rochdale	-	0-0	0-0	-	-	3-2

League Two

	2009-10	2010-11	2011-12	2012-13	2013-14	2014-15
Bristol Rovers v Luton	-	-	-	-	-	-
Cambridge U v AFC Wimbledon	2-2	1-2	-	-	-	0-0
Carlisle v Plymouth	-	1-1	-	-	-	2-0
Exeter v Dag & Red	-	2-1	-	0-1	2-2	2-1
Mansfield v Accrington	-	-	-	-	2-3	0-1
Newport County v Hartlepool	-	-	-	-	2-0	2-2
Northampton v Barnet	1-3	0-0	1-2	2-0	-	-
Notts County v Oxford	-	-	-	-	-	-
Portsmouth v Crawley Town	-	-	-	1-2	-	-
Stevenage v Leyton Orient	-	-	0-1	0-1	0-1	-
Wycombe v Morecambe	-	2-0	-	2-2	1-0	0-1
Yeovil v York	-	-	-	-	-	-

National League

	2009-10	2010-11	2011-12	2012-13	2013-14	2014-15
Braintree v Boreham W	-	-	-	-	-	-
Cheltenham v Kidderminster	-	-	-	-	-	-

Results cover matches from Premier League to National League and Scottish Premiership to League Two

	2009-10	2010-11	2011-12	2012-13	2013-14	2014-15
Chester v Altrincham	-	-	-	-	-	0-2
Dover v Welling	-	-	-	-	-	4-0
Eastleigh v Bromley	-	-	-	-	2-1	-
Forest Green v Torquay	-	-	-	-	-	2-1
Gateshead v Barrow	2-1	3-0	2-0	0-1	-	-
Grimsby v Guiseley	-	-	-	-	-	-
Halifax v Lincoln	-	-	-	-	5-1	3-2
Southport v Wrexham	-	0-1	0-0	1-4	1-2	0-1
Tranmere v Macclesfield	-	-	-	-	-	-
Woking v Aldershot	-	-	-	-	1-2	1-2

Ladbrokes Premiership						
Celtic v Partick	-	-	-	-	1-0	1-0/2-0
Dundee v Dundee United	-	-	-	0-3	-	1-4/3-1
Inverness CT v Ross County	1-3/3-0	-	-	3-1/2-1	1-2	1-1/1-1
Kilmarnock v Hearts	1-2	1-2/2-2	0-0/1-1	1-0/0-1	2-0/4-2	-
Motherwell v Hamilton	1-0	0-1/1-0	-	-	-	0-4/4-0
St Johnstone v Aberdeen	1-0/1-1	0-1/0-0	1-2	1-2/3-1	0-2	1-0/1-1

Ladbrokes Championship						
Alloa v Falkirk	-	-	-	-	0-0/3-0	2-3/1-3
Dumbarton v Rangers	-	-	-	-	-	0-3/1-3
Hibernian v Raith	-	-	-	-	-	1-1/1-1
Livingston v Queen of Sth	-	-	2-2/2-2	-	3-3/1-2	2-2/1-0
Morton v St Mirren	-	-	-	-	-	-

Ladbrokes League One						
Albion v Airdrieonians	-	-	7-2/0-1	-	-	-
Brechin v Forfar	-	0-0/0-1	0-1/2-1	4-1/3-4	2-1/1-5	3-3/2-3
Dunfermline v Cowdenbeath	-	2-1/5-0	-	3-0/1-0	-	-
Peterhead v Stenhousemuir	2-2/0-1	2-2/0-3	-	-	-	1-0/2-0
Stranraer v Ayr	-	-	-	2-0/0-1	1-1/4-0	3-1/1-0

Ladbrokes League Two						
Berwick v Annan	2-1/0-2	2-2/2-3	0-1/1-3	3-1/0-2	4-2/1-4	2-0/2-2
Clyde v Queens Park	-	2-3/0-2	0-2/1-2	0-3/2-3	3-0/1-2	0-2/2-0
East Fife v Elgin	-	-	-	-	-	1-1/3-1
East Stirling v Stirling	-	-	-	3-1/1-1	2-2/1-0	-
Montrose v Arbroath	-	3-0/0-5	-	-	-	1-5/3-0

Saturday January 9th, 2016

League One						
Blackpool v Sheffield United	3-0	-	-	-	-	-
Bradford v Barnsley	-	-	-	-	-	1-0
Bury v Crewe	3-0	3-1	-	2-2	-	-
Colchester v Fleetwood Town	-	-	-	-	-	2-1
Coventry v Walsall	-	-	-	5-1	2-1	0-0
Doncaster v Port Vale	-	-	-	-	-	1-3
Millwall v Scunthorpe	-	3-0	-	-	-	-
Peterborough v Burton	-	-	-	-	-	-
Rochdale v Chesterfield	2-3	-	1-1	1-1	2-2	1-0
Shrewsbury v Oldham	-	-	-	1-0	1-2	-
Swindon v Southend	2-1	-	2-0	-	-	-
Wigan v Gillingham	-	-	-	-	-	-

League Two						
Accrington v Notts County	0-3	-	-	-	-	-
AFC Wimbledon v Carlisle	-	-	-	-	-	1-3
Barnet v Bristol Rovers	-	-	2-0	1-1	-	2-0
Crawley Town v Cambridge U	1-0	3-0	-	-	-	-

Results cover matches from Premier League to National League and Scottish Premiership to League Two

	2009-10	2010-11	2011-12	2012-13	2013-14	2014-15
Dag & Red v Wycombe	-	-	-	3-0	2-0	0-1
Hartlepool v Stevenage	-	-	0-0	0-2	-	1-3
Leyton Orient v Newport County	-	-	-	-	-	-
Luton v Yeovil	-	-	-	-	-	-
Morecambe v Portsmouth	-	-	-	-	2-2	3-1
Oxford v Mansfield	2-0	-	-	-	3-0	3-0
Plymouth v Northampton	-	-	4-1	3-2	1-0	2-0
York v Exeter	-	-	-	1-2	2-1	0-0

National League

	2009-10	2010-11	2011-12	2012-13	2013-14	2014-15
Aldershot v Chester	-	-	-	-	2-0	0-1
Altrincham v Gateshead	3-2	1-1	-	-	-	0-1
Barrow v Tranmere	-	-	-	-	-	-
Boreham W v Cheltenham	-	-	-	-	-	-
Bromley v Southport	-	-	-	-	-	-
Guiseley v Forest Green	-	-	-	-	-	-
Kidderminster v Eastleigh	-	-	-	-	-	1-3
Lincoln v Dover	-	-	-	-	-	1-0
Macclesfield v Halifax	-	-	-	-	2-2	1-1
Torquay v Braintree	-	-	-	-	-	1-5
Welling v Grimsby	-	-	-	-	1-0	0-2
Wrexham v Woking	-	-	-	3-1	2-0	1-2

Ladbrokes League Two

	2009-10	2010-11	2011-12	2012-13	2013-14	2014-15
Arbroath v Elgin	-	2-0/3-5	-	-	-	1-0/3-3
East Fife v Berwick	-	-	-	-	-	2-3/1-4
Montrose v East Stirling	0-3/0-1	0-2/3-0	2-1/3-1	3-1/2-2	2-0/2-0	4-1/0-1
Queens Park v Annan	0-0/3-2	3-0/0-1	0-0/2-0	2-2/2-2	2-5/0-1	0-0/2-0
Stirling v Clyde	1-1/1-0	-	-	0-1/2-0	1-1/4-1	-

Tuesday January 12th, 2016

Premier League

	2009-10	2010-11	2011-12	2012-13	2013-14	2014-15
Aston Villa v Crystal Palace	-	-	-	-	0-1	0-0
Bournemouth v West Ham	-	-	-	-	-	-
Liverpool v Arsenal	1-2	1-1	1-2	0-2	5-1	2-2
Swansea v Sunderland	-	-	0-0	2-2	4-0	1-1

Championship

	2009-10	2010-11	2011-12	2012-13	2013-14	2014-15
Blackburn v QPR	-	-	3-2	-	2-0	-
Brentford v Middlesbrough	-	-	-	-	-	0-1
Bristol City v Preston	4-2	1-1	-	-	1-1	0-1
Derby v Reading	2-1	1-2	0-1	-	1-3	0-3
Huddersfield v Charlton	1-1	3-1	1-0	0-1	2-1	1-1
Hull v Cardiff	-	0-2	2-1	2-2	1-1	-
Ipswich v Leeds	-	2-1	2-1	3-0	1-2	4-1
MK Dons v Burnley	-	-	-	-	-	-
Nottm Forest v Birmingham	-	-	1-3	2-2	1-0	1-3
Rotherham v Brighton	-	-	-	-	-	1-0
Sheffield Weds v Bolton	-	-	-	1-2	1-3	1-2
Wolves v Fulham	2-1	1-1	2-0	-	-	3-0

Wednesday January 13th, 2016

Premier League

	2009-10	2010-11	2011-12	2012-13	2013-14	2014-15
Chelsea v West Brom	-	6-0	2-1	1-0	2-2	2-0
Man City v Everton	0-2	1-2	2-0	1-1	3-1	1-0
Newcastle v Man United	-	0-0	3-0	0-3	0-4	0-1
Southampton v Watford	-	-	4-0	-	-	-
Stoke v Norwich	-	-	1-0	1-0	0-1	-
Tottenham v Leicester	-	-	-	-	-	4-3

Results cover matches from Premier League to National League and Scottish Premiership to League Two

Saturday January 16th, 2016

Premier League	2009-10	2010-11	2011-12	2012-13	2013-14	2014-15
Aston Villa v Leicester	-	-	-	-	-	2-1
Bournemouth v Norwich	-	-	-	-	-	1-2
Chelsea v Everton	3-3	1-1	3-1	2-1	1-0	1-0
Liverpool v Man United	2-0	3-1	1-1	1-2	1-0	1-2
Man City v Crystal Palace	-	-	-	-	1-0	3-0
Newcastle v West Ham	-	5-0	-	0-1	0-0	2-0
Southampton v West Brom	-	-	-	0-3	1-0	0-0
Stoke v Arsenal	1-3	3-1	1-1	0-0	1-0	3-2
Swansea v Watford	1-1	1-1	-	-	-	-
Tottenham v Sunderland	2-0	1-1	1-0	1-0	5-1	2-1

Championship	2009-10	2010-11	2011-12	2012-13	2013-14	2014-15
Blackburn v Brighton	-	-	-	1-1	3-3	0-1
Brentford v Burnley	-	-	-	-	-	-
Bristol City v Middlesbrough	2-1	0-4	0-1	2-0	-	-
Derby v Birmingham	-	-	2-1	3-2	1-1	2-2
Huddersfield v Fulham	-	-	-	-	-	0-2
Hull v Charlton	-	-	-	1-0	-	-
Ipswich v Preston	1-1	2-1	-	-	-	-
MK Dons v Reading	-	-	-	-	-	-
Nottm Forest v Bolton	-	-	-	1-1	3-0	4-1
Rotherham v QPR	-	-	-	-	-	-
Sheffield Weds v Leeds	-	-	-	1-1	6-0	1-2
Wolves v Cardiff	-	-	-	1-2	-	1-0

League One	2009-10	2010-11	2011-12	2012-13	2013-14	2014-15
Blackpool v Scunthorpe	4-1	-	-	-	-	-
Bradford v Oldham	-	-	-	-	2-3	2-0
Bury v Walsall	-	-	2-1	1-1	-	-
Colchester v Sheffield United	-	-	1-1	1-1	0-1	2-3
Coventry v Burton	-	-	-	-	-	-
Doncaster v Gillingham	-	-	-	-	-	1-2
Millwall v Port Vale	-	-	-	-	-	-
Peterborough v Southend	-	-	-	-	-	-
Rochdale v Fleetwood Town	-	-	-	0-0	1-2	0-2
Shrewsbury v Barnsley	-	-	-	-	-	-
Swindon v Crewe	-	-	3-0	4-1	5-0	2-0
Wigan v Chesterfield	-	-	-	-	-	-

League Two	2009-10	2010-11	2011-12	2012-13	2013-14	2014-15
Accrington v Portsmouth	-	-	-	-	2-2	1-1
AFC Wimbledon v Mansfield	2-0	2-1	-	-	0-0	0-1
Barnet v Carlisle	-	-	-	-	-	-
Crawley Town v Notts County	-	-	-	0-0	1-0	2-0
Dag & Red v Northampton	0-1	-	0-1	0-1	0-3	0-2
Hartlepool v Wycombe	1-1	-	1-3	-	1-2	1-3
Leyton Orient v Exeter	1-1	3-0	3-0	-	-	-
Luton v Cambridge U	2-2	2-0	0-1	3-2	0-0	3-2
Morecambe v Yeovil	-	-	-	-	-	-
Oxford v Bristol Rovers	-	-	3-0	0-2	0-1	-
Plymouth v Stevenage	-	-	-	-	-	1-1
York v Newport County	-	2-1	1-1	-	1-0	0-2

Ladbrokes Premiership	2009-10	2010-11	2011-12	2012-13	2013-14	2014-15
Dundee United v Celtic	2-1/0-2	1-2/1-3	0-1/1-0	2-2/0-4	0-1/0-2	2-1/0-3
Hearts v Motherwell	1-0/0-2	0-2/0-0/3-3	2-0/0-1	1-0/1-2	0-1	-
Kilmarnock v Inverness CT	-	1-2/1-1	3-6/4-3	1-2	1-2/2-0	1-2
Partick v Dundee	0-2/0-1	1-0/0-0	0-1/0-0	-	-	1-1

Results cover matches from Premier League to National League and Scottish Premiership to League Two

	2009-10	2010-11	2011-12	2012-13	2013-14	2014-15
Ross County v Aberdeen	-	-	-	2-1	1-0/1-1	0-1
St Johnstone v Hamilton	1-1/2-3	2-0/1-0	-	-	-	0-1

Ladbrokes Championship

	2009-10	2010-11	2011-12	2012-13	2013-14	2014-15
Alloa v Morton	-	-	-	-	2-0/2-0	-
Dumbarton v Queen of Sth	-	-	-	-	0-1/0-3	0-4/0-0
Falkirk v Hibernian	1-3/1-3	-	-	-	-	1-0/0-3
Rangers v Livingston	-	-	-	-	-	2-0/1-1
St Mirren v Raith	-	-	-	-	-	-

Ladbrokes League One

	2009-10	2010-11	2011-12	2012-13	2013-14	2014-15
Airdrieonians v Forfar	-	2-0/3-1	4-4/3-0	-	0-2/5-1	1-2/3-1
Ayr v Cowdenbeath	-	-	-	-	-	-
Dunfermline v Albion	-	-	-	-	-	-
Stenhousemuir v Brechin	1-1/1-2	0-0/1-3	1-1/2-1	3-1/3-3	3-2/4-2	0-2/2-2
Stranraer v Peterhead	-	-	2-1/0-3	-	-	5-0/2-0

Ladbrokes League Two

	2009-10	2010-11	2011-12	2012-13	2013-14	2014-15
Annan v East Fife	-	-	-	-	-	2-1/2-1
Berwick v Arbroath	-	4-1/0-4	-	-	-	1-2/3-1
Clyde v East Stirling	-	1-2/2-0	7-1/3-0	2-1/2-0	1-2/1-0	0-1/1-1
Elgin v Stirling	-	-	-	3-1/1-2	4-0/2-3	-
Queens Park v Montrose	3-2/3-0	1-0/4-1	3-1/5-0	2-2/1-2	0-1/1-1	2-0/4-1

Saturday January 23rd, 2016

Premier League

	2009-10	2010-11	2011-12	2012-13	2013-14	2014-15
Arsenal v Chelsea	0-3	3-1	0-0	1-2	0-0	0-0
Crystal Palace v Tottenham	-	-	-	-	0-1	2-1
Everton v Swansea	-	-	1-0	0-0	3-2	0-0
Leicester v Stoke	-	-	-	-	-	0-1
Man United v Southampton	-	-	-	2-1	1-1	0-1
Norwich v Liverpool	-	-	0-3	2-5	2-3	-
Sunderland v Bournemouth	-	-	-	-	-	-
Watford v Newcastle	1-2	-	-	-	-	-
West Brom v Aston Villa	-	2-1	0-0	2-2	2-2	1-0
West Ham v Man City	1-1	1-3	-	0-0	1-3	2-1

Championship

	2009-10	2010-11	2011-12	2012-13	2013-14	2014-15
Birmingham v Ipswich	-	-	2-1	0-1	1-1	2-2
Bolton v MK Dons	-	-	-	-	-	-
Brighton v Huddersfield	0-0	2-3	-	4-1	0-0	0-0
Burnley v Derby	-	2-1	0-0	2-0	2-0	-
Cardiff v Rotherham	-	-	-	-	-	0-0
Charlton v Blackburn	-	-	-	1-1	1-3	1-3
Fulham v Hull	2-0	-	-	-	2-2	-
Leeds v Bristol City	-	3-1	2-1	1-0	-	-
Middlesbrough v Nottm Forest	1-1	1-1	2-1	1-0	1-1	3-0
Preston v Brentford	-	-	1-3	1-1	0-3	-
QPR v Wolves	-	-	1-2	-	-	-
Reading v Sheffield Weds	5-0	-	-	-	0-2	2-0

League One

	2009-10	2010-11	2011-12	2012-13	2013-14	2014-15
Barnsley v Rochdale	-	-	-	-	-	5-0
Burton v Shrewsbury	1-1	0-0	1-1	-	-	1-0
Chesterfield v Millwall	-	-	-	-	-	-
Crewe v Wigan	-	-	-	-	-	-
Fleetwood Town v Doncaster	-	-	-	-	-	3-1
Gillingham v Peterborough	-	-	-	-	2-2	2-1
Oldham v Bury	-	-	0-2	1-2	-	-
Port Vale v Bradford	2-1	2-1	3-2	0-0	2-1	2-2
Scunthorpe v Colchester	-	-	1-1	1-0	-	1-1

Results cover matches from Premier League to National League and Scottish Premiership to League Two

	2009-10	2010-11	2011-12	2012-13	2013-14	2014-15
Sheffield United v Swindon	-	-	-	2-0	1-0	2-0
Southend v Coventry	-	-	-	-	-	-
Walsall v Blackpool	-	-	-	-	-	-
League Two						
Bristol Rovers v Plymouth	-	2-3	2-3	2-1	2-1	-
Cambridge U v Hartlepool	-	-	-	-	-	2-1
Carlisle v York	-	-	-	-	-	0-3
Exeter v Accrington	-	-	-	2-0	0-1	1-2
Mansfield v Luton	0-0	0-0	1-1	2-2	-	1-0
Newport County v Dag & Red	-	-	-	-	1-2	2-3
Northampton v Morecambe	2-0	3-3	0-2	3-0	0-0	2-1
Notts County v AFC Wimbledon	-	-	-	-	-	-
Portsmouth v Oxford	-	-	-	-	1-4	0-0
Stevenage v Barnet	-	4-2	-	-	-	-
Wycombe v Leyton Orient	0-1	-	4-2	-	-	-
Yeovil v Crawley Town	-	-	-	2-2	-	2-1
National League						
Boreham W v Eastleigh	-	-	-	-	0-3	-
Bromley v Tranmere	-	-	-	-	-	-
Chester v Southport	-	-	-	-	2-2	2-0
Dover v Cheltenham	-	-	-	-	-	-
Forest Green v Braintree	-	-	0-2	4-1	0-2	1-1
Grimsby v Altrincham	-	0-1	-	-	-	0-0
Kidderminster v Guiseley	-	-	-	-	-	-
Macclesfield v Aldershot	1-1	2-0	0-1	-	1-1	0-0
Torquay v Gateshead	-	-	-	-	-	2-2
Welling v Barrow	-	-	-	-	-	-
Woking v Halifax	-	-	-	-	0-0	3-2
Wrexham v Lincoln	-	-	2-0	2-4	0-1	1-1
Ladbrokes Premiership						
Aberdeen v Dundee	-	-	-	2-0/1-0	-	3-3
Celtic v St Johnstone	5-2/3-0	2-0	0-1/2-0/1-0	1-1/4-0	2-1/3-0	0-1
Dundee United v Kilmarnock	0-0	1-1/4-2	1-1/4-0	3-3	1-0/3-2	3-1
Hamilton v Hearts	2-1	0-4/0-2	-	-	-	-
Inverness CT v Partick	2-3/2-1	-	-	-	1-2/1-0	0-4
Motherwell v Ross County	-	-	-	3-2/2-0	3-1/2-1	2-2/1-1
Ladbrokes Championship						
Hibernian v St Mirren	2-1/2-1	2-0/1-1	1-2/0-0	2-1/3-3	2-0/2-3	-
Livingston v Falkirk	-	-	1-1/1-2	2-1/1-2	0-3/0-1	0-1/2-1
Morton v Rangers	-	-	-	-	-	-
Queen of Sth v Alloa	-	-	-	1-0/0-0	0-0/3-1	2-0/1-0
Raith v Dumbarton	-	-	-	2-2/3-2	2-1/1-3	3-1/2-1
Ladbrokes League One						
Albion v Ayr	-	-	-	2-0/1-3	-	-
Brechin v Airdrieonians	-	3-1/1-2	1-1/1-1	-	4-3/1-1	1-1/0-0
Cowdenbeath v Stranraer	-	-	-	-	-	-
Forfar v Stenhousemuir	-	1-1/2-0	2-3/1-2	3-2/3-3	1-2/3-0	3-0/1-0
Peterhead v Dunfermline	-	-	-	-	-	1-1/1-1
Ladbrokes League Two						
Arbroath v Annan	-	0-2/2-1	-	-	-	3-2/1-1
East Stirling v East Fife	-	-	-	-	-	1-1/2-0
Elgin v Berwick	3-3/1-5	1-2/3-2	4-1/4-0	3-1/1-2	2-0/1-3	2-1/3-3
Montrose v Clyde	-	8-1/3-1	4-0/5-0	2-3/1-1	0-2/0-2	0-3/0-1
Stirling v Queens Park	-	-	-	1-2/2-3	3-0/2-2	-

Results cover matches from Premier League to National League and Scottish Premiership to League Two

Tuesday January 26th, 2016

National League

	2009-10	2010-11	2011-12	2012-13	2013-14	2014-15
Altrincham v Woking	-	-	-	-	-	0-3

Saturday January 30th, 2016

Championship

	2009-10	2010-11	2011-12	2012-13	2013-14	2014-15
Blackburn v Fulham	2-0	1-1	3-1	-	-	2-1
Brentford v Leeds	0-0	-	-	-	-	2-0
Bristol City v Birmingham	-	-	0-2	0-1	-	-
Derby v Preston	5-3	3-0	-	-	-	-
Huddersfield v Cardiff	-	-	-	0-0	-	0-0
Hull v Brighton	-	-	0-0	1-0	-	-
Ipswich v Reading	2-1	1-3	2-3	-	2-0	0-1
MK Dons v Middlesbrough	-	-	-	-	-	-
Nottm Forest v QPR	5-0	0-0	-	-	2-0	-
Rotherham v Charlton	-	-	-	-	-	1-1
Sheffield Weds v Burnley	-	-	-	0-2	1-2	-
Wolves v Bolton	2-1	2-3	2-3	2-2	-	1-0

League One

	2009-10	2010-11	2011-12	2012-13	2013-14	2014-15
Blackpool v Gillingham	-	-	-	-	-	-
Bradford v Fleetwood Town	-	-	-	1-0	-	2-2
Bury v Sheffield United	-	-	0-3	0-2	-	-
Colchester v Chesterfield	-	-	1-2	-	-	2-1
Coventry v Scunthorpe	2-1	1-1	-	1-2	-	1-1
Doncaster v Walsall	-	-	-	1-2	-	0-2
Millwall v Crewe	-	-	-	-	-	-
Peterborough v Oldham	-	5-2	-	-	2-1	2-2
Rochdale v Burton	1-2	-	-	0-1	1-1	-
Shrewsbury v Southend	-	1-1	2-1	-	-	1-1
Swindon v Barnsley	-	-	-	-	-	2-0
Wigan v Port Vale	-	-	-	-	-	-

League Two

	2009-10	2010-11	2011-12	2012-13	2013-14	2014-15
Accrington v Bristol Rovers	-	-	2-1	1-0	2-1	-
AFC Wimbledon v Yeovil	-	-	-	-	-	-
Barnet v Portsmouth	-	-	-	-	-	-
Crawley Town v Mansfield	0-2	2-0	-	-	-	-
Dag & Red v Carlisle	-	3-0	-	-	-	4-2
Hartlepool v Exeter	1-1	2-3	2-0	-	0-2	2-1
Leyton Orient v Cambridge U	-	-	-	-	-	-
Luton v Notts County	-	-	-	-	-	-
Morecambe v Newport County	-	-	-	-	4-1	3-2
Oxford v Northampton	-	3-1	2-0	2-1	2-0	1-1
Plymouth v Wycombe	-	-	-	0-1	0-3	0-1
York v Stevenage	1-1	-	-	-	-	0-2

National League

	2009-10	2010-11	2011-12	2012-13	2013-14	2014-15
Aldershot v Kidderminster	-	-	-	-	0-0	0-1
Altrincham v Dover	-	-	-	-	-	2-2
Braintree v Chester	-	-	-	-	3-0	1-3
Cheltenham v Bromley	-	-	-	-	-	-
Eastleigh v Wrexham	-	-	-	-	-	2-2
Forest Green v Macclesfield	-	-	-	1-1	2-3	3-1
Gateshead v Grimsby	-	0-0	1-0	1-1	1-2	1-6
Halifax v Welling	-	-	-	-	3-0	3-0
Lincoln v Guiseley	-	-	-	-	-	-
Southport v Boreham W	-	-	-	-	-	-
Tranmere v Torquay	-	-	-	-	-	-
Woking v Barrow	-	-	-	3-1	-	-

Results cover matches from Premier League to National League and Scottish Premiership to League Two

FIXTURES
2015-16

	2009-10	2010-11	2011-12	2012-13	2013-14	2014-15
Ladbrokes Premiership						
Aberdeen v Celtic	1-3/4-4	0-3	0-1/1-1	0-2	0-2/2-1	1-2/0-1
Dundee v Motherwell	-	-	-	1-2/0-3	-	4-1
Kilmarnock v Hamilton	3-0/1-2	3-0	-	-	-	1-0/2-3
Partick v Dundee United	-	-	-	-	0-0/1-1	2-2
Ross County v Hearts	-	-	-	2-2	2-1/1-2	-
St Johnstone v Inverness CT	-	1-0/0-3	2-0/0-0	0-0/1-0	4-0/0-1	1-0/1-1
Ladbrokes Championship						
Dumbarton v Livingston	-	1-2/0-3	-	3-4/0-3	1-2/2-2	1-0/1-5
Hibernian v Morton	-	-	-	-	-	-
Raith v Queen of Sth	1-0/0-0	0-1/0-1	0-2/3-1	-	2-1/3-2	3-4/3-0
Rangers v Falkirk	4-1/3-0	-	-	-	-	4-0/2-2
St Mirren v Alloa	-	-	-	-	-	-
Ladbrokes League One						
Ayr v Stenhousemuir	-	2-0/4-3	-	1-1/1-2	4-3/2-3	2-3/0-0
Cowdenbeath v Forfar	-	-	3-1/2-0	-	-	-
Dunfermline v Airdrieonians	2-0/2-0	-	-	1-3/1-2	2-1/0-1	3-0/2-2
Peterhead v Albion	-	-	-	-	1-1/2-0	-
Stranraer v Brechin	-	-	-	0-2/3-2	3-0/1-2	2-2/0-2
Ladbrokes League Two						
Annan v Elgin	0-2/3-3	0-1/2-2	1-1/1-1	2-0/2-2	2-1/2-0	3-3/2-3
Berwick v Queens Park	1-0/1-1	1-1/3-1	2-0/1-4	2-0/4-1	4-0/1-0	0-0/1-1
East Fife v Clyde	1-0/1-1	-	-	-	-	0-1/1-1
East Stirling v Arbroath	-	1-3/2-5	-	-	-	2-3/1-0
Stirling v Montrose	-	-	-	1-3/3-1	3-1/2-2	-

Tuesday February 2nd, 2016

	2009-10	2010-11	2011-12	2012-13	2013-14	2014-15
Premier League						
Arsenal v Southampton	-	-	-	6-1	2-0	1-0
Crystal Palace v Bournemouth	-	-	-	-	-	-
Leicester v Liverpool	-	-	-	-	-	1-3
Man United v Stoke	4-0	2-1	2-0	4-2	3-2	2-1
Norwich v Tottenham	-	-	0-2	1-1	1-0	-
Sunderland v Man City	1-1	1-0	1-0	1-0	1-0	1-4
Watford v Chelsea	-	-	-	-	-	-
West Brom v Swansea	0-1	-	1-2	2-1	0-2	2-0
West Ham v Aston Villa	2-1	1-2	-	1-0	0-0	0-0

Wednesday February 3rd, 2016

	2009-10	2010-11	2011-12	2012-13	2013-14	2014-15
Premier League						
Everton v Newcastle	-	0-1	3-1	2-2	3-2	3-0

Saturday February 6th, 2016

	2009-10	2010-11	2011-12	2012-13	2013-14	2014-15
Premier League						
Aston Villa v Norwich	-	-	3-2	1-1	4-1	-
Bournemouth v Arsenal	-	-	-	-	-	-
Chelsea v Man United	1-0	2-1	3-3	2-3	3-1	1-0
Liverpool v Sunderland	3-0	2-2	1-1	3-0	2-1	0-0
Man City v Leicester	-	-	-	-	-	2-0
Newcastle v West Brom	2-2	3-3	2-3	2-1	2-1	1-1
Southampton v West Ham	-	-	1-0	1-1	0-0	0-0
Stoke v Everton	0-0	2-0	1-1	1-1	1-1	2-0
Swansea v Crystal Palace	0-0	3-0	-	-	1-1	1-1
Tottenham v Watford	-	-	-	-	-	-
Championship						
Birmingham v Sheffield Weds	-	-	-	0-0	4-1	0-2
Bolton v Rotherham	-	-	-	-	-	3-2
Brighton v Brentford	3-0	1-0	-	-	-	0-1

Results cover matches from Premier League to National League and Scottish Premiership to League Two

	2009-10	2010-11	2011-12	2012-13	2013-14	2014-15
Burnley v Hull	2-0	4-0	1-0	0-1	-	1-0
Cardiff v MK Dons	-	-	-	-	-	-
Charlton v Bristol City	-	-	-	4-1	-	-
Fulham v Derby	-	-	-	-	-	2-0
Leeds v Nottm Forest	-	4-1	3-7	2-1	0-2	0-0
Middlesbrough v Blackburn	-	-	-	1-0	0-0	1-1
Preston v Huddersfield	-	-	1-0	-	-	-
QPR v Ipswich	1-2	2-0	-	-	1-0	-
Reading v Wolves	-	-	-	-	-	3-3

League One

	2009-10	2010-11	2011-12	2012-13	2013-14	2014-15
Barnsley v Bury	-	-	-	-	-	-
Burton v Bradford	1-1	3-0	2-2	1-0	-	-
Chesterfield v Peterborough	-	-	-	-	-	3-2
Crewe v Rochdale	2-2	-	-	-	-	2-5
Fleetwood Town v Shrewsbury	-	-	-	-	-	-
Gillingham v Swindon	5-0	-	3-1	-	2-0	2-2
Oldham v Blackpool	-	-	-	-	-	-
Port Vale v Coventry	-	-	-	-	3-2	0-2
Scunthorpe v Doncaster	2-2	1-3	-	2-3	-	1-2
Sheffield United v Wigan	-	-	-	-	-	-
Southend v Colchester	1-2	-	-	-	-	-
Walsall v Millwall	2-2	-	-	-	-	-

League Two

	2009-10	2010-11	2011-12	2012-13	2013-14	2014-15
Bristol Rovers v AFC Wimbledon	-	-	1-0	1-0	3-0	-
Cambridge U v Dag & Red	-	-	-	-	-	1-1
Carlisle v Accrington	-	-	-	-	-	1-0
Exeter v Oxford	-	-	-	1-3	0-0	1-1
Mansfield v Morecambe	-	-	-	-	1-2	1-0
Newport County v Barnet	-	-	-	-	-	-
Northampton v York	-	-	-	0-2	0-2	3-0
Notts County v Hartlepool	-	3-0	3-0	2-0	-	-
Portsmouth v Leyton Orient	-	-	-	2-3	-	-
Stevenage v Crawley Town	2-0	-	-	1-2	2-0	-
Wycombe v Luton	-	-	-	-	-	1-1
Yeovil v Plymouth	-	1-0	-	-	-	-

National League

	2009-10	2010-11	2011-12	2012-13	2013-14	2014-15
Barrow v Cheltenham	-	-	-	-	-	-
Boreham W v Kidderminster	-	-	-	-	-	-
Braintree v Gateshead	-	-	3-1	2-1	0-0	1-0
Bromley v Halifax	-	-	-	-	-	-
Chester v Aldershot	-	-	-	-	1-1	1-0
Dover v Southport	-	-	-	-	-	2-2
Grimsby v Woking	-	-	-	5-1	2-2	3-1
Guiseley v Tranmere	-	-	-	-	-	-
Lincoln v Eastleigh	-	-	-	-	-	1-2
Macclesfield v Torquay	2-1	3-3	1-2	-	-	1-0
Welling v Altrincham	-	-	-	-	-	0-1
Wrexham v Forest Green	1-0	2-1	1-2	2-1	2-0	0-0

Ladbrokes League One

	2009-10	2010-11	2011-12	2012-13	2013-14	2014-15
Airdrieonians v Cowdenbeath	-	-	1-5/1-1	0-3/1-1	-	-
Albion v Brechin	-	-	1-2/0-1	1-2/3-1	-	-
Ayr v Peterhead	-	1-1/2-2	-	-	-	3-3/2-4
Forfar v Stranraer	1-0/2-0	-	-	4-0/3-1	1-2/1-0	1-1/1-0
Stenhousemuir v Dunfermline	-	-	-	-	4-5/1-2	1-0/0-1

Ladbrokes League Two

	2009-10	2010-11	2011-12	2012-13	2013-14	2014-15
Arbroath v Stirling	3-4/2-4	-	4-2/2-0	-	-	-
Berwick v East Stirling	0-1/2-2	3-0/1-1	4-2/0-2	3-0/2-0	2-0/1-0	5-0/3-0

Results cover matches from Premier League to National League and Scottish Premiership to League Two

	2009-10	2010-11	2011-12	2012-13	2013-14	2014-15
Clyde v Annan	-	0-2/0-2	0-0/1-1	2-1/2-3	2-1/0-3	1-1/1-0
Montrose v East Fife	-	-	-	-	-	0-4/0-3
Queens Park v Elgin	0-3/0-1	1-1/1-0	6-0/1-3	1-1/0-1	3-3/2-0	2-1/1-1

Tuesday February 9th, 2016
National League
Tranmere v Southport	-	-	-	-	-	-

Friday February 12th, 2016
League One
Burton v Chesterfield	2-2	1-0	-	0-1	0-2	-

Saturday February 13th, 2016
Premier League
Arsenal v Leicester	-	-	-	-	-	2-1
Aston Villa v Liverpool	0-1	1-0	0-2	1-2	0-1	0-2
Bournemouth v Stoke	-	-	-	-	-	-
Chelsea v Newcastle	-	2-2	0-2	2-0	3-0	2-0
Crystal Palace v Watford	3-0	3-2	4-0	2-3	-	-
Everton v West Brom	-	1-4	2-0	2-1	0-0	0-0
Man City v Tottenham	0-1	1-0	3-2	2-1	6-0	4-1
Norwich v West Ham	-	-	-	0-0	3-1	-
Sunderland v Man United	0-1	0-0	0-1	0-1	1-2	1-1
Swansea v Southampton	-	-	-	0-0	0-1	0-1

Championship
Blackburn v Hull	1-0	-	-	1-0	-	-
Brighton v Bolton	-	-	-	1-1	3-1	2-1
Bristol City v Ipswich	0-0	0-1	0-3	2-1	-	-
Charlton v Cardiff	-	-	-	5-4	-	1-1
Derby v MK Dons	-	-	-	-	-	-
Leeds v Middlesbrough	-	1-1	0-1	2-1	2-1	1-0
Nottm Forest v Huddersfield	-	-	-	6-1	1-0	0-1
QPR v Fulham	-	-	0-1	2-1	-	-
Reading v Burnley	-	2-1	1-0	-	2-2	-
Rotherham v Birmingham	-	-	-	-	-	0-1
Sheffield Weds v Brentford	-	1-3	0-0	-	-	1-0
Wolves v Preston	-	-	-	-	2-0	-

League One
Blackpool v Shrewsbury	-	-	-	-	-	-
Colchester v Swindon	3-0	2-1	-	0-1	1-2	1-1
Coventry v Bury	-	-	-	2-2	-	-
Crewe v Walsall	-	-	-	2-0	0-3	1-1
Doncaster v Sheffield United	1-1	2-0	-	2-2	-	0-1
Gillingham v Barnsley	-	-	-	-	-	0-1
Peterborough v Bradford	-	-	-	-	2-1	2-0
Port Vale v Fleetwood Town	-	-	-	0-2	-	1-2
Rochdale v Millwall	-	-	-	-	-	-
Scunthorpe v Southend	-	-	-	-	2-2	-
Wigan v Oldham	-	-	-	-	-	-

League Two
Accrington v Crawley Town	-	-	0-1	-	-	-
AFC Wimbledon v Luton	1-1	0-0	-	-	-	3-2
Dag & Red v Barnet	4-1	-	3-0	1-0	-	-
Hartlepool v Yeovil	1-1	3-1	0-1	0-0	-	-
Leyton Orient v Northampton	-	-	-	-	-	-
Morecambe v Oxford	-	0-3	0-0	1-1	1-1	1-0

Results cover matches from Premier League to National League and Scottish Premiership to League Two

	2009-10	2010-11	2011-12	2012-13	2013-14	2014-15
Newport County v Carlisle	-	-	-	-	-	2-1
Plymouth v Mansfield	-	-	-	-	1-1	2-1
Portsmouth v Bristol Rovers	-	-	-	-	3-2	-
Stevenage v Cambridge U	4-1	-	-	-	-	3-2
Wycombe v Exeter	2-2	-	3-1	0-1	1-1	2-1
York v Notts County	-	-	-	-	-	-

National League

	2009-10	2010-11	2011-12	2012-13	2013-14	2014-15
Aldershot v Tranmere	-	-	-	-	-	-
Altrincham v Lincoln	-	-	-	-	-	1-2
Cheltenham v Welling	-	-	-	-	-	-
Dover v Gateshead	-	-	-	-	-	1-0
Eastleigh v Barrow	-	-	-	-	-	-
Grimsby v Boreham W	-	-	-	-	-	-
Halifax v Forest Green	-	-	-	-	1-0	1-0
Kidderminster v Macclesfield	-	-	-	3-0	2-1	0-2
Southport v Braintree	-	-	0-4	0-2	0-4	0-2
Torquay v Chester	-	-	-	-	-	0-1
Woking v Guiseley	-	-	-	-	-	-
Wrexham v Bromley	-	-	-	-	-	-

Ladbrokes Premiership

	2009-10	2010-11	2011-12	2012-13	2013-14	2014-15
Celtic v Ross County	-	-	-	4-0	2-1/1-1	0-0
Dundee v St Johnstone	-	-	-	1-3/2-2	-	1-1/0-2
Hamilton v Dundee United	0-1	0-1/1-1	-	-	-	2-3
Hearts v Partick	-	-	-	-	0-2/2-4	-
Inverness CT v Aberdeen	-	2-0/0-2	2-1/0-2	1-1/3-0	3-4/0-0	0-1/1-2
Motherwell v Kilmarnock	3-1/1-0	0-1/1-1	0-0	2-2	2-1/1-2	1-1/3-1

Ladbrokes Championship

	2009-10	2010-11	2011-12	2012-13	2013-14	2014-15
Alloa v Rangers	-	-	-	-	-	1-1/0-1
Falkirk v Raith	-	0-0/2-1	2-0/2-3	0-2/1-1	3-1/2-1	0-1/1-0
Livingston v Hibernian	-	-	-	-	-	0-4/1-3
Morton v Dumbarton	-	-	-	3-0/0-3	2-0/3-0	-
Queen of Sth v St Mirren	-	-	-	-	-	-

Ladbrokes League One

	2009-10	2010-11	2011-12	2012-13	2013-14	2014-15
Brechin v Cowdenbeath	3-1/3-3	-	1-0/2-2	-	-	-
Dunfermline v Ayr	3-1/0-1	-	-	-	5-1/3-0	4-2/2-1
Peterhead v Forfar	-	1-2/1-1	-	-	-	3-2/1-0
Stenhousemuir v Airdrieonians	-	1-3/1-0	1-1/0-3	-	1-1/1-2	1-0/0-2
Stranraer v Albion	1-1/2-1	3-2/1-3	-	1-1/3-2	-	-

Ladbrokes League Two

	2009-10	2010-11	2011-12	2012-13	2013-14	2014-15
Annan v Montrose	2-0/0-0	2-2/2-1	2-1/1-2	2-1/1-1	2-1/1-0	2-2/4-3
East Fife v Arbroath	1-1/3-1	-	2-2/1-3	2-1/0-1	2-1/1-0	1-5/2-0
Elgin v Clyde	-	0-1/0-1	0-3/1-1	2-1/4-2	1-0/3-1	1-0/2-0
Queens Park v East Stirling	1-0/2-0	2-0/2-0	2-0/5-1	1-2/5-1	1-3/0-0	3-0/1-1
Stirling v Berwick	-	-	-	6-3/1-0	3-1/2-1	-

Tuesday February 16th, 2016

National League

	2009-10	2010-11	2011-12	2012-13	2013-14	2014-15
Gateshead v Eastleigh	-	-	-	-	-	2-3
Torquay v Halifax	-	-	-	-	-	2-1

Saturday February 20th, 2016

Championship

	2009-10	2010-11	2011-12	2012-13	2013-14	2014-15
Birmingham v Leeds	-	-	1-0	1-0	1-3	1-1
Bolton v QPR	-	-	2-1	-	0-1	-
Brentford v Derby	-	-	-	-	-	2-1

Results cover matches from Premier League to National League and Scottish Premiership to League Two

	2009-10	2010-11	2011-12	2012-13	2013-14	2014-15
Burnley v Rotherham	-	-	-	-	-	-
Cardiff v Brighton	-	-	1-3	0-2	-	0-0
Fulham v Charlton	-	-	-	-	-	3-0
Huddersfield v Wolves	-	-	-	2-1	-	1-4
Hull v Nottm Forest	-	0-0	2-1	1-2	-	-
Ipswich v Blackburn	-	-	-	1-1	3-1	1-1
Middlesbrough v Reading	1-1	3-1	0-2	-	3-0	0-1
MK Dons v Bristol City	-	-	-	-	2-2	0-0
Preston v Sheffield Weds	2-2	-	0-2	-	-	-

League One

	2009-10	2010-11	2011-12	2012-13	2013-14	2014-15
Barnsley v Doncaster	0-1	2-2	2-0	-	0-0	1-1
Bradford v Rochdale	0-3	-	-	2-4	-	1-2
Bury v Colchester	-	-	4-1	1-2	-	-
Chesterfield v Crewe	2-3	5-5	-	-	-	1-0
Fleetwood Town v Scunthorpe	-	-	-	-	0-1	2-2
Millwall v Peterborough	-	-	2-2	1-5	-	-
Oldham v Gillingham	1-0	-	-	-	1-0	0-0
Sheffield United v Port Vale	-	-	-	-	2-1	1-0
Shrewsbury v Coventry	-	-	-	4-1	1-1	-
Southend v Burton	-	1-1	0-1	0-1	1-0	0-0
Swindon v Blackpool	-	-	-	-	-	-
Walsall v Wigan	-	-	-	-	-	-

League Two

	2009-10	2010-11	2011-12	2012-13	2013-14	2014-15
Barnet v AFC Wimbledon	-	-	4-0	1-1	-	-
Bristol Rovers v Morecambe	-	-	2-1	0-3	1-0	-
Cambridge U v York	0-1	2-1	0-1	-	-	0-3
Carlisle v Stevenage	-	-	1-0	2-1	0-0	3-0
Crawley Town v Plymouth	-	-	2-0	-	-	-
Exeter v Newport County	-	-	-	-	0-2	2-0
Luton v Hartlepool	-	-	-	-	-	3-0
Mansfield v Dag & Red	-	-	-	-	3-0	2-1
Northampton v Wycombe	-	1-1	-	3-1	1-4	2-3
Notts County v Leyton Orient	-	3-2	1-2	1-1	0-0	1-1
Oxford v Accrington	-	0-0	1-1	5-0	1-2	3-1
Yeovil v Portsmouth	-	-	-	1-2	-	-

National League

	2009-10	2010-11	2011-12	2012-13	2013-14	2014-15
Altrincham v Guiseley	-	-	-	-	4-1	-
Barrow v Braintree	-	-	0-4	0-1	-	-
Boreham W v Torquay	-	-	-	-	-	-
Bromley v Woking	-	-	-	-	-	-
Forest Green v Eastleigh	-	-	-	-	-	1-1
Gateshead v Aldershot	-	-	-	-	0-0	1-1
Halifax v Grimsby	-	-	-	-	4-0	1-1
Kidderminster v Chester	-	-	-	-	3-1	2-2
Lincoln v Southport	-	-	2-0	1-0	1-0	1-0
Macclesfield v Dover	-	-	-	-	-	1-0
Tranmere v Cheltenham	-	-	-	-	-	2-3
Welling v Wrexham	-	-	-	-	1-1	2-1

Ladbrokes Premiership

	2009-10	2010-11	2011-12	2012-13	2013-14	2014-15
Celtic v Inverness CT	-	2-2	2-0/1-0	0-1/4-1	2-2/5-0/6-0	1-0/5-0
Dundee United v Hearts	2-0/1-0	2-0/2-1	1-0/2-2	0-3/3-1	4-1	-
Kilmarnock v Dundee	-	-	-	0-0/1-2	-	1-3
Partick v Aberdeen	-	-	-	-	0-3/3-1	0-1
Ross County v Hamilton	-	-	1-0/5-1	-	-	0-1/2-1
St Johnstone v Motherwell	2-2/1-2	0-2/1-0	0-3	1-3/2-0	2-0/3-0	2-1

Results cover matches from Premier League to National League and Scottish Premiership to League Two

	2009-10	2010-11	2011-12	2012-13	2013-14	2014-15
Ladbrokes Championship						
Hibernian v Alloa	-	-	-	-	-	2-0/4-1
Morton v Falkirk	-	0-0/2-2	3-2/0-0	1-2/2-0	0-2/1-1	-
Queen of Sth v Rangers	-	-	-	-	-	2-0/3-0
Raith v Livingston	-	-	0-1/0-3	0-0/0-2	1-0/2-4	1-5/0-4
St Mirren v Dumbarton	-	-	-	-	-	-
Ladbrokes League One						
Airdrieonians v Stranraer	-	-	-	-	3-2/1-1	3-3/1-1
Albion v Stenhousemuir	-	-	1-1/1-0	4-4/4-3	-	-
Ayr v Forfar	-	0-1/3-1	-	2-3/2-1	2-0/2-3	2-0/1-0
Brechin v Dunfermline	-	-	-	-	1-1/3-2	1-1/3-0
Cowdenbeath v Peterhead	5-0/1-3	-	-	-	-	-
Ladbrokes League Two						
Arbroath v Queens Park	-	1-0/2-2	-	-	-	1-2/1-1
Clyde v Berwick	-	1-4/2-0	1-4/2-2	2-1/2-1	1-0/3-3	3-3/0-3
East Fife v Stirling	1-2/0-3	-	1-0/1-0	-	-	-
East Stirling v Annan	1-3/3-1	1-5/2-0	1-0/0-4	2-2/1-2	1-1/2-1	0-1/1-3
Montrose v Elgin	1-1/0-4	0-1/1-0	3-0/2-3	2-2/4-1	3-3/0-3	2-3/2-1
Tuesday February 23rd, 2016						
Championship						
Birmingham v Bolton	1-2	2-1	-	2-1	1-2	0-1
Brentford v Wolves	-	-	-	-	0-3	4-0
Bristol City v Brighton	-	-	0-1	0-0	-	-
Burnley v Nottm Forest	-	1-0	5-1	1-1	3-1	-
Derby v Blackburn	-	-	-	1-1	1-1	2-0
Ipswich v Hull	-	1-1	0-1	1-2	-	-
Leeds v Fulham	-	-	-	-	-	0-1
Middlesbrough v Cardiff	0-1	1-0	0-2	2-1	-	2-1
MK Dons v Huddersfield	2-3	1-3	1-1	-	-	-
Preston v Charlton	-	-	2-2	-	-	-
Reading v Rotherham	-	-	-	-	-	3-0
Sheffield Weds v QPR	1-2	-	-	-	3-0	-
National League						
Braintree v Halifax	-	-	-	-	1-0	0-0
Lincoln v Forest Green	-	-	1-1	1-2	2-1	1-2
Southport v Macclesfield	-	-	-	3-2	4-1	1-1
Wrexham v Kidderminster	2-2	2-2	2-0	1-2	0-0	1-0
Saturday February 27th, 2016						
Premier League						
Leicester v Norwich	-	2-3	-	-	-	-
Liverpool v Everton	1-0	2-2	3-0	0-0	4-0	1-1
Man United v Arsenal	2-1	1-0	8-2	2-1	1-0	1-1
Newcastle v Man City	-	1-3	0-2	1-3	0-2	0-2
Southampton v Chelsea	-	-	-	2-1	0-3	1-1
Stoke v Aston Villa	0-0	2-1	0-0	1-3	2-1	0-1
Tottenham v Swansea	-	-	3-1	1-0	1-0	3-2
Watford v Bournemouth	-	-	-	-	6-1	1-1
West Brom v Crystal Palace	0-1	-	-	-	2-0	2-2
West Ham v Sunderland	1-0	0-3	-	1-1	0-0	1-0
Championship						
Blackburn v MK Dons	-	-	-	-	-	-
Bolton v Burnley	1-0	-	-	2-1	0-1	-
Brighton v Leeds	0-3	-	3-3	2-2	1-0	2-0

Results cover matches from Premier League to National League and Scottish Premiership to League Two

	2009-10	2010-11	2011-12	2012-13	2013-14	2014-15
Cardiff v Preston	1-0	1-1	-	-	-	-
Charlton v Reading	-	-	-	-	0-1	3-2
Fulham v Middlesbrough	-	-	-	-	-	4-3
Huddersfield v Ipswich	-	-	-	0-0	0-2	2-1
Hull v Sheffield Weds	-	-	-	1-3	-	-
Nottm Forest v Bristol City	1-1	1-0	0-1	1-0	-	-
QPR v Birmingham	-	-	-	-	1-0	-
Rotherham v Brentford	-	-	-	-	3-0	0-2
Wolves v Derby	-	-	-	1-1	-	2-0

League One

	2009-10	2010-11	2011-12	2012-13	2013-14	2014-15
Blackpool v Bradford	-	-	-	-	-	-
Burton v Walsall	-	-	-	-	-	-
Colchester v Shrewsbury	-	-	-	0-0	1-0	-
Coventry v Fleetwood Town	-	-	-	-	-	1-1
Crewe v Barnsley	-	-	-	-	-	1-2
Doncaster v Millwall	-	2-1	0-3	-	0-0	-
Gillingham v Chesterfield	-	0-2	-	1-1	-	2-3
Peterborough v Swindon	-	5-4	-	-	1-0	1-2
Port Vale v Southend	-	1-1	2-3	1-2	-	-
Rochdale v Sheffield United	-	-	2-5	-	-	1-2
Scunthorpe v Oldham	-	-	1-2	2-2	-	0-1
Wigan v Bury	-	-	-	-	-	-

League Two

	2009-10	2010-11	2011-12	2012-13	2013-14	2014-15
Accrington v Barnet	1-0	3-1	0-3	3-2	-	-
AFC Wimbledon v Oxford	0-1	-	0-2	0-3	0-2	0-0
Dag & Red v Yeovil	-	2-1	-	-	-	-
Hartlepool v Northampton	-	-	-	-	2-0	1-0
Leyton Orient v Crawley Town	-	-	-	0-1	2-3	4-1
Morecambe v Carlisle	-	-	-	-	-	0-1
Newport County v Mansfield	-	1-0	1-0	2-0	1-1	0-1
Plymouth v Notts County	-	1-1	-	-	-	-
Portsmouth v Cambridge U	-	-	-	-	-	2-1
Stevenage v Exeter	-	-	0-0	-	-	1-0
Wycombe v Bristol Rovers	2-1	-	-	2-0	1-2	-
York v Luton	0-0	1-0	3-0	-	-	0-0

National League

	2009-10	2010-11	2011-12	2012-13	2013-14	2014-15
Barrow v Forest Green	1-1	3-0	1-1	2-2	-	-
Cheltenham v Gateshead	-	-	-	-	-	-
Chester v Tranmere	-	-	-	-	-	-
Dover v Lincoln	-	-	-	-	-	1-2
Eastleigh v Woking	-	-	-	-	-	2-2
Grimsby v Southport	-	1-1	0-1	2-2	0-0	0-1
Guiseley v Braintree	-	-	-	-	-	-
Halifax v Boreham W	-	-	-	-	-	-
Kidderminster v Bromley	-	-	-	-	-	-
Macclesfield v Wrexham	-	-	-	2-0	3-2	2-2
Torquay v Altrincham	-	-	-	-	-	2-0
Welling v Aldershot	-	-	-	-	1-0	3-1

Ladbrokes Premiership

	2009-10	2010-11	2011-12	2012-13	2013-14	2014-15
Aberdeen v St Johnstone	2-1/1-3	0-1/0-2	0-0/0-0	2-0	0-0/1-0/1-1	2-0/0-1
Dundee v Inverness CT	2-2/2-2	-	-	1-4/1-1	-	1-2/0-1
Hamilton v Celtic	1-2/0-1	1-1	-	-	-	0-2
Hearts v Kilmarnock	1-0/1-0	0-3/0-2	0-1	1-3/0-3	0-4/5-0	-
Motherwell v Partick	-	-	-	-	1-0/4-3	1-0/0-0
Ross County v Dundee United	-	-	-	1-2/1-0	2-4/3-0	2-3

Results cover matches from Premier League to National League and Scottish Premiership to League Two

	2009-10	2010-11	2011-12	2012-13	2013-14	2014-15
Ladbrokes Championship						
Alloa v Livingston	-	2-2/1-3	-	-	1-0/0-3	1-0/2-2
Dumbarton v Hibernian	-	-	-	-	-	3-6/1-2
Falkirk v Queen of Sth	-	3-1/0-3	1-0/3-0	-	2-1/1-0	1-1/1-1
Raith v Morton	3-0/1-2	1-0/2-2	1-1/5-0	3-3/2-1	2-1/2-1	-
Rangers v St Mirren	2-1/3-1	2-1	1-1/3-1	-	-	-
Ladbrokes League One						
Airdrieonians v Ayr	3-1/1-1	2-2/0-5	-	-	0-1/3-0	3-0/2-0
Dunfermline v Stranraer	-	-	-	-	3-1/3-2	0-1/1-0
Forfar v Albion	2-2/1-1	-	0-2/4-0	4-2/4-2	-	-
Peterhead v Brechin	1-0/0-3	0-5/1-1	-	-	-	1-1/3-0
Stenhousemuir v Cowdenbeath	0-2/0-0	-	3-1/0-2	-	-	-
Ladbrokes League Two						
Annan v Stirling	-	-	-	5-2/0-1	4-4/1-2	-
Arbroath v Clyde	0-3/2-0	3-2/2-0	-	-	-	4-0/3-1
Berwick v Montrose	2-0/0-2	1-0/0-1	1-2/2-2	1-4/4-0	1-1/5-0	2-2/3-3
Elgin v East Stirling	1-2/0-1	0-2/2-0	2-0/3-1	3-4/3-2	0-1/5-0	1-2/0-0
Queens Park v East Fife	-	-	-	-	-	3-0/1-0

Tuesday March 1st, 2016

	2009-10	2010-11	2011-12	2012-13	2013-14	2014-15
Premier League						
Arsenal v Swansea	-	-	1-0	0-2	2-2	0-1
Aston Villa v Everton	2-2	1-0	1-1	1-3	0-2	3-2
Bournemouth v Southampton	-	1-3	-	-	-	-
Leicester v West Brom	1-2	-	-	-	-	0-1
Liverpool v Man City	2-2	3-0	1-1	2-2	3-2	2-1
Man United v Watford	-	-	-	-	-	-
Norwich v Chelsea	-	-	0-0	0-1	1-3	-
Sunderland v Crystal Palace	-	-	-	-	0-0	1-4
West Ham v Tottenham	1-2	1-0	-	2-3	2-0	0-1
League One						
Barnsley v Coventry	0-2	2-1	2-0	-	-	1-0
Bradford v Colchester	-	-	-	-	2-2	1-1
Bury v Peterborough	-	-	-	-	-	-
Chesterfield v Blackpool	-	-	-	-	-	-
Fleetwood Town v Gillingham	-	-	-	2-2	-	1-0
Millwall v Wigan	-	-	-	-	2-1	2-0
Oldham v Port Vale	-	-	-	-	3-1	1-1
Sheffield United v Burton	-	-	-	-	-	-
Shrewsbury v Rochdale	0-1	-	-	-	-	-
Southend v Crewe	-	0-2	1-0	-	-	-
Swindon v Doncaster	-	-	-	1-1	-	0-1
Walsall v Scunthorpe	-	-	2-2	1-4	-	1-4
League Two						
Barnet v Plymouth	-	-	2-0	1-4	-	-
Bristol Rovers v Hartlepool	2-0	0-0	-	-	2-2	-
Cambridge U v Wycombe	-	-	-	-	-	0-1
Carlisle v Leyton Orient	2-2	0-1	4-1	1-4	1-5	-
Crawley Town v Newport County	-	2-3	-	-	-	-
Exeter v Portsmouth	-	-	-	-	1-1	1-1
Luton v Morecambe	-	-	-	-	-	2-3
Mansfield v Stevenage	2-3	-	-	-	-	1-0
Northampton v AFC Wimbledon	-	-	1-0	2-0	2-2	2-0
Notts County v Dag & Red	3-0	1-0	-	-	-	-
Oxford v York	2-1	-	-	0-0	0-1	0-0
Yeovil v Accrington	-	-	-	-	-	-

Results cover matches from Premier League to National League and Scottish Premiership to League Two

	2009-10	2010-11	2011-12	2012-13	2013-14	2014-15
National League						
Aldershot v Grimsby	1-1	-	-	-	0-3	2-1
Bromley v Welling	-	-	-	-	-	-
Eastleigh v Cheltenham	-	-	-	-	-	-
Ladbrokes Championship						
Livingston v Morton	-	-	1-1/0-0	2-2/0-2	2-2/0-1	-
Queen of Sth v Hibernian	-	-	-	-	-	1-0/0-2
Rangers v Raith	-	-	-	-	-	6-1/4-0
St Mirren v Falkirk	1-1	-	-	-	-	-

Wednesday March 2nd, 2016

	2009-10	2010-11	2011-12	2012-13	2013-14	2014-15
Premier League						
Stoke v Newcastle	-	4-0	1-3	2-1	1-0	1-0
Ladbrokes Premiership						
Celtic v Dundee	-	-	-	2-0/5-0	-	2-1/5-0
Dundee United v Aberdeen	0-1	3-1/3-1	1-2	1-1/1-0	1-2/1-3	0-2/1-0
Hamilton v Motherwell	2-2/0-0	0-0	-	-	-	5-0/2-0
Inverness CT v Hearts	-	1-3/1-1	1-1/1-0	1-1	2-0/0-0	-
Kilmarnock v Ross County	-	-	-	3-0	2-0/2-2	0-3/1-2
St Johnstone v Partick	-	-	-	-	1-1/1-1	2-0
Ladbrokes Championship						
Dumbarton v Alloa	1-3/3-1	4-1/2-2	-	-	1-1/4-1	3-1/1-0

Saturday March 5th, 2016

	2009-10	2010-11	2011-12	2012-13	2013-14	2014-15
Premier League						
Chelsea v Stoke	7-0	2-0	1-0	1-0	3-0	2-1
Crystal Palace v Liverpool	-	-	-	-	3-3	3-1
Everton v West Ham	2-2	2-2	-	2-0	1-0	2-1
Man City v Aston Villa	3-1	4-0	4-1	5-0	4-0	3-2
Newcastle v Bournemouth	-	-	-	-	-	-
Southampton v Sunderland	-	-	-	0-1	1-1	8-0
Swansea v Norwich	-	3-0	2-3	3-4	3-0	-
Tottenham v Arsenal	2-1	3-3	2-1	2-1	0-1	2-1
Watford v Leicester	3-3	3-2	3-2	2-1	0-3	-
West Brom v Man United	-	1-2	1-2	5-5	0-3	2-2
Championship						
Birmingham v Hull	0-0	-	0-0	2-3	-	-
Brentford v Charlton	1-1	2-1	0-1	-	-	1-1
Bristol City v Cardiff	0-6	3-0	1-2	4-2	-	-
Burnley v Blackburn	0-1	-	-	1-1	1-1	-
Derby v Huddersfield	-	-	-	3-0	3-1	3-2
Ipswich v Nottm Forest	1-1	0-1	1-3	3-1	1-1	2-1
Leeds v Bolton	-	-	-	1-0	1-5	1-0
Middlesbrough v Wolves	-	-	-	2-0	-	2-1
MK Dons v QPR	-	-	-	-	-	-
Preston v Brighton	-	-	-	-	-	-
Reading v Fulham	-	-	-	3-3	-	3-0
Sheffield Weds v Rotherham	-	-	-	-	-	0-0
League One						
Bury v Bradford	2-1	0-1	-	-	-	-
Coventry v Rochdale	-	-	-	-	-	2-2
Crewe v Burton	2-1	4-1	3-2	-	-	-
Doncaster v Shrewsbury	-	-	-	1-0	-	-
Fleetwood Town v Sheffield United	-	-	-	-	-	1-1
Millwall v Blackpool	-	-	2-2	0-2	3-1	2-1
Oldham v Swindon	2-2	2-0	-	0-2	2-1	2-1

Results cover matches from Premier League to National League and Scottish Premiership to League Two

	2009-10	2010-11	2011-12	2012-13	2013-14	2014-15
Port Vale v Colchester	-	-	-	-	2-0	1-2
Scunthorpe v Gillingham	-	-	-	-	-	2-1
Southend v Chesterfield	-	2-3	-	3-0	3-0	-
Walsall v Barnsley	-	-	-	-	-	3-1
Wigan v Peterborough	-	-	-	-	-	-

League Two

	2009-10	2010-11	2011-12	2012-13	2013-14	2014-15
AFC Wimbledon v Accrington	-	-	0-2	1-2	1-1	2-1
Barnet v Hartlepool	-	-	-	-	-	-
Cambridge U v Exeter	-	-	-	-	-	1-2
Carlisle v Northampton	-	-	-	-	-	2-1
Crawley Town v Morecambe	-	-	1-1	-	-	-
Dag & Red v York	-	-	-	0-1	2-0	2-0
Leyton Orient v Luton	-	-	-	-	-	-
Mansfield v Yeovil	-	-	-	-	-	-
Newport County v Wycombe	-	-	-	-	2-0	0-2
Notts County v Bristol Rovers	-	0-1	-	-	-	-
Plymouth v Oxford	-	-	1-1	0-1	0-2	1-2
Stevenage v Portsmouth	-	-	-	2-1	-	1-0

National League

	2009-10	2010-11	2011-12	2012-13	2013-14	2014-15
Altrincham v Macclesfield	-	-	-	-	-	1-0
Boreham W v Barrow	-	-	-	-	-	-
Braintree v Eastleigh	-	-	-	-	-	1-5
Chester v Bromley	-	-	-	-	-	-
Forest Green v Grimsby	-	3-3	0-1	0-1	2-1	2-1
Guiseley v Wrexham	-	-	-	-	-	-
Lincoln v Aldershot	1-0	0-3	-	-	0-1	3-0
Southport v Halifax	-	-	-	-	2-1	1-0
Torquay v Kidderminster	-	-	-	-	-	2-1
Tranmere v Gateshead	-	-	-	-	-	-
Welling v Cheltenham	-	-	-	-	-	-
Woking v Dover	-	-	-	-	-	6-1

Ladbrokes Championship

	2009-10	2010-11	2011-12	2012-13	2013-14	2014-15
Falkirk v Alloa	-	-	-	-	0-0/3-1	2-1/1-0
Hibernian v Rangers	1-4/0-1	0-3/0-2	0-2	-	-	4-0/0-2
Livingston v Dumbarton	-	2-0/1-1	-	5-0/2-3	1-3/1-2	1-2/1-2
Morton v Queen of Sth	1-2/3-3	2-0/0-4	2-2/2-2	-	0-2/1-1	-
Raith v St Mirren	-	-	-	-	-	-

Ladbrokes League One

	2009-10	2010-11	2011-12	2012-13	2013-14	2014-15
Albion v Peterhead	-	-	-	-	1-2/0-0	-
Brechin v Ayr	-	0-3/1-0	-	2-1/2-1	1-1/2-1	2-4/2-1
Cowdenbeath v Airdrieonians	-	-	2-0/0-0	1-1/3-2	-	-
Dunfermline v Stenhousemuir	-	-	-	-	3-2/0-0	2-0/3-2
Stranraer v Forfar	1-0/2-0	-	-	4-1/0-3	0-4/3-1	1-1/4-2

Ladbrokes League Two

	2009-10	2010-11	2011-12	2012-13	2013-14	2014-15
Annan v Clyde	-	0-2/1-0	1-0/1-0	1-3/0-1	1-2/0-1	2-1/0-1
East Stirling v Montrose	1-0/2-3	2-1/1-2	1-0/3-1	2-2/1-2	2-2/1-2	4-0/0-1
Elgin v East Fife	-	-	-	-	-	1-0/3-5
Queens Park v Berwick	2-0/2-3	0-2/1-0	1-1/2-2	1-1/2-1	0-4/1-3	2-0/2-1
Stirling v Arbroath	2-2/2-2	-	0-1/1-1	-	-	-

Tuesday March 8th, 2016

Championship

	2009-10	2010-11	2011-12	2012-13	2013-14	2014-15
Blackburn v Birmingham	2-1	1-1	-	1-1	2-3	1-0
Bolton v Ipswich	-	-	-	1-2	1-1	0-0
Brighton v Sheffield Weds	-	2-0	-	3-0	1-1	0-1
Cardiff v Leeds	-	2-1	1-1	2-1	-	3-1

Results cover matches from Premier League to National League and Scottish Premiership to League Two

	2009-10	2010-11	2011-12	2012-13	2013-14	2014-15
Charlton v MK Dons	5-1	1-0	2-1	-	-	-
Fulham v Burnley	3-0	-	-	-	-	-
Huddersfield v Reading	-	-	-	-	0-1	3-0
Hull v Brentford	-	-	-	-	-	-
Nottm Forest v Preston	3-0	2-2	-	-	-	-
QPR v Derby	1-1	0-0	-	-	2-1	-
Rotherham v Middlesbrough	-	-	-	-	-	0-3
Wolves v Bristol City	-	-	-	2-1	3-1	-

Saturday March 12th, 2016

Premier League

	2009-10	2010-11	2011-12	2012-13	2013-14	2014-15
Arsenal v West Brom	-	2-3	3-0	2-0	1-0	4-1
Aston Villa v Tottenham	1-1	1-2	1-1	0-4	0-2	1-2
Bournemouth v Swansea	-	-	-	-	-	-
Leicester v Newcastle	0-0	-	-	-	-	3-0
Liverpool v Chelsea	0-2	2-0	4-1	2-2	0-2	1-2
Man United v Crystal Palace	-	-	-	-	2-0	1-0
Norwich v Man City	-	-	1-6	3-4	0-0	-
Stoke v Southampton	-	-	-	3-3	1-1	2-1
Sunderland v Everton	1-1	2-2	1-1	1-0	0-1	1-1
West Ham v Watford	-	-	1-1	-	-	-

Championship

	2009-10	2010-11	2011-12	2012-13	2013-14	2014-15
Blackburn v Leeds	-	-	-	0-0	1-0	2-1
Bolton v Preston	-	-	-	-	-	-
Brighton v Reading	-	-	0-1	-	1-1	2-2
Cardiff v Ipswich	1-2	0-2	2-2	0-0	-	3-1
Charlton v Middlesbrough	-	-	-	1-4	0-1	0-0
Fulham v Bristol City	-	-	-	-	-	-
Huddersfield v Burnley	-	-	-	2-0	2-1	-
Hull v MK Dons	-	-	-	-	-	-
Nottm Forest v Sheffield Weds	2-1	-	-	1-0	3-3	0-2
QPR v Brentford	-	-	-	-	-	-
Rotherham v Derby	-	-	-	-	-	3-3
Wolves v Birmingham	0-1	1-0	-	1-0	-	0-0

League One

	2009-10	2010-11	2011-12	2012-13	2013-14	2014-15
Barnsley v Southend	-	-	-	-	-	-
Blackpool v Coventry	3-0	-	2-1	-	-	-
Bradford v Doncaster	-	-	-	-	-	1-2
Burton v Fleetwood Town	-	-	-	0-1	2-4	-
Chesterfield v Walsall	-	-	1-1	-	-	1-0
Colchester v Wigan	-	-	-	-	-	-
Gillingham v Crewe	-	1-3	3-4	-	1-3	2-0
Peterborough v Port Vale	-	-	-	-	0-0	3-1
Rochdale v Bury	3-0	-	3-0	-	1-0	-
Sheffield United v Oldham	-	-	2-3	1-1	1-1	1-1
Shrewsbury v Scunthorpe	-	-	-	0-1	-	-
Swindon v Millwall	1-1	-	-	-	-	-

League Two

	2009-10	2010-11	2011-12	2012-13	2013-14	2014-15
Accrington v Plymouth	-	-	0-4	1-1	1-1	1-0
Bristol Rovers v Mansfield	-	-	-	-	0-1	-
Exeter v Carlisle	2-3	2-1	0-0	-	-	2-0
Hartlepool v Dag & Red	-	0-1	-	-	2-1	0-2
Luton v Crawley Town	3-0	1-2	-	-	-	-
Morecambe v AFC Wimbledon	-	-	1-2	3-1	1-1	1-1
Northampton v Cambridge U	-	-	-	-	-	0-1
Oxford v Leyton Orient	-	-	-	-	-	-
Portsmouth v Newport County	-	-	-	-	0-2	0-1

Results cover matches from Premier League to National League and Scottish Premiership to League Two

	2009-10	2010-11	2011-12	2012-13	2013-14	2014-15
Wycombe v Stevenage	-	0-1	0-1	-	-	2-2
Yeovil v Notts County	-	2-1	1-0	0-0	-	1-1
York v Barnet	-	-	-	1-2	-	-

National League						
Aldershot v Torquay	0-2	1-0	0-1	1-0	-	2-0
Barrow v Altrincham	0-3	1-0	-	-	1-1	-
Bromley v Guiseley	-	-	-	-	-	-
Cheltenham v Woking	-	-	-	-	-	-
Dover v Tranmere	-	-	-	-	-	-
Eastleigh v Chester	-	-	-	-	-	3-2
Gateshead v Forest Green	3-1	1-1	1-0	1-1	1-1	2-4
Grimsby v Braintree	-	-	1-1	3-0	1-0	1-0
Kidderminster v Halifax	-	-	-	-	2-0	0-0
Macclesfield v Lincoln	0-1	1-1	-	2-1	3-1	3-0
Southport v Welling	-	-	-	-	2-2	1-0
Wrexham v Boreham W	-	-	-	-	-	-

Ladbrokes Premiership						
Aberdeen v Kilmarnock	1-0/1-2	0-1/5-0	2-2/0-0	0-2/1-0	2-1/2-1	1-0
Dundee v Hearts	-	-	-	1-0/1-0	-	-
Inverness CT v Hamilton	-	0-1/1-1	-	-	-	4-2
Motherwell v Dundee United	2-2/2-3	2-1/2-1	0-0/0-2	0-1/0-1	0-4	1-0
Partick v Celtic	-	-	-	-	1-2/1-5	0-3
St Johnstone v Ross County	-	-	-	1-1/2-2	4-0/0-1	2-1

Ladbrokes Championship						
Alloa v Raith	-	-	-	-	1-0/0-1	0-1/0-0
Dumbarton v Falkirk	-	-	-	0-2/0-2	1-1/2-1	0-3/1-0
Hibernian v Livingston	-	-	-	-	-	2-1/2-1
Rangers v Morton	-	-	-	-	-	-
St Mirren v Queen of Sth	-	-	-	-	-	-

Ladbrokes League One						
Airdrieonians v Brechin	-	1-1/2-2	2-3/4-1	-	3-1/2-1	4-0/1-1
Albion v Stranraer	3-1/0-0	1-2/1-0	-	2-1/2-3	-	-
Ayr v Dunfermline	1-0/1-2	-	-	-	2-4/1-1	0-1/0-2
Forfar v Cowdenbeath	-	-	2-2/1-0	-	-	-
Stenhousemuir v Peterhead	2-0/1-1	3-1/4-2	-	-	-	1-2/2-1

Ladbrokes League Two						
Arbroath v East Stirling	-	2-0/3-5	-	-	-	4-0/0-1
Berwick v Stirling	-	-	-	4-1/1-0	1-1/4-0	-
Clyde v Elgin	-	1-1/3-3	1-2/0-2	2-2/1-1	2-1/4-0	2-1/0-2
East Fife v Annan	-	-	-	-	-	1-1/2-1
Montrose v Queens Park	1-2/1-2	1-2/0-2	0-1/3-1	1-1/1-2	1-2/1-0	1-2/2-2

Saturday March 19th, 2016

Premier League						
Chelsea v West Ham	4-1	3-0	-	2-0	0-0	2-0
Crystal Palace v Leicester	0-1	3-2	1-2	2-2	-	2-0
Everton v Arsenal	1-6	1-2	0-1	1-1	3-0	2-2
Man City v Man United	0-1	0-0	1-0	2-3	4-1	1-0
Newcastle v Sunderland	-	5-1	1-1	0-3	0-3	0-1
Southampton v Liverpool	-	-	-	3-1	0-3	0-2
Swansea v Aston Villa	-	-	0-0	2-2	4-1	1-0
Tottenham v Bournemouth	-	-	-	-	-	-
Watford v Stoke	-	-	-	-	-	-
West Brom v Norwich	-	-	1-2	2-1	0-2	-

Results cover matches from Premier League to National League and Scottish Premiership to League Two

	2009-10	2010-11	2011-12	2012-13	2013-14	2014-15
Championship						
Birmingham v Fulham	1-0	0-2	-	-	-	1-2
Brentford v Blackburn	-	-	-	-	-	3-1
Bristol City v Bolton	-	-	-	1-2	-	-
Burnley v Wolves	1-2	-	-	2-0	-	-
Derby v Nottm Forest	1-0	0-1	1-0	1-1	5-0	1-2
Ipswich v Rotherham	-	-	-	-	-	2-0
Leeds v Huddersfield	2-2	-	-	1-2	5-1	3-0
Middlesbrough v Hull	-	2-2	1-0	2-0	-	-
MK Dons v Brighton	0-0	1-0	-	-	-	-
Preston v QPR	2-2	1-1	-	-	-	-
Reading v Cardiff	0-1	1-1	1-2	-	-	1-1
Sheffield Weds v Charlton	-	2-2	0-1	2-0	2-3	1-1
League One						
Bury v Shrewsbury	1-0	1-0	-	2-2	-	1-0
Coventry v Swindon	-	-	-	1-2	1-2	0-3
Crewe v Blackpool	-	-	-	-	-	-
Doncaster v Peterborough	3-1	-	1-1	-	-	0-2
Fleetwood Town v Barnsley	-	-	-	-	-	0-0
Millwall v Sheffield United	-	0-1	-	-	-	-
Oldham v Rochdale	-	1-2	2-0	-	-	3-0
Port Vale v Burton	3-1	2-1	3-0	7-1	-	-
Scunthorpe v Chesterfield	-	-	2-2	-	1-1	2-0
Southend v Gillingham	1-0	2-2	1-0	0-1	-	-
Walsall v Colchester	1-0	0-1	3-1	1-0	0-1	0-0
Wigan v Bradford	-	-	-	-	-	-
League Two						
AFC Wimbledon v York	0-1	1-0	-	3-2	0-1	2-1
Barnet v Oxford	-	2-2	0-2	2-2	-	-
Cambridge U v Yeovil	-	-	-	-	-	-
Carlisle v Wycombe	1-0	-	2-2	-	-	2-3
Crawley Town v Hartlepool	-	-	-	2-2	-	-
Dag & Red v Accrington	3-1	-	2-1	1-1	0-0	4-0
Leyton Orient v Morecambe	-	-	-	-	-	-
Mansfield v Portsmouth	-	-	-	-	2-2	1-2
Newport County v Bristol Rovers	-	-	-	-	1-0	-
Notts County v Exeter	-	0-2	2-1	-	-	-
Plymouth v Luton	-	-	-	-	-	0-1
Stevenage v Northampton	-	0-1	-	-	-	2-1
National League						
Altrincham v Aldershot	-	-	-	-	-	1-0
Barrow v Bromley	-	-	-	-	-	-
Boreham W v Macclesfield	-	-	-	-	-	-
Braintree v Cheltenham	-	-	-	-	-	-
Guiseley v Dover	-	-	-	-	-	-
Halifax v Eastleigh	-	-	-	-	-	0-2
Lincoln v Kidderminster	-	-	0-1	1-0	2-0	0-0
Torquay v Southport	-	-	-	-	-	0-0
Tranmere v Forest Green	-	-	-	-	-	-
Welling v Gateshead	-	-	-	-	2-0	1-1
Woking v Grimsby	-	-	-	0-1	1-2	1-2
Wrexham v Chester	-	-	-	-	0-2	1-0
Ladbrokes Premiership						
Dundee United v Dundee	-	-	-	3-0/1-1	-	6-2/3-0
Hamilton v Partick	-	-	1-0/2-2	1-0/0-2	-	3-3/1-1
Hearts v St Johnstone	1-2	1-1/1-0	1-2/2-0	2-0/2-0	0-2	-

Results cover matches from Premier League to National League and Scottish Premiership to League Two

	2009-10	2010-11	2011-12	2012-13	2013-14	2014-15
Kilmarnock v Celtic	1-0	1-2/0-4/0-2	3-3/0-6	1-3	2-5/0-3	0-2
Motherwell v Aberdeen	1-1	1-1/2-1	1-0/1-0	4-1	1-3/2-2	0-2
Ross County v Inverness CT	2-1/0-0	-	-	0-0/1-0	0-3/1-2	1-3

Ladbrokes Championship

	2009-10	2010-11	2011-12	2012-13	2013-14	2014-15
Falkirk v Rangers	1-3	-	-	-	-	0-2/1-1
Livingston v St Mirren	-	-	-	-	-	-
Morton v Alloa	-	-	-	-	0-2/0-1	-
Queen of Sth v Dumbarton	-	-	-	-	1-2/3-1	3-0/2-1
Raith v Hibernian	-	-	-	-	-	1-3/2-1

Ladbrokes League One

	2009-10	2010-11	2011-12	2012-13	2013-14	2014-15
Brechin v Albion	-	-	1-4/2-1	1-0/2-0	-	-
Cowdenbeath v Dunfermline	-	0-4/0-1	-	0-4/4-2	-	-
Forfar v Ayr	-	4-1/3-2	-	2-1/2-1	0-1/4-2	2-0/1-3
Peterhead v Airdrieonians	-	5-1/2-4	-	-	-	1-1/0-1
Stranraer v Stenhousemuir	-	-	-	1-1/1-1	1-0/1-1	0-2/3-2

Ladbrokes League Two

	2009-10	2010-11	2011-12	2012-13	2013-14	2014-15
Annan v Berwick	1-1/0-1	1-1/2-3	2-2/1-1	3-2/2-2	3-2/4-0	2-0/4-2
East Stirling v Clyde	-	0-0/2-0	1-1/0-1	3-0/3-0	0-1/2-4	1-0/1-2
Elgin v Montrose	0-1/5-2	3-2/1-0	3-1/2-1	6-1/3-2	3-3/2-3	0-1/4-0
Queens Park v Arbroath	-	5-2/1-1	-	-	-	0-2/2-1
Stirling v East Fife	3-0/3-3	-	1-0/0-1	-	-	-

Friday March 25th, 2016

League One

	2009-10	2010-11	2011-12	2012-13	2013-14	2014-15
Barnsley v Scunthorpe	1-1	2-1	-	-	-	1-2
Burton v Oldham	-	-	-	-	-	-
Colchester v Doncaster	-	-	-	1-2	-	0-1
Gillingham v Walsall	0-0	-	-	-	2-2	0-0
Peterborough v Coventry	0-1	-	1-0	-	1-0	0-1
Rochdale v Southend	-	-	-	4-2	0-3	-
Sheffield United v Crewe	-	-	-	3-3	3-1	1-2
Shrewsbury v Port Vale	0-1	2-2	1-0	-	0-0	-
Swindon v Wigan	-	-	-	-	-	-

League Two

	2009-10	2010-11	2011-12	2012-13	2013-14	2014-15
Accrington v Leyton Orient	-	-	-	-	-	-
Bristol Rovers v Cambridge U	-	-	-	-	-	-
Exeter v Barnet	-	-	-	2-2	-	-
Hartlepool v AFC Wimbledon	-	-	-	-	3-1	1-0
Luton v Dag & Red	-	-	-	-	-	3-1
Morecambe v Plymouth	-	-	2-2	2-3	2-1	2-1
Northampton v Newport County	-	-	-	-	3-1	3-0
Oxford v Stevenage	2-1	1-2	-	-	-	0-0
Portsmouth v Notts County	-	-	-	0-2	-	-
Wycombe v Mansfield	-	-	-	-	0-1	2-1
Yeovil v Carlisle	3-1	1-0	0-3	1-3	-	-
York v Crawley Town	2-0	1-1	-	-	-	-

Saturday March 26th, 2016

League One

	2009-10	2010-11	2011-12	2012-13	2013-14	2014-15
Blackpool v Bury	-	-	-	-	-	-
Bradford v Millwall	-	-	-	-	-	-
Chesterfield v Fleetwood Town	-	-	-	1-2	2-1	3-0

National League

	2009-10	2010-11	2011-12	2012-13	2013-14	2014-15
Braintree v Bromley	-	-	-	-	-	-
Cheltenham v Boreham W	-	-	-	-	-	-
Chester v Barrow	-	-	-	-	-	-
Dover v Torquay	-	-	-	-	-	2-2

Results cover matches from Premier League to National League and Scottish Premiership to League Two

	2009-10	2010-11	2011-12	2012-13	2013-14	2014-15
Eastleigh v Welling	-	-	-	-	-	3-1
Forest Green v Aldershot	-	-	-	-	3-1	1-3
Gateshead v Macclesfield	-	-	-	2-2	2-2	2-1
Grimsby v Wrexham	-	2-1	1-3	1-0	3-1	0-1
Halifax v Altrincham	-	-	-	-	-	1-3
Southport v Guiseley	-	-	-	-	-	-
Tranmere v Lincoln	-	-	-	-	-	-
Woking v Kidderminster	-	-	-	2-2	1-0	2-3
Ladbrokes Championship						
Alloa v St Mirren	-	-	-	-	-	-
Falkirk v Livingston	-	-	4-3/2-5	1-2/2-0	4-1/1-1	0-0/2-0
Hibernian v Dumbarton	-	-	-	-	-	0-0/3-0
Morton v Raith	5-0/1-1	0-1/0-0	1-1/1-3	1-0/1-0	1-1/0-0	-
Rangers v Queen of Sth	-	-	-	-	-	4-2/1-1
Ladbrokes League One						
Airdrieonians v Albion	-	-	4-0/1-0	-	-	-
Ayr v Stranraer	-	-	-	2-1/2-1	3-6/5-0	0-2/0-2
Dunfermline v Brechin	-	-	-	-	3-1/2-1	0-0/0-1
Peterhead v Cowdenbeath	0-2/1-0	-	-	-	-	-
Stenhousemuir v Forfar	-	3-0/0-1	2-3/1-2	0-4/2-0	1-1/4-1	0-2/1-3
Ladbrokes League Two						
Berwick v Elgin	2-0/2-1	6-2/4-0	1-1/3-3	0-0/2-1	2-3/2-3	1-1/0-2
Clyde v Arbroath	1-0/0-2	1-1/0-3	-	-	-	2-5/1-1
East Fife v Queens Park	-	-	-	-	-	2-2/0-0
Montrose v Annan	0-0/1-2	1-1/0-1	2-3/1-1	0-0/5-1	0-2/2-1	2-0/2-1
Stirling v East Stirling	-	-	-	1-1/9-1	1-3/2-1	-

Monday March 28th, 2016

League One						
Bury v Gillingham	-	5-4	-	-	-	-
Crewe v Bradford	0-1	2-1	1-0	-	0-0	0-1
Doncaster v Blackpool	3-3	-	1-3	-	1-3	-
Fleetwood Town v Peterborough	-	-	-	-	-	1-1
Millwall v Burton	-	-	-	-	-	-
Oldham v Chesterfield	-	-	5-2	-	-	0-0
Port Vale v Barnsley	-	-	-	-	-	2-1
Scunthorpe v Swindon	-	-	-	3-1	-	3-1
Southend v Sheffield United	-	-	-	-	-	-
Walsall v Shrewsbury	-	-	-	3-1	1-0	-
Wigan v Rochdale	-	-	-	-	-	-
League Two						
AFC Wimbledon v Portsmouth	-	-	-	-	4-0	1-0
Barnet v Luton	-	-	-	-	1-2	-
Cambridge U v Oxford	1-1	-	-	-	-	5-1
Carlisle v Bristol Rovers	3-1	4-0	-	-	-	-
Crawley Town v Exeter	-	-	-	-	-	-
Dag & Red v Morecambe	1-1	-	1-2	1-2	1-1	0-3
Leyton Orient v Hartlepool	1-3	1-0	1-1	1-0	-	-
Mansfield v Northampton	-	-	-	-	3-0	1-1
Newport County v Accrington	-	-	-	-	4-1	1-1
Notts County v Wycombe	-	-	1-1	-	-	-
Plymouth v York	-	-	-	2-0	0-4	1-1
Stevenage v Yeovil	-	-	0-0	0-2	-	-
National League						
Aldershot v Braintree	-	-	-	-	2-1	1-3
Altrincham v Southport	-	1-1	-	-	-	2-0

Results cover matches from Premier League to National League and Scottish Premiership to League Two

	2009-10	2010-11	2011-12	2012-13	2013-14	2014-15
Barrow v Halifax	-	-	-	-	-	-
Boreham W v Dover	-	-	-	-	2-2	-
Bromley v Forest Green	-	-	-	-	-	-
Guiseley v Chester	-	-	-	-	-	-
Kidderminster v Tranmere	-	-	-	-	-	-
Lincoln v Gateshead	-	-	1-0	1-1	0-1	1-1
Macclesfield v Grimsby	0-0	-	-	1-3	1-1	0-1
Torquay v Eastleigh	-	-	-	-	-	2-0
Welling v Woking	-	-	-	-	3-0	1-1
Wrexham v Cheltenham	-	-	-	-	-	-

Tuesday March 29th, 2016

League One

	2009-10	2010-11	2011-12	2012-13	2013-14	2014-15
Coventry v Colchester	-	-	-	2-2	2-0	1-0

Saturday April 2nd, 2016

Premier League

	2009-10	2010-11	2011-12	2012-13	2013-14	2014-15
Arsenal v Watford	-	-	-	-	-	-
Aston Villa v Chelsea	2-1	0-0	2-4	1-2	1-0	1-2
Bournemouth v Man City	-	-	-	-	-	-
Leicester v Southampton	-	-	3-2	-	-	2-0
Liverpool v Tottenham	2-0	0-2	0-0	3-2	4-0	3-2
Man United v Everton	3-0	1-0	4-4	2-0	0-1	2-1
Norwich v Newcastle	-	-	4-2	0-0	0-0	-
Stoke v Swansea	-	-	2-0	2-0	1-1	2-1
Sunderland v West Brom	-	2-3	2-2	2-4	2-0	0-0
West Ham v Crystal Palace	-	-	0-0	-	0-1	1-3

Championship

	2009-10	2010-11	2011-12	2012-13	2013-14	2014-15
Blackburn v Preston	-	-	-	-	-	-
Bolton v Reading	-	-	-	-	1-1	1-1
Brighton v Burnley	-	-	0-1	1-0	2-0	-
Cardiff v Derby	6-1	4-1	2-0	1-1	-	0-2
Charlton v Birmingham	-	-	-	1-1	0-2	1-1
Fulham v MK Dons	-	-	-	-	-	-
Huddersfield v Sheffield Weds	-	1-0	0-2	0-0	0-2	0-0
Hull v Bristol City	-	2-0	3-0	0-0	-	-
Nottm Forest v Brentford	-	-	-	-	-	1-3
QPR v Middlesbrough	1-5	3-0	-	-	2-0	-
Rotherham v Leeds	-	-	-	-	-	2-1
Wolves v Ipswich	-	-	-	0-2	-	1-1

League One

	2009-10	2010-11	2011-12	2012-13	2013-14	2014-15
Barnsley v Oldham	-	-	-	-	-	1-0
Blackpool v Southend	-	-	-	-	-	-
Bradford v Scunthorpe	-	-	-	-	-	1-1
Burton v Bury	0-0	1-3	-	-	2-2	1-0
Chesterfield v Port Vale	0-5	2-0	-	2-2	-	3-0
Colchester v Millwall	1-2	-	-	-	-	-
Gillingham v Coventry	-	-	-	-	4-2	3-1
Peterborough v Crewe	-	-	-	-	4-2	1-1
Rochdale v Doncaster	-	-	-	-	-	1-3
Sheffield United v Walsall	-	-	3-2	1-0	1-1	1-1
Shrewsbury v Wigan	-	-	-	-	-	-
Swindon v Fleetwood Town	-	-	-	-	-	1-0

League Two

	2009-10	2010-11	2011-12	2012-13	2013-14	2014-15
Accrington v Cambridge U	-	-	-	-	-	2-1
Bristol Rovers v Crawley Town	-	-	0-0	-	-	-
Exeter v Plymouth	-	1-0	-	1-1	3-1	1-3
Hartlepool v Mansfield	-	-	-	-	2-4	1-0

Results cover matches from Premier League to National League and Scottish Premiership to League Two

	2009-10	2010-11	2011-12	2012-13	2013-14	2014-15
Luton v Stevenage	0-1	-	-	-	-	2-0
Morecambe v Barnet	2-1	2-2	0-1	4-1	-	-
Northampton v Notts County	0-1	-	-	-	-	-
Oxford v Dag & Red	-	-	2-1	2-3	2-1	3-3
Portsmouth v Carlisle	-	-	-	1-1	-	3-0
Wycombe v AFC Wimbledon	-	-	-	0-1	0-3	2-0
Yeovil v Newport County	-	-	-	-	-	-
York v Leyton Orient	-	-	-	-	-	-
National League						
Aldershot v Barrow	-	-	-	-	-	-
Bromley v Lincoln	-	-	-	-	-	-
Cheltenham v Grimsby	2-1	-	-	-	-	-
Chester v Boreham W	-	-	-	-	-	-
Dover v Halifax	-	-	-	-	-	0-1
Eastleigh v Guiseley	-	-	-	-	-	-
Forest Green v Wrexham	0-2	3-0	1-0	0-0	1-1	0-1
Gateshead v Torquay	-	-	-	-	-	3-1
Kidderminster v Altrincham	3-0	2-1	-	-	-	4-0
Macclesfield v Braintree	-	-	-	2-1	0-1	1-0
Southport v Woking	-	-	-	1-2	1-1	2-5
Tranmere v Welling	-	-	-	-	-	-
Ladbrokes Premiership						
Aberdeen v Hamilton	1-2/1-3	4-0/1-0	-	-	-	3-0
Celtic v Hearts	2-1/2-0	3-0/4-0	1-0/5-0	1-0/4-1	2-0	-
Dundee v Ross County	2-0/0-1	0-0/2-0	1-2/1-1	0-1/0-2	-	1-1
Inverness CT v Motherwell	-	1-2/3-0	2-3	1-5/4-3	2-0/1-2	3-1
Partick v Kilmarnock	-	-	-	-	1-1/1-1	1-1/1-4
St Johnstone v Dundee United	2-3/0-1	0-0	3-3/1-5/0-2	0-0/1-1	3-0/2-0	2-1/1-1
Ladbrokes Championship						
Dumbarton v Morton	-	-	-	1-5/0-3	3-1/2-0	-
Livingston v Alloa	-	3-3/4-0	-	-	3-2/2-0	4-0/0-0
Queen of Sth v Falkirk	-	1-5/0-1	1-5/0-0	-	2-0/1-2	3-0/1-0
Raith v Rangers	-	-	-	-	-	0-4/1-2
St Mirren v Hibernian	1-1	1-0/0-1	2-3/1-0	1-2/0-1	0-0/2-0	-
Ladbrokes League One						
Albion v Dunfermline	-	-	-	-	-	-
Brechin v Stenhousemuir	1-0/2-2	0-0/3-1	2-0/1-0	7-2/1-2	0-1/1-3	1-0/2-1
Cowdenbeath v Ayr	-	-	-	-	-	-
Forfar v Peterhead	-	1-1/2-1	-	-	-	1-0/3-1
Stranraer v Airdrieonians	-	-	-	-	3-1/1-1	1-0/1-0
Ladbrokes League Two						
Arbroath v East Fife	0-1/2-2	-	3-0/2-2	2-0/1-0	2-2/2-1	0-2/1-1
Clyde v Montrose	-	2-0/1-1	1-0/1-2	1-2/1-0	0-3/1-1	1-2/2-0
East Stirling v Berwick	1-0/3-2	0-0/1-0	1-3/2-1	0-1/0-3	1-0/1-1	0-2/0-4
Elgin v Annan	1-1/1-0	2-0/2-3	3-0/1-2	2-2/3-1	2-3/2-3	0-0/4-5
Queens Park v Stirling	-	-	-	2-1/2-2	0-2/0-1	-

Tuesday April 5th, 2016

Championship						
Birmingham v Brighton	-	-	0-0	2-2	0-1	1-0
Brentford v Bolton	-	-	-	-	-	2-2
Bristol City v Rotherham	-	-	-	-	1-2	-
Burnley v Cardiff	-	1-1	1-1	1-1	-	-
Derby v Hull	-	0-1	0-2	1-2	-	-
Ipswich v Charlton	-	-	-	1-2	1-1	3-0
Leeds v QPR	-	2-0	-	-	0-1	-

Results cover matches from Premier League to National League and Scottish Premiership to League Two

	2009-10	2010-11	2011-12	2012-13	2013-14	2014-15
Middlesbrough v Huddersfield	-	-	-	3-0	1-1	2-0
MK Dons v Wolves	-	-	-	-	0-1	-
Preston v Fulham	-	-	-	-	-	-
Reading v Nottm Forest	0-0	1-1	1-0	-	1-1	0-3
Sheffield Weds v Blackburn	-	-	-	3-2	3-3	1-2

Saturday April 9th, 2016

Premier League

	2009-10	2010-11	2011-12	2012-13	2013-14	2014-15
Aston Villa v Bournemouth	-	-	-	-	-	-
Crystal Palace v Norwich	-	0-0	-	-	1-1	-
Liverpool v Stoke	4-0	2-0	0-0	0-0	1-0	1-0
Man City v West Brom	-	3-0	4-0	1-0	3-1	3-0
Southampton v Newcastle	-	-	-	2-0	4-0	4-0
Sunderland v Leicester	-	-	-	-	-	0-0
Swansea v Chelsea	-	-	1-1	1-1	0-1	0-5
Tottenham v Man United	1-3	0-0	1-3	1-1	2-2	0-0
Watford v Everton	-	-	-	-	-	-
West Ham v Arsenal	2-2	0-3	-	1-3	1-3	1-2

Championship

	2009-10	2010-11	2011-12	2012-13	2013-14	2014-15
Bristol City v Sheffield Weds	1-1	-	-	1-1	-	-
Burnley v Leeds	-	2-3	1-2	1-0	2-1	-
Derby v Bolton	-	-	-	1-1	0-0	4-1
Fulham v Cardiff	-	-	-	-	1-2	1-1
Huddersfield v Hull	-	-	-	0-1	-	-
Ipswich v Brentford	-	-	-	-	-	1-1
Middlesbrough v Preston	2-0	1-1	-	-	-	-
MK Dons v Rotherham	-	-	-	-	3-2	-
Nottm Forest v Brighton	-	-	1-1	2-2	1-2	0-0
QPR v Charlton	-	-	-	-	1-0	-
Reading v Birmingham	-	-	1-0	-	2-0	0-1
Wolves v Blackburn	1-1	2-3	0-2	1-1	-	3-1

League One

	2009-10	2010-11	2011-12	2012-13	2013-14	2014-15
Barnsley v Chesterfield	-	-	-	-	-	1-1
Blackpool v Colchester	-	-	-	-	-	-
Bradford v Swindon	-	-	0-0	-	1-1	1-2
Bury v Doncaster	-	-	-	2-0	-	-
Millwall v Shrewsbury	-	-	-	-	-	-
Oldham v Walsall	1-0	1-1	2-1	1-1	0-1	2-1
Peterborough v Rochdale	-	2-1	-	-	-	2-1
Port Vale v Crewe	0-1	2-1	1-1	-	1-3	0-1
Scunthorpe v Burton	-	-	-	-	1-0	-
Sheffield United v Gillingham	-	-	-	-	1-2	2-1
Southend v Fleetwood Town	-	-	-	1-1	2-0	-
Wigan v Coventry	-	-	-	-	-	-

League Two

	2009-10	2010-11	2011-12	2012-13	2013-14	2014-15
Barnet v Leyton Orient	-	-	-	-	-	-
Carlisle v Mansfield	-	-	-	-	-	2-1
Crawley Town v Oxford	1-2	-	4-1	-	-	-
Dag & Red v Portsmouth	-	-	-	-	1-4	0-0
Luton v Accrington	-	-	-	-	-	2-0
Morecambe v Hartlepool	-	-	-	-	1-2	0-1
Newport County v Cambridge U	-	1-1	0-1	6-2	-	1-1
Northampton v Bristol Rovers	-	-	3-2	1-0	0-0	-
Notts County v Stevenage	-	-	1-0	1-2	0-1	-
Plymouth v AFC Wimbledon	-	-	0-2	1-2	1-2	1-1
Yeovil v Exeter	2-1	1-3	2-2	-	-	-
York v Wycombe	-	-	-	1-3	2-0	0-0

Results cover matches from Premier League to National League and Scottish Premiership to League Two

	2009-10	2010-11	2011-12	2012-13	2013-14	2014-15
National League						
Altrincham v Bromley	-	-	-	-	-	-
Barrow v Macclesfield	-	-	-	1-0	-	-
Boreham W v Southport	-	-	-	-	-	-
Braintree v Forest Green	-	-	1-5	3-1	1-1	1-2
Grimsby v Eastleigh	-	-	-	-	-	2-1
Guiseley v Cheltenham	-	-	-	-	-	-
Halifax v Aldershot	-	-	-	-	4-0	1-0
Lincoln v Chester	-	-	-	-	1-1	0-1
Torquay v Tranmere	-	-	-	-	-	-
Welling v Kidderminster	-	-	-	-	1-2	3-0
Woking v Gateshead	-	-	-	2-1	1-2	3-0
Wrexham v Dover	-	-	-	-	-	1-1
Ladbrokes Premiership						
Dundee United v Inverness CT	-	0-4/1-0	3-1/3-0	4-4	0-1/2-1	1-1
Hamilton v Dundee	-	-	1-6/3-1	-	0-3/1-1	2-1
Hearts v Aberdeen	0-3	5-0	3-0/3-0	2-0	2-1/1-1	-
Kilmarnock v St Johnstone	2-1/3-2/1-2	1-1	1-2/0-0	1-2	0-0/1-2	0-1
Motherwell v Celtic	2-3	0-1/2-0	1-2/0-3	0-2/2-1/3-1	0-5/3-3	0-1
Ross County v Partick	2-2/1-2	0-2/0-0	2-2/3-0	-	1-3/1-1	1-0/1-2
Ladbrokes Championship						
Alloa v Hibernian	-	-	-	-	-	2-1/0-1
Falkirk v St Mirren	1-3/2-1/1-1	-	-	-	-	-
Morton v Livingston	-	-	2-1/1-3	2-2/2-1	1-5/2-0	-
Queen of Sth v Raith	1-1/3-0	1-3/0-2	1-3/1-0	-	0-1/1-0	2-0/2-1
Rangers v Dumbarton	-	-	-	-	-	4-1/3-1
Ladbrokes League One						
Airdrieonians v Stenhousemuir	-	1-0/2-2	5-2/0-3	-	0-1/1-1	2-0/2-1
Ayr v Albion	-	-	-	2-1/5-2	-	-
Cowdenbeath v Brechin	0-0/4-0	-	3-1/1-0	-	-	-
Dunfermline v Forfar	-	-	-	-	1-1/0-0	0-0/1-3
Peterhead v Stranraer	-	-	1-3/1-1	-	-	1-4/1-2
Ladbrokes League Two						
Annan v Arbroath	-	1-2/3-0	-	-	-	0-1/2-0
Berwick v Clyde	-	2-1/1-1	0-2/3-0	2-1/3-3	0-1/3-0	4-0/0-0
East Fife v Montrose	-	-	-	-	-	3-0/3-0
East Stirling v Queens Park	1-0/0-3	0-1/3-2	1-3/1-2	0-2/0-2	1-1/1-4	1-3/3-1
Stirling v Elgin	-	-	-	1-4/1-1	1-1/2-2	-

Friday April 15th, 2016

Championship						
Brighton v Fulham	-	-	-	-	-	1-2

Saturday April 16th, 2016

Premier League						
Arsenal v Crystal Palace	-	-	-	-	2-0	2-1
Bournemouth v Liverpool	-	-	-	-	-	-
Chelsea v Man City	2-4	2-0	2-1	0-0	2-1	1-1
Everton v Southampton	-	-	-	3-1	2-1	1-0
Leicester v West Ham	-	-	1-2	-	-	2-1
Man United v Aston Villa	0-1	3-1	4-0	3-0	4-1	3-1
Newcastle v Swansea	3-0	-	0-0	1-2	1-2	2-3
Norwich v Sunderland	-	-	2-1	2-1	2-0	-
Stoke v Tottenham	1-2	1-2	2-1	1-2	0-1	3-0
West Brom v Watford	5-0	-	-	-	-	-

Results cover matches from Premier League to National League and Scottish Premiership to League Two

	2009-10	2010-11	2011-12	2012-13	2013-14	2014-15
Championship						
Birmingham v Burnley	2-1	-	2-1	2-2	3-3	-
Blackburn v Huddersfield	-	-	-	1-0	0-0	0-0
Bolton v Middlesbrough	-	-	-	2-1	2-2	1-2
Brentford v Bristol City	-	-	-	-	3-1	-
Cardiff v QPR	0-2	2-2	-	-	-	-
Charlton v Derby	-	-	-	1-1	0-2	3-2
Hull v Wolves	2-2	-	-	2-1	-	-
Leeds v Reading	-	0-0	0-1	-	2-4	0-0
Preston v MK Dons	-	-	1-1	0-0	2-2	1-1
Rotherham v Nottm Forest	-	-	-	-	-	0-0
Sheffield Weds v Ipswich	0-1	-	-	1-1	1-1	1-1
League One						
Burton v Barnsley	-	-	-	-	-	-
Chesterfield v Sheffield United	-	-	0-1	-	-	3-2
Colchester v Peterborough	-	2-1	-	-	1-0	1-3
Coventry v Millwall	-	2-1	0-1	-	-	-
Crewe v Scunthorpe	-	-	-	1-0	-	2-0
Doncaster v Wigan	-	-	-	-	3-0	-
Fleetwood Town v Oldham	-	-	-	-	-	0-2
Gillingham v Port Vale	-	3-0	1-1	1-2	3-2	2-2
Rochdale v Blackpool	-	-	-	-	-	-
Shrewsbury v Bradford	1-2	3-1	1-0	-	2-1	-
Swindon v Bury	-	-	-	0-1	-	-
Walsall v Southend	2-2	-	-	-	-	-
League Two						
Accrington v Morecambe	3-2	1-1	1-1	2-0	5-1	2-1
AFC Wimbledon v Crawley Town	1-1	2-1	2-5	-	-	-
Bristol Rovers v Yeovil	1-2	2-1	-	-	-	-
Cambridge U v Carlisle	-	-	-	-	-	5-0
Exeter v Northampton	-	-	-	3-0	0-1	0-2
Hartlepool v York	-	-	-	-	2-0	1-3
Leyton Orient v Dag & Red	-	1-1	-	-	-	-
Mansfield v Notts County	-	-	-	-	-	-
Oxford v Luton	2-0	-	-	-	-	1-1
Portsmouth v Plymouth	-	-	-	-	3-3	2-1
Stevenage v Newport County	-	-	-	-	-	2-1
Wycombe v Barnet	-	4-2	-	0-0	-	-
National League						
Aldershot v Boreham W	-	-	-	-	-	-
Bromley v Torquay	-	-	-	-	-	-
Cheltenham v Halifax	-	-	-	-	-	-
Chester v Welling	-	-	-	-	1-3	1-1
Dover v Grimsby	-	-	-	-	-	0-1
Eastleigh v Altrincham	-	-	-	-	-	0-2
Forest Green v Woking	-	-	-	3-1	2-2	2-1
Gateshead v Braintree	-	-	2-2	1-2	1-0	3-1
Kidderminster v Barrow	1-2	2-0	1-2	2-0	-	-
Macclesfield v Guiseley	-	-	-	-	-	-
Southport v Lincoln	-	-	2-2	4-2	0-1	3-3
Tranmere v Wrexham	-	-	-	-	-	-
Ladbrokes Championship						
Alloa v Queen of Sth	-	-	-	1-0/1-2	0-3/0-1	1-1/2-2
Dumbarton v Raith	-	-	-	4-2/1-2	2-4/3-3	2-1/2-2
Hibernian v Falkirk	2-0	-	-	-	-	0-1/3-3
Livingston v Rangers	-	-	-	-	-	0-1/1-1
St Mirren v Morton	-	-	-	-	-	-

Results cover matches from Premier League to National League and Scottish Premiership to League Two

	2009-10	2010-11	2011-12	2012-13	2013-14	2014-15
Ladbrokes League One						
Albion v Cowdenbeath	-	-	3-3/1-0	-	-	-
Brechin v Peterhead	3-0/1-2	4-2/3-1	-	-	-	1-1/2-2
Forfar v Airdrieonians	-	1-2/1-2	3-2/2-3	-	3-3/1-1	1-1/2-0
Stenhousemuir v Ayr	-	3-1/2-1	-	1-1/4-0	1-1/1-1	1-1/1-1
Stranraer v Dunfermline	-	-	-	-	1-2/3-1	1-2/5-1
Ladbrokes League Two						
Annan v East Stirling	0-1/1-0	3-1/2-1	3-0/2-2	5-2/1-2	1-2/2-3	4-3/3-2
Arbroath v Berwick	-	3-2/2-1	-	-	-	2-0/5-0
Clyde v East Fife	1-3/2-1	-	-	-	-	3-1/1-0
Elgin v Queens Park	0-1/0-1	4-2/0-1	2-0/1-1	0-4/3-5	3-2/1-1	1-4/1-2
Montrose v Stirling	-	-	-	3-2/2-2	1-2/0-0	-

Tuesday April 19th, 2016

Championship	2009-10	2010-11	2011-12	2012-13	2013-14	2014-15
Birmingham v Preston	-	-	-	-	-	-
Bolton v Charlton	-	-	-	2-0	1-1	1-1
Brentford v Cardiff	-	-	-	-	-	1-2
Brighton v QPR	-	-	-	-	2-0	-
Bristol City v Derby	2-1	2-0	1-1	0-2	-	-
Burnley v Middlesbrough	-	3-1	0-2	0-0	0-1	-
Ipswich v Fulham	-	-	-	-	-	2-1
Leeds v Wolves	-	-	-	1-0	-	1-2
Nottm Forest v Blackburn	-	-	-	0-0	4-1	1-3
Reading v Hull	-	1-1	0-1	-	-	-
Rotherham v Huddersfield	-	-	-	-	-	2-2
Sheffield Weds v MK Dons	-	2-2	3-1	-	-	-

League One	2009-10	2010-11	2011-12	2012-13	2013-14	2014-15
Barnsley v Peterborough	2-2	-	1-0	0-2	-	1-1
Blackpool v Port Vale	-	-	-	-	-	-
Burton v Wigan	-	-	-	-	-	-
Chesterfield v Doncaster	-	-	-	-	-	2-2
Coventry v Bradford	-	-	-	-	0-0	1-1
Crewe v Colchester	-	-	-	3-2	0-0	0-3
Millwall v Fleetwood Town	-	-	-	-	-	-
Rochdale v Gillingham	-	-	-	1-1	-	1-1
Scunthorpe v Bury	-	-	1-3	1-2	2-2	-
Shrewsbury v Sheffield United	-	-	-	1-2	2-0	-
Southend v Oldham	0-1	-	-	-	-	-
Walsall v Swindon	1-1	1-2	-	0-2	1-1	1-4

League Two	2009-10	2010-11	2011-12	2012-13	2013-14	2014-15
Barnet v Notts County	1-0	-	-	-	-	-
Cambridge U v Morecambe	-	-	-	-	-	1-2
Carlisle v Luton	-	-	-	-	-	0-1
Dag & Red v AFC Wimbledon	-	-	0-2	0-1	1-0	4-0
Exeter v Mansfield	-	-	-	-	0-1	1-2
Hartlepool v Accrington	-	-	-	-	2-1	1-1
Leyton Orient v Plymouth	-	2-0	-	-	-	-
Newport County v Oxford	-	-	-	-	3-2	0-1
Northampton v Crawley Town	-	-	0-1	-	-	-
Stevenage v Bristol Rovers	-	-	-	-	-	-
Wycombe v Yeovil	1-4	-	2-3	-	-	-
York v Portsmouth	-	-	-	-	4-2	0-0

Saturday April 23rd, 2016

Premier League	2009-10	2010-11	2011-12	2012-13	2013-14	2014-15
Aston Villa v Southampton	-	-	-	0-1	0-0	1-1
Bournemouth v Chelsea	-	-	-	-	-	-
Crystal Palace v Everton	-	-	-	-	0-0	0-1

Results cover matches from Premier League to National League and Scottish Premiership to League Two

	2009-10	2010-11	2011-12	2012-13	2013-14	2014-15
Leicester v Swansea	2-1	2-1	-	-	-	2-0
Liverpool v Newcastle	-	3-0	3-1	1-1	2-1	2-0
Man City v Stoke	2-0	3-0	3-0	3-0	1-0	0-1
Norwich v Watford	-	2-3	-	-	-	3-0
Sunderland v Arsenal	1-0	1-1	1-2	0-1	1-3	0-2
Tottenham v West Brom	-	2-2	1-0	1-1	1-1	0-1
West Ham v Man United	0-4	2-4	-	2-2	0-2	1-1
Championship						
Blackburn v Bristol City	-	-	-	2-0	-	-
Cardiff v Bolton	-	-	-	1-1	-	0-3
Charlton v Brighton	1-2	0-4	-	2-2	3-2	0-1
Derby v Sheffield Weds	3-0	-	-	2-2	3-0	3-2
Fulham v Nottm Forest	-	-	-	-	-	3-2
Huddersfield v Birmingham	-	-	-	1-1	1-3	0-1
Hull v Leeds	-	2-2	0-0	2-0	-	-
Middlesbrough v Ipswich	3-1	1-3	0-0	2-0	2-0	4-1
MK Dons v Brentford	0-1	1-1	1-2	2-0	2-2	-
Preston v Burnley	-	1-2	-	-	-	-
QPR v Reading	4-1	3-1	-	1-1	1-3	-
Wolves v Rotherham	-	-	-	-	6-4	5-0
League One						
Bradford v Walsall	-	-	-	-	0-2	1-1
Bury v Millwall	-	-	-	-	-	-
Colchester v Burton	-	-	-	-	-	-
Doncaster v Coventry	0-0	1-1	1-1	1-4	-	2-0
Fleetwood Town v Blackpool	-	-	-	-	-	-
Gillingham v Shrewsbury	-	2-0	0-1	-	1-1	-
Oldham v Crewe	-	-	-	1-2	1-1	1-2
Peterborough v Scunthorpe	3-0	-	-	-	-	1-2
Port Vale v Rochdale	1-1	-	-	2-2	-	1-0
Sheffield United v Barnsley	0-0	2-2	-	-	-	0-1
Swindon v Chesterfield	-	-	-	-	-	3-1
Wigan v Southend	-	-	-	-	-	-
League Two						
Accrington v York	-	-	-	0-1	1-1	2-2
AFC Wimbledon v Leyton Orient	-	-	-	-	-	-
Bristol Rovers v Exeter	1-0	0-2	-	2-0	2-1	-
Crawley Town v Carlisle	-	-	-	1-1	0-0	-
Luton v Newport County	-	1-1	2-0	2-2	-	3-0
Mansfield v Barnet	-	-	-	-	-	-
Morecambe v Stevenage	-	0-0	-	-	-	0-0
Notts County v Cambridge U	-	-	-	-	-	-
Oxford v Hartlepool	-	-	-	-	1-0	0-2
Plymouth v Dag & Red	-	2-1	0-0	0-0	2-1	3-0
Portsmouth v Wycombe	-	-	-	-	2-2	1-1
Yeovil v Northampton	-	-	-	-	-	-
National League						
Aldershot v Southport	-	-	-	-	5-1	1-2
Altrincham v Welling	-	-	-	-	-	0-4
Boreham W v Guiseley	-	-	-	-	-	-
Eastleigh v Tranmere	-	-	-	-	-	-
Forest Green v Halifax	-	-	-	-	2-1	2-0
Gateshead v Bromley	-	-	-	-	-	-
Grimsby v Chester	-	-	-	-	2-1	3-0
Kidderminster v Dover	-	-	-	-	-	0-2
Lincoln v Woking	-	-	-	0-2	2-2	0-2

Results cover matches from Premier League to National League and Scottish Premiership to League Two

	2009-10	2010-11	2011-12	2012-13	2013-14	2014-15
Macclesfield v Cheltenham	1-0	0-2	1-3	-	-	-
Torquay v Barrow	-	-	-	-	-	-
Wrexham v Braintree	-	-	5-1	1-1	2-3	3-0
Ladbrokes Championship						
Dumbarton v St Mirren	-	-	-	-	-	-
Morton v Hibernian	-	-	-	-	-	-
Queen of Sth v Livingston	-	-	0-2/0-4	-	2-2/2-0	1-1/3-1
Raith v Falkirk	-	2-1/1-2	1-0/2-2	2-1/0-0	1-1/2-4	0-0/2-2
Rangers v Alloa	-	-	-	-	-	1-1/2-2
Ladbrokes League One						
Airdrieonians v Dunfermline	1-1/0-1	-	-	1-2/3-3	0-3/2-0	3-1/3-2
Albion v Forfar	1-1/0-1	-	1-0/2-2	2-3/1-2	-	-
Brechin v Stranraer	-	-	-	3-0/2-2	1-1/1-3	1-2/1-3
Cowdenbeath v Stenhousemuir	2-1/1-0	-	2-0/0-0	-	-	-
Peterhead v Ayr	-	2-4/1-2	-	-	-	2-0/2-0
Ladbrokes League Two						
Arbroath v Montrose	-	4-0/4-1	-	-	-	3-1/2-2
Berwick v East Fife	-	-	-	-	-	2-3/0-3
East Stirling v Elgin	1-1/2-0	0-2/2-1	1-1/2-2	1-4/3-2	3-0/3-0	2-1/1-0
Queens Park v Clyde	-	0-1/4-0	3-0/3-0	1-0/4-1	1-1/1-3	1-2/1-1
Stirling v Annan	-	-	-	5-1/2-1	0-2/1-1	-

Saturday April 30th, 2016

Premier League						
Arsenal v Norwich	-	-	3-3	3-1	4-1	-
Chelsea v Tottenham	3-0	2-1	0-0	2-2	4-0	3-0
Everton v Bournemouth	-	-	-	-	-	-
Man United v Leicester	-	-	-	-	-	3-1
Newcastle v Crystal Palace	2-0	-	-	-	1-0	3-3
Southampton v Man City	-	-	-	3-1	1-1	0-3
Stoke v Sunderland	1-0	3-2	0-1	0-0	2-0	1-1
Swansea v Liverpool	-	-	1-0	0-0	2-2	0-1
Watford v Aston Villa	-	-	-	-	-	-
West Brom v West Ham	-	3-3	-	0-0	1-0	1-2
Championship						
Birmingham v Middlesbrough	-	-	3-0	3-2	2-2	1-1
Bolton v Hull	2-2	-	-	4-1	-	-
Brentford v Fulham	-	-	-	-	-	2-1
Brighton v Derby	-	-	2-0	2-1	1-2	2-0
Bristol City v Huddersfield	-	-	-	1-3	-	-
Burnley v QPR	-	0-0	-	-	2-0	2-1
Ipswich v MK Dons	-	-	-	-	-	-
Leeds v Charlton	0-0	-	-	1-1	0-1	2-2
Nottm Forest v Wolves	-	-	-	3-1	-	1-2
Reading v Preston	4-1	2-1	-	-	-	-
Rotherham v Blackburn	-	-	-	-	-	2-0
Sheffield Weds v Cardiff	3-1	-	-	0-2	-	1-1
League One						
Barnsley v Colchester	-	-	-	-	-	3-2
Blackpool v Wigan	-	1-3	-	-	1-0	1-3
Burton v Gillingham	-	1-1	1-0	3-2	-	-
Chesterfield v Bury	1-0	2-3	1-0	-	4-0	-
Coventry v Sheffield United	3-2	0-0	-	1-1	3-2	1-0
Crewe v Doncaster	-	-	-	1-2	-	1-1
Millwall v Oldham	2-0	-	-	-	-	-
Rochdale v Swindon	-	3-3	-	-	-	2-4

Results cover matches from Premier League to National League and Scottish Premiership to League Two

	2009-10	2010-11	2011-12	2012-13	2013-14	2014-15
Scunthorpe v Port Vale	-	-	-	-	-	1-1
Shrewsbury v Peterborough	-	-	-	-	2-4	-
Southend v Bradford	-	4-0	0-1	2-2	-	-
Walsall v Fleetwood Town	-	-	-	-	-	1-0

League Two						
Barnet v Yeovil	-	-	-	-	-	-
Cambridge U v Plymouth	-	-	-	-	-	1-0
Carlisle v Oxford	-	-	-	-	-	2-1
Dag & Red v Crawley Town	-	-	1-1	-	-	-
Exeter v Morecambe	-	-	-	0-3	1-1	1-1
Hartlepool v Portsmouth	-	-	-	0-0	0-0	0-0
Leyton Orient v Mansfield	-	-	-	-	-	-
Newport County v Notts County	-	-	-	-	-	-
Northampton v Luton	-	-	-	-	-	2-1
Stevenage v AFC Wimbledon	0-0	-	-	-	-	2-1
Wycombe v Accrington	-	1-2	-	0-1	0-0	2-2
York v Bristol Rovers	-	-	-	4-1	0-0	-

National League						
Barrow v Wrexham	2-1	0-1	3-1	0-1	-	-
Braintree v Altrincham	-	-	-	-	-	4-2
Bromley v Aldershot	-	-	-	-	-	-
Cheltenham v Lincoln	1-0	1-2	-	-	-	-
Chester v Gateshead	-	-	-	-	1-1	1-0
Dover v Forest Green	-	-	-	-	-	0-0
Guiseley v Torquay	-	-	-	-	-	-
Halifax v Macclesfield	-	-	-	-	2-1	2-2
Southport v Kidderminster	-	2-2	1-2	1-3	1-2	1-0
Tranmere v Grimsby	-	-	-	-	-	-
Welling v Boreham W	-	-	-	-	-	-
Woking v Eastleigh	-	-	-	-	-	1-1

Ladbrokes Championship						
Alloa v Dumbarton	1-3/1-2	0-0/2-3	-	-	1-2/1-5	0-1/3-0
Falkirk v Morton	-	2-1/1-0	1-0/0-2	0-1/4-1	3-1/1-1	-
Hibernian v Queen of Sth	-	-	-	-	-	0-0/0-1
Livingston v Raith	-	-	1-1/4-0	2-1/2-3	3-0/2-0	0-1/0-2
St Mirren v Rangers	0-2	1-3/0-1	2-1	-	-	-

Ladbrokes League One						
Ayr v Airdrieonians	1-1/1-4	1-0/3-1	-	-	2-2/3-0	2-3/0-1
Dunfermline v Peterhead	-	-	-	-	-	3-0/1-1
Forfar v Brechin	-	1-1/2-1	0-0/4-1	1-0/1-4	2-0/1-1	3-1/0-2
Stenhousemuir v Albion	-	-	3-0/1-2	1-0/0-1	-	-
Stranraer v Cowdenbeath	-	-	-	-	-	-

Ladbrokes League Two						
Annan v Queens Park	3-1/0-2	2-1/1-2	5-2/2-3	2-3/2-0	3-2/1-1	0-1/2-0
Clyde v Stirling	0-1/1-2	-	-	2-1/1-2	2-1/1-0	-
East Fife v East Stirling	-	-	-	-	-	3-1/2-1
Elgin v Arbroath	-	3-5/3-2	-	-	-	1-1/2-1
Montrose v Berwick	1-3/1-1	1-1/1-1	3-5/1-1	3-1/1-3	1-1/0-0	2-1/0-2

Saturday May 7th, 2016

Premier League						
Aston Villa v Newcastle	-	1-0	1-1	1-2	1-2	0-0
Bournemouth v West Brom	-	-	-	-	-	-
Crystal Palace v Stoke	-	-	-	-	1-0	1-1
Leicester v Everton	-	-	-	-	-	2-2
Liverpool v Watford	-	-	-	-	-	-
Man City v Arsenal	4-2	0-3	1-0	1-1	6-3	0-2

Results cover matches from Premier League to National League and Scottish Premiership to League Two

	2009-10	2010-11	2011-12	2012-13	2013-14	2014-15
Norwich v Man United	-	-	1-2	1-0	0-1	-
Sunderland v Chelsea	1-3	2-4	1-2	1-3	3-4	0-0
Tottenham v Southampton	-	-	-	1-0	3-2	1-0
West Ham v Swansea	-	-	-	1-0	2-0	3-1
Championship						
Blackburn v Reading	-	-	-	-	0-0	3-1
Cardiff v Birmingham	-	-	1-0	2-1	-	2-0
Charlton v Burnley	-	-	-	0-1	0-3	-
Derby v Ipswich	1-3	1-2	0-0	0-1	4-4	1-1
Fulham v Bolton	1-1	3-0	2-0	-	-	4-0
Huddersfield v Brentford	0-0	4-4	3-2	-	-	2-1
Hull v Rotherham	-	-	-	-	-	-
Middlesbrough v Brighton	-	-	1-0	0-2	0-1	0-0
MK Dons v Nottm Forest	-	-	-	-	-	-
Preston v Leeds	-	1-2	-	-	-	-
QPR v Bristol City	2-1	2-2	-	-	-	-
Wolves v Sheffield Weds	-	-	-	1-0	-	3-0
League Two						
Accrington v Stevenage	-	1-0	-	-	-	2-2
AFC Wimbledon v Newport County	-	2-2	-	-	2-2	2-0
Bristol Rovers v Dag & Red	-	0-2	2-0	0-1	1-2	-
Crawley Town v Barnet	-	-	1-0	-	-	-
Luton v Exeter	-	-	-	-	-	2-3
Mansfield v Cambridge U	2-1	1-0	1-2	3-1	-	0-0
Morecambe v York	-	-	-	2-2	0-0	1-1
Notts County v Carlisle	-	0-1	2-0	1-0	4-1	-
Oxford v Wycombe	-	2-2	-	0-1	2-2	1-2
Plymouth v Hartlepool	-	0-1	-	-	1-1	2-0
Portsmouth v Northampton	-	-	-	-	0-0	2-0
Yeovil v Leyton Orient	3-3	2-1	2-2	3-0	-	0-3

Sunday May 8th, 2016

	2009-10	2010-11	2011-12	2012-13	2013-14	2014-15
League One						
Bradford v Chesterfield	3-0	0-1	-	0-0	-	0-1
Bury v Southend	-	1-0	-	-	1-1	0-1
Colchester v Rochdale	-	1-0	0-0	-	-	1-4
Doncaster v Burton	-	-	-	-	-	-
Fleetwood Town v Crewe	-	-	-	-	-	2-1
Gillingham v Millwall	2-0	-	-	-	-	-
Oldham v Coventry	-	-	-	0-1	0-0	4-1
Peterborough v Blackpool	0-1	-	3-1	1-4	-	-
Port Vale v Walsall	-	-	-	-	1-0	1-1
Sheffield United v Scunthorpe	0-1	0-4	2-1	3-0	-	4-0
Swindon v Shrewsbury	-	-	2-1	2-0	3-1	-
Wigan v Barnsley	-	-	-	-	2-0	-

Sunday May 15th, 2016

	2009-10	2010-11	2011-12	2012-13	2013-14	2014-15
Premier League						
Arsenal v Aston Villa	3-0	1-2	3-0	2-1	1-3	5-0
Chelsea v Leicester	-	-	-	-	-	2-0
Everton v Norwich	-	-	1-1	1-1	2-0	-
Man United v Bournemouth	-	-	-	-	-	-
Newcastle v Tottenham	-	1-1	2-2	2-1	0-4	1-3
Southampton v Crystal Palace	-	-	2-0	-	2-0	1-0
Stoke v West Ham	2-1	1-1	-	0-1	3-1	2-2
Swansea v Man City	-	-	1-0	0-0	2-3	2-4
Watford v Sunderland	-	-	-	-	-	-
West Brom v Liverpool	-	2-1	0-2	3-0	1-1	0-0

Results cover matches from Premier League to National League and Scottish Premiership to League Two

Premier League

Champions	Chelsea
Champions League	Manchester City
	Arsenal
	Manchester United
Europa League	Tottenham
	Liverpool
	Southampton
	West Ham*
Relegated	Hull
	Burnley
	QPR

*Via the Uefa Respect Fair Play ranking

Chelsea's Didier Drogba snaps a quick selfie

Championship

Champions	Bournemouth
Promoted	Watford
Playoff winners	Norwich
Relegated	Millwall
	Wigan
	Blackpool

League One

Champions	Bristol City
Promoted	MK Dons
Playoff winners	Preston
Relegated	Notts County
	Crawley
	Leyton Orient
	Yeovil

League Two

Champions	Burton
Promoted	Shrewsbury
	Bury
Playoff winners	Southend
Relegated	Cheltenham
	Tranmere

Conference Premier

Champions	Barnet
Playoff winners	Bristol Rovers
Relegated	Alfreton
	Telford
	Dartford
	Nuneaton

Conference North

Champions	Barrow
Playoff winners	Guiseley
Relegated	Colwyn Bay
	Leamington
	Hyde

Conference South

Champions	Bromley
Playoff winners	Boreham Wood
Relegated	Farnborough
	Staines Town

Community Shield

Winners	Arsenal
Beaten finalists	Manchester City

FA Cup

Winners	Arsenal
Beaten finalists	Aston Villa

League Cup

Winners	Chelsea
Beaten finalists	Tottenham

Bristol City boss Steve Cotterill shows off the League One trophy and Football League Trophy

Football League Trophy	
Winners	Bristol City
Beaten finalists	Walsall

FA Trophy	
Winners	North Ferriby
Beaten finalists	Wrexham

Scottish Premiership	
Champions	Celtic
Europa League	Aberdeen
	Inverness CT
Relegated	St Mirren

Scottish Championship	
Champions	Hearts
Relegated	Cowdenbeath

Scottish League One	
Champions	Morton
Relegated	Stirling Albion

Scottish League Two	
Champions	Albion

Scottish Cup	
Winners	Inverness CT
Beaten finalists	Falkirk

Scottish League Cup	
Winners	Celtic
Beaten finalists	Dundee United

Scottish Challenge Cup	
Winners	Livingston
Beaten finalists	Alloa

Uefa Super Cup	
Winners	Real Madrid
Beaten finalists	Seville

Fifa Club World Cup	
Winners	Real Madrid
Beaten finalists	San Lorenzo

Champions League	
Winners	Barcelona
Beaten finalists	Juventus

Europa League	
Winners	Seville
Beaten finalists	Dnipro

Mame Biram Diouf's goal against Manchester City at Eastlands set up Stoke for a profitable season

Premier League			
Stoke	+26.70	Man City	-0.35
Swansea	+24.49	Liverpool	-3.35
Crystal Palace	+17.45	West Ham	-3.42
Tottenham	+6.73	Newcastle	-4.57
West Brom	+5.80	Burnley	-5.23
Aston Villa	+4.52	Leicester	-5.29
Southampton	+1.17	Everton	-10.93
Chelsea	+0.87	Hull	-11.94
Arsenal	+0.16	Sunderland	-13.06
Man Utd	-0.31	QPR	-13.20

Championship			
Brentford	+17.64	Cardiff	-2.93
Leeds	+14.75	Nottm Forest	-3.83
Watford	+13.28	Derby	-3.91
Middlesbrough	+9.19	Blackburn	-5.25
Wolves	+8.48	Fulham	-5.30
Norwich	+6.12	Huddersfield	-5.78
Ipswich	+5.90	Bolton	-8.43
Birmingham	+5.36	Rotherham	-12.76
Bournemouth	+3.91	Wigan	-15.86
Charlton	+3.23	Millwall	-15.92
Reading	+0.57	Brighton	-19.65
Sheff Wed	-1.32	Blackpool	-31.75

All profit & loss figures calculated to a £1 level stake at best bookmakers' odds published in the Racing Post on matchday

League One			
Crewe	+18.92	Scunthorpe	+0.92
Bristol City	+14.27	Peterborough	-0.04
Gillingham	+14.17	Port Vale	-0.62
Swindon	+7.28	Chesterfield	-0.66
Crawley	+7.00	Doncaster	-1.35
MK Dons	+6.75	Sheff Utd	-4.02
Rochdale	+5.10	Coventry	-4.90
Preston	+4.98	Yeovil	-5.70
Colchester	+4.78	Walsall	-6.60
Bradford	+3.50	Oldham	-10.23
Barnsley	+3.16	Notts County	-11.40
Fleetwood	+2.49	Leyton Orient	-15.73

League Two			
Morecambe	+21.05	Luton	-0.46
Burton	+19.32	Oxford	-1.70
Dag & Red	+18.62	Northampton	-1.93
Wycombe	+12.27	Hartlepool	-3.17
Bury	+10.47	AFC Wimbledon	-3.70
Southend	+8.17	Carlisle	-3.99
Plymouth	+7.66	Cambridge Utd	-9.05
Exeter	+7.17	Mansfield	-10.73
Newport County	+6.57	Portsmouth	-14.06
Shrewsbury	+5.82	York	-18.20
Stevenage	+5.51	Cheltenham	-19.15
Accrington	+5.32	Tranmere	-19.95

Conference

Macclesfield	+11.87	Lincoln	+0.85
Chester	+10.25	Braintree	+0.39
Eastleigh	+9.28	Woking	-0.25
Southport	+8.22	Torquay	-3.46
Grimsby	+7.91	Nuneaton	-4.05
Altrincham	+7.86	Alfreton	-4.35
Barnet	+6.56	Aldershot	-6.23
Telford	+6.02	Kidderminster	-10.42
Bristol R	+3.35	Gateshead	-12.30
Forest Green	+3.35	Halifax	-12.97
Wrexham	+2.14	Welling	-13.10
Dover	+2.12	Dartford	-17.60

Scottish Premiership

St Johnstone	+26.02	St Mirren	-2.05
Hamilton	+10.62	Partick	-2.75
Inverness CT	+8.49	Ross County	-2.97
Aberdeen	+3.95	Kilmarnock	-3.75
Dundee Utd	+3.95	Motherwell	-7.22
Celtic	+1.11	Dundee	-8.82

Scottish Championship

Hearts	+11.71	Cowdenbeath	-5.10
Hibernian	+7.46	Rangers	-5.20
Queen of Sth	+4.56	Dumbarton	-7.45
Raith	+0.92	Livingston	-11.99
Falkirk	-1.23	Alloa	-18.45

Scottish League One

Morton	+11.98	Peterhead	-0.27
Forfar	+10.16	Stenhousemuir	-6.50
Stranraer	+9.14	Ayr	-7.79
Airdrieonians	+7.20	Dunfermline	-10.97
Brechin	+3.52	Stirling	-20.00

Scottish League Two

East Stirling	+18.65	Clyde	+4.10
Albion	+14.63	Annan	-1.34
Queen's Park	+7.96	Arbroath	-4.66
East Fife	+6.09	Montrose	-5.40
Elgin City	+5.82	Berwick	-10.34

SOCCERBASE.COM

Italian Serie A

Genoa	+16.99	Roma	-3.26
Juventus	+7.71	Napoli	-4.77
Lazio	+2.92	Palermo	-4.82
Verona	+1.90	Parma	-6.17
Chievo	+1.07	Inter	-9.13
Sassuolo	+0.83	Cagliari	-9.79
Sampdoria	-0.16	Milan	-9.80
Udinese	-1.49	Empoli	-12.61
Fiorentina	-2.05	Atalanta	-13.94
Torino	-2.22	Cesena	-16.60

Spanish Primera Liga

Malaga	+21.71	Barcelona	-0.12
Celta Vigo	+7.98	Espanyol	-1.15
Valencia	+6.68	Almeria	-2.20
Seville	+5.50	Getafe	-4.25
Sociedad	+4.56	Villarreal	-5.99
Elche	+3.60	Levante	-6.90
R. Vallecano	+3.45	Eibar	-7.09
Atl Madrid	+1.80	Granada	-13.76
Real Madrid	+0.60	Deportivo	-14.75
Ath Bilbao	+0.02	Cordoba	-20.88

German Bundesliga

Mgladbach	+20.64	B Munich	-2.06
Augsburg	+17.12	Schalke	-2.77
Wolfsburg	+9.33	Hertha Berlin	-3.83
W Bremen	+3.60	Mainz	-7.08
E Frankfurt	+2.02	Freiburg	-7.60
Hannover	+0.85	Hoffenheim	-7.82
B Leverkusen	+0.05	SC Paderborn	-8.96
Cologne	-1.05	Stuttgart	-11.45
Hamburg	-1.73	B Dortmund	-14.71

French Ligue 1

Guingamp	+12.67	Marseille	-1.20
Nice	+12.31	St-Etienne	-1.79
Lorient	+7.55	Lille	-2.98
Bastia	+6.92	Paris St-G.	-3.51
Lyon	+5.20	Rennes	-4.41
Montpellier	+4.19	Evian	-4.67
Bordeaux	+3.59	Toulouse	-4.93
Caen	+2.87	Nantes	-8.40
Monaco	+1.85	Lens	-11.10
Reims	+1.40	Metz	-19.13

Multiple bets

Selections	2	3	4	5	6	7
Doubles	1	3	6	10	15	21
Trebles		1	4	10	20	35
Fourfolds			1	5	15	35
Fivefolds				1	6	21
Sixfolds					1	7
Sevenfolds						1
Full cover	3	7	15	31	63	127

Patent (3 selections, 7 bets) 3 singles, 3 doubles, 1 treble

Trixie (3 selections, 4 bets) 3 doubles, 1 treble

Yankee (4 selections, 11 bets) 6 doubles, 4 trebles, 1 four-fold

Lucky 15 (4 selections, 15 bets) 4 singles, 6 doubles, 4 trebles, 1 four-fold

Canadian (5 selections, 26 bets) 10 doubles, 10 trebles, 5 four-folds, 1 five-fold

Lucky 31 (5 selections, 31 bets) 5 singles, 10 doubles, 10 trebles, 5 four-folds, 1 five-fold

Heinz (6 selections, 57 bets) 15 doubles, 20 trebles, 15 four-folds, 6 five-folds, 1 six-fold

Lucky 63 (6 selections, 63 bets) 6 singles, 15 doubles, 20 trebles, 15 four-folds, 6 five-folds, 1 six-fold

Super Heinz (7 selections, 120 bets) 21 doubles, 35 trebles, 35 four-folds, 21 five-folds, 7 six-folds, 1 seven-fold

Goliath (8 selections, 247 bets) 28 doubles, 56 trebles, 70 four-folds, 56 five-folds, 28 six-folds, 8 seven-folds, 1 eight-fold

Aberdeen...................... *Scottish Premiership* 102
Accrington..................... *League Two* 80
AFC Wimbledon .... *League Two* 80
Airdrieonians .... *Scottish League One*..... 114
Albion .... *Scottish League One*..... 114
Alloa .... *Scottish Championship* 110
Angers .... *French Ligue 1* 156
Annan .... *Scottish League Two* 118
Arbroath....................... *Scottish League Two* 118
Arsenal......................... *Premier League* 24
Aston Villa.................... *Premier League* 25
Atalanta .... *Italian Serie A* 138
Athletic Bilbao.............. *Spanish Primera Liga* .. 150
Atletico Madrid .... *Spanish Primera Liga* .. 150
Augsburg....................... *German Bundesliga* 144
Ayr .... *Scottish League One*..... 114
Barcelona .... *Spanish Primera Liga* .. 150
Barnet .... *League Two* 81
Barnsley .... *League One* 64
Bastia .... *French Ligue 1* 156
Bayern Munich .... *German Bundesliga* 144
Berwick......................... *Scottish League Two* 118
Betis .... *Spanish Primera Liga* .. 150
Birmingham.................. *Championship*............... 48
Blackburn..................... *Championship*............... 48
Blackpool .... *League One* 64
Bologna........................ *Italian Serie A* 138
Bolton .... *Championship*............... 49
Bordeaux...................... *French Ligue 1* 156
Bournemouth................ *Premier League* 26
Bradford....................... *League One* 65
Brechin......................... *Scottish League One*..... 114
Brentford...................... *Championship*............... 49
Brighton....................... *Championship*............... 50
Bristol City .... *Championship*............... 50
Bristol Rovers .... *League Two* 81
Burnley .... *Championship*............... 51
Burton .... *League One* 65
Bury .... *League One* 66
Caen............................. *French Ligue 1* 156
Cambridge United .... *League Two* 82
Cardiff.......................... *Championship*............... 51
Carlisle .... *League Two* 82
Carpi .... *Italian Serie A* 138
Celta .... *Spanish Primera Liga* .. 151
Celtic............................ *Scottish Premiership* 102
Charlton .... *Championship*............... 52
Chelsea .... *Premier League* 27
Chesterfield.................. *League One* 66
Chievo.......................... *Italian Serie A* 138
Clyde............................ *Scottish League Two* 118
Colchester .... *League One* 67
Cologne........................ *German Bundesliga* 144
Coventry .... *League One* 67
Cowdenbeath .... *Scottish League One*..... 115
Crawley......................... *League Two* 83
Crewe........................... *League One* 68
Crystal Palace............... *Premier League* 28
Dag & Red .... *League Two* 83

Darmstadt .... *German Bundesliga* 144
Deportivo .... *Spanish Primera Liga* .. 151
Derby .... *Championship*............... 52
Doncaster .... *League One* 68
Dortmund .... *German Bundesliga* 145
Dumbarton................... *Scottish Championship* 110
Dundee .... *Scottish Premiership* 103
Dundee United .... *Scottish Premiership* 103
Dunfermline................. *Scottish League One*..... 115
East Fife....................... *Scottish League Two* 119
East Stirling .... *Scottish League Two* 119
Ein Frankfurt .... *German Bundesliga* 145
Elche .... *Spanish Primera Liga* .. 151
Elgin............................. *Scottish League Two* 119
Empoli.......................... *Italian Serie A* 139
Espanyol....................... *Spanish Primera Liga* .. 151
Everton .... *Premier League* 29
Exeter........................... *League Two* 84
Falkirk.......................... *Scottish Championship* 110
Fiorentina..................... *Italian Serie A* 139
Fleetwood Town .... *League One* 69
Forfar .... *Scottish League One*..... 115
Frosinone .... *Italian Serie A* 139
Fulham.......................... *Championship*............... 53
Genoa........................... *Italian Serie A* 139
Getafe .... *Spanish Primera Liga* .. 152
GFC Ajaccio .... *French Ligue 1* 157
Gillingham .... *League One* 69
Girona .... *Spanish Primera Liga* .. 152
Granada .... *Spanish Primera Liga* .. 152
Guingamp .... *French Ligue 1* 157
Hamburg....................... *German Bundesliga* 145
Hamilton .... *Scottish Premiership* 104
Hannover .... *German Bundesliga* 145
Hartlepool..................... *League Two* 84
Hearts .... *Scottish Premiership* 104
Hellas Verona .... *Italian Serie A* 140
Hertha.......................... *German Bundesliga* 146
Hibernian...................... *Scottish Championship* 110
Hoffenheim .... *German Bundesliga* 146
Huddersfield .... *Championship*............... 53
Hull.............................. *Championship*............... 54
Ingolstadt .... *German Bundesliga* 146

*Outside the Weston Homes
Community Stadium as
Colchester host Sheffield
United in League One*

Inter .... Italian Serie A 140
Inverness CT.................. Scottish Premiership.... 105
Ipswich............................ Championship................ 54
Juventus........................ Italian Serie A 140
Kilmarnock.................... Scottish Premiership.... 105
Las Palmas.................... Spanish Primera Liga .. 152
Lazio .... Italian Serie A 140
Leeds............................. Championship................ 55
Leicester........................ Premier League 30
Levante .... Spanish Primera Liga .. 153
Leverkusen .... German Bundesliga 146
Leyton Orient .... League Two 85
Lille .... French Ligue 1 157
Liverpool........................ Premier League 31
Livingston .... Scottish Championship 111
Lorient .... French Ligue 1 157
Luton.............................. League Two 85
Lyon .... French Ligue 1 158
Mainz............................. German Bundesliga 147
Malaga .... Spanish Primera Liga .. 153
Manchester City .... Premier League 32
Manchester United .... Premier League 33
Mansfield .... League Two 86
Marseille .... French Ligue 1 158
Mgladbach .... German Bundesliga 147
Middlesbrough .... Championship................ 55
Milan.............................. Italian Serie A 141
Millwall .... League One 70
MK Dons......................... Championship................ 56
Monaco .... French Ligue 1 158
Montpellier .... French Ligue 1 158
Montrose........................ Scottish League Two 119
Morecambe .... League Two 86
Morton .... Scottish Championship 111
Motherwell.................... Scottish Premiership.... 106
Nantes............................ French Ligue 1 159
Napoli .... Italian Serie A 141
Newcastle....................... Premier League 34
Newport County .... League Two 87
Nice................................ French Ligue 1 159
Northampton.................. League Two 87
Norwich.......................... Premier League 35
Nottingham Forest........ Championship................ 56
Notts County .... League Two 88
Oldham .... League One 70
Oxford............................ League Two 88
Palermo.......................... Italian Serie A 141

Paris Saint-Germain .... French Ligue 1 159
Partick............................ Scottish Premiership.... 106
Peterborough.................. League One 71
Peterhead .... Scottish League One..... 115
Plymouth........................ League Two 89
Port Vale......................... League One 71
Portsmouth .... League Two 89
Preston .... Championship................ 57
QPR................................ Championship................ 57
Queen of the South........ Scottish Championship 111
Queen's Park .... Scottish League Two 120
Raith .... Scottish Championship 111
Rangers .... Scottish Championship 112
Reading........................... Championship................ 58
Real Madrid .... Spanish Primera Liga .. 153
Reims .... French Ligue 1 159
Rennes .... French Ligue 1 160
Rochdale .... League One 72
Roma............................... Italian Serie A 141
Ross County .... Scottish Premiership.... 107
Rotherham .... Championship................ 58
Sampdoria....................... Italian Serie A 142
Sassuolo .... Italian Serie A 142
Schalke 04...................... German Bundesliga 147
Scunthorpe .... League One 72
Seville .... Spanish Primera Liga .. 153
Sheffield United............. League One 73
Sheffield Wednesday....... Championship................ 59
Shrewsbury .... League One 73
Sociedad .... Spanish Primera Liga .. 154
Southampton .... Premier League 36
Southend .... League One 74
St-Etienne .... French Ligue 1 160
St Johnstone................... Scottish Premiership.... 107
St Mirren .... Scottish Championship 112
Stenhousemuir .... Scottish League One..... 116
Stevenage........................ League Two 90
Stirling .... Scottish League Two 120
Stoke .... Premier League 37
Stranraer......................... Scottish League One..... 116
Stuttgart.......................... German Bundesliga 147
Sunderland...................... Premier League 38
Swansea .... Premier League 39
Swindon.......................... League One 74
Torino .... Italian Serie A 142
Tottenham...................... Premier League 40
Toulouse.......................... French Ligue 1 160
Troyes .... French Ligue 1 160
Udinese .... Italian Serie A 142
Valencia .... Spanish Primera Liga .. 154
Vallecano .... Spanish Primera Liga .. 154
Villarreal .... Spanish Primera Liga .. 154
Walsall .... League One 75
Watford .... Premier League 41
Werder Bremen .... German Bundesliga 148
West Brom...................... Premier League 42
West Ham........................ Premier League 43
Wigan.............................. League One 75
Wolfsburg........................ German Bundesliga 148
Wolves............................ Championship................ 59
Wycombe .... League Two 90
Yeovil .... League Two 91
York................................ League Two 91

Odds conversion

Odds-on As %	Decimal	Fractional	Decimal	Odds-against As %
50.00%	2.00	Evens	2.00	50.00%
52.38%	1.91	11-10	2.10	47.62%
54.55%	1.83	6-5	2.20	45.45%
55.56%	1.80	5-4	2.25	44.44%
57.89%	1.73	11-8	2.38	42.11%
60.00%	1.67	6-4	2.50	40.00%
61.90%	1.62	13-8	2.63	38.10%
63.64%	1.57	7-4	2.75	36.36%
65.22%	1.53	15-8	2.88	34.78%
66.67%	1.50	2-1	3.00	33.33%
69.23%	1.44	9-4	3.25	30.77%
71.43%	1.40	5-2	3.50	28.57%
72.22%	1.38	13-5	3.60	27.78%
73.33%	1.36	11-4	3.75	26.67%
73.68%	1.36	14-5	3.80	26.32%
75.00%	1.33	3-1	4.00	25.00%
76.92%	1.30	10-3	4.33	23.08%
77.78%	1.29	7-2	4.50	22.22%
80.00%	1.25	4-1	5.00	20.00%
81.82%	1.22	9-2	5.50	18.18%
83.33%	1.20	5-1	6.00	16.67%
84.62%	1.18	11-2	6.50	15.38%
85.71%	1.17	6-1	7.00	14.29%
86.67%	1.15	13-2	7.50	13.33%
87.50%	1.14	7-1	8.00	12.50%
88.24%	1.13	15-2	8.50	11.76%
88.89%	1.13	8-1	9.00	11.11%

Correct scores 2014-15

	Prem	Chmp	Lg1	Lg2	Conf	SCP	SCh	SLg1	SLg2
1-0	37	43	59	77	58	30	16	17	12
2-0	37	40	35	49	39	14	10	17	18
2-1	35	47	44	50	51	17	17	15	20
3-0	19	24	21	21	20	12	10	6	8
3-1	14	21	16	15	25	7	4	8	7
3-2	9	15	16	16	14	3	1	7	2
4-0	4	11	5	6	10	7	5	6	5
4-1	5	7	9	3	6	4	6	1	2
4-2	2	7	3	2	3	1	1	2	1
4-3	1	3	1	0	1	0	0	0	2
0-0	31	46	36	43	36	9	10	5	8
1-1	37	69	69	71	61	25	17	20	18
2-2	22	33	36	22	32	7	9	11	7
3-3	3	8	4	2	8	3	2	3	5
4-4	0	2	0	1	1	0	0	0	0
0-1	40	54	47	53	47	22	14	13	15
0-2	14	23	28	28	31	14	8	17	11
1-2	26	37	44	35	39	24	12	9	9
0-3	5	14	20	7	7	8	7	0	5
1-3	15	15	16	15	21	5	10	7	3
2-3	6	9	14	23	16	4	4	5	7
0-4	1	2	4	0	2	2	5	2	3
1-4	4	3	5	4	3	2	1	2	3
2-4	2	3	1	0	3	0	0	2	0
3-4	0	1	0	1	1	0	1	1	1
Other	11	15	19	8	17	8	12	4	8

Win/draw/win percentages 2014-15

	Prem	Chmp	Lg1	Lg2	Conf	SCP	SCh	SLg1	SLg2
Home	45	41	40	44	43	45	42	45	44
Draw	24	29	26	25	25	19	21	22	21
Away	30	30	33	31	32	36	37	33	35

Unders & overs 2014-15

	Prem	Chmp	Lg1	Lg2	Conf	SCP	SCh	SLg1	SLg2
<1.5	28	26	26	31	26	27	22	19	19
>1.5	72	74	74	69	74	73	78	81	81
<2.5	52	50	50	58	49	50	41	49	46
>2.5	48	50	50	42	51	50	59	51	54
<3.5	74	72	73	79	70	77	66	66	69
>3.5	26	28	27	21	30	23	34	34	31
<4.5	89	87	87	89	87	89	85	85	83
>4.5	11	13	13	11	13	11	15	15	17

Ante-post odds of recent champions

Premier League		Best odds
2014-15	Chelsea	19-10
2013-14	Manchester City	23-10
2012-13	Manchester United	13-5
Championship		**Best odds**
2014-15	Bournemouth	25-1
2013-14	Leicester	14-1
2012-13	Cardiff	12-1
League One		**Best odds**
2014-15	Bristol City	8-1
2013-14	Wolves	4-1
2012-13	Doncaster	14-1
League Two		**Best odds**
2014-15	Burton	16-1
2013-14	Chesterfield	8-1
2012-13	Gillingham	22-1
Conference		**Best odds**
2014-15	Barnet	18-1
2013-14	Luton	9-2
2012-13	Mansfield	5-1
Scottish Premiership		**Best odds**
2014-15	Celtic	1-33
2013-14	Celtic	1-40
2012-13	Celtic	1-25
Scottish Championship		**Best odds**
2014-15	Hearts	7-2
2013-14	Dundee	15-8
2012-13	Partick Thistle	5-1
Scottish League One		**Best odds**
2014-15	Morton	5-1
2013-14	Rangers	1-10
2012-13	Queen of the South	7-2
Scottish League Two		**Best odds**
2014-15	Albion	6-1
2013-14	Peterhead	15-8
2012-13	Rangers	1-20

Asian handicaps

Conceding handicap				Receiving handicap
Result of bet	Result of game	Handicap	Result of game	Result of bet
Win	Win	0	Win	Win
No bet	Draw	Scratch	Draw	No bet
Lose	Lose		Lose	Lose
Win	Win	0,0.5	Win	Win
Lose half	Draw	0.25	Draw	Win half
Lose	Lose		Lose	Lose
Win	Win	0.5	Win	Win
Lose	Draw		Draw	Win
Lose	Lose		Lose	Lose
Win	Win by 2+	0.5,1	Lose by 2+	Lose
Win half	Win by 1	0.75	Lose by 1	Lose half
Lose	Draw		Draw	Win
Lose	Lose		Win	Win
Win	Win by 2+	1	Lose by 2+	Lose
Return stake	Win by 1		Lose by 1	Return stake
Lose	Draw		Draw	Win
Lose	Lose		Win	Win